CASES ON CHURCH AND STATE

IN THE UNITED STATES

Compiled by

Mark De Wolfe Howe

Professor of Law in Harvard University

Harvard University Press
Cambridge, Massachusetts.
1952

Distributed in Great Britain by

GEOFFREY CUMBERLEGE
OXFORD UNIVERSITY PRESS
LONDON

Library of Congress Catalog Card Number 52-5398
Printed in the United States of America

PREFACE

Some three years ago the editor of this collection of materials was called upon to conduct a seminar in American Legal History at the Harvard Law School. Somewhat by chance he found himself directing the attention of the students to problems of church and state in the United States. Out of that beginning grew this collection of cases. The editor is fully aware of the limitations which such a beginning imposed upon the structure of the collection; it meant, firstly, that the materials were chosen for the use of law students, and it meant, secondly, that the cases were to be considered in a course which was committed to an emphasis on an historical method.

Although those limitations would make impossible any pretension that this collection of materials is exhaustive, it was felt that there might be a number of scholars and other readers outside of the law schools who would find this preliminary collection of cases of some utility. It is hoped that before very long a much more complete edition of these materials may be published. Such a volume should, of course, include far more extensive annotations and editorial comment than will be found in this temporary edition. It would also be well, I believe, to include some of the rich materials concerning the relationship between government and religion in the American colonies.

Needless to say the editor will be more than grateful for any suggestions which he may receive from readers as to how this preliminary edition might be made more useful when it later takes its final form.

M. DeW. H.

Cambridge, Massachusetts
November 1951

CONTENTS

	Page
I. The Disestablishment of Established Churches	1
1. Virginia	1
Patrick Henry's Defense of the Baptists	1
The Presbyterian Memorial	3
Madison's Remonstrance	5
Act for Establishing Religious Freedom	7
Jefferson on Christianity and the Common Law	8
Presbyterian Protest against Incorporation of Churches	13
Act Incorporating the Episcopal Church	14
The Repealing Statute	15
Selden v. Overseers of Poor	16
Gallege's Executors v. Attorney General	20
2. Massachusetts	27
Declaration of Rights	28
Barnes v. First Parish	29
Adam v. Howe	35
Baker v. Fales	40
Congregational Protest	47
Hale v. Everett	55
McGinnis v. Watson	78
3. Federal	84
Introductory	84
Madison's Veto Message	85
The Blaine Amendment	86
History according to Everson	88
II. The Church as Corporation	94
New York Statute of 1786	94
Mazaika v. Krauczunas	96
St. Casimir's Polish R. C. Church's Case	102
Canovaro v. Brothers of The Order of Hermits of St. Augustine	105
Robertson v. Bullions	113
Westminster Church v. Presbytery of New York	120
Saint Nicholas Cathedral v. Kedroff	126
III. The Effect of Ecclesiastical Adjudications	153
Smith v. Nelson	153
Gartin v. Penick	158
Watson v. Jones	169
Watson v. Garvin	175
S. S. & B. Live Poultry Corp. v. Kashruth Corp.	182

III. The Effect of Ecclesiastical Adjudications (Continued)

	Page
Burr v. Parish of Sandwich	190
The Rector, etc. v. Melish	191
O'Hara v. Stack	199
Bonacum v. Harrington	202
Gray v. Christian Society	207
Hardin v. Trustees of the Second Baptist Church of Detroit	209
Carter v. Papineau	210
Moyle v. Franz	212
McGuire v. Trustees of St. Patrick's Cathedral	219
Ramon v. Ramon	227

IV. Police Powers 236

Chancellor Kent in the Council of Revision	236
Davis v. Beason	237
Hamilton v. Regents of the University of California	242
United States v. Kauten	247
United States v. Ballard	251
Ex parte Newman	260
Cantwell v. Connecticut	267
Murdock v. Pennsylvania	273
Martin v. Struthers	283
Douglas v. Jeannette	287
(N.Y. Decision on The Miracle)	300
"Pressure Problem" by Elia Kazan	312

V. Education 316

Commonwealth v. Cooke	316
Board of Education v. Minor et al	322
State ex rel. Weiss v. District Board, etc.	329
Scopes v. State	333
Pierce v. Society of Sisters	338
Cochran v. Board of Education	341
Nicholls Jr. v. Mayor and School Committee of Lynn	342
Minersville School District v. Gobitis	346
Board of Education v. Barnette	354
Everson v. Board of Education	360
McCollum v. Board of Education	364
Zorach v. Clauson	375

CHAPTER I

THE DISESTABLISHMENT OF ESTABLISHED CHURCHES

1. VIRGINIA

During the Colonial period the Church of England had a notably preferred position in Virginia. The entire population was compelled to contribute to the support of the Episcopal minister by contributing to his annual salary. The community also provided him with glebe lands. From the early years dissenting groups made frequent protest against these and other preferences. The ministers of the Church of England turned to the English authorities, both ecclasiastical and civil, for protection, and in doing so made commitments of loyalty intolerable to the rebellious elements in the Colony. Church questions thus became, quite inevitably, political questions. The grudging and limited concessions which were occasionally made to dissenting sects, particularly to the Baptists and the Presbyterians, did little to appease their resentment. Nor did the efforts of the Episcopal clergy to eliminate lay control of the hiring, firing, and discipline of the ministry aid the clerical cause with the patriots. (See, in general, Eckenrode, Separation of Church and State in Virginia (1910).)

All of these factors, many of them of great political and ecclasiastical complexity, gave special intensity to the problems of disestablishment in Virginia. Though Patrick Henry, after the revolution was over, showed considerable sympathy for the establishment, it was his voice that first dramatized the issues of church and state. Not only did he support the civil power in 1763 in the famous Parson's Cause, but he had supported the dissenting ministers when they were prosecuted for preaching without license. The dramatics of his performance in defending the unlicensed Baptist preachers are significant of the mood in which problems of church and state were considered during the period of the revolution. The following account of his performance is from Parton's Life of Jefferson 204.

Patrick Henry's Defense of the Baptists

"He (Mr. Henry) entered the court-house while the prosecuting attorney was reading the indictment. He was a stranger to most of the spectators; and being dressed in the country manner, his entrance excited no remark. When the prosecutor has finished his brief opening, the new-comer took the indictment, and glancing at it with an expression of puzzled incredulity, began to speak in the tone of a man who has just heard something too astounding for belief:

" 'May it please your Worships, I think I heard read by the prosecutor, as I entered the house, the paper I now hold in my hand. If I have rightly understood, the king's attorney has framed an indictment for the purpose of arraigning and punishing by imprisonment these three inoffensive persons before the bar of this court for a crime of great magnitude, - as disturbers of the peace. May it please the court, what did I hear read?

Did I hear it distinctly, or was it a mistake of my own? Did I hean an expression as of crime, that these men, whom your Worships are about to try for misdemeanor, are charged with - with - with what?'

"Having delivered these words in a halting, broken manner, as if his mind was staggering under the weight of a monstrous idea, he lowered his tone to the deepest bass; and assuming the profoundest solemnity of manner, answered his own question:

" 'Preaching the gospel of the Son of God!'

"Then he paused. Every eye was riveted upon him, and every mind intent; for all this was executed as a Kean or a Siddons would have performed it on the stage, - eye, voice, attitude, gesture, all in accord to produce the utmost possibility of effect. Amid a silence that could be felt, he waved the indictment three times around his head, as though still amazed, still unable to comprehend the charge. Then he raised his hands and eyes to heaven, and in a tone of pathetic energy wholly indescribable, exclaimed,

" 'Great God!'

"At this point, such was his power of delivery, the audience relieved their feelings by a burst of sighs and tears. The orator continued:

" 'May it please your Worships, in a day like this, when Truth is about to burst her fetters; when mankind are about to be aroused to claim their natural and inalienable rights; when the yoke of oppression that has reached the wilderness of America, and the unnatural alliance of ecclesiastical and civil power is about to be dissevered, - at such a period, when Liberty, Liberty of Conscience, is about to wake from her slumberings, and inquire into the reason of such charges as I find exhibited here to-day in this indictment'-

"Here occurred another of his appalling pauses, during which he cast piercing looks at the judges and at the three clergymen arraigned. Then resuming, he thrilled every hearer by his favorite device of repetition.

" 'If I am not deceived, - according to the contents of the paper I now hold in my hand, - these men are accused of preaching the gospel of the Son of God!'

"He waved the document three times around his head, as though still lost in wonder; and then with the same electric attitude of appeal to heaven, he gasped,

" 'Great God!'

"This was followed by another burst of feeling from the spectators; and again this master of effect plunged into the tide of his discourse:

" 'May it please your Worships, there are periods in the history of man when corruption and depravity have so long debased the human character, that man sinks under the weight of the oppressor's hand, - becomes his servile, his abject slave. He licks the hand that smites him. He bows in passive obedience to the mandates of the despot; and in this state of servility, he receives his fetters of perpetual bondage. But may it please your Worships, such a day has passed. From that period when our fathers left the land of their nativity for these American wilds, - from the moment they placed their feet upon the American continent, from that moment despotism was crushed, the fetters of darkness were broken, and Heaven decreed that man should be free, - free to worship God according to the Bible. In vain were all their offerings and bloodshed to subjugate this new world, if we, their offspring, must still be oppressed and persecuted. But, may it please your Worships, permit me to inquire once more, for what are these men about to be tried? This paper says, for preaching the gospel of the Saviour to Adam's fallen race!'

"Again he paused. For the third time, he slowly waved the indictment round his head; and then turning to the judges, looking them full in the face, exclaimed with the most impressive effect,

" 'What laws have they violated?'

"The whole assembly were now painfully moved and excited. The presiding judge ended the scene by saying,

" 'Sheriff, discharge these men.'

"It was a triumph of the dramatic art. These men were discharged; but not the less in other counties, did zealous bigots pursue and persecute the ministers of other denominations than their own. It was not till the Revolutionary War absorbed all minds, that Baptists ceased to be imprisoned."

The Presbyterian Memorial

Virginia's Declaration of Rights, adopted June 12, 1776, contained the following section concerning religious liberty:

"That religion, or the duty which we owe to our CREATOR and the manner of discharging it, can be directed only by reason and conviction, not by force or violence, and therefore all men are equally entitled to the free exercise of religion according to the dictates of conscience; and that it is the mutual duty of all to practise Christian forbearance, love, and charity towards each other."[1]

The adoption of this Declaration of Rights did not, however, bring an immediate end to the established church. Dissenting sects were quick to protest that action should be taken by the Legislature to abolish the old advantages which the Episcopalian church continued to enjoy. The following petition of the Hanover Presbytery of the Presbyterian Church expressed in characteristic form the grievances of the dissenting sects. (James, The Struggle for Religious Liberty in Virginia (1899) p. 70.)

"October 24, 1776: "A memorial of the Presbytery of Hanover was presented to the House and read; setting forth that they are governed by the same sentiments which have inspired the United States of America, and are determined that nothing in their power and influence shall be wanting to give success to the common cause; that dissenters from the Church of England in this country have every been desirous to conduct themselves as peaceable members of the civil government, for which reason they have hitherto submitted to several ecclesiastical burthens and restrictions that are inconsistent with equal liberty, but that now, when the many and grievous opressions of our mother country have laid

[1]George Mason's original draft of the provision, between "all men" and "conscience" read as follows: "That all men should enjoy the fullest toleration in the exercise of religion, according to the dictates of conscience, unpunished and unrestrained by the magistrate, unless under color of religion any man disturb the peace, the happiness, or safety of society."

this continent under the necessity of casting off the yoke of tyranny and of forming independent governments upon equitable and liberal foundations, they flatter themselves they shall be freed from all the encumbrances which a spirit of domination, prejudice, or bigotry hath interwoven with most other political systems; that they are more strongly encouraged to expect this by declaration of rights, so universally applauded for the dignity, firmness, and precision with which it delineates and asserts the privileges of society and the prerogatives of human nature, and which they embrace as the Magna Charta of the Commonwealth, which can never be violated without endangering the grand superstructure it was destined to support. Therefore, they rely upon this declaration, as well as the justice of the Legislature, to secure to them the free exercise of religion according to the dictates of their consciences; and that they should fall short in their duty to themselves and to the many and numerous congregations under their care, were they upon this occasion to neglect laying before the House a state of the religious grievances under which they have hitherto labored; that they no longer may be continued in the present form of government; that it is well known that in the frontier countries, which are justly supposed to contain a fifth part of the inhabitants of Virginia, the dissenters have borne the heavy burthens of purchasing glebes and supporting the Established clergy, where there are very few Episcopalians either to assist in bearing the expense or to reap the advantage; and that throughout the other parts of the country there are also many thousands of zealous friends and defenders of the State, who, besides the invidious and disadvantageous restrictions to which they have been subjected annually, pay large taxes to support establishment from which their consciences and principles oblige them to dissent, all which are so many violations of their natural rights, and in their consequences a restraint upon freedom of inquiry and private judgment. In this enlightened age, and in a land where all are united in the most strenuous efforts to be free, they hope and expect that their representatives will cheerfully concur in removing every species of religious as well as civil bondage. That every argument for civil liberty gains additional strength when applied to liberty in the concerns of religion, and that there is no argument in favor of establishing the Christian religion but what may be pleaded for establishing the tenets of Mahomet by those who believe the Alcoran; or, if this be not true, it is at least impossible for the magistrate to adjudge the right of preference among the various sects which profess the Christian faith, without erecting a chair of infallibility, which would lead us back to the Church of Rome. That they beg leave farther to represent that religious establishments are highly injurious to the temporal interests of any community, without insisting upon the ambition and the arbitrary practices of those who are favored by government, or the intriguing, seditious spirit which is commonly excited by this, as well as every other kind of oppression, such establishments greatly retard population, and consequently the progress of arts, sciences, and manufactures. Witness the rapid growth and improvements of the northern provinces, compared with this. That no one can deny the more early settlement and the many superior advantages of our country would have invited multitudes of artificers, mechanics, and other useful members of society to fix their habitation among us, who have either remained in the place of their nativity or preferred worse civil government and a more barren field, where they might enjoy the right of conscience more fully than they had a prospect of doing in this; from which they infer that Virginia might now have been the capital of America, and a match for the British arms without depending upon others for the necessaries of war, had it not been prevented by her religious establishment. Neither can it be made to appear that the gospel needs any such civil aid; they rather conceive that, when our blessed Saviour declares his kingdom is not of this world, he renounces all dependence upon State power, and, as his weapons are spiritual, and were only designed to have influence on the judgment and heart of man, they are persuaded that, if mankind were left in the quiet possession of their unalienable religious privileges, Christianity, as in the days of the apostles, would continue to prevail and flourish in the greatest purity by its own native excellence, and under the all-disposing providence of God. That they would also humbly represent that the only proper objects of civil government are the happiness and protection of men in the present state of existence, the security of the life, liberty, and property of the citizens, and to restrain the vicious and encourage the virtuous by wholesome laws, equally extending to every individual; but that the duty they owe their Creator, and the manner of discharging it, can only be directed by reason and conviction, and is nowhere cognizable but at the tribunal of the Universal Judge; and that, therefore, they ask no ecclasiastical establishments for themselves, neither can they approve of them when granted to others, and earnestly entreating that all laws now in force in this Commonwealth which countenance religious dominations may be speedily repealed, that all and every religious sect may be protected in the full exercise of their several modes of worship, and exempted from the payment of all taxes for the support of any church whatever, farther than what may be agreeable to their own private choice, or voluntary obligation."

Madison's Remonstrance

The immediate result of this petition and many similar protests was the adoption of an act which went far to meet the objections of the dissenters. At the October 1776 sitting of the General Assembly a statute was adopted (9 Hening 164) in which it was provided that "all dissenters, of whatever denomination, from the said church [Episcopal], shall . . . be totally free and exempt from all levies, taxes and impositions whatever, towards supporting and maintaining the said church, as it now is or hereafter may be established." The statute went on, however, to provide that "there shall in all time coming be saved and reserved to the use of the church by law established the several tracts of glebe land already purchased" and other properties of the Episcopal churches. The legislature postponed to later solution the question whether a "general assessment" for the support of ministers of all denominations, to be applied in accordance with the religious preference of the individual taxpayer, should be adopted. During the course of the next few years there was much discussion of the issue concerning the "general assessment," with the Presbyterians ultimately joining the Episcopalians in the effort to secure such an assessment, and Patrick Henry also supporting that cause. The opposition was led by James Madison and energetically supported by the

Baptists. A bill was at length drawn up in 1785 making provision for a general assessment for the support of ministers. Its opponents succeeded, however, in having its adoption postponed until the people had been given the opportunity to consider it. In the effort to arouse opposition to the bill the most effective piece of writing was Madison's Remonstrance. That Remonstrance, which was successful, contained the following passages!

"To the Honorable the General Assembly of the Commonwealth of Virginia:

"We, the subscribers, citizens of the said Commonwealth, having taken into serious consideration a bill, printed by order of the last session of General Assembly, entitled "A bill establishing a provision for teachers of the Christian religion"; and conceiving that the same, if finally armed with the sanctions of a law, will be a dangerous abuse of power, are bound, as faithful members of a free State, to remonstrate against it, and to declare the reasons by which we are determined. We remonstrate against the said bill:

"Because we hold it for fundamental and unalienable truth, "that religion, or the duty which we owe to the Creator, and the manner of discharging it, can be directed only by reason and conviction, not by force or violence." The religion, then, of every man must be left to the conviction and conscience of every man; and it is the right of every man to exercise it as these may dictate. This right is, in its nature, an unalienable right. It is unalienable, because the opinions of men depending only on the evidence contemplated by their own minds, cannot follow the dictates of other men. It is unalienable, also, because what is here a right towards man is a duty towards the Creator. It is the duty of every man to render to the Creator such homage, and such only, as he believes to be acceptable to him. This duty is precedent, both in order of time and in degree of obligation, to the claims of civil society. Before any man can be considered as a member of civil society he must be considered as a subject of the Governor of the Universe. And if a member of civil society who enters into any subordinate association must always do it with a reservation of his duty to the general authority, much more must every man who becomes a member of any particular civil socity do it with a saving of his allegiance to the Universal Sovereign. We maintain, therefore, that in matters of religion, no man's right is abridged by the institution of civil society, and that religion is wholly exempt from its cognizance. True it is that no other rule exists by which any question which may divide a society can be ultimately determined but by the will of the majority. But it is also true that the majority may trespass on the rights of the minority.

"Because, if religion be exempt from the authority of the society at large, still less can it be subject to that of the legislative body. The latter are but the creatures and vicegerents of the former. Their jurisdiction is both derivitive and limited. It is limited with regard to the coordinate departments; more necessarily is it limited with regard to the constituents. The preservation of a free government requires not merely that the metes and bounds which separate each department of power be invariably maintained, but more especially that neither of them be suffered to overleap the great barrier which defends the rights of the people. The rulers who are guilty of such encroachment exceed the commission from which they derive their authority, and are tryants. The people who submit to it are governed by laws made neither by themselves nor by an authority derived from them, and are slaves.

"Because it is proper to take alarm at the first experiment on our liberties. We behold this prudent jealousy to be the first duty of citizens and one of the noblest characteristics of the late revolution. The freemen of America did not wait until usurped power had strengthened itself by exercise and entangled the question in precedents. They saw all the consequences in the principle, and they avoided the consequences by denying the principle. We revere this lesson too much soon to forget it. Who does not see that the same authority which can establish Christianity in exclusion of all other religions may establish with the same ease any particular sect of Christians in exclusion of all other sects? That the same authority which can force a citizen to contribute three pence only of his property for the support of any one establishment may force him to conform to any other establishment in all cases whatsoever. . ."

Act for Establishing Religious Freedom

Not only was the adoption of the general assessment act blocked by the remonstrations of Madison and the Baptists, but affirmative action was taken in 1785 towards giving fuller effect to the Declaration of Rights. That action consisted in the adoption of Jefferson's famous Act for Establishing Religious Freedom. (12 Hening 84.)

"I. WHEREAS, Almighty God hath created the mind free; that all attempts to influence it by temporal punishments or burthens, or by civil incapacitations, tend only to beget habits of hypocrisy and meanness, and are a departure from the plan of the Holy author of our religion, who being Lord both of body and mind, yet chose not to propagate it by coercions on either, as was in his Almighty power to do; that the impious presumption of legislators and rulers, civil as well as ecclesiastical, who being themselves but fallible and uninspired men, have assumed dominion over the faith of others, setting up their own opinions and modes of thinking as the only true and infallible, and as such endeavouring to impose them on others, hath established and maintained false religions over the greatest part of the world, and through all time; that to compel a man to furnish contributions of money for the propagation of opinions which he disbelieves, is sinful and tyrannical; that even the forcing him to support this or that teacher of his own religious persuasion, is depriving him of the comfortable liberty of giving his contributions to the particular pastor, whose morals who would make his pattern, and whose powers he feels most persuasive to righteousness, and is withdrawing from the ministry those temporary rewards, which proceeding from an approbation of their personal conduct, are an additional incitement to earnest and unremitting labours for the instruction of mankind; that our civil rights have no dependence on our religious opinions, any more than our opinions in physics or geometry; that therefore the proscribing any citizen as unworthy the public confidence by laying upon him an incapacity of being called to offices of trust and emolument, unless he profes or renounce this or that religious opinion, is depriving him injuriously of those privileges and advantages to which in common with his fellow-citizens he has a natural right; that it tends only to corrupt the principles of that religion it is meant to encourage, by bribing with a monopoly of wordly honours and emoluments, those who will externally profess and conform to it; that though indeed these are criminal who do not withstand such temptation, yet neither are those innocent who lay the bait in their way; that to suffer the civil magistrate to intrude his powers into the field of opinion, and to restrain the profession or propagation of principles on supposition of their ill tendency, is a dangerous fallacy, which at once destroys all religious liberty, because he being of course judge of that tendency will make his opinions the rule of judgment, and approve or condemn the sentiments of others only as they shall square with or differ from his own; that it is time enough for the rightful purposes of civil government, for its officers to interfere when principles break out into overt acts against peace and good order; and finally, that truth is great and will prevail if left to herself, that she is the proper and sufficient antagonist to error, and has nothing to fear from the conflict, unless by human interposition disarmed of her natural weapons, free argument and debate, errors ceasing to be dangerous when it is permitted freely to contradict them:

"II. Be it enacted by the General Assembly, That no man shall be compelled to frequent or support any religious worship, place, or ministry whatsoever, nor shall be enforced, restrained, molested, or burthened in his body or goods, nor shall otherwise suffer on account of his religious opinions or belief; but that all men shall be free to profess, and by argument to maintain, their opinion in matters of religion, and that the same shall in no wise diminish, enlarge, or affect their civil capacities.

"III. And though we well know that this assembly elected by the people for the ordinary purposes of legislation only, have no power to restrain the acts of succeeding assemblies, constituted with powers equal to our own, and that therefore to declare this act to be irrevocable would be of no effect in law; yet we are free to declare, and do declare, that the rights hereby asserted are of the natural rights of mankind, and that if any act shall be hereafter passed to repeal the present, or to narrow its operation, such act will be an infringement of natural right."

Jefferson on Christianity and the Common Law

Jefferson's opinions concerning the relationship between church and state have become of such large moment in recent constitutional decisions that his early, but as yet undated, memorandum concerning the maxim of the English courts that Christianity is part of the common law has considerable importance.

Thomas Jefferson, Inquiry Whether Christianity is a Part of the Common Law (1768?) 1 Jefferson's Reports 137 (1829)

In Quare impedit, in C. B. 34 H. 6. fo. 38, the defendant, Bishop of Lincoln, pleads that the church of the plaintif became void by the death of the imcumbent; that the plaintiff and I. S. each pretending a right, presented two several clerks that the church being thus rendered litigious, he was not obliged, by the ecclasiastical law, to admit either until an inquisition de jure patronatus in the ecclesiastical court; that, by the same law, this inquisition was to be at the suit of either claimant, and was not ex officio to be instituted by the Bishop, and at his proper costs; that neither party had desired such an inquisition; that six months passed; whereon it belonged to him of right to present as on a lapse, which he had done. The plaintiff demurred. A question was, How far the ecclesiastical law was to be respected in this matter by the Common law court? And Prisot c. 5. (sic) in the course of his argument uses this expression, "a tels leis que ils de seint eglise ont en ancien scripture, covient a nous a donner credence; car ceo common ley sur quel touts manners leis sont fondus. Et auxy, Sir, nous sumus obliges de conustre lour ley de saint eglise; et semblablement ils sont obliges de conustre nostre ley, et, Sir, si poiteapperer or a nous que l'evesque ceo adjuger bon, our autrement nemy," &,. It does not appear what judgment was given. Y. B. ubi supra, 3 c. Fitzh. Abr. Qu. imp. 89. Bro. Abr. Qu. imp. 12. Finch mis-states this in the following manner: "to such laws of the church as have warrant in holy scripture, our law giveth credence;" and cites the above case, and the words of Prisot in the margin. Finch's law, B. 1. c. 3. published in 1613. Here we find "ancien scripture" converted into "holy scripture"; whereas it can only mean the antient written laws of the church. It cannot mean the scriptures, 1st.; Because the term antient scripture must then be understood as meaning the Old Testament in contra-distinction to the New, and to the exclusion of that; which would be absurd; and contrary to the wish of those who cite this passage to prove that the scriptures, or Christianity, is a part of the common law. 2nd. Because Prisot says, "ceo (est) Common ley sur quel touts manners leis sont fondes." Now it is true that the ecclesiastical law, so far as admitted in England, derives its authority from the common law. But it would not be true that the scriptures so derive their authority. 3rd. The whole case and argument shew, that the question was, How far the ecclesiastical law in general should be respected in a common law court? And in Bro's Abr. of this case, Littleton says "les juges del Common ley prenda conusans quid est lex ecclesiae vel admiralitatis et hujus modi." 4th. Because the particular part of the ecclesiastical law then in question, viz. the right of the patron to present to his advowson, was not founded on the law of God, but subject to the modification of the law-giver; and so could not introduce and such general position as Finch pretends. Yet Wingate (in 1658) thinks proper to erect this false quotation into a maxim of the common law, expressing it in the very words of Finch, but citing Prisot, Wing. Max. 3. Next comes Sheppard (in 1675) who states it in the same words of Finch, and quotes the Y. B. Finch and Wingate. 3 Shep. Abr. tit. "Religion". In the case of the King and Taylor, Sir Matthew Hale lays it down in these words; "Christianity is parcel of the laws of England." 1 Ventr. 293. 3 Keb. 607. But he quotes no authority. It was from this part of the supposed common law, that he derived his authority for burning witches. So strong was this doctrine become in 1728, by additions and repetitions from one another, that in the case of the King v. Woolston, the

the court would not suffer it to be debated, Whether to write against Christianity was punishable in the temporal courts, at common law? saying it had been so settled in Taylor's case, ante, 2 Stra, 834. Therefore Wood, in his Institute, lays it down, that all blasphemy and profaneness are offences by the common law, and cites Strange ubi supra. Wood. 409. And Blackstone (about 1763) repeats, in the words of Sir Matthew Hale, that "Christianity is part of the laws of England", citing Ventr. and Stra, ubi supra. 4 Bl. 59. Lord Mansfield qualified it a little, by saying, in the case of the Chamberlain of London v. Evans, 1767, that "the essential principles of revealed religion are part of the common law". But he cites no authority, and leaves us at our peril to find out what, in the opinion of the judge, and according to the measure of his foot or his faith, are those essential principles of revealed religion, obligatory on us as a part of the common law. Thus we find this string of authorities when, examined to the beginning, all hanging on the same hook; a perverted expression Prisot's; or on nothing. For they all quote Prisot, or one another, or nobody. Thus, Finch quotes Prisot; Wingate also; Sheppard quotes Prisot, Finch and Wingate; Hale cites nobody; the court, in Woolston's case, cite Hale; Wood cites Woolston's case; Blackstone that and Hale; and Lord Mansfield, like Hale, ventures it on his own authority. In the earlier ages of the law, as in the Year Books for instance, we do not expect much recurrence to authorities by the judges; because, in those days, there were few or none such made public. But in later times we take no judge's word for what the law is, further than he is warranted by the authorities he appeals to. His decision may bind the unfortunate individual who happens to be the particular subject of it; but it cannot alter the law. Although the common law be termed Lex non scripta, yet the same Hale tells us, "when I call those parts of our laws Leges non Scriptae, I do not mean as if all those laws were only oral, or communicated from the former ages to the latter merely, by word. For all these laws have their several monuments in writing, whereby they are transferred from one age to another, and without which they would soon lose all kind of certainty. They are for the most part extant in records of pleas, proceedings and judgments, in books of reports, and judicial decisions, in tractates of learned men's arguments and opinions, preserved from antient times, and still extant in writing". Hale's Com. Law, 22. Authorities for what is common law, may, therefore, be as well cited as for any part of the lex scripta. And there is no better instance of the necessity of holding the judges and writers to a declaration of their authorities, than the present, where we detect them endeavoring to make law where they found none, and to submit us, at one stroke to a whole system, no particle of which, has its foundation in the common law, or has received the "esto" of the legislator. For we know that the common law is that system of law which was introduced by the Saxons, on their settlement in England, and altered, from time to time, by proper legislative authority, from that, to the date of the Magna Charta, which terminates the period of the common law, or lex non scripta, and commences that of the statute law, or the fifth century; but Christianity was not introduced till the seventh century; the conversion of the first Christian King of the Heptarchy, having taken place about the year 598, and that of the last about 686. Here, then, was a space of two hundred years, during which the common law was in existence, and Christianity no part of it. If it ever, therefore, was adopted into the common law, it must have been between the introduction of Christianity and the date of the Magna Charta. But of the laws of this period, we have a tolerable collection, by Lambard and Wilkins; probably not perfect, but neither very defective; and if any one chooses to build a doctrine on any law of that period, supposed to have been lost, it is incumbent on him to prove it to have existed, and what were its contents. These were so far alterations of the common law, and became themselves a part of it; but none of these adopt Christianity as a part of the common law. If, therefore, from the settlement of the Saxons, to the introduction of Christianity among them, that system of religion could not be a part of the common law, because they were not yet Christians; and if, having their laws from that period to the close of the common law, we are able to find among them no such act of adoption; we may safely affirm (though contradicted by all the judges and writers on earth) that Christianity neither is, nor ever was, a part of the common law. Another cogent proof of this truth is drawn from the silence of certain writers on the common law. Bracton gives us a very complete and scientific treatise of the whole body of the common law. He wrote this about the close of the reign of Henry III, a very few years after the date of the Magna Charta. We consider this book as the more valuable, as it was written about the time which divides the common and statute law; and therefore gives us the former in its ultimate state. Bracton, too, was an ecclesiastic, and would certainly not have failed to inform us of the adoption of Christianity as a part of the common law, had any such adoption ever taken place. But no word of his, which intimates any thing like it, has ever been cited. Fleta and Britton, who wrote in the succeeding reign of E. I., are equally silent. So also is Glanvil, an earlier writer than any of them, to wit, temp. H. 2; but his subject, perhaps, might not have led him to mention it. It was reserved then for Finch, five hundred years after, in the time of Charles II., by a falsification of a phrase in the Year book, to open this new doctrine, and for his successors to join full-mouthed in the cry, and give to the fiction the sound of fact. Justice Fortescue Aland, who possessed more Saxon learning than all the judges and writers before mentioned put together, places this subject on more limited ground. Speaking of the laws of the Saxon Kings, he says, "the ten commandments were made part of their law, and consequently were once part of the law of England; so that to break any of the ten commandments, was then esteemed a breach of the common law of England; and why it is not so now, perhaps, it may be difficult to give a good reason." Pref. to Fortescue's Rep. xvii. The good readon is found in the denial of the fact.

Houared, in his Coutumes Anglo-Normandes, I. 87, notices the falsification of the laws of Alfred, by prefixing to them four chapters of the Jewish law, to wit, the 20th, 21st, 22nd and 23rd chapters of Exodus; to which he might have added the 15th of the Acts of the Apostles, v. 23 to 29, and precepts from other parts of the scripture. These he calls Hors d' oeuvre of some pious copyist. This awkward monkish fabrication, makes the preface to Alfred's genuine laws stand in the body of the work. And the very words of Alfred himself prove the fraud; for he declares in that preface, that he has collected these laws from those of Ina, of Offa, Aethelbert and his ancestors, saying nothing of any of them being taken from the scripture. It is still more certainly proved by the inconsistencies it occasions. For example, the Jewish legislator, Exodus, xxi. 12, 13, 14 (copies by the Pseudo Alfred sec. 13) makes murder, with the Jews, death. But Alfred himself, L1. xxvi. punishes it by a fine only, called a weregild, proportioned to the condition of the person killed. It is remarkable that Hume (Append. I. to his History) examining this article of the laws of Alfred, without perceiving the fraud, puzzles himself with accounting for the inconsistency it had introduced. To strike a pregnant woman, so that she die, is death by Exod. xxi. 22, 23, and Pseudo Alfred sec. 19, 20, if of a servant by his master, is freedom to the servant; in every other case, retaliation. But by Alfred L1. xi. a fixed indemnification is paid. Theft of an ox or a sheep, by the Jewish law xxii. Exod. 1, was repaid five fold for the ox, and four fold for the sheep; by the Pseudograph sec. 24, double for the ox, and four fold for the sheep. But by Alfred L1. xvi he who stole a cow and calf, was to repay the worth of the cow and 40s. for the calf. Goring by an ox, was the death of the ox, and the flesh not to be eaten; Exod. xxi. 28. Pseud. Alfr. sec. 21. By L1. Alfr. xxiv. the wounded person had the ox. This Pseudograph makes municipal laws of the ten commandments: sec. 1 - 10, regulate concubinage; sec. 12, makes it death to strike, or to curse father or mother; sec. 14, 15, gives an eye for an eye, tooth for tooth, hand for hand, foot for foot, burning for burning, wound for wound, stripe; sec. 19, sells the thief to repay his theft; sec. 24, obliges the fornicator to marry the woman he has lain with; sec. 29, forbids interest on money; sec. 28, 35, makes the laws of bailment and very different from what Lord Hold delivers in Coggs v. Bernard, and what Sir William Jones tells us they were; and punished witchcraft with death. sec. 30, which Sir Matthew Hale 1. P. C. ch. 33, declares was not a felony before the statl. 1. Jac. c. 12. It was under that statute, that he hung Rose Cullender, and Amy Duny, 16 Car. 2 (1662) on whose trial he declared, "that there were such creatures as witches, he made no doubt at all; for 1st. The scriptures had affirmed so much. 2nd. The wisdom of all nations had provided laws against such persons - and such hath been the judgment of this kingdom, as appears by the act of parliament which hath provided punishments proportionable to the quality of the offence." And we must certainly allow greater weight to this position "that it was no felony till James's statutes," deliberately laid down in his H. P. C., a work which he wrote to be printed and transcribed for the press in his lifetime, than to the hasty scriptum, that "at common law, witchcraft was punished with death as heresy by writ de heretico comburendo," in his methodical summary of the P. C. pa. 6; a work "not intended for the press, nor fitted for it and which he declared himself he had never read over since it was written." Preface. Unless we understand his meaning in that to be, that witchcraft could not be punished at common law as witchcraft, but as a heresy. In either sense, however, it is a denial of this pretended law of Alfred! Now all men of reading know that these pretended laws of homicide, concubinage, theft, retaliation, compulsory marriage, usury, bailment, and others which might have been cited from this Pseudograph, were never the laws of England, not even in Alfred's time; and of course, that it is a forgery. Yet, palpable as it must be to a lawyer, our judges have piously avoided lifting the veil under which it was shrouded. In truth, the alliance between church and state in England, has ever made their judges accomplices in the frauds of the clergy; and even bolder than they are; for instead of being contented with the surreptitious introduction of these four chapters of Exodus, they have taken the whole leap, and declared at once that the whole Bible and Testament, in a lump, make part of the common law of the land; the first judicial declaration of which was by this Sir Matthew Hale, and thus they incorporate into the English code, laws made for the Jews alone, and the precepts of the gospel, intended by their benovolent author as obligatory only in foro conscientiae; and they arm the whole with the coercions of municpal law. They do this, too, in a case where the question was, not at all, whether christianity was a part of the law of England, but simply how far the ecclesiastical law was to be respected by the common law courts of England, in the special case of a right of presentment. Thus identifying Christianity with the ecclesiastical law of England.

Th: Jefferson

Presbyterian Protest Against Incorporation of Churches

During the same time in which the probelm of general assessment was being discussed the Eposcopal churchmen filed in the legislature a bill in which they asked that the Protestant Episcopal Churches in each parish might be incorporated. The Hanover Presbytery of the Presbyterian Church protested this episcopal effort in the following memorial to the Legislature (James, supra, 231):

". . . We have understood that a comprehensive incorporating act has been and is at present in aggitation, whereby ministers of the gospel as such, of certain descriptions, shall have legal advantages which are not proposed to be extended to the people at large of any denomination. A proposition has been made by some gentlemen in the house of delegates, we are told, to extend the grace to us amongst others in our professional capacity. If this be so we are bound to acknowledge with gratitude our obligations to such gentlemen for their inclination to favor us with the sanction of public authority in the discharge of our duty. But as the scheme of the incorporating clergymen, independent of the religious communities to which they belong, is inconsistent with our ideas of propriety, we request the liberty of declining any such solitary honor should it be again proposed. To form clergymen into a district order in the community, and especially where it would be possible for them to have the principal direction of a considerable public estate by such incorporation, has a tendency to render them independent, at length, of the churches whose ministers they are; and this has been too often found by experience to produce ignorance, immorality and neglect of the duties of their station.

"Besides, if clergymen were to be erected by the State into a distinct political body, detached from the rest of the citizens, with the express design of "enabling them to direct spiritual matters," which we all possess without such formality, it would naturally tend to introduce the antiquated and absurd system in which government is owned in effect to be the fountain head of spiritual influences to the church. It would establish an immediate, a peculiar, and for that very reason, in our opinion, illicit connection between government and such as were thus distinguished. The Legislature in that case would be the head of the religious party, and its dependent members would be entitled in all decent reciprocity to a becoming paternal and fostering care. This we suppose would be given a preference, and creating a distinction between citizens equally good, on account of something entirely foreign from civil merit, which would be a source of endless jealousies, and inadmissible in a Republic or any other well directed government. The principle, too, which this system aims to establish is both false and dangerous to religion, and we take this opportunity to remonstrate and protest against it. The real ministers of true religion derive their authority to act in the duties of their profession from a higher source than any Legislature on earth, however respectable. Their office relates to the care of the soul, and preparing it for a future state of existence, and their administrations are, or ought to be, of a spiritual nature suited to this momentous concern. And it is plain from the very nature of the case that they should neither expect nor receive from government any commission or direction in this respect. We hope, therefore, that the house of delegates share so large a portion of that philosophic and liberal discernment which prevails in America at present, as to see this matter in its proper light - and that they will understand too well the nature of their duty, as the equal and common guardians of the chartered rights of all the citizens, to permit a connection of this kind we have just now mentioned to subsist between them and the spiritual instructors of any religious denomination in the State. The interference of government in religion cannot be indifferent to us, and as it will probably come under consideration at the present session of the Assembly, we request the attention of the honorable House to our sentiments upon this head."

Act Incorporating the Episcopal Church

This Presbyterian remonstrance had small success, however, for at the October session in 1784 the Assembly adopted a statute making the Episcopal Minister and vestry of every parish in the state a corporation. (11 Hening 532.) Not only was all property "of the late established church," including glebe lands, vested in these corporations, but control of church affairs was put in the minister and vestrymen. It was specifically provided, however, that the minister should have no veto over the vestry and that a majority vote of the whole should control. The colonial practice by which the vestry was a self-perpetuating body was terminated, and the Episcopal members of each parish were empowered to choose the vestrymen in triennial elections. In that respect, and in others as well, the act subjected the minister and vestrymen to a more democratic form of control than had been known in the Colonial period. The effort of the state to remove itself from theological responsibility was shown in the following paragraph of the statute:

"X. Be it enacted, That all former acts relating to the elections, qualifications, powers, and duties of vestrymen and churchwardens, all former acts for the support of the clergy, all former acts relating to the appointment or qualifications or duties of ministers, all acts enjoining the observance of any particular liturgy or form of worship, the use of any particular catechism or mode of faith, and the observance of fasts and festivals, and all former acts imposing penalties on clergymen for neglecting to keep registers, or neglecting to give notice of any observance, or publishing any law, and every other act or clauses of acts within the purview of this act, are hereby repealed; and all the vestries within this commonwealth, are, on the day before the Monday in next Easter week, declared to be dissolved; and the Protestant Episcopal Church within this commonwealth, are hereby authorized to regulate (in conventions of their church, to be held so often as, and where they think proper, and to consist of a deputation of two persons from each parish, whereof the minister shall always be one, if there be a minister in the parish, and the other person or persons shall be appointed by the vestries) all the religious concerns of that church, its doctrines, discipline, and worship, and to institute such rules and regulations as they may judge necessary for the good government thereof, and the same to revoke and alter at their pleasure. Forty persons so appointed, shall be a convention, and the first meeting may be at the call of any three ministers of the Protestant Episcopal Church. Provided, That no rules or regulations shall be instituted that shall be repugnant to the laws and constitution of this commonwealth, or by which a minister may be received into, or turned out of a parish, contrary to the consent of a majority of a vestry."

The Repealing Statute

Dissenting groups, particularly the Baptists, continued to protest that by the incorporation of Episcopal churches they had secured an unconstitutional preference in Virginia. The result of these insistent protests was that in 1786 the act of 1784 incorporating the Episcopal churches was repealed. In 1799 this repeal was confirmed by the legislature and a number of other less important statutes relating to religious matters were eliminated from the Virginia statutes. The preamble of the act of 1799 fully stated the reasons which prompted the legislature to effect the repeal.

"WHEREAS the constitution of the state of Virginia, hath pronounced the government of the King of England, to have been totally dissolved by the revolution: hath substituted in place of the civil government so dissolved, a new civil government; and hath in the bill of rights, excepted from the powers given to the substituted government, the power of reviving any species of ecclesiastical or church government, in lieu of that so dissolved, by referring the subject of religion to conscience: And whereas the several acts presently recited, so admit the church established under the regal government, to have continued so, subsequently to the constitution; have bestowed property upon that church; have asserted a legislative right to establish any religious sect; and have incorporated religious sects, all of which is inconsistent with the principles of the consistent with the principles of the constitution, and of religious freedom, and manifestly tends to the re-establishment of a national church:"

This legislative statement of policy was translated into broader constitutional terms in 1850, when the Virginia Constitution was amended to provide that the Legislature should never permit the incorporation of "any church or religious denomination." That clause still stands in the Constitutions of Virginia and of West Virginia.

Litigation was the inevitable result of the repeal of the act incorporating the Episcopal churches and of a supplementary statute of 1802 which provided that whenever glebe lands should become vacant through the death or removal of the Episcopal minister the Overseers of the Poor should dispose of them for the benefit of the poor. Chancellor Wythe in an unpublished opinion sustained the constitutionality of the repealing act and of the statute of 1802 and his decision was affirmed by an equally divided court in Turpin v. Locket, 6 Call 113 (1804). The Supreme Court of the United States, on the other hand, determined that the statutes were unconstitutional in Terrett v. Taylor, 9 Cranch 43 (1815). Virginia judges, however, did not accept the opinion of Mr. Justice Story as conclusive. One of the most important cases in which the constitutionality of the statutes was sustained was Selden v. Overseers of the Poor (1830). The opinion of Chancellor Tucker, which was affirmed in the Court of Appeals (11 Leigh 127), discussed at length the historical and legal status of churches and ministers in Virginia. The Chancellor's opinion is printed in full in 2 Tucker's Commentaries (1837), Appendix. Significant portions of that opinion follow.

"And here, in the first place, it is to be observed, that the Church of England, (and, a fortiori, the Episcopal church in Virginia) is not, and never was a common law corporation. The Church of England is not degraded to the rank of a corporation - it is one of the estates of the realm. A bishop, or a parson, is a corporation, says Mr. Blackstone, but the church is not. 1 Bla. Com. 472. . . Still less could the church, in Virginia, constitute a corporation, by common law. If we are to look upon it in any other light than as the creature of the legislature, we must regard it as a scion of the Church of England, which withered on the stem when the parent stock was uprooted by the revolution. In that aspect, it may perhaps, have been considered as forming a part of the diocese of the bishop of London, since all lands in Virginia were held of the crown, as of the manor of East Greenwich. Be this as it may, even that connection was severed by the revolution; and neither before nor since was the Episcopal church, in Virginia, a common law corporation.

"Nor were the Vestries of the parishes corporations by the common law. The vestries of parishes were, originally, only meetings of the ministers, church wardens, and chief men, and every parishoner who was assessed to, and paid church rates, was entitled to sit in the vestry. See Ld. Ray. 1388. 2 Stra. 624. 8 Mod. 52, 351. . .

"But though neither the church itself, nor its vestry and wardens, were corporations, yet bishops and parsons were such by the common law. As such, we are told, they never die. But whether they die or not, in their corporate character, still, upon the natural death of one parson, his place could only be supplied by the presentation, institution, and induction of another. And in like manner, the creation of a bishop, who is to supply a vacancy in the bishoprick, requires election, confirmation, consecration, and installation. 3 Salk. 72. See Also 2 Wils. 181.

"Admitting, then, that bishops and parsons were sole corporations in Virginia, as well as in England, the question recurs - 'How was the vacancy to be supplied, in Virginia, upon the death of the incumbent.'

"First: As to the Bishop. Before the revolution there was no bishop in Virginia; and there never was an arch-bishop among us. At the date of the Declaration of Independence we were without either of these high dignitaries of the church. Nor was the colony of Virginia ever a bishoprick. Bishopricks were by the creation of the crown, and all "the bishopricks in England are of the king's foundation, and he is the patron of them all." Co. Litt. 94. Every new bishop was thus, in fact, a new corporation sole, who could only be created by the crown, or by act of parliament. Nor is it matter of wonder, that this power was retained by the civil authority, instead of being left to the exercise of the church. For this corporation, a bishop becomes upon his installation not only invested with high ecclesiastical powers, but he is endowed with extensive revenues and temporalities, as well as spiritualities. He is, by force of his office of bishop, the ordinary, with jurisdiction over wills and testaments; and, as judge of the ecclesiastical court, has cognizance of matrimonial and other causes pertaining to ecclesiastical law. He has, moreover, the power of ordaining ministers, destined themselves to constitute an inferior corporation, with like immortality to that of the bishop himself, and with the right to hold, for life, the Glebe attached to their parish church, as and for their freehold, with the privilege of exacting tithes, and other ecclesiastical dues.

"With this view of the powers of a bishop when created, and the mode of his creation, we may venture to ask - 'How came Virginia by a bishop?' The answer is, 'She has none.' By courtesy, indeed, certain eminent divines, selected, and so styled by their brethren, are denominated bishops; but legally speaking we have none. Before the revolution, as I have already said, it is not pretended that Virginia had a bishop, or was a bishoprick. After the Declaration of Independence, if the power existed any where to erect this commonwealth into a bishoprick, and to create this new corporation, (a bishop,) with all his common law powers and attributes, that power must have been vested in the legislature alone. Could it have been in the archbishop of Canterbury, by whom, I presume, the late most estimable Mr. Madison was consecrated? or can it now be in the bishops of adjoining states, who have consecrated the present venerable Bishop Moore, and his most highly respected suffragan?

"To suppose such a power in the dignitaries of the Church of England, is at war with the whole principles of the revolution. That revolution broke the power of the British king. It dissolved forever his authority over this commonwealth. The political union of the two countries was at an end. Neither parliament nor king had any longer power here. And if the sceptre of the monarch cannot reach across the Atlantic, can the crozier of the archbishop? If its powers are wrested from the state, do they still remain vested in the church, which in England clings to it like a parasitical plant, thus forming in effect a part of that very government whose yoke has been thrown off? Such pretensions are too monstrous to find an advocate; and, accordingly, I do not understand it to be contended, even by the most zealous votary of the church, that those whose virtues and acquirements have elevated them to the dignity of bishops, in the Episcopal church here, are recognized as such by law. They are entitled, indeed to our highest respect as holy men; and to our veneration as pious ministers of the gospel; but like the bishops of the Methodist church, they are only bishops by courtesy. Their only power is in the voluntary submission of the members of their society; their only authority is derived from the regulation of conventions; (bodies equally unknown to the law with themselves;) their only influence is the powerful influence of religion, sustained and enforced by their virtues of piety; by their learning, their eloquence, and their zeal. To the law they are unknown, except that, like the humblest of the ministers of the most humble dissenting congregation, they are protected from insult and contumely when engaged in religious service. They are invested with the power of solemnizing marriages, and they are excluded from participation in the legislative power. In every other aspect they are, legally speaking, non entities, (or I would rather say, non existences,) without rights, without privileges, without duties, capacities, or incapacities.

"We come next to the case of the Parson. The first requisites to constitute a parson are, by common law, a parish and a church. Without these, there can be no parson; for a parson is "one who is in holy orders, who hath full possession of all the rights of a parochial church, and he is so called because he is persona ecclesia." Co. Litt. 300. 1 Bla. Com. 385. Now it is obvious, that, at the first settlement of Virginia, there were no parishes. Those which have been laid off derived their existence from legislative provision alone. Consequently, there could not have been any such thing as a parson in Virginia, until parishes were established by the legislature; and hence, it is obvious, that the ministers recognized by law, before the revolution, derived their existence, not from the common law, but immediately from the statute law.

"Parishes, however, having been at length established, and the ecclesiastical system of England forming part of the common law, it is probable that the appointment of ministers to particular parishes, might have constituted that sole corporation denominated 'a parson,' if all the other requisites of the common law could have united in him. Moreover, Glebes having been purchased, the possession of them, I presume, would have vested in the incumbent parson, and his successors; for, according to the common law, the corporation could never die. But in order to do all this, it was necessary that there should be a common law parson. A legislative minister would not constitute the sole corporation known to the common law as the parson of the parish. Let us then see what were the requisites to the creation of a common law parson.

"1. The first was holy orders; and, by the ecclesiastical law, a priest, (so the parson was called before induction,) could only be ordained by a bishop. For this doctrine, it is believed, the clergy of the Protestant Episcopal church, at this day, very strenously contend, though it is as strenuously opposed by the members of other congregations. It is not my purpose to enter upon the consideration of this litigated question, in any other than a legal point of view. In that aspect, there can be no doubt that ordination, by a bishop, was, at common law, required to constitute a priest, and a priest so ordained was necessary to constitute a parson.

"From this position it may not be improper, at once, to deduce these corollaries:

1. That, since the revolution, there cannot have been any priest ordained in Virginia, according to the common law. For as there is no bishop in Virginia - as English bishops cannot now ordain Virginia priests - and, as even legally speaking, there can be no priest except through Episcopal ordination, it is impossible there should have been a legally ordained priest in Virginia since the revolution.

2. This consequence will equally follow, whether the act of 1661, ch. 3, be considered as repealed or not. That act provided that 'no minister should be admitted to the church, except such as could produce a testimonial or ordination by a bishop in England!' For my own part, I do not hesitate to affirm that this act was repealed ipso facto by the revolution. It lashed us to the ecclesiastical polity of Great Britain. It made us, in so far a ramification of the church of England; of that church the members of which were all united in one common head - the king; who has been recognized, ever since the reformation, as the supreme head of the church. And when lashings were cut away, which bound us to the state, we were also cut loose forever from the church. When the head was cut off, I cannot conceive that this member, (the Episcopal church in Virginia) thus lopped from the parent stock, continued in existence, and still less that its union with the Church of England so far remained as to require or to justify ordination of their bishops. But be this as it may, the consequence is the same. If the law be repealed then there can be no legal ordination in Virginia, at this time, for want of a bishop. If the law be not repealed, then it may be safely affirmed that there is not, at this time, a legally ordained minister under it, in the state of Virginia; as I presume there is not now living a single minister who received his ordination from the hands of an English bishop. . .

"The second requisite to the creation of a parson is presentation. This belonged to the patron in England, but was given by the act of 1748, ch. 28, to the vestries, whose appointment was first directed in 1661. And as the vestries were elected by the parishoners, the parsons, instead of being presented by a patron, (as at common law,) was in effect mediately elected by the People, in direct hostility with common law principles.

"The third requisite to the creation of a parson, is institution; and this is, when the bishop invests the minister with the spiritual part of the benefice; 1 Burns Ecc. L. 148; saying to him, 'Instituo te rectorum talis ecclesiae cum cura animarum accipe curam tuam et meam.' Co. Litt. 344. This ceremony of institution might also have been performed by the bishop under the Episcopal seal.

"The last requisite to the creation of a parson was induction. It was this which made the parson complete incumbent, and fixed the freehold in him, 4 Rep. 79., Plow. 529, and this was performed by a mandate from the bishop to the archdeacon, who usually commissioned some clergyman to do it for him. 1 Bl. Com. 391. From this it is obvious that no power, foreign to this commonwealth, could have the power of creating them sole corporations, since such power could give them, indirectly, a power over landed estates of the country. . .

"This short recurrence to the antiquated law of this subject, will serve to shew that there never could have been, in Virginia, such a corporation sole, as a common law parson; and certainly there never can be now, without the aid of some legislative act. . .

"The truth is, the whole ecclesiastical system, in Virginia though connected before the revolution with the establishment of the Church of England, was evidently built up by the early practices of the settlers, or by legislative regulation. It is a statutory system, in contradistinction to a common law system. It was a public civil institution, ordained by the government for public purposes, instead of being a private ecclesiastical establishment; or, like the Church of England, a co-ordinate and co-equal estate of the realm.

"This view of the subject will enable us to form proper conceptions of the legal characters of preachers of the gospel. They were, before the revolution, statutory ministers, not common law parsons. By an early act, places of worship were ordered to be set apart, in each plantation, and ministers were directed to perform divine service to the people. This was among the first steps in the establishment of this Public Institution, for the purpose of inculcating the principles of genuine piety and morality among the people of each division of the colony. Then it was provided that ministers should be ordained by a bishop in England, and be presented by the vestry, and inducted by the Governor. The vestry were to be elected by the parishoners, and were empowered to purchase Glebes with public funds, to be raised by levy on all persons, of whatever denomination, in the parishes; and in like manner to erect houses, &c. for the comfortable accommodation of the minister of the parish. For his support a certain compensation, fixed by law, was to be raised by levy on all the parishioners; but no tithes were provided for him, for these seem to have been regarded as alien to the system.

"These positions, then I consider as established.

1. That the common law ecclesiastical system was, in effect, abolished; and a statutory system substituted by the colonial legislature.

2. That the system, such as it was, was a public institution, established for great public purposes, and sustained by public funds. . ."

Gallego's Executors v. Attorney General
Court of Appeals of Virginia 1832, 3 Leigh 450

Carr, J. This case involves several very important questions, which I shall consider in the order they were discussed at the bar.

First, then, as to the charities. The attorney general filed an information and bill, to have them applied to the objects for which they were bequeathed, and to enforce the execution of the trusts in respect to them; and the chancellor considering them good and valid, decreed them. It was contended in the argument that this degree was erroneous, because the devise and bequests were vague and indefinite, and therefore void. Let us examine this. The pecuniary legacies of 4000 dollars are, in effect, given to the roman catholic congregation, but for the building and support of a chapel; and the ground is given to trustees to permit the roman catholics to build a church on, for the use of themselves, and all persons of that religion, residing in Richmond. The bare statement seems sufficient to shew, that under the general rule, as applicable to ordinary legacies, these would be void. Who are the beneficiaries? the roman catholic congregation residing in Richmond. And who are they? Suppose you name them to-day: are those the same persons who constituted the congregation yesterday? or who will constitute it tomorrow? will none remove from, or come to Richmond, to reside? Will none be converted to or from the roman catholic religion? For it is to the roman catholic congregation for the time being, that the legacies are given. This however is a point which need not be pressed; for it was not pretended, that they could be supported, as legacies to individual persons. But it was strongly insisted, that as charitable legacies they were entitled to the aid of the protection of a court of equity; and the practice of the english courts, in similar cases, was referred to in proof of the position. The course of decisions in England was admitted on the other side, but it was contended, that they rested entirely on the statute of charitable uses, 43 Eliz. and did not at all belong to the ordinary powers of a court of equity. This was the only serious question. I certainly shall not discuss it; for I find this completely done to my hand, by chief justice Marshall, in the case of The Baptist Association v. Hart's ex'ors. (4 Wheat. 1 (1819)). The cases cited and examined, and the reasons given by him, prove, conclusively to my mind, that in England, charitable bequests, where no legal interest is vested, and which are too vague to be claimed by those for whom the beneficial interest was intended, cannot be established by a court of equity, either exercising its ordinary jurisdiction, or enforcing the prerogative of the king as parens patriae, independently of the statute 43 Elizabeth; and as that statute, if ever in force here, was repealed in 1792, I conclude that charitable bequests stand on the same footing with us, as all others, and will alike be sustained, or rejected, by courts of equity. I think the bill of the attorney general must be dismissed. . .

Tucker, P. It cannot be denied, that the principal question in this case, is one of the deepest interest and importance. It is worthy of the diligent research and great ability which have been devoted to the discussion of it, and will justify the enlarged view which may be found necessary in the decision: I mean the question as to the charities.

It is contended, on the one hand, that these several bequests are void and ineffectual, for uncertainty as to the beneficiaries who are to take under them: and, on the other, that they are good as bequests to charitable purposes, which the law will support, and which the court of chancery, upon the general principles of its equitable jurisdiction, will enforce at the instance of the attorney general.

There is no principle supposed to be more perfectly settled in reference to conveyances, than that every deed must have sufficient certainty as to the grantee who is to take under it. If there be such uncertainty as to the grantee, that it cannot be know distinctly who is to take by the grant, it is ipso facto void, for that uncertainty. This, it would seem to me, was not merely a principle of common law, but the dictate of common sense; and hence this defect is equally fatal, whoever may be the grantor; for it is a defect, not of power in him, but growing out of the utter impossibility of effectuating the grant, by reason of the undefined character of the grantee. The absurdity of such a grant cannot be better exposed, than by an attention to its operation in this very case, if it could be supposed to be valid. It is obvious that the bequest here, though for building a church, is a bequest to the roman catholic congregation in Richmond; and it is equally obvious that the testator designed no individual benefit to the members of that congregation: yet, as the society or congregation is not incorporated, it may well be asked, who are to be regarded as the beneficiaries entitled to the advantage of this bequest. Who can present himself as a claimant of this aid designed for the roman catholic religion? If membership of the congregation is to be the test of right, then the title will be in a continual state of flux. What belongs to A. today will by his removal from Richmond, or apostacy from the church, cease to be his tomorrow; whereas B. by removal to the city, or conversion to the church, might, by the converse of the principle, acquire tomorrow, a right which he has not today. Moreover, who would be the legally constituted triers of the fact of conversion or apostacy, whereby one man is to gain, or another is to lose, the interest in the property? Who, indeed, constitute the society? Whom does the law recognize, or the testator designate, as having the power to decide this essential question? Are all who have been baptised in the church, within the operation of the will? or will those only who are received as partakers of its most solemn ordinances? These, and a multitude of like difficulties, present themselves to the notion of any grant or conveyance to a religious society, or to trustees for their use. For, in the eye of the law, the intervention of a trustee does not remove a single difficulty. There is not more necessity for a properly defined grantee, in a deed, than for cestui que trust capable of taking, and so defined and pointed out, that the trust will not be void for uncertainty. In short, there cannot be a trust without a cestui que trust; and if it cannot be ascertained who the cestui que trust is, it is the same thing as if there were none.

These principles, it is confidently believed, are the general principles of the common law upon this subject. If there are exceptions to these principles, those exceptions may without doubt be shewn. A diligent search has led me to the conviction, that there was no case at common law, in which a bequest or a trust of this indefinite character, could be supported; and the learned counsel on both sides, have acknowledged, that they have been unable to discover any case anteriour to the statute 43 Elizabeth, in which the validity of such bequests or trusts has been distinctly recognized by the courts. It ought, therefore, perhaps, to suffice to rest the argument here; since if under the general principle the bequest would be void, it is incumbent upon those who claim to be protected by an exception, to establish that exception. Accordingly, it is contended, that gifts for charitable uses, furnish an exception: and when it is answered, that indefinite charities received their whole force and efficacy from the statute 43 Elizabeth, it is confidently replied that charities existed, and were recognized by law, anteriour to that statute; that the statute itself affords evidence of the fact; that it ought not to be regarded as an enabling statute, or as creative of an original power not before existing, but as affording new and additional facilities for the administration of charities of a particular description. It is indeed further contended, that, by the common law, the king, as parens patriae, had the teneral superintendence of charities, which he exercised by the keeper of his conscience the lord chancellor; that, whenever it was necessary, the attorney general, at the relation of some informant, field an information in the court of chancery, to have the charity established; that the exercise of this jurisdiction by that court, was by virtue of its general judicial functions, and of its extraordinary equitable jurisdiction, which has been transferred to the courts of equity in Virginia; that this authority, of the king, as parens patriae, is inherent in all governments, and therefore vested in this; that it embraces the protection of infants, lunatics and idiots, and the execution of charities, and that this inherent authority is devolved upon the courts of chancery in Virginia, the nature of whose jurisdiction and powers are peculiarly adapted to its judicious and faithful exercise. In this general, and I own, very imperfect view of the outlines of the argument for the charities, it is sufficiently obvious that there are many grave and important questions involved. A hasty review of some of them, however, must suffice here. ...

Upon the whole, I am well satisfied, that the whole of the doctrine of the english courts in reference to indefinite charities, springs from the statute of 43 Elizabeth, which is not in force in Virginia. Whether that statute ever was in force here, has been made a question in the cause. I incline to think it may have been, at least according to the construction which was given to it, and which considered it not as merely constituting a commission for inquiring into breaches of charitable trusts, but as greatly enlarging, if not as opening an entirely new field for the exercise of benevòlence. Though local in its provisions in some respects, it was general in its operation in others. If it ever was in force, however, it was repealed in the year 1792, in the general repeal of english statutes. That repeal was no rash or unadvised act. By an act of the session of 1789, ch. 9, followed by the act of 1790, ch. 20, a commission, consisting of six gentlemen of the most distinguished acquirements, was appointed, whose duty was, among other things, "to prepare bills upon the subject of such english statutes, if any there were, which were suited to this commonwealth, and had not been enacted in the form of Virginia laws." The committee of revisors proceeded to the discharge of the duty confided to it, and the result was the act of 1792, by which all english statutes then in force, were declared to be repealed; the legislature reciting that, at that session, it had specially enacted such of them as appeared worthy of adoption. The repeal of this statute must, therefore, be looked upon as an advised act of legislation, and in the same light as if it had been specially repealed by its title.

I have already taken occasion to remark, that, if there were any recognized charities of an indefinite character at common law, the broad language of the statute of Elizabeth comprehended them. In so far as it did comprehend them, it reduced only to the form of a statute, what was law before the statute; and our legislature, in repealing it, must be regarded as having repealed not its mere naked words, but the principle which they involved. Although, therefore, it should be admitted that certain indefinite charities were recognized at common law yet as the statute also comprehended them, and was itself repealed, the common law was repealed eodem flatu with the statute. In this aspect of the case, it is unnecessary to decide whether, if an english statute prior to the 4 James I. which repealed the common law, be itself repealed, the common law is thereby revived; notwithstanding the provision 1 Rev. Code, ch. 41 §2. and notwithstanding the common law principle so repealed, was not at the settlement of the colony, nor ever since the law of Virginia.

If I have been correct in this course of argument, there can be no pretense for the enforcing of the charities under this will of Mr. Gallego, as they were void at common law, and are not entitled to the protection of the statute of the 43 Elizabeth. Be this as it may, I must have argued to little purpose, and chief justice Marshall must for once have been also singularly unfortunate, if what has been said has not at least shown, that it is a matter of very serious doubt, whether the power to enforce charities ever did exist independent of the statute. If it be a matter even of doubt, to what conclusion must we come? I am deliberately of opinion, that in that case, a just respect to the policy of the legislature, in relation to religious charities especially; a prudent caution on our part, in assuming doubtful powers; a due sense of the infinite difficulty and embarrassment, which must attend the search after the common law doctrines anterious to the statute of Elizabeth; and a just view of the danger of reviving those obsolete doctrines; - must determine us to leave the subject to the wisdom of the legislature itself. A few remarks on these topics, will close this part of my opinion.

No man at all acquainted with the course of legislation in Virginia, can doubt, for a moment, the decided hostility of the legislative power to religious incorporations. Its jealousy of the possible interference of religious establishments in matters of government, if they were permitted to accumulate large possessions, as the church has been prone to do elsewhere, is doubtless at the bottom of this feeling. The legislature knows, as was remarked by the counsel, that wealth is power. Hence, the provision in the bill of rights; hence, the solemn protest of the act on the subject of religious freedom; hence, the repeal of the act incorporating th episcopal church and of that other act which invested the trustees appoint by religious societies with power to manage their property; hence too, in part, the law for the sale of the glebe lands: hence the tenacity with whicl applications for permission to take property in a corporate character (even the necessary ground for churches and graveyards) have been refused. The legislature seems to have been fearful, that the grant of any privilege, however trivial, might serve but as an entering wedge to greate demands. Nor did this apprehension of the dangers of ecclesiastical establishments, spring up for the first time with our republican institutions. The history of ages had attested the proneness of such establishments to vast accumulations of property, and the statute book of England is loaded with statutes of mortmain, which were rendered necessary by the rapacity of the clergy, at least in the early periods of the church. So long as there have been church establishments, with power to receive and accumulate property, so long has the tendency to such accumulation been manifested distinctly. The history of the papal see, and of the religious houses under its dominion, is but a history of the cupidity of monks and devotees, veiled under the sacred garb of our holy religion. The vast domains of the clergy acquired by the catholic establishment of France, are known to us all. From the fatal source, among others, sprung a revolution, which deluged the fairest country in Europe in blood, and, in its horrible progress, spread desolation over adjoining states, and shook the civilized world to its centre. And in protestant England, fenced around as it has been with mortmain acts, we see a church establishment possessed of overgrown wealth and power, less devoted to the cause of genuine religion, than to pamper the luxury and indolence of the high dignitaries of the church. With these examples before our eyes, it is not wonderful that our statesmen have been cautious. They have been wise in their caution. The evil has not sprung from particular creeds, or the pecularities of a confession of faith. It grows out of the very nature of the thing. The church, if made capable to take, while it is continually acquiring, from the liberality of the pious, or the fears of the timid, or the credulity of the ignorant, never can part with any thing; and thus, like those sustaining powers in mechanics, which retain whatever they once have gained, it advances with a step that never retrogrades. The natural cupidity of the human heart, is watched by the devotee himself, with the less jealousy in his pursuit after acquisitions for the church, since he believes it to be purified from the dress of selfishness, and sanctified by the holy object of his ambition. Thus it is, that however humble in its beginning, accumulation is the natural result of the power vested in any religious society to acquire property. The same influence which enables it to gain from the state its first insignificant privileges, will secure to it, from time to time, new though apparently inconsiderable accessions; until at last the power will be acquired which legislative jealousy has apprehended. Property, indeed, it need not ask of the legislature. The power to take and accumulate, alone, is necessary: all time has shewn, that the influence of feelings of devotion will do the rest. I speak of those feelings which exist without any undue influence from the pastor of the society. But, if we go farther, and suppose it possible, that those abuses which once have existed, may exist again, the progress will be more rapid, though not more certain. "What (says the accomplished sir Samuel Romilly) is the authority of a guardian, or even of a parent, compared with the power of religious impressions under the ascendancy of a spiritual adviser, with such an engine to work upon the passions; to inspire (as the object may be best promoted) despair or confidence; to alarm the conscience by the horrors of eternal misery, or support the drooping spirits, by unfolding the prospect of happiness which is never to end."

Such, I conceive, are the general grounds, upon which rests the legislative policy, in relation to the power of acquiring and holding property by religious societies. We have seen, too, a similar policy evinced as to charities generally, in striking at the root of them all, by the repeal of the statute of Elizabeth. It is not (to use the language of one of the counsel) that charity is banished from Virginia. Its benign and salutary influence may warm and animate every heart, and lead to a generous munificence, as the daily habit of our lives, without exposing the state to the evils which have always flowed from what are called conveyances in mortmain. It is not necessary here to detail those evils. But it is relevant to observe, that conveyances in mortmain to corporations, were not more calculated to produce a pernicious locking up of property, than charitable bequests of this indefinite character. A corporation may be dissolved, and the property may be again taken up into the general circulation, by reverting to the donor. But these charities never die. There is no means of putting an end to them in the lapse of ages; for according to this celebrated doctrine of cy pres, if the original object should fail, the attorney general and the master in chancery go to work to digest another scheme, cy pres the original intention of the donor. Such was the case with the charity to William & Mary college. Experience has justified these complaints, and accordingly about one hundred years ago, the parliament of G. Britain found itself compelled to pass the statute of 9 George 2. .. It is at this moment when the country whose laws we have adopted, has partly receded from the wretched policy of permitting the whole property of society to be swallowed up in the insatiable gulph of public charities, that we are called upon to reanimate the pernicious principle, which they now deprecate, and which with us has been sleeping in inaction, for nearly two centuries and an half. And this too, when we have put off the panoply of the mortmain acts, by the general repeal of them in 1792. It is said, indeed, that the legislature may pass the necessary laws for regulating these charitable gifts, and thus prevent the evils that might flow from the unlimited permission of them. But I think, under the existing doubts which hang around the subject, and after the lapse of centuries, during which the law respecting charities, if it ever existed here, has been silent and quiescent, it behoves the judiciary to leave to the legislature, the duty of waking it into life.

This leads me to remark, lastly, that the occasion calls for a prudent caution on the part of the judiciary in the assumption of this jurisdiction. We have already seen, that no cases are to be found, no guide is afforded, as to the course pursued by courts of equity in respect to charities anteriour to the statute of Elizabeth, if they ever took cognizance of them. But it is said that the king as parens patriae, from the earliest times had the power to superintend and enforce charities: that this power was exercised by him through the lord chancellor, the keeper of his conscience: that it was so exercised, not under a specially delegated authority, but by virtue of his general judicial functions or extraordinary jurisdiction in matters of equity: that this authority of the parens patriae is inherent in all governments, and therefore in this; and is developed upon the court of chancery here, whose jurisdiction is general over all matters in chancery, and is peculiarly adapted to the judicious administration of the law of charities. I shall content myself with referring to the conclusive argument of the chief justice, 4 Wheat. 47. for the position, that the jurisdiction of the chancellor of England over charities, is a branch of the prerogative, and not a part of the ordinary powers of the chancery court, in the exercise of its equitable jurisdiction. The authorities to which he refers are entirely satisfactory upon the point. If this be so, it is sufficiently obvious, that the act which established the court of chancery in Virginia, cannot have transferred to that court this branch of the prerogative. The powers conferred by that act are judicial in their character, and not such as belonged to the chancellor of England, as the keeper of the conscience of the king, as representing his person, and administering, as his agent, his prerogatives and duties. Admitting then, as we well may, the superintending power of the crown, as parens patriae, over charities, and admitting that this power is inherent in the sovereignty, I will ask upon what ground shall we arrogate it to the judicial branch of the government? That there inheres in every sovereign power, a right and a duty to protect those who have no other protector, as infants and lunatics, cannot be denied: and that there is an inherent power also in the sovereign, to declare that vague and indefinite charities shall be administered, if, in its wisdom, it shall so decree, is equally undeniable. But it remains to be proved, that this power is judicial, and not legislative: it remains to be proved, that the flowers of royal prerogative, which have fallen from the crown of England, have devolved upon the chancellors here. In this government of prescribed and limited powers, no public functionary, no organ of the sovereign power, no department, can assume a power which is not to be found in the law or the constitution. They constitute the commission under which alone authority can be duly exercised. It was in this view, very truly said, that this branch of the royal prerogative, if it had not been withered by the repeal of the statute, would have developed upon the legislature. That body is the parens patriae, under our system, and it would have remained for it to point out the organ which should administer its important function. My own opinion is, decidedly, that it does not now belong to the judiciary, even if it has existence any where in relation to charities. They must first be established, to call this guardian power into existence; and I have endeavored to shew, that there is nothing, now recognized by law in relation to charities, upon which it can operate; for definite charities are but trusts which equity will execute by virtue of its ordinary jurisdiction, and with which, even in England, the attorney general cannot interfere; and indefinite charities are not recognized by law, and cannot therefore be enforced, either with or without his aid.

The result of this view of the subject is, that the interlocutory order of the chancellor must be reversed, and the bill of the attorney general dismissed...

2. MASSACHUSETTS

During the course of the 18th century, Massachusetts was concerned with problems essentially similar to those which had bothered the Virginians on the eve of the Revolution. Of course the fundamental difference was that in Virginia the Episcopal Church was an established church, whereas in Massachusetts the state's preference was for the Congregational churches. Throughout most of the Province of Massachusetts Bay all were compelled to make payments for the support of the parish minister; since all parishes were predominantly congregational in faith, this meant that public aid for the Congregational churches was in fact provided. In Boston, however, the ministry got its entire support from the voluntary contributions of the members of the several churches. The first significant change in law with respect to these problems occurred in 1727 when the legislature adopted the so-called "Five-Mile Act," providing that taxes collected from Episcopalians who attended an Episcopal church within five miles of their place of residence should be applied to the support of their Episcopal minister. (2 Province Laws 459.) During the course of the century the benefits of this statute were extended to other denominations. The Quakers, who opposed entirely the payment of ministerial salaries, were granted a total exemption from ministerial taxes.

When Massachusetts adopted her first Constitution in 1780, she dealt with problems of religious freedom and the relations of church and state in the opening sections of the first article in the Declaration of Rights. Those provisions did not, as had been the case in Virginia, bring about a basic change in policy; they seem to have done little more than codify accepted practices and principles. The provisions in question were as follows:

Declaration of Rights

"I. All men are born free and equal, and have certain, natural, essential, and unalienable rights; among which may be reckoned the right of enjoying and defending their lives and liberties; that of acquiring, possessing, and protecting property; in fine, that of seeking and obtaining their safety and happiness.

"II. It is the right as well as the duty of all men in society, publicly, and at stated seasons, to worship the SUPREME BEING, the great creator and preserver of the universe. And no subject shall be hurt, molested, or restrained, in his person, liberty or estate, for worshipping GOD in the manner and season most agreeable to the dictates of his own conscience; or for his religious profession or sentiments; provided he doth not disturb the public peace, or obstruct others in their religious worship.

"III. As the happiness of a people, and the good order and preservation of civil government, essentially depend upon piety, religion and morality; and as these cannot be generally diffused through a community, but by the institution of the public worship of GOD, and of public instructions in piety, religion and morality: Therefore, to promote their happiness, and to secure the good order and preservation of their government, the people of this Commonwealth have a right to invest their Legislature with power to authorize and require, and the Legislature shall, from time to time, authorize and require, the several towns, parishes, precincts, and other bodies politic, or religious societies, to make suitable provision, at their own expence, for the institution of the public worship of GOD, and for the support and maintenance of public Protestant teachers of piety, religion and morality, in all cases where such provision shall not be made voluntarily.

"And the people of this Commonwealth have also a right to, and do, invest their Legislature with authority to enjoin upon all the subjects an attendance upon the instructions of the public teachers aforesaid, at stated times and seasons, if there be any on whose instructions they can conscientiously and conveniently attend.

"Provided notwithstanding, That the several towns, parishes, precincts, and other bodies-politic, or religious societies, shall, at all times, have the exclusive right of electing their public teachers, and of contracting with them for their support and maintenance.

"And all monies paid by the subject to the support of public worship, and of the public teachers aforesaid, shall, if he require it, be uniformly applied to the support of the public teacher or teachers of his own religious sect or denomination, provided there be any on whose instructions he attends; otherwise it may be paid towards the support of the teacher or teachers of the parish or precinct in which the said monies are raised.

"And every denomination of Christians, demeaning themselves peaceably, and as good subjects of the Commonwealth, shall be equally under the protection of the law: And no subordination of any one sect or denomination to another shall ever be established by law."

Although the provisions of the Declaration of Rights seemed on their face, to put all denominations on an approximately even footing, the interpretation which the courts gave to those provisions denied the equality which the Declaration had promised. The basis and scope of the denial were indicated in the Barnes case. The legislative effort to create equality, and the judicial response to that effort, are shown in the Adams case.

Barnes v. First Parish
Supreme Judicial Court of Massachusetts, 1810
6 Mass. 401

This was an action of assumpsit, brought to recover of the defendants a sum of money, which had been assessed, by the proper officers of the said parish, on the polls and estates of James Buxton and Amos Knight, as their ministerial taxes for the years 1798 to 1805, inclusive, for the support of the Congregational minister settled in said parish; the said Buxton and Knight having been, during said years, inhabitants of said parish; which sum the plaintiff demands, that it may be applied to his support and maintenance, as the Protestant teacher of a religious society in said town of Falmouth, alleged to be of different denomination from that of the Congregational society composing said parish, viz., Universalists; said Buxton and Knight being also alleged to have belonged to the said society, whereof the plaintiff is alleged to be the teacher, as aforesaid.

Upon the trial of the cause, which was had upon the general issue, before Thatcher, J., October term 1897, the plaintiff's counsel having proved the payment to the defendants of the taxes demanded in the declaration, and a proper demand of them by the plaintiff before the date of the writ, offered to prove to the jury by witnesses, that the plaintiff was, and had been for several years, including the years before named, a public teacher, as aforesaid, of the society aforesaid, in said Falmouth, and was, about seven years previous to the trial, by the wish and consent of said society, placed and ordained over them as their teacher, (although the mode of ordination was not stated,) and so continued; although the said society has never been incorporated by any act of the legislature.

But the judge rejected the proof so offered as improper and inadmissible, inasmuch as such facts could only be proved by record; and accordingly no further proof was afterwards offered in the cause. And the judge instructed and directed the jury, that as the said society, over which the plaintiff was alleged to be ordained, was not a town, parish, precinct, or body politic, or religious society incorporated within the meaning of the constitution and laws of this commonwealth, the said action could not in law be maintained. The jury returned a verdict for the defendants, pursuant to the said direction. The opinion and direction aforesaid were excepted to by the counsel for the plaintiff; and the exceptions being allowed by the judge, the action stood over for the opinion of the whole Court thereon; and was argued at the May term, 1808, and again at the last May term, by Mellen for the plaintiff and Longfellow for the defendants. ..

PARSONS, C. J. The plaintiff claims to be a public teacher of piety, religion, and morality, within the third article of the declaration of rights prefixed to the constitution of this commonwealth, but of a sect of Christians different from the inhabitants of the first parish in Falmouth, and publicly instructing several of the said inhabitants, who are of the same sect with himself, who usually attend on his preaching, and who have directed their taxes, paid for supporting public worship in the parish, to be paid over for his support; and he has instituted this suit to recover those taxes of the parish.

Not pretending to be the public teacher of any incorporated religious society obliged by law to maintain a public teacher, to maintain the issue on his part, he offered evidence, that in fact he was the teacher of a voluntary society of Universalists, who usually attended on his instruction. This evidence was rejected by the judge, on the ground that no person could maintain this action but a Protestant teacher of piety, religion, and morality, of some incorporated religious society; and to this rejection the plaintiff excepts.

The legal effect of evidence of this kind, in cases of this nature, has been often a subject of discussion; and among judges there have been different opinions. The subject certainly requires a diligent examination, exempt, as far as possible, from the influence of any prepossessions, or preconceived opinions. For this purpose, we shall consider the motives which induced this people to introduce into the constitution a religious establishment, the nature of the establishment introduced, and the rights and privileges it secured to the people, and to their teachers. If these points shall be clearly and justly explaine, it will then be easy to infer the principles by which the present action must be decided.

The object of a free civil government is the promotion and security of the happiness of the citizens. These effects cannot be produced, but by the knowledge and practice of our moral duties, which comprehend all the social and civil obligations of man to man, and of the citizen to the state. If the civil magistrate in any state could procure by his regulations a uniform practice of these duties, the government of that state would be perfect.

To obtain that perfection, it is not enough for the magistrate to define the rights of the several citizens, as they are related to life, liberty, property, and reputation, and to punish those by whom they may be invaded. Wise laws, made to this end, and faithfully executed, may leave the people strangers to many of the enjoyments of civil and social life, without which their happiness will be extremely imperfect. Human laws cannot oblige to the performance of the duties of imperfect obligation; as the duties of charity and hospitality, benevolence and good neighborhood; as the duties resulting from the relation of husband and wife, parent and child; of man to man, as children of a common parent; and of real patriotism, by influencing every citizen to love his country, and to obey all its laws. These are moral duties, flowing from the disposition of the heart, and not subject to the control of human legislation... Civil government, therefore, availing itself only of its own powers is extremely defective; and unless it could derive assistance from some superior power, whose laws extend to the temper and disposition of the human heart ... wretched indeed would be the state of man under a civil constitution of any form ...

When it is remembered that no man is compellable to attend on any religious instruction, which he conscientiously disapproves, and that he is absolutely protected in the most perfect freedom of conscience in his religious opinions and worship, the first objection (that the constitution sanctions persecution) seems to mistake a man's conscience for his money and to deny the state a right of levying and appropriating the money of the citizens, at the will of the legislature, in which they all are represented. But as every citizen derives the security of his property, and the fruits of his industry, from the power of the state, so, as the price of this protection, he is bound to contribute, in common with his fellow-citizens, for the public use, so much of his property, and for such public uses, as the state shall direct. And if any individual can lawfully withhold his contribution, because he dislikes the appropriation, the authority of the state to levy taxes would be annihilated; and without money it would soon cease to have any authority. But all moneys raised and appropriated for public uses, by any corporation, pursuant to powers derived from the state, are raised and appropriated substantially by the authority of the state, and the people, in their constitution, instead of devolving the support of public teachers on the corporations, by whom they should be elected, might have directed their support to be defrayed out of the public treasury, to be reimbursed by the levying and collection of state taxes. And against this mode of support, the objection of an individual, disapproving of the object of the public taxes, would have the same weight it can have against the mode of public support through the medium of corporate taxation. In either case, it can have no weight to maintain a charge of persecution for conscience's sake. The great error lies in not distinguishing between liberty of conscience in religious opinions and worship, and the right of appropriating money by the state. The former is an unalienable right; the latter is surrendered to the state, as the price of protection.

The second objection is, that it is intolerant to compel a man to pay for religious instruction, from which, as he does not hear it, he can derive no benefit. This objection is founded wholly in mistake. The object of public religious instruction is to teach, and to enforce by suitable arguments, the practice of a system of correct morals among the people, and to form and cultivate reasonable and just habits and manners; by which every man's person and property are protected from outrage, and his personal and social enjoyments promoted and multiplied. From these effects every man derives the most important benefits; and whether he be, or be not, an auditor of any public teacher, he receives more solid and permanent advantages from this public instruction, than the administration of justice in courts of law can give him. The like objection may be made by any man to the support of public schools, if he have no family who attend; and any man, who has no lawsuit, may object to the support of judges and jurors on the same ground; when, if there were no courts of law, he would unfortunately find that causes for lawsuits would sufficiently abound.

The last objection is founded upon the supposed antichristian conduct of the state, in availing itself of the precepts and maxims of Christianity, for the purposes of a more excellent civil government. It is admitted that the Founder of this religion did not intend to erect a temporal dominion, agreeably to the prejudices of his countrymen; but to reign in the hearts of men, by subduing their irregular appetites and propensities, and by moulding their passions to the noblest purposes. And it is one great excellence of his religion, that, not pretending to worldly pomp and power, it is calculated and accommodated to meliorate the conduct and condition of many under any form of civil government.

The objection goes further, and complains that Christianity is not left, for its promulgation and support, to the means designed by its Author, who requires not the assistance of man to effect his purposes and intentions. Our constitution certainly provides for the punishment of many breaches of the laws of Christianity, not for the purpose of propping up the Christian religion, but because those breaches are offences against the laws of the state; and it is a civil, as well as a religious duty of the magistrate, not to bear the sword in vain. But there are many precepts of Christianity, of which the violation cannot be punished by human laws; and as obedience to them is beneficial to civil society, the state has wisely taken care that they should be taught, and also enforced by explaining their moral and religious sanctions, as they cannot be enforced by temporal punishments. And from the genius and temper of this religion, and from the benevolent character of its Author, we must conclude that it is his intention that man should be benefited by it in his civil and political relations, as well as in his individual capacity. And it remains for the objector to prove, that the patronage of Christianity by the civil magistrate, induced by the tendency of its precepts to form good citizens, is not one of the means by which the knowledge of its doctrine was intended to be disseminated and preserved among the human race.

The last branch of the objection rests on the very correct position that the faith and precepts of the Christian religion are so interwoven, that they must be taught together; whence it is inferred that the state, by enjoining instruction in its precepts, interferes with its doctrines, and assumes a power not intrusted to any human authority. If the state claimed the absurd power of directing or controlling the faith of its citizens there might be some grounds of objection. But no such power is claimed. The authority derived from the constitution extends no further than to submit to the understandings of the people the evidence of truths deemed of public utility, leaving the weight of evidence, and the tendency of those truths, to the conscience of every man. [The argument if logically applied] would prohibit the state from providing for public instruction in many branches of human knowledge which naturally tend to defeat the arguments of infidelity ...

As Christianity has the promise not only of this, but of a future life, it cannot be denied that public instruction in piety, religion, and morality, by

Protestant teachers, may have a beneficial effect beyond the present state of existence. And the people are to be applauded, as well for their benevolence as for their wisdom, that, in selecting a religion whose precepts and sanctions might supply the defects in civil government, necessarily limited in its power, and supported only by temporal penalties, they adopted a religion founded in truth; which in its tendency will protect our property here, and may secure to us an inheritance in another and a better country ...

The last point for our consideration is, whether this establishment, according to the true intent and design of its provisions, will, or will not, enable the plaintiff to maintain his claim to the money he demands.

The objection against his claim is substantially this: that the constitution has not provided in any way for the legal support of any teacher of piety, religion, and morality, unless he be a public Protestant teacher of some incorporated religious society. It is admitted by the parties, that the plaintiff is a Protestant teacher of a voluntary society not incorporated, and which is under no legal obligation to elect or support a teacher; that he and his hearers are of a denomination of Christians different from that of the inhabitants of the first parish in Falmouth; and all other facts, necessary to support the action, may be presumed.

After a consideration of these facts, we are all of opinion that the constitution has not authorized any teacher to recover, by action at law, any money assessed pursuant to the third article of the declaration of rights, but a public Protestant teacher of some legally incorporated society; and that the objection must prevail. The societies, who may be enjoined to elect and support teachers of this description, are described as "towns, parishes, precincts, or other bodies politic, or religious societies" which last expression is merely explanatory of the words, "bodies politic," and confines them to bodies politic incorporated to act as religious societies. If we are to consider the words "religious societies" as descriptive of a class of societies not included in the words "bodies politic," the consequence would be, that all bodies politic, for whatever purposes incorporated, would be obliged to elect and maintain a teacher of religion - a consequence too absured to be admitted. Indeed, the words "religious societies" must, from the nature of the duty imposed on them, necessarily mean societies having corporate powers; because, without those powers, the duty cannot be legally performed, a voluntary association having no legal authority to assess money on all the members, or to compel payment, or to elect a teacher by a vote of the greater part.

The plaintiff's claim is endeavored to be supported by the fourth paragraph of the third article, in which it is declared that "all moneys paid by the subject to the support of public worship, and of the public teachers aforesaid, shall, if he require it, be uniformly applied to the support of the teacher of his own religious denomination, on whose instruction he attends." And it is contended, that in this paragraph two descriptions of teachers are included - the first referring to the teachers of incorporated societies provided for in the first paragraph, and the latter embracing teachers of any voluntary society, who in fact, have a teacher, although not obliged to elect and support one. We are, however, satisfied, that in every part of the third article, but one class of public teachers is contemplated, and which is particularly described in the first paragraph; and that, whenever teachers are mentioned, such teachers alone are intended, who by law are entitled to support. For, although the constitution contemplates different denominations of Protestant Christians, yet no religious societies are referred to, unless incorporated; and no teachers are mentioned as existing, who are not entitled to a maintenance.

If the construction which was contended for was right, then a Roman Catholic teacher might maintain an action similar to the plaintiff's. But in the case of Matignon vs The Inhabitants of Newcastle, in the county of Lincoln, decided some years since by this Court in Suffolk, it was determined, that the teacher mentioned in the latter part of the fourth paragraph so far referred to the first paragraph, as that he must be a Protestant teacher. And if a reference must be made to any part of the description, we know not why it must not be made to the whole of it, as the article has drawn no line of distinction.

In the latter part of this fourth paragraph, the teachers to whom the money may be applied, are described as public teachers. But a public teacher must be a teacher of some public, and not of any private religious society. And what society must be deemed a public society, is certainly a question of law, whether it be settled by a judge or by a jury. When, therefore, the facts describing the nature or circumstances of any society, are established by evidence, from those facts the law must conclude whether the society be, in legal contemplation, public or private. Now, if the society be not incorporated, what rules are prescribed by law, by which its character may be defined? Does it depend on the number of the associates, or on the notoriety of the association? If on the former, what number is sufficient? If on the latter, what degree of notoriety is necessary? On these points the law is silent. But there is a legal principle applicable to this subject, and which can at all times be applied with certainty. A public society is a society known in law, formed by the public authority of the state; and a private society is formed by the voluntary association of private persons, the powers of which are derived from the individual consent of each member...

The last paragraph of the third article has also been pressed upon us. It provides that "every denomination of Christians, demeaning themselves peaceably, and as good subjects of the commonwealth, shall be equally under the protection of law; and no subordination of one sect or denomination to another shall ever be established by law."

In our opinion, this paragraph has no relation to the subject before us. Its object was to prevent any hierarchy, or ecclesiastical jurisdiction of one sect of Christians over any other sect; and the sect of Roman Catholics are as fully entitled to the benefit of this clause, as any society of Protestant Christians. It was also intended to prevent any religious test, as a qualification for office. Therefore those Catholics, who renounce all obedience and subjection to the pope, as a foreign prince or prelate, may, notwithstanding their religious tenets, hold any civil office, although the constitution has not provided for the support of any public teacher of the Popish religion. ...

This construction, which we find ourselves obliged to give to the constitution on this subject, is agreeable to the construction adopted by the legislature, as expressed in the statute of 1799, c. 87, before cited. Thus all citizens, except Quakers, are obliged to contribute to the support of public teachers; and when any member of any society, but of a different sect, shall request to have his taxes paid to the teacher of his own sect, but of another society, his request cannot prevail, but on his producing a certificate signed by his public teacher, and by a committee of the society, purporting in substance such facts as entitle him to the obtaining of his request; and the assessors of the society in which he dwells may afterwards omit him in their assessments.

This construction is not denied; but it is argued that the legislature cannot, by any construction, control the constitution. This is true; but where any part of the constitution is of doubtful construction, the opinion of the legislature deserves to be heard, and is entitled to due consideration. And in the present case, their construction appears to us to be correct. Certainly no conclusion can be drawn from it, that the statute intended to exempt any citizen, except Quakers, from contributing to the support of some public Protestant reader.

It is our opinion that the verdict do stand, and the judgment be rendered upon it.

Adams v. Howe
Supreme Judicial Court of Massachusetts, 1817
14 Mass. 340

PARKER, C. J. By the special verdict in this case, it appears that the plaintiff in error was exempted from ministerial taxes, according to the provisions of the Stat. 1811, c. 6,[1] he having regularly obtained and filed with the proper officer of the town a certificate of his membership in a Baptist society in the town of Barre, and such a society being found to exist. It is true that it also appears that the society of which he was a member was not incorporated; and that their minister or teacher was not settled over that society, but only engaged to preach to them one Sabbath in a month, he being, in fact, a stated minister of another society in another town. But these latter facts are immaterial, provided the statute has legal force and validity; for it expressly puts corporate and unincorporated societies upon the same footing, and makes no distinction between such as have an ordained minister specially settled over them, and such as are occasionally taught by preachers who may be ordained at large, or as ministers of other parishes, devoting a part of their labors and services to them.

The true and only question, then, arising in this case is, whether the statute before cited is contrary or repugnant to the principles of the constitution, and so of no binding force upon the Court. And after a careful examination of the declaration of rights prefixed to the constitution, where

---

[1]The relevant section of the act provided as follows: "All monies paid by the citizen to the support of public worship or of public teachers of religion shall, if required by the citizen, be uniformly applied to the support of the teacher of his own sect or denomination, provided there be any on whose instruction he usually attends, as well where the teacher is of an unincorporated as of a corporate religious society."

alone the subject is treated of, we do not find that the legislature is restricted in the manner contended for by the counsel for the defendants in error.

We are well aware of the great inconveniences, and the injury to public morals and religion, and the tendency to destroy all the deceny and regularity of public worship, which may result from a general application of the indulgence granted by the legislature, in that statute, to all persons who may choose to associate, and withdraw themselves from the regular and established religious societies in towns and parishes, which, being by law obliged to support public teachers, may thus have their means and power so much dimished as to render that duty oppressive and burdensome. But our duty is to give effect to such acts of the legislature as they have the constitutional authority to make, without regarding their evil tendency or inexpediency. Subsequent legislatures may correct the proceedings of their predecessors, which may be found to have been improvident or pernicious. And if a law, however complained of, is suffered to remain unrepealed, the only legal presumption is, that it is the will of the community that such should be the law.

We proceed to show why the statute in question may be considered as constitutional; and to show that there is no decided case which in any manner contravenes the opinion which we feel ourselves bound to adopt; that the judgment of the Circuit Court of Common Please is erroneous, and must be reversed.

We must premise, that so much respect is due to any legislative act, solemnly passed, and admitted into the statute-book, that a court of law, which may be called upon to decide its validity, will presume it to be constitutional, until the contrary clearly appears; so that in any case of the kind substantially doubtful, the law would have its force. The legislature is, in the first instance, the judge of its own constitutional powers; and it is only when manifest assumption of authority, or misapprehension of it, shall appear, that the judicial power will refuse to execute it. Whenever such a case happens, it is among the most important duties of the judicial power to declare the invalidity of an act so passed.

The act of the legislature now in question is supposed to be unconstitutional, in providing for the exemption of persons from taxation to the support of ministers, or public teachers of piety, religion, and morality, in the towns or parishes within which they may dwell, if they belong to a religious society of a different persuasion, whether that society be incorporated or not. In order to ascertain whether, for this cause, the act is unconstitutional, we must examine the constitution, to see whether there is any restriction upon the legislature in this respect.

The framers of the constitution, and the people who adopted it in the articles of the declaration of rights, which respect religion and public worship, undoubtedly intended to secure and establish the orderly and regular preaching of the gospel in towns and parishes, and public incorporated societies; and the decent and suitable maintenance of persons of learning and piety, to be set apart as public teachers of religion and morality. This is obvious from the frequent use of the word public, as applicable to worship, and to ministers and teachers.

Another great object was, to secure and establish the most perfect and entire freedom of opinion, as to tenets of religion, and as to the choice of the mode of worship.

It was difficult to establish any fundamental rules upon the subject, and they did not attempt it; but contented themselves with declaring the public sentiment upon the subject, and enjoining upon the legislature the importance of providing, from time to time, such laws as should carry these great objects into effect. It was believed that the future guardians of the moral and religious character of the state, and of the rights of conscience among the people, would be at all times regardful of these important concerns, and would establish such wholesome regulations as would comport with the solemnity of the subject and the true interests of the people.

It is therefore declared, in the third article of the declaration of rights, "That the people have a right to invest their legislature with power to authorize and require, and the legislature shall from time to time authorize and require, the several towns, parishes, precincts, and other bodies corporate and politic, and religious societies, to make suitable provision, at their own expense, for the institution of the public worship of God, and for the support and maintenance of public Protestant teachers of piety, religion, and morality, in all cases where such provision shall not be made voluntarily."

And it is further declared in the same article, "that the people of this commonwealth have a right to, and do, invest their legislature with authority to enjoin upon all their subjects an attendance upon the instructions of the public teachers aforesaid at stated times and seasons, if there be any on whose instructions they can conscientiously and conveniently attend."

The right of choosing and contracting with their own teachers is, then, declared to belong to the public bodies before mentioned; that the money paid by the subject for the support of public worship shall be applied to the support of a teacher of his own denomination, if there be any one upon whom he attends; and that there shall be no subordination or superiority of one sect or denomination over any other.

Three great objects appear to have been the influential causes of the solemn declaration of the will of the people: 1. To establish, at all events, liberty of conscience and choice of the mode of worship; 2. To assert the right of the state, in its political capacity, to require and enforce the public worship of God; 3. To deny the right of establishing any hierarchy, or any power in the state itself, to require conformity to any creed or formulary of worship.

The restrictions upon the legislature are against any exercise of authority which might contravene the rights of conscience or the choice of forms of worship, and against the establishment of any national or state creed, or form of worship, to which those who conscientiously disagreed should be obliged to conform, or suffer any inconvenience from nonconformity. The mode of securing these essential points is left entirely to the legislature, and confidence was reposed in them to maintain them by equal and wholesome laws.

That part of the declaration which enjoins it upon the legislature to exact the support of religious institutions, and attendance upon public worship, is merely directory. - If no law had been passed pursuant to it, there could be no penalty upon the citizen for not obeying the clear expression of the public will; nor is there any way of coercing a legislature to carry into effect these important requisitions. So the mode, also, of executing the will of the people, in this particular, is left entirely to the legislature; and although laws may be passed which have a contrary tendency, and which, in their consequences, may injure, instead of promoting, the public worship, yet the legislature is to judge; and even their erroneous construction of the design of the people, as expressed in the said declaration, must have legal effect so far as they are not manifestly repugnant to the principles of the constitution.

This being the character of the legislative power on this all-important subject, we are at a loss to conceive how it can be restrained, when it is professedly exercised for the purpose of enlarging, instead of diminishing, the rights of the citizen on the subject of religious worship. Great responsibility rests upon the legislature, and also upon the people, in delegating power to those who have almost unlimited authority. If they, with a view to secure the rights of conscience, pass laws, within the letter of the constitution, which may have a tendency injuriously to affect the regular public worship, it is not for the judiciary power to control their course.

The mischief to be dreaded is the breaking up of the parochial religious establishments, by authorizing any number of individuals to withdraw themselves, in the easy and loose way which is provided in this act. But they have the authority, and they have continually exercised it, to incorporate parts of parishes, and even individuals, as poll parishes; and by this means to diminish the resources of the religious communities from which such corporations are taken. They may incorporate five, ten, or twenty people for this purpose; and there seems to be no more constitutional difficulties in the way of vesting societies unincorporated, and the members of them, with the same privileges.

This may be an abuse of power, for which they are amenable to their constituents; but these acts are not therefore void. It is certainly unjust to leave the standing parishes liable to penalties, if they do not maintain a minister, and not to impose any duty of the kind upon those whom they have exempted from the common burden. But in this they merely neglect their duty; and this neglect does not affect the validity of the acts which they may choose to pass...

It has been supposed that, according to the principles stated in the case of Barnes vs. The Inhabitants of the First Parish in Falmouth, 6 Mass. 401 (1810), this legislative act is clearly repugnant to the constitution of the state. But no such inference can be drawn from that case. The question to be settled there was, whether the minister of an unincorporated society could maintain an action against the parish, for the taxes paid by one of his hearers. The action was founded altogether upon the supposed constitutional right of the minister, in behalf of his hearer; and no legislative act had then been passed tending to vary or affect the natural and obvious meaning of the terms of the articles of the declaration of rights before cited; it being clear by those articles that the privilege of appropriating money paid to another use than that of the town or parish into whose treasury it was paid applied only when the appropriation was to be made to the use of a teacher of a public society, and that by a public society was intended one known and incorporated. The plaintiff in that suit could not prevail.

That decision was correct; and it was probably to avoid the effect of it that the legislature passed the law in question. It nowhere appears in the learned and elaborate opinion delivered in that case, that the power of the legislature over the subject was questioned. On the contrary, the following expressions may be considered as an admission of that power. The chief justice observed, "that it seems a mistake to suppose that the legislature cannot grant any further relief in particular cases, which in its discretion it may consider as deserving relief."

Such relief had been before granted to Quakers, in whose favor no exception had been made by the constitution. The same right exists with respect to Baptists, or those of any other denomination different from that which prevails in the town of which they are inhabitants; and it may be applied in favor of Congregationalists, where they are a minority, and dissent from the established worship of the town, or Episcopalians, or any other sect, who may unite and form themselves into a separate society.

Whether it is expedient to give legislative sanction to a system so destructive to regular and orderly worship, we again say we are not to judge. We are, however, satisfied that there is nothing in the constitution which prohibits this exercise of power.

One of the objections to the effect of the exemption of the plaintiff in error is, that the society, of which he is a member, had no settled minister; but hired one only for one Sabbath in a month. But here, again, the legislature has authorize this; not having required, as essential to an exemption, that there should be any minister at all, but only a society and a committee...

But the statute of 1811 makes no such requisition; expressly giving the right to the preacher on whom the party taxed shall attend, whether he be ordained at large, or over a particular society; or whether he divide his labors among twenty different societies, or confine them entirely to one. The provision of the act is too broad to exclude the members of any society, large enough to choose a committee, from the enjoyment of its privileges; and it does not appear that even attendants upon public worship any where is necessary to secure the exemption.

Judgment reversed.

The process of disestablishment in Massachusetts was noticeably hastened by the successes of the Unitarian movement. Despite the efforts of the Congregational ministers to retain the loyalty of the people the majority of Congregationalists in many communities became Unitarians. That shift of faith brought in its wake numerous controversies between the champions of the old orthodoxy and the new religion. The Supreme Judicial Court wás finally confronted by the problem of adjusting the conflicting rights of the two elements. It is hardly necessary to say that the decision in Baker v. Fales brought vigorous and prolonged protest from the Congregationalists.

Baker v. Fales
Supreme Judicial Court of Massachusetts, 1820
16 Mass. 492

PARKER, C. J. This is replevin of certain bonds and other money securities, and of certain records and documents, alleged to belong to the first church in Dedham, of which church the plaintiffs aver themselves to be deacons.

The defendant, in this first plea, denies the property to be in the plaintiffs, and issue is joined on this point.

In his second plea, he denies that the plaintiffs are deacons of the first church in Dedham, and issue is also joined upon this point. Both issues on trial by the jury, have been found, under the direction of the judge who sat on the trial, for the plaintiffs; and a new trial is moved for, on account of the supposed misdirection of the judge in matters of the law, and also on account of the admission of some evidence and the rejection of other, contrary to the motion of the defendant's counsel at the trial. On the hearing before the whole Court, the argument of counsel has been confined altogether to the matters of law, arising out of the direction of the judge; so that no notice will now be taken of the questions which relate to the evidence, other than to say that we see no objection to the decisions of the judge upon those questions as they arose.

The two issues of fact, which were submitted to the jury, resolve themselves into one and the same point; so that it is not now necessary to consider them separately, nor have they been so considered by the counsel in their argument. If the plaintiffs are not the deacons of the first church in Dedham, they are not entitled to the possession of the articles repleived; if they are such deacons, then, as the articles are agreed to belong, for certain purposes, to the proper representatives of that church, the plaintiffs are constituted by law, the proper persons to sue for, and have the custody of, them. But this question, though simple in its form, necessarily led into a wide field of argument, and must be pursued in the same manner, in order that the reasons of the opinion which the Court have adopted, may be clearly and distinctly seen and understood.

One branch of the charge of the judge is, "that, although the grants of land and donations to the church in Dedham purport to be for the use of the church, yet the church could not hold the same as a corporation, never having been incorporated as a body politic; and that said lands, and other property, did vest in the deacons of said church by virtue of the statute of 1754; and that the deacons were to hold the same in trust for supporting the ministry, and for defraying charges relating to public worship; and that, by the true construction of that statute, and other acts relating to the same subject, said grants and donations must be considered as made for the whole town of Dedham, for the purpose of supporting and maintaining public worship. That, after the erection of new parishes in said town, said property remained for the use of the remaining part of said town, which, thereupon, constituted the first parish in said town."

There is nothing in this part of the charge which obviously affects the question, whether the plaintiffs are deacons of the first church in Dedham;

but it will be seen, in the sequel, that the correctness or incorrectness of the principles laid down by the judge is essential in the consideration of the question between the parties. The defendant, as well as the plaintiffs, claims to be the deacon of the first church in Dedham, and contends that the property, out of which the securities sued for grew, belonged to the church as an ecclesiastical body, without any connection with the parish, and that the conveyances were originally to the use of the church, without any trust in favor of the parish. If this position can be maintained, it will materially affect the question whether the plaintiffs, who were appointed deacons by those members of the church who remained and acted with the parish, had thereby acquired any right in the property; and so it is necessary to determine the legal character of the grants to the church in Dedham...

[The Court here determined that the early grants "to the Church in Dedham" were to be interpreted as conveyances to the church, as trustee for the benefit of the parish in which it was situated.]

Hitherto we have gone upon the ground that, at the time when the earliest of these grants were made, there was a body of men in Dedham, known by the name of the Dedham Church, distinct from the society of Christians usually worshipping together in that town; and, even upon this hypothesis, we are satisfied that the church was intended to take nothing in the lands granted but estates in trust; and that, as the particular trusts intended must have been the providing for the public worship of God in Dedham, the inhabitants at large of that town, as parishioners or members of the religious society, were the proper cestui que trusts, because the effect of the grants was to relieve them from an expense they would otherwise have been obliged to bear, or forego all the benefits of a Christian ministry. But, in reverting to the history of those times, reason will be found to doubt the application of the term church as used in the grants, in the precise and limited sense in which it is now used.

Probably there was no very familiar distinction, at that time, between the church and the whole assembly of Christians in the town. We have had no evidence that the inhabitants were divided into two bodies, of church and society, or parish, keeping separate records, and having separate interests; but if the fact be otherwise than is supposed, there is no doubt that most of the inhabitants of the town were church members at that time. In the year 1631, ten years only before the earliest of these grants, it was provided, by a colonial law, that no inhabitants should have the political rights of a free man, unless he were a member of some orthodox church. The presumption is violent, then, that almost if not quite all of the adult inhabitants of Dedham, and other towns, were church members, and a grant to the church, under such circumstances, could mean nothing else than a grant to the town; except that a designation of the use of the property might be inferred from the denomination of the grantee. That this was the state of things, will not be doubted by those who look into the ancient tracts and writings respecting the churches in New England. Before the migration of our ancestors to this country, it is believed a Congregational church was, as it was in the earliest times of Christianity, an assembly of Christians meeting together in the same place, for the public worship of God, under the same minister or ministers. Mr. Wise, a writer on this subject, defines a particular church to be "a society of Christians meeting together in one place, under their proper pastors, for the performance of religious worship and the exercising of Christian discipline, united together by covenant," as most of those undoubtedly were who composed that society. Parochia, or parish, he says, signifies, in a church sense, a competent number of Christians dwelling near together, and having one bishop, pastor, &c., or more set over them. Therefore, parish, in this sense, is the same with a particular church or congregation; and this, he observes, is plainly agreeable with the sense, custom, and platform of the New England churches: a whole diocese is one parish, it not exceeding, in ancient times, the bounds of a parish or a small town, or a part of a town...

... From this account of the ancient state of things, it may well be conceived, that a person intending to give property to pious uses, and particularly for the support and maintenance of public worship, within the first half century after the migration of our ancestors, would denominate the donees - the church, meaning the whole society of worshipping Christians; and if his donation should be afterwards applied to the use of a few Christians, who had constituted themselves the church, instead of the whole society, his bounty would be perverted. The later grants from the proprietors were undoubtedly made for the same purposes, and with the same intentions; for, there being then but one church and one Christian society in Dedham, the proprietors, or the clerk who made the record, would be likely to adopt the phraseology which had been before used; and these grants should have the same construction as the earlier ones, although the distinction between church and town, or parish, might then have been known.

Considering, then, that the land granted was for the beneficial use of the assembly of Christians in Dedham, which were no other than the inhabitants of that town who constituted the religious society, within which the church was established, these inhabitants were the cestui que trusts, and the equitable title was vested in them, as long as they continued to constitute the assembly denominated the church in the grants.

Since the grants were made, parishes have been set off in the town, and other churches have been established within these parishes; but a residuum has always been left, which, by the statutes of the government and the decisions of the courts, have thus become the first parish, and have lawfully succeeded to all the rights vested in the inhabitants of the town, of a parochial nature, which have not been parted with in some legal form. In 1754, the legislature, having found that much property had been given to churches, with intention that the same should be held in perpetual succession, constituted the deacons a corporation with the power of holding the property, for the purpose of executing therewith the will of the donors. ...

And we are now brought to the question, whether the plaintiffs have proved themselves to be deacons of the same church, to which the grants were originally made, for the trusts before mentioned.

Until the invitation was given to Mr. Lamson (the present officiating minister in the first parish in Dedham), the church and congregation appear to have acted in unison, and the funds held by the church arising from the grants of land, which have been considered, have been, from time to time, applied, as needed, to the support of the minister, and to defray other charges relating to public worship. This was in conformity to the spirit of the trust, and is a sufficient explanation in itself of the kind of interest which the church claimed in the property. On the dismission of the Rev. Mr. Bates from the pastoral charge of the church and congregation in Dedham, at his own request, the unhappy dissension arose, which has terminated in a dismemberment of the society, and a litigation about the property. Mr. Lamson was elected by the parish, at a regular parish meeting, to be the successor of Mr. Bates. The church refused to concur in the choice; a majority of this body disapproving of his religious tenets, or for other causes. The parish, with the minority of the church, invited a respectable council, consisting of the ministers of several churches and delegates, who advised to the ordination of Mr. Lamson over the parish, and who, accordingly, ordained him, notwithstanding the remonstrance of a majority of the members of the church, who finally seceded from the parish, and never, since the ordination of Mr. Lamson, have attended public worship there, but have, in another place within the territorial limits of the parish, attended public worship, and had the ordinances administered to them as a church.

After the ordination of Mr. Lamson, a church meeting was called, at which the members who acted with the parish attended; and they voted to remove from office the former deacons, who seceded with the majority of the old church, and elected the plaintiffs in their stead.

The members who seceded claim still to be the first church in Dedham, and the successors of the church to which the property was given in trust; and the defendant claims to be the deacon of that church, and as such, claims a right to hold the property.

In whatever light ecclesiastical councils or persons may consider the question, it appears to us clear from the constitution and laws of the land, and from judicial decisions, that the body, which is to be considered the first church in Dedham, must be the church of the first parish in that town, as to all questions of property which depend upon that relation...

If a church may subsist unconnected with any congregation or religious society, as has been urged in argument, it is certain that it has no legal qualities, and more expecially that it cannot exercise any control over property which it may have held in trust for the society with which it had been formerly connected. That any number of the members of a church who disagree with their brethren, or with the minister, or with the parish, may withdraw from fellowship with them, and act as a church in a religious point of view, having the ordinances administered and other religious offices performed, it is not necessary to deny; indeed, this would be a question proper for an ecclesiastical council to settle, if any should dispute their claim. But as to all civil purposes, the secession of a whole church from the parish would be an extinction of the church; and it is competent to the members of the parish to institute a new church, or to engraft one upon the old stock if any of it should remain; and this new church would succeed to all the rights of the old, in relation to the parish. This is not only reasonable, but it is conformable to the usages of the country; for, although many instances may have occurred of the removal of church members from one church or one place of worship to another, and no doubt a removal of a majority of the members has sometimes occurred, we do not hear of any church ceasing to exist, while there were members enough left to do church service. No particular number is necessary to constitute a church, nor is there any established quorum, which would have a right to manage the concerns of the body. According to the Cambridge Platform, ch. 3, § 4, the number is to be no larger than can conveniently meet together in one place, nor, ordinarily, fewer than may conveniently carry on church work. It would seem to follow, from the very structure of such a body as this, which is a mere voluntary association, that a diminution of its numbers will not affect its identity. A church may exist, in an ecclesiastical sense, without any officers, as will be seen in the Platform; and, without doubt, in the same sense a church may be composed only of femes covert and minors, who have no civil capacity. The only circumstance, therefore, which gives a church any legal character, is its connection with some regularly-constituted society; and those who withdraw from the society cease to be members of that particular church, and the remaining members continue to be the identical church. This is analogous to the separation of towns and parishes - the effect of which, by law, is, to leave the original body politic entire, with its powers and privileges undiminished, however large may be the proportion which secedes. And so it is of all voluntary societies, having funds to be disposed of to charitable uses in any particular place. A refusal of a majority of the members to act would devolve all power over the subject upon those who might choose to persevere. Numerous fire societies, and other voluntary associations having funds, have acted upon this principle...

The consequences of the doctrine contended for by the defendant, will glaringly show the unsoundness of the principle upon which the argument is founded. The position is that, whenever property is given to a church, it has the sole control of it, and the members, for the time being, may remove to any other place, even without the commonwealth, and carry the property with them.

Now, property bestowed upon churches has always been given for some pious or benevolent purpose, and with a particular view to some associated body of Christians. The place in which the church is located, is generally had in view by the donor, either because he there had enjoyed the preaching of the gospel and the ordinances or because it was the place where his ancestors or his family and friends had assembled together for religious purposes. These associations will be found to be the leading motive for the particular direction which his charity has received. If he gives to a church for the general purpose of promoting piety, or for the use of the poor of the church, he generally designates the body by the place where it is accustomed to worship. Thus, if a donation were made to the Old South church, Parkstreet church, Brattlestreet church, or any other that might be thus designated by local qualities, it must be supposed that the donor had in view the society of Christians worshipping in those places; and as his donation is intended to be perpetual, that he had regard to the welfare of successive generations, who might become worshipping Christians and church members in the same place. If the whole society should find occasion to remove to some other place in the same town, the identity might be preserved, and the bounty enjoyed as he intended it. But if the church alone should withdraw, and unite itself to some other church, or to a new and different congregation, it would be defeating his intentions to carry the property with them, and distribute the proceeds in a community for the members of which he may have never entertained any particular feelings of kindness...

It being, as we think, established that the members of the church, who withdrew from the parish, ceased to be the first church in Dedham, and that all the rights and duties of that body, relative to property intrusted to it, devolved upon those members who remained with and adhered to the parish; it remains to be considered whether the plaintiffs were duly chosen deacons of that church, and so became entitled to the possession of the property, as the trustees under the statute of 1754, as stated by the judge in his charge to the jury...

The objection to the settlement of Mr. Lamson rests altogether upon the supposition that there could be no legal settlement and ordination, unless the church, as a distinct body from the parish or congregation, had assented to his call, and concurred in the proceedings preliminary to his settlement; and it is upon this ground, also, that the ordaining council are supposed to have had no authority in the matter, they being invited by the parish and a minority of the members of the church, but not by the church itself, to which body, it is alleged, belongs solely the right of convening a council upon such occasions.

That the proceedings of the parish and the council were not conformable to the general usage of the country, cannot be denied. But the parish allege, in vindication of their departure from this usage, their constitutional right to elect and contract with their minister, exclusively of any concurrence or control of the church; and the necessity they were under to proceed as they did, because the church had refused to concur with them in the choice, and in the invitation to the ordaining council. That the parish have the constitutional right contended for, cannot be questioned by those who will pursue the clause of the third article of the Declaration of Rights, upon which this claim is asserted. It is there provided, "that the several towns, parishes, precincts, and other bodies politic or religious societies, shall at all times have the exclusive right of electing their public teachers, and of contracting with them for their support and maintenance." This is too explicity to admit of cavilling or to require explanation, as every constitutional provision for the security of civil or religious liberty ought to be. All preexisting laws or usages must bow before this fundamental expression of the public will; and however convenient or useful it might be to continue the old form of electing or settling a minister, whenever a parish determines to assert its constitutional authority, there is no power in the state to oppose their claim...

We consider, then, the non-concurrence of the church in the choice of the minister, and in the invitation to the ordaining council, as in no degree impairing the constitutional right of the parish. That council might have refused to proceed, but the parish could not by that have been deprived of their minister. It was right and proper, as they could not proceed according to ancient usage, because of the dissent of the church, to approach as near to it as possible by calling a respectable council, and having their sanction in the ordination. And it was certainly wise in that council, finding that the points of disagreement were such as would be likely to cause a permanent separation, to yield to the wishes of the parish, and give their sanction to proceedings which were justified by the constitution and laws of the land. They ordained him over the parish only; but, by virtue of that act, founded upon the choice of the people , he became not only the minister of the parish, but of the church still remaining there, notwithstanding the secession of a majority of the members. Mr. Lamson thus became the lawful minister of the first parish in Dedham, and of the church subsisting therein; and he had a right to call church meetings, and do all other acts pertaining to a settled and ordained minister of the gospel. The church had a right to choose deacons, finding that the former deacons had abdicated their office, and thus no legal objection is found to exist against their right to maintain this action. . .

[The Chief Justice here reviewed the historical process by which the authority to call a minister had passed from the churches to the towns.]

But still instances of disagreement must have now and then occurred, and the public sentiment was gradually verging towards the broad and liberal principle, which was adopted in the constitution; a principle, in reference to religious privileges, correspondent with that which was established in relation to civil rights, that the citizen who contributed towards the support of the government, should have a share in the election of those who were to administer the government.

The right is now, by a fundamental law, which cannot be repealed, vested in the body politic, which is made liable to the duty, and for the support.

Churches, as such, have no power but that which originally belonged to them, and which was recognized in the provincial statute of 1692, and again in the statute of the commonwealth of 1800, viz., of divine worship and church order and discipline. They still retain, by courtesy, the practice of nominating to the congregation, and there is seldom any disagreement. As long as this privilege shall be discreetly exercised, without doubt it will continue. We are not desirous of impairing it, but being called upon to declare the law of the land on a question of property, it is not in our power to yield to prejudices, however long they may have endured, or however useful, in the opinion of some, may be their continuance.

It has been suggested, that the usage of churches has been so general and constant, ever since the adoption of the constitution, that it may now be set up as law, although contrary to the Declaration of Rights. But constitutional privileges can never be lost by mere non-user. Neither individuals, nor aggregate bodies, nor the government itself, can prescribe against the rights of the citizen, with respect to any privilege secured by the constitution.

Indeed, we apprehend those are mistaken, who imagine that the cause of religion would be served, public worship promoted, or instruction in piety, religion and morality more extensively encouraged, by restoring to the churches the power they once enjoyed, of electing the minister without concurrence of the people or congregation, or by the aid of a council which they might select to sanction their choice. Nothing would tend more directly to break up the whole system of religious instruction; for the people never would consent to be taxed for the support of men in whose election they had no voice. It is an undoubted fact, that the male members of the churches form but a small part of the corporation which makes the contract, and is obliged to perform it; and it is not at all consistent with the spirit of the times, that the great majority should, in this particular, be subject to the minority. To arrogate such a power, would be to break up, in no distant period, every parish in the commonwealth.

The authority of the church should be of that invisible, but powerful nature, which results from superior gravity, piety, and devout example. It will then have its proper effect upon the congregation, who will cheerfully yield to the wishes of those who are best qualified to select the candidate. But as soon as it is challenged as a right, it will be lost. The condition of the members of a church is thought to be hard, where the minister elected by the parish is not approved by them. This can only be because they are a minority; and it is one part of the compensation paid for the many blessings resulting from a state of society. A difficulty of this nature surely would not be cured by returning to the old provincial system of letting the minority rule the majority; unless we suppose that the doctrines of a minister are of no consequence to any but church members. Besides, in the present state of our laws, and as they are likely to continue, there is no hardship, although there may be some inconvenience; for dissenting members of the church, as well as of the parish, may join any other church and society, or they may institute a new society; so that they are neither obliged to hear nor to pay a minister, in whose settlement they did not concur. It is true, if there are any parish funds, they will lose the benefit of them by removal; but an inconvenience of this sort will never be felt, when a case of conscience is in question.

Having established the points necessary to settle this cause, viz., that the property sued for belongs to the first church in Dedham, sub modo; that is, to be managed by its deacons under the superintendence of the church, for the general good of the inhabitants of the first parish, in the support of the public worship of God, - that the members of the church now associated and worshipping with the first parish, constitute the first church, - and that the plaintiffs are duly appointed deacons of that church; it follows that the verdict of the jury is right, and that judgment must be entered accordingly.

Congregational Protest

Congregationalist indignation over the decision of Baker v. Fales was intense and articulate. An ecclesiastical council which in 1823 was convened in Groton to give its advice with respect to a conflict between church and parish as to the choice of a minister, rejected the decision entirely and urged its repudiation by the parties to the dispute. In the course of its "Result" the following specific arguments were made:

"1. It has been decided that 'the only circumstance which gives a church any legal character, is its connexion with some legally constituted society, and those who withdraw from the society cease to be members of that particular church, and the remaining members continue to be the identical church.'

"But though it may be true that the churches of Massachusetts have in fact existed, within the limits of a town or parish, (for where else could they exist since the entire territory of the State is thus divided,) it may not be true that the legal existence of the church depended on her civil location within some town or parish. There is no such condition expressed in the ancient laws, and the historical evidence leads to a conclusion directly the reverse of this. It was a dependance of the church on the State, that endangered her purity, and controlled her perfect liberty, which induced our Fathers to abandon their country, and pass the ocean, and face the wilderness, that they might establish churches dependant upon no power, but the authority and protection of heaven. They would not have the church depend for her existence, or rights, upon any earthly powers, civil or ecclesiastical. Their fundamental maxim was, that the church is a spiritual community, dependant upon God only for her existence. They felt the denial to the church of the right of electing her pastor, and complained at being obliged to pay for the support of a minister, forced upon them by a civil designation, against their will. And now, coming to this wilderness, on purpose to establish churches independent of the civil power, did they make them dependant for their very existence in law upon their connexion with a civil body; when it was precisely such a power in England, as is now given to towns and parishes, that drove them into exile? Annoyed by indiscriminate communion, and going into the wilderness to establish churches independent of all power but that of heaven; did they forget their errand, and frame laws recognizing the church only upon condition of such an alliance with a secular association, as they had come hither to avoid? Did they commit to those whom the law should make voters, in town or parish meeting, all the sacred interests of that kingdom which is not of this world; the high responsibility of maintaining purity of doctrine and discipline, and of propagating the religion of Jesus Christ throughout the earth?

"Our Fathers opposed, strenuously, all dependance of local churches upon any external power whatever, civil or ecclesiastical. And though, acting in their civil capacity, they required the town to aid the church, it was as an ally, while they precluded the least civil interposition or control of the church, by the town or the State. The churches existed for eighty years before the towns and parishes were allowed any voice in the election of a pastor; and then the right came in the form of a concession, on the part of the churches, and a compromise, in consideration of the aid furnished by taxation, for the support of the Gospel. And now, did the church depend for her existence and protection in law, upon her alliance with towns and parishes, when she had, for almost an hundred years, enjoyed absolute independence, and was, in fact, the primary institution, for whose sake our Fathers came hither, and to whom these civil associations were made subservient, without the least shadow of alliance, or power of interference, and which were afterwards received into partnership, upon the specific condition, that each should enjoy a concurrent vote in the election of a pastor? ...

"Besides, the churches may have been incorporated really, though informally. Whatever community is recognised as having a legal existence, possesses all the powers which are implied in the terms of legal recognition. And upon this principle, whoever reads the ancient laws of Massachusetts, might almost as well doubt whether the towns were supposed to possess the power of corporations for civil purposes, as whether the churches were supposed to possess the power of holding and managing property for religious uses.

"If it was not the intention of the civil power, that the churches should hold property as corporations, it is incredible that no legal intimation to the contrary was ever made, in the face of such constant and immemorial usage. But if the government did consider the churches as corporations, to hold property for religious uses, then the consent and usage of one hundred and fifty years, is of equal validity, as an express act of acquiescence of parties to a contract, in respect to subjects which might originally appear questionable, is also very justly held to be evidence, that those subjects were originally intended to be comprehended in the compact."

"Our Fathers were republicans; but it was not for the enjoyment of civil liberty, chiefly, that they came hither. It was to establish churches according to the Gospel, and independent of civil and ecclesiastical domination; and all their civil arrangements were subordinate to the interests of the church, as the means are subordinate to the end. It was Zion, which they preferred above their chief joy, for which the civil power legislated, and around which the military power encamped, and for which the prayers of both were fervently and constantly offered. To a great extent, the wars of New England were religious wars. It was the fear of Popery, which roused her so often to lavish her treasure and pour forth her best blood, and which, in times of disaster, arrayed her in sackcloth, and multiplied days of humiliation and prayer. The political sky of the world was explored by our Fathers, with reference to its aspect upon the churches of New England, and it might almost as well be said, that the sun was unknown to astronomers, until the year 1754, as that the churches of New England were not substantially corporations, known in law, until that time. The following considerations would seem to place the subject beyond all reasonable doubt.

"The Jewish church, which stood high in the estimation of our Fathers, had enjoyed eminently the rights of property, and though not a model for imitation, would naturally lead them to take it for granted that the Christian church might, for religious purposes, do the same thing.

"The Christian Church, from the time she enjoyed civil protection, had ever been, also in some form or other, in the possession of property for religious purposes. It was commonly in the hands of the clergy, and often grossly perverted; but the right of the church to hold and appropriate property, was doubtless, by such immemorial usage, made familiar to them.

"In the Church of England, of which they had once been members, they had been accustomed to witness the same thing.

"It is not strange, therefore, that no act of incorporation should be found in the early statutes. The church being the primary institution, and all laws and civil institutions being established in subservience to her prosperity, it did not occur to our Fathers, that she could need an act of incorporation. They took for granted her corporate existence, as much as they did their own existence. Nor were they singular in this; many of our most valuable civil institutions, grew up from use, until they came at length into some legal form. The House of Representatives derives its existence from no charter, or formal legal enactment; but grew up silently, from the capacity of a humble committee of consultation, to a powerful legislative body. Hence we find the laws continually recognising the church, in terms which imply substantially a corporate existence, until, as legal accuracy became more indispensable, they gave her technically, what she had possessed from the beginning substantially, a legal corporation...

"But it is said, that, whatever may have been the rights of the churches before the constitution of 1780, that instrument has impaired them, and enlarged those of towns and parishes; that the exclusive power of electing the minister, is now given to towns and parishes, in language 'too explicit to admit of cavilling, or to require explanation, and that all pre-existing laws and usages must bow before this fundamental expression of the public will.'

"To this decision, we can by no means accede.

"1. Because the rights of the churches, supposed to be impaired by the constitution of 1780, are corporate rights, recognised in law, and enjoyed from the beginning; and which a mere "bill of rights" can no more take away, than it can take away the rights of any other pre-existing corporation, and bestow them upon some other corporation.

"2. Because, to our apprehension, the evidence is conclusive, that the people who adopted the constitution, had no intention to impair the rights of the churches, and did not understand the instrument in accordance with the legal construction which has since been given to it. And

"3. Because it is not the natural construction, according to the obvious import of terms, and the established laws of interpretations.

"The passage in question, is the third article of the bill of rights, and is as follows, viz. 'That the several towns, parishes, precincts, and other bodies politic, or religious societies, shall at all times, have the exclusive right of electing their public teachers, and of contracting with them for their support and maintenance.'

"Now if this article admits of two constructions, one of which enroaches upon rights over which it had no power, and does violence to the known opinions and feelings of the times, by destroying institutions of unparalleled utility, sacred by age; and another, which corresponds with the rights of the churches, and the known sentiments of the age, and upholds institutions of immemorial utility, it cannot be doubted which is the true construction.

"1. The churches, at the time the constitution was adopted, were, and had been, corporations, with the rights of holding property, for religious purposes, and with the right of a concurrent vote in the election of their pastors.

"In the beginning they existed, most certainly, independent of any alliance with towns or parishes, and with the rights of electing their pastors.

Their alliance afterwards with towns and parishes, was the result of a compromise, made by the churches, as the primary institutions, with towns and societies, admitting them, for peace [sic] sake and their aid in taxation, to the right of a concurrent vote with the churches in the election of a pastor. With this right of pastoral election, by a concurrent vote with towns and parishes, and the power of corporations, always exercised and expressly conferred in the year 1754, the churches came down to the year 1780; when, as the construction imports, these rights of the churches were taken away, and bestowed on towns and parishes. And were taken away, too, 'by a bill of rights,' which, strictly speaking, is neither law nor constitution, but a recognition of certain elementary principles of the social compact. Laws are mutable, and sometimes unjust. Communities, therefore, have thought proper to throw around particular fundamental principles, the guardianship of a bill of rights. But if, in the enumeration of a bill of rights, one part of the community is enriched by the spoils of the other, could this bill of fraud become a bill of rights? What if late decisions had discovered that the bill of rights somewhat enlarged the rights of the eastern half of Massachusetts, and so far impaired those of the western, as to make them wholly dependant on the will of the capital and the region round about, for every civil immunity? Could such injustice in principle, carry with it the force of law? How, then, can the Congregational churches be stripped of their rights, by a 'bill of rights,' whose object it is to protect from the caprice of legislation the great principles of the social compact, among which the rights of conscience and of incorporations are most sacred?

"It has been decided, that 'every law, which takes away rights vested agreeably to existing laws, is retrospective, and is generally unjust, and may be oppressive. That the legislature may enact retrospective laws, respecting remedies, but not respecting the rights of parties.'

"But the third article of the bill of rights, as construed by the courts, is a retrospective law, obliterating rights of the most sacred character, but for the prospect of enjoying which, our Fathers had never come hither, and this goodly land had not been blessed with such holy institutions; rights bought repeatedly with blood, and enjoyed for almost two centuries. Now, though the law of 1754 had not ratified and confirmed the antecedent usages of the churches, and though a simple "non user" may not divest existing corporations of their rights, yet the unopposed usage of two centuries, may suffice to afford evidence of the concurrence of all concerned, and make rights as unequivocal, as acts of incorporation could do. For the books have decided, that 'the long acquiescence of parties to a contract, in respect to subjects which might originally appear questionable, is also very justly held to be evidence, that those subjects were originally intended to be comprehended in the compact...' "

In a Congregationalist periodical, Spirit of the Pilgrims, vol. 2, pp. 379-82, a review of several publications relating to the issues in Baker v. Fales was published in 1829. The effort to show that the churches had always been considered to be corporations was made in the following passage:

"But let us consider the language which, at different periods of our history, has been applied to churches. In the early settlement of the country, the formation of churches was frequently called their 'incorporation.' Mr. Cotton speaks of the church as "a spiritual political body.' They are spoken of in the Platform as 'political churches.' Mather calls the church 'a sacred corporation.' Mr. Wise repeatedly terms the churches 'incorporate bodies.' The late Governor Sullivan represents the church as, in a certain point of view, 'a civil society,' and 'a civil corporation.' The Editor of Winthrop speaks of 'each of our churches as a body corporate.' And what is more to the purpose than either, and, in our view, decisive - in the statute of 1754, reenacted in 1786, but a few years after the adoption of the Constitution, churches are expressly denominated bodies politic. In the section which limits 'the income of church grants,' it is provided 'that the income to any one such body politic' - the very phrase of the Constitution 'shall not exceed three hundred pounds per annum.'

"But we have an argument, if possible, more conclusive than this. We are able to show, that in the discussions attendant upon the formation and adoption of the Constitution, the 'religious societies' spoken of in the third article, were understood to mean Churches; so that to churches, as well as to 'towns, parishes, precincts,' &c. is secured, by the Constitution, 'the exclusive right of electing their public teachers.'

"It appears from the Boston Gazette of May 22, 1780, that the minority in Boston offered eight distinct objections to the third article in the bill of rights. The third of these objections was as follows: - 'The people have no right to invest the legislature with power to 'authorize and require religious societies,' &c. because, By Religious Societies, We Are To Understand The Churches of Christ, which churches can receive no authority, nor be subject to any requisition of any legislature under heaven.' - In the return from Framingham, we find this objection quoted and adopted in precisely the same words - We find the same, also, in the return from Holliston.

"In the return from Ashby, we find the following objection to the article under consideration. 'The third article says, the people of this Commonwealth have a right to invest their legislature with power to make laws that are binding on religious societies, as such, (as we understand it), which is as much as to say, We will not have Christ to reign over us - that the laws of his kingdom are not sufficient to govern us - that the prosperity of his kingdom is not equally important with the kingdoms of this world - and that the ark of God stands in need of Uzza's hand to keep it from falling to the ground. But let us attend seriously to this important truth, that I will build My Church upon this rock, and the gates of hell shall not prevail against it. Now where resides this power? In Christ only - or in the legislature?' - From the reasoning as well as language of this objection, it is impossible not to perceive, that the phrase, religious societies, in the third article, was understood as including churches.

"We quote the following from the Independent Chronicle of April 6, 1780, 'Another part of the article which ought to be rejected with abhorrence is this, "The legislature shall have poqer to authorize and require religious societies to support the public worship of God, and the teachers of religion." By religious societies, I suppose we are to understand the churches of Christ,' &c.

"Of the same bearing is the following from the Independent Ledger of June 12, 1780. 'My antagonist,' (an advocate for the third article,) 'attempts to get along by saying that the legislature have a right to require Religious Societies or Churches to perform a civil duty. To which I reply, that the legislature may require the members of churches, considered as citizens, or in their civil capacity, to perform a civil duty. But as members of churches, or in their religious character, they have no authority over them.'

"In the controversy between Governor Sullivan and the late Dr. Thacher of Boston, agitated in 1784, Mr. S. expressed the opinion that 'the custom of the country,' according to which the church preceded the parish in the 'choice of the minister as their pastor, was done away by the declaration of rights;' to which Mr. Thacher replies, 'Ministers did not suppose that there would be such a total change in the system of their church government, as Mr. S. hath suggested; Neither Had This Gentleman Himself Ideas of This Nature at That Time,' (the time of the adoption of the Constitution,) 'unless I am much mistaken,' Mr. Thacher then proceeds to say, an 'idea hath been to this day entertained of the necessity of the concurrence of the church with a society in the choice of a minister.' pp. 16, 20.

"To the quotations here made, and to the conclusion inevitable growing out of them, what will Mr. L. reply? He has expressly admitted, as all must admit, that if, in 1780, churches were known and understood to be 'bodies politic or religious societies, they are within the provisions of the Constitution. And we have produced proof upon proof, from the returns of towns, from the discussions attendant upon the adoption of the Constitution, from the testimony of eye and ear witnesses, that the religious societies spoken of in the Constitution were then understood, on all hands, to include the churches.

"In further proof of the same general conclusion, we here present another class of testimony, extracted from letters which have been received in consequence of the recent discussions relating to this subject. The first is from the late venerable Dr. Dana of Ipswich, dated April 13, 1827.

" 'I have a perfect remembrance of what passed in 1780, when the Constitution was pending. After the frame of it was voted in Convention, it was sent to all the towns for their adoption, with such variations as two thirds of them might wish for. It was read in town meeting where I live, and a committee appointed to consider it and report. I was on that committee. Besides this, it was read publicly, and considered by parts for several days. Explanations were likewise given, as they were desired, by a venerable member who had attended the Convention. At all these meetings I was present. But at none of them all did I meet with one intimation, or expressed apprehension, of such a king of exclusive right of towns, parishes, &c. as we are now called to believe in. In fact, had we then believed that such an exclusion of the church was intended, it is past conjecture, that nine-tenths of this ancient town would have rejected it. Nor is it believed that it was with such an understanding, that the Convention itself agreed, or could have agreed in it. In every view, their silence on the subject is conclusive evidence.

Respectfully,

J. Dana.' "

"The following is from a venerable and highly respectable layman, of Groton, (Mass.) dated Nov. 1827.

" 'I was twenty-eight years of age, and had been a member of the church eight years, when the Constitution of this Commonwealth was framed. I well remember the concern which religious people appeared to feel about the third article of the bill of rights; but those members of the Convention with whom I conversed assured me, that though the word church was not used in said article, it was included or meant by the words, "religious societies," and, as such, was recognised in the closing part of the first section, and its duty made sufficiently plain; and in the proviso following, its right of choosing its own pastor sufficiently secured; - that the rights and usages of the church were so far from being lessened or invaded, that they were not meddled with at all, but were considered as left altogether secure, as they always had been. It was my understanding, that the Convention considered the rights of the church as above their limits, as out of their power, and as above the power of human legislation or jurisdiction; therefore, they left the rights of the church out of the question, leaving her to the full enjoyment of her own rights and usages. And the closing section of the aforesaid article was considered as affording or securing the protection of law to a church, as a religious society, as well as to towns and other corporate bodies.

Wm. Nutting.' "

"To these, we may add the certificate of one of the aged and worthy ministers of Newton (Mass.), dated June, 1829.

" 'In reply to the question you propose, allow me to state, that from 1776 to 1781, the date of my settlement in the ministry, I resided chiefly in Boston, my native place. I was there during the sittings of the Convention who framed the Constitution of Massachusetts, and often attended for the purpose of hearing their debates. And I can assure you that I heard nothing, either in Convention, or abroad among the people at that day, so far as I can recollect, which led me to suspect that any part of the Constitution was designed to take from the churches their natural and immemorial right of choice in the election of their Pastors.

Respectfully yours,

W. Greenough.' "

The disestablishment of Congregationalism had followed in New Hampshire essentially the same course as that indicated in the preceding cases from Massachusetts. New problems of policy and of political theory came to the surface in the opinions of the New Hampshire judges in Hale v. Everett and were faced by Lowrie, J. in Pennsylvania in McGinnis v. Watson. Those issues, in another context, were considered in Harold Laski's early essay, "Notes on Ecclesiastical Trusts," 36 Canadian Law Times 190 (1916).

Hale v. Everett

Supreme Court of New Hampshire, 1868

53 N. H. 9

[In these proceedings in equity the plaintiffs, members of The First Unitarian Society of Christians in Dover and owners of pews in its meeting house, had alleged that the defendant wardens of the Church were permitting Francis E. Abbott, a renegade Unitarian, to preach theistic and non-Unitarian doctrine in the meeting house of the Society. The majority of the Supreme Court of New Hampshire granted them injunctive relief. The decree of the Court forbade the defendant wardens to permit Abbott "or any other person, to preach or inculcate in the meeting-house of said society doctrines subversive of the fundamental principles of Christianity, as generally received" by the denomination of Christians known as Unitarians and further forbade the "denial of the doctrine that the Scriptures of the Old and New Testaments do contain a divine revelation given by inspiration of God." The decree included other prohibitions of a similar sort. The opinion of the majority was written by Sargent J. and filled 84 pages of the reports; the dissenting opinion of Doe, J. covered 143 pages.]

SARGENT, J. This society in Dover was formed and organized on the 28th day of August, 1827, and has continued to the present time under the same organization. The purpose and design of forming the society was set forth in the articles of agreement, as follows: "Believing that the public worship of God has a salutary influence upon society, by awakening and diffusing moral and religious affections, and considering there are many persons in the place who are unprovided with such means of religious instructions and accommodations for public worship as are most congenial with their own convictions of truth and duty, - therefore, the subscribers, for their mutual and better accommodation in the premises, do hereby unite and form themselves into a religious society by the name and style of The First Unitarian Society of Christians in Dover, and do hereby agree to be governed, in their associate capacity, by such rules and by-laws as said society may from time to time establish. Such persons as are desirous of uniting with them may become members of said society by subscribing this agreement"...

This society thus constituted, and having voluntarily assumed this name, the leading and most important words in which were, and were designed to be, so expressive of the most fundamental doctrines of the sect of which, and of which alone, its members were to be composed, on the 6th day of November, 1826, met and voted, - "that, in the views of the society, it is expedient that there should be a house built for the accommodation of its members, in their public worship; that there be a committee formed for raising by subscription the sum of $10,000, for the purpose of purchasing a lot of land, and thereon building a house for the above purpose; and that that sum be divided into 100 shares of $100 each"; and a committee was at the same time appointed to superintend said subscription.

The required amount was thus raised by subscription, and a lot of land was bargained for; and during the year 1828 a meeting-house was commenced thereon, said house fronting on Locust street, in said Dover, the land and house all being paid for by the money thus subscribed. After the house was commenced, the land, including the house, was conveyed, by the Dover Manufacturing Company, June 10, 1828, to five persons, - H., C., A., P., and O., - all of Dover, and their successors, as "trustees of said society", to be held by them "in trust for the use of the stockholders or proprietors of the meeting-house to be erected thereon, their heirs and assigns, and under such regulations, condition, and restrictions for the sale and occupancy of the pews in said house, and for the use, care, custody, and control of said house as may be prescribed by a majority of the votes of said stockholders at any time previous to the sale or disposal of the pews in said house."

A meeting of said stockholders or subscribers was duly called and holden at said Dover, on the 6th day of March, 1829, prior to the sale of any of the pews in said house; and among other things it was voted, 1st, "That the general custody of said house shall be under the control of The First Unitarian Society of Christians in Dover." Then, after various other regulations, they provided that a pew tax shall be paid on the 1st day of April annually, "to be appropriated for the support of religious worship in said house, under the direction of the First Unitarian Society of Christians in Dover," and, also, that the pews be sold subject to these conditions.

A public sale of the pews in said house was holden March 17, 1829, when said pews were sold and conveyed, with all the privileges and appurtenances incident to the pews in said house, and subject to all their liabilities, agreeably to the regulations and conditions as adopted by said stockholders for the sale of said pews.

It appears that such vacancies as have occurred in the board of trustees of said society have been duly filled by new elections, and that Eri Perkins and others are the present trustees, and the proper successors of the original grantees of the land, who now hold it, with the meeting-house thereon, subject to the same trusts as contained in the original deed...

This society was formed under and by virtue of an act of the legislature of this state, entitled "An act empowering religious associations to assume corporate powers." Approved July 3, 1827, N. H. Laws (1830) 462. This was substantially a reenactment of the act of 1819, 2 N. H. Laws (1824) 44; and this act of 1810 was in amendment of the law of 1791, entitled "An act for regulating towns and the choice of town officers" - N. H. Laws (1815) 243; and this law of 1791 was passed under and in conformity with the provisions in our state constitution of 1783, which provisions remained unchanged in the constitution of 1792, which is still in force.

Let us then examine such parts of our constitution as bear upon this subject, and we shall find it convenient to select a group together several articles of part first of the bill of rights, and also of part second of the constitution, each of which we may need to examine by itself and in connection with the others, as throwing light upon the questions involved in this case.

These articles in the constitution of 1783 were not changed in the revision of 1792, but remain the same in both, and continue unchanged to the present time. They are as follows:

"Part First

"Bill of Rights

..."Art. IV. Among the natural rights, some are in their very nature unalienable, because no equivalent can be given or received for them. Of this kind are the Rights of Conscience.

"Art. V. Every individual has a natural and unalienable right to worship God according to the dictates of his own conscience and reason; and no subject shall be hurt, molested, or restrained in his person, liberty, or estate, for worshipping God in the manner and season most agreeable to the dictates of his own conscience, or for his religious profession, sentiments, or persuasion, provided he doth not disturb the public peace, or disturb others in their religious worship.

"Art. VI. As morality and piety, rightly grounded on evangelical principles, will give the best and greatest security to government, and will lay in the hearts of men the strongest obligations to due subjection; and as the knowledge of these is most likely to be propagated through a society by the institution of the public worship of the Deity, and of public instruction in morality and religion; - therefore, to promote these important purposes, the people of this state have a right to empower, and do hereby fully empower, the legislature to authorize from time to time the several towns, parishes, bodies corporate, or religious societies within this state to make adequate provision, at their own expense, for the support and maintenance of public Protestant teachers of piety, religion, and morality.

"Provided, notwithstanding, That the several towns, parishes, bodies corporate, or religious societies shall at all times have the exclusive right of electing their own public teachers, and of contracting with them for their support and maintenance; and no person of any one particular religious sect or denomination shall ever be compelled to pay toward the support of the teacher or teachers of another persuasion, sect, or denomination.

"And every denomination of Christians, demeaning themselves quietly, and as good subjects of the state, shall be equally under the protection of the law; and no subordination of any one sect or denomination to another shall ever be established by law."

The other provisions of the constitution, that need to be considered in connection with the above, are the following:

"Part Second

"Form of Government

"Art. V. And, further, full power and authority are hereby given and granted to the said general court, from time to time, to make, ordain, and establish all manner of wholesome and reasonable orders, laws, statutes, ordinances, directions, and instructions, ether with penalties or without, so as that the same be not repugnant or contrary to this constitution, as they may judge for the benefit and welfare of this state, and for the governing and ordering thereof, and of the subjects of the same.

"Art. XIV. Every member of the house of representatives * * * shall be of the Protestant religion, and shall cease to represent such town, parish, or place, immediately on his ceasing to be qualified as aforesaid.

"Art. XXIX. Provided, nevertheless, That no person shall be capable of being elected a senator who is not of the Protestant religion * * *.

"Art. XLII. The governor shall be chosen annually, in the month of March * * *. And no person shall be eligible to this office * * * unless he shall be of the Protestant religion.

"Art. LXI. * * * and the qualifications for councillor shall be the same as for senator."

It is sufficiently plain that, by these last four provisions, a religious test is instituted as a qualification for holding certain civil offices. Every member of the house of representatives "shall be of the Protestant religion." No person shall be capable of being elected a senator or councillor "who is not of the Protestant religion." And no person shall be eligible to the office of governor "unless he shall be of the Protestant religion." Something more is evidently intended by these expressions than that a man should simply not be a Roman Catholic in order to hold these offices. The requirement is not negative, but positive and affirmative. It is not that these offices may be filled with those who are not Roman Catholics, or who are not pagans, or Jews, or Mohammedans, but only by those who are of the Protestant religion. This is so in every case; each provision requires a positive and affirmative qualification in order to hold the office. A Mohammedan is not a Roman Catholic; but he cannot hold these offices, or either of them, because he is not of the Protestant religion, as the law requires he should be. So of the Jew; so of the pagan. The same would be true of an infidel; he is not a Roman Catholic, but he is not of the Protestant religion, because, to be a Protestant he must be a Christian; to be of the Protestant religion, he must be of the Christian religion. The term Christian embraces and includes both Roman Catholic and Protestant alike; and, to be of the Catholic or Protestant religion, a person must first be of the Christian religion...

An infidel - one who does not believe the Bible, or that Jesus Christ was the true Messiah, "the Christ of God," can no more be a Protestant than he can a Roman Catholic, because he lacks the first and chief qualifications of either, viz., a belief in Christianity; for while he, with the Protestant, denies the authority of the pope, he differs from both in not believing the Bible, or in Jesus Christ and his religion. The infidel and the pagan stand alike; they are both anti-Catholic, and equally anti-Protestant. They each lack the first element necessary to make them either Catholic or Protestant, and that element is Christianity. Jews believed in the Old Testament, and not in the New. Mohammedans receive the whole Bible in a sense, but receive and acknowledge the Alcoran as of higher authority, and accept Mohammed as a greater prophet than Jesus. Neither believes the system of Christianity, as taught in the New Testament. They are both, alike, anti-Catholic and anti-Protestant, for the reason that they are both anti-Christian. A Roman Catholic is a Christian who admits the authority of the pope; a Protestant is a Christian who denies that authority; and no one not a Christian can be either a Catholic or a Protestant, any more than a man can be a Jew (religiously) who does not believe in Moses or the Pentateuch, or than he could be a Mohammedan who did not believe in Mohammed or the Alcoran. Since the days of Luther, Romanists and Protestants have constituted, and still constitute, the two great divisions of Christianity in western Europe and America...

Under the constitution, religious sects or denominations were recognized, which were then only distinguished by their names, the names being sufficiently indicative of the doctrines of the sect: "Roman Catholics" was the name of one sect, "Presbyterians" of another, "Quakers" of another. A society which should take for its name "The First Society of Roman Catholics in C," or "The First Society of Presbyterians in C," or "The First Society of Quakers in C," would be understood as made up of persons of the sect which the name of the society indicated; and if a donation of a church had been made to certain persons in trusts for a certain use, which use was to be forever subject to the control of The First Society of Roman Catholics in C, or of The First Society of Quakers in C, the trust would have been held to be subject to the control of such of the society, and such only, as adhered to the fundamental doctrines of the society as indicated by the name, even though they might be a minority of those who at first were numbered among its members; that a majority of the original society, if they had abandoned the principles and doctrines of the sect, would not be known as a society of Romanists or Quakers, for the purpose of administering such trust. So of the Methodists, after, by special statute, they were recognized and declared to be a distinct religious sect. The name indicated the belief of the sect. The name in that case would also indicate that the church polity, or plan of church government, was different from that of the Congregationalists, just as the term Episcopalian or Presbyterian would indicate, in each, a different polity from the Congregations; and after the acts of 1819 and 1827, which took away from towns all power to act as parishes or to support religious teachers, and gave to the different religious sects, and denominations of Christians, and to them alone, the right to form religious societies, they retained all the powers and rights which they had before as sects, and acquired the additional powers of a corporation for certain limited purposes.

While the authority was granted to towns by the legislature to raise money to support the ministry and to build meeting-houses, these towns, being simply municipal corporations, could not be made sectarian or denominational; while under the acts of 1819 and 1827, as we have seen, all religious societies were to be assumed to be, sectarian and denominational; and they might adopt a sectarian and denominational name, which should describe and declare their faith, and at the same time answer as its corporate name; or they might adopt a general corporate name merely, having no reference to the faith or doctrines of the sect to which they belonged, and then they would, of course, make a declaration of their doctrines, or creed, or confession, in their articles of association. ...

Under this condition of things, this society was formed by a distinct religious sect, by a particular denomination of Christians, and, instead of assuming a name which should merely answer as a corporate name in which to transact business, but which should not have any reference to the peculiar sect that had formed the society, they assumed a name, which, while it answered for a legal corporate appellative, should also express, as definitely as language could be made to do, the peculiar creed or doctrines of the sect or denomination which formed the society. It was to be a "Unitarian society of Christians." Both these words in the name are as strongly expressive of the fundamental doctrines of the sect as words could be; and it would be assumed in such a case, without any evidence, that the name was adopted for the purpose of expressing the peculiar and fundamental doctrines of the sect that formed the society; and that this would be so understood by everybody.

Therefore, when a trust was created in certain persons, for the benefit or use of this society, or for the use of others, to be under the control of this society by its denominational name, but its distinctive sectarian appellative, it must be understood that the donor or founder of the trust had in view that fact; and that when he constituted his trust or use, and made it subject to the control of this society, he had in view, and referred more particularly to, its sectarian and denominational qualities than to any other. ... Now, suppose such a society should, in the course of time, become equally divided; just half its members should secede from the faith and doctrines of the sect which formed the society, and the other half should adhere to such faith and doctrines, and each half should separately undertake to control the use of the house according to its own religious views, and the views of the two divisions were antagonistic, and the court were called on to enforce the trust: can there be a doubt that equity would require that the control of the house should be given to the division which adhered to the original faith? Would not that be carrying out the wishes and intentions of the original founders of the trust? But, suppose that the party which had seceded from the faith of the denomination should outnumber the other by one or more, could that change the reason of the case or its controlling equities? Would it not be the duty of a court of equity to look beyond the mere form of the thing to its material substance, and to say, in such a case, that the portion of the religious society, who adhered to the faith of the sect that founded the society, were entitled to control the use of the house, rather than the portion who, being still members of the society in form, had renounced the faith of the sect which formed, and whose fundamental doctrines had given name to, the society? ...

We will next examine the main charge in the bill, viz., that Mr. Abbott has apostatized from the Christian faith and become a disbeliever in Christianity, and also in Unitarianism; and that he is now occupying said church, not as a public teacher of Christianity, but as an open opposer of Christianity - as an avowed deist or theist, disowning Jesus Christ as the Messiah, and his religion as the only true religion; and charging that said Abbott is now neither a Unitarian nor a Christian.

Mr. Abbott remained with this society, as pastor or religious teacher, till April 1, 1868, when, by his resignation, that relation terminated. Towards the latter part of his preaching, he made statements that "Jesus

Christ was like other men, with no more authority," and compared Christ with Garrison and other good men; that he doubted whether there was more than one pulpit in Boston that he (Abbott) would be allowed to occupy; stated that he was looked upon as a "rebel" in his theology ...; that he considered Christ a mere man, and falible like other men; that Christ was not the Messiah, and that if he (Christ) believed himself to be the Messiah, he was mistaken ...; that the New Testament showed that Christ did claim to be the Messiah, but that he (Abbott) believed the Messiah had not come, and would not come...

He went on in this way, step by step, until he openly declared himself not a Christian, nor a Unitarian, so far as Unitarianism was based upon Christianity or the recognition of Christ as the Messiah; proclaimed himself a theist, and preached his theistical doctrines to such an extent as to give great dissatisfaction to the members of the church and society, - in consequence of which his subscription list fell off until he was advised by his friends to resign, which he at once did; and by arrangement, his term of service terminated April 1, 1868...

The reformation has in fact gone far beyond Luther and Calvin, as the articles of faith, and more particularly the doctrinal preaching of the Lutheran and Calvinistic churches of the present day, will show. But, while they have changed and modified the old formulas of doctrine and introduced new ones, they will uniformly adhere to the doctrine of John Robinson - that all religious truth is to be made known and received "from the written word of God." That is the source of all religious light and truth. If new developments of truth are to be looked for, they are to be expected to be made known from that source alone. By this standard all new truth is to be tried; it is to be examined, considered, and compared with other scriptures of truth, and must be proved to be founded upon, and emanate from the written word of God, before it is received. Upon this point all denominations of Christians, now termed evangelical, are agreed. This in fact was the doctrine of the reformation - the great doctrine which was the foundation and chief corner-stone of the reformation - that the Bible alone was, and was to be, the only source of all true religious light, and of all revealed religious truth; and that every doctrine in theology, as well as every course of life, is to be tried by this test and judged by this standard; in fact, Lutherism and Calvinism are only excellent so far as they embody the real teachings and doctrines of the Bible.

That was the faith of the puritans; that is generally the faith of their descendants. A few only have apostatized, and believe with Mr. Abbott and some of his associates and followers, in a religion "that acknowledges no leader, is loyal to no master, imitates no exemplar, looks to no redeemer, needs no saviour, knows no Christ...

DOE, J., dissenting - ... The decree is a perpetual injunction upon all the members of this corporation and the whole world. It forever prohibits the preaching and inculcating of doctrines subversive of Unitarianism in "the meeting-house of said society." The doctrines of the Trinity and the vicarious atonement are peculiarly and entirely subversive of the fundamental principles of Unitarianism. Any Trinitarian minister, missionary, agent, or other person, who should on a single occasion, on any day of the week, occupy this house for the purpose of preaching and inculcating either of those doctrines; and every member of the corporation who should "allow, suffer, or permit" any person, at any time, or in any form or manner, to preach and inculcate either of those doctrines in this house, would be liable to fine and imprisonment for the criminal offence of violating this decree. If Mr. Abbott should become a Methodist or Baptist, he could not, in this house, endeavor to convert his former parishioners, even upon their own unanimous invitation, without incurring the same penalty. And if all the members of this corporation should become orthodox, and should, "in the meeting-house of said society," listen to an orthodox sermon on the vicarous atonement, every one of them would be guilty of a flagrant breach of the injunction. Banishment from their own meeting-house is to be the punishment of their conversion. It may be a serious question whether the choir or congregation can safely sing the Trinitarian doxology. If a Trinitarian minister (contrary to usage) should exchange pulpits for a Sunday with a minister of this parish, the former will need to prepare himself with extreme caution for a perilous service. It would be strange if another temple could be found in any country more thoroughly fortified against orthodox doctrines than is "the meeting-house of said society" by the decree made in this case.

The carefully chosen language of the decree seems to vouch for the theological soundness of Unitarians as Christians, and to elevate them to a certain ecclesiastical position among other sects, which they have not been able to acquire by their own unaided exertions. Undoubtedly they are, in law, the peers of any other sect; but whether they are Christians, in the technical, ecclesiastical, Trinitarian sense, entitled, as theological equals, and by virtue of the genuineness of their Christianity, to the Christian fellowship of other sects, is a question upon which it is not our official duty to intimate an opinion.

The decree forbids this parish ever to "permit" any person to preach in its meeting-house "who preaches and inculcates a disbelief in the doctrine of the Lordship and Messiahship of Jesus Christ, as taught by him in the New Testament Scriptures, or a disbelief in Jesus Christ as the great head of the church, or of his divine mission and authority as a religious teacher, as thus taught by him." This prohibition is a clear assumption of ecclesiastical jurisdiction. It is a decision that the doctrines mentioned were taught by Christ: we cannot enforce the decree without deciding what doctrines were "taught by him" on those subjects; and the power of deciding what he taught on all subjects. If we can authoritatively establish what are the doctrines of the Lordship of Christ, his Messiahship, his headship of the Church, and his divine mission and authority as a religious teacher, "as taught by him," - if it is our duty to settle theology to that extent, it is our duty to settle the whole body of theology for every parish in the state. It is supreme ecclesiastical authority, maintained by the civil power, that is asserted...

It is necessary to remember that this society is a New Hampshire lay corporation, and not an English ecclesiastical one; that the peculiarities of the latter, and the ecclesiastical courts, ancient clerical prerogatives and religious abuses of amalgamated church and state, are not here; and that the idea of ecclesiastical immutability, generated by or embodied in foreign political institutions, has no place in our law. "Ecclesiastical corporations are where the members that compose it are entirely spiritual persons, - such as bishops; certain deans and prebendaries; all archdeacons, parsons, and vicars, which are sole corporations; deans and chapters at present, and formerly prior and convent, abbot and monks, and the like bodies aggregate." 1 Bl. Com. 470. Our "incorporated societies are not to be regarded as ecclesiastical corporations in the sense of the English law, which were composed entirely of ecclesiastical persons and subject to the ecclesiastical judicatories, but as belonging to the class of civil corporations, to be controlled and managed according to the principles of the common law, as administered by the ordinary tribunals of justice." Robertson v. Bullions, 11 N. Y. 243, 251. "Public teachers of religion and morality, chosen by a corporate body, are to every purpose civil officers of the state, as much so as schoolmasters and magistrates. * * Public instruction in religion and morality, within the meaning of our constitution and laws, is, to every purpose, a civil and not a spiritual institution. * * The minority must submit to the judgment of the majority." Muzzy v. Wilkins, in the county of Hillsborough, May, 1803; 4 Chief Justice Smith's MSS. Reports 65, [Smith, 1].

Congregationalism, in its broad and general meaning, is a form of church polity, a system of ecclesiastical organizations, the essential peculiarly of which is, that it maintains the independence of each congregation or society, in all matters of ecclesiastical government, discipline, doctrine and practice, including the right of the majority to change its religion, to choose its ministers, and to inaugurate them, or employ them without any inaugural ceremonies, as it sees fit. It may be connected with any form of doctrine and any mode of worship. Baptists, Universalists, Unitarians, and Trinitarian Congregationalists are different divisions of the Congregational denomination, or different denominations of Congregationalists. The Dublin case, 38 N. H. 459, 459, 516-538; Muzzy v. Wilkins, p. 35; Henderson & a. v. Erskine, in Cheshire, October 1802; 5 New American Cyclopedia 606; Baird's Religion in America 555-564; Lawrence's N. H. Churches 11; Wayland's Baptists 14; Hutch. Coll. 482, 500. "This constitution of church government was adapted to the constitution of civil government, both as popular as can well be conceived." 1 Hutch. Hist. Mass. 371, 372.

The definition of Congregationalism was forcibly illustrated in Henderson & a. v. Erskine and in other cases, more than sixty years ago, when towns were parishes, and, as such, had power to elect public teachers of piety, religion, and morality, and to support them by taxation. The constitution provides that no person of one sect or denomination shall be compelled to pay toward the support of the religious teacher or teachers of another persuasion, sect, or denomination. Towns, in which the majorities were Trinitarian Congregationalists, elected Trinitarian Congregational religious teachers, and taxed Universalists as well as others to support them; and the courts held that Universalists were Congregationalists, and must pay the ministerial taxes. Those decisions were manifestly wrong in this: they were based solely on the indisputable proposition that Universalists are Congregationalists, in disregard of the two other propositions equally indisputable and equally important, that Universalists are one of several Congregational sects, and that religious liberty is the object of the constitutional provision. In 1804 the Freewill Baptists, in 1805 the Universalists, and in 1807 the Methodists, applied to the legislature for relief from the tax-paying consequences of being held not to be a religious sects distinct from the puritans, and procured the passage of resolutions declaring them to be religious sects entitled to the constitutional privilege. Whether they were religious sects, within the meaning of the constitution, or not, was a judicial and not a legislative question; but, by the unconstitutional and void resolutions of the legislature, the erroneous decisions of courts, juries, towns, and town officers were practically reversed. In holding Universalists, whom they regarded as infidels, to be liable, as Congregationalists, to Congregational taxation, the puritans illustrated the broad idea of Congregationalism as a system of ecclesiastical government without any theological limitations...

...Article VI of part I of the constitution, which was adopted in 1783 and took effect in 1784, provides that the legislature may authorize "the several towns, parishes, bodies corporate, or religious societies, within this state, to make adequate provision, at their own expense, for the support and maintenance of public Protestant teachers of piety, religion, and morality.

"Provided, notwithstanding, That the several towns, parishes, bodies corporate, or religious societies, shall at all times have the exclusive right of electing their own public teachers, and of contracting with them for their support and maintenance."

And this article was retained in the constitution of 1792. It does not confer any power that the legislature would not have if this article had been omitted. The legislature could authorize towns or other parishes to support ministers, under those general grants of legislative power by which it passes acts of incorporation, and a great variety of other statutes Concord R. R. v. Greely, 17 N. H. 47, 53; Company v. Fernald, 47 N. H. 444, 458. But the provision, that all parishes shall at all times have the exclusive right of electing their own public teachers, is the provincial system of parochial freedom, incorporated in the organic law of the state beyond the reach of legislative action. Whatever sectarian ties of advisory councils, ecclesiastical fellowship, or theological harmony, or other limitations of parochial autonomy, were associated with the idea of Congregationalism in the minds of theologians, no such limitations were inserted in the constitution. So far as Congregationalism was a system of independent parochial government, the ecclesiastical supremacy of the majority of each parish, and an embodiment of the fundamental principle of free institutions, it was adopted as the ecclesiastical system of the state. So far as it was a system of theology, it could not be adopted without establishing a state religion; - a state religion in any other sense than a religion of parochial independence, was not established, but was prohibited...

In the early part of the present century, large numbers of Trinitarian societies became Unitarian, in Maine, New Hampshire, Massachusetts, Rhode Island, and Connecticut. There were more than one hundred cases of this apostasy in Massachusetts. The defection occurred in all the old orthodox Congregational societies in Boston except one, and probably in half the towns in eastern Massachusetts... It naturally produced a bitter and prolonged controversy. A vast amount of time and thought and zeal was spent upon it. A mass of literature in newspapers, pamphlets, and volumes accumulated, presenting both sides of the controversy, in all its details, in every possible light. Ellis's Half Century of the Unitarian Controversy 3; The Dublin case, 38 N. H. 537. The most eminent legal talent that this country has produced was employed by the Trinitarians to maintain their rights of property. Suits were brought and judgments rendered; but it seems that no one, in court or out of court, ever questioned the constitutional right of apostasy, or the right of an apostate society to retain and use its meeting-house and all its corporate property for preaching and inculcating doctrines subversive of its former faith...

When this Dover corporation was formed and its house built, very few parishes in America had been organized by Unitarians; they were essentially a denomination of apostate parishes, who, by their apostasy, in substance of doctrine, had lost their ecclesiastical standing and fellowship without losing their corporate property or any of their corporate rights; and the amount of such property was very large. According to the history of this sect, culminating in the decree in the present case, while the law upholds apostasy in carrying property from other religions to Unitarianism, it does not allow apostasy to carry property from Unitarianism to other religions. The theory, that the constitution and the parochial unsectarian independence guaranteed by the constitution can be abolished by the sectarianism of the member of a parish, is a novel and startling one. It did not occur to such a constitutional lawyer as Webster (sorely pressed as he was for arguments against that independence, and losing the memorable Dedham case for want of such arguments), but was left to be invented by the thrifty ingenuity of these plaintiffs, as the peculiar privilege and exclusive protection of Unitarians against loss from parochial apostasy, after what it had won, by that practice... The result is a Unitarian monopoly of parochial apostasy. The plaintiffs are not barred, in law, from setting up this claim, by the doctrine of estoppel: whether they and their sect are morally estopped is a religious question, of which this court has no jurisdiction...

There is a strong intrinsic improbability that the founders of our institutions overlooked the practical necessity of allowing for some variations in all ecclesiastical affairs. The Catholic church, more stable in doctrine than the Protestant bodies that have withdrawn from it or from others in that line of secession, and exhibiting a constancy nearly equal to that of its Jewish predecessor, or of Mohammedanism or other steadfast religions, now teaches, in its schools, astronomical principles which it formerly condemned as fatal theological heresies, to be extirpated by fire. Draper's Intellectual Development of Europe 443, 513, 520. "What is theologically true in religion, it is agreed on all hands that the court are not competent to decide; nor have they power to determine what is really and intrinsically substantial and essential in matters of doctrine." The Dublin case, 38 N. H. 509. But in the cases of Bruno and Galileo, and throughout Christendom, astronomical doctrines now admitted to be erroneous were held by the church to be essential. And the doctrines of the sovereignty of the church over the state, and of the unlawfulness of receiving compensation for the use of money loaned, once maintained, are now practically abandoned by the same church. "A large proportion, perhaps the majority of the members of the Lutheran church, believe no more in the doctrines of Luther than in the doctrines of Confucius. * * I do not believe that any denomination of Christians exists, which, for so long a period as the Baptists, have maintained so invariably the truth of their early confessions. * * It is difficult at the present day to conceive to what extent the doctrine of the limited atonement, and the views of election which accompanied it, were carried" among the Baptists. "Within the last fifty years a change has gradually taken place in the views of a large portion of our brethren. At the commencement of that period, Gill's Divinity was a sort of standard, and Baptists imbibing his opinions were what is called almost hyper-Calvinistic. A change commenced upon the publication of the writings of Andrew Fuller, * * which, in the Northern and Eastern states, has become almost universal." Wayland's Baptists 15, 18, 19. "In a late edition of Neal's History of the Puritans, it is stated that in almost all the Presbyterian congregations there has taken place a change of opinions, and that they have swerved from the doctrines of their forefathers, and have now become advocates of very different tenets." Attorney-Gen. v. Pearson, 7 Sim. 290, Portions of the Common Prayer of the English Church are not now generally accepted in the original sense by the learned laity or clergy of England or America. 4 Hume's Hist. Eng. 503; 1 Works of John Adams 40; Stanley's Life and Correspondence of Dr. Arnold of Rugby, Letter No. CCXI. The constructions lately introduced by the supreme ecclesiastical tribunal of that church in England are sufficiently liberal to admit some who are substantially Catholics, some who are really Unitarians, and an infinite variety of others. Universalism changes with the rest. Greeley's Recollections 74. Among some sects the old formularies remain, with an understanding that each individual enjoys a large liberty in putting his own interpretation upon them. Within the strictest nominal uniformity there is immense diversity. The most rigid standards of orthodoxy have an undefined and uncertain degree of flexibility. Explicit creeds, upheld by the acts of parliament, conform themselves to the apostacies of the people...

The Calvinistic doctrine of predestination, whatever it originally was in general principle, and however it was applied to infants or adults, has been rejected or essentially modified in Calvinistic churches since the time of Calvin. 1 Lecky's Hist. Rationalism, ch. iv., part 1; 10 Works of John Adams 67. It has been greatly changed since the organization of the old puritan parishes of New Hampshire. Not one of them would now endure the doctrine of its founders. The preaching that first mustered them, would now disband them. Calvin and Edwards are the two great Calvinists of history; their religion was Calvinism. The New England Calvinism of today is a very different religion. There are many parishes in this state that once held the faith of Calvin and Edwards: let them be decreed to return to it, and they would be extinguished, or the decree would be reversed. The length of the process of doctrinal elimination or transformation is immaterial. It was going on in 1783, as it is now; and it was a striking illustration of the necessity of parochial liberty brought to the knowledge of the authors of the constitution by study, tradition and observation. They did not intend, in establishing parochial independence, to authorize the court to disperse the old Calvinistic parishes by requiring them to adhere to their original doctrine in regard to infants or adults...

When Edwards preached, - "The God who holds you over the pit of hell, much as one holds a spider or some loathsome insect over the fire, abhors you, and is dreadfully provoked", - and "The sight of hell-torments will exalt the happiness of the saints for ever. It will not only make them more sensible of the greatness and fulness of the grace of God in their happiness, but it will really make their happiness the greater, as it will make them more sensible of their own happiness: it will give them a more lively relish of it; it will make them prize it more when they see others who were of the same nature, and born under the same circumstances, plunged in such misery, and they so distinguished. Oh! it will make them sensible how happy they are!" - he inculcated ideas of the divine government that were prevalent in and before his time, but have since been generally modified. Whether any particular or general changes in theological or ecclesiastical affairs are for the better or for the worse, are questions which the court, being by law incapable of officially entertaining their private religious opinions, are not authorized to consider; but perpetual change establishes a probability that change was contemplated and provided for in the constitutional grant of parochial power.

Every sect has a legal right, while nominally retaining an ancient creed "for substance of doctrine," to change it in everything that is legally, logically, or practically the substance of it. But to say that such changes as have occurred in Calvinism do not affect it "for substance of doctrine," is to indulge in a style too hyperbolical for the practical purposes of the law, however useful it may be for other purposes. They who resist the changes of the present, may be tempted to deny the changes of the past; to yield to the temptation would weaken their cause; so far as the success of their resistance is concerned, it would be worse for them to be convicted of gross and inexcusable ignorance or insincerity, than to confess themselves guilty of progress. Every reading and thinking person, gathering information, and exercising his faculties without bigotry or prejudice, believes that the tendency is, and for a long time has been, to a religion more humane and rational (according to human tests) than that of former times. Whether the movement is towards truth or towards error, and whether it is the duty of religious teachers to accelerate the current, or to float along with it, or to stem it, it is not the duty of the court to deny a notorious fact of history, or to construe the constitution in defiance of the fact, in full view of which, and in conformity to which, the constitution established parochial independence...

The parochial power of electing public teachers is granted or guaranteed by the constitution. Whether the constitution creates, establishes, and grants it, or recognizes, declares, and guarantees it, is immaterial. There can be no objection, in this case, to calling it a power granted. As the power is granted by the constitution, which is the supreme law, we are not at liberty to look anywhere for a limitation of the constitutional power, except in the constitution itself. And when we examine the constitution to see what bounds are fixed around this parochial power, we find in the proviso in which the power is granted no limitation whatever. The language is, - "Provided, notwithstanding, that the several towns, parishes, bodies corporate, or religious societies shall at all times have the exclusive right of electing their own public teachers, and of contracting with them for their support and maintenance." The grant is absolute and unqualified; but the clause immediately preceding the proviso empowers the legislature to authorize parishes "to make adequate provision at their own expense for the support and maintenance of public Protestant teachers of piety, religion, and morality." No question of teaching practical piety, practical religion, or practical morality arises in this case; and, in respect to doctrinal religion and theological theories, whatever reasons there may be for holding the grant of elective power to be entirely unqualified, it cannot be claimed that it is qualified in any other manner, or to any other extent, than by the word "Protestant". And, if it be conceded for the purposes of this case that it is qualified by that word, the question arises, What is the meaning of "Protestant" in the constitution? ...

The original historical meaning of the word is significant. The first Protestants acquired the name in Germany, when a Catholic decree prohibited innovation in religion. Certain persons "entered a solemn protest against the decree, as unjust and impious. On that account they were distinguished by the name of Protestants - an appellation which hath since become better known and more honorable by its being applied indiscriminately to all the sects, of whatever denomination, which have revolved from the Roman see." 2 Prescott's Robertson's Charles V 208... "Hence arose the denomination of Protestants, which from this period has been given to those who renounce the superstitious communion of the Church of Rome." 4 Mosheim's Ecc. Hist. 72. And the sects of deists and theists, of the class of Thomas Jefferson, Benjamin Franklin, Ethan Allen, Gov. Plumer, and the defendant Abbott, have revolted from it, by seceding from other Protestant sects whose ecclesiastical genealogy runs through a series of revolts and secessions more or less numerous, back to the Catholic church. The Protestant party was organized for the purpose of resisting certain doctrines and practices of Catholicism in church and state; and the whole force of the Protestant name, in its popular as well as its etymological signification, lies in its expression of hostility to Rome.

Protestantism is the Protestant religion - the religion of Protestants. As a system of theology, it is positive and negative - positive in its acceptance of affirmative doctrine, negative in its rejection of Catholicism. Mere negation is not a system of theology; and, as a system of theology, and for some ecclesiastical purposes, Protestantism is more than a negation of Catholicism. What its positive theological limits are, is a question upon which theologians are divided. The prevailing ecclesiastical opinion is, that Unitarianism is outside of those limits; and if the court hold that the constitutional parochial power of electing public teachers is limited by the Protestant test, and interpret the test as if it were used for a purpose of technical, positive theology, according to the clear weight of theological authority applicable to the execution of such a purpose, the decree is precisely the opposite of what it should be: it should suppress Unitarianism, instead of suppressing all doctrines subversive of Unitarianism. Fortunately for the plaintiffs and all other Unitarians, the Protestant test of the constitution is a legal and not an ecclesiastical one, and is founded on political and not on theological reasons. Inadequate for a theological system as a mere negation is, it is amply sufficient for the purpose of a legal official test. And Protestantism, as a negation of Catholicism, is the Protestant test of the constitution, - the legal test inherited by us and our ancestors, in this and in the old country, for many generations...

The practical construction given to the constitution by the men who framed it, and their contemporaries, and their successors inheriting their opinions, is to be considered... The practical construction shows that the Protestant test is an anti-Catholic test and nothing else, or that, in its widest possible sweep, it does not disable for unbelief any non-Catholic who has, directly or indirectly, recently or remotely, by his own action or the action of his ancestors, become separated from the Roman Catholic church.

The constitution containing the Protestant test went into operation in June, 1784. In March, 1785, William Plumer was elected to the house of representatives. He was then well known as a deist or theist (the difference between deism and theism is not material in this case), who had been a zealous Baptist preacher though not ordained, and had traversed the state in that capacity, but had apostatized before he ceased from preaching. The circumstances and extent of his apostasy were notorious, and calculated to excite opposition. He was re-elected to the house in 1788, 1790, 1791, 1797, 1798, 1800, and 1801, and was several times speaker of that body. By election to the United States senate in 1802, he was withdrawn from state office. He was a member and president of the state senate in 1810 and 1811, and was governor in 1812, 1816, 1817, and 1818. His deism was openly avowed and never recanted. He became a politician, and did not give unnecessary offence by assailing the religion of others; but his deism was known throughout the state to be as settled and confirmed as that of Jefferson. His biographer speaks of him as an inquirer after truth. He was such an inquirer as Jefferson. He inquired after truth all his life; but during his last seventy years he found nothing that he believed to be religious truth but deism, and this fact was universally and distinctly understood by the people of the state. He first held Protestant office at the age of twenty-six, before the organization of political parties, when there could be no motive to screen him from the constitutional test so recently adopted, when his exemption could not be allowed by any change in public opinion, or by personal influence, or on the ground of military service, or any peculiar merit, and when his extraordinary apostasy called for the application of the test if it had been understood that it disabled any but Catholics. He was afterwards the leader of his party, and repeatedly its candidate for the highest office, and often successful in contests far more acrimonious than any that have since occurred. And yet no attempt was ever made to exclude him from the legislature, and, throughout his long and active public life, though he was constantly and vehemently opposed on the ground of his infidelity as well as for political reasons, it is certain that it was not understood that he was constitutionally disqualified for Protestant office.

And, from 1785 to the present time, there has been in the legislature a succession of similar precedents, sufficient to show the universal understanding that the test is merely anti-Catholic. Within a few years past, Catholics have held the representative office, in known contravention of the constitution; but this has resulted from a change of public opinion as to the necessity and propriety of excluding them. The test would have been enforced against them in 1785; or, if such men as Lafayette and Carroll had been citizens of the state and admitted to the legislature, the test would have been understood to be waived in their favor; but no waiver of it would have been thought necessary for Jefferson and Franklin. It has always and universally been as well understood that, under the test, all others were eligible, as that Catholics were not. And to hold that every non-Catholic in the state is disqualified for the offices of governor, councillor, senator, and representative, who does not come up to some other standard of theological soundness, is a revolutionary decision. Men still live who, with a majority of their fellow-citizens, repeatedly elected Plumer to the Protestant office of chief magistrate. These venerable men will be startled by the change now made, that his holding the highest office in their gift was a violation of the constitution. They will be surprised by such a manifestation of the irreverent and innovating spirit of the present generation. They will wonder how the settled constitutional principles and practices of the fathers could be subverted in a case of religous persecution.

If Judge Woodbury had delivered his opinion on this point from the bench, he could hardly have stated it more explicitly than he did in his speech against the test in the constitutional convention of 1850, when he said, - "This test crept into the constitution originally under a temporary impulse. * * Tradition says, and I probably had it in early life from the venerable parent of the member from Epping (Mr. Plumer), - that parent the Nestor of the politicians of that generation, and sole survivor of the convention of 1781, - that the provision was inserted in 1784 to repel taunts which had been flung out by some, after the French alliance, that there was to be an alliance also with the French religion, and the establishment of it here. The provision fell then still-born so few Catholics existed in the state. * * If any soreness against Catholic persecutions of the puritans abroad mingled with this, and rendered prejudice stronger with some against erasing the test, they ought, for more recent persecution by Laud and the Episcopalians in England, to have excluded them also. But it was right to exclude neither. * * There is now no dread of French influence or French religion. * * It is likewise contrary to all sound experience and reason to say, as we do, that Catholics may vote but not be voted for. * * So it is inconsistent to * * agree, as we do, in the constitution of the Union, that Catholics may be fit and safe for members of congress, senators, cabinet officers, yea, presidents, and yet denounce them as unfit and unsafe at home to represent one hundred and fifty polls in one of our small townships. * * Why not as well explicitly say, and not do it covertly, that none but Protestants are fit for a republic? Why not say that Catholic Maryland is unfit? Catholic Ireland? Catholic France? * * Indeed, this test debars man from what we allow to the degraded African, as he is eligible here to hold office as well as to vote. * *

The Protestant himself cannot now vote here for a Catholic. * * In most Catholic countries Jesuitism is banished and the inquisition abolished, and the pope himself has become quite a reformer and republican. * * What sect did Sidney, or Locke, or Jefferson, or Madison think fit to be trusted with legislative power?" 1 Woodbury's Writings 486, 487, 504...

The common law, so far as it is adapted to our institutions and circumstances, and not repugnant to the rights and liberties contained in the constitution, remains in force until altered and repealed by the legislature. Constitution of N. H., Part II, art. 90; Lisbon v. Lyman, 49 N. H. 582. If religious inequality, operating in any way to the disadvantage of deists or theists, had been a rule of the common law, it would not be in force here, because it would be inconsistent with free institutions. But it is not a rule of the common law. In that system of jurisprudence there is nothing that gives Trinitarians or Unitarians, on account of the legal superiority of their religion, any advantage over a deist or theist in a court of justice. By the common law adopted in the constitution, or the constitution interpreted by common law analogies, Abbott is not disabled.

Christianity, in the sense of a system of theology miraculously revealed, and distinguished from natural religion, is not the basis nor any part of the common law. "Reason is the life of the law; nay, the common law itself is nothing else but reason; which is to be understood of an artificial perfection of reason, gotten by long study, observation, and experience, and not of every man's natural reason. * * This legal reason est summa ratio." The common law "is the perfection of reason." Co, Lit. 97, b. "Nothing is law that is not reason." Coggs v. Bernard, Ld. Raym. 909, 911. And whatever may be the definition of legal reason, it certainly does not include miraculous revelation. What is true in law, and what is substantial and essential in legal principle, the court are authorized to decide. But, as was said in The Dublin case, 38 N.H. 510, 573, "what is theologically true in religion it is agreed on all hands that the court are not competent to decide; nor have they power to determine what is really and intrinsically substantial and essential in matters of doctrine." Burr v. First Parish in Sandwich, 9 Mass. 298; Field v. Field, 9 Wend. 401; Miller v. Gable, 2 Denio 517. The court was authorized to determine all the principles of the common law in force in this state; the court are not authorized to determine a single principle of Christianity; therefore, in contemplation of law, the principles of Christianity are no part of the principles of the common law. If Christianity were in any sense, theoretically or practically, a part of the common law of New Hampshire, it would be the right and duty of this court to decide what Christianity is, and to enforce it as law, and as other laws are enforced, by the whole power of the state placed in our hands for the purpose. That would be law, which a majority of the court (if a majority could agree on the subject) should hold to be "theologically true in religion." At one time Trinitarianism would be law; at another, Unitarianism; today, Methodism; tomorrow, Catholicism. If the court should go back to 1783 for a standard, they must choose between Quakerism, Calvinism, Universalism, and other religions. If they resorted to the earliest technically Christian period of the common law, they would adopt ancient Catholicism with the scientific doctrines of the theology of that age. Whatever theological law, permanent or fluctuating, were established, it would be enforced by the court, not only upon Mr. Abbott, but upon the whole population of the state; for the common law is uniform in its operation, and exempts no privileged classes. Without adopting a system of theology as law, Mr. Abbott could not be persecuted at common law: nothing but his theology is complained of as unlawful...

And it is no disparagement of the law to say that miraculously revealed Christianity is not a part of it, as it is no depreciation of a physical science or a mechanical art to say that miraculous revelation is no part of it. Every institution, art, and science is not ordained for the accomplishment of all the purposes of creation: some are assigned to one work, some to another: if each is equal to its office, it is sufficient. The common law is not designed to be either a civil agency of the church, or an ecclesiastical institution of the state. It does not claim either a divine or a human authority to propagate or patronize any system of theology, to enforce or interpret the divine law, or to control or regulate the relations between mankind and the supreme government of the universe. "An orange-woman stops up the pavement with her wheelbarrow, and a policeman takes her into custody. A miser who has amassed a million, suffers an old friend and benefactor to die in a workhouse, and cannot be questioned before any tribunal for his baseness and ingratitude. Is this because legislators think the orange-woman's conduct worse than the miser's? Not at all. It is because the stopping up of the pathway is one of the evils against which it is the business of the public authorities to protect society; and heartlessness is not one of those evils." Macaulay's Essay on Church and State, Ed. Rev., Apr. 1839. Upon views of this kind, it was stipulated in the treaty with Tripoli, in 1786, that, "as the government of the United States is not in any sense founded on the Christian religion," no pretext arising from religious opinions should ever interrupt the harmony existing between the two countries. And such are the views taken by the common law, which, unperverted by the union of church and state, is adopted in the constitution of New Hampshire, and which, by its principles and analogies, supports the general doctrine of religious equality, and requires the construction of the Protestant test that disables no man for his theology...

Narrow, technical definitions of Christianity abound in sectarian controversies, and in the history of united church and state, at levels of civilization lower than that of New Hampshire in 1783. Eleven years before the settlement of New Hampshire, Bartholomew Legatt and Edward Wightman were burned in England for being guilty of that Unitarianism which the decree in this case undertakes to perpetuate. The writs *de haeretico comburendo* issued in their cases are given in 2 How. St. Tr. 731-738. The writ for burning Legatt, directed to the sheriffs of London, contained a preamble, reciting, among other things, that "the reverend father in Christ, John, bishop of London," had certified that "in a certain business of heretical pravity," "with the advice and consent as well of the reverend bishops and other divines as also of men learned in the law in judgment sitting and assisting," he had decreed Legatt "to be an obdurate, contumacious, and incorrigible heretic, and rotten, contagious member, to be cut off from the church of Christ and the communion of the faithful," and had left him "as a blasphemous heretic to our secular power to be punished with condign punishment, as by the letters patent of the said reverend father in Christ, the bishop of London, in this behalf thereupon made, is certified unto us in our chancery." The mandatory clause of the writ runs thus: We command you that you cause the said Bartholomew Legatt, being in your custody, to be publicly committed to the fire, before the people, in a public and open place, at West Smithfield, for the cause aforesaid, and the said Bartholomew Legatt to be really consumed in the said fire, in detestation of said crime, and for an example to other Christians lest they fall into the same crime." Concerning the execution of Legatt, an orthodox historian writes, - "in this very Smithfield how many saints, in the Marian days, suffered for the testimony of Jesus Christ! Whereas, now one therein dieth in his own blood for denying him. * * Refusing all mercy, he was burned to ashes. * * Oh, that he might be the last to deserve" such manner of death. 2 How. St. Tr. 730. It is not by sectarian precedents and ecclesiastical authorities of this kind that the language of the constitution is to be interpreted...

The true construction of the constitution is that which makes every parish theologically independent of the state, and leaves the pulpit of every parish in the control of the parish, free from the thological correction of secular tribunals. The constitution, like the common law adopted by it, is neither a medical theory (Boardman v. Woodman, 47 N. H. 148, 150) nor a theological system. It is human law, reverently recognizing the inviolability of religion; not impiously usurping the direction of spiritual affairs; permitting no executive, legislative, or judicial encroachment upon the kingdom that is not of this world; meddling not, and allowing no earthly power to meddle, with those rights for the exercise of which, men, in their individual, parochial, and ecclesiastical capacities and relations, are responsible only to the divine government. Upon these fundamental and acknowledged principles of the constitution, the word "Christians," in Article VI of the bill of rights, does not give the court any spiritual jurisdiction, or any temporal power to invade the province or infringe the liberty of the church; and therefore is not an ecclesiastical criterion or religious limitation which the court is to apply, and is not used in any theological sense which the court is to enforce. It does not authorize the court to demolish parochial independence, erect a hierarchial system of license and prohibition, and appropriate the ecclesiastical sovereignty. It does not force the law to profrane the territory of the church, nor subject religion to the dishonor and degradation of nominal and actual insignificance...

The next and last question is, whether there is any sectarian trust or limitation attached to "the meeting-house of said society," - whether the use of the meeting-house of the parish is confined within any narrower theological lines than those of parochial power. The answer to this question it is not difficult to find or to grasp. A meeting-house, or the control of a meeting-house, given, without restriction, to an independent parish, is given to parochial independence. That is the leading ideas in what remains of the case to be considered.

It is perfectly easy for persons giving their own private property to a religious use, to limit that use, and devote the property to a particular faith. Princeton v. Adams, 10 Cush. 129; Guild v. Richards, 16 Gray 309. They need no professional assistance or technical learning to supply them with a peculiar phraseology. Any intelligible language will answer the purpose. They can have no difficulty in saying, in some comprehensible form, that they intend the dissemination of the thirty-nine articles of the English church, or the Westminster Catechism; the doctrines of Luther, or Loyola, of Edwards or Channing, or Jefferson; the tenets held by some sect at a certain time, or such as it may hold from time to time in the course of its existence in a changing world. If they intend a theological limitation, they will express it; and then the court may be called upon to decide, by legal rules settled by the wisdom of ages, not what the true faith is, but what limitation is expressed by the words used. The Dublin case, 38 N. H. 510, 563. But when the builders of a meeting-house carefully avoid imposing any theological limitation, and put it under the unrestricted parochial control of an independent parish, as was done in this case, they devote it to the independence of the parish, and a judicial imposition of a sectarian limitation is a plain breach of trust...

An individual may convey his property in trust, for any stipulated legal use, personal or corporate, private or public, special or general, ecclesiastical, sectarian, educational, or commercial. And "it would be the duty of this court, on a proper application, to see that the trust was executed according to the intention of the donor, provided that his intention was expressed so plainly that it could be legally ascertained. When the intentions of the donor, as to the religious opinions which he means shall be supported, are expressed in general terms, and the disputed construction of those terms depends on an examination of religious doctrines and the history of theological opinion and controversy, the inquiries upon which the court are obliged to enter are of an unusual and embarrassing character. What is theologically true in religion, it is agreed on all hands that the court are not competent to decide; nor have they power to determine what is really and intrinsically substantial and essential in matters of doctrine. The difficulty of considering in legal tribunals questions which depend on such inquiries has led courts to act upon the rule that they will not interfere with the application which a trustee has made of a fund given to a religious use, upon the ground that the donor intended to limit the application of the fund, unless the intention to exclude the opinions to the support of which the fund has been applied has been plainly expressed by the donor. Courts of law are, by their habits and constitution, ill fitted for the investigation of such questions; and it will not be supposed that the founder of a religious charity intended the trustee, whom he selected to administer his charity, should be called to account in the legal tribunals for a misapplication of the funds to the support of religious opinions different from those intended, unless he has used appropriate and explicity terms excluding the doctrines to which the fund has been applied." The Dublin case, 38 N. H. 509.

Under the recent decision of this court, in The Dublin case, a sectarian limitation must be expressed in plain, appropriate, and explicit terms; and the sectarian sentiments of individuals cannot be shown, by extraneous evidence, to control or vary a writing in such a case as this. "It is a general rule that corporations must take and grant by their corporate name." 2 Kent Com. 292; 1 Bl. Com. 475; Bac. Abr. Corporations (C), 1; Angell & A. on Corp., sec. 99; Co. Lit. 250 a. n. (a). An intention to impose a sectarian limitation, in a transfer of the control of property to a corporation, is not plainly, appropriately, and explicitly expressed by designating the corporation by its corporate name, when it would be inconvenient to designate it in any other way, and when its name does not express its constitutional nature or the extent of its constitutional power, when it is an independent and not a sectarian corporation. It is usual, in assignments, appointments, deeds, wills, leases, and licenses, to describe the assignee, appointee, grantee, devisee, lessee, and licensee by name. The use of a circumlocution as a substitute for the name would be a freak in which no one, knowing the name, would be likely to indulge. It would be unprecedented, useless, and troublesome. The omission of the name would be so extraordinary that it is impossible, from the presence of the name, to infer a special intent to create a sectarian limitation. When such a limitation can be imposed only by plain and explicit terms, and when the name is used for the purpose of identifying the independent parish, the name, necessarily used for that purpose, is not an explicit declaration of another and totally different purpose, to wit, the creation of a sectarian limitation...

Whatever views the plaintiffs may entertain of the proper grounds of judicial decision, they repudiate the spirit of Unitarian Christianity, as set forth by its American apostle. "It is necessary that religion should be held and professed in a liberal spirit. Just as far as it assumes an intolerant, exclusive, sectarian form, it subverts instead of strengthening the soul's freedom, and becomes the heaviest and most galling yoke which is laid on the intellect and conscience. Religion must be viewed, not as a monopoly of priests, ministers, or sects, not as confering on any man a right to dictate to his fellow-beings, not as an instrument by which the few may awe the many, not as bestowing on one a prerogative which is not enjoyed by all, but as the property of every human being, and as the great subject for every human mind. It must be regarded as the revelation of a common Father, to whom all have equal access, who invites all to the like immediate communion, who has no favorites, who has appointed no infallible expounders of his will, who opens his works and word to every eye, and calls upon all to read for themselves, and to follow fearlessly the best convictions of their own understanding. Let religion be seized on by individuals or sects, as their special province; let them clothe themselves with God's prerogative of judgment; let them succeed in enforcing their creed by penalties of law or penalties of opinion; let them succeed in fixing a brand on virtuous men, whose only crime is free investigation; and religion becomes the most blighting tyranny which can establish itself over the mind. You have all heard of the outward evils which religion, when thus turned into tyranny, has inflicted; how it has dug dreary dungeons, kindled fires for the martyr, and invented instruments of exquisite torture. But, to me, all this is less fearful than its influence over the mind. When I see the superstitions which it has fastened on the conscience, the spiritual terrors with which it has haunted and subdued the ignorant and susceptible, the dark, appalling views of God, which it has spread far and wide, the dread of inquiry which it has struck into superior understandings, and the servility of spirit which it has made to pass for piety, - when I see all this, the fire, the scaffold, and the outward inquisition, terrible as they are, seem to me inferior evils. I look with a solemn joy on the heroic spirits who have met freely and fearlessly pain and death in the cause of truth and human rights. But there are other victims of intolerance, on whom I look with unmixed sorrow. They are those who, spellbound by early prejudice, or by intimidations from the pulpit and the press, dare not think; who shrink from the seekers after truth as from infection; who deny all virtue which does not wear the livery of their own sect; who, surrendering to others their best powers, receive unresistingly a teaching which wars against reason and conscience; and who think it a merit to impose, on such as live within their influence, the grievous bondage which they bear themselves. How much to be deplored is it, that religion, the very principle which is designed to raise men above the judgment and power of man, should become the chief instrument of usurpation over the soul. Is it said that, in this country, where the rights of private judgment, and of speaking and writing according to our convictions, are guaranteed with every solemnity by institutions and laws, religion can never degenerate into tyranny; that here its whole influence must conspire to the liberation and dignity of the mind? I answer, we discover little knowledge of human nature, if we ascribe to constitutions the power of charming to sleep the spirit of intolerance and exclusion. Almost every other bad passion may sooner be put to rest; and for this plain reason, that intolerance always shelters itself under the name and garb of religious zeal. Because we live in a country where the gross, outward, visible chain is broken, we must not conclude that we are necessarily free. There are chains not made of iron, which eat more deeply into the soul. An espionage of bigotry may as effectually close our lips and chill our hearts, as an armed and hundred-eyed police. There are countless ways by which men in a free country may encroach on their neighbors' rights. In religion, the instrument is ready made and always at hand. I refer to opinion, combined and organized in sects, and swayed by the clergy. We say we have no inquisition. But a sect skilfully organized, trained to utter one cry, combined to cover with reproach whoever may differ from themselves, to drown the free expression of opinion by the denunciations of heresy, and to strike terror into the multitude by joint and perpetual menace, - such a sect is as perilous and palsying to the intellect as the inquisition. It serves the ministers as effectually as the sword. The present age is notoriously sectarian, and therefore hostile to liberty. One of the strongest features of our times is the tendency of men to run into associations, to lose themselves in masses, to think and act in crowds, to act from the excitement of numbers, to sacrifice individuality, to identify themselves with parties and sects. At such a period, we ought to fear and cannot too much dread lest a host should be marshalled under some sectarian standard, so numerous and so strong as to overawe opinion, stifle inquiry, compel dissenters to a prudent silence, and thus accomplish the end, without incurring the odium, of penal laws. We have indeed no small protection against this evil, in the multiplicity of sects. But let us not forget that coalitions are as practicable and as perilous in church as in state; and that minor differences, as they are called, may be sunk, for the purpose of joint exertion against a common foe. Happily, the spirit of this people, in spite of all narrowing influences, is essentially liberal. Here lies our safety. The liberal spirit of the people, I trust, is more and more to temper and curb that exclusive psirit which is the besetting sin of their religious guides.'' 4 Channing's Works 85...

These questions concern interests of greater consequence than the doctrinal sermons to be preached, by leave of the court, in the meeting-house of this parish. They comprise the inquiry whether this is an ecclesiastical court, with papal or prelatic powers and general jurisdiction in parochial heresy, liable to be called upon by parochial minorities to dictate the theology of every pulpit, superintend the clergy, and regulate the ordinances of religion. They involve the independence of every parish in the state, the parochial privilege of choosing public teachers, the sovereign prerogatives of electing and being elected to executive and legislative office, and the comprehensive birthright of religious freedom and equality. When such investigations are forced upon the court, and natural, unalienable rights, established institutions of society, and first principles of free government are attacked, under whatever pretexts or with whatever disclaimers the attack may be made, it becomes necessary to resist, with firmness proportioned to the vigor and audacity of the assault.

A division of society into two ranks, a theological aristocracy on one side, a lower caste on the other, the former wielding all the instruments of the law and all the power of the government to degrade men of the faith of Jefferson, Franklin, Ethan Allen, or Governor Plumer; commanding what doctrines shall not be preached; suppressing the freedom of the pulpit; abolishing the rights of property given to independent religious uses; and confiscating such property for the use of a state religion, - all this is as repugnant to the plain and vital principles of the constitution, as to the sense and spirit of the people who made the constitution. The governmental work of that generation has been sufficiently extolled for eighty-five years past as a triumphant vindication of human rights, affording a sure protection against ecclesiastical oppression in particular and perpetuating through the state such refuge as Wheelwright found for a season at Exeter in exile for conscience's sake. That work must be undone, and a degenerate age must be ready to welcome the return of the worse despotisms, before a system of religious caste can be introduced. When an infidel does not stand as well in law before the tribunals of justice as a Christian, in any sense of the word, our free institutions are a failure. To sneer at free-thinkers or free thought is to make a thoughtless use of free speech, and to scoff at a privilege which we are bound to protect. The constitution does not assume to create religious rights or to distribute them. It reverently recognizes and maintains them as original and universal, as rights which human government can neither grant nor withhold, which are not of human tenure, and which no man can give up. A single unresisted infringement, established as a precedent, subjugates the weak, and leaves them at the mercy of the strong. Every man and every parish is liable to hold unpopular theological opinions. And when the right to hold and inculcate such opinions is not sacred, and the violation of it is not sacrilege; when the constitutional defences of that right are dismantled, and it is left with no better security than the generosity and tolerance of an ecclesiastical court, or the caprice of a ruling class; when freemen are reduced to the consolation of remembering that the writ for burning heretics is obsolete, and of hoping that civilization will not suffer it to be revived, - the theory of our government is exploded and its original authority at an end.

Unless Abbott's religion is unconstitutional, the majority of this Dover parish, in allowing him to preach it "in the meeting-house of said society," did what they had an obvious constitutional right to do. We cannot adjudge his faith to be a heretical departure from a state religion until we destroy the constitution, establish a state religion, and annex a supreme bishopric to the judicial office. If we can condemn this man as a heretic, and his religion as an offence against the state, or as legally inferior to any other, we can anathematize and outlaw any other person, and any other form of religion. Abbott's cause, strenuously opposed in the field of theology, becomes, in law, the common cause of religious liberty, and the indestructible interest of mankind. The decree cannot be aimed at him until it batters down constitutional bulwarks, erected by our ancestors for the defense of a possession, which, through ages of suffering and struggle, cost too much, and, after being long enjoyed in apparent safety, has been found worth too much, to be voluntarily surrendered.

McGinnis v. Watson

Supreme Court of Pennsylvania, 1861
41 Pa St. 9

LOWRIE, C. J. - About 1803, the Unity Congregation, belonging to the Associate or Seceder Church of North America, purchased a lot of ground in Venango township, Butler county, and erected a meeting-house upon it, and there continued to worship God in unity until 1858. Then the Seceder Synod of North America, by a very large majority, and after many years' consideration, formed a union with the Associate Reformed Synod; and a majority of the Unity Congregation, and the Shenango Presbytery, to which it belongs, have approved of the union thus formed. A minority of the congregation, and several ministers of the Associate Church, disapprove of it, and the minority of the congregation claim the lot and meeting house. Which party is entitled to it? The Common Pleas decided in favour of the minority: is this right?

Our fundamental law on this subject is written in the Constitution, Art. 9, s 3. All men have a natural and indefeasible right to worship Almighty God according to the dictates of their own consciences, and no human authority can, in any case whatever, control or interfere with the rights of conscience.

Of course this law was not intended to exempt any religious society from the respect that is due to the organization and moral and social order of the state, or from the necessity of holding its land under the state, and according to its laws. But it does mean, that, for its own internal order, and for the mode in which it fulfils its functions, it is to be a law unto itself, or have its law within itself, provided it keep within the bounds of social order and morality. This is the same rule that the law applies to individuals in their contracts about legitimate business. Their contracts and their own interpretation of them, so far as they are engaged, are the elements out of which we derive the law of the case which they present for our decision.

In its most general form, therefore, our question is: Judging this congregation by its own order, was its union with the Associate Reformed Church, and incorporation into the United Presbyterian Church, regular?

But this raises another question: How far is the congregation bound by the act of its Synod? Religious societies are not free, if they may not choose their own form or organization. They may organize as independent churches, and then their law is found in their own separate institutions, customary or written. Or they may organize as associated churches, and then their law is to be found in their own rules, and in those of the associated organism. When persons join a church belonging to such a general organism, they assent to its laws, and are entitled to the implication that the affairs of the church are to be managed according to them. This result of our law and of the relations of associates in churches, is so clear, obvious, and necessary, that we need not dwell upon it.

It has, however, a qualification already alluded to in general, which ought, perhaps, to be more specially stated. If the general organism extend over several states, it may require much more than ordinary charity, prudence, and discretion in directing its legislation and action so as to preserve its sphere of influence and usefulness in its integrity. If it should make terms of communion, or adopt a course of ecclesiastical action in any form, that is hostile to the policy of one or more of the states embracing its churches, it may induce a perfectly lawful division; for no state can help to sustain an organism that it judges to be hostile to its own principles, and none of its citizens can be presumed by law to have intended to concede authority for such hostile action. It was under the influence of this principle that our American churches separated from their mother churches in England, Scotland, and Holland before and after our revolution, without being chargeable with secession. It has also divided many of our churches, between north and south, or excluded them altogether from any foothold in the south. The Church of Rome was in many instances saved from such a division, by submitting to laws, as in England, or by entering into concordats with states, by which its ecclesiastical action was greatly restrained by subjection to civil law.

We state this limitation merely by way of precaution; for it is not needed in this case. But, subject to this limitation, our question may now be more specially stated thus: Has the act of union of the Associate and the Associate Reformed Synods been so conducted, that, judged by the law of this congregation, and of the general organism to which it belongs, it can now be properly declared to be a member of the United Presbyterian Church? The congregation was divided by the act of union; and that part of it which is acting in harmony with its own law must be approved and sustained by the state law. That one of them has obtained a charter of incorporation, has no influence on the question, and is not pretended to have. The title depends upon the legitimate, orderly, and regular maintenance of the organized congregation, or succession of associate owners.

We desire it to be noticed that, in this statement of the question, we adopt fully the view of Lord Chancellor Eldon in the case of The Attorney-General v. Pearson, 3 Meriv. 400, relative to the usage or customs of the congregation, as the law of the case; while we do not adopt his view in treating it as a trust created by the vendor, and to be used according to his intention. No doubt there are cases where such titles are really trusts, by reason of donations for special purposes; but this is not so often found in cases of church property as in gifts for charitable uses. Questions of this kind have often been obscured by treating them as trusts by the grantor. It is quite natural to call them so, because the rights under them have been usually enforced in equity as trusts. They are analogous to trusts strictly so called, but not identical with them in every aspect. As between the trustees holding the legal title, and the congregation holding the equitable title, they are trusts. But as between the congregation and any other person, they are simply titles...

In Craigdallie v. Aikman, 1 Dow's Parl. Rep. 1, Lord Eldon laid down the rule that a congregation's title depends upon its adherence to the opinions and principles in which it had originally united, and this has been followed and repeated in many cases. But we should grievously misapply this rule if we should interpret it as meaning that no congregation can change any material part of its principles or practices without forfeiting its property. This would be imposing a law upon all churches that is contrary to the very nature of all intellectual and spiritual life; for it would forbid both growth and decay; not prevent, for that is impossible. The guaranty of freedom to religion, forbids us to understand the rule in this way.

And all history forbids it. Let us be indulged in so much detail, in the illustration of this, as is necessary to make the principle clear by means of the facts which it has produced. Many of the principles of human action depend so closely upon the peculiar development of a given people that they are not susceptible of clear illustration, except by instances and cases drawn from the conduct, life, and history of that people. But on the other hand, very many of them are so common to all humanity that any illustration of them must be inadequate that does not embrace a side sphere of human conduct both in time and space.

The principle is, that all intellectual or spiritual growth involves some change or development of opinions, principles, and practices, and therefore some change in the systems which are constituted of those opinions, principles, and practices; for these are the elements of systems, and decide their character. And the fact is, that from the very origin of Christianity, such a change has been continually going on in the Christian Church, in all its branches, congregations, and members, without producing a forfeiture of the property held even by those in which the change has been most decided. Changes in principles and practice are not incompatible with legitimate social succession, but are necessary elements of its normal progress. All denominations admit that all others must change in the progress towards union, even though they may suppose their own system too perfect to undergo any change...

We must, of course, look at this question as statesmen and jurists, and not as theologians. Whatever may be the limits that theologians may fix for the growth of the church in form or principles, we can fix none until the law can decide what particular church is perfect. All history reveals the church to us as an institution that is continually educating, developing, and changing society, and changing with the changes it produces, and this right to change is part of its freedom. No doubt many religionists think that no change can ever go so far as to justify the rejection of their peculiar customs; though to other intelligent men they may appear absurd. Such persons would expect us to prohibit all change in their practice or to declare it illegitimate. A case among the Russian dissenters may illustrate what might be thus fixed by civil law, at least until the law of nature would interfere for our relief. With them the change of the calendar, blessing with two fingers uplifted instead of three, using two instead of three syllables in uttering the name Jesus, pronouncing hallelujah three times instead of once, shaving the beard, and improving the mediaeval chants and service-books by modernizing the language, were considered as damnable heresies, and as justifying separation. The state cannot visit regular and orderly changes in religion with forfeiture of rights without condemning the Reformation, and setting itself up as judge of religious controversies, which with us is always disclaimed.

No doubt the consciences of many are offended by the changes which they witness around them, and very often this is so when those changes constitute a real and valuable progress. Such changes often operate very hardly upon those who fall in the rear of the social movement; but no law can cure this, which many individuals and classes feel as an evil. The progress of the race cannot be stopped because there are many who cannot keep up with it. No man or generation of men can stop it, for nature will vanquish all obstructions and do its work.

From all this it seems very plain that we must judge these people and their acts, relative to this dispute, by the ecclesiastical laws, usages, customs, and principles which were accepted among themselves before the dispute began, and ascertain which party if right, tried by that standard. One of the most obvious of those principles is the authority of the church to legislate upon its doctrines, forms, and practice; a principle legitimately descended to them from the Church of Scotland, and maintained in full vigour by them ever since...

No doubt, most men who are instrumental in the enactment of regulations that seem to them of great social importance, have very large ideas relative to the permanence or perpetuity of their institutions; but this cannot make them perpetual. However much they may intend to bind posterity by them, they must fail if posterity does not find them adapted to its times and circumstances. Human nature respects its inherited institutions, and this is one of God's provisions to secure social order and to save us from anarchy. But such an inheritance is never received without some modification, whether it be made unconsciously or by design. And since intentions can never be equivalent to facts, and are so proverbially fallible and insecure; surely the intentions and hopes of one generation are not to be taken for the actual facts, usages, and customs of several succeeding ones. Though these intentions of perpetuity do often appear, yet they do not constitute the actual law that rules through successive generations...

All these objections proceed upon the assumption of a degree of strictness and rigidity which the law cannot appreciate. Apices juris non sunt jura. Our ideals of strictness are never the actual law of any society, except in times of excitement on the subject to which they relate. Extremes never represent the true living law of any people, though they may represent that towards which it is growing, or, that which it has outgrown. It is a plain law of nature that time and peace wear off the acerbities and extreme points that grow up in all social divisions, and we are not authorized to counteract this result. Union among churches is a perfectly legitimate part of their purpose and of their freedom, and mutual concession is part of the natural law of it, which we cannot direct or limit.

We need not inquire how far the Basis of Union relaxes the former strictness on the subject of communion, psalmody, convenanting, and bearing testimony; for, if the objections are true in fact, there may have been good reasons for doing so, and of this the presbyteries and synods were their constitutional judges. They may have judged that the strictness which was generated in times of great intellectual collisions, was not the normal condition of affairs; that the requistion of an intelligent acceptance of the Confession of Faith, Catechisms, Covenants, Narrative, and Testimony, as a condition of membership, might seem like requiring people to be thorough theologians before being received as disciples; that, in logical phrase, the more comprehensive is their system of principles, the less extensive it must be; the more doctrines it makes essential, the fewer people can accept it; the more exacting the bond, the fewer will come under it; and that, though an intelligent joining in bearing testimony against the errors and sins of those around them and of past generations, may secure a very considerable acquaintance with the history of doctrines and of church controversy, yet it may be carried to such an extreme as to beget a very large amount of pride and censoriousness, and substitute a mere legalism for religious principles. However this may be, they have adopted a testimony on all these subjects, which they have deemed sufficient, and we find in it no such departure from ancient usages as entitles us to condemn their decision. We cannot condemn such proceedings as unlawful without deciding that there can be no unions of the church without a forfeiture of civil rights, and that the law almost compels the perpetuation of divisions.

Many judicial decisions very properly make such questions as those turn upon the fact of identity; but, as this term itself stands in need of explanation, we have not hitherto made much use of it. The foregoing discussion, however, prepares us now for a reasonably precise understanding of it, with the assistance of a very few additional suggestions. The analogies of identity of mere dead matter would not help us much, for it is living identity we are dealing with. A few of these may aid us:

That acorn: follow the idea of identity in it. Future generations may point to that old oak some centuries old, with many of its branches gone, and decay commenced, and say: there it is. That helpless infant: the next generation may point to a Newton or a Washington, with his mature growth, and his immense accretions of intellectual power, and moral majesty, and social influence, and say: there he is.

But it is rather identity of social life that we want to understand. All social life involves a common participation in spiritual acquisitions, a mutual giving and receiving of moral and mental influences according to the capacities and opportunities of each individual, and a social and individual growth thereby. All institutions, to be social at all, must be adapted to this giving and receiving of influence, and must share in the social growth; educational institutions that have not this adaptation must die by their own success. And yet they must have organic form that will give them force and save them from being merged in the common mass. To be social institutions without this adaptation, and participation, and growth, is a contradiction in terms, as much, though not so obvious, as to say that the radii of a circle are unequal.

It is essential, therefore, to social institutions that they grow with society, and in adaptation to its intelligence and wants, and times and circumstances, and in so far as they fail in this, they detract from their social identity and social life, and begin to decay. Of course, for such departure we can have no measure, and therefore no definite law; but the natural law is not hard to discover. Thousands of institutions have died out because of this want of reciprocity with a growing society. Thousands of government have failed and disappeared for the same reason. Too often they represent mere social form, while all the social life is in the people alone. All organization, political or social, that consult only their own wills, and that oppress or condemn society because it will not accept what they decree to be benefits, and in the form in which they choose to confer them, must necessarily be rejected by society when it can obtain substitutes.

Yet the people remain and preserve their social identity in all these changes of government. We cannot deny the identity of the Transalpine Gauls with the modern French, because of the many subjugations, and revolutions, and changes of government and religion which they have undergone in the last twenty centuries; nor that of the Anglo-Saxons with the English, because of similar changes. All such changes are but the accidents of the social life, the continuity of which constitutes its identity.

It will readily be seen that we are not here announcing any positive law of civil society, but simply endeavouring, it may be unsuccessfully, to illustrate a fundamental principle of social law. Philosophy and history may trace out these social principles in long periods; but such a task is beyond the demands of legal administration, its duty being best fulfilled by keeping itself in harmony with the common order of society for the time being. It must regard the forms and accidental principles of social organisms much more than history and philosophy do, because they are of great importance in the short periods to which legal actions refer, and because history and philosophy investigate, while the law regulates, the course of events. They may recognise social identity wherever they can trace a continued social unity, however great may be the variety and changes of its forms and principles. Law deals with short periods in its administration, and with individuals and societies under government, and expects to find social unity continued without any violent rupture of forms or departures from principles, and yet makes all reasonable allowances for development according to principles, and with due respect for customary forms. Let these thoughts pass for what they are worth in themselves. If they do not illustrate the subject, they are good for nothing here.

Doubtless there may be cases wherein the change complained of as a violation of social identity is conducted according to all the forms of order that are recognized in a given society, and yet it may be of such a character, or be produced by such unfair means, or by such partisan agitations, as not to be entitled to the support of the law in its equitable administration of justice. Or the general organism may so fall into anarchy that the subordinate organisms can have no peace or prosperity under its rule, and then a separation may be justified in equity. It may allow secession in such cases, because it has no adequate remedy; while in mere civil relations it cannot admit its own inability. But we forbear to give any special opinion on supposed cases of this kind. In this case there is nothing of the sort. We can hardly imagine a case that could have been more patiently, deliberately, charitably, and thoroughly considered, and it was almost unanimously decided.

We might have decided this case by saying, that there is nothing in the plaintiff's evidence that shows that the action complained of, judged by the constitution and usages of the Seceder Church, was brought about by any excess of authority on the part of the presbyteries and synod. But we have preferred to treat the case as if the burden of proof was on the defendants, and show affirmatively that the proceeding is in harmony with the authority usually admitted to belong to those bodies...

3. FEDERAL

Introductory

When the Federal Constitution, without the first ten amendments, was submitted to the States for adoption, frequent objection was made to the absence of a Bill of Rights limiting Federal power. Some of the more orthodox opponents of the Constitution objected to the provision in Article VI that "no religious Test shall ever be required as a Qualification to any Office or public Trust under the United States," but that objection nowhere was of major significance. With respect to the absence of any specific provision limiting Congressional power in matters of religion the fears in Virginia were of greater consequence than elsewhere. In view of the frequency with which the opinions of Jefferson and Madison have been referred to in connection with problems of religious liberty it is worth remembering what Madison said in the Virginia ratifying convention in reply to Patrick Henry's objection that religious freedom was not guaranteed in the proposed Constitution. "Is a bill of rights a security for religion?", asked Madison. "Would the bill of rights, in this state, exempt the people from paying for the support of one particular sect, if such sect were exclusively established by law? ... This freedom arises from that multiplicity of sects which pervades America, and which is the best and only security for religious liberty in any society; for where there is such a variety of sects, there cannot be a majority of any one sect to oppress and persecute the rest." (3 Eliot's Debates 330.)

Despite these doubts of Madison's, the Bill of Rights, added to the Federal Constitution, opened with the specific pronouncement: "Congress shall make no law respecting an establishment of religion, or prohibiting the free exercise thereof ..." Until after the Civil War the significance of this provision, as a source of limitation on Federal and State power had relatively little importance. Jefferson believed that it made impossible a Presidential proclamation of Thanksgiving (see Blakely,

American State Papers 174) and Madison, agreeing to that view, also considered that it made the appropriation of Federal funds for the payment of chaplains illegal (id. p. 201). In 1850 and again in 1854 memorials were submitted to Congress by religious and other groups urging that the appointment of chaplains should be abandoned. (See Johnson, Chaplains of the General Government (1856) passim). Adverse committee reports, however, led to the rejection of these proposals. (33rd Cong. 1st Sess. H. of R. Rep. #124; 31st Cong. 1st Sess., H. of R., Rep. #171.) See, Elliott v. White, 23 F2 997 (1928). Cf. Moulton and Myers, Report of 1832 in Blau, Cornerstones of Religious Freedom in America (1949), 141. Another issue in which the constitutional provision was much involved concerned proposals that the United States mails should not be carried on Sundays. As a result of the famous report of Congressman Richard M. Johnson (Blakely, p. 245) the effort to prohibit such carriage failed.

Madison's Veto Message

During the 3rd Session of the 11th Congress an act incorporating the Protestant Episcopal Church in the Town of Alexandria in the District of Columbia was adopted by Congress. President Madison, however, returned the bill with the following veto message (22 Annals of Congress 982-83):

"To the House of Representatives of the United States:

"Having examined and considered the bill, entitled 'An Act incorporating the Protestant Episcopal Church in the town of Alexandria, in the District of Columbia,' I now return the bill to the House of Representatives, in which it originated, with the following objections:

"Because the bill exceeds the rightful authority to which Governments are limited, by the essential distinction between civil and religious functions, and violates, in particular, the article of the Constitution of the United States, which declares, that 'Congress shall make no law respecting a religious establishment.' The bill enacts into, and establishes by law, sundry rules and proceedings relative purely to the organization and polity of the church incorporated, and comprehending even the election and removal of the Minister of the same; so that no change could be made therein by the particular society, or by the general church of which it is a member, and whose authority it recognises. This particular church, therefore, would so far be a religious establishment by law; a legal force and sanction being given to certain articles in its constitution and administration. Nor can it be considered, that the articles thus established are to be taken as the descriptive criteria only of the corporate identity of the society, inasmuch as this identity must depend on other characteristics; as the regulations established are generally unessential, and alterable according to the principles and canons, by which churches of that denomination govern themselves; and as the injunctions and prohibitions contained in the regulations, would be enforced by the penal consequences applicable to a violation of them according to the local law:

"Because the bill vests in the said incorporated church an authority to provide for the support of the poor, and the education of poor children of the same; an authority which being altogether superfluous, if the provision is to be the result of pious charity, would be a precedent for giving to religious societies, as such, a legal agency in carrying into effect a public and civil duty."

In the House of Representatives Mr. Wheaton expressed his disagreement with the views of the President (id. 984-85).

"Mr. Wheaton said he differed widely from his colleague (Mr. Pickman) as to the importance of the bill now under consideration. He did not imagine that they were to assume the objections of the President to be valid and of course to dismiss the bill. They had a duty to perform as well as the President. He had performed his duty in the case presented for consideration. And would gentlemen assume it as a correct position because the bill was objected to by the President that the House ought not to act understandingly? This was not a correct principle. In his view the objections made by the President to this will were altogether futile. Mr. W. said he did not consider this bill any infringement of the Constitution. If it was, both branches of the Legislature, since the commencement of the Government, had been guilty of such infringement. It could not be said, indeed, that they had been guilty of doing much about religion; but they had at every session appointed Chaplains, to be of different denominations, to interchange weekly between the two Houses. Now, if a bill for regulating the funds of a religious society could be an infringement of the Constitution, the two Houses had so far infringed it by electing, paying or contracting with their Chaplains; for so far it established two different denominations of religion. Mr. W. deemed this question of very great consequence. Were the people of this District never to have any religion? Was it to be entirely excluded from these ten miles square? He should be afraid to come if that were to be the case. The want of time was no sufficient reason against giving this subject a mature consideration. What was done ought to be well done. For these reasons he was in favor of the bill lying on the table."

In the House the required two-thirds majority could not be secured to pass the bill over the President's veto (id. 998).

The Blaine Amendment

After the Civil War, and after the adoption of the 14th Amendment and while the embers of the Know Nothing Movement were still burning, the Republican party became active in a national effort to safeguard the system of public school education from what was considered to be a Catholic threat. The fear was derived in part from the Catholic efforts to eliminate Bible reading from public school exercises and in part from the Catholic insistence, after that objective had been achieved, that the public schools were Godless in character. Those who feared the direction which Catholic effort was taking often quoted passages from the Encyclical of Pope Pius IX of December 1845. The Pope had there condemned the views of those persons who "assert that 'the best condition of human society is that wherein no duty is recognized by the government of correcting by enacted penalties the violators of the Catholic religion, except when the maintenance of public peace requires it.' " The Pope had then gone on to quote the reflections of Gregory XVI on the "insanity" which maintains that "liberty of conscience and worship is the right of every man; and that this right ought, in every well-governed state, to be proclaimed and asserted by law; and that the citizens possess the right of being unrestrained in the exercise of every kind of liberty, by any law, ecclesiastical or civil, so that they are authorized to publish and put forward openly all their ideas whatsoever, either by speaking, in print, or by any other method." Pius had appended to his Encyclical a syllabus of the "principal errors of our time." These errors, as he described them, included the following:

"45. The entire direction of public schools in which the youth of Christian states are educated ... may and must appertain to the civil power, and belong to it so far that no other authority whatsoever shall be recognized as having an right to interfere in the discipline of the schools, the arrangement of the studies, the taking of degrees, or the choice and approval of the teacher.

"47. The best theory of civil society requires that popular schools, open to the children of all classes ... should be free from all ecclesiastical authority, government, and interference and should be fully subject to the civil and political power, in conformity with the will of the rulers and the prevailing opinions of the age.

"48. This system of instructing youth which consists in separating it from the Catholic faith and from the power of the Church, and in teaching exclusively or at least primarily the knowledge of natural things and the earthly ends of social life alone, may be approved by Catholics.

Responding to the Republican demand that the public schools should be rendered entirely secure from sectarian influences, President Grant in his message to Congress of December 7, 1875, made the following recommendation:

"... I suggest for your earnest consideration, and most earnestly recommend it, that a constitutional amendment be submitted to the legislatures of the several States for ratification, making it the duty of each of the several states to establish and forever maintain free public schools adequate to the education of the children in the rudimentary branches within their respective limits, irrespective of sex, color, birthplace, or religions; forbidding the teaching in said schools of religious, atheistic, or pagan tenets; and prohibiting the granting of any school funds or school taxes, or any part thereof, either by legislative, municipal, or other authority, for the benefit or in aid, directly or indirectly , of any religious sect or denomination, or in aid or for the benefit of any other object or nature or kind whatever." (7 Richardson, Messages, 332, 334.)

Following this Presidential suggestion James G. Blaine immediately presented to Congress a Joint Resolution proposing the following amendment to the Federal Constitution:

"No State shall make any law respecting an establishment of religion or prohibiting the free exercise thereof; and no money raised by taxation in any State for the support of public schools, or derived from any public funds therefor, or any public lands devoted thereto, shall ever be under the control of any religious sect or denomination; nor shall any moneys so raised or lands so devoted be divided between religious sects or denominations. This article shall not vest, enlarge, or diminish legislative power in the Congress."

In the Senate not only was Blaine's proposed amendment extensively debated, but an alternative considerably broader in its scope, was discussed. The requisite two-thirds majority was not secured, however, for either proposal and the effort to secure a constitutional amendment failed. The Senate debate is reported in Congressional Record, 44th Congress, 1st Session, Part 6, pp. 5580-95. (See also, Ames, Proposed Amendments to the Constitution (vol. ii, Rep. Am. Hist. Soc. for 1896), p. 277.) It is constitutionally significant that no Senator suggested that the use of state funds for denominational education was already prohibited by the provisions of the 1st and 14th Amendements? See, "The Blaine Amendment and the Bill of Rights," 64 Harv. L. Rev. 939 (1951).

One other issue with respect to the use of public funds for denominational education came to a head in the 1890's. It concerned the allocation of money in the Federal treasury for Indian schools operated by the Catholic Church. The issue is briefly outlined in Desmond, The A. P. A. Movement (1912), Chapter 10. The issue was first dealt with by Congress and ultimately by the Supreme Court of the United States in Quick Bear v. Leup, 210 U. S. 50 (1908).

History according to Everson

The fullest judicial examination of the history and purpose of the 1st Amendment is in the dissenting opinion of Mr. Justice Rutledge in Everson v. Board of Education, 330 U. S. 1, 28 (1947). The following passage from that opinion, with its footnotes omitted, gives an historial account to which none of the Justices seems to have disagreed. Cf. Corwin in 14 Law & Contemp. Prob. 3 (1949). See also concurring opinion of Desmond, J. in Zorach v. Clauson, infra.

Mr. Justice Rutledge, with whom Mr. Justice Frankfurter, Mr. Justice Jackson and Mr. Justice Burton agree, dissenting.

"Congress shall make no law respecting an establishment of religion, or prohibiting the free exercise thereof ..." US Const, Am Art 1.

"Well aware that Almighty God hath created the mind free; ... that to compel a man to furnish contributions of money for the propagation of opinions which he disbelieves, is sinful and tyrannical; ...

"We, the General Assembly, do enact, That no man shall be compelled to frequent or support any religious worship, place, or ministry whatsoever, nor shall be enforced, restrained, molested, or burthened in his body or goods, nor shall otherwise suffer, on account of his religious opinions or belief ..."

I cannot believe that the great author of those words, or the men who made them law, could have joined in this decision. Neither so high nor so impregnable today as yesterday is the wall raised between church and state by Virginia's great statute of religious freedom and the First Amendment, now made applicable to all the states by the Fourteenth. New Jersey's statute sustained is the first, if indeed it is not the second breach to be made by this Court's action. That a third and a fourth, and still others will be attempted, we may be sure. For just as Cochran v. Louisiana State Bd. of Edu. 281 US 370, 74 L ed 913, 50 S Ct 335, has opened the way by oblique ruling for this decision, so will the two make wider the breach for a third. Thus with time the most solid freedom steadily gives way before continuing corrosive decision.

This case forces us to determine squarely for the first time what was "an establishment of religion" in the First Amendment's conception; and by that measure to decide whether New Jersey's action violates its command. The facts may be stated shortly, to give setting and color to the constitutional problem.

By statute New Jersey has authorized local boards of education to provide for the transportation of children "to and from school other than a public school'' except one operated for profit wholly or in part, over established public school routes, or by other means when the child lives "remote from any school.'' The school board of Ewing Township has provided by resolution for "the transportation of pupils of Ewing to the Trenton and Pennington High Schools and Catholic Schools by way of public carrier...''

Named parents have paid the cost of public conveyance of their children from their homes in Ewing to three public high schools and four parochial schools outside the district. Semiannually the Board has reimbursed the parents from public school funds raised by general taxation. Religion is taught as part of the curriculum in each of the four private schools, as appears affirmatively by the testimony of the superintendent of parochial schools in the Diocese of Trenton.

The Court of Errors and Appeals of New Jersey, reversing the Supreme Court's decision, 132 NJL 98, 39 A2d 75, has held the Ewing board's action not in contravention of the state constitution or statutes or of the Federal Constitution, 133 NJL 350, 44 A2d 333. We have to consider only whether this ruling accords with the prohibition of the First Amendment implied in the due process clause of the Fourteenth.

I.

Not simply an established church, but any law respecting an establishment of religion is forbidden. The Amendment was broadly but not loosely phrased. It is the compact and exact summation of its author's views formed during his long struggle for religious freedom. In Madison's own words characterizing Jefferson's Bill for Establishing Religious Freedom, the guaranty he put in our national charter, like the bill he piloted through the Virginia Assembly, was "a Model of technical precision, and perspicuous brevity.'' Madison could not have confused "church'' and "religion'', or "an established church'' and "an establishment of religion.''

The Amendment's purpose was not to strike merely at the official establishment of a single sect, creed or religion, outlawing only a formal relation such as had prevailed in England and some of the colonies. Necessarily it was to uproot all such relationships. But the object was broader than separating church and state in this narrow sense. It was to create a complete and permanent separation of the spheres of religious activity and civil authority by comprehensively forbidding every form of public aid or support for religion. In proof the Amendment's wording and history unite with this Court's consistent utterances whenever attention has been fixed directly upon the question.

"Religion'' appears only once in the Amendment. But the word governs two prohibitions and governs them alike. It does not have two meanings, one narrow to forbid "an establishment'' and another, much broader, for securing "the free exercise thereof.'' "Thereof'' brings down "religion'' with its entire and exact content, no more and no less, from the first into the second guaranty, so that Congress and now the states are as broadly restricted concerning the one as they are regarding the other.

No one would claim today that the Amendment is constricted, in "prohibiting the free exercise'' of religion, to securing the free exercise of some formal or creedal observance, of one sect or of many. It secures all forms of religious expression, creedal, sectarian or nonsectarian, wherever and however taking place, except conduct which trenches upon the like freedoms of others or clearly and presently endangers the community's good order and security. For the protective purposes of this phase of the basic freedom, street preaching, oral or by distribution of literature, has been given "the same high estate under the First Amendment as ... worship in the churches and preaching from the pulpits." And on this basis parents have been held entitled to send their children to private, religious schools. Pierce v. Society of Sisters, 268 US 510, 60 L ed 1070, 45 S Ct 571, 39 ALR 468. Accordingly, daily religious education commingled with secular is "religion" within the guaranty's comprehensive scope. So are religious training and teaching in whatever form. The word connotes the broadest content, determined not by the form or formality of the teaching or where it occurs, but by its essential nature regardless of those details.

"Religion" has the same broad significance in the twin prohibition concerning "an establishment." The Amendment was not duplicitous. "Religion" and "establishment" were not used in any formal or technical sense. The prohibition broadly forbids state support, financial or other, of religion in any guise, form or degree. It outlaws all use of public funds for religious purposes.

II.

No provision of the Constitution is more closely tied to or given content by its generating history than the religious clause of the First Amendment. It is at once the refined product and the terse summation of that history. The history includes not only Madison's authorship and the proceedings before the First Congress, but also the long and intensive struggle for religious freedom in America, more especially in Virginia, of which the Amendment was the direct culmination. In the documents of the times, particularly of Madison, who was leader in the Virginia struggle before he became the Amendment's sponsor, but also in the writings of Jefferson and others and in the issues which engendered them is to be found irrefutable confirmation of the Amendment's sweeping content.

For Madison, as also for Jefferson, religious freedom was the crux of the struggle for freedom in general. Remonstrance, 15, Appx hereto. Madision was coauthor with George Mason of the religious clause in Virginia's great Declaration of Rights of 1776. He is credited with changing it from a mere statement of the principle of tolerance to the first official legislative pronouncement that freedom of conscience and religion are inherent rights of the individual. He sought also to have the Declaration expressly condemn the existing Virginia establishment. But the forces supporting it were then too strong.

Accordingly Madison yielded on this phase but not for long. At once he resumed the fight, continuing it before succeeding legislative sessions. As a member of the General Assembly in 1779 he threw his full weight behind Jefferson's historic Bill for Establishing Religious Freedom. That bill was a prime phase of Jefferson's broad program of democratic reform undertaken on his return from the Continental Congress in 1776 and submitted for the General Assembly's consideration in 1779 as his proposed revised Virginia code. With Jefferson's departure for Europe in 1784, Madison became the Bill's prime sponsor. Enactment failed in successive legislatures from its introduction in June, 1779, until its adoption in January, 1786. But during all this time the fight for religious freedom moved forward in Virginia on various fronts with growing intensity. Madison led throughout, against Patrick Henry's powerful opposing leadership until Henry was elected governor in November, 1784.

The climax came in the legislative struggle of 1784-1785 over the Assessment Bill. See Supplemental Appendix hereto. This was nothing more nor less than a taxing measure for the support of religion, designed to revive the payment of tithes suspended since 1777. So long as it singled out a particular sect for preference it incurred the active and general hostility of dissentient groups. It was broadened to include them, with the result that some subsided temporarily in their opposition. As altered, the bill gave to each taypayer the privilege of designating which church should receive his share of the tax. In default of designation the legislature applied it to pious uses. But what is the utmost significance here, "in its final form the bill left the taxpayer the option of giving his tax to education."

Madison was unyielding at all times, opposing with all his vigor the general and nondiscriminatory as he had the earlier particular and discriminatory assessments proposed. The modified Assessment Bill passed second reading in December, 1784, and was all but enacted. Madison and his followers, however, maneuvered deferment of final consideration until November, 1785. And before the Assembly reconvened in the fall he issued his historic Memorial and Remonstrance.

This is Madison's complete, though not his only, interpretation of religious liberty. It is a broadside attack upon all forms of "establishment" of religion, both general and particular, nondiscriminatory or selective. Reflecting not only the many legislative conflicts over the Assessment Bill and the Bill for Establishing Religious Freedom but also, for example, the struggles for religious incorporations and the continued maintenance of the glebes, the Remonstrance is at once the most concise and the most accurate statement of the views of the First Amendment's author concerning what is "an establishment of religion". Because it behooves us in the dimming distance of time not to lose sight of what he and his co-workers had in mind when, by a single sweeping stroke of the pen, they forbade an establishment of religion and secured its free exercise, the text of the Remonstrance is appended at the end of this opinion for its wider current reference, together with a copy of the bill against which it was directed.

The Remonstrance, stirring up a storm of popular protest, killed the Assessment Bill. It collapsed in committee shortly before Christmas, 1785. With this, the way was cleared at last for enactment of Jefferson's Bill for Establishing Religious Freedom. Madison promptly drove it through in January of 1786, seven years from the time it was first introduced. This dual victory substantially enede the fight over establishments, settling the issue against them. See note 33.

The next year Madison became a member of the Constitutional Convention. Its work done, he fought valiantly to secure the ratification of its great product in Virginia as elsewhere, and nowhere else more effectively. Madison was certain in his own mind that under the Constitution "there is not a shadow of right in the general government to intermeddle with religion" and that "this subject is, for the honor of America, perfectly free and unshackled. The government has no jurisdiction over it..." Nevertheless he pledged that he would work for a Bill of Rights, including a specific guaranty of religious freedom, and Virginia, with other states, ratified the Constitution on this assurance.

Ratification thus accomplished, Madison was sent to the first Congress. There he went at once about performing his pledge to establish freedom for the nation as he had done in Virginia. Within a little more than three years from his legislative victory at home he had proposed and secured the submission and ratification of the First Amendment as the first article of our Bill of Rights.

All the great instruments of the Virginia struggle for religious liberty thus became warp and woof of our constitutional tradition, not simply by the course of history, but by the common unifying force of Madison's life, thought and sponsorship. He epitomized the whole of that tradition in the Amendment's compact, but nonetheless comprehensive, phrasing.

As the Remonstrance discloses throughout, Madison opposed every form and degree of official relation between religion and civil authority. For him religion was a wholly private matter beyond the scope of civil power either to restrain or to support. Denial or abridgment of religious freedom was a violation of rights both of conscience and of natural equality. State aid was no less obnoxious or destructive to freedom and to religion itself than other forms of state interference. "Establishment" and "free exercise" were correlative and coextensive ideas, representing only different facets of the single great and fundamental freedom. The Remonstrance, following the Virginia statute's example, referred to the history of religious conflicts and effects of all sorts of establishments, current and historical, to suppress religion's free exercise. With Jefferson, Madison believed that to tolerate any fragment of establishment would be by so much to perpetuate restraint upon that freedom. Hence he sought to tear out the institution not partially but root and branch, and to bar its return forever.

In no phase was he more unrelentingly absolute than in opposing state support or aid by taxation. Not even "three pence" contribution was thus to be exacted from any citizen for such a purpose. Remonstrance, 3. Tithes had been the lifeblood of establishment before and after other compulsions disappeared. Madison and his coworkers made no exceptions or abridgments to the complete separation they created. Their objection was not to small tithes. It was to any tithes whatsoever. "If it were lawful to impose a small tax for religion, the admission would pave the way for oppressive levies." Not the amount but "the principle of assessment was wrong." And the principle was as much to prevent "the interference of law in religion" as to restrain religious intervention in political matters. In this field the authors of our freedom would not tolerate "the first experiment on our liberties" or "wait till usurped power had strengthened itself by exercise, and entangled the question in precedents." Remonstrance, 3. Nor should we.

In view of this history no further proof is needed that the Amendment forbids any appropriation, large or small, from public funds to aid or support any and all religious exercises. But if more were called for, the debates in the First Congress and this Court's consistent expressions, whenever it has touched on the matter directly, supply it.

By contrast with the Virginia history, the congressional debates on consideration of the Amendment reveal only sparse discussion, reflecting the fact that the essential issues had been settled. Indeed the matter had become so well understood as to have been taken for granted in all but formal phrasing. Hence, the only enlightening reference shows concern, not to preserve any power to use public funds in aid of religion, but to prevent the Amendment from outlawing private gifts inadvertently by virtue of the breadth of its wording...

CHAPTER II

THE CHURCH AS CORPORATION

The problems which were presented in Virginia when the Episcopal Church sought, obtained, and later lost its charter of incorporation have already been touched upon above. In other states there was less fear that the incorporation of churches would result in the establishment of a particular religion and it had become a common practice for the legislature, by special act, to incorporate churches and religious societies. Such charters characteristically included rather detailed provisions concerning the control of the "temporalities" of the society. It was usual to specify with some particularity how the powers should be divided between the congregation, the vestry, the wardens, and the minister. Not unnaturally the provisions with respect to such matters varied with the denomination of the society being incorporated.

New York Statute of 1786

In 1786 New York enacted an important statute providing for the incorporation of "churches, congregations and religious societies" (1 Jones & Varick Revision 104). This Act was the first general incorporation statute to be adopted in any of the states and, as such, had a considerable influence in other states. Its most significant portions were as follows:

"Whereas by the Thirty-eighth Article of the Constitution of the State of New York, it is ordained, determined and declared, that the free Exercise and Enjoyment of religious Profession and Worship, without Discrimination or Preference should forever thereafter be allowed within this State to all Mankind, Provided that the Liberty of Conscience, thereby granted, should not be so construed as to excuse Acts of Licentiousness ... And whereas many of the Churches, Congregations and religious Societies in this State (while it was a Colony) have been put to great Difficulties to support the public Worship of God, by reason of the illiberal and partial Distributions of Charters of Incorporation to religious Societies, whereby many charitable and well-disposed Persons have been prevented from contributing to the Support of Religion, for Want of Proper Persons authorized by Law, to take charge of their pious Donations, and many Estates purchased and given for the Support of Religious Societies, now rest in private Hands, to the great Insecurity of the Society, for whose Benefit they were purchased or given and to the no less Disquiet of many of the good People of this State: And whereas it is the Duty of all Wise, Free and Virtuous Governments, to countenance and encourage Virtue and Religion, and to remove every Lett or Impediment to the Growth and Prosperity of the People, and to enable every religious Denomination to provide for the Decent and Honorable Support of Divine Worship agreeable to the Dictates of Conscience and Judgment;
1. Be it therefore enacted by the People of the State of New York, represented in Senate and Assembly, and it is hereby Enacted by the Authority

of the same, That from and after the passage of this Act, it shall and may be lawful to and for the Male Persons of full Age, belonging to any Church, Congregation or religious Society not already established within this State, or which may at any Time hereafter be within the same, to assemble and meet together, at the Church, Meeting-House or other Place where they statedly attend for Divine Worship, and then and there by Plurality of Voices, to elect, nominate and appoint any Number of discreet and prudent Persons of their Church, Congregation or Society, not less than three or exceeding nine in Number as Trustees, to take the charge of the Estate and Property belonging to their respective Churches, Congregations or religious Societies, and to transact all Affairs relative to the Temporalities of their respective Churches, Congregations or Societies: That at such Election, every Male Person of full Age who has statedly worshipped with the said Church, Congregation or Society, and has formerly been considered as belonging thereto, shall be entitled to a Voice at such first Election."

The trustees thus elected were to: "... have, hold, use, exercise and enjoy, all and singular the Churches, Meeting-Houses, Parsonages ... thereunto belonging, with the Hereditaments and Appurtenances heretofore by the said Church, Congregation or Society held, occupied or enjoyed...to the sole and only proper Use and Benefit of them the said Trustees and their Successors for ever, in as full, firm and ample a Manner in the Law, as if the said Trustees had been legally incorporated."

Further provisions were made in the statute under which the trustees were given exclusive control of the money of the Society, but were charged with the responsibility of filing triennial financial accounts with the judges of the state. The salary of the minister was, under the statute, to be voted by the members of the corporation, not by the trustees. No religious society was permitted to hold property producing an income in excess of 1200 pounds a year. In 1813 this general act was amended to make provisions for certain denominations, including the Episcopal Church, but its fundamentals remained unchanged.

One of the most difficult periods which the Catholic Church went through in this country was in the first half of the 19th century. The basic source of its difficulties was the fact that the New York method of organizing religious societies, with control over the "temporalities" vested in laymen, spread to other states. The hierarchical organization of the Catholic Church made this method of control quite impossible, for the traditional system of Church government allowed the laymen a very small share of power. In a number of states priests defied their bishops, gained the support of the congregation, and sought to upset entirely the normal methods of ecclesiastical administration. The story of the Church's struggle is ably told in Dignan, _A History of the Legal Incorporation of Catholic Church Property in the United States_ (1935). See also, Tourscher, _The Hogan Schism_ (1930); Guilday, _The Catholic Church in Virginia_ (1924); Brown, _The Canonical Juristic Personality_ (1927).

A considerably later phase of this problem of adjusting American law and Roman Canon law arose in Pennsylvania at the beginning of this century.

Mazaika v. Krauczunas
Supreme Court of Pennsylvania, 1911
233 Pa. 138

Opinion by Mr. Justice Stewart, October 9, 1911:

Either the deliverances of this court as reported in 221 Pa. 213, and 229 Pa. 47, with respect to the ownership of church property and congregational power in connection therewith, have been seriously misapprehended, or the present proceeding is a clear attempt to circumvent the law as we have there declared it. In the first of the cases referred to, Krauczunas v. Hoban, the effort was on the part of the ten lay members of the congregation, duly chosen trustees of the legal title to the church property, to compel a reconveyance to them of the title by Bishop Hoban who had previously been designated trustee of the title for a special purpose which had been fully accomplished. The effort of these trustees was resisted, not on the ground that the congregation was without statutory right to choose its own trustee or trustees for the purpose indicated, or that the election of these particular trustees was in any way irregular, but distinctly on the ground that any such election, except as it resulted in the choice of the bishop of the diocese in which the property was located, offended against the rules and regulations of the Catholic church. To make this clear it is only necessary to quote a single finding of fact, and the conclusion derived therefrom, on which the lower court rested its dismissal of the plaintiffs' bill. The finding was as follows: "The Canons of the Roman Catholic Church provide and require that the title to the property of the Roman Catholic Congregation which is under the jurisdiction of the Roman Catholic Bishop of the Diocese in which the Congregation has its place of worship, must be in the ordinary, or, in the present case, in the Bishop of the Diocese." This was the conclusion derived: "If a congregation is formed for the purpose of religious worship according to the faith and rites of the Catholic church, and has accepted the pastor assigned to it by the bishop of the diocese, has placed itself under the authority of the bishop and submitted itself to his authority in all ecclesiastical matters, the title to its property must be taken and held as provided by the Canons of the Catholic Church. The property acquired by the congregation under such circumstances is the property of the church, and is subject to its control and must be held in the manner directed by its laws. ... The title to the real estate described in plaintiffs' bill is properly and legally vested in the defendant, Rt. Rev. Michael J. Hoban, Bishop of Scranton, as trustee for St. Joseph's Lithuanian Catholic Congregation, in accordance with the laws and usages of the Catholic Church." Referring to this language, in our review of the case, we said: "It will be seen from this that what was a controversy over an unimportant result - the right to substitute one dry, passive trustee of a legal title for another - was made to involve a question of ownership of property. ... Conveyance to the Church is not pretended; nor is forfeiture on the part of the congregation. Nothing is asserted in this connection but ecclesiastical rules and regulations, which, except as they are aided by legal conveyance, are ineffectual to divest any owner of his property. But more than this the position taken by the defendant and sustained by the court, is in direct opposition to the law, whose supremacy, over all ecclesiastical rules and regulations, when rights of property are concerned, is not to be questioned. The Act of April 26, 1855, P. L. 328, sec. 7, provides that 'whensoever any property, real or personal, shall hereafter be bequeathed, devised or conveyed to any ecclesiastical corporation, bishop, ecclesiastic, or other person, for the use of any church, congregation, or religious society, for religious worship or sepulture, or the maintenance of either, the same shall not be otherwise taken and held, or enure, than subject to the control and disposition of the lay members of such church, congregation, or religious society, or such constituted officers or representatives thereof, etc.' We accordingly sustained the appeal, and ordered that Bishop Hoban reconvey the church property to the plaintiffs as trustees. It is to be remarked in this connection that these trustees, because of their attempt to vindicate their right under the law, had been excommunicated by the bishop (Appendix, p. 233). Nevertheless the bishop complied with the decree of the court, and made conveyance of the title; he followed it up, however, with an episcopal interdict which closed the doors of the church against the congregation. This interdict reads as follows: "The members of St. Joseph's Congregation; Greeting - The court had decided that the Catholic Bishop of Scranton must hand over to a band of excommunicated apostates the deed of the Catholic Church of St. Joseph's. As the church cannot be used for any other worship than Catholic Worship, and as it is intolerable to hold Catholic services in a church controlled by members who despise the Church and Her laws, and who have lost their Catholic Faith, I am exceedingly pained to be obliged to place the Lithuanian Catholic Church of St. Joseph's under interdict until the members of the congregation shall turn these faithless men out and place the Church once more under the care of the Bishop of the Diocese of Scranton, according to the laws of the Catholic Church. I now declare that the Lithuanian Catholic Church of St. Joseph's, North Main Avenue, in this city of Scranton, is hereby placed under Interdiction from midnight of Sunday, May 31 - June 1, 1908, and that no Catholic services of any kind shall be held therein, nor shall any Catholic enter therein without incurring ecclesiastical censure, until the Interdict shall be removed." (signed) "Michael John Hoban, Bishop of Scranton." Simultaneously with the proclamation of this edict a meeting of the congregation was called, elsewhere than in the church, to determine how the title to the property was to be held. We are not now concerned with the factional differences which disturbed that meeting, and resulted in a separate meeting of the dissentients, except to say that the latter repudiated the action attempted at the meeting regularly called, and declined to reconvey the title to the bishop. The present bill was filed to enforce compliance. A protracted hearing resulted, the one issue being the regularity in the proceedings and membership of the meeting which declared for a reconveyance to the bishop. In the course of two or three days - we use the language of the chancellor before whom the case was heard - it became apparent that if the question were to be decided by review of the action taken at that meeting, the result would be unsatisfactory or doubtful. It was consented to by the individual litigants that an election should be held in open court, conducted by the chancellor. Such election was held, covering several days, and resulted, according to the findings of the chancellor, in the election of Bishop Hoban as trustee. A decree followed requiring a reconveyance of the title to him. On appeal to this court, Mazaika v. Krauczunas, 229 Pa. 47, we held that the election before the chancellor in open court was without effect for reasons therein stated at length, and which need not be repeated here, and we accordingly set aside the decree and remitted the record, the case to be proceeded with as though the election in court had not been held. The case was thereupon proceeded with in due form, with like conclusions upon the issues raised by the original bill and answer, and we have this present appeal from a decree requiring a reconveyance to the "Rt. Rev. Michael J. Hoban, Bishop of Scranton, as trustee for St. Joseph's Lithuanian Catholic Congregation of the city of Scranton." If the case rested simply on the findings of fact and conclusions of the learned chancellor with respect to the regularity of the proceedings in the meeting of the congregation at which Bishop Hoban was declared to have received a majority of the votes cast, while much that there occurred is open to criticism, we would not feel justified in prolonging this unprofitable controversy by a reversal. But there are other admitted facts which have a significance not to be overlooked. In this we make no reference to the excommunication of the appellants as a punishment for their appeal to the law of the land for a vindication of the right of the congregation they represented to the control of its property, nor to the episcopal edict which followed at once upon our decision, depriving the congregation of the privilege of Christian worship according to its faith and practice in its own sanctuary until such time as it chose to elect the bishop of the diocese the trustee of the legal title to its property. We will assume that these acts were within episcopal authority under the polity of the Roman Catholic Church, however much they may be at variance with the policy of our civil law which regards with condemnation all interference with freedom of elections. No one is heard complaining in regard to them, and they concern us here only as they help to an understanding of the real purpose of the meeting of the congregation whose action in the election of Bishop Hoban as trustee has been sustained by the court below. The resolution embodying the action of the meeting was as follows: "Whereas, it is deemed advisable and proper, and it is also the desire of the members of St. Joseph's Lithuanian Catholic Congregation of the city of Scranton, Pennsylvania, to vest the title to all the property of said St. Joseph's Lithuanian Catholic Congregation of the city of Scranton, Pennsylvania, in Rt. Rev. Michael J. Hoban, Bishop of Scranton, as trustee for said St. Joseph's Lithuanian Catholic Congregation, in accordance with the laws, rules and usages of the Catholic Church in the diocese of Scranton and state of Pennsylvania.

"Now, therefore be it resolved, That all the property of said St. Joseph's Lithuanian Catholic Congregation is, and is hereby declared, subject to the jurisdiction of the Catholic Church and the Catholic Bishop of Scranton, and be it further

"Resolved that Rt. Rev. Michael J. Hoban, Bishop of Scranton, be, and is hereby chosen and designated trustee for said St. Joseph's Lithuanian Catholic Congregation of the city of Scranton, Pennsylvania, to hold as such trustee all the property of said Congregation, and the title thereto in accordance with the laws, rules and usages of the Catholic Church in the Diocese of Scranton and state of Pennsylvania." The significance of the language here employed can be fully understood only as we recall what was said by this court in Krauczunas v. Hoban, supra, the language of the interdict of the bishop closely following upon our decision, and the rules and regulations of the Catholic church with respect to the property of the congregation as defined by Bishop Hoban in his testimony in the case. In the case referred to we distinctly held that the case was one involving the right of property, and that the law governing was not to be found in the rules and regulations of the general ecclesiastical system, but in the statute of April 26, 1855, P. L. 328, wherein it is declared that property "devised or conveyed to any ecclesiastical corporation, bishop, ecclesiastic or other person, for the uses of any church, congregation, or religious society for religious worship, or sepulture, or the maintenance of either, the same shall not be otherwise taken and held, or enure, than subject to the control and disposition of the lay members of such church, congregation or religious society, or such constituted officers or representatives thereof." The contention of the bishop there was that he had a right to hold the title to the property under the Catholic system, vurtute officii. This view having prevailed with the court below we sustained the appeal, and expressly held that the position taken "is in direct opposition to the law whose supremacy over all ecclesiastical rules and regulations, when the rights of property are concerned, is not to be questioned." We further held that the conveyance to the appellees in that case constituted an executed legal estate in the congregation, and created a dry, passive trust which gave the trustees neither interest in the estate, nor power to control it or direct its management in any way; that trustees in such case become simply the depository of the legal title and nothing more. We refer in this connection to only so much of the interdict as decreed that it shall continue in force "until the members of the Congregation shall turn out these faithless men (the acting trustees) and place the Church once more under the care of the Bishop of the Diocese of Scranton according to the laws of the Catholic Church." We make no question here of the authority of the bishop under the rules of the church for this coercive decree. It was nevertheless a manifest attempt to deny to the congregation freedom of action with respect to property of which, under the law of the land, it was sole owner; notwithstanding, the bishop, as he himself asserts, was acting strictly in line with his episcopal duty and prerogative. He had testified that as bishop of the diocese he had control and disposition of the church property under the general laws of the church. He was asked "Whether under the ecclesiastical law of the Catholic Church the lay members had the right of control and dispostition of the property, or whether the bishop had the right?" His answer was as follows: "Under the general law of the church the lay people have not the right to control." He was again asked, "Under the law of the church, the ecclesiastical law, have the members of the church the right to hold the property as trustee for the congregation?" His answer was, "No, they have not." In this reflected light we may see the real significance of the language used in the resolution declaring for the election of Rt. Rev. Bishop Hoban, "to hold as trustee all the property of said Congregation and the title thereto in accordance with the law, rules and usages of the Catholic Church in the Diocese of Scranton;" that is to say, even to a denial to the congregation of the chief incident of its ownership, control of the property which is its own under the laws of the state of Pennsylvania. In the case above cited we took occasion to explain, in the hope that it would end this prolonged controversy, that a trust in such cases gives to the trustee neither interest in the estate, nor power to control it or direct its management in any way; that it creates no duty for the trustee to perform, and leaves nothing to his discretion; that he is simply the passive, silent depository of the legal title and nothing more. In view of the plain words of the statute thus called to their attention as to the exclusive right of property in the congregation; the unquestioned sovereignty of the law where rights of property are involved, the legal inhibition against the bishop, qua bishop, exercising control of the church property, the positive conflict in this respect between the rules and regulations of the Catholic church and the statute laws of the state, what other conclusion can be reached than that the action of the meeting of the congregation, as expressed in the resolution we have referred to, and at which it is claimed Bishop Hoban was elected trustee, was a clear attempt to invest that particular ecclesiastic with an authority over the congregational property which the law expressly forbids? If no other purpose was intended than to elect Michael J. Hoban, in his private and natural capacity - the only capacity in which under the law he was compentent to hold the legal title as trustee - was it for the purpose of identification that he was described as "Rt. Rev. Michael J. Hoban, Bishop of the Diocese of Scranton?" We should likely so conclude, were this all; but this is preceded by the express declaration that all the property of this congregation is to be subject to the jurisdiction of the Catholic church and the Catholic Bishop of Scranton, and followed by the equally express declaration that the bishop is to hold as such trustee all the property of said congregation, and the title hereto, in accordance with the laws, rules and usages of the Catholic church which invested him with absolute control. If it be said that the purpose back of the action is irrelevant in a proceeding of this character, where the formal requirements have all been met in the matter of the call for the meeting, and in the general conduct of the election, our reply is, that the application here is for equitable interference, not in a matter resting in contract, but in a matter having to do with the general policy of the law and express statutory regulation as well, and for so much the greater reason the familiar maxim applies, that equity will respond only as the suitor comes with clean hands. Need we argue the proposition that the suitor comes not with clean hands in such case when the unmistakable purpose of his coming is to accomplish something which the law forbids? Let us make this plain even though it be only to repeat, What the law does not expressly allow to such trustee, it forbids. The office of trustee simply of legal title is not created by ecclesiastical authority, but created by the law; such trustee can exercise no control whatever over the property held in trust; being an officer created by law, and answerable only to the law, he can derive neither authority nor power from any other source. His duties, privileges, authority and responsibility qua trustee, can neither be enlarged nor impaired by ecclesiastical interference, and any attempt to so interfere would be quite as illegal as though forbidden in express terms.

But suppose we are mistaken in attributing to the congregational meeting that elected Bishop Hoban a purpose to circumvent the law, it follows then that the election was made under a total misapprehension of the law regulating ownership of church property and the rights of the congregation therein. The fact of conflict between the rules and regulations of the Catholic church and the laws of the state in this regard, remains. It is idle to dispute such fact; it is too patent to be questioned, and further discussion of it would be but wasted effort. If in ignorance of its rights on the one hand, and the law's restriction on the other, the congregation by a majority of votes took the action on which these appellees base their claim, should the court lend its aid to compel compliance? Were contractual rights involved we might feel constrained to do so; but we are embarrassed by no such consideration. No possible prejudice can come to any individual or interest by our withholding our sanction to the decree in this case. If St. Joseph's Lithuanian congregation desires Michael J. Hoban, whether described by his episcopal office or not, to be the custodian of the legal title to their church property, let them so declare by a majority vote of the adult male membership at a meeting regularly called, and their choice will not only be respected by the courts, but will by them be enforced if necessary. In either case no other purpose or understanding can be imputed than that the individual so chosen is to hold his office by virtue of the law, with no power of control whatever except what the law confers. However he may thereafter attempt interference with control of the property by the congregation, his action in this regard will be referred to his episcopal office and its legality adjudged accordingly, without regard to his trusteeship of the legal title.

It is urged that the decree from which the appeal is taken does not and cannot subject the church property to the control of the legal title. This is quite true; but the decree, except as it gives effect to the purpose of the congregation as expressed in the resolution which prevailed and which was the basis of its action, must be held extrajudicial, inasmuch as it substitutes for the will of the congregation in the matter of the selection of a trustee, the power of the court. The presumption may not be violent that the congregation would have elected Bishop Hoban trustee to hold under the law, but the court cannot presume that. That he was to hold it under the rules and regulations of the church, in view of what we have said, must be regarded as a condition of his election, which the court had no right to suppress or to ignore.

The eighth assignment of error was the refusal of the court to instruct in accordance with the ninth request for conclusions of law. The instruction asked for was as follows: "The action of the alleged meeting of June 8, 1908, embodied in the resolution claiming to have been adopted by the meeting, and upon which plaintiffs based their right to the relief prayed for in their appeal was illegal, and not binding upon the congregation for the reason that its purpose was to put the control and disposition of the property of the congregation in the Bishop of the Diocese under the laws of the Catholic Church, the same being in conflict with the laws of Pennsylvania.'" For the reasons above stated we are of opinion that this point should have been affirmed. We accordingly sustain the appeal. The decree of the court requiring the defendants to execute, acknowledge and deliver a proper deed of the premises described in the plaintiff's bill held in trust by them for St. Joseph's Lithuanian Catholic Congregation of the city of Scranton to Rt. Rev. Michael J. Hoban, Bishop of Scranton, as trustee for St. Joseph's Lithuanian Catholic Congregation of the city of Scranton is reversed, and it is ordered that the appellees pay the costs of this proceeding.[1]

St. Casimir's Polish R. C. Church's Case
Supreme Court of Pennsylvania, 1922
273 Pa. St. 494

Opinion by Mr. Justice Schaffer, March 27, 1952:

Prior to March 1, 1920, petitioners were members of St. Casimir's Polish Roman Catholic Church of Shenandoah. If appellee's position is sustained, thereafter they ceased to be members, and for that reason had no standing to present to the court below the petition which gives rise to this controversy.

St. Casimir's Church had a large congregation, almost a thousand in number. March 1, 1920, the duly constituted authorities of the Catholic Church divided the parish in which it belonged, and directed that all of its members on one side of the newly established boundary line should be members of St. Stanislaus' Church, another Catholic church in Shenandoah, which was created as a new parish; the effect of this, under the canons of the church, was to transfer the petitioners and several hundred other members of the first named church from membership in it to membership in the latter.

After this action was taken by the church authorities, the former congregation of St. Casimir's Church called a meeting which was attended by a large majority of its members, the bulk of them being those transferred to membership in St. Stanislaus' Church, who by formal announcement entered their protest against what had been done by the church authorities, elected appellants trustees of the church, and resolved that proceedings should be instituted to have the title to the church property transferred from the archbishop of the diocese in which the church was located, who held the title, to the elected trustees of the church. Accordingly the petition we are now considering was presented to the court below, the prayer of which was that the appellants, petitioners, be appointed trustees of the legal title of the church property, in trust for the congregation of the church, in the place and stead of the archbishop.

An answer was filed by Cardinal Dougherty, Archbishop of Philadelphia, in which, among other things, it was set up that the "petitioners are not residents of St. Casimir's parish, but are all residents of St. Stanislaus' parish; and that as nonresidents of St. Casimir's parish, they have no right to assert any claim to ownership or control of the property of St.

[1]In 1935 the statute of 1855 discussed in the principal case was repealed. Act of June 20, 1935, P.L. 353; Pa. Stat. Ann. (Purdon Supp. 1936) Tit. 10, Sec. 81. See, 4 U. of Pittsburgh L. Rev. 76 (1937).

Casimir's parish," and praying for the dismissal of the petition. After hearing, the petition was dismissed by the court below, which held that the proper ecclesiastical body of the church, empowered to make the division, had divided St. Casimir's parish, that this action by the church authorities was binding on the courts, and that under the laws, customs and usages of the Roman Catholic Church, those members of St. Casimer's Church residing within the boundary lines of the newly established St. Stanislaus' parish, ipso facto, by the order of division, ceased to be members of the former and became members of the latter, without any voice thereafter over the temporal affairs of the original parish, or power or authority over any of the church property therein. The petitioners have appealed from the order dismissing their petition.

Appellants' position is that, as members of St. Casimir's Church, they, and the others affected by the division, have rights in the property of that church, of which they cannot be deprived by the act of the church authorities in dividing the parish and consigning them to membership in another church; they contend that the question is a temporal one, affecting the title to the real estate of the church and not in its nature spiritual or ecclesiastical, and that under the Act of 1855 and its supplements and amendments, they have a standing to petition the court to establish their rights.

If the petitioners are members of St. Casimir's Church, they are parties in interest, and therefore entitled to call the powers of the court into action to appoint trustees to take over the legal title to the church property (Petition of Trustees of St. Joseph's Lithuanian Roman Catholic Church, filed herewith (the preceding case): Burton's Appeal, 57 Pa. 213; St. George's Church Petition, 244 Pa. 410). This brings us to the critical inquiry in the case. Is church membership a temporal or spiritual matter; does the decision as to who are and who are not members of any given church lie within the domain of the tribunals of the State or of the Church? Appellants concede that if the question involved is ecclesiastical and spiritual, it is solely within the jurisdiction of the church authorities.

It was testified in appellee's behalf, without contradiction, that under the canon law of the Roman Catholic Church, after the division of a parish, the members of the respective parishes, thus created, have no right to determine for themselves to which church they belong, that those within the respective parishes belong to the church within that parish, and the persons of one parish have no jurisdiction over the affairs of the other. Appellants admit that, under the laws of the Church, the proper authorities made the division of the parish and that, ecclesiastically, the effect of the division was to sever appellants from membership in St. Casimir's Church. "In Pennsylvania the term 'parish' has no especial legal signification, it is used merely in its general sense. In English ecclesiastical law, it has been used to designate the territory committed to the particular charge of a parson or priest. In the absence of a state church here, however, the status of a parish is rendered comparatively unimportant; if used in ecclesiastical divisions, it has just such importance and particular significance as may be given it under ecclesiastical regulations": Tuigg v. Treacy, 104 Pa. 493, 498.

Mr. Justice Simpson, delivering the opinion in Furmanski v. Iwanowski, 265 Pa. 1, at page 5, after reviewing our earlier cases dealing with the subject of church laws and the binding effect in certain instances of the decisions of duly constituted church tribunals, thus laid down the broad, controlling, legal principle: "In matters relating to a church or other voluntary organization its members are bound by and required to conform to its laws. ... Where it has appropriate tribunals to decide what are the scope and effect of its laws their decisions duly made are binding on the members unless in violation of the law of the land." In Watson v. Jones, 80 U. S. 679 (one of the most famous church disputes in the country's history), it was said, at page 728: "The right to organize religious associations to assist in the expression and dissemination of any religious doctrine, and to create tribunals for the decision of controverted questions of faith within the association, and for the ecclesiastical government of all the individual members, congregations and officers within the general association, is unquestioned. All who unite themselves to such a body, do so with an implied consent to this government and are bound to submit to it. But it would be a vain consent and would lead to the total subversion of such religious bodies, if any one aggrieved by one of their decisions could appeal to the secular courts and have them reversed. It is of the essence of these religious unions, and of their right to establish tribunals for the decision of questions arising among themselves, that these decisions should be binding in all cases of ecclesiastical cognizance, subject only to such appeals as the organism itself provided for."

Appellants treat the question before us, as one of property rights in the church vested in them, but the difficulty this meets with is, that there can be no property rights in church property, save through membership in the congregation, and this essential cord of membership, to tie themselves to the church property, petitioners do not now possess.

Appellants would invoke the Act of April 26, 1855, P. L. 330, and its supplements and amendments, relating to the right of a congregation to control church property, to sustain their position, contending that a temporal right was infringed by the division of the parish. We know of no legislation which gives to a member of a congregation a property right in his membership therein. His rights in the church property flow from his membership. We are not in any way impairing the principle announced in Krauczunas v. Hoban, 221 Pa. 213, that church property belongs to the congregation of the church. The difficulty here is that appellants are no longer members of the congregation.

Counsel have not referred us to any Pennsylvania case on the precise point we are dealing with - whether church membership is temporal or ecclesiastical matter - nor has our own research developed one; but we have discovered that the subject has received consideration in other jurisdictions. It was held in Waller v. Howell, 45 N. Y. Supp. 790, that the question of church membership is entirely ecclesiastical and involves no rights which the civil courts can recognize. In Shannon v. Frost, 3 B. Monroe 253, at 258, the Supreme Court of Kentucky said: "Our only judicial power in the case arises from the conflicting claims of the parties to the church property and the use of it. .. We cannot decide who ought to be members of the church, nor whether the excommunicated have been, justly or unjustly, regularly or irregularly, cut off from the body of the church. We must take the fact of expulsion as conclusive proof that the persons expelled are not now members of the repudiating church; for, whether right or wrong, the act of excommunication must, as to the fact of membership, be law to this court.

For every judicial purpose...we must consider the persons who were expelled by a vote of the church, as no longer members of the church, or entitled to any rights or privileges incidental to or resulting from membership therein...Every member of that church has a beneficial interest in the property thus conveyed, so long as he or she shall continue to be a member, but no longer. It is only as a constituent element of the aggregated body or church, that any person can acquire or hold, as a cestui que trust, any interest in the property thus dedicated to that church...The judicial eye of the civil authority of this land of religious liberty, cannot penetrate the veil of the church, nor can the arm of this court either rend or touch that veil for the forbidden purpose of vindicating the alleged wrongs of the excinded members. When they became members they did so on the condition of continuing or not, as themselves and their church might determine. In that respect they voluntarily subjected themselves to the ecclesiastical power, and cannot invoke the supervision or control of that jurisdiction by this or any other civil tribunal. Then, not being now members of the church to whose use the ground was conveyed, the appellants seem no longer to be entitled to any beneficial interest in that property, nor to any other right which this court can either enforce or recognize." In our own case of German Reformed Church v. Seibert, 3 Pa. 282, we held that as a person excommunicated from the church ceases to be a member, he loses his right as a corporator of the church. In Wheelock v. First Presbyterian Church of Los Angeles, 51 Pacific Repr. 841, the Supreme Court of California decided that the division of a local Presbyterian church into two organizations by an act of a presbytery, according to the recognized ecclesiastical law of the Presbyterian Church, is binding upon the local church and upon the civil courts whenever material to pending litigation.

Our conclusion, both from reason and authority, must be that, as a result of the division of St. Casimir's parish, appellants lost their membership in its church and all interest in its property; they, therefore, had no right which the court below could sanction as prayed for in their petition, which the court properly dismissed.

The assignments of error are overruled and the order dismissing the petition is affirmed at the cost of appellants.

Canovaro v. Brothers of The Order of Hermits of St. Augustine
Supreme Court of Pennsylvania, 1937
326 Pa. St. 76

Opinion by Mr. Chief Justice Kephart, March 22, 1937:

The Parish of the Church of Our Lady of Good Counsel, sometimes known as the Church of Our Mother of Good Counsel, was created in Philadelphia in 1889 by and under the authority of the Roman Catholic Church. It had fixed lines and its communicants generally were of Italian origin. The Brothers of the Order of St. Augustine purchased some land in the parish, the legal title being taken in the name of the Order. A church with a rectory was erected on a portion of it under the auspices and in accordance with the ritual of the Roman Catholic Church and was used exclusively for Roman Catholic services under Roman Catholic rules, regulations and canons. A parochial school was also established for Roman Catholic educational purposes under the Franciscan Sisters. The funds to build and pay for the church and school were derived in part from contributions, donations and collections from the parishioners and others. At the time of this action there was outstanding a mortgage of $60,000 against the property, secured by the bond of the Order of St. Augustine.

The Parish was the seat of a branch of the Order of St. Augustine, having therein a monastery. This Order, under the Ordinary or Archbishop, took charge of the church, supplying it with a pastor approved by the Ordinary and teachers for the schools free from any control whatever by the communicants of the church, who were the lay members of the Church of Our Lady of Good Counsel. The parish was instituted, in spirit at least as a parish for Italian people. The church was located close to two other Catholic churches, St. Paul's and St. Nicholas of Tolentino, and on May 5, 1933, the Ordinary, who is the Archbishop of the Diocese of Philadelphia, deeming the church building not in keeping with the standard fixed by this Roman Catholic Church in size and structure, and for canonical reasons, issued a decree dismembering the parish. At the same time the Ordinary petitioned the Vatican to approve the removal of the Seat of the Order of St. Augustine to another parish, that of St. Nicholas of Tolentino. This act received the approval of the Pope and was recognized by the Superior General of the Order of St. Augustine, who resides in Rome. The dismembered parts of the parish were merged with St. Paul's parish, which has a much more beautiful church, only two blocks away, and with other adjoining parishes. According to the laws of the church all parochial property in the dismembered parish, including the church and school with the land on which they were erected, though held in the name of the Order, was the property of the Roman Catholic Church under the control and disposition of the Ordinary.

Rev. Dr. Hickey, Assistant General of the Order, appearing for defendant, testified that the Order recognized the validity of the dismemberment decree by the Ordinary and stated that, under the canon law of the church, it caused the church and rectory property, held in the name of the Order, to come under the control and disposition of the Ordinary for the religious and charitable uses to which it had been dedicated. While the dismemberment decree was being carried into effect, the plaintiffs, members of the Church of Our Lady of Good Counsel, protested against such action and appealed to Pope Pius XI at Rome. They dispatched a cable asking him to intervene and restore the status quo. An appeal was also made to the Apostolic Delegate at Washington. The action of Cardinal Dougherty, dismembering the parish, was sustained by the Pope, and the objectors were called upon to obey the Cardinal's decree made in the exercise of the rights and authority conferred upon him by the canons of the church.

Plaintiffs, as members of the Church of Our Lady of Good Counsel, but claiming to be an unincorporated association independent of the Roman Catholic Church, then filed this bill in equity, alleging the Church and school properties were impressed with a trust to be used as an Italian church and school, and that the title was taken in defendant Order's name upon that understanding and agreement. They averred that the Order was no longer in sympathy with the purposes and objectives for which the school and church properties were purchased and maintained, and was about to convey the real estate to third parties in direct violation of the trust agreements. They asked the court below to place the property under the control of the lay members, "its rightful owners," to enjoin defendant Order from conveying, selling, encumbering or transferring the premises, to decree that the property should be held by the defendant Order in trust for the plaintiff lay members for the purposes for which it was given, and to direct the Order to convey the premises to the lay trustees in accordance with these purposes. Complete answers were filed. The court below, after a full hearing, dismissed the bill, and this appeal followed.

The court below held that as the plaintiffs were no longer members of the dismembered parish they had no standing to assert any rights in the property, and to grant the requested relief would be inequitable, since it would divert the property from the use for which it had been dedicated.

At the hearing appellants endeavored unsuccessfully to show by parol evidence that they, as a separate organization, made an agreement or entered into an understanding with the Order of St. Augustine whereby the property was to be held perpetually by the Order for the religious and educational purposes of the Italian people of the parish, and that their association was independent of the Roman Catholic Diocese of Philadelphia, but under the jurisdiction of the Order of St. Augustine. Even if this parol evidence had been admitted (see Act of April 22, 1856, P. L. 532, Section 4), and had been sufficient in quantity and quality, it would have placed appellants just as securely under the governance of the Roman Catholic Church as if they were a secular church in the parish. Appellee Order is altogether a Roman Catholic organization subject to the control and discipline of that Church. Any church controlled or held by it, is under the jurisdiction of the church through the Ordinary, and such property used for church or school purposes is subject to the Roman Catholic canons, unless, perhaps, the trust purposes are embodied in a writing which provides otherwise.

But, as the record shows, no such independent association ever existed in this parish. On the contrary, it appears that the religious services and the administration of the parochial property were at all times under the control and jurisdiction of the Roman Catholic Church. These church uses existed from the date of the church's erection in 1889 to 1933, when dismemberment occurred. The members were exclusively of the Roman Catholic faith.

Under the canons of the church there can be no such thing as a separate and independent church organization within the Roman Catholic Church, whereby property may be acquired and held in opposition to its laws, canons, rules and regulations, and at the same time be subject to its supervision and control. To create such a status would require special authority from the church itself. There must be evidence that the Order with which the supposed agreement was made had power to enter into such an agreement hostile to church laws and that the church itself accepted the agreement. Any church organization claiming the protection, benefits and assistance of the Roman Catholic faith and laws directly, or through one of its bodies, such as the defendant Order, is and must be subservient to its laws, canons, rules and regulations. It cannot in one breath claim life from the church, and the benefit of the faith that it follows with the protection granted under its laws, and, in the next breath deny its allegiance to the body under which it serves. Its very practices deny such conclusion. Nor can it, in opposition to church laws, set up a trust in property acquired through church contributions, donations and gifts, unless it was specifically reserved in writing. The impulse or motive of the donors in giving was the spirit and love of the church generally, to promote the Catholic faith under its protection, not because of any so-called independent association or any of the members who composed it. It was given for the purpose of advancing the worship of God according to the faith and discipline of the Roman Catholic Church and for no other purpose.

Appellants' counsel, realizing the great burden his clients assumed to establish an independent association, in his argument before us planted his rights on a different basis and argued that the provisions of the Act of April 26, 1855, P. L. 328, Section 7, covered his case. By so doing, he acknowledged his clients to be communicants and members of the Roman Catholic faith. Taking up the case from this viewpoint, appellants earnestly contend that the decree of the court below removed control of the church property from the lay members in contravention of the Act of 1855.

There can be no question that under the Act of 1855 church property was held subject to the control and disposition of lay members, but it could not be diverted from the purposes, uses and trusts imposed through its dedication for religious purposes. The fulfillment of the trust was to be accomplished under the rules, regulations and laws of the church as governing and controlling.[1] The act expressed the settled policy of the State, with respect to the tenure of property held by religious societies, existent for years and steadily observed without question: Krauczunas v. Hoban, 221 Pa. 213, 225. The amendatory Act of May 20, 1913, P. L. 422, was construed in Zernosky v. Kluchinsky, 278 Pa. 99, 104, to be no more than a clarification of the accepted meaning of the Act of 1855. But this right of control and disposition of church property was in the lay members by virtue of their membership, and only by those having that status could any right be claimed ...

Inasmuch as the church in which appellants claim membership is a subordinate body of the Roman Catholic Church, it follows that their rights and obligations as members are governed by the laws of that denomination since the voluntary act of joining the church subjects them to its rules and regulations: Krecker v. Shirey, 163 Pa. 534, 551; Zernosky v. Kluchinsky supra. The Roman Catholic canons and the decisions of the

---

[1]Citations omitted.

appropriate tribunals and officials of the church are decisive of the issues here raised, unless in contravention of the law of the land: St. Casimir's Polish R. C. Church's Case, supra, at pp. 498, 599; Furmanski v. Iwanowski, 265 Pa. 1, 5, 6; Krecker v. Shirey, supra, at p. 551.

The canons empower the Ordinaries to divide or dismember parishes when canonical reasons exist, notwithstanding the unwillingness of the rectors and members. The finding of the court below, that the Ordinary in dismembering the parish acted in accordance with the authority vested in him by the canons, is amply supported by evidence. Furthermore, the validity of the decree is not disputed by appellee Order, and, on appeal to the Pope, was upheld by him. Under the church law the effect of dismemberment was to cause the parish to cease to exist and to transfer its members to adjoining parishes. There were no longer any members of the original parish. The order of dismemberment was binding on the parish members. Division, dismemberment or suppression of parishes, and the effect thereof on membership are purely ecclesiastical matters, dependent upon the church law as administered by the appropriate authorities and tribunals. See St. Casimir's Polish R. C. Church's Case, supra, at p. 501. The effect of the dismemberment of the parish and the transfer of appellants' membership therefrom to other parishes was to deprive them of all rights as members in the church property of the parish from which they were transferred. Church membership is an ecclesiastical matter, not temporal. There is no property right in membership, and there could be no property rights in lay members except through their membership in the congregation ...

It is earnestly contended by appellants that the Ordinary, in dismembering the parish entirely, did by indirection that which the Act of 1855 intended should not be done directly, as his decree of dismemberment left no members of the Church of Our Lady of Good Counsel with a voice in the future control and disposition of the church property. The sole factual distinction between this case and the St. Casimir case is that in the latter the parish was not completely extinguished, only part of its membership being transferred to another parish by the change in the boundary line. In the instant case the parish has been entirely dismembered, and, as a result, it not only has no members but no longer exists as a parish. In reply to the contention that the purpose of dismemberment was merely to avoid the Act of 1855, we point out that there is nothing in the record to justify the inference that the underlying motive was to divest lay members of control of church property in circumvention of the statute. We cannot view either the cause of dismemberment or its effect other than in the light of the action of the church authorities as found by the chancellor. The decree of dismemberment was a proper exercise of the authority vested in the Archbishop by the Roman Catholic rules and made in pursuance of just and canonical reasons. The actuating reasons for dismemberment, as testified to by Bishop O'Hara, were proper for the consideration of the Archbishop, and were amply sufficient to justify action within the canons of the church. The decision of the proper ecclesiastical tribunals in this respect must be accepted by the civil courts unless it violates the civil law or is plaintly in disregard of the church canons, even though it touches directly upon property rights which fall within the jurisdiction of civil courts. "When a civil right depends upon an ecclesiastical matter, it is the civil court and not the ecclesiastical which is to decide. But the civil tribunal tries the civil right, and no more, taking the ecclesiastical decisions out of which the civil right arises as it finds them": Watson v. Jones, 13 Wall. 679, 730

Under the controlling church law, therefore, appellants are no longer members of the parish in which they seek to control the property and are without standing to maintain a bill in equity to enforce such property rights. However, it is not necessary to base our decision on this ground and to hold definitely that lay control can be entirely suppressed indirectly by the dismemberment of a parish for canonical reasons. Whatever merit there may be to appellants' argument is vitiated by the Act of June 20, 1935, P. L. 353, Section 1, which is amendatory of Section 7 of the Act of 1855, and materially and substantially changes the law concerning the control of church property.

Turning to the Act of 1935, the extent and effect of the change brought about by it is immediately made clear when its provisions are contrasted with the Acts of 1855 and 1913 preceding it. The Act of 1855 vested in the church laity absolute control and disposition of church property subject to the uses for which it was lawfully dedicated. The Act of 1935 provides that whenever any property has heretofore been or shall hereafter be conveyed for the use of any church, congregation or religious society having a controlling power according to the rules of such church, congregation or religious society, "which control and disposition shall be exercised in accordance with and subject to the rules and regulations, usages, canons, discipline and requirements of the religious body, denomination or organization to which such church, congregation or religious society shall belong." The Act is comprehensive enough to include all property, real or personal, of churches, congregations or religious societies acquired by gift, purchase, grant or devise.

The long established and deeply imbedded policy of entrusting the ultimate power of control and disposition of church property to the laity subject to the uses for which it was dedicated was uprooted by the Act of 1935. Its provision prohibiting the diversion of property from the purposes or trusts for which it was lawfully dedicated is similar to that of the Act of 1855, and by its express terms it applies to all property acquired by churches either prior or subsequent to its enactment. The effect of this statute is to make supreme the internal rules, regulations and usages of religious societies respecting the control of their property. The civil law no longer requires control to vest in lay members, but permits each individual church or society to determine for itself in what authorities this power shall vest. Property control, as well as all other ecclesiastical matters, is now governed by church law, since the impediment imposed thereto by the civil law has been removed. Churches are now no longer differentiated from other voluntary organizations in this respect. The Act of 1935 recognizes the binding effect of the internal laws of religious societies regarding the power of control and disposition of church property.

Does the Act of 1935 because of its retrospective character take property without due process of law, and divest church lay members of vested property rights? The fact that it is retrospective in itself does not render it unconstitutional: Adle v. Sherwood, 3 Wharton 481. We there said: "A retrospective law, which does not impair the obligation of a contract, nor is in its nature ex post facto, is constitutional." See also Paliaret's Appeal, 67 Pa. 479, 485. But if a legislative act operates to divest a vested right by virtue of its retrospective effect, it amounts to a taking of property without due process of law, unless it is a valid exercise of some fundamental power, as the police power, taxing power, or power of eminent domain: White, Constitution of Pennsylvania (1907), p. 117. The legislature cannot arbitrarily interfere with or destroy private property rights: Norman v. Heist, 5 W. & S. 171; Wolford v. Morgenthal, 91 Pa. 30.

A consideration of the constitutionality of this act requires a study of the character of the interest which lay members had in church property prior to 1935, so that it may be determined whether they had such a property right as entitles them to protection under the constitution.

Prior to the Act of 1855 property held or acquired by a voluntary association as a religious sect, denomination or congregation to be used for religious worship or education, governed by the doctrines of any particular church, faith or denomination, was subject to the control and disposition of the congregation according to the church rules and regulations. The control vested in the lay members. It had long been a settled rule in Pennsylvania where land is conveyed for the use of a religious society, even though the conveyance be in trust, that the transfer operates to vest absolute legal title in the congregation, subject to the limitation that the property may not be diverted from the uses for which it had been lawfully dedicated. This rule was predicated on the Act of February 6, 1731, 1 Sm. L. 192, Sec. 2, which conferred upon religious societies the legal capacity to hold land...

The question arises as to what is meant by the expressions "fee simple," "absolute ownership," "grant to the society itself," "title," and others of a similar nature, which appear throughout the cases in describing the interest of the congregation in church property. Do they mean that the lay members took the property free of all restraints? Obviously not, since such interpretation would lose sight of the fact that they are limited in the use of the property to the purposes for which it was dedicated. All the acts, including that of 1935, prohibit "the diversion of any property from the purposes, uses and trusts to which it may have been heretofore lawfully dedicated, or to which it may hereafter be lawfully dedicated..." It is quite aparent that in effect the lay members held title merely as trustees in a limited sense and were vested with the power of control and disposition of the church property solely in that capacity. A particular church of a given faith or sect as a local congregation is a part of the larger religious faith or sect which comprises the entire church or denomination. The local or parish church cannot divorce or separate itself from the mother church, set up a new independent organization and by so doing retain the ownership of the local church or congregational property: Dochkus v. Lithuanian B. Society, supra, at p. 29. In no event can the members utilize the property in a manner foreign to the principles, customs and rules of the church to which it has been conveyed, even though a majority or the entire congregation express their approval of such action: Krecker v. Shirey, supra. Neither can it, or a majority of its members, sever its connection or separate itself from the ecclesiastical body by and through which it was endowed with faculties, which enabled it to organize as part of the church family in subordination to the givèn authority of the church, and its laws, and retain any property rights. While the ownership of church property vested in a particular congregation, its use was dedicated to the church generally, not specifically to a local congregation with the power to sell it and divide the proceeds among themselves. The lay members held title subject to the uses, purposes and benefits for which it was given, acquired or devised. In this respect it was subject to the church laws, canons and regulations. Furthermore when a religious society becomes inactive or extinct, its property is not subject to division among its members and does not revert to the original grantors. See Act of May 17, 1921, P. L. 861, Section 1. A dissenting minority of one, or the intervention of the church generally can prevent any spoliation of such uses: Nagle v. Miller, 175 Pa. 157; Kicinko v. Petruska, 259 Pa. 1.

Consequently, nothing is clearer than the fact that the property interest of the lay members was in no sense absolute prior to 1935. They merely had the power of control and disposition over the property to be exercised in harmony with and submission to the principles, rules and canons of their church. This did no more than clothe them with some of the attributes of trustees. The restricted use to which they could put the property negatives "absolute ownership" in them. This term has been used in a loose sense and is inextricably coupled with the prohibition against diversion of the property. Taken by itself it conveys an erroneous impression of the extent of the interest of the lay members in church property. In short, the effect of the Act of 1855, was purely to preserve to them their right to act as "trustees," and prevent any interference with this right by the church law. The policy of the law was to vest in the lay members, as "trustees," the power of control and disposition of the property, and nothing more ...

Furthermore it is fair to assume that where a gift is made to a religious society with knowledge that under an existing statute the property will be controlled by the congregation as "trustees," the donor intends that in the future the right of control is to be subject to the will of the legislature in the absence of the expression of any intent to the contrary. In this respect Philadelphia v. Fox, 64 Pa. 169, is helpful. That case involved certain charitable, testamentary trusts, among them the trusts created by Girard's Estate, appointing the City of Philadelphia as trustee. Subsequent to their creation a statute was passed vesting their administration in the "Board of Directors of City Trusts." The constitutionality of this statute was attacked on the ground that it deprived the municipality of its vested right to administer and control the trusts. This court, speaking through Justice Sharswood, ruled it constitutional, holding that the trusts were created subject to the control of the legislature with full knowledge that the trustees were merely agents of the legislature acting under a revocable power, and that the city, as trustee of the charities, cannot set up a vested right to have the trust continued in the form in which it was created.

It has long been recognized that a religious and educational use is a charitable use. In Price v. Maxwell, 28 Pa. 23, this court stated, at p. 36: "A charitable use is not always a religious one, but we know of no religious use, which could be recognized at all as free from superstition, that is not included in the definition of a charitable use." Considered in this light, there can be no doubt of the right of the legislature to take measures which they deem necessary to the proper enforcement of the trust. In Philadelphia v. Fox, supra, at pp. 182 and 183, there is the following quotation from Girard v. Phila., 7 Wallace 14: " 'It cannot admit of a doubt,' says Mr. Justice Grier, 'that where there is a valid devise to a corporation, in trust for charitable purposes, unaffected by any question as to its validity because of superstition, the sovereign may interfere to enforce the execution of trusts, either by changing the administrator if the corporation be dissolved, or, if not, by modifying or enlarging its franchises, provided the trust be not perverted, and no wrong done to the beneficiaries.' " Therefore, for the above mentioned reasons, the Act of 1935 does not constitute a divestment of a vested right and applies with full force to all property acquired by religious societies either prior or subsequent to its enactment.

The order of the court below dismissing the bill is affirmed at appellants' cost.

Robertson v. Bullions
New York Court of Appeals, 1854
11 New York 243

SELDEN, J. The defendants not having appealed from any portion of the decree of the supreme court, so much of that decree as declares that Dr. Bullions had been deposed from the ministry, and that the trustees could not rightfully appropriate the funds of the corporation to his support, while he continued so deposed, without the consent of all the members of the corporation, and as prohibits such appropriation for the future, is to be regarded as final and conclusive. This court can only review those parts of the decree from which an appeal is taken. (Kelsey v. Western, 2 Coms. 500) It is not, however, to be inferred from this portion of the decree, that the supreme court intended to affirm the views of the trust, insisted upon by the complainants; because that part of the decree of the vice chancellor which declares the nature of the trust, was expressly reversed and annulled by the supreme court. The whole case therefore, except so far as it is involved in the simple prohibition in regard to the support of Dr. Bullions, is before this court; and in determining the questions which must necessarily be here decided in respect to the removal of the trustees, and their obligation to account, it becomes indispensable to pass to some extent upon the powers, duties and functions of trustees of religious corporations, the tenure by which they hold the corporate property, and the nature of the trusts committed to their charge.

Two distinct views have been taken of the nature of the corporations formed pursuant to the statute of this state providing for the incorporation of religious societies. According to one of these views the society itself does not become incorporated, but only its trustees. The individuals composing the society, the persons associated for the purpose of religious worship, form no part of the corporation, and are not to be regarded in any sense as corporators, but simply as members as well after as before incorporation, of a voluntary association, without unity, except such as may be produced by the assent of its members to its own self-imposed rules and regulations. The trustees in this aspect, constitute a body corporate entirely separate and distinct from the society, created for the sole purpose of receiving and holding the legal title to the property, and devoting it to the purposes and objects of the society, which is supposed to retain its distinctive characteristics as a mere voluntary association, in no degree merged in the corporation, even in respect to its temporal and secular concerns. The consequence of this view of the subject would be, that the trustees of a religious corporation are not to be regarded as the managing officers and agents of the society, clothed with the aggregate powers of the corporators, representing their interests and entrusted with a discretionary charge of their temporal affairs, as in other corporations, but their relations to the society are those simply of a trustee to his cestui que trust, as understood in equity. Were this view established, its effect would probably be, to devolve upon the courts of equity the administration of the entire property of religious corporations throughout the state, a jurisdiction bringing with it as its inevitable concomitant, inumerable judicial inquiries into modes of faith, shades of religious opinion, and all those subtleties which attend the diversities of religious belief.

The other view assumes that the society itself is incorporated; that the previous voluntary association is merged in the corporation, so far as its secular affairs merely are concerned; that the trustees are not the body corporate itself, but merely its officers, to whom is committed the custody of its property, and the management of its concerns; that the members of the association form the constituent body, the legal entity which is represented by the trustees, and that the latter are clothed with the customary discretionary powers which appertain to the managing officers of all civil corporations; modified it is true in some degree, by the mixed nature of the body which they represent, and the peculiar objects of the incorporation.

The argument by which the former of these views is sustained, rests mainly upon that clause in the third section of the act authorizing these incorporations, which, after providing for the election of these trustees, declares, not that the society, but that such trustees and their successors shall by virtue of the act, be a body corporate, by the name or title expressed in the certificate. But while I do not deny the force of this and the other arguments adduced in support of this construction of the act, I nevertheless insist that the arguments against it are too strong to be resisted. In the first place, such a construction is adverse to the universal popular sentiment in respect to the law in question. To prove this I need only refer to the names adopted by the various religious societies upon becoming incorporated. The following list was taken promiscuously from the records of religious corporations in Monroe county, viz: Churchville Presbyterian Society. First Congregational Society of Mumford, Associate Reformed Association of Beulah. Adams' Basin Free Church Society.

Baptist Church and Society of Sweden. Society of Christian Brethren in Rochester. St. Peter's Presbyterian Congregation, Rochester. Fifth Presbyterian Society and Congregation of Rochester.

Of the great number of religious corporations in the county almost all bear names similar in character to these. The trustees are sometimes, though rarely named.

The founders of these corporations must have supposed, that it was the society of congregation that was incorporated. I hazard nothing in saying, that this has been the general understanding throughout the state, ever since the passage of the acts in question.

But this view of the nature of religious corporations is not only opposed to the general sentiment of the people, but is repugnant also to judicial construction so far as any has ever been given to the acts in question. In the case of The Baptist Church, &c., v. Witherell, (3 Paige, 296) Chancellor Walworth treats, throughout, the society as corporators, and the trustees as the mere officers of the corporation ... The same view is taken in the subsequent case of Lawyer v. Cipperly, (7 Paige, 281) So in the case of Miller v. Gable, in the late court of errors, (2 Denio, 492) Gardiner, president of the court, speaks of trustees as "the representatives" of the congregation and of the members of the latter, as corporators. It is clear therefore that if the popular understanding of the act authorizing religious corporations be an error, it is one in which the most enlightened of our courts and judges have participated ...

It cannot, I think, be necessary to pursue this subject further, although there are other portions of the statute which equally conflict with the view, that the trustees and not the society constitute the body corporate. I think it clear, therefore, that the views which appear to have been generally entertained by both courts and people upon this subject are correct; that the societies are themselves incorporated; that their members are the corporators, and the trustees the managing officers or the corporation.

What then are the powers, rights and obligations of this class of corporate officers, and to what extent has this court jurisdiction over them? These questions are to be answered in view of the statute authorizing the incorporation of these societies, and the rules which regulate other corporations of the same legal character, and their officers; and not with reference to those peculiar principles which are applied to trusts by courts of equity. These officers are trustees in the same sense with the president and directors of a bank, or of a railroad company. They are the officers of the corporation to whom is delegated the power of managing its concerns for the common benefit of themselves and all other corporators; and over whom the body corporate retains control, through its power to supersede them at ever recurring election ...

It follows from this view, that the supreme court were entirely right in holding, in this case, that these incorporated societies are not to be regarded as ecclesiastical corporations, in the sense of the English law, which were composed entirely of ecclesiastical persons, and subject to the ecclesiastical judicatories; but as belonging to the class of civil corporations to be controlled and managed according to the principles of the common law, as administered by the ordinary tribunals of justice.

The question then arises, to what extent had the late court of chancery jurisdiction and control over the officers of civil corporations, in respect to the performance of their official duties? This question was ably discussed by Chancellor Kent, in Attorney General v. Utica Insurance Company (2 John. Ch. 371). He there held, that the court of chancery did not possess any general supervisory control over corporations of this character, and inclined to the opinion that the court had no jurisdiction whatever, even in a case of abuse by a corporate trustee, or other officer of his trust, by a perversion or misapplication of the funds of the corporation ...

This brings us to the consideration of the alleged trust in the present case. In the view I take of the case, it is unnecessary to inquire as to the effect of the deed of July, 1786, or whether a court of equity would sustain the right of the congregation to an equitable fee under that deed, agreeably to the obvious intent of the parties, or compel a further assurance to effectuate that intent; but I shall consider the case as though all the rights, either legal or equitable, of the congregation or its trustees, derived under the first deed, were fully merged in the second. Under this deed the persons named became seised of an estate in fee, which they held subject to the trust expressed in the deed, until the congregation became incorporated in 1826. What then was the effect of that incorporation upon the title to this property, and upon the trusts under which it was held? We are saved the necessity of inquiring whether the title actually passed to the corporation; because, the counsel on both sides concede that such was the effect of incorporating the congregation.

A question arises as to the construction of the clause in the deed limiting the trust. If by members "in full communion," &c., is intended members of the church, or the body of covenanted professors of a certain faith, as distinct from other members of the association, which I suppose to be its true interpretation, then prior to the incorporation the title to the property was held not for the benefit of the congregation at large, but for the exclusive use and benefit of the members of the church of a particular connection.

What effect then had the transfer of the title to the corporation upon this trust? This involves the inquiry, whether trustees of a religious corporation can take a trust for the exclusive benefit of a portion of the body, whose interests they represent, and whose officers they are. In the case of Williams v. Williams, decided by this court in January last, it was held that the trustees of such a corporation might take a bequest in trust for the support of a minister, that being one of the general objects for which the corporation existed. Denio, J., in that case says: "The object of this bequest is, the support of a minister, which is one of the most prominent of the objects for which these corporations are created. It is not essential to the validity of a bequest to a religious corporation, that it should be given generally, for all the purposes for which it may be legally used, or for any to which the trustees may see fit to devote it. This is apparent from the language of the provision as well as from the reason of the case. These corporations are authorized to take property, for the use of the society, 'or other pious uses,' which plainly shows that a benefactor may apply his bounty to the whole, or any one or more of the various purposes for which the corporation are authorized to hold property.'' (MS. Opinion.) The learned judge in this passage nowhere intimates, that the trustees of an entire corporation can take and hold property for the sole benefit of a portion of the members of that corporation, and exclude the other members from all participation in its use. His language, in my view, tends strongly to repel any such conclusion. He says they are authorized to take property for the use of the society: and that they may take it for any of the objects for which the corporation, that is, of course, the corporation as an entirety, was created. It would be difficult, I think, to maintain, that it would be compatible with the office and duties of trustees of a religious corporation, they they should take and hold and administer the revenues of property, from the benefits of which a portion of the corporators must be excluded. It would prove an entering wedge of division, the force of which even Christian charity and forbearance would scarcely be able to resist. But the unanswerable objection to such a trust is, that it is not authorized by the statute, and is inconsistent with its general scope and object, as well as with its terms.

It follows from this that when the title to the property in question passed, as it is conceded it did, to the trustees of the corporation, by the voluntary act of all the parties interested either as trustees or beneficiaries, the trust, if its character was such as we have supposed, was merged; or was at least transmuted into a trust, for the benefit of the entire corporation. No question arises here in regard to the effect of this change, as between the trustees and the original grantor or his heirs. The exclusive trust in favor of members of the church of a particular faith, if such a trust existed, being thus at an end, the title stands as though it had been conveyed to the trustees for the use and benefit of the corporation generally.

But it is said that the nature of the trust may be ascertained, not only from the language of the deeds by which the property is conveyed, but may be inferred from the tenets, faith and practice of the creators of the fund; and hence that it is to be inferred in this case, that a trust was intended in favor of those only who adhered to the principles and practices of the Associate Synod of North America. This doctrine, if it means any thing more than, that where the language of the deed is ambiguous it may be explained by proof of the surrounding circumstances, I deny. It is at variance with well established principles, and rests, as I conceive, upon no sound and reliable common law authority. In the first place, conditions and limitations are not to be raised by inference or argument. (See 4 Kent's Com. 132) The law favors the free and untrammeled alienation of property, simplicity in its title, and freedom in its use; especially in this country: and every presumption is against the existence of limitations, restrictions or qualifications ...

But, were it otherwise, and were we to infer in this case, either from the evidence on this subject, or from what appears upon the face of the deed, or any other source, that a trust was intended in favor of persons of a particular religious faith; then I hold it to be clear, that a religious corporation in this state can be the recipient of no such trust, for the reason, that its execution would be entirely inconsistent with the provisions of the act, authorizing such incorporations ...

But such a trust would be still more repugnant to the provisions of section 8. By that section the salary of the minister is put absolutely, and at all times, under the control of a majority of the congregation. The trustees have no control over the subject, but are imperatively required to ratify and pay the salary fixed by the majority. ... It would be in vain for any donor of property or funds to the congregation, to prescribe the religious faith of the minister to whose support the avails should be devoted; for, until the salary should be fixed by a majority of the congregation, not one dollar of the revenues of the society could be appropriated by the trustees to its payment.

The whole act shows, that it was the intention of the legislature to place the control of the temporal affairs of these societies in the hands of the majority of the corporators, independent of priest or bishop, presbytery, synod, or other ecclesiastical judicatory. This is the inevitable effect of the provision giving to the majority, without regard to their religious sentiments, the right to elect trustees, and to fix the salary of the minister. The courts clearly cannot disfranchise and corporator who possesses the qualifications prescribed by the statute.

Suppose then, the majority in a particular congregation choose to change entirely their form of worship; how are they to be controlled? Should the court assume in the exercise of its jurisdiction over trusts to direct the trustees to employ a minister of a particular faith, the whole object of the direction might be defeated, by the employment of a minister wholly unacceptable to those who procured the interference of the court; and even if the court went so far as to direct whom they should employ, still the majority would have the right to fix the salary, and the court would clearly have no power to control such majority in the exercise of this discretion, which the statute confides wholly to them. The act has in truth accomplished what the public sentiment in this country would seem to demand, that is, the entire separation of the functions of the ecclesiastical and temporal judicatories, and has limited the former to their proper sphere of control over the spiritual concerns of the people. If this statute is properly construed, we shall have fewer examples of temporal courts engaged in the inappropriate duty of deciding upon confessions of faith, and shades of religious belief and points of doctrine too subtle for any but ecclesiastical comprehension.

The courts have not hitherto fully considered the broad distinction that exists between a voluntary association which may adopt such rules and regulations and such mutual obligations not inconsistent with law, as it may see fit, and a corporation whose powers and functions are prescribed by statute. If a society wishes to devote its property to an unchangeable form of worship and to tie down its members to a Procrustean bed of creeds and confessions of faith, it must remain a voluntary association, and not commit the management of its affairs to a corporation.

I by no means deny that a grantor of property to the trustees of a religious corporation may annex such conditions to the grant as he may choose, not inconsistent with law; and that the trustees may take the property subject to the conditions. For instance, property may be conveyed to them to be held so long as the society continues in a certain ecclesiastical connection; or so long as it supports a minister of a certain faith; and this condition if explicit and clear and free from all doubt or obscurity would be good.[1] An uncertain condition would be void.

The title of the trustees under such a deed would be good so long as a majority of the corporators chose to abide by the condition; and when that was departed from, their title would be forfeited.[2] This is widely different from a trust, which is to be enforced in opposition to the will of the majority.

It follows from these principles, that neither presbytery or synod had any control over the Associate Congregation of Cambridge in respect to the minister whom they should employ. That depended upon the trustees and a majority of the congregation. His deposition or excommunication had nothing whatever to do with the right of the congregation to employ him, so far as the administration of its temporalities was concerned; although it might subject them or some portion of them to spiritual censure or ecclesiastical penalties ...

It may be well briefly to recapitulate here the principal points which I have attempted to maintain. They are -

1. That this court cannot review those portions of the decree of the supreme court not appealed from. 2. That a religious corporation under our statute, consists not of the trustees alone, but of the members of the society. That the society itself is incorporated, and not merely the trustees, and its members are the corporators. 3. That the relation of the trustees to the society is not that of a private trustee to the cestui que trust; but they are the managing officers of the corporation, and trustees in the same sense in which the president and directors of a bank or of a railroad company are trustees, and are invested in regard to the temporal affairs of the society, with the powers specifically conferred by the statute, and with the ordinary discretionary powers of similar corporate officers. 4. Than an incorporated religious society, under our law, does not belong to the class of ecclesiastical corporations in the sense of the English law; which were composed entirely of ecclesiastical persons; and subject to the ecclesiastical judicatories; but are to be regarded as civil corporations, governed by the ordinary rules of the common law. 5. That if it be granted that courts of equity, by virtue of their general jurisdiction over trusts, may exercise some degree of control over the trustees of a religious corporation in cases of gross abuse of their trust; yet, they have no power to remove those officers, who derive their offices directly from the enactments of the legislature; nor have they power to prescribe qualifications for electors of such trustees, other than those prescribed by the statute. 6. That the trustees of a religious corporation under our statute, cannot take a trust for the sole benefit of members of the church as distinguished from other members of the congregation, nor for the benefit of any portion of the corporators to the exclusion of others, no trust being authorized by the statute except for the use and benefit of the whole society. 7. That where in a deed executed to

---

1 See, however, the later decision of the Court of Appeals in Levy v. Levy, 33 N. Y. 97 (1865).

2 But see the later decision of the Court of Appeals in Gram v. Evangelical Society, 36 N. Y. 161 (1867)

trustees for religious purposes, the use is expressed in general and not in specific terms, it cannot be inferred from the religious tenets and faith of the grantor, that it was intended to limit the use to the support of the particular doctrines which he professed or the religious class to which he belonged: although if the language creating the trust be ambiguous, evidence of the surrounding circumstances, and among them perhaps of the faith of the donor, may be received, as in other cases, to aid in its construction. 8. That the trustees of a religious corporation in this state cannot receive a trust limited to the support of a particular faith, or a particular class of doctrines, for the reason that it is inconsistent with those provisions of the statute which give to the majority of the corporators, without regard to their religious tenets, the entire control over the revenues of the corporation.

The decree of the supreme court should be affirmed.

Westminster Church v. Presbytery of New York
New York Court of Appeals, 1914
211 N. Y. 214

WILLARD BARTLETT, Ch. J. This is an action in ejectment. The complaint alleges that the plaintiff is a religious corporation organized under the laws of this state; that on or about the 17th day of March, 1908, it owned in fee simple certain described premises in the city of New York on West Twenty-third street, near the corner of Seventh avenue, in the borough of Manhattan; and that the defendant on or about the 18th day of March, 1908, unlawfully entered into said premises and ousted the plaintiff therefrom without right or authority of law, and continues unlawfully to withhold possession of the same from the plaintiff. The answer denies the allegation of unlawful entry and sets up two separate defenses. The first defense is that the Westminster Presbyterian Church of West Twenty-third Street sometime prior to January 1, 1908, was in pecuniary and spiritual turmoil in consequence of which it was duly dissolved by the Presbytery of New York, which thereupon took possession and charge of the church building, and has conserved the same, in consequence of which the plaintiff is at present merely a naked church corporation with a board of trustees holding over until such time as under the lawful directions of the Presbytery of New York the ultimate disposition of the property may be provided for. The second defense is the pendency of an action in equity in the Supreme Court wherein the Trustees of the Presbytery of New York are the plaintiffs and the Westminster Presbyterian Church of West Twenty-third Street is the defendant, in which the Presbytery seeks to compel the trustees to convey to the Trustees of the Presbytery the property in controversy. There was a supplemental answer averring that subsequent to the original joinder of issue a period of two years had elapsed since the dissolution of the church by the Presbytery as set out in the original answer; and that thereafter the Presbytery acting in accordance with section 16 of the Religious Corporations Law had decided that the Westminster Presbyterian Church of West Twenty-third Street was extinct, which decision empowered the Presbytery to take possession of the temporalities and property belonging to such church and manage the same.

The case has been twice tried. Upon the first trial a verdict was directed in favor of the plaintiff upon the ground that its title to the property in question was undisputed, and that the Trustees of the Presbytery of New York had no legal right to take and administer the property under the circumstances alleged in the answer. The judgment entered upon that verdict was reversed by the Appellate Division, and upon the trial which now comes up for review, a verdict was directed in favor of the defendant. The judgment upon this last verdict has been affirmed by the Appellate Division, the presiding justice dissenting.

The real property which is the subject-matter of this action originally belonged to the Eighth Avenue Presbyterian Church, to which it was conveyed by two deeds dated February 28th, and recorded on March 16th, 1853.

In the same year the corporate name of the Eighth Avenue Presbyterian Church was changed to the West Twenty-third Street Presbyterian Church under and pursuant to the provisions of chapter 323 of the Laws of 1853.

By an order of the Supreme Court made on April 19, 1889, the West Twenty-third Street Presbyterian Church was consolidated with the Westminster Presbyterian Church under the corporate name of the Westminster Presbyterian Church of West Twenty-third Street (the plaintiff herein). In the petition of the Westminster Presbyterian Church for this consolidation it is stated that the petitioner "is connected with the Presbytery of New York and is subject to its advice and control."

The defendant took possession of the property in controversy on March 17, 1908. It was stipulated on the trial that the value of the property on that date was $300,000, subject to a mortgage of $60,000 and such liens as might appear on the trial.

As to the plea that another action is pending for the same cause, it appears that in the action thus mentioned the Trustees of the Presbytery are the plaintiffs while the Westminster Presbyterian Church of West Twenty-third Street is the defendant. To render such a plea available the other action must be one in which the present plaintiff is the plaintiff and the present defendant is the defendant. "If the party who interposes such defence is a plaintiff in such other action it is no defence although for the same cause." (Walsworth v. Johnson, 41 Cal. 61.) "The very foundation of such a defence is the maxim *nemo debet bis vexari*; and manifestly this can have no application when the first suit is brought, not by, but against, the person who is the plaintiff in the second action." (Id.)

Before the enactment of chapter 79 of the Laws of 1875 and chapter 110 of the Laws of 1876 "it had been settled that a religious corporation held its temporalities wholly free from the denomination of any ecclesiastical authority, and by a tenure so independent that it could change its creed and denominational character without losing its hold upon its property. Doubtless the acts of 1875 and 1876 were intended to restrain, in some degree, that sort of diversion of church property from one sect to another, for the provision is that the trustees shall hold and administer it according to the rules and usages of the denomination to which the church members of the corporation belong, and shall not divert it to the support of some other disconnected institution." (Matter of First Presbyterian Soc. of Buffalo, 106 N. Y. 251, 254.)

The amendments thus referred to by Judge Finch in the case cited have been continued in effect with slight changes in form through various statutes down to the existing Religious Corporations Law (Cons. Laws, ch. 51) and now appear in section 5 of that act.

I am of the opinion that the plaintiff corporation having been formed in 1889 by the consolidation of two preexisting church corporations is subject to the obligation first imposed by the act of 1875, and continued ever since, to administer its property in accordance with the discipline, rules and usages of the religious denomination with which the corporation is connected, namely the Presbyterian church.

The statute under which the West Twenty-third Street Presbyterian Church was consolidated with the Westminster Presbyterian Church in 1889 was chapter 167 of the Laws of 1880. That act provided that when the prescribed order of consolidation had been made and entered according to the practice of the Supreme Court, "the said corporations shall be united and consolidated into one corporation by the name designated in the order, and it shall have all the rights and powers, and be subject to all the obligations of religious corporations under the act to which this is supplementary, and the acts amendatory thereof and supplementary thereto." The act from which this language is quoted was an amendment of chapter 176 of the Laws of 1876, and referring thereto for the purpose of ascertaining what were the obligations to which the consolidated corporation became subject upon the entry of the order of consolidation, we find the following provisions: "The rector, wardens and vestrymen, or the trustees, consistory or session of any church, congregation or religious society, incorporated under any of the laws of this state, shall administer the temporalities thereof and hold and apply the estate and property belonging thereto, and the revenues of the same, for the benefit of such corporation according to the rules and usages of the church or denomination to which said corporation shall belong; and it shall not be lawful to divert such estate, property or revenue to any purpose, except the support and maintenance of any church or religious or benevolent institution or object connected with the church or denomination to which such corporation shall belong."

This provision, so far as it commands the administration of the property of a religious corporation in accordance with denominational rules and usages, is substantially the same as the existing provision contained in section 5 of the Religious Corporations Law.

From the foregoing statement it is apparent that the two corporations which were consolidated in 1889 voluntarily consented to become component parts of a consolidated corporation whose trustees should be obligated to administer its temporalities and apply its estate and property according to the rules and usages of the Presbyterian church; and, having taken this action voluntarily and without constraint, each of the preexisting corporations must be deemed to have relinquished and abandoned any right which it might previously have possessed under the law as it existed when such corporation was originally organized, to administer its property irrespective of denominational considerations. In other words, whatever the West Twenty-third Street Presbyterian Church, as the successor of the Eighth Avenue Presbyterian Church, might have done with its real estate if it had never merged its existence with the Westminster Presbyterian Church, as soon as such merger was effected it became liable to the law affecting religious corporations in force at the time of the merger, which law prescribed the administration of its temporalities, including the management of its real estate, in accordance with denominational usage. This conclusion takes out of the present case any question as to the power of the legislature to subject to denominational control the property acquired by a religious corporation prior to the time when the laws of New York first provided for such control; for, as we have seen, the corporation which originally owned the property in controversy consented of its own free will to a change in its corporate character which involved subjection to denominational control in the future.

The Trustees of the Presbytery of New York constitute an ecclesiastical governing body having control over the several Presbyterian churches in the county of New York, including the plaintiff. (Religious Corporations Law, § 15.) As such it has assumed to dissolve the Westminster Presbyterian Church of West Twenty-third Street. Its decree of dissolution, however, could extend no further than the ecclesiastical or spiritual side of the plaintiff's organization; for the Religious Corporations Law confers no power upon such a governing body, or anybody else, to dissolve a religious corporation, considered as a legal entity, in the county of New York. (Religious Corporations Law, § 18.) That county is expressly excepted from the operation of the section cited.

The law of the state of New York prescribing, as it has done ever since 1875, that the temporalities of a religious corporation shall be administered in accordance with denominational usage, contemplates the co-existence of a church in the spiritual sense and a church in the legal sense, working together toward the same beneficient ends. When, however, the superior governing body having authority over the ecclesiastical organization decrees its dissolution, there still remains the legal entity - that is to say, the trustees of the corporation are left in charge of its property, but without any spiritual body to maintain services or carry on religious work therein. The church as a legal corporate entity remains; the church in a spiritual sense is dissolved and gone. What becomes the duty of the trustees under such circumstances? They hold the property subject to denominational uses, notwithstanding the dissolution of the spiritual church. The Presbytery cannot oust them from office by dissolving the spiritual church. It may, however, by virtue of its control in ecclesiastical matters, insist that the trustees continue to administer the property for denominational purposes, and if they fail to do so, undoubtedly it would have a standing in a court of equity to enforce action on the part of the trustees to that end.

The Trustees of the Presbytery ousted the plaintiff from the church property in this case and took possession thereof in the first instance under the claim that the Presbytery had the right to do so by virtue of the decree of ecclesiastical dissolution. Subsequently, after two years had elapsed, the Presbytery sought to justify the ouster and its possession on the ground that it had decided the church to be extinct under section 16 of the Religious Corporations Law. In short, the Presbytery has compelled a non-user of the property by a corporation which was in active being, containing at least 94 voting members, one-half of whom voted against dissolution, and then by reason of such non-user for a period of two years asserts the right itself to appropriate and use the corporate real estate. A deed of land to a religious corporation is not worth much if it can thus readily be nullified.

In my opinion, the provisions of the Religious Corporations Law relating to the property of extinct churches has no application whatever to such a case as is presented by this record. The facts which constitute extinction within the meaning of the statute are plainly defined in section 16. According to that section a church has become extinct "if it has failed for two consecutive years next prior thereto, to maintain religious services according to the discipline, customs and usages of such governing body, or has had less than thirteen resident attending members paying annual pew rent, or making annual contribution toward its support." The failure to maintain religious services therein mentioned does not mean an enforced failure due to mandate of the Presbytery itself. It implies rather the inability to carry on the ordinary services by reason of diminished income and attendance and similar causes. Whatever it means, it clearly was not designed to authorize an enforced extinction such as has been attempted in the present case.

Upon the trial of the action the plaintiff proved all the facts necessary to make out a prima facie case in ejectment. It proved title, possession and ouster by the defendant. No defense was established sufficient to justify the direction of a verdict in favor of the defendant. The corporation had not been dissolved, for the Presbytery could not dissolve it; the decision that the church had become extinct was not warranted by the evidence, and hence, as the case stood when all the proof was in, the plaintiff was entitled to a verdict. The plaintiff having the legal title to the property was entitled to the possession thereof so far as appeared from any evidence properly in the record. If, as the defendant asserts, the trustees of the plaintiff corporation are not administering the property in accordance with denominational usage, the Presbytery has an adequate remedy in equity to compel them to do so; its assertion in that respect does not warrant the defendant in taking away the church edifice from the plaintiff with a strong hand pending the decision of that issue in a court of equitable jurisdiction.

In the opinion of the Appellate Division it is said: "We must accept without questioning the resolution of the Presbytery dissolving the church as a religious body. Thereafter the trustees and other rebellious members of the congregation could not administer the property of the congregation 'in accordance with the discipline, usages, laws and books of government' of the church, for they instantly ceased to be such trustees and members respectively, and it was their duty to accept letters of dismission and become communicants of some other congregation of the same denomination." I cannot agree with the proposition that the trustees of the corporation instantly ceased to be such by reason of the dissolution of the church by the Presbytery. They still remained in law trustees of the real estate and were obligated at all events to care for that property pending a determinating as to its future administration by other trustees, if others should thereafter be appointed or elected whose duty it would be to administer the property in accordance with denominational usage. The error which, as it seems to me, pervades the disposition made of this case in the courts below, is the idea that the Presbytery could take away from the Westminster Presbyterian Church of West Twenty-third Street all authority and control of its trustees over its real property, and by hostile action appropriate that property to such uses as it saw fit without any legal proceeding to that end, and wholly by the exercise of the ecclesiastical jurisdiction of the Presbytery. This view might be correct if the statute permitted the dissolution of the corporation as distinguished from the dissolution of the church by the mandate of the Presbytery; but, as has already been pointed out, under the law the Presbytery has no power to dissolve the corporation.

Subdivision 2 of section 69 of the Religious Corporations Law provides that if any trustee of an incorporated church to which the article applies, ceases to be a member of the church his office shall be vacant; and the contention in behalf of the defendant is, that inasmuch as all the members of the Westminster Presbyterian Church of West Twenty-third Street ceased to be such upon its dissolution by the Presbytery, the trustees were also all removed from office by the Presbytery's decree of dissolution. This, I think would be a forced application of the statutory provision cited, which plainly was not designed to enable the supervising governing body having ecclesiastical authority over a church, to turn out all its legally chosen trustees for the purpose of gaining control of its real property. The provision is merely intended to apply to vacancies occurring from time to time by reason of changes in membership, as when a member of one congregation leaves the church to unite with another.

In 1899, prior to the commencement of the present action in ejectment, the Trustees of the Presbytery of New York began a suit in equity against the Westminster Presbyterian Church of West Twenty-third Street and its trustees, for an injunction to restrain them from transferring or disposing of any of the real of personal property of the church and to compel them to convey the same to the Presbytery. The defendants successfully demurred to the complaint in that suit, but the judgment in their favor upon the demurrer was reversed by the Appellate Division with leave to the defendants to withdraw their demurrers and answer. They did not avail themselves of this leave, however, but made default in pleading, whereupon a final judgment was entered against them on April 22, 1911, declaring that the Presbytery of New York had duly dissolved the Westminster Presbyterian Church of West Twenty-third Street by appropriate ecclesiastical proceeding and enjoining the defendants from transferring or disposing of any of the real or personal property of the church unless they should convey it to the Trustees of the Presbytery or to a successor church duly constituted by that body. Leave was granted in this final judgment to apply at the foot thereof for the appointment of a suitable person as trustee to convey the property; and by a subsequent order, granted on June 7, 1911, there was added at the foot of the judgment, upon notice to the defendants and against the opposition of their attorney, a clause appointing the New York Trust Company to make, execute and deliver to the Trustees of the Presbytery of New York a conveyance of the church property. It is said in the brief for the respondent that this judgment, whether appealed from or not, will doubtless stand as a final adjudication on the equitable rights of the parties in the premises. The record does not contain the pleadings in that equity suit or disclose what were the precise issues involved therein, but enough appears from the language of the judgment itself to show that the court which rendered it must have assumed the existence of the power on the part of the New York Presbytery to dissolve the church corporation - a power which, as has already been shown, it does not possess. The judgment in the equity suit was not rendered until long after the first trial of the present action. If the defendant had intended to rely upon it as a bar it should have been set up as such in a second supplemental answer. It does not appear to have been offered as a bar or as an estoppel, and it could not properly have been received as such without having been pleaded as a defense. (Krekeler v. Titter, 62 N. Y. 372.) The conclusiveness of the judgment as evidence is limited to the facts thereby adjudicated. It is not perceived that it establishes any fact which operates to divest the Westminster Presbyterian Church of West Twenty-third Street of its title to the property in controversy. As a declaration of legal conclusions the judgment has no evidentiary effect. Under the circumstances it is not available to the defendants as an obstacle to the maintenance of the present action.

The judgment should be reversed and a new trial granted, with costs to abide the event.

WERNER, HISCOCK, COLLIN, CUDDEBACK, HOGAN and CARDOZO, JJ., concur.

Judgment reversed, etc.

Saint Nicholas Cathedral v. Kedroff.

New York Court of Appeals, 1950
302 N. Y. 1

CONWAY, Judge.

In 1903, a church was built at 15 East 97th Street in New York City, title to which was held by a corporation, created in 1899 under the Religious Corporations Law of this State and named "Russian Orthodox St. Nicholas Church in New York." The church was constructed with funds supplied partly from abroad and partly from local contributions and it was dedicated to the use of the members of the local congregation of the Russian Orthodox Church in New York City established in 1893. Two years later in 1905, the See of the Russian Orthodox Diocese of North America and the Aleutian Islands was transferred from San Francisco to New York and St. Nicholas Church became a cathedral occupied by the ruling bishop of the North American Diocese and dedicated to the use of all the members of the diocese as a central place of worship of the Russian Orthodox Church in North America. This cathedral is the subject of the present controversy. Simply stated, it is our duty in this action to identify the true and proper beneficiaries at the present time of such dedication of the cathedral so that there may be proper administration of this religious trust. In approaching that task, it is vital to our inquiry that we understand the history and organization of the Russian Orthodox Church, and the origins of its difficulties in modern times as disclosed in the record here and the record in Kedrovsky v. Rojdesvensky, 242 N. Y. 547, which was submitted to us upon the argument.

The Russian Orthodox Church is one of that loosely knit group which generically is referred to as the Eastern Confession or the Eastern Orthodox Church—an allusion to the rupture of the eastern and western portions of the Catholic church in 1054. The Russian church originally was subject to the Patriarch of Constantinople but acquired greater autonomy when Constantinople fell to the Turks and the Metropolitan of Moscow was no longer appointed by the Patriarch of Constantinople but was elected by the Russian bishops. Finally, express recognition of the "autocephaly," i.e., the complete independence, of the Russian church came in the 16th century when the Metropolitan of Moscow was raised to the dignity of Patriarch. The Patriarch ruled the church until 1700 when Peter the Great forbade the election of a new Patriarch and established the Most Sacred Governing Synod, consisting of a Procurator appointed by the Czar, and several metropolitans and bishops, to govern the church in place of the Patriarch. This form of church government continued for over two hundred years until 1917.

During that period, the Russian Orthodox Church conducted missionary activities in many parts of the world. A mission was established in 1793 in the then Russian territory of Alaska, and spread down the Pacific coast. In 1870, the mission had grown to the extent that the Diocese of Alaska and the Aleutian Islands was created with its See at San Francisco. Since it extended from Alaska through Canada to San Francisco, we shall refer to it herein as the North American Diocese or as the diocese.

A New York City congregation of the Russian Orthodox Church was established in 1893, incorporated in 1899, as already noted, and completed St. Nicholas Church in 1903. In 1905, when the See of the diocese was moved from San Francisco to New York the church became a cathedral occupied, in accordance with the rules of the church, by the ruling bishop of the diocese. Throughout that period, the paramount jurisdiction of the Most Sacred Governing Synod in Russia over the North American Diocese was recognized and unquestioned.

Such was the condition of the Russian Orthodox Church and its North American Diocese until 1917—the year of the Kerensky revolution in Russia.

Following the overthrow of the czarist regime, a great "Sobor" or convention of the Russian Orthodox Church was called. This sobor of 1917-18, it is conceded here by all parties, had indisputable canonicity and validity. The sobor re-established the Patriarchate and elected thereto Patriarch Tikhon, the "arch-prelate" and "head of Church Administration," the first such since Peter the Great. The Patriarch, as the head of the Sacred Synod and of the Supreme Church Council, constituted the Supreme Church Authority and ruled the Russian Orthodox Church. Other enactments of the sobor provided a procedure for the local election of diocesan bishops and the confirmation of such election by the Supreme Church Authority. It also provided that the Patriarch might call a sobor every three years and that he should preside over it. No sobor was ever called by Patriarch Tikhon (and he was the only one with power to do so) prior to his death in 1925.

Up to 1917, the ruling archbishop of the diocese had been appointed by the central church authorities. Tikhon himself, later to be Patriarch, was the diocesan archbishop from 1905 to 1907. Archbishop Platon succeeded him and ruled until 1914 when he returned to Russia and Archbishop Evdokim came in his stead. Archbishop Evdokim remained until 1917 when he too returned to Russia. All three duly appointed archbishops, in conformity with the rules of the Russian church, used and occupied St. Nicholas Cathedral as their administrative headquarters and as a place of worship. Those three archbishops were in proper and direct canonical succession and as to that there is no controversy.

Archbishop Evdokim's departure in 1917 marked the beginning of the difficulties which have ever since beset the diocese. No discussion of the Russian Orthodox Church since 1917 is possible without constant reference to the political conditions upon which its character and its existence depended. In March of 1917, the Provisional Government of Kerensky replaced the czarist regime. The Kerensky Government itself was soon overthrown by the so-called Bolsheviki led by Lenin in the famous "October Revolution." Prior to his downfall, Kerensky, as noted, had authorized the convocation of the great sobor of the Russian Orthodox Church, which was in session through the latter part of 1917 and up to February of 1918 and which named Tikhon as Patriarch. Upon their accession to power, the Bolsheviki, in accordance with the then acknowledged and asserted principles of communism, attempted by every means at their command to destroy religion in Russia. In the years following 1917, church property was confiscated, clergymen were killed, exiled or imprisoned, and Patriarch Tikhon himself, old and in poor health but a useful symbol, too valuable to be destroyed, was confined under house arrest and later imprisoned.

This frontal attack upon the church continued for five years. In November of 1920, however, at the height of the persecution, Patriarch Tikhon issued his now famous ukase No. 362 of 1920. This document contained "instructions to the Diocesan Bishops for the case that a given Diocese be severed from the highest Church Administration, <u>or in case the latter's activity stop.</u>" (Emphasis supplied.) It was provided in part that "if the highest Church Administration * * * would for any reason discontinue their church-administrative activity," the diocesan bishop, either with the bishops of neighboring dioceses or, it that were not possible alone, should "assume the full hierarchical power" and "do everything possible to regulate the local church life, and if necessary * * * organize the diocesan administration suitable to conditions created." Other paragraphs provided for the continuation of such local administration of the church if the discontinuance of activity of the highest church administration "should acquire a protracted or even permanent character." Finally, it was provided that "all measures that were taken locally in accordance with the present instructions * * * must be submitted for confirmation later to the Central Church Authority when it is reestablished."

The apparent forebodings of Patriarch Tikhon, which prompted this ukase, proved accurate, for in the spring of 1922 he was arrested and imprisoned. The Russian Government, then for its own purposes, as later became evident, permitted a group of priests to visit Tikhon and they procured from him a letter authorizing the transfer of certain business papers of the church tó a named archbishop (Agathangel) who was to be his representative. Instead of doing that, the recipients of the letter—members of a radical group styling themselves the "Living" or "Renovated" church—declared themselves to be the Supreme Authority of the Russian Orthodox Church and purported to authorize and summon the pseudo-sober of 1923. Patriarch Tikhon later referred to them as "ambitious and wilful men" who took advantage of the situation "to usurp the highest clerical power of the Orthodox Russian Church which did not belong to them," and he denounced their statements as "nothing but lies and deception." It is now conceded here that this was a schism which is now extinct. Nevertheless, while Tikhon was still in prison, this schismatic group purported to call another sobor of the church although power so to do resided only in the Patriarch Tikhon, as we have seen. There is evidence that they were aided and abetted in their plan by the Russian Government which permitted them to proceed while killing, arresting or exiling those members of the church who objected. This new pseudo-sobor met in 1923. Tikhon was roundly and vehemently condemned by all the speakers. The patriarchate was dissolved and Tikhon, reviled and denounced as an apostate and traitor, was unfrocked. The church created by the pseudo-sobor of 1923 was called the "Living Church" or the "Renovated Church." It was schismatic and had no canonical validity. That fact, it should again be noted, is conceded by all the interested parties here.

The turmoil and the turbulence with which the Russian Orthodox Church was beset in Russia was not without its echoes in this country. Bishop Alexander of Canada became acting head of the diocese by designation of Archbishop Evdokim (see 302 N. Y. 6). Several conventions were held in this country at which the status and fate of the North American Diocese were discussed and measures were proposed to preserve it from disintegration or the usurpation of pretenders. Archbishop Platon, who had ruled the diocese from 1907 to 1914, in proper canonical succession, returned to this country in 1921. He succeeded in restoring peace and order in the diocese, and prominent churchmen of the diocese urgently petitioned Patriarch Tikhon to reappoint him formally as archbishop of the diocese. This was just before Tikhon was actually imprisoned. While he was technically at liberty, his visitors in Moscow were being watched and interrogated carefully, and his correspondence, especially with Americans, was systematically searched. The American entreaties regarding Archbishop Platon were relayed to the Patriarch by a representative of the Y.M.C.A. who was in Moscow. The Patriarch, in the presence of another witness, Bishop Pashhovsky, assured him that Platon would be appointed the ruling bishop of the diocese and that he would issue papers to that effect. The Patriarch asked that Platon be notified immediately, but it was agreed that it would not be possible at that moment to put the appointment in writing because of the constant surveillance of the civil authorities and the fear that any such communication, if seized, would endanger the safety or the life of the Patriarch. The Patriarch's intention and will were transmitted to Archbishop Platon by the Y.M.C.A. representative and Bishop

Pashhovsky. Alexander, the acting archbishop, recognized in writing Platon's appointment as ruling bishop of the diocese, as did the bishops of the church outside Russia. Tikhon was imprisoned by the Soviet Government immediately after making this oral appointment. A diocesan convention was held at Pittsburgh in October, 1922, and after investigating the situation Platon was acknowledged as the ruling bishop. Platon accordingly took possession of St. Nicholas Cathedral and exercised administrative supervision over the diocese.

Patriarch Tikhon was released from prison in the latter part of 1923, after the pseudo-sobor of that year had completed its work. Under date of September 20, 1923, from a monastery, he signed an order directed to Platon advising him that, with the concurrence of the Sacred Synod, "having taken cognizance of the situation of the American Church we deemed it necessary to appoint you to rule the North American Church."

Meanwhile, one John Kedrovsky, a priest of the Russian Orthodox Church in this country, had, in 1918, commenced an action in this State on behalf of himself and other priests against the association or corporation known as the Archbishop and Consistory, which was a managing and advisory group handling the affairs of the diocese. In that complaint Kedrovsky asserted that he was one of the clergy of the Russian Orthodox Greek Catholic Church of North America; that it was a religious denomination of about 300 churches with about 300,000 members organized in various unincorporated parishes or bodies throughout North America; that his lawful archbishop was Archbishop Evdokim (Meschersky) who had departed from the United States for Russia about August 6, 1917, and had since remained there; that Alexander (Nemolovsky) was then a bishop of the church in Canada and had been assuming to act as the acting archbishop of the church pursuant to a cablegram from the lawful Archbishop Evdokim but that in truth no such appointment had been made by Archbishop Evdokim and that Alexander was therefore a usurper.

After the institution of that action, but before trial, the aforementioned pseudo-sobor of 1923 was held in Moscow. It created the "Living Church" or "Renovated Church," which, as noted, is now conceded to have been schismatic and uncanonical. Kedrovsky, the same priest who in his 1918 action had asserted that he was subject to Archbishop Evdokim as the true archbishop of the North American Diocese, procured from this "Renovated Church" certain credentials in the latter part of 1923. One document purported to consecrate him as North American archbishop and to excommunicate and condemn Archbishop Platon. The other documents contained Kedrovsky's formal appointment as archbishop of the North American Diocese and a full power of attorney to act for the church.

In March, 1924, he commenced another action, this time asserting that he was the lawful archbishop of the North American Diocese, in order to gain control of St. Nicholas Cathedral, the subject premises in the case at bar, which he then conceded had been possessed by Bishop Alexander in 1919 "as the de facto or acting archbishop." As noted Archbishop Platon was occupying the cathedral in 1924 by virtue of his oral appointment by Patriarch Tikhon and the written confirmation thereof in September, 1923.

In March of 1924, immediately prior to the institution of the cathedral action by Kedrovsky, a document dated, February, 1924, appeared in the newspapers here purporting to have been issued by the Patriarch Tikhon accusing Platon of engaging "in public acts of Counter-Revolution directed against the Soviet power and of disastrous consequences to the Orthodox Church." It provided for the dismissal of Platon "from the day on which this Present Decision is announced to him," by a new ruling bishop who was to be chosen. The publication of this decree, dated less than five months after the patriarchal order confirming Platon and the legal action instituted by Kedrovsky, caused bewilderment among the members of the diocese. A North American sobor was called and held at Detroit in April of 1924 to consider the situation, excerpts from the minutes of which appear in the record.

It was pointed out that the North American Diocese, for a good many years, had been "cut off from the highest organ of the administration of the Russian Church" and that that situation made operative the above-quoted ukase of 1920 providing for local administration and election of bishops. The sobor then adopted resolutions asking Platon to head the administration of the church. Another resolution emphatically stated it to be the will of the sobor "not to break at all the spiritual ties and communion with the Russian Church, but always to pray for her good." The "final regulation" of the status of the North American church was to be left to "a future Sobor of the Russian Orthodox Church which will be legally convoked, legally elected, will sit with the participation of representatives of the American Church under conditions of political freedom, guaranteeing the fullness and authority of its decisions for the entire Church, and will be recognized by the entire Oecumenical Orthodox Church as a true Sobor of the Russian Orthodox Church."

The second or 1924 action brought by John S. Kedrovsky reached us two years before the 1918 action brought by him. In that 1924 action there was evidence as to most of the facts already detailed. However it was not there conceded as it is now that the "Renovated Church" had been schismatic in origin and had been later absorbed by or merged with the pariarchal church nor that the 1923 sobor was not considered as having complied with canonical requirements because it was not convened pursuant to a call by the Patriarch and the Holy Synod. Moreover, in that action there was not before the court ukase No. 362 of 1920 of Patriarch Tikhon. The Appellate Division Kedrovsky v. Rojdesvensky, 214 App. Div. 483, stated that "The validity of Kedrovsky's appointment really depends upon the validity of the second Sobor that of 1923 as it is called." 214 App.Div. at page 487. It then found (contrary to what is now conceded to be the fact) that the sobor was properly called and that the "Renovated Church," created by it, had the power to appoint Kedrovsky as the ruling bishop of the North American Diocese. When the appeal from that decision reached us we treated it as one involving only questions of fact as to whether (1) there was a governing body of the church and whether (2) that governing body had recognized Kedrovsky as archbishop of the church. We determined that there was evidence to sustain the findings of the Appellate Division on both of those points. We thereupon affirmed the judgment, one Associate Judge being recorded as absent.

Kedrovsky v. Rojdesvensky, 1926, 242 N.Y. 547. The control of all phases of Russian life by the Government was not as apparent in 1924 as it is a quarter of a century later and on the surface, at least, the case appeared to be a proper one for the application of the rule that in an ecclesiastical dispute involving a denominational church, the decision of the highest church judicatories will be accepted as final and conclusive by the civil courts, Trustees of Presbytery of N. Y. v. Westminster Presbyterian Church of West Twenty-Third St. 222 N. Y. 305, 315; Watson v. Jones, 13 Wall. 679, 724-727, Religious Corporations Law, §§ 4, 5.

Two years later there was presented the original or 1918 action commenced by Kedrovsky, as a priest of the patriarchal church, on behalf of himself and all others similar situated. It had been brought against the "Archbishop and Consistory of the Russian Orthodox Greek Catholic Church, alleged corporation", and others. Archbishop Platon (Rojdesvensky) was again an appellant. In that action a receiver pendente lite had been appointed and the judgment at Special Term directed that the defendant Platon and other defendants deliver over to such receiver, who in turn was directed to deliver to plaintiff John S. Kedrovsky, all the properties and deeds thereto held by Bishop Alexander and conveyed by him to the general board of trustees by the exhibit dated June 7, 1921, which listed and enumerated all of the 135 church properties in the 19 States and the Territory of Alaska heretofore referred to. That judgment was unanimously affirmed by the Appellate Division, Kedrovsky v. Archbishop & Consistory of Russian Orthodox Greek Catholic Church, 220 App. Div. 750. We, however, granted leave to appeal. The decision of the Appellate Division there was correct and unassailable if by our affirmance in Kedrovsky v. Rojdesvensky, 242 N.Y. 547, supra, we had adopted the view that the properties of the North American Diocese were required to be administered by an appointee of the central authorities of the patriarchal church as it then existed in Russia, whatever the status and characteristics of the church there might be, and that Kedrovsky had been validly appointed by such authorities. We, however, declined so to consider our earlier affirmance in the cathedral case two years before. Realizing that the legitimate claims of the North American Diocese, whose temporary autonomy had but recently been declared, were entitled to consideration under the circumstances disclosed, we unanimously reversed the judgments below. Kedrovsky v. Archbishop & Consistory of Russian Orthodox Catholic Church, 1928, 249 N.Y. 75.

We pointed out that the title to the properties "was either in Archbishop Nemolovsky (Alexander) for the benefit of the faithful of the church within his diocese, or in the defendants (Platon and the general board of trustees) to whom he attempted to transfer his trusts * * * or in the faithful of the church themselves." 249 N. Y. at page 77, 162 N.E. at page 589. We further noted that in none of those views was title in the members of the Consistory, then headed by Kedrovsky. Then, taking cognizance of the doubt as to Kedrovsky's status as archbishop by appointment of the "Renovated Church," and of the declaration of administrative autonomy by the American church at Detroit in 1924, we said 249 N.Y. at pages 77-78, 162 N.E. at page 589: "In view of the dissensions that have arisen, the Supreme Court may well conclude that the title should be vested in some other trustee who may be relied upon to carry out more effectively and faithfully the purposes of this religious trust. Carrier v. Carrier, 226 N.Y. 114. Whether such trustee should be the plaintiff, who is the present Archbishop or the incorporated Archbishop and Consistory, or some one else, we do not now determine. This question is one to be passed upon by the Supreme Court in its discretionary supervision of the conduct of trustees. That discretion has not been exercised by any judgment yet pronounced. * * *''

That 1928 decision by this court thus recognized that the difficulties of the Russian Orthodox Church in this country differed substantially from the situations presented in the Westminster and Watson cases (supra), and that those cases were not helpful in the solution of the problem. The problem, indeed, was one which strained the limits of judicial power, and we deemed it proper to return the case to the Supreme Court leaving it to that court, after full consideration of the facts, in the exercise of its discretionary power, to achieve a result whereby the faithful of the Russian Orthodox Church in this country might enjoy their accustomed religious temporalities under the supervision of trustees who might "be relied upon to carry out more effectively and faithfully the purposes of this religious trust."

While this litigation was in progress, the Soviet sponsored "Renovated Church" was the only one permitted to function in Russia, the central office of the patriarchal church being suppressed by the Government. Despite this State assistance, the "Renovated Church" had no popular following and few adherents outside its own clergy. In a few years it joined with and was absorbed by the patriarchal church. For two years, after Tikhon's death in 1925, there was no Patriarch of the Russian Orthodox Church. Then in 1927, one Sergius, the Metropolitan of Moscow, made peace with the Soviet Government and concluded an agreement with it under which the central office of that church was permitted to reopen, after acknowledging its "loyalty" to the Government and promising to secure similar written pledges of loyalty from the clergy of the church abroad. No election to fill the office of Patriarch was permitted. Instead, Sergius was appointed the acting locum tenens of the patriarchal throne. Unsuccessful discussions subsequently ensued with a view toward reuniting the North American metropolitan district with the patriarchal church.

Under the leadership of Metropolitan Platon following the creation of the administratively autonomous metropolitan district by the Detroit sobor of 1924, to which reference will be made hereafter, the church grew and prospered. With the exception of schismatics such as Kedrovsky, who was recognized by no one but who occupied St. Nicholas Cathedral by virtue of the decision and injunction of 1924, the North American church followed Metropolitan Platon. In 1933, the Acting Locum Tenens, Sergius, dispatched one Benjamin (Fedchenkoff) to the United States in order to take over the administration of the metropolitan district from Platon, whose proclamation of autonomy was declared to be "null and void." Sergius also purported to excommunicate Platon and all the clergy and laymen who followed him, until they submitted themselves to the jurisdiction of the patriarchal Exarch Benjamin (in America) or directly to the

Acting Locum Tenens (in Moscow). Finally in 1934, Sergius appointed his ambassador, Benjamin, as "permanent Ruling Bishop of the Russian North American Diocese." The text of the order contains a recital that Benjamin had "organized in New York a Diocesan Council and that our North American Diocese has begun official existence." (Emphasis supplied.) This would appear to be a significant admission that the former North American Diocese, which had by that time become a metropolitan district, had achieved practical administrative autonomy and that it was necessary for the Russian church to organize a new diocese. By 1945, the number of parishes which recognized the new diocese set up by Benjamin in 1934, and which we must assume, in view of the provisions of the Religious Corporations Law since 1875, were organized for the purpose of adhering to such new diocese set up by Benjamin was only 13, while those adhering to the autonomous metropolitan district were said to total 358.

Platon died in 1934 and another sobor of the American church convened at Cleveland. Bishop Theophilus (Pashkovsky) was elected as ruling bishop and has served as such since. The temporary autonomy of the North American metropolitan district created in 1924 was reaffirmed, and rules for the administration of parishes were adopted. Another sobor at New York in 1937 again confirmed the temporary autonomy of the North American metropolitan district. The central church authorities in Moscow immediately issued a decree suspending and excommunicating Bishop Theophilus.

In 1934, John S. Kedrovsky, the schismatic, also died, but his son, Nicholas, continued to occupy the St. Nicholas Cathedral, even though by that time the "Renovated Church" had ceased to exist. Nicholas remained there until 1944, when he too died, and possession of the cathedral passed informally to his brother, John, who claimed to be a priest by virtue of an ordination of the "Renovated Church."

In 1940, the status of the metropolitinate again came before this court in Waipa v. Kushwara, 259 App.Div. 843, motion for leave to appeal denied 283 N.Y. 780. That was a suit to oust a priest from a Russian Orthodox Church in Yonkers, N. Y. He had been suspended by Archbishop Theophilus of the metropolitan district and in the civil action brought against him, he defended on the ground, among others, that Benjamin, the appointee of the Moscow Patriarchate and not Archbishop Theophilus, the elected metropolitan, had the power and authority to administer the affairs of the church here. The lower courts rejected that contention, finding authority for the creation of the administrative autonomous metropolitan district in the ukase of 1920 of Patriarch Tikhon which was to continue "until such time as the existing civil authorities * * * would cease interfering with the church." (N.Y.L.J., Jan. 6, 1940, p. 97, col. 5.) We denied leave to appeal.

Following the invasion of Russia by German in 1941, the Soviet Government, fighting for survival, apparently found it expedient to permit a somewhat broadened area of activity to the Russian Orthodox Church in that country. Then, following the death of Sergius in 1944, it consented to the convening of a sobor at Moscow in January of 1945. The news which was permitted to seep out of Russia after 1941 encouraged the hope in the members of the metropolitan district that unity might again be found.

Suddenly, without advance notice, an invitation was received for the North American church to be represented at the new sobor in Moscow. Four delegates were hurriedly chosen—three clergymen and one layman, the attorney for the church—who made preparations to travel to Alaska, from which place the Russian Government was to provide transportation to Moscow. After two of the clergymen had started, the Soviet Government cancelled the visa of the attorney on the pretext that entry was permitted only to clerical persons—a restriction which was not observed with reference to the delegation from Yugoslavia. The two clergymen who had already left were met by a Russian airplane which was to carry them to Moscow. Instead, they were landed in Siberia and transferred to a train to continue their journey. As a result, they arrived in Moscow ten days after the sobor had adjourned.

They found that one Alexy had been named Patriarch of the Russian Orthodox Church, and they presented to him a report of the church in North America and a request for the lifting of the spiritual separation on terms of autonomy. In return, they were handed a prepared document, the so-called ukase of February, 1945, for delivery to Metropolitan Theophilus. The terms of this ukase were not acceptable to the North American church. Instead of the necessary autonomy, the ukase provided for the calling of a sobor in America to be presided over by an archbishop sent from Russia. The sobor was to be required to declare in the name of the church "its abstention from political activities against the U. S. S. R. and give corresponding orders to all parishes." There was no comment or provision concerning the status of Metropolitan Theophilus, the elected head of the North American church. Instead, the sobor was to be required to elect a new person to be head of a new metropolitan district. Two representatives of the then Moscow Patriarchate were reccommended as candidates for the position, and the right was reserved to refuse confirmation of the person chosen "if he be considered unsuitable by the Patriarchy, for any motivated reason whatsoever." There was an intimation that "some extended powers" might be given to the person so chosen and confirmed, "but the right to confirm candidates for bishop, the right to reward the clergy with higher titles, and the right of appeal as regards bishops, clergy and others, remain with the Moscow Patriarchy."

A council of the bishops of the North American metropolitan district met in May, 1945, and decided that the terms proposed in the ukase of February, 1945, were not acceptable.

The attempts at reconciliation having met with failure, the metropolitan district decided to commence this action to recover possession of St. Nicholas Cathedral, which by custom and rule had always been the See of the Russian Orthodox Church in North America and the residence and place of worship of the ruling bishop of the church in North America. Technically, the plaintiff in this action is the corporation, "Saint Nicholas Cathedral of the Russian Orthodox Church of North America." When the land for the proposed cathedral was acquired in 1899, title was taken in the name of a religious corporation organized pursuant to the Religious Corporations Law of 1895, L.1895, ch. 723, § 50, which provided that the incorporators of such Orthodox churches should be, by virtue of office, the Russian Ambassador and the Counsul General. This corporation, so formed, retained title until 1925, with the exception of one year (1916-17) when title was temporarily placed in the name of the then ruling Archbishop Evdokim to whom John S. Kedrovsky, when he brought his 1918 action, was subject as a priest and whom he, in his complaint, recognized as the true head of the North American Diocese.

In 1925, a special act of the New York State Legislature, L.1925, ch. 463, created the plaintiff corporation, composed of Metropolitan Platon and others of the metropolitan district, to which the old or 1899 corporation transferred the cathedral property. The deed was signed by the Russian Consul General, but not by the other statutory incorporator, the Russian Ambassador, as we did not then recognize the Russian Government in that country. That necessary defect was cured, and all such deeds validated by a subsequent act of our Legislature. L.1942, ch. 206. Moreover, the corporate existence of the plaintiff corporation was specifically confirmed by still another act of our Legislature, L.1945, ch. 817, "notwithstanding any nonuser by said corporation of its corporate rights, privileges and franchises or the lapse of any period of time during which said corporation was inactive." The plaintiff corporation, accordingly, is the present owner of the record title to St. Nicholas Cathedral. This is not, however, the ordinary ejectment action, in which proof of such title and of an ouster would constitute ground for relief. Since 1875, ch. 79, our Legislature has provided for the denominational control and administration of church properties and temporalities. See Religious Corporation Law, Consol.Laws, c. 51, § 5. The corporate owner of the title thus holds the property in trust for the religious body for whose use it was dedicated. Plaintiff does not dispute this trust theory, but on the contrary relies upon it. Plaintiff has endeavored to prove that the beneficial use of the property today rightfully belongs to the Russian church in America, Religious Corporations Law, § 105, which was forced to declare its administrative autonomy at the Detroit sobor of 1924 in order to preserve and adhere to those principles and practices fundamental to the Russian Orthodox faith, free from the influence of an atheistic and antireligious foreign civil government.

The action, as stated, was commenced against John Kedroff, the second son of John S. Kedrovsky, in April, 1945. Apparently fearful of his anomalous status, as a cleric of a concededly extinct church (the "Renovated Church"), Kedroff made overtures to Benjamin, the representative of the Moscow Patriarchate, and in October, 1945 was reordained by Benjamin and thereupon surrendered the cathedral premises to Benjamin, as head of a new diocese of a different church. We must remember that Benjamin never possessed or occupied the cathedral until after the commencement of this action on April 9, 1945, against the defendant Kedroff. Benjamin was not originally a party herein because he was not an occupant of the cathedral but was later permitted to intervene. Kedroff, the second son of Kedrovsky, was but a priest of the schismatic "Renovated Church" and thus could not have defended this action as an occupant of the cathedral. He therefore went to Benjamin, recognized him as the "Chief Church Authority," and said "Ordain me all over again" and had himself reordained as a priest by Benjamin in what must have been the latter's new diocese. When Benjamin did so reordain Kedroff as a priest, the latter "gave" the cathedral to Benjamin according to Benjamin's counsel here. Thereafter, in order to obtain an adjournment in this action, Benjamin stipulated to and did give up possession of the cathedral on June 6, 1947. At the time of the trial, when he was called by the plaintiff only, Benjamin was living at 38 Halsey Street in Brooklyn. Benjamin was therefore an occupant of the cathedral only from October, 1945, a time subsequent to the commencement of this action, until June 6, 1947.

Kedroff had interposed a general denial to plaintiff's complaint. After Benjamin, following such surrender by John Kedroff, took over the cathedral, he was permitted to intervene and interposed the present amended answer setting up four affirmative defenses. Only the first need concern us here. The second, third and fourth defenses, i.e., nonuser and lack of authority in plaintiff, the Statute of Limitations and laches, respectively, were either ignored, abandoned or found in plaintiff's favor below. There was little or no discussion concerning them and they have been effectively eliminated from the case. The first affirmative defense sets up Benjamin's appointment and his asserted right to occupy the cathedral by virtue of such appointment to that office.

Before this action was commenced a new article of the Religious Corporations Law, 5-C, was passed by both houses of the New York Legislature. It was subsequently signed by the Governor. This legislation had a conclusive effect upon the issues presented in the case at bar and will be discussed at length below. Quite apart from this legislative action with respect to the specific dispute here involved, we think that, as a matter of common law as intimated by our 1928 decision in Kedrovsky v. Archbishop & Consistory of Russian Orthodox Catholic Church, 249 N.Y. 75, 162 N.E. 588, supra, there was ample basis and room for an exercise of the discretionary power of the Supreme Court over the conduct of trustees, in favor of the North American metropolitan district. We think that in the light of historical facts and the evidence in the records before us, the conclusion would have been fully warranted that the leaders of the North American metropolitan district are the trustees "who may be relied upon to carry out more effectively and faithfully the purposes of this religious trust," 249 N.E. at pages 77-78, 162 N.E. at page 589, i.e., who may administer the temporalities of St. Nicholas Cathedral for the benefit of the faithful for whose use it was originally dedicated.

The courts below, in granting judgment herein to defendants, did not determine, in the exercise of their discretion, whether defendants could be relied upon to carry out faithfully and effectively the purposes of the religious trust. The Westminster and Watson cases, supra, were cited and the conclusion drawn that St. Nicholas Cathedral must be occupied by an archbishop appointed by the central authorities in Moscow and that Benjamin, who was so appointed, was therefore entitled to the possession of the cathedral. This, we think, was error. The determinative issue in the case, apart from the action of the Legislature with respect to the problem, was whether there exists in Moscow at the present time a true central organization of the Russian Orthodox Church capable of functioning as the head of a free international religious body. If the Moscow patriarchal throne has been resurrected by the Soviet Government solely as a means of influencing opinion at home and abroad, and if it may now operate on an international scale, not as a true religious body, but only as an extension or implementation of Russian foreign policy, then it is clear that the North American metropolitan district and not the appointee or ambassador of the central authorities in Moscow, is the proper trustee to manage for the benefit of the faithful in this hemisphere those religious temporalities dedicated to the use of the Russian Orthodox Mission and Diocese prior to 1924 when it became an administratively autonomous metropolitan district. Religious Corporations Law, # 105.

We know that a nominal church organization exists in Russia, but that it not enough. We are told—by the only witness called by the defendants and one who supplied the only testimony to this effect—that "from 1925 to date, the Church has received greater liberty and is functioning freely as an Orthodox Church, without interference by the civil authorities, and the political views held by the authorities, and any atheistic sentiment that they may have in no way interferes with the unhampered activities of the Russian Orthodox Church." (Emphasis supplied.) On the other hand, plaintiff urges that, willingly or not, the Moscow patriarchy is unable to conduct "church-administrative activity" except as an arm of the Russian Government to further its domestic and foreign policy; that that is a fact publicly recognized by our President and our State Department; and that it is attested to an demonstrated in the records submitted to us by (1) the imprisonment of Patriarch Tikhon, (2) the suppression of the patriarchal church during the days of the State-supported schism of the "Renovated Church" and (3) by the later re-establishment of an enfeebled patriarchate, when the "Renovated Church" had served its purpose, willing to pledge its loyalty to the Russian State and to attempt to exact a similar pledge from clergy abroad. Having in mind the warning of Lord Coleridge, in Lumley v. Gye (2 El. & Bl. 216, 167), "Judges are not necessarily to be ignorant in Court of what every one else, and they themselves out of Court, are familiar with," we feel we must accept the historical statements contained in the dissenting opinion of Mr. Justice Van Voorhis, below: "* * * In recent public pronouncements the State Department, and our representatives in the United Nations, have frequently recognized and denounced the suppression of human rights and basic liberties in religion as well as in other aspects of life, existing in Soviet Russia and in all of its satellite states. The President of the United States has publicly characterized such efforts as a campaign to turn religion into a tool of the state (Armistice Day Address, November 11, 1949)." 276 App.Div. 309, 330.

Everyone agrees that the Russian Orthodox Church has continuously existed down through the centuries, for no communicant would concede that the suppression of the church by the Soviet Government had ever destroyed the patriarchy as a spiritual symbol of the spiritual unity of the church as distinguished from its temporalities. Moreover, members of the North American metropolitan district admittedly revere and respect the office of the patriarchy, whatever may be their feelings as to the merits of the current incumbent of the office. This devotion is traditional and serves as a common bond for the members of the Russian Orthodox

Church, as distinguished from the members of other Orthodox churches in various countries which have recognized as their spiritual heads at various times the Patriarchates of Constantinople, of Alexandria, of Antioch, of Serbia and of Jerusalem. Recognition of the Moscow patriarchy by the North American metropolitan district in that sense is by no means a disavowal of the position steadfastly maintained by it down to the present day, viz., that the beloved patriarchy has been absorbed by the Russian Government and its action deprived, during the period of such domination, of any religious significance.

In short, we think that further inquiry might well have been made into the present status of the patriarchate in Russia and we think the Supreme Court should have determined, in the exercise of its discretion, whether Benjamin, the appointee of the central church authorities in Moscow, or Metropolitan Theophilus, the archbishop of the North American metropolitan district, was the proper person to administer the temporalities of St. Nicholas Cathedral and whether he was the proper trustee "who may be relied upon to carry out more effectively and faithfully the purposes of this religious trust (Carrier v. Carrier, 226 N.Y. 114)." Kedrovsky v. Archbishop & Consistory of Russian Orthodox Catholic Church, 249 N.Y. 75, 77-78, supra. That was not done because it was thought that the cases of Watson v. Jones, 13 Wall. 679, supra, and Trustees of Presbytery of N. Y. v. Westminster Presbyt. Church, 222 N.Y. 305, supra, required a decision in favor of defendants and that the earlier case of Kedrovsky v. Rojdesvensky, 242 N.Y. 547, supra, was determinative of some phases of the problem. Our views on this aspect of the controversy would require reversal and the ordering of a new trial so that the Supreme Court might exercise its discretion along the lines herein indicated. It is unnecessary, however, to discuss that further, for there is another ground requiring reversal here and judgment in favor of plaintiff and the North American metropolitan district which it represents.

We refer, of course, to the authoritative and unambiguous action finally taken by the New York State Legislature in 1945 and 1948 with respect to the controversy which has now occupied the attention of our courts for a quarter of a century.

If there were any doubt as to the proper determination of the case along common-law lines, it has been completely eliminated by the Legislature. In April of 1945, L. 1945, ch. 693, the Governor signed a bill adding a new article 5-C to the Religious Corporations Law consisting of four sections, two of which, sections 105 and 107, are presently material. In 1948, L. 1948, ch. 711, important amendments were made to these sections which will be noted later. In the first section, § 105, the Legislature defined the "Russian Church in America" (i.e., the North American church as we have referred to it above) and carefully traced its origin. The first paragraph of section 105, as it reads today, is as follows: "The 'Russian Church in America,' as that term is used anywhere in this article, refers to that group of churches, cathedrals, chapels, congregations, societies, parishes, committees and other religious organizations of the Eastern Confession (Eastern Orthodox or Greek Catholic Church) which were known as (a) Russian American Mission of the Russian Orthodox Church from in or about 1793 to in or about 1870; (b) Diocese of

Alaska and the Aleutian Islands of the Russian Orthodox Church from in or about 1870 to in or about 1904; (c) Diocese of North America and the Aleutian Islands (or Alaska) of the Russian Orthodox Church from in or about 1904 to in or about 1924; and (d) Russian Orthodox Greek Catholic Church of North America since in or about 1924; and were subject to the administrative jurisdiction of the Most Sacred Governing Synod in Moscow until in or about 1917, later the Patriarchate of Moscow but now constitute an administratively autonomous metropolitan district created pursuant to resolutions adopted at a general convention (sobor) of said district held at Detroit, Michigan, on or about or between April 2nd to 4th, 1924."

The second paragraph of section 105, defines what is meant in the statute by the phrase "Russian Orthodox church." This is used as a word of art and is used generally to denote the particular local buildings or organizations of the Russian Orthodox faith as distinguished from the spiritual church. The statutory definition reads as follows: "A 'Russian Orthodox church,' as that term is used anywhere in this article, is a church, cathedral, chapel, congregation, society, parish, committee or other religious organization founded and established for the purpose and with the intent of adhering to, and being subject to the administrative jurisdiction of said mission ((a) above), diocese ((b) and (c) above) or autonomous metropolitan district ((d) above) hereinabove defined as the Russian Church in America." It is to be noted that the words "Russian Orthodox church" refer not only to those church buildings and religious organizations founded and established for the purposes and with the intent of adhering to, and being subject to the autonomous North American metropolitan district since 1924, but also to those properties and organizations adhering and subject in the past to the Russian Mission from 1793 to 1870, and the North American Dioceses from 1870 to 1904 and from 1904 to 1924.

These definitions, in turn, make the meaning and intent of section 107 clear. With them in mind, the following command of the Legislature in section 107 is abundantly plain:

"1. Every Russian Orthodox church in this state, whether incorporated before or after the creation of said autonomous metropolitan district and whether incorporated or reincorporated pursuant to this article or any other article if the religious corporations law, or any general or private law, shall recognize and be and remain subject to the jurisdiction and authority of the general convention (sobor), metropolitan archbishop or other primate or hierarch, the council of bishops, the metropolitan council and other governing bodies and authorities of the Russian Church in America, pursuant to the statutes for the government thereof adopted at a general convention (sobor) held in the city of New York on or about or between October 5th to 8th, 1937, and any amendments thereto and any other statutes or rules heretofore or hereafter adopted by a general convention (sobor) of the Russian Church in America and shall in all other respects conform to, maintain and follow the faith, doctrine, ritual communion, discipline, cannon law, traditions and usages of the Easter Confession (Eastern Orthodox or Greek Catholic Church).

"2. * * *

"3. The trustees of every Russian Orthodox church shall have the custody and control of all temporalities and property, real and personal, belonging to such church and of the revenues therefrom and shall administer the same in accordance with the by-laws of such church, the normal statutes for parishes of the Russian Church in America approved at a general convention (sobor) thereof held at Cleveland, Ohio, on or about or between November 20th to 23d, 1934, and any amendments thereto and all other rules, statutes, regulations and usages of the Russian Church in America." (Dates in Arabic; emphasis supplied.) Little, if anything, is left for the courts to construe in the face of such a clear manifestation of intent. St. Nicholas Cathedral, the subject property herein, is indisputably a "Russian Orthodox church", as defined in the statute. It was built in 1903 and dedicated as a cathedral in 1905, in connection with the establishment of the Diocese of North America and the Aleutian Islands, which as we have seen, is listed in the first paragraph of section 105. It is a "cathedral * * * founded and established for the purpose and with the intent of adhering to, and being subject to the administrative jurisdiction of said mission, diocese or autonomous metropolitan district hereinabove defined as the Russian Church in America." (Emphasis supplied.) As such, it is within the purview of subdivision 1 of section 107 and must be subject to the jurisdiction and authority of the governing bodies of the North American church. Likewise, pursuant to subdivision 3 of section 107, the trustees of the St: Nicholas Cathedral Corporation must administer the cathedral in accordance with the by-laws, the normal statutes for parishes of the Russian Church in America as therein defined.

Special Term attempted to construe the statute, as it stood in 1945, in such a manner as to make it applicable only to those new parishes, founded and established after 1924 for the express purpose of adhering to the Russian Church in America. Whether the court's construction was justified under the then wording of the statute is not before us, for after the decision at Special Term, and obviously as a result of it, the Legislature amended the statute to read in its present form, above quoted. In order that there might not be any doubt that the 1945 legislation was intended to apply to a property, such as St. Nicholas Cathedral, the second paragraph of section 105, defining "Russian Orthodox church," was amended so that there was included within its compass any cathedral "founded and established for the purpose and with the intent of adhering to, and being subject to the *administrative jurisdiction of said mission, diocese or autonomous metropolitan district hereinabove defined* as the Russian Church in America." (New matter italics.) Likewise, subdivision 1 of section 107, which provides that every such Russian Orthodox church in this State shall "recognize and be and remain subject to the jurisdiction and authority" of the Russian Church in America, was amended to provide that such Russian Orthodox churches were within its coverage "whether incorporated *before or after the creation* (1924) *of said autonomous metropolitan district.*" (New matter italics.) These significant amendments, enacted within a month after Special Term's decision, illustrate beyond cavil that the decision of that court did not correspond with the intent of the Legislature, which immediately interpreted and explained its prior enactment.

Nevertheless, the majority in the Appellate Division, while conceding that plaintiff was entitled to the benefit of the statute in its amended form, failed properly to appreciate and give meaning to what we consider to be the plain legislative intent. It said in part 276 App.Div. at page 317: "In other words, it appears to us that it (§ 107) was intended to mean that any church heretofore or hereafter incorporated for the purpose of adhering to the American church must be subordinate to the rules and the decisions of the authorities of the governing bodies of that church (the American church, the autonomous metropolitan district, created in 1924)." Such a view gives no meaning to the change made by subdivision 1 of section 107 by the 1948 amendment. That amendment excised the three words ("heretofore or hereafter") which we have italicized in the above quotation, and substituted the words: "before or after the creation of said autonomous metropolitan district (in 1924) * * *." The following quotation from subdivision 1 of section 107 shows in brackets the words eliminated by the 1948 amendment and indicates by italicizing the words substituted by that amendment: "Every Russian Orthodox church in this state, whether (heretofore or hereafter) incorporated before or after the creation of said autonomous metropolitan district * * * shall recognize and be and remain subject to the jurisdiction and authority of * * * the Russian Church in America * * *." The Legislature quite clearly made the amendment after the decision at Special Term herein so as to remove the possibility of a construction such as that adopted by the Special Term and later the Appellate Division, that the statute was limited in its operation to churches incorporated after 1924. If, as the Appellate Division construed it, the statute were limited to churches "incorporated for the purpose of adhering to the American church", that would mean that it could only apply to churches founded and established after 1924, since that was the year in which the autonomous metropolitan district, denominated by the Appellate Division, the American church, was created. Yet sub-division 1 of section 107 clearly states that it is to apply to Russian Orthodox churches "whether incorporated before or after the creation of said autonomous metropolitan district", i.e., before or after 1924. The only construction which gives meaning to all the language in sections 105 and 107 is that the statute was intended to apply to those Russian Orthodox churches founded and established before 1924 for the purpose of adhering and being subject to the North American Mission or North American Diocese, and to those Russian Orthodox churches founded and established after 1924 for the purpose of adhering and being subject to the autonomous metropolitan district. The majority in the Appellate Division further intimated that to read the statute literally would result in an interference in ecclesiastical concerns not within the competency of the Legislature. The latter suggestion is the only one which requires discussion, for, as already indicated, the intent of the Legislature (as distinguished from its competency) is unmistakable.

The primary purpose of the Religious Corporations Law is to provide for an orderly method for the administration of the property and temporalities dedicated to the use of religious groups and to preserve them from exploitation by those who might divert them from the true beneficiaries of the trust. Prior to 1875, when the Legislature provided for denominational control of the temporalities of religious corporations, the majority of the members of a religious corporation could change its denominational character and devote the church property to an entirely different religious faith than that for which it was originally dedicated. Robertson v. Bullions, 11 N.Y. 243, 163-164; Petty v. Tooker, 21 N.Y. 267; Gram v. Prussia Emigrated Evangelical Lutheran German Soc., 36 N.Y. 161. For the public good, the Legislature decreed that the trustees of religious corporations, irrespective of the wishes of the majority of the local congregation, must administer the temporalities in accordance with the discipline, rules and usages of the ecclesiastical body, if any, to which the corporation was subject. Religious Corporations Law, § 5. As a broad guide this rule undoubtedly has worked well, but it is by no means a constitutional doctrine not subject to change or modification by the same Legislature which announced it, in cases where literal enforcement would be unreasonable and opposed to the public interest. The Legislature, in the exercise of its extensive and acknowledged power to act for the common welfare, may find as a fact that a situation has arisen of such novelty and uniqueness that existing law is incapable of performing its avowed function—the preservation of religious temporalities for the use of their original and accustomed beneficiaries. If the Legislature find as a fact that, because of drastically changed circumstances, the accustomed beneficiaries of religious properties are thus threatened with their loss, and if there be a basis for such finding, we perceive no constitutional objection to a legislative attempt to trace and identify, as of today, the authentic group entitled to the administration of such properties.

That, as we see it, is all that the Legislature has done in the above-quoted provisions of article 5-C. The Legislature has made a determination that the "Russian Church of America" was the one which, to use our words in 249 N.Y. at pages 77-78, 162 N.E. at page 589, was the trustee which "may be relied upon to carry out more effectively and faithfully the purposes of this religious trust (Carrier v. Carrier, 226 N. Y. 114)" by reason of the changed situation of the patriarchate in Russia. No purpose would be served by repeating all the circumstances which forced the North American church to declare its temporary autonomy, and the process by which the Moscow Patriarchy has been subjugated by the Russian Government and used as its tool. All that has been detailed fully above. These facts must be deemed to have been found by and to have been within the actual knowledge of the Legislature when it decided to act in 1945 and 1948. Even assuming that we, as judges, are prevented from recognizing these facts, it cannot be successfully contended that the Legislature is required to labor under such unrealistic handicap.

The Legislature of the State of New York, like the Congress of the United States, in addition to the general knowledge of its members, has access to vast sources of information to assist it in determining the need and scope of new statutory law. Every new piece of legislation is the result of certain factual premises, whether they be expressed or tacit. In gathering the material for these premises, and in evaluating conflicting data, the Legislature is not bound by any formal rules. It has the widest latitude of inquiry. It cannot, and does not, close its eyes to any legitimate avenue of knowledge.

The courts have always recognized that it is the province of the Legislature to make the underlying findings of fact which give meaning and substance to its ultimate directives. The courts have traditionally refused to consider the wisdom or technical validity of such findings of fact, if there be some reasonable basis upon which they may rest.

Thus, in passing upon matters of legislative intent and competence, the courts do not merely read the bare end product of the legislative labors. They read the statute in the light of the state of facts which were found by the Legislature, and which prompted the enactment. Then, and only then, can the courts intelligently approach their assigned tasks.

A recent pertinent example of such judicial recognition of the extent of the power of the legislative body to find the facts in a situation involving communist activity is found in American Communications Ass'n, v. Douds, 339 U.S. 382. There, the noncommunist oath provision in the National Labor Relations Act, 29 U.S.C.A. § 151 et seq., was upheld, not because any such oath requirement was generally within the power of Congress, but because the specific evil, the existence of which Congress was assumed to have reasonably found as a fact, was such that some infringement upon traditional liberties was justifiable. The case illustrates well that enactments which might seem unconstitutional on their face may yet be sustained if the factual background found by the legislative body warranted an extended exercise of its powers. The case is noteworthy, too, in that it rejects the fallacious contention that the legislative body cannot go behind a carefully constructed facade to ascertain the real motives, ends and techniques of communist activity. It recognizes, as we must recognize in the instant case, that problems created by the extension of Soviet communist activity in this country are sui generis, and can only be dealt with intelligently on that basis.

As Justice Jackson said in his opinion 339 U.S. at page 423, n. 1,: "Of course, it is not for any member of this Court to express or to act upon any opinion he may have as to the wisdom, effectiveness or need for this legislation. Our 'inquiries, where the legislative judgment is drawn in question, must be restricted to the issue whether any state of facts either known or which could reasonably be assumed affords support for it.' United States v. Carolene Products Co., 304 U.S. 144, 154," (Emphasis supplied.) See, also, Powell v. Com. of Pennsylvania, 127 U.S. 678, 685; O'Gorman & Young v. Hartford Fire Ins. Co., 282 U.S. 251, 257-258; Szold v. Outlet Embroidery Supply Co., 274 N.Y. 271, 278.

The judicial technique of ascertaining the legislative finding of fact supporting a particular enactment is shown in Justice Jackson's opinion in the Douds case, supra, 339 U.S. at page 424-433. He wrote, 339 U.S. at page 424, 70 S.Ct. at page 696:

"From information before its several Committees and from facts of general knowledge, Congress could rationally conclude that behind its political party facade, the Communist Party is a conspiratorial and revolutionary junta, organized to reach ends and to use methods which are incompatible with our constitutional system. A rough and compressed grouping of this data would permit Congress to draw these important conclusions as to its distinguishing characteristics." (Then follows a footnote containing a long list of books and articles.) * * *

"It rejects the entire religious and cultural heritage of Western civilization, as well as the American economic and political systems. This Communist movement is a belated counter-revolution to the American Revolution, designed to undo the Declaration of Independence, the Constitution, and our Bill of Rights * * *." 339 U.S. at page 425.

The Legislature of the State of New York, like the Congress, must be deemed to have investigated the whole problem carefully before it acted. The Legislature knew that the central authorities of the Russian Orthodox Church in Russia had been suppressed after the 1917 revolution, and that the patriarchate was later resurrected by the Russian Government. The Legislature, like Congress, knew the character and method of operation of international communism and the Soviet attitude toward things religious. The Legislature was aware of the contemporary views of qualified observers who have visited Russia and who have had an opportunity to observe the present status of the patriarchate in the Soviet system. The Legislature realized that the North American church, in order to be free of Soviet interference in its affairs, had declared its temporary administrative autonomy in 1924, pursuant to the ukase of 1920, while retaining full spiritual communion with the patriarchate, and that there was a real danger that those properties and temporalities long enjoyed and used by the Russian Orthodox Church worshippers in this State would be taken from them by the representatives of the patriarchate. On the basis of these facts, and the facts stated (supra) and no doubt other facts we know not of, our Legislature concluded that the Moscow Patriarchate was no longer capable of functioning as a true religious body, but had become a tool of the Soviet Government primarily designed to implement its foreign policy. Whether we, as judges, would have reached the same conclusion is immaterial. It is sufficient that the Legislature reached it, after full consideration of all the facts.

It is clear, therefore, that the plaintiff corporation and the autonomous metropolitan district which it represents, must prevail in this action in accordance with the legislative finding and mandate and be reinvested with the possession and administration of the temporalities of St. Nicholas Cathedral.

The judgments below should be reversed, with costs in all courts, and judgment directed for the plaintiff.[1]

DESMOND, Judge (dissenting).

None of us, of course, deny that the present Russian Government is frankly and grossly anti-religious and irreligious. But judicial recognition of that well-known fact is of no help in deciding this lawsuit. We are dissenting here because we strongly feel that this decision is an unlawful intrusion into the internal affairs of a religious body contrary to first principles of American government, violative of the First Amendment's guaranty of freedom of religions from such governmental interference, and in conflict with the controlling decisional law as set forth in _Watson_ v. _Jones_, 13 Wall. 679, and _Westminster Presbyt. Church of West Twenty-Third Street_ v. _Trustees of Presbytery of N.Y._, 211 N.Y. 214. For the decision about to be made is just this: that the judicial and

[1] A concurring opinion of Froessel, J. is omitted.

legislative branches of the Government of this State have the power (and that the New York State Legislature has exercised the power) to oust from the archdiocesan cathedral of the Russian Orthodox Church in New York City, a prelate (defendant Benjamin) who has been appointed archbishop of that archdiocese by the Patriarch of Moscow, supreme head of that church. No other decision reaching such a result can be found in the books.

In aid of clarity we set down these indisputable and uncontested propositions:

1. The Russian Orthodox Church is a "general" or centrally organized church, see Watson v. Jones, supra, 13 Wall. at page 722, under whose law and discipline the Patriarch of Moscow, as its supreme head, has the power of appointing archbishops.

2. Defendant Benjamin was appointed by the Patriarch as archbishop of the Diocese of North America and the Aleutian Islands, and that appointment is now in effect.

3. The Russian Orthodox Cathedral in New York City, is the see church of the archdiocese, and, accordingly, defendant Benjamin, as the duly appointed archbishop, is entitled to possess and occupy that cathedral as his see church.

4. Plaintiff-appellant, a New York corporation, holds title to the cathdral property but, under New York law, that title is in trust for the religious purposes of the Russian Orthodox Church, and for no other purpose, Westminster Presbyt. Church of West Twenty-Third Street v. Trustees of Presbytery of N. Y., 211 N.Y. 214, 233, supra.

5. Plaintiff, in seeking to exclude defendant Archbishop Benjamin from possession of the cathedral, is acting under the control of, and in the interest of, a dissident or schismatic group of Russian Orthodox Catholic individuals and parishes, which group, formed at Detroit in 1924, refuses to recognize the authority and primacy of the Patriarch of Moscow.

6. Under the law of New York, see Religious Corporations Law, § 5, religious denominations, such as the world-wide Russian Orthodox Church, have denominational control over their constituent churches, parishes or branches, and the constituents cannot escape such control by secession, Trustees of Presbytery of N. Y. v. Westminster Presbyt. Church, 222 N.Y. 305, 315 118 N.E. 800, 803.

7. The appointment of Archbishop Benjamin, as an official act of the highest Russian Orthodox Church authority, was a decision on a denominational matter of internal church government, and as such is final, and absolutely binding on the civil courts of this State, Watson v. Jones, 13 Wall. 679, 727, 729, supra.

The sum of those plain propositions is this: that Archbishop Benjamin's possession of the cathedral is not subject to control by any civil authority or by any judgment of a civil court, and that no civil court may decree to the independent or nonconformist group (which controls plaintiff corporation), possession of that cathedral, hostile to the authority and action of the mother church, Watson v. Jones, supra, 13 Wall. at page 734.

What bases, then, are announced for the direction by this court that a judgment issue which will remove defendant Benjamin from his cathedral?

As we understand it, those asserted grounds are two: first, that the Moscow Patriarchate is not in fact functioning as the true central organization of the Russian church but is a mere agency or instrumentality of the Soviet regime; and, second, that article 5-C of the New York Religious Corporations Law has, by legislative fiat, ousted the patriarchal appointee, and turned the cathedral over to the schismatics. The first of those bases amounts to a new finding by this court, without evidentiary support in this record, and in the face of contrary testimony, and express contrary findings by both courts below. The second basis gives to article 5-C a construction not reasonably supported by its language, or by its history, or by any reasonable or discoverable legislative intent—a construction which, furthermore, makes the statute unconstitutional. We now take up these matters in turn.

The finding, or determination, now being made by the majority of this court as a basis for reversal, is that the presently ruling Patriarch of Moscow is not, and should not, be treated as, the true central head of the church, but that he is a mere fellow traveler on the communist road, serving not God but the Soviet Caesar. Interestingly enough, plaintiff itself seems not to cast so cold an eye on the Patriarch, since the record abounds with protestations by the "American," or schismatic Orthodox Russians, of their filial loyalty and devotion to the Patriarch, whom they regard as a virtuous and venerable spiritual leader. Aside from that, and confining ourselves within the strict bounds of our own jurisdiction we, the Court of Appeals, have, of course, no power or right to adjudicate that the incumbent is no true Patriarch but a mere usurper or pretender. We dissenters refuse so to do, not from any mere naivete as to Russia and communism, but as a necessary conclusion from the record in this lawsuit. At the very most, we have here the attempted determination of a fact, vigoriously denied by witnesses, and found to the contrary by the courts which have jurisdiction to pass on facts.

It is suggested that common sense, or general knowledge, makes it appropriate for us to take judicial notice that Patriarch Alexy is not acting independently but is obeying commands of his communist masters. Perhaps he is, for all we know, but his motivation is no proper subject of judicial notice. Many years ago our predecessors warned us against taking judicial notice in such uncertain fields. See Baxter v. McDonnell, 155 N.Y. 83, 93. And, even if we could, somehow or other, get sure knowledge that the Patriarch's appointment of this archbishop was made for the most unholy reasons, or because of the meanest accommodation to brute power, we still could not, as a court, strike down the appointment or refuse to give it credit. The Patriarch, like all men, must account for his stewardship, but not to the New York courts.

The long and the short of it is that this is an ecclesiastical matter, to which, be their answer right or wrong, the ecclesiastic superiors have the final answer. "* * and civil courts, if they should be so unwise as to attempt to supervise their judgments on matters which come within their jurisdiction, would only involve themselves in a sea of uncertainty and doubt, which would do anything but improve either religion or good morals". Connitt v. Reformed Prot. Dutch Church of New Prospect, 54 N.Y. 551, 562. We are not talking about the powers of courts or of government to keep from our shores persons dangerous to our institutions, be they churchmen or laymen, or to deal with such persons when and if they violate our laws. No one has testified that Archbishop Benjamin is such a subversive, and, if he were, the New York courts would hardly be the place, or an action of ejectment the method, to arrange for his deportation from our shores. The United States Government has never withdrawn recognition of the Russian Orthodox Church and its Patriarch. See Ponce v. Roman Catholic Apostolic Church in Porto Rico, 210 U.S. 296, 318.

We turn now to the statute which seems to be appellant's chief reliance. Article 5-C of the Religious Corporations Law, consisting of four sections, §§ 105-108, was enacted in 1945, L. 1945, ch. 693, and amended in 1948, L. 1948, ch. 711. Its language follows the general pattern of several other articles in the same law. On its face there is no indication that it had any purpose other than that of any other special or general law incorporating a religious society or sect or church, that is, "to give an organization for public worship legal rights, and to impose on it legal obligations as a corporate body." Van Buren v. Reformed Church of Gansevoort, 61 Barb. 495, 197; Petty v. Tooker, 21 N.Y. 267, 271. Incorporation of a church is the method by which the municipal law recognizes a church's present existence. Obviously, such a statute cannot be a device for transferring property from one faction to another, or for subjecting centrally organized churches to the control of seceding groups. Neither of those two general statements will be contradicted, and yet we are told that the passage by the New York legislature, in 1945, or article 5-C, and its amendment in 1948, had the precise and intended effect of freeing the whole Russian Orthodox religious community in America from its traditional submission to its supreme hierarchical head, of outlawing in New York so much of that community as remained submissive to the Patriarch, of putting the whole group and all its properties under the control of the new schismatic "Russian Church in America", and, specifically, of mandating the ouster of the patriarchically appointed archbishop and the substitution of a rival claimant, not so appointed. We confidently assert that there is nothing in the statute itself to suggest such a legislative coup, that there is much to show that such was not the legislative purpose, and that the statute, if so intended or so construed, is plainly unconstitutional.

The first section, 105, in article 5-C is headed "Definitions." It is not in form or in meaning a preamble or legislative finding of fact. It defines two terms used elsewhere in the article: "Russian Church in America" and "Russian Orthodox church." The long, one-sentence definition of the first of those terms says that, as used in the article, it means those churches, cathedrals, parishes, etc., which were known as the Russian American Mission of the Russian Orthodox Church from 1793 to 1870, then known as the Diocese of Alaska, etc., from 1870 to 1904, then as the Diocese of North America and the Aleutian Islands from 1904 to 1924, and which have been known as the Russian Orthodox Greek Church of North America since 1924, and which were subject to the administrative jurisdiction of the Most Sacred Governing Synod in Moscow until 1917, later the "Patriarchate of Moscow," but which "now constitute an administratively autonomous metropolitan district created pursuant to resolutions adopted at a general convention (sobor) of said district held at Detroit, Michigan, on or about or between April second to fourth, nineteen hundred twenty-four." A "definition" of a term is a precise statement of its meaning. Nothing could be more precise than the statement (above summarized) which the Legislature thus gave us of what the Legislature meant by the use, in article 5-C, of the term "Russian Church in America." The definition describes, by reciting its history, the particular "group" of churches intended to be affected by the article. So read, the definition cannot possibly mean anything but this; that the "group" of churches or parishes thus recognized by the Legislature under the name "Russian Church in America," were those particular churches and parishes which were formerly part of the unified body called at successive times first the "Russian American Mission," then called the "Diocese of Alaska and the Aleutian Islands," then styled the "Diocese of North America and the Aleutian Islands" and which have been called the "Russian Orthodox Greek Catholic Church of North America" since 1924—in other words, the secessionists. To make that totally clear, the Legislature added to its "definition" a statement that it meant those churches, cathedrals or parishes which, though formerly subject to the Moscow Patriarch, had created themselves into an autonomous metropolitan district (or diocese) in April, 1924. On the trial, the witnesses agreed that not all the American parishes of the Russian Orthodox Church have gone over to the new "American" church. The definition describes those who did so cross over. The second "definition" in section 105 (of "Russian Orthodox church") says that term means a church, cathedral, etc., founded and established with the purpose and intent of adhering to the new metropolitan district.

The next section 106, of article 5-C sets forth the formalities for incorporation of a "Russian Orthodox church" as defined in section 105. Section 107, as amended in 1948, prescribes the method of government, by the new "Russian Church in America" of "every Russian Orthodox church in this state," whether incorporated before or after the creation of the new "autonomous metropolitan district." Appellant seizes upon the words "Every Russian Orthodox church in this state" as meaning, literally, every Russian Orthodox parish, church or cathedral, whether or not it has seceded, and whether or not it desires to retain its traditional ties with the Patriarch. Of course, the words must be limited as defined in section 105, which says precisely what they are to mean, when "used anywhere in this article."

Section 108, headed "Reincorporation of existing corporations" authorizes the reincorporation "under the provisions of this article," of any "heretofore incorporated Russian Orthodox church." Such a provision would be useless and meaningless if the Legislature had, by the previous sections of the article, put every Russian Orthodox church and parish, automatically, into the new, dissident, "Russian Church in America." Indeed, if so strange and ruthless a plan had been intended by the Legislature, section 105 itself ("Definitions") would have been meaningless and unnecessary since, with all included, there would be no need for any definition or limitation.

Article 5-C, we think, is so plain and clear as not to need or permit any construction beyond the patent meaning of its simple words, Matter of Rathscheck's Estate, 300 N.Y. 346, 350, 90 N.E.2d 887, 889. But if construction were permissible, every known canon of construction would lead to the same result: that the Legislature could not have intended this as a statute of outlawry, ouster, or disestablishment. Words in a statute are to receive their natural and obvious meaning; the general purpose and spirit of the law is to be kept in mind; objectionable consequences, injustice and unreasonableness are to be avoided; acts will not be so construed as to accuse the Legislature of a purpose to do harm (see McKinney's Cons. Laws of N. Y., Book 1, Statutes, §§ 94, 141, 143, 146, 148, 151, and cases cited for these propositions). A bad result suggests a wrong construction. People ex rel. Beaman v. Feitner, 168 N.Y. 360, 366. We find another aid to construction in the very practical ideal that the busy New York Legislature which enacted over 1,200 laws in 1945, and which had no committee reports or debates as to article 5-C, was entitled to believe that this law meant what it said, without hidden purposes.

And one of the most urgent of all the canons of construction is this one: that a statute must be construed, when possible, "in manner which would remove doubt of its constitutionality, and possible danger that it might be used to restrain or burden freedom of worship or freedom of speech and press." People v. Barber, 289 N.Y. 378, 385. Put another way, the rule is that the construction, if at all possible, must be such as not only to avoid unconstitutionality but to avoid grave doubts thereof, Matter of Cooper, 22 N.Y. 67, 87, 88; Kovacs v. Cooper, 336 U.S. 77, 85; Tauza v. Susquehanna Coal Co., 220 N.Y. 259, 267; People v. Realmato, 294 N.Y. 45,50; United States v. Jin Fuey Moy, 241 U.S. 394, 401. How can there be any dispute but that this article 5-C, if read so as to take this archbishopric from the control of the central church and give it to appellant's group, is unconstitutional? Watson v. Jones, supra, does not use the precise word "unconstitutional" but the opinion, contrasting American with old world systems (see page 728 et seq. of 13 Wall.' says that "In this country the full and free right to entertain any religious belief to practice any religious principle" finds expression in the American rule of law that the determinations of the tribunals and judicatories of a centrally organized church are absolutely binding on the civil power. The modern Supreme Court in Everson v. Board of Education of Erving Tp., 330 U.S. 1, 13, has cited Watson v. Jones, supra, as authority for the proposition tha the First Amendment provides "protection against governmental intrustion on religious liberty" through statutes. It is no answer to this charge of unconstitutionality that there is here in dispute a "property right" only as to the use of a building. "* * * when rights of property are dependent upon the questions of doctrine, discipline, or church government, the civil court will treat the determination made in the highest tribunal within the church as controlling" Baxter v. McDonnell, 155 N.Y. 83, 101, supra, citing Watson v. Jones, supra; and Connitt v. Reformed Prot. Dutch Church of New Prospect, supra; see Gonzalez v. Roman Catholic Archbishop of Manila, 280 U.S. 1, 16.

We pause to remark on the notable similarity between the present case and Watson v. Jones, supra. A controversy over slavery split the

Presbyterian Church in Kentucky in the 1860's; dissension over communism ideologies and Soviet controls played their part in the internecine warfare which broke out among the American members of the Russian Orthodox Church. A faction withdrew from the central control in the Presbyterian Church; plaintiff's faction here divorced themselves from their supreme hierarch. In Watson v. Jones the Supreme Court, holding the Presbyterian controversy to be "a case of division or schism in a church" 13 Wall. at page 717, as is surely true of our case, made the classic statement of law which runs from page 722 to the end of the long opinion. The holding as between the dissenters and the central organization was summarized thus: "They (the schismatics) now deny its authority, denounce its action, and refuse to abide by its judgments. They have first erected themselves into a new organization, and have since joined themselves to another totally different, if not hostile, to the one to which they belonged when the difficulty first began. Under any of the decisions which we have examined, the appellants, in their present position, have not right to the property, or to the use of it, which is the subject of this suit" at page 734.

Going back to the statute (art. 5-C) and its supposed effect here, we have, fortunately, the strongest kind of proof from the Religious Corporations Law itself that the Legislature never intended for article 5-C the meaning and result now ascribed to it. In 1943, ch. 145 of that year, the Legislature, two years before it was set up article 5-C, had enacted a new article XV of the Religious Corporations Law and had, concurrently, amended subdivision 3 of section 15 of the Religious Corporations Law. That 1843 legislation described and recognized a "federation" of the "four primary Orthodox Greek Catholic jurisdictions in America," being the churches, congregations, etc., recognized by the "apostolic historic Orthodox Patriarchates of Constantinople, Antioch, Moscow and Serbia (Yugoslavia)." Among other things, that 1943 law described the processes whereby new congregations adhering to the four historic patriarchates could be newly incorporated or reincorporated as member churches of the federation. The significance for us is this: as late as 1943, the Legislature was thus legislating as to those churches which were under the government of the Moscow Patriarch. The Governor of New York, after signing the bill, made it clear that he so understood its import. In a speech at Buffalo (see Public Papers of the Governor, 1943, p. 550) Governor Dewey said: "For more than 180 years members of the Greek Church have been on what is now American soil. We find in the records that as long ago as 1763 a native of the Aleutian Islands was converted by a devout and hardy missionary from Russia. Nineteen years later the Holy Synod sent a mission of eight monks to Alaska and in 1794 they established missionary headquarters on the Kodiak Island. Three years later the hierarchy of the Greek Church consecrated a Bishop of Alaska, but he perished at sea before he could ever reach his diocese. The living successor of the reverend prelates who succeeded him is The Most Reverend Metropolitan Benjamin of New York. It is an interesting historic fact, particularly in these days, that his full title is Metropolitan of the Archdiocese of the Aleutian Islands and North America."

The Most Reverend Metropolitan Benjamin whom the Governor thus saluted as the successor to the historic line of Orthodox prelates in America was our defendant Benjamin.

Thus we see that in 1943, by article XV and the amendment to section 15, the Legislature dealt with those Orthodox churches which remained loyal to the Patriarch and in 1945 and 1948, through article 5-C, gave its attention and recognition to the new, nonconformist "American Church." There is no slightest sign that the Legislature intended the later statutes to repeal the earlier. We should not strain to discover a repeal by implication but must read these statutes as harmonious parts of a whole and assume that the Legislature in 1945 knew what it had done in 1943. Matter of Cooper, 22 N.Y. 67, 88, supra; Chase v. Lord, 77 N.Y. 1, 18; Matter of Tiffany, 179 N.Y. 455, 457; Matter of Timmis, 200 N.Y. 177, 181; Betz v. Horr, 176 N.Y. 83, 88; Morris Plan Ind. Bank of N.Y. v Gunning, 295 N.Y. 324, 331. "The intent and purpose of the legislative commands must be found from the statutes relating to the same general subject-matter taken as a whole." Betz v. Horr, supra, 276 N.Y. at page 88. "If, by any fair construction, whether strict or liberal, a reasonable field of operation can be found for both acts, that construction should be adopted. In other words, if the old and the new law, by any reasonable interpretation, can stand together, there is no repeal by implication." Matter of Tiffany, supra, 179 N.Y. at page 457. The Legislature in 1943 dealt with the patriarchal church, in 1945 with the American church, and there is no repugnance, inconsistency or overlapping of the two sets of statutes.

A final comment:

In the long run, communist repression and abuse of religion will make religion stronger, for "the blood of the martyrs is the seed of the Church." And so with government interferences with churches in our country. But with us the loser will be a traditional principle of American government; that the inner affairs of religious bodies are no concern of the State.

The judgment should be affirmed, with costs.

LEWIS, DYE and FROESSEL, JJ., concur in opinion by CONWAY, J.

LEWIS, CONWAY and DYE, JJ., concur in separate opinion by FROESSEL, J.

DESMOND, J., dissents in opinion in which LOUGHRAN, C. J., and FULD, J., concur.

Judgments reversed, etc.

CHAPTER III

THE EFFECT OF ECCLESIASTICAL ADJUDICATIONS

Smith v. Nelson
Supreme Court of Vermont, 1846
18 Vermont 511

[A majority of the congregation of a Presbyterian church in Vermont, which fell within the immediate jurisdiction of the Presbytery of Vermont and ultimately of the Associate Synon of North America, had refused to accept as valid and binding a decree of excommunication and deposition which the Synod had entered against a Presbyterian minister, Dr. Bullions. The congregation had also disregarded supplementary orders of the Synod by which the ministry over the Vermont congregation had been declared vacant, and its minister, Mr. Pringle, had been deposed. In the Supreme Court of Vermont it was held that the local congregation was free to disregard the orders of the Synod and that it could continue to hold and administer property which had been bequeathed to the Congregation in earlier and more peaceful times. In the course of the opinion of Mr. Chief Justice Williams he wrote as follows.]

In recurring to the proceedings of the congregation, different presbyteries, and synod, which have been brought to our notice, as well as the effect they are to have on the subject in controversy, and the authorities which have been read, it becomes necessary to examine the foundation of ecclesiastical law, the powers of their judicatories, the effect of their sentences in this country, as compared with the same in Great Britain, and also the striking difference, which exists between them in that country and this, which will necessarily require different determinations on subjects apparently similar, when brought before the courts in Great Britain, or in this State.

In England the ecclesiastical law and ecclesiastical courts are established by legitimate authority and become a part of the law of the land. By the common law, the King is the head of the church; which means, that all ecclesiastical power and authority is established by him, and by and under law. No canons can be made, except by his consent. Ecclesiastical courts and ecclesiastical law are adopted, as part of the common law. Their proceedings are according to the forms of the civil law, and the King may pardon all offences, within the jurisdiction of the spiritual courts. The courts of common law have and exercise a superintendence over their proceedings, and may keep them within their jurisdiction, and control them by writ of mandamus, prohibition, &c. The authorities for this may be found in Caudrey's Case, 5 Co. 1; 3 Com., Tit. Ecclesiastical persons; 7 Com., Tit. Prerogatives, D. 8-10, 17; Bishop of St. Davids v. Luch, 1 Ld. Raym. 447, 539. The sentences of these courts are there entitled to the same consideration, as the sentences of any other inferior tribunal. Their decisions are final and conclusive on all subjects within their jurisdiction; but as I have said, they may be controlled and examined into by the courts of law. Thus a prohibition will issue, when they take cognizance of matters clearly within the jurisdiction of the temporal courts, and also when they proceed on matters not sufficient to justify proceedings, either in a temporal or spiritual court. 39 E. C. L. 548. The government and jurisdiction of the church in Scotland are also established by authority of parliament. Abridgment of Acts of Parliament, Pardovan 225.

In this State the case is wholly different. We have no religious establishment, no ecclesiastical law, or courts, established by any authority. All their laws are wanting in this essential requisite, to give them any authority, that they are not "prescribed by the supreme power in a State." And though they may form constitutions, enact canons, laws, or ordinances, establish courts, or make any decisions, decrees of judgments, yet they can have only a voluntary obedience, cannot affect any civil rights, immunities, or contracts, or alter or dissolve any relations, or obligations, arising from contracts. When their proceedings are to be examined by ordinary tribunals of justice, their power is a phantom, and they can receive no other consideration, than the regulations of any other voluntary associations, formed for trifling, or grave and important, purposes. Obedience to the requisitions of any ecclesiastical societies may be required, under the penalty of spiritual censures; but this is the only penalty incurred by disobedience; and whether one submits to, or defies, the proccedings of any ecclesiastical court, or any censures passed by them, depends on his conviction of the regularity, or irregularity, of their proceedings. In short, they can only affect the conscience of the individual; how far they affect this, he must be the judge.

It is not to be inferred by this, that I am indifferent to the subject of ecclesiastical organization, government, or discipline. As an individual I should be disposed to submit to all regulations, not inconsistent with my duty to a higher power, and should examine their proceedings with great consideration and care, before I should venture to question their propriety. But in a court of justice, sworn to administer justice according to law, I cannot recognize any constitution, laws, ordinances, or sentences of any ecclesiastical tribunal, or of any voluntary society, as having any efficacy or power over the civil rights, immunities, or contracts of individuals. In Cullen v. Duke of Queensbury, Lord Thurlow said, of a voluntary society, that he could convince the parties, they had no laws and constitutions. And Lord Eldon spoke with contempt and alarm of a lodge of freemasons, who affected a corporate character, and exhibited their laws, forms and constitutions upon record. And of these voluntary associations, though they frequently make constitutions and pass by-laws, which they declare are not to be altered, except in a certain way, or manner, as by the concurrence of two thirds, or at two different meetings, &c., yet their constitution and laws may at any time be altered, or abrogated, by the same power which created them, and the vote of any subsequent meeting, abrogating, or altering, such constitution, though passed only by a majority, has as much efficacy, as a previous vote establishing them. A constitution for a voluntary society may be proper, as an organization, but it has none of the powers or requisites of a constitution in political bodies, which emanates from a higher power than the legislature, and always is supposed to be enacted by a power superior to the legislature, and hence, is unchangeable, except by the body which established it; but that body can change it at pleasure. It is idle, however, for such societies to talk of constitutional restrictions, or absolute or unlimited power, either in conventions, associations, presbyteries, or synods.

There cannot, in this country, be attributed to the decisions of a synod, or the decisions of any ecclesiastical judicatory, either infallibility, or freedom from error, nor can they claim rightfully unlimited obedience; and when it is attempted to give to their adjuciations the same effect, as is given to the sentence of ecclesiastical courts in England, or the superior courts of common law, the attempt must be unavailing; even the limits of the obedience which is due to the church courts of the associate church, to which all these parties belong, from the members of the denomination, and for a disobedience to which the party may be subject to church censures, is by no means accurately defined. Mr. Goodwillie, in his testimony, says, the church courts have not sovereign, arbitrary and absolute power; that if their decisions are not agreeable to the word of God, they are not to be received; and that every many has a right to judge for himself concerning their determinations. Mr. Reid considers the decisions of church courts as binding, provided such decisions are not contrary to the word of God. He makes a distinction between such as affect personal cases, and such as affect doctrines and matters of faith. Mr. Anderson considers them as absolutely binding, and rejects the distinction between decisions on matters of faith and doctrine, and decisions in personal or public matters. In the declaration and testimony of the Associate Presbytery, adopted in 1784 and revised in 1813, Art. 10, sec. 5, par. 3, it is expressly declared, that their decisions, if not agreeable to the word of God, are not to be received; and the right of every man to judge for himself, concerning the determinations of church judicatories, is expressly recognized. In the proceedings before the Vice-Chancellor of the State of New-York, between Stevenson and Dr. Bullions, I find Mr. Anderson claimed, that, if Dr. Bullions had a seat in the presbytery in a trial then pending, he should claim, in the event of the decision being against him, that the proceeding was vitiated by Dr. Bullions' having a seat; and at the time of the secession of the Associate Church from the General Assembly in Scotland, in 1733, by Erskine and others, in their review of the proceedings of the judicatories again them, they say, "We are indeed bound at our ordination to subject ourselves unto the judicatories of the church; but it is not an absolute subjection that we engage unto," not a "blind and implicit obedience;" and they proceed to declare, that the same vows, which bound them formerly to communion, equally bound them to secede. Non nobis tantas componere lites. We can only observe, that the doctrine of passive obedience and non-resistance, which was exploded in that last century, cannot find favor, at this day, in a court of justice. These different and discordant views of the duty of submission, and indeed the whole controversy in this case, show how impossible it is for a court of law to endeavor to fix any standard, by which to determine and regulate the duty of obedience to the proceedings of any voluntary associations, whether for civil or ecclesiastical purposes, and how unsafe and improper it would be, to consider any church as vacant, and the relation of minister and church, or congregation dissolved, against the consent of both, by the sentence, or decree, of an ecclesiastical court, to which, at the most, only a voluntary obedience can be required.

It is, however, claimed, in this case, that there is an implied contract between a minister and his people, that he should continue in the same ecclesiastical connection; and that, Mr. Pringle having been suspended from the exercise of his ministry, the contract between him and his people is dissolved, and the congregation cannot be entitled to any funds, given or appropriated for the support of a minister; that the intent of the testator was to give this legacy to the congregation at Ryegate, as a part, or branch, of the associate church of the United States; and that, as the associate church have, according to the rules of discipline, deprived Mr. Pringle of the character of minister, no benefit can be had from this legacy for his support. This involves the consideration of the subject of such implied contract, the intent of the testator, and the proceedings of the different presbyteries and of the synod, according to their rules of discipline and church government, and, as a branch of the first inquiry, the right of secession.

With respect to any implied contract between a minister and his people, it may be remarked of this, as well as of any other contract, that we cannot add any thing by implication to the express terms of the contract itself. The parties may make conditions and qualifications, as they deem necessary. It may be true of this, as of all other agreements for future services, that there must continue and remain an ability to perform, or the party failing may be subject to the consequences attached to a breach of an obligation. When a minister ceases to be able to perform his ministerial duties, in consequence of any immorality, or a church censure for such immorality, it may afford a sufficient reason for the parties mutually to dissolve the relation, or for one of them to treat the contract as forfeited and rescinded by the other. But when both parties to the contract are satisfied, and neither desires the relation to be dissolved, it is not for this court, at the instance of others, not parties to the contract, to seek for understandings and implications, by which to avoid it, or to inquire, whether it would conduce to the satisfaction of others, to have a more acceptable minister, or one more closely connected with the denomination to which he belongs...

There is still remaining a question of importance in this case, which has been elaborately argued, and to which the attention of the court has been directed, that is, whether, according to the rules of discipline of the associate church, Mr. Pringle has been properly suspended and deposed from the ministry. It seems to be necessary, that the court should decide this question, as it may be and has been claimed, that, if he is regularly deposed, the avails of the legacy in question ought either to be decreed to the minority adhering to the synod, or divided between those who adhere to him and those who adhere to the synod. The court approach this question with some diffidence, as we have not the aid of previous acquaintance with the rules of church government and discipline recognized in this denomination of christians and as the cases, which may be found in our English reports, have no relation to ecclesiastical organization and proceedings, as they exist in this country.

But examining the proceedings of the judicatories, which have been had in the case under consideration, by the rules applied to ecclesiastical courts in Great Britain, we should, without much hesitation, come to the conclusion, that the proceedings, which have been had in relation to the presbytery of Vermont and Mr. Pringle, are irregular, arbitrary and wholly void. To excommunication in England certain civil disabilities are attached. To aid in carrying into effect a sentence of excommunication, a writ de excommunicato capiendo may issue out of chancery, which has been said by some to be a writ grantable ex debito justitiae, by others ex gratia. This writ is said to be a liberty, or privilege, peculiar to the church of England, above all the realms of christendom, as being more sure and effectual, than any other aid of the secular power afforded elsewhere. When a person was taken and in custody on such writ, the regularity of the proceedings of the court passing such sentence might be inquired into on habeas corpus; 1 Salk. 293; and the party be relieved, if the proceedings were irregular. In 12 Co. 76 it was held, that, if a man be excommunicated by the bishop wrongfully and against law, he shall have a writ out of chancery, directed to the bishop, commanding him to assoil him, that is, to release, or absolve him. In the case of Beaurain v. Scott, 3 Camp. 388, the defendant, as Vicar General of the Bishop of London, had excommunicated the plaintiff for not appearing as guardian ad litem to his son. For this excommunication an action was sustained against the defendant, notwithstanding he acted as judge of the ecclesiastical court, because the court had no authority to compel the plaintiff, against his will, to be guardian ad litem, and also for some irregularity in their proceedings. On these questions evidence was given, and the effect of the evidence left to the jury. In Beaurain's Case, 16 Vessey 346, the court of chancery sustained jurisdiction of a motion for a writ to issue to the bishop, commanding him to absolve a person, who had been excommunicated for a cause, for which, by the law, they had no authority to excommunicate. These cases show, that the proceedings of an ecclesiastical court in England may be examined into collaterally, and that the sentence of such court is not as conclusive, as has been claimed for the adjudications of the synod in this case. [Discussion of Scottish cases is omitted.]

These cases show, that the proceedings of an ecclesiastical court in England and Scotland may be inquired into collaterally, and that, when they proceed illegally, even those who pronounced their decrees are not exempt from responding for any damages, which an individual may sustain in consequence of their illegal acts. And surely, if the proceedings of an ecclesiastical tribunal, known to the law, may be a subject of inquiry in the courts of Great Britain and Scotland, and the parties injured may have redress in the civil courts by action, the proceedings of any self-constituted ecclesiastical tribunal, not recognized as a part of our jurisprudence, may be examined, disregarded and declared void, whenever the subject comes before our courts of law, whether directly or collaterally. The proceedings of the synod, or of any other ecclesiastical tribunal in this country, as a court of the last resort, are not to be held conclusive and absolute, when they come in question in courts of law...

Gartin, &c. v. Penick, &c.
Court of Appeals of Kentucky, 1868
5 Bush 100

Judge Robertson delivered the opinion of the majority of the court:

This litigation between conflicting sections of a once harmonious, but now discordant body of Presbyterians, involves fundamental principles in church and State peculiar to our own jurisprudence, and essential to the purity of religion and to the civil liberty contemplated by the Constitutions of the Anglo-American Union and States.

As early as the year 1828, a Presbyterian Church, called the "Bethel Union," was organized in Marion county, Kentucky. In the year 1857, the appellant, B. N. Penick, who was a member of that church, conveyed to Chandler and others, in trust for its use, several acres of land, on which it erected a new house of worship. That dedication was to "The Bethel Union Church" without any other description or limitation. At that time this church was affiliated with the "New School" organization of Presbyterianism. The deed of 1857, duly acknowledged and recorded, was burnt with the records of the clerk's office in the year 1863; and Penick, in the year 1865, made, without authority, another conveyance of the same house and ground to other trustees for the use of the "Bethel Union Church, adhering to the General Assembly." Nearly a year after the conveyance of 1857, the members of the "Bethel Union" unanimously joined the "Old School" organization.

Until about the year 1861, the members of this church appear to have harmonized as a fraternal unit in the use of the church property, and afterwards to have continued, though rather discordantly, the joint use of it, until the year 1867, when certain "deliverances," and other disturbing acts of the General Assembly, hereafter to be considered, had culminated in a partial disruption of the Presbyterian Church as a national unity. After that catastrophe, the appellee, Penick, and about half of the other members of the "Bethel Union," adhered to the General Assembly, and the appellant, Gartin, and his associated, cooperated with the protesting party. Penick and his concurrent associates asserted and strove to maintain a right to the exclusive use of the church property, while Gartin and his party, asserting the like right, proposed, as a compromise, an equal and alternate enjoyment of the property. This conflict resulted in this appeal by both parties to the civil tribunals of the State; and here, without now noticing the voluminous pleadings and testimony, it is sufficient to say, that the circuit court adjudged to the appellees the exclusive use of all the property of the "Bethel Union" Church; and that, by this appeal, the appellants seek a reversal of that judgment.

In revising the case, this court, in the logical and necessary order of consideration, must first dispose of the controverted question of jurisdiction by the civil power of the State, and which both parties acknowledged by invoking its intervention.

A church, like every other organized body of citizens, must be consolidated by an organic law; and, under and according to the Constitution of the United States, the organic law of the Presbyterian Church is a fundamental compact, voluntarily made between all the members of the unincorporated association, for the guidance and protection of each constituent church and member, and necessarily inviolable by any delegated power of the aggregate church. Its supremacy over all representative organs deriving their authority from it, and therefore subordinate to it, was the great end, and must be the necessary consequence of its adoption. It defines the sphere of the "General Assembly," as the organized representative of all the members of the Presbyterian Church, as a Christian nationality, subordinate to the political sovereignty of the civil union, which is as supreme over members of churches as over any other citizens. Hence, all acts of the General Assembly not sanctioned by its own, as well as the Federal Constitution, are, like ultra-constitutional acts of Congress, void; and that which is void can impose no obligation, even on the conscience. As no act of an agent is the act of the principal, except so far as it was authorized by the charter or other contract of delegation, so the constituent body in either church or State is not bound by any act of its organic representative - legislative, judicial, or executive - unauthorized by its charter of authority. No such unauthorized act of Congress or of the General Assembly can be law; and it is even a misnomer to call it, as it is loosely called, "an unconstitutional law," instead of an unconstitutional act; for, being as much a legal nullity as if it had never been enacted, it is, in no sense, law, which is necessarily supreme.

The political government is founded on the civil Constitution; the ecclesiastical, on the Bible; but the Bible and the Constitution harmonize in aim and in spirit, and religion and politics should go hand in hand together, each equally free, and neither presuming to control the other in its legitimate sphere. This is the true, and only true, illustration of the modern maxim, that church and State should be kept separate. It is the vital principle of both civil and religious liberty, and its universal prevalence would secure liberty, purify religion, and promote the welfare of mankind.

In the administration of this dual government, justly styled North American, let the political power confine itself to secular, and the ecclesiastical to spiritual interests and concerns, and all may be well, as anticipated by our fathers; and these fundamental doctrines are recognized alike by the Bible and by the Constitution, and are also ratified by the organic law of the Presbyterian Church of these United States...

The 2d section of the 31st chapter of the Confession of Faith, as a part of the organic law of the church, defines the jurisdiction of synods and councils, and confines it to controversies of faith and cases of conscience, rules for public worship and government of the church, and "complaints in cases of maladministration," and, repudiating any other than moral coercion, prescribes "reverence and submission" as the only sanctions of "their decrees and determinations, if consonant with the word of God"; and the third and fourth sections are as follows:

3d. "All synods or councils, since the Apostles' times, whether general or particular, may err, and may have erred; they are not to be made the rule of faith or practice, but to be used as a help in both."

4th. "Synods and councils are to handle or conclude nothing but that which is ecclesiastical, and are not to intermeddle with civil affairs which concern the Commonwealth, unless by humble petition in cases extraordinary, or by way of advice for satisfaction of conscience, if they be thereunto required by the civil magistrate."

The political constitutions of the National and each of the State governments recognize, in various modes, these fundamental principles and doctrines of both church and State; and thus we may see that all our organic institutions harmonize on this delicate and interesting subject. Consequently, to a rational mind as free as a tabula rasa, there can be no plausible doubt that the General Assembly, as the head of the Presbyterian Church, can have no reasonable pretense for attempting control over any civil right or duty; and that no department of the civil power has any semblance of authority to secularize the church, or interfere with the acts of the General Assembly in constitutionally exercising its ecclesiastical jurisdiction; but the organic law of the church, like that of the State, being a contract between all the parties to it, and the members of the church being entitled, as citizens, to the protection of the paramount constitution of the State against all wrongful breaches of their contracts, the civil tribunals must have some rightful jurisdiction over the constitution of the church as a contract not less obligatory than any other contract between competent parties; and those tribunals must have jurisdiction also to protect a member of the church against unconstitutional invasion of his fundamental right to personal liberty and security, whenever attempted by his ecclesiastical government inconsistently with either its own constitution or that of the political government. A contrary assumption would magnify the General Assembly beyond the sphere of its own organic law, and install it as an arbitrary, infallible, and final power above all constitutional restraint; and would thus exile members of the church from the guardianship of the civil and only supreme human power, which is bound to protect them as well as all other citizens in their property and personal liberty; but, as they joined the church with a knowledge of its defined powers, and as the civil power cannot interfere in matters of conscience, faith, or discipline, they must submit to rebuke or excommunication, however unjust, by their adopted spiritual advisers and ecclesiastical rulers. So far the jurisdiction of the General Assembly is exclusive and final; but it has no such jurisdiction over property, nor any authority to imprison a member of the church, whose locomotive liberty as a citizen must be protected by the civil power against all ecclesiastic or other usurpation.

Having thus drawn the line imperfectly, but, as we think, truly, between civil and ecclesiastical power and jurisdiction, we may be content with making it more luminous and certain by a reference to a few adjudged cases in Scotland and England corroborating our general theory, and substantially confirmed by many American adjudications which we need not cite. All those cases involved the principles which control this case...

Without more elaboration, we conclude that our jurisdiction in this case is sufficiently established by policy, principle, and authority...

The second question to be now considered is less important, but more difficult, than the first just disposed of in this opinion. Whether the appellants or the appellees, as now constituting separate churches, are entitled to the exclusive or alternate use of the property claimed by each party, depends on the essential identity of one or both of them with the

Bethel Union Church to whose use that property was dedicated...

From the pleadings and proofs, the judicial deduction is inevitable that the appellants and the appellees, as now organized, constitute separate and antagonistic churches, each claiming to be the church to which the property in litigation was dedicated; and, consequently, the question now to be decided is one of identity, involving in its solution the equitable title to property dependent on contract, which this court must, when, as in this case, appealed to, interpret and uphold as well between ecclesiastical as civil bodies, or any other parties. The contract is purely civil, and not ecclesiastical, and the usufructuary rights resulting from it depend on the laws of the land, and not on the arbitrium of the General Assembly of the Church, which has no civil power; but within the limits of the political and ecclesiastical constitutions, has supreme and final jurisdiction over church doctrines and discipline. The jurisdiction of the civil tribunals over church property does not, therefore, conflict with the exclusive jurisdiction of the General Assembly in the plenitude of its ecclesiastical power, either legislative or judicial...

From their first connection with that council until the churches, as well as the States, had become distracted by the late civil convulsion, the members of the Bethel Union Church had been signally blessed by Christian fraternity and concord, and without disturbance, harmonized with the General Assembly; but the stultifying passions excited by that revolutionary commotion developed a general demoralization, as contagious in our ecclesiastical as in our political councils. In the rapid progress of moral deterioration, Congress and the General Assembly, each representing the Union section of the belligerents, seemed to cooperate, pari passu, in proscribing the revolting section and its sympathizers everywhere, and each body assumed undelegated powers especially for enforcing "loyalty" and the abolition of slavery. Antecedently to that elemental war, fanatical abolitionists had, by premature and lawless disturbance of that domestic institution of many of the States, frenzied the popular mind and jeoparded the Union; and many professors of Christianity had sympathized with them in their reckless crusade, in defiance of the prophetic warnings of the most eminent and philantropic of American Christians and statesmen...

In the year 1845, the following question was propounded to the General Assembly: "Do the Scriptures teach that the holding of slaves, without regard to circumstances, is a sin, the rununciation of which should be made a condition of membership in the Church of Christ?" And the Assembly answered that question in the following words: "It is impossible to answer the question in the affirmative without contradicting some of the plainest declarations of the word of God. That slavery existed in the days of Christ and his Apostles, is an admitted fact; that they did not denounce the relation as sinful, as inconsistent with Christianity; that slaveholders were admitted to membership in the churches organized by the Apostles; that, whilst they were required to treat their slaves with kindness, and, if Christians, as brethren in the Lord, they were not commanded to emancipate them. The Assembly cannot, therefore, denounce the holding of slaves as necessarily a heinous and scandalous sin, calculated to bring on the Church of Christ the curse of God, without charging the Apostles of Christ with conniving at sin, introducing into the church such sinners, and then bringing upon them the curse of the Almighty." We will also see whether late Assemblies have not tattered and torn this graceful cap.

These noble principles and prudent sentiments seem to have been faithfully observed by the Assembly until the year 1861; and, had that observance been continued until now, it might have been better for the Union, better for peace, better for both races, white and black, and much better for the cause of pure and evangelical religion. But that elevated neutrality in politics, which had eminently characterized the General Assembly in successive agitations of slavery, nullification, national bank, annexation of Texas, and other disturbing questions, yielding at last to the spirit of the civil war, the General Assembly, sitting in Philadelphia in the year 1861, so far fell from grace as to inaugurate its political partisanship, by a resolution pledging its devotion to the Union, and its support of the Frederal administration in its efforts to put down the rebellion. The Synods of Kentucky, Missouri, New Jersey, and Pennsylvania, and many Presbyteries, recorded their disapprobation of that initial "deliverence" as unconstitutional and pregnant with mischief. The language of the Kentucky protest, moulded by two of her most distinguished Doctors of Divinity, the Rev. R. J. Breckinridge and E. P. Humphrey, was as follows: "This Synod contents itself with the expression of its grave disapprobation of this action of the General Assembly, which the Synod judges to be repugnant to the word of God, as that word is interpreted in our Confession of Faith."

The Synod of Missouri resolved, "that the action of the General Assembly, in relation to the political condition of the country, was unscriptural, unconstitutional, unwise, and unjust; and we, therefore, solemnly protest against it, and declare it of no binding force whatever upon the synod, or upon the members of the Presbyterian Church within our bounds"...

While President Lincoln's proclamation of emancipation had aggravated the horrors of the war, and perverted it from a defense of the Union into a military crusade against slavery, the General Assembly of 1864, without disguise, boldly entered the political field, and espoused the cause of extirpating that domestic institution at once by force and in blood. It then made the following declarations: "The Assembly, in the name of the Presbyterian Church, expresses her thanks to Almighty God that the President of the United States has proclaimed the abolition of slavery within most of the rebellious States, and has decreed its extinction by military force. He has ordered the enlistment of soldiers and those formerly held as slaves in the national armies. It is the President's declared policy not to consent to the reorganization of civil government within the seceded States upon any other basis than that of emancipation."

"Our communion must also be mindful of the fact that now, while multitudes of these freedmen are taught the use of arms, and have been trained in military tactics, and inspired with the thought that they are now called of God to conquer for their people a position among the races of mankind," &c.

How far these extraordinary declarations of presumptuous dogmas, which have long vexed enlightened jurists and philanthropists, were consistent with the Constitution or the Bible, or wise economy or humanity, this court will not presume to say; but it must say, that they signalized the Assembly as an intermeddling and revolutionary partisan in an unconstitutional, unholy, and bloody work of abolition by armies, and even servile war and insurrection.

The Assembly of 1865, after the close of the war, ordered all Presbyteries to examine southern applicants for admission into the church on the subjects of the rebellion and slavery, and to reject all who should admit their agency in the revolt, or their belief that slavery is an ordinance of God, unless "they give evidence of repentance for their sin and renounce their error." It also endorsed all the acts of the administration during the war, and specially approved the military intervention of General Rosecrans in the organization of Presbyterian courts in Missouri, and published, what might have been expected, that "the spirit of true worship has almost fled from the sanctuary;" and of that decay of the Christian spirit of faith and love, the belligerent conduct of the Assembly itself, contrary to both the ecclesiastical and civil constitutions, was not only proof, but an efficient cause.

As might have been expected, if the free and self-poised spirit of true Christianity still lived in the Presbyterian Churches, many of them remonstrated against the political interferences and intolerant proscriptions by the Assembly, as manifested by most of the foregoing "deliverances."

The most conspicuous of these protests was an argumentative document called "The Declaration and Testimony," signed by a multitude of Kentucky Presbyterians, and adopted by the Presbytery of Louisville in September, 1865. After arguing to prove the unconstitutionality of some of the Assembly's deliverances since 1861, and especially those of 1864 and 1865 on loyalty and slavery, this famous protest concludes in the following language:

"We declare our deliberate purpose, trusting in God, who can save by few as well as by many, to use our best endeavors to bring back the church of our fathers to her ancient purity and integrity, upon the foundation of the Apostles and Prophets, and under the banner of our only King, Priest, and Prophet, the Lord Jesus Christ. In this endeavor we pledge ourselves to assist and cooperate with each other. And, by the grace of God, we will never abandon the effort, no matter what sacrifices it may require us to make, until we shall either have succeeded in reforming the church and restoring her tarnished glory, or, failing in this, necessity shall be laid on us, in obedience to apostolic command, to withdraw from those who have departed from the truth. Compelled to this course, we will go, bearing with us the true Presbyterian Church, with her doctrine, order, worship, and freedom, as they have been given her by the Divine Head, and transmitted from generation to generation by the hands of saints, confessors, and martyrs."

The General Assembly of 1866 condemned that document "as a slander against the Presbyterian Church, schismatical in its character and aims, and its adoption by any of our church courts as an act of rebellion against the authorities of the General Assembly;" and, arraigning the signers and Presbytery at Louisville for trial at the next General Assembly, resolved, that "until their case is decided, they shall not be permitted to sit as members of any church court higher than the Session;" and also declared, that if any Presbytery should, during that suspension, enrol any such person, it should be "ipso facto dissolved."

The Assembly of 1867 required the remonstrants to make humiliating acknowledgments as a sine qua non to their restoration; and declared that all who should refuse to make such concessions should "be dropped from the roll, as having voluntarily withdrawn from the jurisdiction of the Presbyterian Church of the United States of America, under the care of the General Assembly; and they shall thenceforth be regarded as being no longer ministers in or members of said Presbyterian Church."

There were then in Kentucky six Presbyteries, one hundred and sixty-three churches, one hundred and eight ministers, and nearly twelve thousand members of the Presbyterian denomination; and of these, only thirty-two ministers, twenty-eight church, and about eighteen hundred members, adhered to the General Assembly; the residue, consisting a very large majority, unwilling to submit to what they held to be unscriptural and unconstitutional orders of the General Assembly, united on the "Declaration and Testimony" platform, and were, for this heroic recusancy, and for imputed insubordination and contempt, irregularly exscinded without trial. A recital of all the intermediate proceedings by all parties is deemed useless in the decision of this case. They will betray the same unsanctified temper.

The appellees, submitting to the General Assembly, and recognizing its asserted powers, continued under its assumed jurisdiction; but the appellants, uniting with the non-conformists, reorganized themselves as the Bethel Union under the auspices of the excommunicated party. These conflicting communities of a dissevered church no longer communed together; but by amicable arrangement, each party occupied the same house of worship on alternate days - the appellants on the first and third, and the appellees on the second and fourth Sabbaths of each month; but finally, the appellees, claiming the exclusive use of it, attempted to exclude the appellants altogether; and this litigation is the monstrous offspring of that unrighteous conflict.

"The Declaration and Testimony" was neither insubordinate nor contemptuous, unless it be insubordinate to act according to religious conscience, and contemptuous to vindicate the act by decent argument and hold appeal to the Bible, to the example of the Founder of Christianity, and to the principles of the Constitution of the United States, and to that of the Presbyterian Churvh founded expressly on the revealed will of God, all of which are supreme over the will of the General Assembly. Entertaining the opinions and principles which the remonstrants professed, they not only had a moral and constitutional right to protest, as they did, but would have been guilty of recreance from their sacred duty had they, by servile submission to a false notion of the infalibility and supremacy of the Assembly, sacrilegiously stifled conscience, and prostituted religion at the shrine of usurped power. Right or wrong in their sentiments, they preferred the martyrdom of excommunication to typocritical recantation and unconscientious co-operation in what they felt to be a wrongful perversion of free religion to an illicit connection with turbulent politics, and thereby adulterating both civil and ecclesiastical government; but for this manifesto and a consistent adherence to it, the Assembly renounced all connection with them. This it had the constitutional power to do, without civil remedy for any abuse of that mere power. Nevertheless, if its acts which were complained of were unconstitutional, and therefore void, the expulsion cannot affect property which the civil tribunals are bound to protect. Then, were any of those acts unconstitutional? We think that they were demonstrably so. But we deem it sufficient to illustrate this conclusion by the deliverances of 1864-'5 on loyalty and slavery. These, at all time, would have been unauthorized interferences with civil affairs; but the crisis aggravated their flagrancy. The seceding States asserted the doctrine of paramount allegiance to the individual States; the non-seceding claimed it for the Union; and this conflict of radical principles was an efficient cause of the insurrectional war. This difference in theory was not less sectional than the war itself. Each section denounced as treason what was loyalty in the other; and even in the Union sections there were various notions of loyalty to the National Government. While many rightly considered devotion to the Constitution as the only true loyalty, a majority treated it as disloyalty when not subservient to all the acts of the Federal administration, constitutional or unconstitutional, right or wrong.

The sentiment on the subject of slavery was also essentially sectional, and was the proximate cause of the war. One party considered it a sin, and, treating it as a crime, advocated its extinction at any time, under all circumstances, and by all possible means. Many of the pro-slavery party tolerated it as legal, and others considered it a providential blessing to the black race, by translating barbarous and hopeless Africans to America, where they were rescued from the worst form of slavery, and secured from the doom of sacrifice, always imminent in their native country, and were gradually civilized and Christianized for their own exaltation and for the regeneration of their fatherland. They also thought that, when the white and black races co-exist on the same territory in such relative proportions as in this country, the security of both races required the subordination of the black to the white race, and that such subordination could not be secured otherwise than by slavery in some form; that, in the providence of God, those races are immiscible without great deterioration of the Caucasian blood and degradation of society; that the Union would never have been formed had not its architects conceded to each State the exclusive right to control all its domestic relations; and that, therefore, the Federal Government had no right, in any mode, to interfere with the institution of slavery; that the abolition of slavery, to be tolerable, must be spontaneous and gradual; and that the immediate and forcible emancipation of four millions of slaves would be a greater curse to both races than American slavery could be felt to be by any considerate abolitionist; and this was the opinion of Henry Clay, a lifetime emancipationist, and also of Abraham Lincoln, who, though zealously anti-slavery, yet, not two weeks before the promulgation of his emancipation proclamation, published that he had no power to abolish slavery, and that if he had, he would not do it suddenly or forcibly, which he would apprehend as a greater evil than slavery itself.

Now, whatever may have been intended, the deliverances of the Assembly on loyalty, which it defined as co-operation with the Government in whatever it might do, and on the abolition of slavery at once, and even by servile war, must have tended to widen the breach, aggravate and prolong the war, and retard restoration; and there can be no candid pretense for saying that, by this conduct, so inflammatory and inopportune, the General Assembly did not try to guide civil affairs, and unconstitutionally intermeddled with vital questions in all-absorbing politics.

We will not debate so plain a question. The inevitable conclusion is, that the General Assembly itself forced the dismemberment of the Presbyterian Church by acts which are void for want of higher authority; and, consequently, even if the appellants held their interest in the church property by the tenure of adherence to the Assembly, a severance of that connection by the unauthorized acts of the Assembly cannot affect the title to the property. They are still, in every essential element of identity, the same "Bethel Union Church" as always hitherto. There might be more reason for saying that the General Assembly has lost its own identity. It is certainly not what it was always before the civil war. By its belligerent anti-slaveryism and political propagandism, it forced a division of one American and once homogeneous church into two sectional and alien churches, and the disruption of the union between itself and many dissenting churches of the Northern section; and its changed conduct has, without any constitutional amendment, practically made vital innovations in its Confession of Faith and its constitution of government. In this way, and by its excinding resolution of 1867, it compelled a dissolution of all ties of government and allegiance between itself as organic head of the church, and the appellants as a reorganized and independent church. If the title to the church property had been granted on the condition of continued connection with the General Assembly, still, if that union has been dissolved by the unconstitutional acts of the Assembly, the condition has become impossible, and the property, liberated from the condition, may be held just as if there had never been such a limitation; and upon the foregoing considerations we adjudge that it may be so held now, even if the title should depend on the conveyance of 1865; but, as before suggested, the only valid title was passed by the deed of 1857, which contained no such condition; and in either aspect of the title, the reorganized church of the appellants, still called "Bethel Union," no having, as before decided, lost its essential identity, the final conclusion is, that the appellants, as now organized in a church capacity, have a right to use the property of the "Bethel Union" Church; but whether the appellees are entitled to any use, we cannot decide on the issue made between the litigants, whereby the appellants claim only one half of the use, as stipulated by compromise.

Wherefore, the judgment of the circuit court is reversed, and the cause remanded, with instructions to secure to the appellants, by all proper means, the undisturbed use of the church for one half of the time which may be dedicated to religious services.

CHIEF JUSTICE WILLIAMS, concurring in the judgment of the majority of the Court - ...

It may, perhaps, be proper to observe, that, as this slavery agitation in the church tribunals has been disastrous to the church, especially to the southern branch, so its agitation in the civil courts will likely be the Trojan horse that will develop within its citadel a most devouring enemy to the southern churches of all denominations.

If civil courts, regarding church constitutions and organizations as civil contracts, look into the action of church tribunals, and pronounce them violations of such contracts, and, therefore, null, there will scarcely be an adjudicated question by such tribunals that may not be reviewed in a secular court, in one aspect or another, and under one pretext or another; and, of all other things this is most to be dreaded and shunned by the southern churches of all denominations.

In all the Federal domain south of Kentucky, to what Caesar can they with confidence apply? Do the southern churches which identified themselves with the cause of the "Confederate States" desire that the civil courts, organized upon the negro-voting population of their States, could have jurisdiction to examine their church action, and test its validity by their church constitution as a civil contract? And is the destiny of these churches to be handed over to such civil courts that a few Presbyterian Churches in Kentucky may have the protecting care of her civil courts? Except Kentucky, Maryland, and Delaware, to which of the thirty-six Supreme Courts of the American States would these churches look with confidence? Which of fifty District Courts of the United States, or, soon to be erected, nine United States Circuit Courts, would they prefer to their own tribunals? If church constitutions are to be regarded as civil contracts, and, therefore, cognizable in the civil courts, when the Form of Government, Discipline, Articles of Faith, and Church History shall be considered by these southern courts, and the rights of the Presbyterian Churches, in connection with the General Assembly, adhering to the Confederate States, shall be by them reviewed and adjudicated, who can predict the fatal result to those churches; but, were the sad consequences which may flow from such cognizance by those civil courts to stop with them, the result would not be so melancholy, since, by the action of their friends, this devouring power has been invoked; but in this great civil maelstrom will be engulfed all other churches and denominations - the Methodist, Baptist, Episcopalian, Catholic, and Christian, and all others, for, when the jurisdiction of the civil courts over the church constitutions and organizations, as civil contracts, is once firmly fixed, there will be but few questions, immediately or remotely affecting individual rights in church property, which may be adjudicated in ecclesiastical courts, that may not also be reviewed by the civil courts, and thus the independence of church courts will be destroyed, the freedom of the church from the State become a mere myth, and the church tribunals will have to defer to the decisions of the civil courts on their own constitutions and laws, instead of being referred to as true expounders of their own church constitution and doctrines, all of which will finally prove equally disastrous to church and State; and when the most eminent divines and highest church judicatures of both divisions of this church, and both ecclesiastical jurisdictions, assert the power and act upon the subjects of slavery and loyalty, how a civil court can deny to them this power, I am at a loss to know...

It is remarkable that not a single case in Kentucky, until the late case of Watson v. Avery, 2 Bush, 336, ever suggested or determined the rights of church litigants on the idea that church constitutions, creeds, etc., were to be regarded as civil contracts; and not a single case, either American or British, which I have seen, has predicated their rights on any such principle...

What church is now willing to surrender its claim to divine origin, and place the same upon the basis of mere civil contracts between men? Are even the Presbyterians of the South willing to concede this? Churches claiming divine origin can no more place their church constitution, laws, and powers on the basis of civil contracts than can they so place the holy word of God. If it is not a government authorized by, and derived its power from, the Holy Scriptures and God, their author, then it is merely the work of men, and may be truly regarded as a civil contract, in the same light that human governments and constitutions are...

There is a material and significant distinction between our statute of 1814, under which all previous decisions of this court as to the right of joint participation by contending parties have been heretofore made, and our Revised Statutes of 1850, and which must govern this case, because the original deed has since been made.

The provisions of the statute of 1814, in case of a division or schism for other cause than immorality, were that nothing in said act should be construed to "authorize said trustees to prevent either of the parties so divided from using the house or houses of worship for the purposes of devotion;" nor were they to be construed "to authorize the minority of any church having seceded from, or been expelled, or excommunicated, to interfere in any manner in their appointments for preaching or worship with any appointments for similar purposes, which may have been made by the body or major part of such church or congregation."

As was said by this court in Gibson et al. vs. Armstrong [B. Mon. 481] "the trustees were prohibited from using their authority under the statute to prevent either party from a proportioned use," because, as before said in the same case, they might be identified with one of the parties; but it did not mean to declare a right; whereas, by the Revised Statutes, it is positively and peremptorily enacted that the trustees "shall permit each party to use the church"; and the next subdivision provides that the "excommunication of one party by the other shall not impair such right, except it be done bona fide on the ground of immorality." It is, therefore, palpable, that the latter enactment declared a legal right in all members, when a division or schism occurs, for anything else than immorality, to still continue in the enjoyment of the benefits of the trust, according to the numbers of each party. The restricted operation of the statute of 1814, as construed by the courts, rendered it almost inoperative and useless, which was doubtless intended to be remedied by the revision, not only in the change of language on this subject, coupled with an express declaration of right, but also by that provision which declares that courts shall give it a liberal construction to make it accomplish the objects designed.

This statute is just in its provisions, wise in its policy, and should have a liberal construction to secure its equitable benefits. I have no doubt as to its proper application in this case, and therefore, concur in the reversal of the judgment; and am for a direction to the court below to reject the present and to set up the destroyed deed; and further, to secure to each party the alternate use of the church property pro rata, according to the number of communicant members adhering to each party at the time of their separation.

Watson v. Jones
Supreme Court of the United States, 1871
13 Wall. 679

[Statement of facts: Within the Walnut Presbyterian Church in Louisville, Kentucky, two factions similar to those in controversy in Gartin v. Penick, supra, had developed during the Civil War and Reconstruction period. Representatives of the two factions had each claimed that they were entitled to the possession and control of the properties of the Walnut Presbyterian Church, and a suit in equity had been brought in the Kentucky courts resulting in a decision in favor of those persons who had denied the authority of the General Assembly. Thereupon the present suit was brought in a Circuit Court of the United States, its jurisdiction being founded upon diversity of citizenship. There it had been held that the determination of the General Assembly of the Church was conclusive on the civil courts. That decision was affirmed in the Supreme Court of the United States. The concluding portion of the opinion of Mr. Justice Miller, for a majority follows.]

The questions which have come before the civil courts concerning the rights to property held by ecclesiastical bodies, may, so far as we have been able to examine them, be profitably classified under three general heads, which of course do not include cases governed by considerations applicable to a church established and supported by law as the religion of the state.

1. The first of these is when the property which is the subject of controversy has been, by the deed or will of the donor, or other instrument by which the property is held, by the express terms of the instrument devoted to the teaching, support, or spread of some specific form of religious doctrine or belief.

2. The second is when the property is held by a religious congregation which, by the nature of its organization, is strictly independent of other ecclesiastical associations, and so far as church government is concerned, owes no fealty or obligation to any higher authority.

3. The third is where the religious congregation or ecclesiastical body holding the property is but a subordinate member of some general church organization in which there are superior ecclesiastical tribunals with a general and ultimate power of control more or less complete in some supreme judicatory over the whole membership of that general organization.

In regard to the first of these classes it seems hardly to admit of a rational doubt that an individual or an association of individuals may dedicate property by way of trust to the purpose of sustaining, supporting, and propagating definite religious doctrines or principles, provided that in doing so they violate no law of morality, and give to the instrument by which their purpose is evidenced, the formalities which the laws require. And it would seem also to be the obvious duty of the court, in a case properly made, to see that the property so dedicated is not diverted from the trust which is thus attached to its use. So long as there are persons qualified within the meaning of the original dedication, and who are also willing to teach the doctrines or principles prescribed in the act of dedication, and so long as there is any one so interested in the execution of the trust as to have a standing in court, it must be that they can prevent the diversion of the property or fund to other and different uses. This is the general doctrine of courts of equity as to charities, and it seems equally applicable to ecclesiastical matters.

In such case, if the trust is confided to a religious congregation of the independent or congregational form of church government, it is not in the power of the majority of that congregation, however, preponderant, by reason of a change of views on religious subjects, to carry the property so confided to them to the support of new and conflicting doctrine. A pious man building and dedicating a house of worship to the sole and exclusive use of those who believe in the doctrine of the Holy Trinity, and placing it under the control of a congregation which at the time holds the same belief, has a right to expect that the law will prevent that property from being used as a means of support and dissemination of the Unitarian doctrine, and as a place of Unitarian worship. Nor is the principle varied when the organization to which the trust is confided is of the second or associated form of church government.. The protection which the law throws around the trust is the same. And though the task may be a delicate one and a difficult one, it will be the duty of the court in such cases, when the doctrine to be taught or the form of worship to be used is definitely and clearly laid down, to inquire whether the party accused of violating the trust is holding or teaching a different doctrine, or using a form of worship which is so far variant as to defeat the declared objects of the trust. In the leading case on this subject, in the English courts, of the Attorney-General v. Pearson, (2 Merivale, 353) Lord Eldon said, "I agree with the defendants that the religious belief of the parties is irrelevant to the matters in dispute, except so far as the King's Court is called upon to execute the trust." That was a case in which the trust-deed declared the house which was erected under it was for the worship and service of God. And though we may not be satisfied with the very artificial and elaborate argument by which the chancellor arrives at the conclusion, that because any other view of the nature of the Godhead then the Trinitarian view was heresy by the laws of England, and any one giving expression to the Unitarian view was liable to be severely punished for heresy by the secular courts, at the time the deed was made, that the trust was, therefore, for Trinitarian worship, we may still accept the statement that the court has the right to enforce a trust clearly defined on such a subject.

The case of Miller v. Gable (2 Denio, 492) appears to have been decided in the Court of Errors of New York on this principle, so far as any ground of decision can be gathered from the opinions of the majority of the court as reported.

The second class of cases which we have described has reference to the case of a church of a strictly congregational or independent organization, governed solely within itself, either by a majority of its members or by such other local organism as it may have instituted for the purpose of ecclesiastical government, and to property held by such a church, either by way of purchase or donation, with no other specific trust attached to it in the hands of the church than that it is for the use of that congregation as a religious society.

In such cases where there is a schism which leads to a separation into distinct and conflicting bodies, the rights of such bodies to the use of the property must be determined by the ordinary principles which govern voluntary associations. If the principle of government in such cases is that the majority rules, then the numerical majority of members must control the right to the use of the property. If there be within the congregation officers in whom are vested the powers of such control, then those who adhere to the acknowledged organism by which the body is governed are entitled to the use of the property. The minority in choosing to separate themselves into a distinct body, and refusing to recognize the authority of the governing body, can claim no rights in the property from the fact that they had once been members of the church or congregation. This ruling admits of no inquiry into the existing religious opinions of those who comprise the legal or regular organization; for, if such were permitted, a very small minority, without any officers of the church among them, might be found to be the only faithful supporters of the religious dogmas of the founders of the church. There being no such trust imposed upon the property when purchased or given, the court will not imply one for the purpose of expelling from its use those who by regular succession and order constitute the church, because they may have changed in some respect their views of religious truth.

Of the cases in which this doctrine is applied no better representative can be found than that of Shannon v. Frost (3 B. Monro, 253) where the principle is ably supported by the learned Chief Justice of the Court of Appeals of Kentucky.

The case of Smith v. Nelson (18 Vermont, 511) asserts this doctrine in a case where a legacy was left to the Associate Congregation of Ryegate, the interest whereof was to be annually paid to their minister forever. In that case, though the Ryegate congregation congregation was one of a number of Presbyterian churches connected with the general Presbyterian body at large, the court held that the only inquiry was whether the society still exists, and whether they have a minister chosen and appointed by the majority and regularly ordained over the society, agreeably to the usage of that denomination. And though we may be of opinion that the doctrine of that case needs modification, so far as it discusses the relation of the Ryegate congregation to the other judicatories of the body to which it belongs, it certainly lays down the principle correctly if that congregation was to be treated as an independent one.

But the third of these classes of cases is the one which is oftenest found in the courts, and which, with reference to the number and difficulty of the questions involved, and to other considerations, is every way the important.

It is the case of property acquired in any of the usual modes for the general use of a religious congregation which is itself part of a large and general organization of some religious denomination, with which it is more or less intimately connected by religious views and ecclesiastical government.

The case before us is one of this class, growing out of a schism which has divided the congregation and its officers, and the presbytery and synod, and which appeals to the courts to determine the right to the use of the property so acquired. Here is no case of property devoted forever by the instrument which conveyed it, or by any specific declaration of its owner, to the support of any special religious dogmas, or any peculiar form of worship, but of property purchased for the use of a religious congregation, and so long as any existing religious congregation can be ascertained to be that congregation, or its regular and legitimate successor, it is entitled to the use of the property. In the case of an independent congregation we have pointed out how this identity, or succession, is to be ascertained, but in cases of this character we are bound to look at the fact that the local congregation is itself but a member of a much larger and more important religious organization, and is under its government and control, and is bound by its orders and judgments. There are in the Presbyterian system of ecclesiastical government , in regular succession, the presbytery over the session or local church, the synod over the presbytery, and the General Assembly over all. These are called, in the language of the church organs, "judicatories," and they entertain appeals from the decisions of those below, and prescribe corrective measures in other cases.

In this class of cases we think the rule of action which should govern the civil courts, founded in a broad and sound view of the relations of church and state under our system of laws, and supported by a preponderating weight of judicial authority is, that, whenever the questions of discipline, or of faith, or ecclesiastical rule, custom, or law have been decided by the highest of these church judicatories to which the matter has been carried, the legal tribunals must accept such decisions as final, and as binding on them, in their application to the case before them.

We concede at the outset that the doctrine of the English courts is otherwise. In the case of the Attorney-General v. Pearson, cited before, the proposition is laid down by Lord Eldon, and sustained by the peers, that it is the duty of the court in such cases to inquire and decide for itself, not only what was the nature and power of these church judicatories, but what is the true standard of faith in the church organization, and which of the contending parties before the court holds to this standard. And in the subsequent case of Craigdallie v. Aikman, 2 Bligh 529, the same learned judge expresses in strong terms his chagrin that the Court of Sessions of Scotland, from which the case had been appealed, had failed to find on this latter subject, so that he could rest the case on religious belief, but had declared that in this matter there was no difference between the parties. And we can very well understand how the Lord Chancellor of England, who is, in his office, in a large sense, the head and representative of the Established Church, who controls very largely the church patronage, and whose judicial decision may be, and not unfrequently is, invoked in cases of heresy and ecclesiastical contumacy, should feel, even in dealing with a dissenting church, but little delicacy in grappling with the most abstruse problems of theological controversy, or in construing the instruments which those churches have adopted as their rules of government, or inquiring into their customs and usages...

In this country the full and free right to entertain any religious belief, to practice any religious principle, and to teach any religious doctrine which does not violate the laws of morality and property, and which does not infringe personal rights, is conceded to all. The law knows no hersy, and is committed to the support of no dogma, the establishment of no sect. The right to organize voluntary religious associations to assist in the expression and dissemination of any religious doctrine, and to create tribunals for the decision of controverted questions of faith within the association, and for the ecclesiastical government of all the individual members, congregations, and officers within the general association, is unquestioned. All who unite themselves to such a body do so with an implied consent to this government, and are bound to submit to it. But it would be a vain consent and would lead to the total subversion of such religious bodies, if any one aggrieved by one of their decisions could appeal to the secular courts and have them reversed. It is of the essence of these religious unions, and of their right to establish tribunals for the decision of questions arising among themselves, that those decisions should be binding in all cases of ecclesiastical cognizance, subject only to such appeals as the organism itself provides for.

Nor do we see that justice would be likely to be promoted by submitting those decisions to review in the ordinary judicial tribunals. Each of these large and influential bodies (to mention no others, let reference be had to the Protestant Episcopal, the Methodist Episcopal, and the Presbyterian churches), has a body of constitutional and ecclesiastical law of its own, to be found in their written organic laws, their books of discipline, in their collections of precedents, in their usage and customs, which as to each constitute a system of ecclesiastical law and religious faith that tasks the ablest minds to become familiar with. It is not to be supposed that the judges of the civil courts can be as competent in the ecclesiastical law and religious faith of all these bodies as the ablest men in each are in reference to their own. It would therefore be an appeal from the more learned tribunal in the law which should decide the case, to one which is less so.

We have said that these views are supported by the preponderant weight of authority in this country, and for the reasons which we have given, we do not think the doctrines of the English Chancery Court on this subject should have with us the influence which we would cheerfully accord to it on others.

We have already cited the case of Shannon v. Frost, supra, in which the appellate court of the State where this controversy originated, sustains the proposition clearly and fully. "This court," says the Chief Justice, "having no ecclesiastical jurisdiction, cannot revise or question ordinary acts of church discipline. Our only judicial power in the case arises from the conflicting claims of the parties to the church property and the use of it. We cannot decide who ought to be members of the church, nor whether the excommunicated have been justly or unjustly regularly or irregularly cut off from the body of the church."

In the subsequent case of Gibson v. Armstrong (7 B. Monro, 481), which arose out of the general division of the Methodist Episcoapl Church, we understand the same principles to be laid down as governing that case, and in the case of Watson v. Avery (2 Bush, 332) the case relied on by the appellants as a bar, and considered in the former part of this opinion, the doctrine of Shannon v. Frost is in general terms conceded, while a distinction is attempted which we shall consider hereafter. [The review of other American cases, accord, is omitted.]

The Court of Appeals of Kentucky, in the case of Watson v. Avery, before referred to, while admitting the general principle here laid down, maintains that when a decision of an ecclesiastical tribunal is set up in the civil courts, it is always open to inquiry whether the tribunal acted within its jurisdiction, and if it did not, its decision could not be conclusive.

There is, perhaps, no word in legal terminology so frequently used as the word jurisdiction, so capable of use in a general and vague sense, and which is used so often by men learned in the law without a due regard to precision in its application. As regards its use in the matters we have been discussing it may very well be conceded that if the General Assembly of the Presbyterian Church should undertake to try one of its members for murder, and punish him with death or imprisonment, its sentence would be of no validity in a civil court or anywhere else. Or if it should at the instance of one of its members entertain jurisdiction as between him and another member as to their individual right to property, real or personal, the right in no sense depending on ecclesiastical questions, its decision would be utterly disregarded by any civil court where it might be set up. And it might be said in a certain general sense very justly, that it was because the General Assembly had no jurisdiction of the case. Illustrations of this character could be multiplied in which the proposition of the Kentucky court would be strictly applicable.

But it is a very different thing where a subject-matter of dispute, strictly and purely ecclesiastical in its character - a matter over which the civil courts exercise no jurisdiction - a matter which concerns theological controversy, church discipline, ecclesiastical government, or the conformity of the members of the church to the standard of morals required of them, becomes the subject of its action. It may be said here, also, that no jurisdiction has been conferred on the tribunal to try the particular case before it, or that, in its judgment, it exceeds the powers conferred upon it, or that the laws of the church do not authorize the particular form of proceeding adopted; and, in a sense often used in the courts, all of those may be said to be questions of jurisdiction. But it is easy to see that if the civil courts are to inquire into all these matters, the whole subject of the doctrinal theology, the usages and customs, the written laws, and fundamental organization of every religious denomination may, and must, be examined into with minuteness and care, for they would become, in almost every case, the criteria by which the validity of the ecclesiastical decree would be determined in the civil court. This principle would deprive these bodies of the right of construing their own church laws, would open the way to all the evils which we have depicted as attendant upon the doctrine of Lord Eldon, and would, in effect, transfer to the civil courts where property rights were concerned the decision of all ecclesiastical questions.

And this is precisely what the Court of Appeals of Kentucky did in the case of Watson v. Avery. Under cover of inquiries into the jurisdiction of the synod and presbytery over the congregation, and of the General Assembly over all, it went into an elaborate examination of the principles of the highest judicatory of that church in the United States, both on the jurisdiction and the merits; and, substituting its own judgment for that of the ecclesiastical court, decides that ruling elders, declared to be such by that tribunal, are not such, and must not be recognized by the congregation, though four-fifths of its members believe in the judgment of the Assembly and desired to conform to its decree.

But we need pursue this subject no further. Whatever may have been the case before the Kentucky court, the appellants in the case presented to us have separated themselves wholly from the church organization to which they belonged when this controversy commenced. They now deny its authority, denounce its action, and refuse to abide by its judgments. They have first erected themselves into a new organization, and have since joined themselves to another totally different, if not hostile, to the one to which they belonged when the difficulty first began. Under any of the decisions which we have examined, the appellants, in their present position, have no right to the property, or to the use of it, which is the subject of this suit.

The novelty of the questions presented to this court for the first time, their intrinsic importance and far-reaching influence, and the knowledge that the schism in which the case originated has divided the Presbyterian churches throughout Kentucky and Missouri, have seemed to us to justify the careful and laborious examination and discussion which we have made of the principles which should govern the case. For the same reasons we have held it under advisement for a year; not uninfluenced by the hope, that since the civil commotion, which evidently lay at the foundation of the trouble, has passed away, that charity, which is so large an element in the faith of both parties, and which, by one of the apostles of that religion, is said to be the greatest of all the Christian virtues, would have brought about a reconciliation. But we have been disappointed. It is not for us to determine or apportion the moral responsibility which attaches to the parties for this result. We can only pronounce the judgment of the law as applicable to the case presented to us, and that requires us to affirm the decree of the Circuit Court as it stands.

Watson, et al. v. Garvin, et al.
Supreme Court of Missouri, 1873
54 Missouri 353

ADAMS, Judge, delivered the opinion of the court.

This was an action in the nature of a bill in equity, brought by the plaintiffs in the St. Charles Circuit Court, claiming to be the only beneficiaries of certain church property, consisting of a house of worship and a parsonage in the city of St. Charles. They allege that they alone constitute the congregation of the First Presbyterian church of St. Charles, and that the defendants, who at one time formed a part of the congregation, had voluntarily withdrawn from the church, but still held the property, to the exclusion of the plaintiffs. The defendants deny all the allegations of the petition, and charge the facts to be that they and the plaintiffs together constituted the congregation entitled as beneficiaries to the use of the church, up to the time of the dissensions growing out of the action of the General Assembly in its deliverances on the subject of slavery and "loyalty". They deny that they have prevented the plaintiffs from the occupancy of the church jointly with themselves, and charge that the plaintiffs have voluntarily withdrawn and formed an independent congregation. They deny that this independent organization, as such, are beneficiaries entitled to the property in dispute.

The leading facts are, that in the year 1818, a Presbyterian congregation was formed in the town of St. Charles, called and known as the First Presbyterian church of St. Charles. This organization, according to the Confession of Faith and Form of Government of the Presbyterian Church, consisted of persons who had been baptized into the Church and had united together for religious worship. The judicatory of this church was a pastor and two ruling elders, called the session. Under the constitution of the Presbyterian Church, this congregation, with others, united together and formed a presbytery, called the St. Louis Presbytery, and this presbytery and others formed a Synod, and these presbyteries sent their commissioners to the General Assembly. And so in this way the First Presbyterian Church of St. Charles was a part of, and subject to the control of the General Assembly. This General Assembly divided into two General Assemblies in 1837, known as Old School and New School, and the church of St. Charles became united to the Old School.

The deeds under which the property in dispute is held, conveyed it to trustees, "in trust for the congregation of the First Presbyterian Church of St. Charles." There were two deeds; one made in 1833, and the other in 1857, confirming the title conveyed by the first deed. There is nothing in either deed which requires that the congregation should be under the control of any superior judicatory. The facts, however, show that this congregation continued in connection with the St. Louis Presbytery and the General Assembly (Old School) until it was exscinded in the manner hereinafter set forth.

From the commencement of the late war of rebellion, and during its prevalence, the General Assembly (Old School) at its annual meetings made deliverances on the subject of slavery and loyalty, declaring the obligations of the church in this regard. A large minority of the church, in different States considered these deliverances of the General Assembly unconstitutional; that is to say, that the church, as a church, according to its written Confession of Faith and Form of Government, had no authority to make deliverances on purely political and civil matters. This minority protested against these deliverances, and issued a paper called the "Declaration and Testimony", inveighing against the conduct of the majority. This paper gave great offense to the majority, and they took steps for punishing the offenders, which resulted in an ex parte decree rendered by the General Assembly, without the form of trial, declaring in effect that the accused ministers should not be allowed to sit in any church judicatory higher than the session, and that if they, or any of them, should be enrolled as entitled to a seat by any presbytery, such presbytery should, ipso facto, be dissolved, and the members adhering to the General Assembly were thereby authorized and directed to take charge of the presbyterial records, to retain the name, and exercise all the authority and functions of the original presbytery until the next meeting of the General Assembly.

Twenty-two members of the congregation of the First Presbyterian church of St. Charles, being the plaintiffs in this suit, formed a new congregation, with a minister and ruling elders, and betook themselves to another place of worship, leaving the remainder of the congregation, consisting of forty-nine members, a minister and ruling elders, in possession of the church and parsonage. This action was taken by the minority because the majority had expressed their adhesion to the doctrines of the paper known as "The Declaration and Testimony". Both of these congregations sent their respective representatives to the St. Louis Presbytery, which had been formed on the plan directed by the General Assembly by excluding the "Declaration and Testimony members." This presbytery received the delegates sent by the plaintiffs and excluded those sent by the defendants, and made a decree to the effect that the plaintiffs were the real and only congregation composing the First Presbyterian Church of St. Charles, and that the congregation made up of the defendants was not the First Presbyterian Church of St. Charles, or any part of it.

The Circuit Court decreed the property to the use of the plaintiff, excluding the defendants from the same. The defendants appealed to the Sixth District Court, which affirmed the judgment of the Circuit Court, and from this judgment of affirmance the defendants appealed to this court. At the March Term, 1871, this court, then consisting of three judges, reversed the judgments of the District and Circuit Courts, Judge Bliss delivering the opinion of the court. A motion was made for a rehearing and this motion was sustained, and the case was set for a rehearing and continued on the docket for that purpose till the March Term, 1873, when it was re-argued and submitted to the court, and has been under advisement till the present time.

It is proper to state that the court, under a new constitutional amendment, has been re-organized, with two additional judges; and that, as now organized, it consists of five judges, only one of whom was on the bench when the first opinion was delivered. Although we concur in the result arrived at by the court in its former opinion, the importance of the principles involved demands that the court, as now organized, should briefly present the grounds of its assent, and the points passed on by us.

1. At the threshold of this inquiry, we are met with the startling proposition that, in cases like this, the judgment or decrees of ecclesiastical judicatories are final and conclusive, and that the civil courts have no authority in the premises, except to register these decrees and carry them into execution. It is to be regretted that loose expressions, by elementary writers, and also by judges in delivering their opinions, have given too much foundation for this false doctrine. Even the Supreme Court of the

United States, in Watson vs. Jones, 13 Wallace, 679, gives prominence to this idea by making it the chief foundation of their opinion. That court seemed to think the judges not sufficiently learned in ecclesiastical law to pass on such questions, and that the ecclesiastical courts, being better qualified than themselves, ought to be allowed to be the exclusive judges.

The civil courts are presumed to known all the law touching property rights; and if questions of ecclesiastical law, connected with property rights, come before them, they are compelled to decide them. They have no power to abdicate their own jurisdiction and transfer it to other tribunals. If they are not sufficiently [sic] advised concerning the questions that arise, it is their duty to make themselves acquainted with them, in all their bearings, and not to blindly register the decrees of tribunals having no jurisdiction whatever over property.

The true ground why civil courts do not interfere with the decrees of ecclesiastical courts, where no property rights are involved, is not because such decrees are final and conclusive, but because they have no jurisdiction whatever in such matters, and cannot take cognizance of them at all, whether they have been adjudicated or not by those tribunals. This principle forms the foundation of religious liberty in Republican governments. The civil authorities have no power to pass or enforce laws abridging the freedom of the citizen in this regard, and hence, in matters purely religious or ecclesiastical, the civil courts have no jurisdiction.

A deposed minister or an excommunicated member of a church, cannot appeal to the civil courts for redress. They can look alone to their own judicatories for relief, and must abide the judgment of their highest courts as final and conclusive. But when property rights are concerned, the ecclesiastical courts have no power whatever to pass on them so as to bind the civil courts. If they expel a member from his church, and he feels himself aggrieved in his rights of property by the expulsion, he may resort to the civil courts, and they will not consider themselves precluded by the judgment of expulsion, but will examine into the case to see if it has been regularly made upon due notice, and if they find it to be duly made, they will let it stand, otherwise they will disregard it, and give the proper relief. In most cases, no doubt, the judgment will be found to be sufficiently regular to fix the status of the expelled member and to warrant the civil courts in denying the desired relief.

2. This controversy had its origin in the deliverance of the General Assembly regarding slavery and loyalty. If this venerable body had no authority in their ecclesiastical capacity, to make the deliverances in question, the subsequent acts of the church judicatories growing out of them, must be treated as nullities, at least as far as property rights are concerned.

It must be conceded on all hands that questions of slavery and loyalty are merely political and civil, and not ecclesiastical or religious in their nature; and yet it is true as a matter of fact, that during the late war between the States, the highest judicatories of most of the churches, both North and South of the federal lines, bent before the storm of passion that swept over the country and engaged in the strife by entering upon their records deliverances in aid of their respective civil authorities.

Had these judicatories any power in their ecclesiastical capacities to do this is the question raised by this record for us to decide. The Presbyterian Church has always been considered, and no doubt is, one of the orthodox Protestant churches, and as such forming a part of the spiritual kingdom of Christ upon earth. Christ authoritatively declared that His kingdom was not of this world. His disciples, as such, owe allegiance alone to Him as the great Head of the Church. As citizens of a republic or subjects of a monarchy or empire, their civil allegiance was due to their respective governments. But the kingdom of Christ is wholly independent of civil governments. This spiritual kingdom has existed and continued to flourish for almost nineteen centuries. While civil governments of all kinds have arisen and lived for a season and then crumbled and faded away, the kingdom of Christ has stood amidst the throes of revolutions; and in the sure hope and faith of its subjects, it will stand till the end of time, and spread throughout all the regions of the earth, until every knee shall bow in humble submission to His holy will. As the Presbyterian Church is a part of this spiritual kingdom, it had no right as such to interfere in civil matters. But the Presbyterian Church also has a written constitution which their ecclesiastical judicatories have no authority to violate. They are as much bound by the provisions of this constitution as the supreme law of the church, as the State and Federal governments are by their respective constitutions.

The written constitution of the Presbyterian Church contains this section: "IV. Synods and councils are to handle or conclude nothing, but that which is ecclesiastical; and are not to intermeddle with civil affairs which concern the commonwealth, unless by way of humble petition in cases extraordinary; or by way of advice for satisfaction of conscience, if they be thereunto required by the civil magistrate." (See Confession of Faith, chap. 31, sec. 4, pp. 159-60.)

In explanation of this section, which is found word for word in the Confession of Faith of the Westminster Assembly of divines, the Rev. Robert Shaw, whose work is considered as a standard authority, says:

"While our Confession denounces any Erastian interference in matters purely spiritual and ecclesiastical, it no less explicitly disavows all popish claims, on the part of the synods and councils of the church, to intermeddle with civil affairs unless by way of petition in extraordinary cases, or by way of advice when required by the civil magistrate. Our reformers appear to have clearly perceived the proper limits of the civil and ecclesiastical jurisdiction, and to have been very careful that they should be strictly observed. 'The power and policy ecclesiastical,' say they, 'is different and distinct in its own nature from that power and policy which is called civil power, and appertaineth to the civil government of the commonwealth; albeit they be both of God and tend to one end, if they be rightly used, viz; to advance the glory of God and to have godly and good subjects. Diligence should be taken chiefly by the Moderator, that only ecclesiastical things be handled in the Assemblies, and that there be no meddling with anything pertaining to civil jurisdiction.' Church and State may co-operate in the advancement of objects common to both, but each of them must be careful to act within its own sphere, the one never intermeddling with the affairs that properly belong to the province of the other." (See Exposition of the Confession of Faith, p. 337.)

The meaning of the section commented on by Rev. Robert Shaw seems to be sufficiently obvious from its own language, but this authoritative exposition puts at rest any possible doubt as to its true intent. In my judgment it prohibited the General Assembly from making the deliverances under review; and they are therefore nullities so far as property rights are concerned. In pronouncing upon these deliverances, we impute no intentional wrong to that reverend and learned body of divines; we hold them in the highest esteem, and regard them as incapable of any such thing.

3. But if this act of the General Assembly and the excinding decree pronounced against the defendants, be treated as within the scope of ecclesiastical authority, such excision surely ought not to have the legal force of cutting off the property rights of the defendants. The penalty decreed against the offending ministers by the General Assembly did not excommunicate them as church members, nor depose them from their ministerial office. They were declared to be incapable of sitting in any church judicatory higher than the session. But they still held their commissions under which they might "Go into all the world and preach the gospel," receive members into the church, and administer the usual rites to that end, and form congregations of Presbyterians for religious worship.

The exscinding decree against the defendants, cut them off in a body from the higher judicatories of the church, but did not excommunicate them, nor in any manner touch them as individual members of the church or congregation. They occupy in that respect precisely the same attitude they did when they joined the church and made up the congregation. At the time the exscinding decree was pronounced they undoubtedly were beneficiaries entitled to the property in dispute. When this congregation was cut off, their property was cut off with them. If they had money in their treasury to pay their minister or other expenses of the church, that money was cut off with them, and still remained their property subject to their disposition; and in like manner the church edifice and parsonage remain theirs as they were before the excision. If this ipso facto self-executing decree had the effect of destroying existing property rights, it could only do so by overriding the plain provisions of the bill of rights of our State and Federal constitutions, which declare in substance that no person can be deprived of his property without due process of law; and that private property cannot be taken for public use without a just compensation; and that means, that private property cannot be taken at all except for public use and then only on payment of a just compensation. How could the existing property rights of the defendant be transferred from them to the plaintiffs without the form of trial, and without any power in the judicatory to act on such rights? It would seem to be a ridiculous farce to hold that the plaintiffs being a part of the original congregation could separate themselves into a distinct organization and then have themselves declared by an ex parte decree the exclusive owners of the property. If that could be done by a part of a congregation, why could it not be done by strangers to the congregation or emmissaries from other States erecting themselves into a Presbyterian congregation and then calling themselves by the same name and having themselves pronounced by the Presbytery the only genuine congregation, entitled to the treasure and property of the old congregation. Courts of justice are made to protect parties in the enjoyment of their rights of person and property, and not to destroy them by upholding such contrivances. But the deeds themselves, by which the property in dispute is held, show the rights of these parties. It was to be held for the use of the congregation - that is, for the members of the church composing the congregation. They can only cease to be members by voluntarily withdrawing, or by excommunication. They have not withdrawn, nor have they been excommunicated. They are still Presbyterians of the same faith and forming a part of the original congregation; and as such are entitled as beneficiaries under those deeds to their interest in the property.

I have not considered it necessary to cite adjudged cases in support of the points here discussed. On questions growing out of church dissensions, the authorities are numerous and contradictory and it would be a useless task to try to reconcile them as each depends so much on its own facts and surroundings. Judge Bliss has referred to the main leading cases in his opinion and I am satisfied with his review of them. But Watson vs. Jones, supra, had not been determined at the time Judge Bliss filed his opinion. That case is relied on by the learned counsel for plaintiffs as controlling authority and therefore demands our notice.

In the first place this case originated in Kentucky, and was pending in the courts of that State under the name of Fulton vs. Farley, which had been decided by the Court of Appeals under the name of Watson vs. Avery, 2 Bush., 332. The Louisville Chancery Court had possession of the property in dispute, and it was in the hands of a receiver of that court. The Court of Appeals of Kentucky, had also decided the case of Gartin vs. Penick, 5 Bush., 110, and passed on the principles involved in both of these cases. And yet the Supreme Court of the United States, two judges dissenting and the chief-justice not sitting, did not seem to feel any embarrassment in assuming jurisdiction of the case pending in the State Courts and to overrule, two well considered opinions of the Kentucky Court of Appeals (Watson vs. Avery, 2 Bush., 332, and Gartin vs. Penick, 5 Bush., 110.) I have always understood the law to be that when two courts have concurrent jurisdiction, the one which first assumes jurisdiction has the sole right to decide the whole controversy. Any other rule would lead to insuperable difficulties and conflicts. If the Court of Chancery at Louisville, had possession of the case, as it undoubtedly had, how could the Circuit Court of the United States take jurisdiction of the same case, simply because some of the beneficiaries lived in another State? The residence of the parties is sufficient to give the Federal courts jurisdiction where nothing intervenes to prevent it. But can a Federal court oust the jurisdiction of a State Court which has already attached? Can jurisdiction be taken by halves or parts? Must it not go to the whole controversy in courts of chancery, before it can attach at all? How can a decree rendered in a Federal court in this sort of case nullify the decree of the State Court? It can only be done by blotting out what little remains of the vestiges of State rights.

But if the Federal Supreme Court had any jurisdiction, it was certainly not superior to the Court of Appeals. In the light of the law, as I understand it, the Kentucky Court of Appeals was the only court of the last resort in those cases. Where the jurisdiction of the Federal Courts grows out of the residence of the parties, they act as auxiliary to or in aid of the State Courts. Therefore, the Federal Supreme Court in Watson vs. Jones, cannot be regarded in the light of a court of last resort. In fact it was its duty under the law to be controlled by the principles which had been decided by the Court of Appeals, and to register its decrees instead of those of the ecclesiastical tribunals. If we allow the decrees of ecclesiastical tribunals to affect property rights, surely such courts in the State of Kentucky are inferior to the Court of Appeals, which is the only court of last resort in that State and has the right to pass ultimately upon the judgments of all the inferior tribunals. "No good lawyer can entertain any doubt that the church courts are to be regarded as subordinate in all respects and wholly dependent upon the rules of law established by the decisions of the highest State tribunals. The extent of the jurisdiction of all inferior courts must be dependent upon the final decision of the Courts of Appeals. Any other rule must lead inevitably to intricable confusion." As the Court of Appeals in Kentucky is the only court of last resort in this class of cases, its opinions ought to be regarded as better authority than those of the Federal Supreme Court. Besides, in point of talents and ability, the Kentucky Court of Appeals deservedly stands high, and its opinions in the cases referred to are supported by a weight of reasoning which the Federal Supreme Court did not seem able to overturn.

For these reasons I do not consider the case of Watson vs. Jones sufficient authority to control the action of this court.

Judgments reversed and petition dismissed. The other judges concur, except Judge Wagner, who dissents. Judge Napton was not present at the argument, but concurs in this opinion.[1]

Wagner, Judge, dissenting.

I am unable to distinguish this case from Watson vs. Farris, (45 Mo., 183) and Watson vs. Jones, (13 Wall., 679), and believing as I do that those cases assert correct expositions of the law, I am therefore constrained to dissent from the opinion above announced.

S. S. & B. Live Poultry Corp. v. Kashruth Corporation
Supreme Court of New York, New York County, 1936
158 Misc. 358

McCOOK, J. A Bronx poultry dealer (business corporation), catering almost entirely to the orthodox Jewish trade, claims in this action that it has been injured and is faced with ruin through the conduct of defendant (a membership corporation). The Kashruth Association of Greater New York, Inc. is accused, in effect, of conspiring with two other groups, not

---

[1]See, accord, Boyles v. Roberts, 222 Mo. 613(1909). The Watson and Boyles cases were both overruled in Hayes v. Manning, 263 Mo. 1 (1914).

not sued, to interfere with plaintiff's contractual rights by procuring religious edicts prohibiting the faithful from buying, and the plaintiff from selling, ritually slaughtered fowl without certain forms of supervision and means of identification not required by the Jewish law, notably the plumba or seal. The chief and most effective weapon specified as employed is a so-called issur or prohibitory decree dated November 5, 1934, promulgated by one of the other two groups mentioned, namely, a large number of orthodox rabbis, and supported on the business side by the second group, a union of schochtim or ritual slaughterers, being Local 440. The relief asked against the defendant Kashruth Association, alone, is for recission of a contract and an injunction with incidental damages.

The complaint has elsewhere been held sufficient (N.Y.L.J. July 17, 1935, p. 168) and we need not discuss in what category this action falls. Plaintiff has attempted to show that the requisite steps to the end sought were not taken; that a committee of twenty-three, also described as the Beth Din (court) or Little Sanhedrin, which first drafted and approved the issur, was improperly appointed and convened; that the orthodox rabbis of the community received inadequate notice, and that the issur itself was so informal, so improperly prepared for, adopted, promulgated and enforced, as to violate the law of the Jews applicable to such a matter. Obviously, therefore, the evidence received by this Supreme Court of the State of New York purporting to establish the facts upon which that question of Jewish law is predicated, and the point of law itself, should be the first subject of consideration.

In this connection it may be explained that while the orthodox Jews, like other Jews, recognize, accept and obey the laws of the country in which they reside, they consider it their religious duty at all times to settle their differences according to their own law.

A brief description of the Jewish system of laws (the Torah) is necessary because of the many references to its various parts by witnesses and counsel. First in time came the five books of Moses, the Prophets and the Writings, three groups constituting what is known as the written law. Next, the Mishna, codifying and developing what preceded, until about year 250 of the Christian era. Then the so-called oral law, the Gemarra (Talmud), reduced to writing in approximately the year 500. The Geonim or Sages followed, with further amplifications, until about the Twelfth century. From that date to the present the Responsa literature, namely, commentaries by recognized rabbis throughout the world, complete the chain. The law of the Jews is essentially racial, tribal or national. Since the government was a theocracy, from one point of view this whole legal system may be called religious. Speaking more exactly, it is divisible into two parts, one public and strictly religious, because concerning the relations between man and God, the other essentially private and secular, as controlling the relations between man and man.

One of the oldest enactments, pronounced by Moses himself 3,400 years ago, relates to food. The dietary laws are mandatory in form, and traditionally regarded as a cornerstone of the faith. What may be eaten is denominated "kosher," an adjective whose corresponding noun is kashruth. From time immemorial the religious duty of every orthodox Jew, and preeminently of the rabbi has been obey, enforce and safeguard the principle of kashruth. Every detail originally mentioned has been repeatedly passed upon by commentators. Some of the specifications may seem strange to the Gentile observer, but on closer examination are found based upon either hygient for the people or mercy for the humbler creatures.

Since the wholesomeness of an article of food is of obvious importance, its selection, inspection and preparation are to be closely scrutinized. Animals must be handled and killed only in a certain way and under rabbinic directory supervision. Ritual slaughtering or schechita is performed by a schochet. (The issur upon examination relates to the slaughtering of poultry alone.) Since continuous attendance by any one rabbi at any one market is impossible, certain duties are delegated to subordinate supervisors. Each of these three, rabbi, schochet and supervisor, is regarded as filling a sacred office. By reason of the issur a new functionary, the plumberer or seal affixer has been designated, usually in the person of a supervisor.

The history of the case may be summarized by the following chronology, all in 1934:

July and August - A series of meetings in the City Hall and elsewhere, called at the request of a committee of fifty orthodox rabbis chosen by the mayor or the president of the board of aldermen, and attended by rabbis and laymen, schochtim, poultry men and commision merchants, discusses alleged abuses in the slaughter and sale of poultry, the economic situation of the participants, and the need of reform. The mayor appoints a lay mediator who holds conferences with different groups. The committee of fifty selects a committee of twelve on ways and means.

August 30 - The mediator reports with recommendations.

September 25 - Meeting of the so-called United Rabbinate, a loosely organized assembly of the rabbis of Greater New York hears and discusses the mediator's report and adopts resolutions approving the principle of the issur and calling for the appointment of a Beth Din or court.

October 4 - The committee of twelve, after a meeting with the defendant's representatives, appoints a committee of three, which selects and notifies a Beth Din of twenty-three.

October 9 - First session of the Beth Din of twenty-three, which after discussion of the situation decides to prepare an issur.

October 20 - Issur drafted, submitted, discussed, revised and adopted by Beth Din of twenty-three.

October 22 - Meeting of market men and rabbis. Issur discussed but without agreement.

October 24 - Meeting of the Rabbinical Board of Greater New York, the largest local association of rabbis. Issur adopted by Beth Din of twenty-three approved.

October 29 - Meeting of the United Rabbinate of the City of New York, with a roll call of 219 recorded as present at the opening. The issur is read, discussed, voted upon and adopted.

November 5- By general invitation and upon public announcement, the issur is promulgated in Norfolk Street Synagogue.

Late in November - The schochtim are called together and accept the issur.

Much criticism has been voiced of the notice given for these various occasions. Several means were adopted, including, notably, mailed letters, word of mouth and advertisement in the Jewish press. In particular the defendant proved full notice of the general meetings for rabbis of September twenty-fifth and October twenty-ninth, which marked, respectively, the official institution of proceedings looking to an issur, and their close in the adoption of the issur presented by the Beth Din. The combination of written notice and publication in newspapers with a circulation among those peculiarly interested of approximately 226,146, presumably read by three times that number of orthodox Jews, advised the religious community, including the rabbis, of an intention to take measures for the enactment of the form and kind of religious ordinance which was finally adopted. No interested party had an excuse for ignorance of what was going on. Applying criteria accepted in corresponding circumstances under our own law and rules, I find that adequate notice was given at each important stage to all concerned.

Plaintiff has gone so far as to assert that, independent of actual or constructive notice, the proceedings thus far were defective unless every congregation in Greater New York be shown to have participated in them, either by its rabbi or through a lay representative duly authorized for the purpose. No reliable authority for such assertion is produced. To be sure, this court entertained some expert testimony to that general effect, but it broke down under cross-examination, either because detached from its context or contrary to the weight of evidence or both. Certainly present day jurisprudence would regard the imposition of any such obligation as incompatible with the practical administration of justice.

Plaintiff has emphasized the failure of the United Rabbinate itself to appoint the court which drew up and adopted the issur, but has failed to indicate any provision of the Jewish law compelling it. Final judgment was rendered, not by the Beth Din of twenty-three, which in effect was an intermediate adviser, but by the whole body of rabbis present when the vote of the United Rabbinate was taken. The court received no testimony in the sense of hearing outside witnesses because not required to do so.

Too much attention has perhaps been given to the matter of testimony and other specific evidence before this committee or court, too little to a situation which amounted to an agreed statement of facts, so that the presentation of proof was relatively unimportant. As a result, of course, the chief function of the Beth Din became that of law-finding rather than fact-finding.

Under the Jewish authorities we discover nothing to prevent members of the court from being judges and witnesses also, and like the other tribunal of the United Rabbinate, it could apparently accept hearsay evidence. There were no parties to the proceedings we are now engaged in scrutinizing and, therefore, bias or prepossession, assuming any were found, was no bar to sitting in judgment. There is already seen to exist a great and fundamental difference between the trial of a religious question and the litigation of a controversy between man and man. Impartial, as between what he deems right and what he deems wrong, a pious Jew could scarcely be in the former case; ex hypothesi, he must take sides.

This Supreme Court has before it no evidence that up to the date of the issur the plaintiff was a party to the proceedings or singled out in any way for personal attack. It was a defendant only in the sense that during the conduct of a public religious cause like this every member of the community, including the rabbis themselves, was deemed worthy of criticism because such conditions had been so long permitted to obtain.

The law of the Jews, like most laws, presupposes a judge free from sordid motives connected with the case. Possibly a few members of the two principal tribunals which passed upon the main question had unworthy individual motives, but that is far from discrediting either body. Here again must always be borne in mind the distinction, already referred to, between the purely religious and the personal types of trial. Besides, motive is a very difficult matter to analyze and weigh. Every rabbi is potentially a judge. Like any other human being, in order to live and function, he needs food, clothing and shelter and, therefore, money, though supposed as a judge to disregard and even despise such considerations. It would be too much to expect him as a man to ignore a prospect (which, by the way, does not appear to have been fully realized) of wider employment at better pay; and it would be quixotic to press such a point against his qualifications as a judge. To do so would be senselessly to impugn the motives of all rabbis and impair their dignity. The absurdity of attempting to impose any such narrow standard or test appeared upon the trial before this Supreme Court in listening to the testimony of the learned clergy. Will any one venture to say that the plaintiff's experts showed more disinterestedness than those called by defendant?

No serious flaw, then, appears in the procedure so far, and we turn to the formal and substantial regularity of the decree itself.

The plaintiff's witnesses asserted that this is the first issur promulgated within the memory of living man, but its counsel brought out on the cross-examination of one of defendant's witnesses what looks like inconsistent evidence. Recourse at great length was had to the earlier authorities. It would be fruitless to give these citations pro and con, and the court contents itself with finding that the plaintiff, upon whom the burden of proof rested, has been unable to show that the document in suit was irregular in form. The best view appears to be that while issurim are usually found to have been ultimately reduced to writing, that fact is attributable to the advisability of identifying and perpetuating an important oral proclamation. So regarded, the writing, and the vertification by signature of witnesses, become matters of proof, technically superfluous if, as here, other proof is available.

In substance, the issur, after reciting the facts found, the principles maintained and the conclusions reached, forbids the faithful from selling or buying poultry not slaughtered and sealed in accordance with its terms, prohibits schochtim, under penalty of disqualification, from participating in schedule of any kind unless agreeably to the issur, urges rabbis to conform, nullifies the rulings of non-conformers, and proclaims them rebel sons. These provisions, and particularly the ones which can be classified as bans, are strongly attacked. The answer in each instance is subtantially the same - that the duty of rabbis to safeguard or hedge the faith, and thus schechita has never been questioned; that even confiscation, and thus any lesser penalty, including what has, in the form of a (later) fixed price for the seal of one cent, been characterized as a tax, is authorized when found necessary in the course of providing such safeguard; that the permanence and seeming finality of the prohibition and the ban are justified by similar necessity and have precedents behind them; that previous opportunity was given all to conform; that some did conform in advance and those who did not, as for example the schochtim, and the plaintiff itself, had later opportunity to acquiesce as evidenced by the agreements they signed. The plaintiff's authorities as to the right of repentance do not apply. There is testimony in addition to the effect that even now, were the United Rabinate or the Beth Din to be convinced that an error or injustice had been committed, an appeal for reconsideration is still in order.

Perhaps the participation of the defendant in the preliminary proceedings and its appointment (in the issur) as secular agent of the United Rabbinate and the court for enforcing the edict require brief separate attention. It is proper under the Jewish law to name such a secular agent, and especially this non-religious corporation, as the arm of a religious body? The defendant's witnesses say yes, if justified by necessity, and that this necessity has been established. The plaintiff has not established the contrary and so fails on this point.

More than fourteen months have passed since the issur was proclaimed to New York Jewry as the law of the community. A relatively small proportion of the rabbis have placed themselves in opposition meantime but none of them rose on October twenty-ninth to register dissent, though some may have left the room. Even plaintiff's chief expert witness actively participated in the ceremony on November fifth. Solemnly garbed for the purpose he convoked the assemblage in his own synagogue and offered opening prayer for the success of the venture. True, considerable difference of opinion was from the first expressed as to the wisdom and policy of enforcing the seal requirement, but no evidence has been offered that in October or November, 1934, the least objection was made by any responsible person to the regularity of the procedure adopted or the validity of the decree. I conclude that the technical objections interposed for the present trial are afterthoughts. On the whole case I hold that the result was at the time acquiesced in, and it seems to have been approved to the present day by a concensus of lay and clerical opinion. This result is entirely consistent with the view of Samuel, the son of Mayer, and 150 other rabbis of early days, cited by plaintiff, in decreeing that rabbis shall not ban "unless by the consent of the community".

One point remains for consideration: the claim of monopoly by the defendant. One who enters the field of the kosher trade assumes certain obligations, not usual in other lines; so much is admitted by the plaintiff, who concedes that supervision by rabbis is a prerequisite and is firmly established in New York law, having been enacted into our Penal Law (§§ 425, 435-a, 435-b). Kosher poultry costs more than non-kosher. It would be inequitable to permit its sale by any one as kosher unless in truth kosher. Whether it is so or not is a religious matter for the rabbis to determine. An overwhelming majority of them support the issur. The plaintiff cannot obtain the advantages of his business without assuming the disadvantages which necessarily accompany it. In the very nature of things, kashruth must be a monopoly in the hands of those best qualified to administer it. By definition and tradition those persons are the rabbis and their decree is final. Such is the effect of the evidence in this case.

Unless flagrant and obvious violation of Jewish law is shown, this Supreme Court will not go behind it.

"In all cases of doubt, when there is not clearly an absence of jurisdiction, the decisions of church judicatories as to their own jurisdiction in ecclesiastical matters should receive great weight." (Connitt v. Reformed Protestant Dutch Church of N. Prospect, 54 N. Y. 551, 561.)

The law of this State is that: "The courts at no time assume to dictate or to interpret ecclesiastical doctrine, and such matters, whether discretionary or mandatory, are left to the ecclesiastical bodies. The court will not review the exercise of any discretion on the part of a superior church nor inquire whether its judgment or that of a subordinate is justified by the truth of a case. It will only inquire whether the organization's officer or tribunal has the power to act, not whether he or it is acting rightly." (Harlem Church, etc., v. Greater N. Y. Corp., etc. 145 Misc. 508, 511; revd. on other grounds, 245 App. Div. 292; modfd. by the Court of Appeals, 269 N. Y. 18.)

This is equally applicable to infringement of property rights. Baxter v. McDonnell (155 N. Y. 83) states: "Judge Bradley, in the court below, conceded that the plaintiff was bound by the determination of that tribunal so far as related to the matter of discipline and ecclesiastical rules, laws and customs of church government; and when rights of property are dependent upon the questions of doctrine, discipline or church government, the civil court will treat the determination made in the highest tribunal within the church as controlling." (See, also, opinion of Rugg, C. J., in Cohen v. Silver, 277 Mass. 230.)

Plaintiff feels itself aggrieved in its civil rights by the fraud, constraint and duress said to have been exercised by defendant corporation. It must fail by virtue of the principles of equity prevailing in this Supreme Court, to which it applies for relief. What basis is there for a claim of damages? There was no fraud for the reasons already discussed under the head of bias. ... There is no duress unless it be first established that defendant arrogated to itself rights which it did not possess, whereas I have held it to possess full rights to do all it attempted. Had there been but one organization instead of two, all the acts complained of would clearly be the result of steps taken by a religious body. That the rabbinate saw fit to administer enforcement and collect funds through a membership corporation does not change the situation. On the contrary, it shows a laudable purpose of separating the spiritual from the mundane, a laudable willingness to subject its business affairs to visitation by the State courts. The Kashruth Association, Inc., being empowered in its charter to enforce compliance with the New York law by prosecuting offenders against the so-called kosher laws, cannot, says the plaintiff, attempt to apply compulsion by any other means. This does not follow. To begin with, by deliberately making the earlier agreement with the defendant, then repudiating it, the S. S. & B. Live Poultry Corporation placed itself in an inconsistent position. Since it does not here defend an action for breach of contract brought by the Kashruth Association, rescission may not avail, the very history of the matter demonstrating the weakness of the plea. The S. S. & B. Live Poultry Corporation is dependent upon the principle of kashruth for the success of its business. It has defied defendant on the ground that the latter had violated the Jewish law in applying the principle at plaintiff's expense. As this Supreme Court has refused to recognize that claim and found defendant's acts done in accordance with the Jewish law, it must further hold the plaintiff entitled to no relief whatever. The answer to plaintiff's complaint of injustice is that there is no injustice. If plaintiff does not like the result of having disagreed with the views of the orthodox Jews there remain the plain alternatives of either once more complying or abandoning the field of kosher poultry sales.

There is another reason for denying the plaintiff relief. Its last rebuttal witness testified that the association of market men, of which plaintiff's president and chief lay witness is a director, have already taken the matter into its own hands and determined to proceed as it sees fit, discarding the issur and disregarding the United Rabbinate. Their plan provides for independent supervision, for which they have retained seven rabbis, of whom four as experts testified for the plaintiff. This court is asked to overturn an issur, carefully prepared, duly authorized and valid in substance and form, and give the stamp of approval to one of the very persons who organized what is at best their own method of accomplishing the same end. Equity will not come to their assistance by indirection, will give no affirmative relief, and leaves them where it finds them.

We have heard the procedure characterized as a revolution in Jewish practice through the adoption and use of divers means, including secular ones, to a religious end; the abandonment, at least for the occasion, of a congregational for a diocesan organization, and of an individualistic for a collective method of supervision and enforcement. Suffice it to say that this is the business of the orthodox Jews, not of the people of the State of New York. Weighty considerations of policy have been argued, as, for example, the difficulties and dangers attendant upon prohibition, supported by penalties, of acts in themselves harmless, such as the purchase and sale of food killed and handled in accordance with the dietary law, unless it bears the defendant's seal. Enough to reply that this court may not examine such questions, which are matters for the orthodox Jew to settle for himself according to his own law and his own judgment. The people of this State and Nation have made many experiments upon matters vital to our very existence, and may freely continue to do so whenever that is not forbidden by our fundamental laws. We should be indignant were any official, without showing such a constitutional barrier, to deny us the right to make mistakes while pursuing our favorite practice of trial and error. Of course, a similar privilege belongs to all religious bodies within their province, and not least to the Jews, whose polity is democratic as well as theocratic. We have no right to consider even whether the tribunals concerned gave too much attention to the evils found and the need of reform, too little to a statesmanlike consideration of the wisdom of the means to be adopted. If perchance the rabbinate have unwittingly imposed upon the laity burdens too heavy to be borne, they will find it out, and may indeed be assisted by facts elicited upon this trial and not previously known.

The court regrets the failure of an attempt to effect a settlement, continued for several days, and the necessity, after a long and bitter struggle between the parties, of awarding victory without peace.

Judgment for defendant. Settle findings and decree accordingly.[1]

Burr v. Parish of Sandwich

In Burr v. Parish of Sandwich, 9 Mass. 277 (1812) it was held that a minister who had been dismissed by the Parish, in accordance with the recommendation of an ex parte ecclesiastical council, summoned to consider the controversy after notice to the minister, could not recover from the Parish for breach of contract. Mr. Chief Justice Parsons, in the course of the opinion for the Court, discussed the tripartite relationships between the parish, the church and the minister.

"Now, a parish and church are bodies with different powers. A regularly gathered Congregational church is composed of a number of persons, associated by a covenant or agreement of church fellowship, principally for the purpose of celebrating the rites of the supper and of baptism. They elect deacons; and the minister of the parish is also admitted a member. The deacons are made a corporation, to hold property for the use of the church, and they are accountable to the members. The members of a church are generally inhabitants of the parish; but this inhabitancy is not a necessary qualification for a church member. This body has no power to contract with or to settle a minister, that power residing wholly in the parish, of which the members of the church, who are inhabitants, are a part. The parish, when the ministerial office is vacant, from an ancient and respectable usage, wait until the church have made choice of a minister, and have requested the concurrence of the parish. If the parish do not concur, the election of the church is a nullity. If the parish concur, then a contract of settlement is made wholly between the parish and the minister, and is obligatory only on them. The proceedings of the church, so far as they relate to the settlement, are only a nomination of a minister to the parish, which may be concurred in or rejected. This view of the subject must be confined to parishes created by the general laws of the land, and not extended to parishes incorporated specially with different powers.

"When, therefore, the parish should have a reasonable claim to a dissolution of their contract with the minister, on grounds proper to be inquired into by an ecclesiastical council, if the church, who have no pecuniary interest in this contract, could, by refusing their assent to the convening of a council, justify the minister in rejecting the offer of a mutual council, the parish would be without remedy. The parish could not legally dissolve the contract by their own vote, for a difference with their minister merely relating to points of doctrine, because a court of law has no means of deciding on those points. The minister refusing to join in

---

[1] Cf., People v. Gordon, 258 App. Div. 421 (1940); Cohen v. Eisenberg, 173 Misc. 1089 (1940).

calling a mutual council, the parish could not proceed to choose one ex-parte, because the non-concurrence of the church would be a sufficient cause of his refusal.

"If, therefore, this cause of refusal, assigned by the plaintiff, were to be adjudged sufficient, the consequence would be, either that the parish had no remedy, which would be unreasonable; or that they might dissolve the ministerial contract by their own vote, thus reducing the office of a minister to a mere tenure at will, which would be repugnant to the nature of the office, and the intent of the parties when the contract was made; or disputes in theology must come into courts of law for decision, when the law has not furnished the jury with weapons of polemic divinity. The conclusion is, therefore, necessary, that no interference of the church can justify the minister in refusing a mutual council; and this last cause assigned, resting on the non-concurrence of the church, cannot be admitted as sufficient."

The Rector, Church Wardens and Vestrymen of the Church of the Holy Trinity in the City of Brooklyn, et al. v. John H. Melish, et al.
Supreme Court of New York, Kings County, 1949
194 Misc. 1006

STEINBRINK, J. (orally) This is an action in equity in which the plaintiffs seek relief, and in which the defendants, other than the Bishop, ask for counterrelief. The unfortunate controversy which has arisen here has found its way into courts because the parties themselves could not resolve their differences.

In order to determine the legal rights of the parties to this litigation, and growing out of their unfortunate differences, it is necessary to consider questions fundamental in their nature and character. The consideration of these questions is essential in order to acquire a true conception, not only of the meaning and purposes of a government, but the rights and duties of churches of all denominations and of those affiliated with the churches, and the relation one bears to the other. A true understanding of these fundamental principles makes easy of solution all questions arising under, by, or through our statutes, the decisions under them, and the canons of the church. Complexity finds its simple solvent and confusion its order in the light of the knowledge of right fundamentals.

The differences, disputes, or dissensions in Holy Trinity Church had their origin a little more than a year and a half ago, when at least one of the Vestrymen complained concerning the activities of the assistant minister.

As early as January 19, 1948, a regular meeting of the Vestry was held, the proceedings of which are set forth at length in Exhibit 18, and in these minutes there was states that a resolution had been offered, which is embodied in full in the minutes, with certain recitals of the adverse criticism which had grown in volume, and concluded with a declaration "that it is the feeling of the Vestry that Reverend William Howard Melish should resign as Assistant Minister of this Church." The minutes further recite that at the request of the Rector, a motion was made and carried that the proposed resolution be tabled, but before those present - and it included all of the Vestrymen, eleven, in addition to the Rector - the opinion was expressed, and the court is quoting "That certain of the outside activities of the Assistant Rector were most detrimental to the interests of Holy Trinity," and there follows the names of all eleven Vestrymen.

Later, on March 16, 1948, another regular meeting of the Vestry was held. These minutes are in evidence as Exhibit 20, and here, there is a recital that "Mr. Bell read a letter addressed to the members of the Parish reporting the action of the Vestry at its meeting on January 19, 1948, in unanimously disapproving certain outside activities of the Assistant Rector, and further requesting an expression of opinion from the Parish in this matter." The motion was made and seconded that the letter be sent out.

After discussion, the Rector refused to put the motion to a vote and stated that the meeting was adjourned, although no motion to that effect had been made. The Rector and Assistant Rector thereupon absented themselves from the meeting, and having done so, all of the remaining Vestrymen proceeded to choose a chairman and continued the meeting. They then, on motion which was carried, directed that theParish secretary furnish a list of the members of the Parish to any member of the Vestry in order to facilitate the addressing of the envelopes.

On April 10, 1948, another regular meeting of the Vestry was held... At this meeting the minutes recorded that the clerk of the Vestry presented a report on the answers received from the Vestry's letter, which was mailed March 30, 1948. The total number of letters sent was 384 to 552 individuals. Answers received as of April 20th, the day of the meeting, were 306, or a return of 55%, and of those received, 156, or 53%, of those expressing opinions, stated that the outside activities of the Assistant Rector were detrimental to the church. Fourteen expressed no opinion. A large minority expressed a contrary opinion.

At this meeting, the Rector announced that he had received a petition signed by 206 expressing their support of the Rector's stand. It did not appear, however, that the petition met the issues posed by the Vestry's letter. ...

These matters were brought to the attention of the Bishop of the Diocese, and on December 8, 1948, he, under the canons, visited the Church of the Holy Trinity. His conference with the Rector and the Assistant Rector, he has already testified to. The difficulties were not solved.

Thereafter, on January 17, 1949, another meeting, a regular meeting of the Vestry, was held,...and after disposing of more or less inconsequential matters, routine matters which naturally come before the governing boards of all churches, there was a statement on dissension. The Senior Warden presented a review of the situation in the Parish as it had been developing for a considerable period of time. In the course of that statement, the Senior Warden embodied in it the observation that "We have now come to the cross-roads. It is evident to my way of thinking that something must be done as there is serious dissension in the Parish, and it is my belief that this lack of harmony and cooperation will continue to exist under the administration of the clergy now in office."

Further, he said, "More than a majority of the members of the Vestry have reached the conclusion that in view of all the circumstances both Ministers should resign for the good of the Parish, and in making a suggestion to this effect they would like to discuss suitable provisions for the comfort and needs of the Rector upon his retirement. It will help so much if an amicable settlement can be reached."

Then there was a discussion, and after the discussion, a resolution was put to the meeting, the Rector having declined to do so, and this resolution, which appears in full in the minutes to which the court has already referred, bears repetition now:

"Whereas, the Vestry of the Church of the Holy Trinity, Brooklyn, New York, desires a separation and dissolution of the pastoral relations of the Rector, and the parties not being in agreement respecting such separation and dissolution; and

"Whereas, the Vestry has offered to pay the Rector upon his retirement an amount equal to the pension which he will be entitled to receive; and

"Whereas, the Rector has declined to resign his Parish and has seen fit not to accept the terms offered;

"Now, Therefore, Be It Resolved, that the giving of the notice in writing and the filing of the petition required by Section 2, Canon 46 of the Church, respecting a separation and dissolution of the pastoral relations, be authorized; such separation and dissolution of the pastoral relations, if granted, to be effective on the date fixed by the Bishop and Standing Committee.

"Be It Further Resolved, that the notice and petition shall be in such form as may be approved by a majority of the members of the Vestry."

There was no dissent in the Vestry to this resolution.

On January 21, 1949, the petition of the Vestrymen to the Bishop for the dissolution of the pastoral relationship was presented...

The petition having been presented, the matter came to the Bishop's official attention, and on February 3, 1949, the standing committee's decision to hold a hearing on the Vestrymen's complaint was made, and they fixed February 15 for the hearing...

When the matter was presented to the Bishop, acting under the canons, his was the right to pass upon the matter himself or to call in the standing committee to counsel and advise him. This latter, he did.

Under the rules and canons governing the church in the Diocese of Long Island, the standing committee is composed of four clerics - I think they are referred to as Presbyters - and four laymen. It was on their advice that the hearing of February 15th was fixed.

Prior to that, however, the standing committee, mindful of its greater obligation to try to restore peace to troubled ranks, counseled the Bishop that prior to formal reference to it of this complaint, that he, the Bishop, should make attempt to settle the differences, pursuant to canon 46. His efforts in this regard came to naught, with the result that it was necessary to hold a hearing.

The hearing was held, covering two entire days, February 15, 1949, and February 16, 1949, at Garden City.

At this hearing, all parties were represented. Evidence was offered, not only for and on behalf of and by the Vestrymen, but also on behalf of the Rector and the Assistant Minister, though neither one, having properly acted on the advice of counsel, testified before the standing committee.

On this hearing before the standing committee, the minutes of which cover some 120 or more pages, there was not only testimony, but there were offered in evidence quite a number of exhibits. These exhibits amplify those matters of complaint or grievance on the part of the Vestrymen which are embodied in the complaint. They are to the effect, and the court does not propose to cover every one of them, that the Assistant Minister was in a measure neglecting his churchly duties in favor of outside political activities and was given warnings concerning the matter and was requested, that is, the Rector was requested by the Vestry to take appropriate action, but failed to do so.

There was offered in evidence an article in "The Churchman," which was written by the Assistant Minister as early as July, 1943, entitled, "Religion and Anti-Soviet Propaganda." The Assistant Minister was chairman of the Executive Committee of the Brooklyn Non-Partisan Legislative Conference, held the latter part of February, 1944, to promote legislation favorable to Soviet Russia, in association with others whose names we need not now record, since they are already in the complaint, but at least two of whom are avowed communists.

In November, 1944, he was the author of an article which appeared in the "Daily Worker," urging clergymen to read: "Teheran, Our Path in War and Peace," by Earl Browder, who was the National Secretary of the Communist Party. I shall skip over a few of these, because, as I have already observed, nothing is to be gained by detailing each item.

In March, 1946, he sponsored, according to the exhibit, the "Win the Peace Conference," which advocated sharing atomic energy with Russia and opposed American aid to democratic European countries.

The assistant Minister, as the standing committee found, was until just about a month ago, chairman of the National Council of American-Soviet Friendship, which had been described by the Attorney General of the United States as one of the subversive, if not communistically dominated, agencies functioning in this country.

It appeared at that hearing before the standing committee that the Assistant Minister's activities had received wide publicity, in much of which he was referred to as the Assistant Minister or Associate Rector of Holy Trinity Church, and it was alleged that his activities have been repeatedly identified in the public's mind with the church.

Then, before the standing committee, many of these matters were again reviewed, not only through the oral testimony of witnesses, but through the exhibits there offered, some of which, if not all, have already been referred to and are contained in the records of this case.

It goes without dispute that when, on March 6, 1948, one of the Vestry, acting for the Vestry, asked for the mailing list, that, under instructions of the Rector, it was refused. The reason for refusal at that time was that there was in the course of preparation the usual Easter appeal, and that, therefore, the list at that time could not be made available. Nevertheless, at that subsequent meeting, to which reference has already been made, the clerk of the Vestry reported that the Vestry's letter to the Parish had been mailed on March 30, 1948. The results of that inquiry were also reported to the standing committee and evidence of it submitted to the standing committee. After the Vestry meeting of May 17, 1948, the summer intervened, and the matter was then, in the interim, discussed with the standing committee of the Diocese, and it was as a result of that discussion that the visitation by the Bishop followed. This visitation was in accordance with canon 43 of the General Canons governing the Protestant Episcopal Church, and appears in that canon which relates to "Of Duties of Bishops."

After the hearings were concluded before the standing committee they made their reports. That appears in Exhibit 7 in evidence. It bears date February 24, 1949, and concludes with a resolution recommending that for the reasons stated in the second specification contained in the written notice given the Bishop of January 21, 1949, the standing committee "advise and consent that the judgment herein be a recommendation that the pastoral relation between the Church and the Reverend John Howard Melish shall be dissolved and that his titles be relinquished by the clergyman, and that the pastoral relation between the parties shall cease and determine at a time and upon terms specified in said judgment."

On February 24, 1949, there was a meeting of the standing committee, attended by four cleric members and the four lay members. All were present. The secretary was instructed to present to the Bishop of the Diocese the communication and resolution appended thereto.

Thereafter, the Bishop, acting within his powers granted by the General Canons of the Church, and specifically, the canons governing the Diocese of Long Island, set forth the judgment.

It was as follows: "It is our judgment that the pastoral relation between the Church of the Holy Trinity, Brooklyn, and the Reverend John Howard Melish, D. D., L. L. D., shall cease and determine on the Fourth Day of April, 1949, and that the Wardens and Vestrymen of said Church shall execute and deliver to the said The Reverend John Howard Melish, D. D., L. L. D., or to us on his behalf, an agreement imposing on the Vestry of said Church an obligation to pay him annually, in quarterly installments, a sum equal to the amount which he shall receive in each year during his life from the Church Pension Fund, approved by us according to Canon 27 of the Diocese and that his title of Rector of said Church be relinquished by said Clergyman." This was dated March 2, 1949.

Immediately thereupon, the Bishop issued his proclamation which, opening with prayer, recited that his own approach to the whole case had been intentionally pastoral, and that his concern was chiefly with the welfare of the spiritual life of the church as a whole, and with that of the priests involved in the matter in particular. He then quoted from the standing committee's report. He also quoted from the Offices of Instruction in the Book of Common Prayer, and here it might be entirely in order to refer to that Book of Common Prayer, which is in evidence as Exhibit 4, and which, at page 543, embodies the vows of a priest in the following language which is part of the ordination.

By the Bishop: "Will you maintain and set forward as much as lieth in you, quietness, peace, and love, among all Christian people and especially among them that are and shall be committed to your charge?' '

And the answer: "I will do so, the Lord being my helper."

And then the Bishop propounds the following question: "Will you reverently obey your Bishop, and other Chief Ministers who, according to the Canons of the Church, may have the charge and government over you; following with a glad mind and will their godly admonitions and submitting yourself to their godly judgments," and the answer by the priest taking the vow is, "I will so do, the Lord being my helper."

This proclamation, mild in its terms, gave effect canonically to the judgment which, in turn, was based on the recommendation of the standing committee.

On February 26, 1949, a petition of a self-constituted committee within the church presented to the Rector a writing subscribed by a so-called chairman and a co-chairman of the committee to retain the Rector, and to which was appended a notice that a special meeting would be held on Monday evening, March 7, 1949, for the purpose of a hearing on the charges against the Vestrymen, the nine Vestrymen who, in the performance of their duties, had filed the complaint with the Bishop.

I speak and try to speak kindly concerning this, and with restraint. Here were reputable men serving their church, who, doing their duty as they saw fit by their God and by their church, were sustained by the standing committee and by the Bishop, and yet, because of what they did - whether swayed by passion or prejudice or a natural affection for their Rector - were to be summarily removed because they had done their duty.

On March 4th, a formal protest was made to the Rector by the then members of the Vestry who were to be called on the carpet...

On March 7th there was presented a protest,...against what was sought to be done as against these nine Vestrymen.

It was a demand to the Rector that the statement therein contained be read at the meeting.

Nevertheless, since they intended to hold that meeting on the night of March 7, 1949, the Vestrymen, as was their right, retained counsel, in their own name and in the name of the church of which they were Vestrymen.

The meeting was held. I shall not comment on the good taste of that meeting, for the decision of the Bishop of this Diocese had already been rendered.

And then followed the purported removal of the nine Vestrymen by those who attended this meeting.

Here I pause to observe that in this court's opinion that meeting had no validity whatever, for it is provided in the Religious Corporations Law of this State, in subdivision 3 of Section 43 (as amd. by L. 1935, ch. 140), as follows: "Special meetings of the Protestant Episcopal parish or church heretofore or hereafter incorporated may be held on any secular day fixed by the vestry."

The Vestry did not fix the time for the holding of this meeting. And it begs the question to say that it would have done no good to have made a request or demand of the Vestry, since they were the very ones whom it was sought to remove.

A church is not a stock corporation, and the rules applicable under the General Corporation Law cannot be invoked here. If the demand or request had been made of the vestry, and if the vestry refused, there were other methods by which a meeting could be compelled. But I say respectfully that this meeting was no different from a rump convention which arises because dissidents withdraw and set up their own organization for action.

After this meeting on March 7th they then determined to hold another meeting, on March 14, 1949, to elect new Vestrymen for those who had ostensibly been ejected from office, even including Vestrymen whose regular terms had not expired nor were about to expire.

And when notice of this proposed meeting of March 14, 1949, came to the attention of the Vestrymen, they took action. It was then that this court issued its preliminary restraining order pending hearing and determination of the application for an injunction pendente lite.

On March 30, 1949, the proposed agreement directed by the Bishop was reduced to writing. It conforms with the judgment and the proclamation of the Bishop with reference to the Rector's pension rights, and other matters...

On April 4, 1949, a certificate, under the hand and seal of the Bishop, was delivered, which declared the dissolution of Dr. John Howard Melish's pastorate of Holy Trinity Church. From that moment on Dr. Melish ceased to be the Rector of Trinity Church, unless it be found that everything that had gone before was for some reason illegal or invalid.

That there were disputes, serious differences, and dissensions in this church, no one can doubt. And no one, not even my old and long-time friend, Dr. Melish, regrets it more sincerely than I do.

However distasteful the duty may be to a judge, he must nevertheless face the facts and the law, and he must, in keeping with the oath which he took, perform his duty; for while Dr. Melish and his son are ministers in the church, we judges are ministers in the temple of justice. We cannot make the law unless the question is new. We must follow the law once that law has been fixed for us by our higher tribunals.

I turn now to decisions of our courts which are germane.

In the case of Connitt v. Reformed Protestant Dutch Church of New Prospect (54 N. Y. 551, 560-561) beginning at the bottom of page 560, our highest court has made this pronouncement. "The relation of a pastor to his congregation, and the manner in which he discharges his duties, involving the spiritual welfare of his congregation and to some extent the character of the church organization to which he is attached, are subjects of ecclesiastical jurisdiction. Whether a man shall be ordained as a minister, whether a pastor shall be called, dismissed, suspended or deposed, and whether his pastoral relation to any particular congregation shall be continued or terminated, are ecclesiastical matters, to be disposed of, in the Reformed Church, in the ecclesiastical judicatories in an ecclesiastical way."

There is further and even higher authority for what has just been stated. It is to be found in Watson v. Jones reported in 80 United States Reports (13 Wall.) There is no need to quote from this at length, because it has been cited with approval many times by the courts of this State. It appears at page 679.

There is, however, in that case one paragraph and observation which I desire to quote, because it expresses my own deep and sincere feeling in this matter. It appears at page 730. The court said: " 'The structure of our government has, for the preservation of civil liberty, rescued the temporal institutions from religious interference. On the other hand, it has secured religious liberty from the invasion of the civil authority.' "

If ever we depart from this it will be a sorry day for America, for then the basic principle of the separation of church and State will be at an end.

The founders of our Republic recognized this when into our Constitution they wrote those sixteen pregnant words: "Congress shall make no law respecting an establishment of religion, or prohibiting the free exercise thereof." (U. S. Const. 1st Amendt.) This must forever remain one of the foundation stones of our Nation. When that stone crumbles, the Nation will crumble with it...

Still later there was an unfortunate controversy within the ranks of the Catholic Church, and that reached our own Court of Appeals.

Said the court in that case (Baxter v. McDonnell, 155 N. Y. 83) at page 101:

"Here the plaintiff asks the civil courts to examine and pass upon questions growing out of his relations to the church and the bishop, as one of the priests of the diocese.

"In such a case, when it appears that the whole controversy had once been submitted by the parties to the ecclesiastical tribunal which the church itself has organized for that purpose, the civil courts are justified in refusing to proceed any further. The decision of the church judicatory may and should then be treated as a bar to the action and good defense in law."

Further (pp. 101-102): "A priest or minister of any church by assuming that relation necessarily subjects his conduct in that capacity to the laws and customs of the ecclesiastical body from which he derives his office and in whose name he exercises his functions, when he submits questions concerning his rights, duties and obligations as such priest or minister to the proper church judicatory, and they have been heard and decided according to the prescribed forms, such decision is binding upon him and will be respected by the civil courts. The decisions of the courts in this country are substantially in accordance with this view", citing quite a number of cases...

This, then, is the law of this case. There is no material issue of fact in the case whatever, none that I have been able to discover.

The records make clear what the facts are, and no one has disputed them. Meanings of words here or there, or inferences to be drawn from them, are not at all germane.

The plaintiffs had a perfect right to resort to a court of equity to restrain injury to themselves or to protect the property of the church, for this involved a civil right.

There must be a decree here which will confirm the judgment and decree of the Bishop.

I repeat that from April 4, 1949, Dr. Melish ceased to be the Rector of this church.

I shall make no observation, though I hold a very strong and firm opinion, concerning the annual meeting subsequently held. That will undoubtedly be disposed of in some other forum at some other time.

There will be judgment for the plaintiffs as prayed for in their complaint.

The defendants' prayer for judgment or cross claims will be denied and dismissed; except that there will be judgment in favor of the defendant De Wolfe on this counterclaim. And since this involves a church which has a long and honorable history in this community, no costs will be granted to either party.

Let the judgment be settled on notice.[1]

O'Hara v. Stack
Supreme Court of Pennsylvania, 1879
90 Pa. St. 477

Mr. Justice Mercur delivered the opinion of the court, October 6th, 1879.

This bill was filed by the pastor and eight members of the congregation and pewholders of the Church of the Annunciation, in Williamsport. It prayed substantially that the bishop is restrained by injunction from removing or attempting to remove the appellee as pastor of said church, and also against prohibiting him from exercising priestly functions in Williamsport; and further asked, that he be restored to his rights and emoluments as they had previously existed and been enjoyed by him. Upon their own petition, and by leave of the court, all the complainants, except the appellee, withdrew before answer was filed. When the learned judge came to enter a decree he found the relations and attachments of the congregation towards the appellee had so changed, and the wise and prudent conduct of its present pastor had so secured its confidence and regard, that he thought it unwise to disturb the existing relations. He therefore refused restoration. He decreed that the removal of the appellee as pastor of the church, and also the prohibition and disfranchisement, forbidding him to exercise any priestly functions in Williamsport, were unlawful; yet, in a spirit of conciliation and compromise, he restricted the liability of the bishop to pay costs, so far as to exempt him from the payment of any bill of the appellee. From that decree, thus imposing a part of the costs on him, the bishop has taken this appeal.

The practical question before us is so narrow, that we deem it unnecessary to discuss the numerous matters involved in the bill and answer. The single question we will consider is whether the appellant has just ground to complain of the decree. The rules and discipline of the church, the cause of religion and the good order of society, justly authorize the bishop to remove a preist from his charge for cause, and to transfer him from one parish to another, as he may deem proper. In this case the appellee was not transferred to another parish. Whether without any specific

[1]The judgment of Steinbrink, J. was affirmed: 276 App. Div. 1088; 301 N.Y. 679, and certiorari was denied by the Supreme Court of the United States, 71 S.Ct. 495.

accusation against a pastor, and without giving him any opportunity for hearing or trial, the bishop can remove him from his charge, without assigning him to any other, and prohibit him from exercising all priestly functions, present grave questions. The appellee is a regularly ordained priest of the Roman Catholic Church. In 1866 he was duly appointed, by the bishop of the diocese, to the charge of this congregation of non-German Catholics. He continued its pastor until the 5th of November 1871. By letter of that date, Bishop O'Hara, the appellant, wrote the appellee, saying:

"Rev. Sir: Your administration of the affairs connected with the Church of the Annunciation has been such that I feel myself compelled to remove you, and leave the church vacant. And I now forbid you to exercise any priestly functions in Williamsport, even to say mass. This prohibition binds sub gravi. You may call on me at Scranton, and I will inform you of my further intention in your regard."

On the same day, the bishop also wrote to the Rev. J. Koeper, pastor of the Church of St. Bonifacius, in Williamsport, informing him that the sheriff had an execution against the Church of the Annunciation, so that it was liable to be sold, and enclosed his money to pay the execution. He further proceeded to say; "You will also take charge of all things connected with that church, such as vestments, furniture, books, &c. and keep them under your custody. They remain in the house and church, but you will keep the key. You may baptize and attend the sick, but nothing else. I am much pained to adopt this severe course, but the state of things in that congregation is such that I would consider myself wanting in duty to allow it to continue any longer."

In pursuance of this direction, Mr. Koeper took possession of the registers of baptism and of marriage and a sacred vessel of the church, and also of the set of keys that were in the possession of the secton, but not of the set of keys in the possession of the appellee. Afterwards, the latter opened the church, addressed the congregation and stated his purpose to contest the legality of the bishop's action.

About one week thereafter he filed this bill.

The letter of the 5th November complains in general terms of his administration of affairs connected with the church, but charges no specific act, either of omission or of commission, showing in what particular it was not satisfactory. He is not informed whether the complaint refers to spiritual or to temporal affairs. It gives no information sufficient to enable him to answer and refute the complaint. It neither gives, nor indicates any intention of giving, him permission to inquire the reasons for his summary removal. At one and the same moment a vague charge is made, the edict issues and the sentence pronounced. The answer of the appellant avers no specific cause for the removal, and the evidence fails to disclose any.

In pursuance of the bishop's permission to call on him at Scranton, the appellee did so. The uncontradicted testimony of the latter in regard to that interview is; "I saw Bishop O'Hara in his residence on or about the 9th November 1871, but he neither made definite his charge nor gave any trial, nor revoked his letter, but wishes me to resign my parish at Williamsport, making vague promises and stating general conditions of a better one if I would resign."

It is a maxim of fundamental law that no man shall be condemned without a hearing. A hearing assumes notice of the specific grounds of complaint, and a reasonable opportunity for answering them. In all matters of faith and of doctrine churches are left to speak for themselves. When rights of property are in question, civil courts will inquire whether the organic rules and forms of proceeding prescribed by the ecclesiastical body have been followed: Nopp et al v. St. Mark's Lutheran Church of Butler, not yet reported; Kerr's Appeal, 8 Norris; and if followed whether they are in conflict with the law of the land. Any rule or proceeding whereby a man's property is swept away from him without a hearing, trial or judgment, or the opportunity of making known his rights therein, is not according to the law of the land within the meaning of the 9th sect. of the Declaration of Rights: Brown v. Hummel, 6 Barr 86; McAuley's Appeal, 27 P. F. Smith 397.

Had the appellee such a right of property in the revenues of his church and in his profession as to authorize a court of equity to inquire into the matter of his removal? He had no specific salary. His income was derived from rent of the pews, Sunday collections, subscriptions and offerings. The Roman Catholic Church makes the support of its pastors one of the commandments of the church. Its precept requires the members of the congregation to contribute to the support of their pastor. It is declared to be a sin of omission, to omit anything willingly, which is commanded by God or his church. While the precise sum the appellee might receive, could not be ascertained in advance; yet the sum of which he was in the actual receipt was so large, that it is not alleged to have been inadequate to his proper support. A man's profession is his property. The appellee was not only deprived of his right of property as pastor of that particular church; but he was also prohibited from exercising any priestly functions, as a means of support, elsewhere. The literal reading of the order forbade the exercise of such functions in Williamsport. Inasmuch, however, as he had been assigned to no other parish, the effect was, to close the doors of every parish against him. The strong arm of the church was laid upon him. All means of support were denied to him, and a stigma was case on his reputation. The sub gravi of the prohibition was a reminder that his administration was of so grave a character, that any disobedience to the order of prohibition, would be a grievous sin. The harshness of the bishop's conduct was well designated in his letter to Mr. Koeper, as "this severe course."

The Act of 16th June 1837, and its supplement of the 14th February 1857, expressly give Courts of Common Pleas of the several counties of the Commonwealth, the supervision and control of unincorporated societies or associations. In granting injunctions, not only acts contrary to law, may be enjoined, but also those contrary to equity: Stockdale v. Ullery, 1 Wright 486.

Then, without reviewing the conflicting opinions as to the ecclesiastical power given to the bishop to deny to a priest the exercise of all priestly functions, without assigning any cause, we cannot assent to the doctrine that the pastor's right of property may thus be stricken down, and he be prohibited from following his profession, without accusation, and opportunity for a hearing and trial. If it is not contrary to the laws of the church, which we are not prepared to admit, it is contrary to the supreme law of the land. The appellant has no just cause to complain of the decree.

Decree affirmed, and appeal dismissed at the costs of the appellant.

Mr. Justice Trunkey filed a dissenting opinion, in which Mr. Justice Sterett concurred.

A motion was subsequently made for a re-argument, which was refused, Chief Justice Sharswood, on the 19th of January 1880, delivering the following opinion:

The motion for re-argument is refused. I desire to add for myself that I think that the learned counsel of the appellant have misapprehended the opinion and decision in the case. I did not and do not understand that it settled anything as to the powers and rights of the bishops of the Roman Catholic Church over the priests. The only decree of the court below adverse to the appellant was that upon the subject of costs. In courts of equity costs are in the sound discretion of the chancellor. They do not necessarily fall on the losing party as they do at law. It appeared to me that whether the appellant had or had not the power which he assumed and exercised over the appellee, that in reason and good conscience he was bound to make known to him the ground of his proceeding, that neither he nor the church might be left to conjecture that it was conduct which affected his character as a clergyman. In concurring in the decree of affirmance, all that I meant to decide and all I think that was meant to be decided was that under the special circumstances of the case, the judge below exercised a sound discretion when he refused to impose all the costs upon the appellee.

Motion refused.[1]

Bonacum v. Harrington
Supreme Court of Nebraska, 1902
65 Neb. 832

POUND, C. Thomas Bonacum, as bishop of the Roman Catholic Church for the diocese of Lincoln, brought this suit against Lewis J. Harrington to obtain an injunction restraining the latter from exercising the powers or faculties of parish priest in the parish of Orleans in said diocese, in contravention of the action of plaintiff, as such bishop and as the governing authority of the church in said diocese, withdrawing his faculties and depriving him of his authority as such parish priest, and from acting or assuming to act in that capacity, exercising the functions of which he had been deprived, or excluding the regularly appointed priest of said parish from the church property therein, or interfering with him in the exercise of his office. A decree was rendered dismissing the suit, from which the bishop appeals.

The controversy involves the interpretation and application of several paragraphs of the decrees of the third plenary council of Baltimore, shown by the evidence to be an authoritative statement of the rules, cus-

[1]Later proceedings arising out of the same controversy are reported in Stack v. O'Hara, 98 Pa. St. 213 (1881).

toms, canons and discipline of the Catholic church in this country. It appears in evidence that the church distinguishes between priests who belong to and are incorporated in a diocese, and those who are proper to some other diocese, but are in process of acquiring a new situs. With respect to the latter, a further distinction is made between secular clergy, the ordinary parish priests, and regular clergy, those who are members of religious orders and have taken special vows. Thus much is conceded by all parties. It is also conceded that the bishop may not deprive or dismiss a priest who has become incorporated in his diocese except upon due trial, after notice and opportunity to defend. With respect to priests who have not been incorporated in the diocese, the evidence appears to show that the bishop may not incorporate them in the first instance when they come to him, but must receive them upon probation for a period of three or five years, as he may determine, after which he may incorporate them by formal act, or may allow them to become incorporated by non-action.

In the case of regular clergy who have taken vows, it is provided that the bishop shall not admit them, even to the preliminary probation in the first instance, unless they have already become secular priests before they come to him; but on producing letters of secularization and after making secret investigation as to the character and qualifications of the priest, he may transmit the result of his investigation to the authorities at Rome, who may finally complete the secularization, whereupon the ordinary process of incorporation will ensue. A written agreement between the bishop and Father Harrington is in evidence, in which it is set forth that the latter is received as a "guest" of the diocese, and that in case the bishop determines to receive him on probation the period thereof shall be five years. It is also agreed that the bishop, for reasons of which he shall be the sole judge, may at any time prior to the expiration of the period of probation refuse to incorporate the defendant, and dismiss him. The bishop contends that under the customs and law of the church in this country there is a recognized practice of receiving priests from other dioceses as guests, without taking them on probation, and without their acquiring any rights to be incorporated until so taken; and he insists that Father Harrington was received in this capacity only, and that he at no time permitted the latter to enter upon the stipulated five-year period of probation, or to become incorporated. He also claims that the necessary steps toward complete secularization have never been gone through with, and consequently that Father Harrington, as a member of a religious order, was not entitled to be received on probation. On the other hand, Father Harrington asserts that the paragraphs relied upon by the bishop as his authority for receiving clergymen as guests of the diocese, refer to what he calls "borrowed priests" or priests loaned by one bishop to another for a temporary purpose, and have no application to his case. He also insists that by virtue of certain letters of secularization, introduced in evidence, he was eligible to be received on probation and was so received and produces some written statements of the bishop, which tend to show that he was regarded as on a permanent footing in the diocese. The bishop contends that the letters of secularization produced are merely a necessary preliminary to the procedure provided for full secularization, and points to a paragraph of the church laws which might be so construed. The lower court, construing the several paragraphs of the church law in evidence, seems to have held that Father Harrington, having been in the diocese a little longer than five years, had become presumptively incorporated, and was entitled to the mode of trial provided for incorporated priests, so that the bishop could not dismiss him or refuse to receive him after a secret investigation, as in the case of those who had not acquired a permanent situs.

The laws and decrees of the church in evidence presuppose a considerable knowledge of the canon law, and their interpretation by a court, which has no knowledge and can not take judicial notice of that system, must necessarily be very unsatisfactory, in the absence of more complete and explicit expert evidence than is before us in this case. The books in evidence, and the witnesses who testified with regard to them, take many things for granted, for which the court is ignorant, and we should feel greatly embarrassed were it necessary for us to attempt to construe them. Such an endeavor, indeed, would amount to nothing less than making law for the church. In order to reach a sound construction on controverted points, the court should be able to enter into and give effect to the reason and intention of the lawgivers; it must know the general spirit of the organization and its attitude towards its governing authorities, whether it construes the laws relating to their powers liberally or strictly; and it must consider the construction, if any, which usage and common consent has determined. We have only to turn to the annotations of our public statute books to see that scarcely less law is made by construction and interpretation than by direct legislative enactment. In such a case as this there would be great danger that the ideas of the court would run counter to those of the fathers of the church, and make laws by construction which were never intentionally adopted. We think we are relieved of the duty of so doing under the decision of this court in Pounder v. Ashe, 44 Nebr. 673. It is in evidence that the bishop is the governing authority of the Catholic church in his diocese. He is said to be the "supreme pastor, the supreme teacher, the supreme governor". It is his duty, under the laws and discipline of the church, to administer the regulations above mentioned, and, in so doing, necessarily to construe and interpret them. His decision is to be final and conclusive, except as reviewed by his ecclesiastical superiors at Rome. Under such circumstances, we do not think we ought to attempt to review his decision, or put ourselves in his place and determine for the church the meaning of its rules and canons. In Pounder v. Ashe, supra, it was settled, after elaborate review of the authorities, that courts will not review judgments or acts of the governing authorities of a religious organization with reference to its internal affairs, for the purpose of ascertaining their regularity or accordance with the discipline and usages of such organization. This case and that are very much alike. In Pounder v. Ashe the controversy related to the action of a conference, which was the governing authority of a religious organization in this jurisdiction, depriving a clergyman of his office and dismissing him; and the question presented was which of two distinct sections of the book of discipline of said organization was to be applied to his case. The conference proceeded under one section, and he claimed its action was irregular, because it should have proceeded under the other. At the first hearing this court reviewed the action of the conference, determined that it proceeded under the wrong section, and rendered judgment accordingly. Pounder v. Ashe, 36 Nebr. 564. But upon rehearing the court altered its position, refused to review the action of the superior church authorities, and granted an injunction against the deprived clergyman. Pounder v. Ashe, 44 Nebr. 672. In this case the questions are whether the provisions relating to the incorporation of secular priests, or instead those relating to members of religious orders, were proper to be applied, and what character and effect belonged to the letter of secularization produced by the defendant. The construction of the provision by virtue whereof the bishop claims the right to receive priests as guests of the diocese is also in issue. It is manifest that these questions are of exactly the same nature, in their substance, as those before the court in Pounder v. Ashe.

For the purpose of the rule announced in Pounder v. Ashe, we think it can make no difference whether the governing authority of a religious denomination is confided to one man or to a synod or conference, nor whether the mode of procedure permitted to such person is in accord with the ordinary course of investigations or trials among laymen. Each religious organization must determine its own polity, and be the judge of its own laws. While Anglo-Saxon notions of fair play may lead us to look with disfavor upon secret investigations and summary determinations by one person, we must not forget that contentious methods of investigation are largely English, and that the Roman system, from which the Roman church has derived its procedure, has always been and still is to a large degree inquisitorial. However much we may think that open and public proceedings and hearings upon due notice ought to be had in every investigation of every sort of charge or issue, we must remember that it is not our province to impose our views as to such matters upon religious denominations. We must not forget that ideas and methods which may seem strange to us are often older than those which, from familiarity, we are prone to think part of the order of nature, and that large bodies of men have been governed by them, and are still governed by them, in the internal affairs of the Roman church, without questioning their entire propriety. When the governing authority of a religious denomination has deprived one of its clergymen of his authority to officiate as such, he may be enjoined from making use of church property in that capacity, or under color of the functions of which he has been deprived. Pounder v. Ashe, 44 Nebr. 672. No other remedy is adequate or practicable in such a case. The denomination at large, of which the local congregation forms a part, has generally contributed, and did contribute in this instance, a large portion of the funds and property wherewith the local society is maintained. If the property and the proceeds of such funds may be diverted from the purpose for which they were contributed and administered in contravention of the discipline, doctrines and canons of the denomination, it is obvious that a wrong is perpetrated not without an analogy to a breach of trust. After the decision of this court in Pounder v. Ashe the question is not an open one. The remedy of the deprived clergymen is to be found within the organization itself. So long as the judgment or act of his superiors and of the governing authority of the church relates merely to its internal affairs and to church discipline, and he is not deprived or sought to be deprived of any property rights, he has no standing in court to procure a review of the proceedings dismissing him. In Pounder v. Ashe the court said: "Mr. Ashe as a member, and also a minister, and from all the evidence, a bright and active one, must be presumed to have been fully acquainted with the discipline and rules and regulations, and the right of the association to try him in the manner it did, if charges were preferred against him, including that of the duty of the committee to adjudicate the question of under which section and paragraph of the rules the charges must be heard and determined, and when he joined the church and entered its ministry, having assented to them, and having thus selected and agreed to the tribunal and its powers and jurisdiction, in so far as it affects him alone and his rights to exercise his office as minister and as a member of the association, the civil courts can not and will not examine the proceedings of the trial committee provided by the discipline, to ascertain whether it has in all things acted in accordance with the rules of the church, or construe the disciplinary laws of the association and take upon them the work of a review or retrial of the case and render in it such verdict or judgment as from the court's construction of the laws of the church, should have been announced." These remarks are very pertinent to the case at bar. It may be Father Harrington's misfortune that under the discipline of the society of which he has voluntarily become a member he was subject, under certain contingencies, to be dismissed upon secret investigation, and for reasons of which the bishop was the sole judge. It may be his misfortune that he has devoted his concededly great abilities to the work of a society in which the supreme authority in each diocese is so largely delegated to one man. But having identified himself with such a denomination, his remedy is either to appeal to the proper ecclesiastical superior of the bishop, or, if so advised, to sever his connection with the organization. It is true, he claims to have appealed. But he produces no evidence thereof, and in fact refuses to state how he appealed, or in what manner proceedings by way of appeal are pending. And, even if he had established an appeal, he has introduced nothing to show that the effect thereof would be to supersede the action of the bishop.

Certain members of the local congregation formed a corporation under the general provisions of the statute with reference to religious societies, and intervened claiming rights in the church property in controversy. No relief was granted by the decree, and we do not think it necessary to direct any decree with reference to the petition of intervention. Where a local church congregation is a member of a general organization, having rules for the government and conduct of all its adherents, congregations and officers, the judgments of the general organization, through its governing authority, so long as they relate exclusively to church affairs and church cases, are binding upon such local organizations, and will not be re-examined by the courts. Pounder v. Ashe, supra. In this case the property has been conveyed to the bishop, as representative of the general church organization, and was contributed and was so conveyed for the purposes of religious worship in accordance with the doctrine and discipline of the Roman Catholic Church. Persons claiming under said denomination and not pretending in any way to hold adversely thereto, or have any title of their own, except as members thereof, may be enjoined from using such property contrary to the determination of the governing authority of the church. This proposition likewise is settled in Pounder v. Ashe. In that case rival parties of a congregation claimed to represent the true doctrine and discipline of the church, and the one attempted to exclude the other from such property, and to administer it contrary to the determination of the conference. The court granted an injunction, as we think properly, because the question was not one of title or possession, but purely one of the administration of trust property in accordance with the terms of the trust. The bishop has prayed for no injunction against the interveners, and they have obtained no relief against him. If they claim merely as members of the local congregation and in subordination to and under the church, it is obvious that they are bound by his determination, or the determination of his ecclesiastical superiors. If they claim by some independent title, or claim adversely to the church, or to the trust represented by the bishop as its governing authority in this jurisdiction, the bishop's remedy would be by forcible entry or ejectment.

In conformity with the rules established by this court in Pounder v. Ashe, we recommend that the decree of the district court be reversed and the cause remanded with directions to enter a decree enjoining and restraining the defendant, Harrington, from exercising the powers or faculties of parish priest in or upon the property of said parish of Orleans in contravention of the orders of the bishop, and from exercising therein the functions of which he has been deprived by the bishop, or excluding such person as the bishop shall appoint regularly as priest of said parish from the church property in the petition described, or interfering with him in the exercise of his office. Further than that we do not think an injunction ought to run. Any contests over possession under claim of title, as distinguished from the administration of the church property in accordance with its discipline, laws and canons, must be decided in proper proceedings at law.

Barnes and Oldham, C. C., concur.

Gray v. Christian Society
Supreme Judicial Court of Massachusetts, 1884
137 Mass. 329

HOLMES, J. At a meeting of the Christian Society [a corporation], held on October 12, 1881, a vote was passed to sell the society's house of worship and to remove elsewhere. At a meeting held on October 28, a motion declaring such sale inexpedient was defeated. Enough persons to have changed the result on each vote were present, who were opposed to the sale of the church, and who wished to vote; but they were prevented from voting by the presiding officer, acting in conjunction with the defendant Goodwin and others. The main question is whether these persons had a right to vote.

The answer depends upon the effect to be given to article 11 of the by-laws of the society, passed May 5, 1880. It is not now argued that the persons concerned did not become members of the society under the previous by-law of 1853, and we have no doubt that they did. The question is narrowed, therefore, to whether they have ceased to be members by force of the present article 11.

This article is as follows: "Any member who shall either cease to regularly worship with the society, or who shall fail to contribute to the support of its public worship for the term of one year, shall have his or her name dropped from the list of members." The judge before whom the cause was tried ruled in terms that this was valid, and, interpreted as we interpret it, we assume both that it was so, and that it applied to existing as well as future members. Taylor v. Edson, 4 Cush. 522. Dawkins v. Antrobus, 17 Ch. D. 615, 634.

In Taylor v. Edson, it was assumed, without argument or mention, that if the by-law there in question was valid, and applied to existing members, the defendant did right in refusing to receive the vote of a person who had not paid his annual subscription of five dollars. The by-law provided that persons owning or hiring pews, who "shall subscribe and pay annually for the support of public worship a sum not less than five dollars. ... shall be deemed members of this parish, subsequent to such subscription and payment and during its continuance, and no longer." It might well be contended, on this language, that membership of the society was only from year to year, and that payment of the subscription for the current year was a condition precedent to membership and the right to vote. It will also be noticed, that the sum to be paid was fixed and that therefore there could not ordinarily arise any question whether the condition had been complied with.

The defendant's by-law, on the other hand, does not create a membership from year to year, and a failure to contribute to the support of public worship for a year stands on the same footing as ceasing regularly to worship with the society, as a breach of a condition subsequent for which the "member" "shall have his or her name dropped from the list of members." By the very words of the by-law, a membership is assumed to exist of which the party is to be deprived. He is to be deprived, once for all, by one act, that of dropping his name from the list. If there were no other ground for the conclusion, this would be enough to satisfy us that membership was not determined by mere omission on the member's part. And, if an act is necessary, it is clear that it must be a vote of the society, just as a vote of the society is necessary under article 10 for the approval of a member. No other person or body is empowered to do it; certainly not the moderator of a meeting. Commonwealth v. Pennsylvania Beneficial Institution, 2 S. & R. 141. Delacy v. Neuse River Nav. Co. 1 Hawks, 274, 279. Sibley v. Carteret Club, 11 Vroom, 295.

But, again, the grounds on which a member is to be deprived of his membership are both of them indefinite, involving questions of, more or less, possible disputes of fact, and certain differences of judgment. Not only is the number of time a man has attended, or the amount he has contributed, to be settled, but then comes the question whether the facts amount to ceasing regularly to worship with the society, or to a substantial failure to contribute. These questions are not to be decided by a moderator when a person offers his vote. They are judicial questions, to be determined by the society, after giving the member notice and an opportunity to be heard. The necessity of complying with these requirements of common justice has been so uniformly asserted, that only a few cases need be cited in addition to those last referred to, to show how unwilling courts have been to admit that charters, by-laws, or rules could be intended to deprive a man of his membership without a hearing. Dean v. Bennett, L. R. 6 Ch. 489. Fisher v. Keane, 11 Ch. D. 353, 359. Queen v. Saddlers' Co. 10 H. L. Cas. 404. Innes v. Wylie, 1 Car. & K. 257, 263. State v. Adams, 44 Mo. 570, 586.

As there had been no hearing, and no vote of the society that their names should be dropped from the list, the persons who were prevented from voting were wrongfully prevented...

Hardin v. Trustees of the Second Baptist Church of Detroit
Supreme Court of Michigan
51 Michigan 137

COOLEY, J. The preliminary objection to the maintenance of this action is so unmistakably fatal that there can be no occasion or excuse for considering any other.

The plaintiff, who, previous to February 2, 1881, was a member in good standing of the Second Baptist Church of Detroit, brings suit against the defendant to recover damages for having been on that day unwarrantably and without trial upon charges expelled from membership. The suit is against the corporate body known in law as "The Trustees of the Second Baptist Church of Detroit," and which was organized by voluntary association under authority conferred by the Revised Statutes of 1838. The provision contained in that Code is substantially the same which has always existed in this State, and which is simple and easily understood. Persons desirous of forming themselves into a religious society sign articles of association for the purpose, agree upon a name, elect trustees and put their articles on record when duly perfected. They thereby become a corporation by the name agreed upon, and may take, hold and convey property and exercise the ordinary functions of corporate bodies. The associates are not necessarily professors of any particular belief or faith, or members of any church; and corporate succession is kept up by conferring the privileges of corporators on all who regularly attend worship in the society and contribute to its support. And the trustees who are to manage the temporal affairs of the corporation may or may not be church members.

Connected with the corporation the statute contemplates that there will be a church, though possibly this may not be essential. In this case there is one. The church has its members who are supposed to hold certain beliefs and subscribe some covenant with each other if such is the usage of the denomination to which the church is attached. The church is not incorporated, and has nothing whatever to do with the temporalities. It does not control the property or the trustees; it can receive nobody into the society and can expel nobody from it. On the other hand, the corporation has nothing to do with the church except as it provides for the church wants. It cannot alter the church faith or covenant, it cannot receive members, it cannot expel members, it cannot prevent the church receiving or expelling whomsoever that body shall see fit to receive or expel. This concise statement is amply sufficient to show that this suit has no foundation. The corporation is sued for a tort which it neither committed nor had the power to prevent, and which has occurred in a proceeding where the interference of the corporation would have been an impertinence.

But it is said that the church is an integral part of the corporation; or rather that it is the corporation in its spiritual capacity. Its being an integral part of the corporation proves nothing: counties, towns and school-districts are integral parts of the State, but the State is not for that reason liable for their torts. And as to spiritual capacity, the corporation has none; it is given capacity in respect to temporalities only. If the corporation had assumed to expel this plaintiff from the church, she might treat its action with contempt. But as she makes no complaint of wrongful corporate action, we must assume that the corporation has never invaded her rights. If the church has done so, the church alone is culprit.

The distinction between church and corporation in these cases is sufficiently explained in the following authorities: Baptist Church v. Witherall 3 Paige 296: s. c. 24 Amer. Dec. 223; Lawyer v. Cipperly 7 Paige 281; Robertson v. Bullions 11 N. Y. 243; Bellport v. Tooker 29 Barb. 256, and 21 N. Y. 267; Burrel v. Associate Reformed Church 44 Barb. 282; Miller v. Gable 2 Denio 492; Ferraria v. Vasconcellos 31 Ill. 25; Calkins v. Cheney 91 Ill. 462; Keyser v. Stansifer 6 Ohio 363; Shannon v. Frost 3 B. Mon. 253; German etc. Cong. v. Pressler 17 La. Ann. 127; O'Hara v. Stack 90 Penn. St. 477; Sohier v. Trinity Church 109 Mass. 1; Walrath v. Campbell 28 Mich. 111. See also Hale v. Everett 53 N. H. 9.

The judgment must be affirmed with costs.

The other Justices concurred.

Carter v. Papineau
Supreme Judicial Court of Massachusetts, 1916
222 Mass. 464

BRALEY, J. The evidence would have amply warranted the jury in finding that the defendant Papineau as priest in charge declined to administer to the plaintiff the rite of "Holy Communion" or to permit her to partake thereof, and that by his authority and order she had been refused admission on the Lord's day to the building in which religious services were being held. It is contended that for these acts he and the defendant Lawrence, bishop of the diocese, are responsible in damages, and that the verdicts in their favor were ordered wrongly.

The record shows that the Protestant Episcopal Church of America, of which the parties are members, has a body of canons or ecclesiastical law of its own, by which the plaintiff upon baptism and confirmation agreed to be bound, and under which her rights of worship must be determined. Fitzgerald v. Robinson, 112 Mass. 371. Grosvenor v. United Society of Believers, 118 Mass. 78. By the "Rubric in the Order for the Administration of the Lord's Supper, or Holy Communion" the "minister" is given authority to refuse the rite to any one whom he knows "to be an open and notorious evil liver, or to have done any wrong to his neighbours by word or deed." By "Canon 40. Of Regulations Respecting the Laity," Section II, "When a person to whom the Sacraments of the Church have been refused, or who has been repelled from the Holy Communion under the Rubrics, shall lodge a complaint with the Bishop, it shall be the duty of the Bishop, unless he see fit to require the person to be admitted or restored because of the insufficiency of the cause assigned by the Minister, to institute such an inquiry as may be directed by the Canons of the Diocese or Missionary District, and should no such Canon exist, the Bishop shall proceed according to such principles of law and equity as will insure an impartial decision, but no Minister of this Church shall be required to admit to the Sacraments a person so refused or repelled, without the written direction of the Bishop."

The plaintiff has not availed herself of this right of appeal to the only personage having the requisite ecclesiastical authority to review her standing as a member and communicant or to pass upon her ceremonial rights in accordance with the principles of "law and equity". Grosvenor v. United Society of Believers, 118 Mass. 78, 91. The letter of her counsel to the bishop, to which no reply appears to have been made, cannot be considered as an appeal which had been denied. It contains only recitals of all her grievances, for the rectification of which his friendly intercession is requested.

But if an appeal had been taken properly and the decision had been adverse, the plaintiff would have been remediless, for in this Commonwealth her religious rights as a communicant are not enforceable in the civil courts. Fitzgerald v. Robinson, 112 Mass. 371, 379. Canadian Religious Association v. Parmenter, 180 Mass. 415, 420, 421. For the same reason it is unnecessary to decide whether at common law, as the plaintiff contends, a member of the Church of England could sue if unjustifiably denied participation in the communion. See Rex v. Dibdin, (1910) P. D. 57; Thompson v. Dibdin, (1912) A. C. 533.

Nor can the action be maintained for defamation. Undoubtedly she suffered mental distress, and the omission was in the presence of the other communicants. The plaintiff, however, was not publicly declared to be "an open and notorious evil liver," or to be a person who had done wrong to her neighbors by word or deed. The act of "passing her by" without comment was within the discipline or ecclesiastical polity of the church, and does not constitute actionable defamation of character. Farnsworth v. Storrs, 5 Cush. 412, 415. Fitzgerald v. Robinson, 112 Mass. 371. Morasse v. Brochu, 151 Mass. 567. See R. L. c. 36, §§ 2, 3.

The action for exclusion from the church building also must fail. It appears that upon being informed by the constable employed for the purpose that she could not enter, the plaintiff made no attempt to pass, but acquiesced and obeyed the order. The elements of an assault are absent. No intimidation was used, or unjustifiable coercion exercised. By Canon 16, to which the plaintiff subjected herself, control of the worship and spiritual jurisdiction of the mission, including the use of the building for religious services, was in Papineau as the minister in charge, "subject to the authority of the Bishop."

We are not asked to review the action of an incorporated religious society owning property where a member has been expelled without being notified of the charges and given an opportunity to be heard, as in Gray v. Christian Society, 137 Mass. 329, nor is any question of a trust in which the plaintiff has a beneficial interest involved. It is not shown that she had any rights of property in the building, the furnishings, or in any contract relating thereto, or that Papineau was actuated by malice or ill will. The manner and time of admission having been within his control primarily, the acts of temporary exclusion are not reviewable at law or in equity. Fitzgerald v. Robinson, 112 Mass. 371. Grosvenor v. United Society of Believers, 118 Mass. 78. Canadian Religious Association v. Parmenter, 180 Mass. 415, 421. Watson v. Jones, 13 Wall. 679.

The remaining exception is to the admission in evidence of a letter of Papineau to the plaintiff, which the jury could find he endeavored to hand to her before communion began, but which she refused to take. It forbade her to partake "until you satisfy me, or my successor or superiors of your repentance and amendment." The letter was not in the nature of a self-serving declaration. The jury, from Papineau's testimony that he laid it on a seat in front of her with the request "I want you to read that before the service goes on," and from the fact that after the service the letter was not found, could say that the plaintiff took it and became aware of the contents. Its admission furthermore could not have prejudiced the plaintiff, as the church canons did not require the giving of any notice.

The relation of the defendant Lawrence to the proceedings may be noticed briefly. It is contended that he approved what had been done, and that, as the acts of his subordinate were tortious, he became a joint wrongdoer by ratification. Dempsey v. Chambers, 154 Mass. 330. But, as Papineau did not exceed or abuse his powers, no tort had been committed. The result is that in each case the exception must be overruled.

So ordered.

Moyle v. Franz

Appellate Division, Second Department, 1944
267 App. Div. 423

Per Curiam. Upon a prior appeal in this libel action this court affirmed an order denying a motion to dismiss the complaint under rule 106 of the Rules of Civil Practice. (Moyle v. Rutherford, 261 App. Div. 986.)

The action is predicated upon the publication by defendants in The Watchtower, a semi-monthly magazine, of two defamatory articles concerning the plaintiff. At the close of the case a motion to dismiss the second cause of action as against the individual defendants was granted upon the ground that they were not shown to have been connected with the publication of the article "Snares." The jury returned a verdict against all the defendants on the first cause of action for $5,000 in actual damages and $10,000 in punitive damages; and against the corporate defendants on the second cause of action for an additional $5,000 in actual damages and an additional $10,000 in punitive damages.

The trial court charges the jury that it was the law of the case that the statements sued upon were libelous. No exception was taken to the court's charge in that respect and no request was made to have the trial court charge otherwise. Upon this appeal the appellants have restricted their arguments to the defenses which they urged upon the trial. They claim that the evidence proved the truth of the defamatory statements; that the statements were qualifiedly privileged and made without malice; and that the awards of actual and punitive damages were excessive.

In considering the merits of the appellants' arguments, we have been guided by their express disclaimer of any desire to obtain a new trial by reason of any errors that may have been committed by the trial court. In part the disclaimer reads: "If defendants have not disproved these charges and established their defenses as a matter of law, they do not desire a new trial."

We are unable to agree with either alternative of the appellants' various contentions that each of their defenses is sustained by the "undisputed evidence or overwhelming preponderance of evidence." As to damages, we find that there was sufficient proof from which malice could be inferred and upon which an award of punitive damages could be based.

In the dissenting opinion dismissal of the complaint is recommended upon the ground that the statements were absolutely privileged and that the jury, in effect, decided upon the propriety of the language used by a religious society in characterizing what it considered misconduct by one of its members. We do not intend to detract from the right of a duly constituted religious or ecclesiastical tribunal to deal with matters subject to its jurisdiction, nor from its privilege to publish the results of its proceedings in an official organ. The jury in this case was instructed that a religious organization had the privilege of publishing such matters in its official magazine. The privilege is, however, not absolute but qualified. The jury was so instructed. Neither upon the trial nor before this court have the appellants contended that their publications were absolutely privileged. In their requests for special findings and in their requests to charge they specifically described their defense as one of qualified privilege. The qualified privilege of a religious society to publish matters of interest to its members may be destroyed by showing excessive publication or other evidence of malice. (Pecue v. West, 233 N. Y. 316, 321-322; 33 Am. Jr., Libel and Slander, § 188, p. 179; 17 R. C. L., Libel and Slander, § 90, p. 344; and see Murray v. Brancato, 290 N. Y. 52, 58.) Evidence was adduced from which the jury could have found that there was excessive publication. It was testified that The Watchtower was distributed to all persons willing to pay its subscription price and not merely to persons interested in the affairs of the appellants' organization. The jury could, therefore, have inferred that The Watchtower was a magazine of general circulation rather than one restricted to persons having a mutual interest in the statements published. The jury was also entitled to infer malice from the tenor of the articles, from the fact that several defamatory statements had been published, and from the evidence that without knowledge, or with only fragmentary knowledge of the incidents to which their signed statement related, most of the individual defendants had acquiesced in defamation of the plaintiff. It is, therefore, impossible to hold as a matter of law that the defendants acted in good faith and without malice. Nor do we find these propositions established by the "undisputed evidence or over-whelming preponderance of evidence."

The jury's verdict, however, was grossly excessive, and should be reduced to $7,500 on each cause of action.

The judgment should be reversed on the facts and a new trial granted, with costs to abide the event, unless within ten days from the entry of the order hereon the plaintiff stipulate to reduce the amount of the verdict on the first cause of action from $15,000 to $7,500, and the amount of the verdict on the second cause of action from $15,000 to $7,500, in which event the judgment as so reduced is affirmed, without costs. The other denying defendants' motion for a directed verdict should be affirmed, without costs.

CARSWELL, J. (dissenting). This litigation had its genesis in a letter written by Moyle, the plaintiff, to Rutherford, the head of a religious society. It was followed by disciplinary action or expulsion of the plaintiff from the Society. The letter and rejoinders thereto were published and this action for libel eventuated. Plaintiff has recovered heavy compensatory and punitive damages. Defendants appeal from the judgment therefor.

The contentions of the defendants are clothed in legal terminology commingled with a distinctive type of religious vernacular. They do not stress a principle that should be determinative of this litigation. It is that all matters arising out of ecclesiastical relations or the administration of the affairs of a spiritual or religious group are to be determined solely by the governing authority in the religious group. To insure unimpaired the integrity of this principle, courts will not inquire into or concern themselves, directly or indirectly, with conflicting contentions relating to the practice or to the administration of the doctrinal affairs of religious groups, or the merits of or grounds for the imposition of discipline for claimed violations of duties owing to a religious group by a member thereof. This principle was enforced against a minister in Connitt v. R. P. D. C. of N., Prospect (54 N. Y. 551); against a priest in Baxter v. McDonnell (155 N. Y. 83); against a nun in Noonan v. Gibbons (253 App. Div. 837); and in support of a rabbinical adjudication in S. S. & B. L. P. Corp. v. Kashruth Assn. of G. N. Y., Inc. (158 Misc. 358). To be sure, courts will enforce civil rights possessed by those in ecclesiastical relationships, but they are not astute to perceive such rights when they are claimed to emergy from conflicts between a member of a spiritual or religious group and its governing authority in respect of practices, doctrine or dogma, or conduct claimed to be in violation thereof. This course recognizes the impropriety of courts by their action impinging upon religious doctrine, or administration relating thereto, or disputes germinating therefrom. Any other course would be productive of public mischief and bring obloquy to all religion by the parading of criminations and recriminations which should be disposed of in camera by duly constituted officials.

The applicability of this principle became manifest on the first day of the trial when plaintiff put in evidence a publication of defendants of September 1, 1939, of which no mention is made in his complaint. It revealed that plaintiff had been actually ousted (not merely recommended for ouster) from the Society upon a final adjudication of "unfaithfulness". The subject matter of the publications of which plaintiff complains was unfaithfulness. One merely gave some of the details of the basis of the disciplinary action.

The defendants might well have directed the court's attention to the significance of this September 1, 1939, exhibit, and the court might have a sua sponte, or on request, exercised its inherent power to control the order of proof and limit the evidence to this primary and controlling factor. This would have obviated, as irrelevant, the adducing of evidence during many days of the trial as to the truth or untruth of plaintiff's letter and defendants' publications, and avoided the public mischief attendant upon such a spectacle. The course pursued resulted in a jury, in effect, passing judgment upon unfamiliar religious doctrine, religious administration, and discipline relating thereto. The jury, in effect, determined the propriety of the conduct of the affairs, spiritual and internal, of a religious society and the right of a religious society to use Scriptural terms to characterize misconduct relating to its religious practices, doctrine or administration, which, in the judgment of its duly constituted authorities, merited discipline.

Defendants are entitled to the full benefit of this pertinent principle even though some of their ideas meet with disfavor and their conduct toward some members of the community is irritating and exasperating. We are not concerned with this latter phase so long as they merely exercise fundamental rights under the law and keep their conduct within prescribed legal limits. The benefit of this principle should not be denied to them because they are inept in invoking it or because they function in a manner different from other conventionally organized or orthodox groups. This principle is indispensable to the independence of all religious groups.

We need only concern ourselves here with certain unchallenged facts. The individual defendants belong to and are directors of a society known as Jehovah's Witnesses. They follow a primitive form of practice and profession of Christianity under theocratic auspices. They disclaim being a sect or a cult. Each member of the Society becomes a "minister" or a "Witness." By joining it he or she voluntarily agrees to submit himself or herself to the existing government thereof. The Society divides itself into groups, each of which is referred to as a "family" with a distinctive name. Each member, or as he is called, each "Witness," foregoes pecuniary gain and dedicates all his native and acquired earthly skills to the religious society as part of his all-inclusive duty to advance the "kingdom interests" as a "Witness" or a "minister." One of these groups located in Brooklyn is known as the Bethel Family.

Plaintiff as a Jehovah's Witness, an ordained minister, and a lawyer, became a member of the Bethel Family. He was assigned to legal work for the group. An incident relating to a certain court proceeding occurred, which with seeming justification, subjected him to reproach. Legal work was not his exclusive field, as he at all times acted as a "minister" or a "Witness" like the others. He decided to cease to be a member of the Bethel Family as of September, 1, 1939, and on July 21, 1939, wrote a long letter to Rutherford, the head of the Society, who is since deceased. In that letter he criticized and slurred the conduct of Rutherford and other members of that family group. He had the letters delivered to Rutherford and immediately left on a vacation. On about sixteen occasions between July 21, 1939, and September 1, 1939, he distributed the letter or the substance thereof to various members of this religious society throughout the country. Meanwhile, on August 8, 1939, Rutherford called a meeting of the Board of Directors at the Bethel Family. The delay in so doing was due to certain members being on vacation. Plaintiff was invited and attended the meeting. The letter of plaintiff was read at that meeting. Plaintiff was asked to justify his animadversions. The meeting became a sort of trial of plaintiff respecting his assertions in the letter and his conduct as a "Witness" acting for other "Witnesses" in certain court proceedings. During the meeting a resolution was adopted by the Board recommending the expulsion of plaintiff. Rutherford, the head of the Society, adopted the recommendation and directed plaintiff to leave the Bethel Home at once. He did so. As the letter referred to conduct of the entire Bethel Family, it was then read to the entire group, which numbered more than two hundred, and they were informed of the disposition made in respect of plaintiff.

In a magazine called The Watchtower, published by a non-stock corporate defendant owned by this religious society, the defendants, on September 1, 1939, published a notice, which stated that plaintiff was no longer with the Society and that this was due to "his unfaithfulness to the kingdom interests, and to those who serve the kingdom." It also stated inter alia that the Board of Directors by unanimous vote on August 8, 1939, had recommended that the president sever plaintiff's connection with the Society and that this had been done.

Up to this point the defendants' conduct was clearly within their legal rights under the doctrine above stated. It was further sanctioned by well-settled authority respecting the propriety of publication of the severance of such relations and the reasons therefor in the exercise of absolute privilege. (Barrows v. Bell, 73 Mass. 301; Fairchild v. Adams, 65 Mass. 549); Farnsworth v. Storrs, 59 Mass. 412; Cranfill v. Hayden, 22 Tex. Civ. App. 656) If this right did not exist, an unfaithful minister or priest would be able to do untold damage to the religious group or church that ousted him. The only way mischievous activities of such an adjudged recreant can be frustrated or neutralized is by publishing, to those to whom his disrupting or unauthorized activities are directed, the reasons for his ouster, so that they may evaluate his representations or his claimed authority to speak on behalf of or to the church or group, in the light of findings of unfaithfulness made by the duly authorized body or official.

After September 1, 1939, plaintiff appeared at various meetings in the West of members of this religious society and publicized his reasons for leaving the Bethel Family. His explanations reflected unfavorabley upon the conduct thereof and after September 1, 1939, he circulated fifty or more copies of his July 21, 1939, letter to members of various congregations of the defendant religious society who requested it, and to about eighteen who apparently made no request therefor. This conduct evidently precipitated a meeting of the defendants on September 21, 1939, at which an article prepared by Rutherford was read and signed by the individual defendants. It was entitled "Information" and it was later, on October 15, 1939, published in the defendants' magazine called The Watchtower. This article restates part of what had been done on August 8, 1939, in reference to the plaintiff's July 21, 1939, communication and also refers to plaintiff's conduct in circulating that letter (which was referred to as a libel), and asserts that plaintiff, who had been entrusted with confidential matters of the Society, "assaults and maligns those who trusted him" (having reference to his July 21, 1939, letter) just as Judas had proved his unfaithfulness to Christ Jesus. It makes no mention of plaintiff as a lawyer. This article, in substance, adds nothing to the ultimate effect of the publication of September 1, 1939, of which plaintiff did not complain, because that article stated that plaintiff had been ousted by reason of "unfaithfulness to the kingdom interests, and to those who serve the kingdom," meaning the Society and the "Witnesses."

When plaintiff became a member of this religious Society he voluntarily obligated himself to submit to and abide by the government thereof, and to devote all his talents, native and acquired, not only as a "Witness" or ordained minister but also his incidental or acquired skill as a lawyer, to the faithful service and welfare to the Society and his associate "Witnesses." When the authorized body of the Society, exercising unquestioned jurisdiction, found him guilty of unfaithfulness, it made an adjudication upon him as an ordained minister or as a "Witness," that is to "those who serve the kingdom." The September 1, 1939, publication and findings based on the August 8, 1939, meeting referred to in the October 15, 1939, publication, were that plaintiff was ousted because of "his unfaithfulness to the kingdom interests (that is, the Society of which he was a member), and to those who serve the kingdom," that is, as a "Witness' and lawyer to his associate "Witnesses." This determination of the Society is conclusive upon the courts, since no recognized vitiating element is invoked. It was a conclusive adjudication against plaintiff in respect of the July 21, 1939, letter and the unfaithful character of his conduct generally as a "Witness."

By widespread circulation of the July 21, 1939, letter plaintiff precipitated on October 15, 1939, a republication of part of the decision of the governing body published September 1, 1939. This republication, in amplified form, in no wise added in substance to the effect of the original publication or findings of the governing body. In fact this later publication was milder than was the one of September 1, 1939. It left unsaid that he had been expelled. It merely indicated that his expulsion had been recommended. It repeated in different language that he had been "unfaithful" by the use of the term "Judas," which is merely a synonym for "unfaithfulness," or the personification of that quality. To say, in effect, that he was like Judas is merely to say in a more colorful way, or with the use of a Scriptural term, what had been said in a prosaic way, in the unchallenged September 1, 1939, decision and publication - that he had been unfaithful to the kingdom and to those who serve the kingdom. The original publication of September 1, 1939, was absolutely privileged under the authorities. The absolute privilege which permitted the first publication stems from the same reason which accords absolute privilege to the republication. That the republication of a part of the basis of the September 1, 1939, article was likewise absolutely privileged became clear when plaintiff's proof relating to the September 1, 1939, article showed that his expulsion had occurred because of the facts stated in the October 15, 1939, article. It was first made known in plaintiff's proof, on the first day of the trial, that there was this September 1, 1939, publication not mentioned in the complaint.

Plaintiff's conduct necessitated the detailed and clarified republication. He professed to be desirous of not creating dissension in this religious Society. His pretensions in this regard are not borne out by the undisputed fact that he circulated the July 21, 1939, letter or the substance thereof, both before and after the publications of September 1 and October 15, 1939. He was seeking cooperation of a rival group which was formerly part of the defendant Society. He was, during these periods, with his July 21, 1939, letter sowing the seeds of distrust, dissension and disunion among other groups in the defendant Society. To explain or neutralize his activities, defendants were entitled, under the cases cited (supra), ot have recourse to a clarified publication of the official basis of the decision resulting in plaintiff's ouster.

This analysis of the pertinent undisputed activities of these individuals may make unnecessary a decision as to whether or not, apart from absolute privilege, there was an actionable libel in the article of October 15, 1939. The fact that no libel was seasonably asserted by suit in respect of the article of September 1, 1939, supports the view that the publication of October 15, 1939, was not a libel since it is a mere amplification of a phase or basis of the earlier publication. It is my view, view, without reference to the September 1, 1939, article, that the October 15, 1939, article is absolutely privileged. When considering this phase, an observation of Lord Cockburn in a kindred situation (Koenig v. Ritchie, 3 F. & F. 413) has pertinency: "I own I cannot feel much sympathy for a man, who, having been the first to make an appeal to public opinion, when he is answered in the same manner by a counter appeal, changes the tribunal which he has himself selected, and invokes the arm of the law."

Plaintiff continued his activities after October 15, 1939, in spreading his July 31, 1939, letter and Rutherford wrote and had published on November 15, 1939, in defendants' The Watchtower another article entitled "Snares". It is a homily, permeated with the distinctive didactic vernacular of this Society. It makes no mention of or reference of plaintiff. It might properly be read as an admonition to other "Witnesses" doing legal work. In another setting it would not attract attention. In the abstract it reproved any person who, while consecrated as a "Witness," acts as a lawyer for another "Witness" in a fashion which indicated "unfaithfulness to the kingdom." It merely declares the propriety of a finding of unfaithfulness against any person who, as a "Witness," is unfaithful in his incidental conduct as a lawyer while functioning as a "witness" on behalf of another consecrated person or "Witness." There is no case which authorizes a court or a jury or a nonmember of this Society to pass judgment on the propriety of a pronouncement of abstract doctrine of this Society, or any other religious group, in its official organ, which makes no mention to plaintiff. Even if the observations be heretical or unsound or in bad taste (none of which here appears) in the eyes of nonmembers, the right to publish them is absolute, and no private right of action may be founded thereon. The writing of the article may have been inspired by plaintiff's conduct, but that has no legal significance. From the earliest time, general or abstract religious and philosophical meditations and observations have been inspired by particular instances of conduct. It has never been considered a proper function of courts to police abstract theological polemics.

If the article be deemed applicable only to plaintiff because he thinks it accurately describes his conduct, it adds nothing to the publications of September 1, 1939, and October 15, 1939. Those publications concretely referred to plaintiff and involved an adjudication of his unfaithfulness to the religious Society of which he was a part. This November 15, 1939, article merely dealt in the abstract with the same type of unfaithfulness. It did so with no mention of the plaintiff, who had been the subject of a permissible publication with reference to him as a "Witness," under a decision by the Board of a religious Society and the action of its President.

We need not consider plaintiff's circulation after the November 15, 1939, publication, of over 1,500 copies of his July 21, 1939, letter, or the extent it illumines his claimed lack of desire to disrupt the Society...

The judgment should be reversed on the law and the facts, with costs, and the complaint dismissed on the law, with costs. The appeal from the order should be dismissed, without costs.

McGuire v. Trustees of St. Patrick's Cathedral

Supreme Court of New York, 1889

54 Hun 207

. . . The action has been brought to secure the interment of the remains of John McGuire, deceased, in Calvary Cemetery, Queens County, in the State of New York. The cemetery was acquired and controlled by the defendants under an act of legislature conferring that power upon the trustees of St. Patrick's Cathedral. The intestate died on the 19th of February, 1888, and an application was made for his interment in the cemetery, which was refused by the Trustees, under the direction of the clerical authorities of the Catholic church. In his lifetime the intestate, for the sum of money mentioned in it, received the following receipt and agreement:

"No. 726 "Calvary Cemetery

"New York, Nov. 22, 1870

"266 Mulberry Street.

"Received from John McGuire, ten dollars, being the amount of purchase-money of a grave two feet by eight in Calvary Cemetery, with privilege to erect a head-stone thereon.

"D. Brennan,

"Supt. of Office of Calvary Cemetery.

"Grave 9, Plot F, Section 8, Range 56."

And prior to his own decease the grave mentioned in the instrument was actually located, and the remains of his wife were interred therein. The grave, as it was located, was sufficient in capacity for the interment of more than two dead bodies, and the object of the action, as well as of the application to the authorities controlling the cemetery, was to secure the interment of the remains of the intestate in the same grave...

Barret, J. [After holding that the alleged agreement was not specifically enforceable in equity, proceeded as follows]

I have thus considered this case precisely as though the rights of property claimed by the plaintiff had come from a secular cemetery. But, when we consider that the transaction was with a strictly denominational cemetery, the weakness of the plaintiff's equity is still more strikingly apparent. The record contains an express admission by the plaintiff on the allegations in the answer, that the cemetery lands in question were set apart and consecrated with appropriate religious ceremonies, by the ministry of a priest or priests of the Roman Catholic church, for the exclusive purpose of the burial of the remains of persons who may die in communion with that church. McGuire was a Catholic. As such, he entered the denominational domain. As such, he obtained the receipt in question from the denominational cemetery office. What transpired at the time he so obtained that receipt, is, as we have already seen, entirely unknown. What may safely be affirmed, however, is that he sought burial privilege in a denominational cemetery, thus consecrated to the exclusive purpose of the burial of those dying in communion with the church. That denominational rule must certainly be implied (as part of the agreement) from the receipt, and the surroundings under which it was sought and obtained.

It is as though the receipt has read: Received, from John McGuire ten dollars, being amount of purchase-money of a grave two feet by eight in the ground of Calvary Cemetery, which has been consecrated for the exclusive purpose of the burial of the remains of persons who may die in communion with the Roman Catholic church.

That is the parol agreement, the only one which can possibly be implied. The plaintiff, too, recognized this, for he averred in this complaint that McGuire died in the Catholic faith and in communion with the church. And it was only when, upon the trial, the difficulty of proving, affirmatively, the latter assertion weighed upon him that he struck it from his complaint and claimed that it was superfluous. Now, who is to determine whether McGuire died in that communion? Mr. Justice Daniels admits that it is the hierarchy, but he thinks that the chosen judges of the church must proceed according to the principles of the common law; that they can only act upon evidence (as applicable to church law); that the accused is entitled to a hearing; and that if those "first principles" which govern in the ordinary administration of justice are ignored, the authorities of the church exceed their jurisdiction when they decree that the holder of the receipt died out of communion with the church. With great respect and diffidence, I venture to differ with the conclusion.

In my judgment, McGuire contracted for the exclusive jurisdiction of the church with regard to the question of communion. Spiritual questions are solely for the determination of the church authorities. Over their action in the domain of church discipline or excision the civil courts exercise no revisory power. (Shannon v. Frost, 3 B. Monroe, 253) There the court said: "We cannot decide who ought to be members of the church, nor whether the excommunicated have been justly or unjustly, regularly or irregularly, cut off from the body of the church. We must take the fact of expulsion as conclusive proof that the persons expelled are not now members of the repudiating church, for, whether right or wrong, the act of excommunication must, as to the fact of membership, be law to this court"...

On the same principle the decision that McGuire, although a Catholic, did not die in communion with the church, was final and conclusive until reversed, not by the civil courts, for they have no jurisdiction under a constitutional system which happily separates church and State, but by the highest authorities of the church itself. To attempt to exercise jurisdiction in such matters upon the plea of want of jurisdiction in the church authorities of first instance, would be the entering wedge whereby the symmetry of our governmental system with regard to church and State might readily be destroyed. And, after all, what do we question when looking into the Ordinary's jurisdiction, but his procedure?

Shall we go further and decide that he has no jurisdiction, within his sphere, to decree that a Roman Catholic died out of communion with the church, because the testimony upon which he acted was unsupported by an oath? Must he also notify the next of kin, or the executor or administrator of a proposed hearing, produce his witnesses in their presence, permit them to cross-examine and then to produce their own witnesses: Is he without jurisdiction if he deny them counsel; And all this while the deady body is awaiting his decision. Where does the right to question the jurisdiction begin, and where does it end?

It seems to me that the Ordinary's jurisdiction in spiritual matters cannot be questioned by the civil courts at all. He may act upon the best light he can obtain, however informal the source, and we cannot review his judgment, however out of touch with common-law principles may have been his means of ascertainment. If the ordinary acts capriciously or arbitrarily, there is an appeal to Rome. If the appellant is there again defeated, it will be time enough to inquire whether he has or has not contracted for the possibility of such injustice, and whether, even then, the facts and the law applicable thereto would warrant a court of equity in entering the spiritual domain to redress a mixed temporal and spiritual wrong. For we cannot overlook the fact, which pervards this entire controversy, that it is not the mere right to be buried in two foot by eight of ordinary earth which the plaintiff seeks to enforce, but plainly the right to be so buried in consecrated earth. It is thus the spiritual right which, in substance, he asks us to enforce; that is, the agreement, so to speak, for consecration predicated upon communion. The rest is but a temporal incident. The world is all before this plaintiff to secure for his testator mere burial. The secular cemeteries, with their regular and binding deeds, were open to McGuire, and are yet open to his representatives. But that is not what is required or desired. What the plaintiff insist upon is the burial of McGuire in the same consecrated earth where the body of his wife now rests. That, however, is something which the civil courts are powerless to compel, under such a contract or understanding as that which here forms the basis of the plaintiff's rights and of this action.

The Guibord case (Brown v. Cure of Montreal, L. R., 6 Privy Council App. 157), for which the learned counsel from the appellant quotes so fully, has no conceivable application here. That case proceeded upon rules referable to a system in which church and State are blended. Under that system, a British subject is entitled to burial in his parish churchyard without regard to contractual locality, and the question of his right to such burial is essentially for the civil courts, in the exercise of their quasi ecclesiastical jurisdiction. The Privy Council, in opening the discussion, declared that the question to be decided was "the right of Guibord to interment in the ordinary way in the cemetery of his parish. It may be observed that the Cure and Marguilliers are not proprietors of the parochial cemetery in the sense in which a parson in England is the owner of the freehold of the churchyard, that is to say, subject to the right of the parishioner to be buried therein."

In that case the church authorities offered to permit Guibord's burial in that part of the cemetery which was unconsecrated. But the court determined that he was entitled to be buried in the consecrated part, and even queried whether they might not command the church to so bury him with its ordinary and appropriate religious rights and service. "The payment of dimes to the clergy of the Roman Catholic church," said the court, "by its lay members and the rateability of the latter in the maintenance of parochial cemeteries are secured by law and statutes. These rights of the church must beget corresponding obligations, and it is obvious that this state of things may give rise to questions between the laity and clergy which can only be determined by the Municipal Courts."

Even the observations made by Lord Phillimore, that "if this church were to be regarded merely as a private and voluntary religious society, resting only on a consensual basis, courts of justice are still bound, when due complaint is made that a member of the society has been injured as to his rights in any matter of a mixed, spiritual and temporal character, to inquire into the laws or rules of the tribunal or authority which has inflicted the alleged injury," must be taken as applicable to the parish churchyard system, that is, to the parish churchyard or cemetery of any private and voluntary religious society in the kingdom, resting only on a consensual basis. The general right of a British subject, a member of such society, to burial in its parish churchyard or cemetery is thus held to be a matter for consideration and adjudication by the courts construing the laws or rules of such consensual society. Throughout the case there is not a suggestion of contractual relation nor of a right to burial in any particular plot. It was simply a judicial review, authorized by the law of England, of the action of the Roman Catholic church in Canada; and thereupon the Privy Council examined the laws of the church and held that its authorities had erred. We have no such system of jurisprudence here. In this, I must be permitted to say we are fortunate, for while human nature is what it is there must always be more or less of religious faction, with its intensity of bitterness, in every theological establishment, however well disciplined and authoritative.[1]...

Daniels, J. (dissenting):

By the language of the instrument, and the location of the grave, his representative was entitled to insist upon the right of the intestate to burial in it if he had observed the laws and discipline of the church, under whose authority the property was acquired and controlled. The instrument as it was issued, and the grave was located, created a privilege or license as it was without conveying a title to the land. (Kincaid's Appeal. 66 Penn. 411; _Page_ v. _Symonds_, 63 N.H., 17; _People ex rel. Coppers_ v. _Trustees_, 21

[1]A concurring opinion of Van Brunt, P. J. is omitted.

Hun. 184.) And the administrator was empowered to secure this interment, if the intestate had complied with the laws of the church controlling the cemetery, up to the time of his decease. (2 Blackstone's Com., 508; Williams v. Williams, 20 L.R., Ch. Div., 659.) And that was the view which was adopted and followed in the decision made at the Special Term. For it was there held by the court that the plaintiff, as the personal representative of the deceased, was vested with whatever right existed to enforce the contract to be implied from or contained in this instrument. The action accordingly did not fail because of any infirmity in the right of the plaintiff as the personal representative to maintain it, if that could be done legally, upon the facts made to appear by the evidence.

Upon the trial of the action accepted compilations of the laws of the church were proved and read in evidence, and these laws or regulations defined and declared the causes for which the interment of a deceased person might be forbidden in the consecrated cemetery and grounds of the church; and, so far as they existed and were applicable to this subject, they were required to be observed in the determination of the controversy which has arisen concerning the right of the deceased to burial in this cemetery. By these laws or regulations it was necessary that the deceased should have been during his life a member of the Catholic church. If he were not such a member, then his personal representative could claim no right to the interment of his remains in these grounds. (Dwenger v. Geary, 133 Ind., 106.) But the right to the interment of remains was not denied for want of any compliance on the part of the deceased with this regulation or requirement. Neither could it have been, for it was stated positively by the daughter of the deceased, who was sworn as a witness upon the trial of the action, that her father was a member of the Catholic church in his lifetime, and she was no further interrogated as to the correctness of this statement made by her. It appears to have been accepted as truthful, and it was assumed, during the progress of the trial, that he was a member of this church; and the complaint, as it is contained in the case, asserts that to have been the fact, for no more was stricken out, on the application of the plaintiff, than the statement that he died in full communion with the church, leaving the complaint as it now forms a part of the case with the allegation that he did die in the faith of the Roman Catholic Church; and it was not for want of any additional evidence as to this fact that the interment of the remains in the cemetery was denied by the authorities of the church or by the trial court.

But that denial appears to have proceeded upon the conclusion adopted by the court that it properly belonged, under the usages and discipline of the church, to the decision of the Ordinary or the Bishop of New York to determine whether the deceased was entitled to be buried in this cemetery; and the Ordinary having made a decision adversely to this right, upon evidence sufficient to give him jurisdiction to act, the remains were not entitled to burial in the consecrated ground of the cemetery.

It is undoubtedly the law that the courts will not review conclusions or decisions of the ecclesiastical authorities of the church relating to mere matters of faith, practice or discipline. (Dutch Church v. Bradford, 8 Cow., 457; People ex.rel. Dilcher v. German, etc., Church, 53 N.Y., 103; Shannon v. Frost, 3 B. Monroe, 253; German, etc., Church v. Seibert, 3

Barr (Penn.), 282, 291.) But this exclusive authority vested in the church is not applicable to the disposition or determination of rights or interests in property, or those derived from contracts lawfully entered into. As much as that was stated in Bouldin v. Alexander (15 Wall. 131.) And it necessarily follows, from the nature of the transactions through which rights or interests in property by virtue of contracts may be created, that they are to be governed by the secular law, as they are distinguishable from ecclesiastical subjects, and may only be divested, impaired or forfeited by reason of some act or circumstance upon which the right or contract has been made dependent, or for the violation of rules or regulations which, by the sanction and intention of the parties, have been made applicable thereto. Rights of this description are recognized and protected by the general law of the State, and that has carefully defined the manner in, and the causes for, which they may be lost or forfeited. And under that law, if the deceased, as a matter of fact, had violated or failed to observe any of the laws or regulations of the church applicable to and controlling this contract, then the plaintiff could not claim or insist upon his interment in this cemetery.

But neither one of these rules or regulations vested the clerical authorities of the church with jurisdiction to determine this right of interment in such a manner as to conclude the party entitled to insist upon the observance of this agreement. No hearing whatever has been provided for, or took place before the vicar-general, by whose order the interment of the remains in these grounds was forbidden. But he acted solely upon information which he had received from no directly responsible source, in reaching the conclusion that the deceased had forfeited his right to this burial. This was done, according to his own testimony, upon mere information; not a safe subject to be relied upon in any case for the determination of rights of property or contract, and the determination was made without any notice to, consultation with, or hearing of any person entitled to represent the deceased or to controvert the correctness of the information received by this clerical official. And under these circumstances the law will not permit a determination arrived at in this manner, to forfeit the right which the deceased may have secured through this instrument to burial in the consecrated cemetery of the church. The legal principle, on the contrary, has been declared to be that "there is nothing which our law denounces more explicitly than the adjudication of the rights of a party without offering him an opportunity of being heard in his defense." People ex rel. Waldron v. Soper (3 Seld., 428,431) and Loubat v. Le Roy (40 Hun, 546), follow and enforce this principle.

The determination which, in fact, was made in this manner, proceeded upon information that the deceased had died in the Academy of Music, at a meeting addressed by Dr. McGlynn, who had been excommunicated from membership in the Catholic church, and that he was, in reality, a confederate and abettor of this deposed priest. The vicar-general had been informed that McGlynn had abused and denounced the Pope, and it was considered a scandal for any good Catholic to be present at his meetings. His own testimony is that he did not know the deceased, but that he had "heard that he had been applauding Dr. McGlynn in abusing the Pope a few minutes before his death."

Upon his cross-examination he testified that it was a public fact that the deceased had died there. Thereupon the following questions were put to and answered by the witness: Q. I was not there; I did not see him die; you say it came up from the trustees; by what means? A. The undertaker called upon them. Q. How do you know? A. The clerk told me. Q. His name? A. Mr. Brennan. Q. Where did he tell you so? A. Oh, I can't remember the exact spot. Q. When did he tell you so? A. Either the day after his death or the following day. Q. What was said? A. Simply the fact that he died at the Academy of Music. Q. And on that you issued the order forbidding the burial? A. I did, sir.

These reports, with the exception of that as to the fact of the deceased dying at the Academy of Music, were of a loose and unreliable character, and could not legally have been the basis of binding action by the vicar-general. They were in no sense so authentic as to warrant or justify the conclusion that the deceased approved of the actions or expressions of McGlynn, or applauded any remarks or imputation made by him, at the meeting in this manner referred to, or at any other, and afforded no grounds of jurisdiction upon which he could legally or properly act in declaring the right of the deceased under this contract to have been forfeited by any misconduct on his part. The evidence was not of such a nature as to be acted upon, and therefore, afforded no jurisdiction over the subject-matter, and the want of jurisdiction, or the power to act, may be questioned in the courts by legal proceedings whenever the legality of the action taken shall be brought in controversy. (Ferguson v. Crawford, 70 N.Y. 253, 257; Cagwin v. Town of Hancock, 84 id., 532, 541; Craig v. Town of Andes, 93 id. 405.) And to afford jurisdiction by way of support for quasi judicial determination, it must proceed upon at least colorable evidence of the fact. But here no such, or, indeed any, evidence was supplied, and this, as well as the circumstances that the consideration given to the subject was wholly without notice, or an opportunity to be heard by any person interested in protecting the right of the deceased against these aspersions, rendered the determination which was made, inoperative for the want of authority over it.

But beyond this, according to the laws and regulations of the church, which have been made a part of the evidence in the case, the deceased could not be deprived of the right to burial in this cemetery by a simple determination that it had been forfeited or lost by him, for the laws of the church have made this disability to depend entirely, where the deceased shall have been a member of the Catholic church, upon some act, misconduct or omission of the deceased. These laws and regulations have in no manner provided that the right to burial in the cemetery, under an instrument of this description, can be taken away merely by the dictum or decision of a member of the church hierarchy. But the right to such burial by these laws has been declared to be lost, or forfeited, only by reason of actual misconduct on the part of the person in whose behalf it may in this manner be claimed. It is a penalty imposed for misconduct either by means of affirmative acts or delinquent omissions to act on the part of the deceased. Among the causes for which burial in consecrated ground may be refused are the fact that the deceased died a public sinner, or that he failed to perform some affirmative duty forming a part of his obligations as a member of the church, or had committed some act of scandalous misconduct. The law of the church in these and other matters attaches the loss or forfeiture to the act itself, or to the delinquency of the party, and not to a mere dictum or determination of any member of the clerical authority of the church; and to bring this case within these laws it was necessary, therefore, that the deceased should be shown, as a matter of fact, by way of defense to the action, to have violated, or become chargeable with, some act of misconduct prohibited by them, thereby forfeiting, under their authority, his right to burial in the consecrated ground of the church. But no such proof in any form has been included in or made a part of this case.

The evidence concerning the conduct of the deceased was obtained from witnesses either related to or knowing him well, and seeing him at meetings of the Anti-Poverty Society, and of the parishioners of the church of which McGlynn had previously been the pastor. But no witness testifies to the fact that he was present on any occasion when McGlynn addressed the people who were assembled, or that he in any manner had applauded, or approved of his conduct or sentiments, or the principles which he endeavored to maintain. And upon the occasion when he was at the Academy of Music, the proof is positive, from at least two witnesses, whose evidence is not contradicted, that he died half an hour before the proceedings of the meeting had commenced, and before Dr. McGlynn made his appearance. All that was shown against him was that he was present at the meetings already referred to, but not when Dr. McGlynn was either officiating or making any remarks or allusions whatsoever. There was no evidence that upon any occasion he had either misconducted himself or neglected any of his duties or obligations as a member of the Roman Catholic church. And that was the view which was adopted by the judge presiding at the trial, for, by his fifteenth finding, he found the facts to be "that the said John McGuire did not at any time after the said 22d day of November, 1870, violate any of the rules or regulations for the management of the said cemetery and interments therein, theretofore mady by the defendants, nor any laws of the Roman Catholic church theretofore made respecting the burial of the bodies of its deceased members."

And in this state of the evidence, as it cannot be affirmed that he had violated any rule or regulation of the Catholic faith, it follows that he did not forfeit his right to burial in this cemetery. If upon a mere mistaken view of the facts produced by unfounded reports, which is all that was before the vicar-general, this right of burial may be forfeited, then no security can certainly exist for the protection of any person acquiring and paying for this privilege of burial. For even the most correct religious deportment may be sacrificed by the malignant and untruthful reports of persons misrepresenting the acts, conduct or sentiments of deceased persons. Instead of the right being maintained, as the law requires it to be, as one of a proprietary character, it may then be overthrown or forfeited after the decease of the party securing it, without any available means of avoiding the result. No Catholic, whatever his standing may be, will be entirely removed from this danger, if upon mere reports, turning out as they have in this instance to be untruthful and unfounded, he can be deprived of burial in the consecrated ground of his church by the action of one of its officials induced by reliance upon such reports. The only safety which exists is that already indicated, in reliance upon and maintaing the laws of the church itself, which require not rumors or information, but that actual misconduct or the omission to observe specific obligations shall be proven to have taken place before a contract or instrument of the description of that, for a good consideration, delivered to the deceased, shall be forfeited or avoided. That proof is wholly wanting in this case, and the judgment should be reversed and a new trial ordered, with costs to the plaintiff to abide the event.

Ramon v. Ramon

Domestic Relations Court of New York City, 1942
34 N.Y. Supp.2nd 100

O'BRIEN, Justice

This is a proceeding wherein the petitioner wife seeks from the respondent-husband support for herself and the child of the parties.

Respondent admits his liability for the support, but asserts that the child of the parties is not being reared and educated in the Catholic religion, all in violation of an ante-nuptial contract and agreement made between the parties. The petitioner is a Protestant. The respondent is a Roman Catholic.

The child now eight years of age is baptized a Roman Catholic. Up to recently the child attended a Roman Catholic Parochial school and had been brought up in the Catholic religion.

Differences having recently arisen between the parties, the petitioner left the home of the respondent and went to live with her mother. Simultaneously she removed the child from the Catholic school, entered her in a public school and sent her to a Protestant Church, which she attended at the time of this hearing and also to the Sunday school connected with it.

The respondent objects to this upon the ground that this is a violation of a contract and agreement made by the respondent with the petitioner prior to their marriage, by which the petitioner, formally and in writing, agreed that any children of the marriage would be brought up in the Catholic religion.

The petitioner concedes that the petitioner and respondent prior to their marriage and in the presence of witnesses signed a written agreement, in conformity with the rule and the Canon Law of the Roman Catholic Church, the substance of which agreement was as follows: "All children of either sex born of the proposed marriage would be baptized and educated in the Catholic religion," and that she, the petitioner, "would not hinder nor obstruct in any manner whatsoever the respondent in the exercise of his religion."

Upon this agreement the respondent married the petitioner with a Catholic ceremony performed by a Catholic priest. Under the Canon Law of the Catholic Church no priest, in the absence of such an agreement, can officiate at a marriage between a Catholic and a non-Catholic. Canon 2319-2375.

Subsequent to the birth of the child, the petitioner consented to its Catholic baptism. Accordingly, the child was prepared, godparents were selected, and with the knowledge and consent of the petitioner the child was taken to the Catholic Church where the baptismal ceremony was performed.

The godparents, in accordance with the Canon Law of the Catholic Church, assumed the obligation and personally pledged themselve to see to it that their godchild would be instructed in the Catholic religion and that they would take an interest in the spiritual welfare of the child "in perpetua," and that they would see to it that during its whole life the child would live up to the principles of the Catholic faith. Canon 769.

Following the ceremony the godparents returned to the home of the petitioner and respondent, where the godparents and the child's parents dined together, the repast having been prepared for the occasion by the petitioner.

The question now before the Court is whether this pre-nuptial agreement contains all the elements of an enforceable valid contract.

The Domestic Relations Court is not vested with jurisdiction in divorce or separation actions. By reason of its broad summary powers, however, its decisions in effect, in some cases and under some circumstances, can relieve the husband or wife of practically all marital obligations except the actual severance of the matrimonial status.

The decisions heretofore regarding the religious education of children have been mainly in cases following the death of one or both parents, where contests have arisen between relatives over the religious education of the surviving children.

In the Domestic Relations Court, the care, education, home surroundings and religious training of children are frequently the subject of bitter parental controversy in cases of "mixed marriages."

Section 81 of the Domestic Relations Law gives both parents equal powers, rights and duties in regard to them.

Hence, by reason of the importance of the issues it becomes not only appropriate but indeed imperative to review briefly the nature, primary purposes and obligations of marriage, its historic direction and control, as well as the legal and enforceable aspects of such individual rights of the parties, as may retain their contractual character, as property rights during the existence of the matrimonial status.

In the Harvard Law Review, Volume 29, page 498, in an article entitled "The Parental Right to Control the Religious Education of a Child," appears this timely and critical observation: "Our Courts have been remarkably free from litigation over the religious education of children. It is only in very recent years that it is beginning to make its appearances."

"Most of the States - even a State so important as New York - are still without any decisions on the subject from a court of last resort. Such litigation as has arisen has either been decided by sidestepping the religious aspects of the controversy altogether, and resting the decision on some other grounds entitling one or the other party to custody of the infants or, too often in more or less slip-shod fashion, the court has treated the matter as if it were a novel issue to be decided as law of the first impression or has fallen into an undiscriminating citation of an English authority to justify some particular disposition of the case under consideration." Harvard Law Review, Vol. 29, page 498.

"In England, * * * as early as 1590," continues the Harvard Law Review, at page 485, "the Elizabethan government aimed at the supression of Catholic education by enacting that only schoolmasters who repaired to the Established Church might be maintained."

"From time to time further laws were passed to render more effectual the suppression of Catholic education, until by 1699, it was a crime punishable by perpetual imprisonment for any Papist to keep school or assume the education of youth."

"Naturally, during this period, in the face of such public sentiment and of such laws there was little or no litigation in the courts of England on the part of the Catholic parents to protect any parental rights in relation to their children." Harvard Law Review, Vol. 29, page 485.

It is apparent, therefore, that the decisions of the English Courts can furnish no helpful guide to American jurisprudence in the determination of cases involving the religious rights of either parents or children.

Our New York courts have issued a caution against relaince upon a foreign law in cases involving the rights of parents over infants. "Any foreign system of law is always to be invoked with discretion. Positive law, or the law of this time and place, is in practice always paramount in the administration of justice, and there is great danger in exploiting a legal theory by reference to the law of other times and places which, if ingeniously used, may furnish justification for the most opposed juridical rules." (Italics those of the Court) Matter of Wagner, 75 Misc. 419, at page 429, 135 N.Y.S. 678, at page 686.

The ante-nuptial agreement made by respondent and petitioner clearly contemplated the preservation of the spiritual rights and status of the respondent and those of his prospective children. These rights though spiritual and intangible became for all purposes just as real, protective and enforcible as pertained to any physical property...

Marriage is a natural right. It was not created by law. It existed before all law. Marriage is a right of personality. By the marriage ceremony these obligations became the vested rights of the personality of the respondent embraced in the law of the land, and defined as the rights of personality.

The reciprocal duties of husband and wife constitute property. "These reciprocal rights may be regarded as the property of the respective parties, in the broad sense of the word property, which includes things not tangible or visible, and applies to whatever is exclusively one's own." Jaynes v. Jaynes, 39 Hun 40, at page 41.

An epitome of the decisions heretofore made by the courts of this State limited and detailed only to the extent necessary to make clear the general policy appears appropriate to this memorandum.

In the case of Weinberger v. Van Hessen, 260 N.Y. 294, 183 N.E. 429, 430, an infant-plaintiff sued upon an agreement that if the custody of the infant, then residing in Holland, was surrendered and the infant brought to New York where the defendant would be permitted "to direct his education and control his religious and moral upbringing, the defendant would, during his natural life, support him and direct his moral education and training - the defendant at all times to have access to the infant so that he might enjoy his companionship and society." The Court said: "Suit may be maintained under the contract by plaintiff. * * * Agreements between parents for a particular sort of religious upbrining have in general been held valid in this country."

In Matter of Mancini, 89 Misc. 83, 151 N.Y.S. 387-389, a Catholic orphaned child was placed by its elder sister, then residing in Italy, in charge of a Protestant minister in New York, under a pledge that the child would be brought up a Catholic. The oldest brother applied for custody, alleging that this pledge was violated by placing the child in a Presbyterian home and while there the child attended the Presbyterian Church.

The physical well being of the child was properly and excellently maintained, but the Surrogate declared: "Of course, this conduct, however well meant, is incompatible with the discipline of the Catholic Church, and it is regarded by the infant's family as a breach of the compact before mentioned." The minister agreed to correct that course of conduct and the child's own wishes were to remain with him and his wife. It was pointed out that the child had been taken from poor surroundings and want, to greater physical comfort and more affluent environment. "But," declared the Surrogate, "I will not forget that the religious status of the child before me is that of a Catholic child, and I think the law governing the action of the courts, under such circumstances as those now disclosed to me, is fairly well determined. * * *"

"To Catholics, in particular, the education of an infant," said the Court, "leading as it does to their indissolvable marriage law, and their family relations founded on a subordination and respect to elders, the education I say of their infants in their own way is regarded by them as of paramount importance. It is evident that the preference of a Catholic family in regard to the education of a Catholic child cannot be overlooked by the court in the selection of a guardian for a Catholic child. * * *" Matter of Mancini, 89 Misc. 83, 151 N.Y.S. 387. . .

The recognition by our American courts of the right of the Catholic party as a matter of sound public policy to determine the religious upbringing of the children, with or without an ante-nuptial agreement, may arise from an instinctive and tacit recognition of three fundamental concepts, to wit: (1) Antenuptial agreements providing for the religious education of children, are exclusively a Catholic rule. (2) The Roman Catholic Church is the only Christian Church which holds marriage, and has always held it to be indissoluble and a Sacrament. Ency. Brit. Sacrament; also Methodism, Presbyterians, and other denominations, Book of Common Prayer, Art XXV; Koresic v. Grand Carniolian Slovenian Catholic Union of United States of America, 138 Kan. 261, 25 P.2d 355; Madden on Divorce and Separation, page 256. (3) The procreation of offspring under the natural law being the object of marriage, its permanency is the foundation of the social order.

Indissolubility of marriage and prohibition of "mixed marriages" are not mere sectarian rules but are deeply rooted in the consciousness and history of mankind. Indeed, it would be a challenging omission in this memorandum if reference were not made to their age old historic origin and enforcement.

It must be borne in mind that the ante-nuptial contract in issue was founded upon and rooted in a living system of jurisprudence ante-dating even the common law, that all embracing system known as the Canon Law.

The Canon Law was founded on the Bible; on the writings of the Fathers in which was contained the authorized interpretation of the Biblical texts and the tradition of the Church; on the custom of the Church which was always recognized as a source of law and which down to the end of the 18th Century was the constituent element of the Common Law. Sir William Holdsworth's History of English Law, Pub. Little Brown Co. 1938.

It was the Canon Law which made Christian States of European nations, directly or indirectly modified their constitutions, and profoundly inspired and motivated international and civil law throughout Christendom. Moreover, it made Christianity the law of the land in many European countries, in England and partly in the United States. New International Ency. Vol. IV, 2nd Ed.

"The elevated condition of woman is due to the Canon Law, prescriptions which the Church enforced in all nations converted to Christianity." International Ency. 1906 Ed.

"The history of the law of marriage in this Country traces its origin back to the ancient Canon Law, which consisted of the decrees of the various Popes and was the basis of the matrimonial law in England, and has been recognized there ever since the establishment of Christianity in the year 605." Reaves v. Reaves, 15 Okl. 240, 82 P. 490, 2 L.R.A., N.S., 353 at page 359.

"In the earliest Hebrew history endogamy prevails." Jewish Ency. "Marriage" From Father Abraham to Pope Pius XII, from the dawn of Israel to modern Jewry a consistent and inflexible prohibition of "Mixed Marriages" is recorded upon the pages of Holy Writ, the history of Christendom and of Jewish history.

The book of Genesis records the command of Abraham to his favorite and trusted servant, whom he sent out to seek a wife for his son Isaac: "And I will make thee swear by the Lord, the God of Heaven and the God of the earth, that thou shalt not take a wife unto my son of the daughters of the Canaanites among whom I dwell. But thou shalt go unto my country and to my kindred, and take a wife unto my son Isaac." Genesis Ch. XXIV, 3,4.

And the bitter protest of Rebekah; "And Rebekah said to Isaac, I am weary of my life, because of the daughters of Heth; if Jacob takes a wife of the daughters of Heth * * * what good shall my life do me?" Genesis XXVII, 46.

Later came the law of Moses, a peremptory interdiction of marriage with the Canaanites: "Neither shalt thou make marriages with them; thy daughter thou shalt not give unto his son, nor his daughter shall thou take unto they son." "For they will turn thy son from Me." Deuteronomy VII, 3,4.

And as further and increasingly frequent intermarriage threatened to disintegrate and even to destroy Israel, the alarmed Priest and Prophet Ezra denounced this practice: "And Ezra the priest stood up and said unto them, 'Ye have transgressed, and have taken strange wives to increase the trespass of Israel.'" Ezra X, 10,11.

"Now therefor give not your daughters unto their sons, neither take their daughters unto your sons." Ezra IX, 12. "And they entered * * * into an oath to walk in God's law * * * and that we would not give our daughters unto the people of the land, nor take their daughters for our sons." Nehem. X, 29,30.

This sound principle has been recognized and maintained until this day and is clearly expressed in these words: "Intermarriage is not countenanced by modern Judaism * * * due * * * to a conviction that unity of religion is essential to the happiness of the home." Jewish Ency. Vol. 5, page 626.

The Roman Catholic Church likewise from the very inception of her existence forbade the marriage of Catholics to non-Catholics. At the Council of Elvira, A.D. 305, the early Christian Fathers adopted this Canon; "Haeretici si se transferre noluerint ad ecclesiam catholicam, nec ipsis catholicas dandas esse puellas." ("It has pleased us to decree that if heretics are unwilling to become members of the Catholic Church, Catholic girls need not be given them.")

The dogma of indissolubility of the marriage required for its supporting foundation a unity of belief by both parties in its sacramental character. A necessary corollary was the rule forbidding the marriage between Christians and heretics, i.e., one accepting but part of the Christian doctrine.

From the Council of Elvira, 305 A.D., more than 1600 years have rolled on. In unbroken continuity two hundred and sixty two Popes have consistently maintained this rule. On December 31, 1930, Pope Pius XI, in his encyclical on Christian marriage, reaffirmed the age old rule concerning mixed marriages. "Everywhere and with the greatest strictness the Church forbids marriage between baptized persons one of whom is a Catholic and the other a member of a schismatical or heretical sect," declared the Pontiff, "And if there is added to this, the danger of falling away of the Catholic party and the perversion of the children, such a marriage is forbidden also by Divine Law." Encyclical Pope Pius XI, on Christian Marriage; 62 Cod. Jr. Can. c. 1060.

This dogma enters into the very essence of the ante-nuptial agreement, for the reason that a Catholic ceremonial marriage binds the Catholic party for life. Matthew XIX, 6; Corinthians VII, 10-27; Mark X, 9; Catholic Encyclopedia - Marriage; Canon Law.

But the non-Catholic party is not bound for life, since the non-Catholic Churches do not hold marriage to be a Sacrament, holding it but a union, which, even though entered into with a religious ceremony, may be dissolved by the non-Catholic spouse for many causes, without any religious, and with little social disability.

The Catholic party is not only forbidden to remarry under pain of excommunication, but the Sacramental bond of matrimony of the Catholic party remains undissolved notwithstanding the civil freedom granted to him by a divorcê court. Matthew XIX, 9; Canon Law.

And, where the non-Catholic party obtains a divorce, the Catholic married with a Catholic ceremony still remains bound. He or she cannot marry during the lifetime of her first spouse. Mark X, 11, 12; Luke XVI, 18; Catholic Ency. on Divorce.

By a Catholic ceremony the non-Catholic attains the safety and permance of a life union and the resulting stability and unity of the family, the husband, the wife and the children, shielded from the lure and peril of divorce now eating its corroding destruction into the vitals of America.

To every Catholic ex-communication among other things means the instant severance of membership in the Catholic Church. It involves the loss of its multifarious ministrations and rituals, the deprivation of all of its Sacraments, ostracism from the Catholic society and exclusion from "Christian burial." This last drastic penalty the Catholic contemplates with dread. Indeed, even under the Jewish law, "to be denied burial was the most humiliating indignity that could be offered to the deceased." Jewish Ency. Vol. III, page 432.

"Marriage is regarded by the law as a valuable consideration and marriage or promise of marriage is sufficient consideration for a promise." Williston on Contracts, 1936 Ed., Vol. 1, Sec. 110, page 376; New York Law Contracts, Clark, Vol. 1, page 458.

"A contract is a promise or set of promises, for the breach of which the law gives a remedy, or the performance of which the law in some way recognizes as a duty." Williston on Contracts, 1936 Ed., Vol. 1, Sec. 1, page 1.

"In its original application the term 'Consortium' was used to designate a right which the law recognizes in a husband growing out of a marital union, to have performance by the wife of all duties and obligations in respect to him which she took on herself when she entered into it." Hence, the ante-nuptial agreement of petitioner became upon the respondent's marriage to her, an inseparable part of the "Consortium," a duty the fulfillment of which lay in the mind and will of the petitioner. Jaynes v. Jaynes, 39 Hun 40.

"Agreements between parents relating to the religious training of their children are generally upheld." Williston on Contracts, Sec. 1744a note, page 4939; Weinberger v. Van Hessen, 260 N.Y. 294, 183 N.E. 429.

The respondent had the legal, equitable and constitutional right to protect, to preserve and to maintain inviolate his membership in the Roman Catholic Church. He had the undoubted right to enter into any agreement which would insure to him the continued enjoyment of its privileges and its protection, the religious and moral inspiration and the spiritual tranquility which he felt it inspired.

He had the right to determine that in his married life he would continue as formerly to abide by its rules, obligations and discipline. He had the right to seek to preserve this advantage for his children, the issue of the marriage, the same privileges, contacts and inspiration which he as a father considered essential to his and to their happiness and well being. In People ex rel. Rich v. Lackey case, 139 Misc. 42, 248 N.Y.S. 561, this latter principle developing into the sanction of law is clearly impregnate.

He had the right to choose for a spouse one who, though not a Catholic, would at least agree not to interfere in the exercise by him of his solemn religious duties, the most important of which would be to see that his children were brought up in the Catholic faith, and to see that they would attend Mass, to partake of the Sacraments, and to faithfully undertake and discharge all of the Catholic duties, inseparable in a Catholic home. For it is important to note that it was only by a concurrence with these obligations, that the respondent's membership in the Catholic Church could be insured and continued. Canon 2316-1219. "A Practical Commentary on the Code of the Canon Law," Paragraphs 1284-1285; Woywood, Vol. II, pp. 59, 60, 467, 471, 472; Canon 1258, 2316-2319, 2229.

Relying on this solemn promise by which the petitioner agreed to protect and preserve this right, respondent married the petitioner and irrevocably and for life changed his status from the single to the married state.

Not only was the status of the respondent changed, but the godparents, under the provisions of the Canon Law, assumed also a new and irrevocable spiritual status and impediments, the details of which need not to be outlined here. Canon 768.

The law favors ante-nuptial agreements and they will be enforced in equity according to the intention of the parties. Strebler v. Wolf, 152 Misc. 859, 273 N.Y.S. 653.

In Johnston v. Spicer, 107 N.Y. 185, at page 191, 13 N.E. 753, 755, the Court said; "Antenuptial contracts * * * are favored by the courts, and will be enforced in equity according to the intention of the parties whenever the contingency provided by the contract arises."

In the case of De Cicco v. Schweizer, 221 N.Y. 431, at page 438, 117 N.E. 807, at page 810, L.R.A. 1918E, 1004, Ann. Cas. 1918C, 816, as said by Mr. Justice Cardozo: "The very formality of the agreement suggests a purpose to affect the legal relations of the signers." (Mr. Justice Crane concurred in the same case) "the marriage having taken place, the settlement (contract) became binding. * * * 'if he induce a person to act upon a particular promise, with a particular view, which affects the interests in life of his own children and of the persons who become united to them, this court will not permit him afterwards to forego his own words, and say that he was not bound by what he then promised.'" (221 N.Y. pages 440, 441, 117 N.E. pages 810, 811) (Parenthesis those of Court.)

Section 53 of the Domestic Relations Law provides, "a contract made between persons in contemplation of marriage, remains in full force after the marriage takes place."

This deep-rooted allegiance of the vast number of Catholics toward the Roman Catholic Church and the general attitude and determination not to leave its embracing and protective shelter is a matter of common knowledge.

The growth of liberty has frequently experienced a powerful acceleration through some controversy, the profound and far-reaching importance of which is entirely beyond the thought of those immediately involved.

The instant case is one of those. In it is involved the relation of the law and the Constitution in preservation of the right of freedom of religious worship. It happens that the respondent seeking herein the protection of the right to the exercise of religious freedom contained in the ante-nuptial contract is a Catholic. But the principle invoked operates to bulwark the right to the exercise of religious freedom of persons of all religions, for its application extends to all.

Since the courts, as already pointed out, have repeatedly decreed the Catholic education of a child with or without an ante-nuptial agreement and without any formal direction on the part of the deceased Catholic parent, with what greater force should such judicial direction issue, where there is a written agreement and a living parent stands before the Court demanding its fulfillment.

From a consideration of the case, and the decisions herein cited, these rules of law are clearly established: (a) An ante-nuptial agreement providing for the Catholic faith and education of the children of the parties, in reliance upon which a Catholic has thereby irrevocably changed the status of the Catholic party, is an enforceable contract having a valid consideration; (b) the Court will take judicial notice of the religious and moral obligations of the parties; (c) the spiritual and Catholic training of a child amid religious persons or institutions of its own faith is paramount over any material considerations; (d) a holding that religious training of children may be dispensed with until they reach maturity upon the theory that they then may adopt any or no religion as they deem fit, is repugnant to our American background and traditions; (e) a court and especially the Domestic Relations Court is bound to approve the demand of a Catholic parent that its child be given a Catholic education and a Catholic upbringing in a Catholic home or institution, Domestic Relations Court Act, Art. 3, Sec. 88; (f) the Court will take judicial notice that the Roman Catholic Church is the only church whose members are bound by its laws even to the penalty of excommunication of the Catholic party who permits non-Catholic training and education of their children; (g) the fact that a child, in violation of the ante-nuptial contract, has for a period of time been brought up in some other religion than that fixed in the ante-nuptial agreement, is not sufficient ground to deprive the respondent of his rights to have the child educated in the religion fixed by the ante-nuptial contract.

It is clear that the respondent is entitled to have the child brought up in the religion agreed upon in the ante-nuptial contract. It is equally apparent that the child being baptized Catholic is entitled to and must receive the training and education of that faith.

The Court is informed that since the beginning of this proceeding the parties have placed the child in a Catholic boarding school and the respondent has assumed the obligation of paying for the child's maintenance and tuition therein. This arrangement of the petitioner and respondent is submitted to this Court for approval.

Accordingly, the said arrangement is hereby approved and the respondent is ordered and directed to pay the child's board, tuition and maintenance at the said Catholic boarding school as aforesaid. Judgment accordingly.[1]

---

[1]Concerning the constitutionality of legislation authorizing courts in divorce and separation cases to call in ministers to aid in effecting reconciliation, see People ex rel. Bernat v. Bicek, 405 Ill. 510 (1950).

CHAPTER IV

POLICE POWERS

Chancellor Kent in the Council of Revision

In 1818 the Legislature of New York adopted a Special Act by which a marriage between Eunice Chapman and her husband James Chapman was dissolved. The reason for granting her the requested relief was that her husband had become a member of the Society of Shakers. The statute came, in the normal course, to the Council of Revision for its consideration. The Council, in an opinion by Chancellor Kent (Street, Council of Revision 381, 386), condemned the statute on several grounds. The third ground stated by the Chancellor was as follows:

"The Council object to this bill because they deem it inconsistent with the thirty-eighth article of the Constitution of this State, which ordains 'that the free exercise and enjoyment of religious profession and worship, without discrimination or preference, shall forever hereafter be allowed within this State to all mankind; provided that the liberty of conscience shall not be so construed as to excuse acts of licentiousness, or justify practices inconsistent with the peace and safety of the State.'

"By the second section of the bill now under consideration, it is enacted 'that in all cases where any husband or wife, having any child or children of the marriage, shall hereafter separate the one from the other, and shall or have attached him or herself to the said Shakers, and shall also take or have taken with him or her such child or children, being under age, the Chancellor or any Judge of the Supreme Court may award the charge and custody of such child or children to that parent who shall not have joined the said Society of Shakers.'

"By the existing general law of this State, applicable alike to all classes of men excepting slaves, the guardianship, custody and control of infant children belong exclusively to the father, who, by the same general law, is also entitled to the service of his infant children without accountability.

"Under the provisions of this bill, the father may be divested of these precious and import rights, for the sole and avowed cause that he has become a member of the Society of Shakers.

"The special regulation is in the nature of a penalty, and in the opinion of the Council, it is practically making a discrimination, and giving a preference, whereby the equality of civil rights (as between persons of different religious professions) is essentially impaired.

"If the Legislature can constitutionally deprive a man of his parental rights, merely because he is a Shaker, they have an equal right for the same cause to disfranchise him of every other privilege, or to banish him or even to put him to death. If the principle be admitted, it must rest in discretion alone how far it shall be carried in the measure of punishment.

"There is no evidence that the Society of Shakers are guilty of any acts of licentiousness, or any practices inconsistent with the peace and safety of this State; and although we may lament what to us appear absurd errors in their religious creed, yet, so long as they preserve the character which they now possess for sobriety, industry and peaceful habits, the Council cannot regard them as having forfeited the protection secured by that article of the Constitution. To justify such an act of denunciation, the danger to 'the peace and safety of this State' must be not merely speculative, remote and possible, bu imminent and certain.

"To condemn a religious tenet by legislative authority is to assume a power hitherto unknown in our statute book; and upon the most mature reflection, the Council are of opinion that it would be not only unprecedented in the annals of our State, but highly dangerous and alarming in its consequences.

"In regard to the people called Shakers, the only possible apprehension of danger to the State on account of their religious faith and practice arises from the tenet that sexual intercourse is sinful; and it is worthy of remark that if they practice according to that belief, the very cause from which danger is apprehended, to wit, celibacy, is the very reason why that sect cannot be propagated to any dangerous extent. The supposed evil, therefore, carried along with it an effectual remedy.

"The absurdity of that tenet is so plain and obvious as to prove an antidote and security against any serious danger of its prevalence; provided the excitement of persecution be not added to that of fanaticism. It may be pitied as a delusion, but it ought not to be regarded as a crime...

<u>Davis</u> v. <u>Beason</u>
Supreme Court of the United States, 1890
122 U. S. 333

In April 1889, the appellant, Samuel D. Davis, was indicted in the District Court of the Third Judicial District of the Territory of Idaho, in the county of Oneida, in connection with divers persons named, and divers other persons whose names were unknown to the grand jury, for a conspiracy to unlawfully pervert and obstruct the due administration of the laws of Territory, in this that they would unlawfully procure themselves to be admitted to registration as electors of said county of Oneida for the general election then next to occur in that county, when they were not entitled to be admitted to such registration, by appearing before the respective registrars of the election precincts in which they resided, and taking the oath prescribed by the statute of the State, in substance as follows: "I do swear (or affirm) that I am a male citizen of the United States of the age of twenty-one years (or will be on the 6th day of November, 1888); that I have (or will have) actually resided in this Territory four months and in this county for thirty days next preceding the day of the next ensuing election; that I have never been convicted of treason, felony, or bribery; that I am not registered or entitled to vote at any other place in this Territory; and I do further swear that I am not a bigamist or polygamist; that I am not a member of any order, organization or association which teaches, advises, counsels or encourages its members, devotees or any other person to commit the crime of bigamy or polygamy, or any other crime defined by law, as a duty arising or resulting from membership in such order, organization or association, or which practises bigamy, polygamy or plural or celestial marriage as a doctrinal rite of such organization; that I do not and will not, publicly or privately, or in any manner whatever teach, advise, counsel or encourage any person to commit the crime of bigamy or polygamy, or any other crime defined by law, either as a religious duty or otherwise; that I do regard the Constitution of the United States and the laws thereof and the laws of this Territory, as interpreted by the courts, as the supreme laws of the land, the teachings of any order, organization or association to the contrary notwithstanding, so held me God," when, in truth, each of the defendants was a member of an order, organization and association, namely the Church of Jesus Christ of Latter-Day Saints, commonly known as the Mormon Church, which they knew taught, advised, counselled and encouraged its members and devotees to commit the crimes of bigamy and polygamy as duties arising and resulting from membership in said order, organization and association, and which order, organization and association, as they all knew, practised bigamy and polygamy, and plural and celestial marriage as doctrinal rites of said organization; and that in pursuance of said conspiracy the said defendants went before the registrars of different precincts of the county (which are designated) and took and had administered to them respectively the oath aforesaid.

The defendants demurred to the indictment, and the demurrer being overruled they pleaded separately not guilty. On the trial which followed on the 12th of September, 1889, the jury found the defendant, Samuel D. Davis, guilty as charged in the indictment. The defendant was thereupon sentenced to pay a fine of $500, and in default of its payment to be confined in the county jail of Oneida County for a term not exceeding 250 days, and was remanded to the custody of the sheriff until the judgment should be satisfied.

Soon afterwards, on the same day, the defendant applied to the court before which the trial was had, and obtained a writ of habeas corpus, alleging that he was imprisoned and restrained of his liberty by the sheriff of the county; that his imprisonment was by virtue of his conviction and the judgment mentioned and the warrant issued thereon; that such imprisonment was illegal; and that such illegality consisted in this: 1, that the facts in the indictment and record did not constitute a public offence, and the acts charged were not criminal or punishable under any statute or law of the territory; and, 2, that so much of the statute of the territory as provides that no person is entitled to register or vote at any election who is "a member of any order, organization, or association which teaches, advises, counsels, or encourages its members, devoteed, or any other person to commit the crime of bigamy or polygamy, or any other crime defined by law, as a duty arising or resulting from membership in such order, organization, or association, or which practises bigamy or polygamy or plural or celestial marriage as a doctrinal rite of such organization" is a "law respecting an establishment of religion," in violation of the first Amendment to the Constitution and void.

The court ordered the writ to issue, directed to the sheriff, returnable before it, at three o'clock in the afternoon of that day, commanding the sheriff to have the body of the defendant before the court at the hour designated, with the time and cause of his imprisonment, and to do and receive what should then be considered concerning him. On the return of the writ, the sheriff produced the body of the defendant and also the warrant of commitment under which he was held, and the record of the case showing his conviction for the conspiracy mentioned and the judgment thereon. To this return, the defendant admitting the facts stated therein, excepted to their sufficiency to justify his detention. The court, holding that sufficient cause was not shown for the discharge of the defendant, ordered him to be remanded to the custody of the sheriff. From this judgment the defendant appealed to this court. Rev. Stat. § 1909...

Mr. JUSTICE FIELD, after stating the case, delivered the opinion of the court.

On this appeal our only inquiry is whether the District Court of the Territory had jurisdiction of the offence charged in the indictment of which the defendant was found guilty. If it had jurisdiction, we can go no farther. We cannot look into any alleged errors in its rulings on the trial of the defendant. The writ of habeas corpus cannot be turned into a writ of error to review the action of that court. Nor can we inquire whether the evidence established the fact alleged, that the defendant was a member of an order or organization known as the Mormon Church, called the Church of Jesus Christ of Latter-Day Saints, or the fact that the order or organization taught and counselled its members and devotees to commit the crimes of bigamy and polygamy as duties arising from membership therein. On this hearing we can only consider whether, these allegations being taken as true, an offence was committed of which the territorial court had jurisdiction to try the defendant. And on this point there can be no serious discussion or difference of opinion. Bigamy and polygamy are crimes by the laws of all civilized and Christian countries. They are crimes by the laws of the United States, and they are crimes by the laws of Idaho. They tend to destroy the purity of the marriage relation, to disturb the peace of families, to degrade woman and to debase man. Few crimes are more pernicious to the best interests of society and receive more general or more deserved punishment. To extend exemption from punishment for such crimes would be to shock the moral judgment of the community. To call their advocacy a tenet of religion is to offend the common sense of mankind. If they are crimes, then to teach, advise and counsel their practice is to aid in their commission, and such teaching and counselling are themselves criminal and proper subjects of punishment, as aiding and abetting crime are in all other cases.

The term "religion" has reference to one's views of his relations to his Creator, and to the obligations they impose of reverence for his being and character, and of obedience to his will. It is often confounded with the cultus or form of worship or a particular sect, but is distinguishable from the latter. The first amendment to the Constitution, in declaring that Congress shall make no law respecting the establishment of religion, or forbidding the free exercise thereof, was intended to allow every one under the jurisdiction of the United States to entertain such notions respecting his relations to his Maker and the duties they impose as may be approved by his judgment and conscience, and to exhibit his sentiments in such form of worship as he may think proper, not injurious to the equal rights of others, and to prohibit legislation for the support of any religious tenets, or the modes of worship of any sect. The oppressive measures adopted, and the cruelties and punishments inflicted by the governments of Europe for many ages, to compel parties to conform, in their religious beliefs and modes of worship, to the views of the most numerous sect, and the folly of attempting in that way to control the mental operations of persons, and enforce an outward conformity to a prescribed standard, led to the adoption of the amendment in question. It was never intended or supposed that the amendment could be invoked as a protection against legislation for the punishment of acts inimical to the peace, good order and morals of society. With man's relations to his Maker and the obligations he may think they impose, and the manner in which an expression shall be made by him of his belief on those subjects, no interference can be permitted, provided always the laws of society, designed to secure its peace and prosperity, and the morals of its people, are not interfered with. However free the exercise of religion may be, it must be subordinate to the criminal laws of the country, passed with reference to actions regarded by general consent as properly the subjects of punitive legislation. There have been sects which denied as a part of their religious tenets that there should be any marriage tie, and advocated promiscuous intercourse of the sexes as prompted by the passions of its members. And history discloses the fact that the necessity of human sacrifices, on special occasions, has been a tenet of many sects. Should a sect of either of these kinds ever find its way into this country, swift punishment would follow the carrying into effect of its doctrines, and no heed would be given to the pretence that, as religious beliefs, their supporters could be protected in their exercise by the Constitution of the United States. Probably never before in the history of this country has it been seriously contended that the whole punitive power of the government for acts, recognized by the general consent of the Christian world in modern times as proper matters for prohibitory legislation, must be suspended in order that the tenets of a religious sect encouraging crime may be carried out without hindrance.

On this subject the observations of this court through the late Chief Justice Waite, in Reynolds v. United States, are pertinent. 98 U. S. 145, 165, 166. In that case the defendant was indicted and convicted under section 5352 of the Revised Statutes, which declared that "every person having a husband or wife living, who marries another, whether married or single, in a Territory, or other place over which the United States have exclusive jurisdiction, is guilty of bigamy, and shall be punished by a fine of not more than five hundred dollars, and by imprisonment for a term not more than five years." The case being brought here, the court, after referring to a law passed in December, 1788, by the State of Virginia, punishing bigamy and polygamy with death, said that from that day there never had been a time in any State of the Union when polygamy had not been an offence against society cognizable by the civil courts and punished with more or less severity; and added: "Marriage, while from its very nature a sacred obligation, is, nevertheless, in most civilized nations a civil contract, and usually regulated by law. Upon it society may be said to be built, and out of its fruits spring social relations and social obligations and duties, with which government is necessarily required to deal. In fact, according as monogamous or polygamous marriages are allowed, do we find the principles on which the government of the people, to a greater or less extent, rests." And, referring to the statute cited, he said: "It is constitutional and valid as prescribing a rule of action for all those residing in the Territories, and in places over which the United States have exclusive control. This being so, the only question that remains is, whether those who make polygamy a part of their religion are excepted from the operation of the statute. If they are, then those who do not make polygamy a part of their religious belief may be found guilty and punished, while those who do must be acquitted and go free. This would be introducing a new element into criminal law. Laws are made for the government of actions, and while they cannot interfere with mere religious belief and opinions, they may with practices. Suppose one believed that human sacrifices were a necessary part of religious worship, would it be seriously contended that the civil government under which he lived could not interfere to prevent a sacrifice? Or, if a wife religously believed it was her duty to burn herself upon the funeral pile of her dead husband, would it be beyond the power of the civil government to prevent her carrying her belief into practice? So here, as a law of the organization of society under the exclusive dominion of the United States, it is provided that plural marriages shall not be allowed. Can a man excuse his practices to the contrary because of his religious belief? To permit this would be to make the professed doctrines of religious belief superior to the law of the land, and in effect to permit every citizen to become a law unto himself. Government could exist only in name under such circumstances." And in Murphy v. Ramsey, 114 U.S. 15, 45, referring to the act of Congress excluding polygamists and bigamists from voting or holding office, the court, speaking by Mr. Justice Matthews, said: "Certainly no legislation can be supposed more wholesome and necessary in the founding of a free, self-governing commonwealth, fit to take rank as one of the coordinate States of the Union, than that which seeks to establish it on the basis of the idea of the family, as consisting in and springing from the union for life of one man and one woman in the holy estate of matrimony; the sure foundation of all that is stable and noble in our civilization; the best guaranty of that reverent morality which is the source of all beneficent progress in social and political improvement. And to this end no means are more directly and immediately suitable than those provided by this act, which endeavors to withdraw all political influence from those who are practically hostile to its attainment."

It is assumed by counsel of the petitioner, that because no mode of worship can be established or religious tenets enforced in this country, therefore any form of worship may be followed and any tenets, however destructive of society, may be held and advocated, if asserted to be a part of the religious doctrines of those advocating and practising them. But nothing is further from the truth. Whilst legislation for the establishment of a religion is forbidden, and its free exercise permitted, it does not follow that everything which may be so called can be tolerated. Crime is not the less odious because sanctioned by what any particular sect may designate as religion. ... [The court then determined that the territorial legislature was entitled to prescribe the qualifications of voters.]

The judgment of the court below is therefore

Affirmed.

Hamilton v. Regents of the University of California
Supreme Court of the United States, 1934
293 U. S. 245

Mr. JUSTICE BUTLER delivered the opinion of the Court.[1]

This is an appeal under § 237 (a), Judicial Code, 28 U. S. C. § 344 (a), from a judgment of the highest court of California sustaining a state law that requires students at its university to take a course in military science and tactics, the validity of which was by the appellants challenged as repugnant to the Constitution and laws of the United States.

The appellants are the above-named minors, and the fathers of each as his guardian ad litem and individually. They are taxpayers and citizens of the United States and of California. Appellees are the regents constituting a corporation created by the State to administer the university, its president, and its provost. Appellants applied to the state supreme court for a writ of mandate compelling appellees to admit the minors into the university as students. So far as they are material to the questions presented here, the allegations of the petition are:

In October, 1933, each of these minors registered, became a student in the university and fully conformed to all its requirements other than that compelling him to take the course in military science and tactics in the Reserve Officers Training Corps, which they assert to be an integral part of the military establishment of the United States and not connected in any way with the militia or military establishment of the State. The primary object of there establishing units of the training corps is to qualify students for appointment in the Officers Reserve Corps. The courses in military training are those prescribed by the War Department. The regents require enrollment and participation of able-bodied male students who are citizens of the United States. These courses include instruction in rifle marksmanship, scouting and patrolling, drill and command, musketry, combat principles, and use of automatic rifles. Arms, equipment and uniforms for use of students in such courses are furnished by the War Department of the United States Government.

These minors are members of the Methodist Episcopal Church and of the Epworth League and connected religious societies and organizations. For many years their fathers have been ordained ministers of that church. The Southern California Conference at its 1931 session adopted a resolution:

"With full appreciation of the heroic sacrifices of all those who have conscientiously and unselfishly served their country in times of war, but

---

[1]Footnotes are omitted. A concurring opinion by Cardozo, J. is also omitted.

with the belief that the time has come in the unfolding light of the new day for the settlement of human conflicts by pacific means, and because we as Christians owe our first and supreme allegiance to Jesus Christ. Because the Methodist Episcopal Church in the General Conference of 1928 has declared: 'We renounce war as an instrument of national policy.' Because our nation led the nations of the world in signing the Paris Peace Pact, and the Constitution of the United States, Article 6, Section 2, provides that: 'This Constitution and the laws of the United States which shall be made in pursuance thereof and all treaties made under authority of the United States shall be the Supreme Law of the Land.' Thus making the Paris Pact the supreme law of the land which declares: 'The high contracting parties agree that the settlement of all disputes or conflict - shall never be sought except by pacific means.'

"Therefore we, the Southern California Conference, memorialize the General Conference which convenes in Atlantic City in May, 1932; to petition the United States Government to grant exemption from military service to such citizens who are members of the Methodist Epsicopal Church, as conscientiously believe that participation in war is a denial of their supreme allegiance to Jesus Christ."

And in 1932 the General Conference of that Church adopted as a part of its tenets and discipline:

"We hold that our country is benefited by having as citizens those who unswervingly follow the dictates of their consciences... Furthermore, we believe it to be the duty of the churches to give moral support to those individuals who hold conscientious scruples against participation in military training or military service. We petition the government of the United States to grant to members of the Methodist Episcopal Church who may be conscientious objectors to war the same exemption from military service as has long been granted to members of the Society of Friends and other similar religious organizations. Similarly we petition all educational institutions which require military training to excuse from such training any student belonging to the Methodist Episcoapl Church who has conscientious scruples against it. We earnestly petition the government of the United States to cease to support financially all military training in civil educational institutions."

And the Southern California Conference at its 1933 session adopted the following:

"Reserve Officers' Training Corps - Recalling the action of the General Conference asking for exemption from military service for those members of our church to whom war and preparation for war is a violation of conscience, we request the authorities of our State Universities at Berkeley, Los Angeles and Tucson, to exempt Methodist students from the R.O.T.C. on the grounds of conscientious objection, and we hereby pledge the moral and official backing of this Conference, seeking such exemption, provided that it be understood that no conscientious objector shall participate in the financial profits of war. The Secretary of the Conference is asked to send copies of this paragraph to the governing boards of these institutions."

Appellants, as members of that church, accept and feel themselves morally, religiously and conscientiously bound by its tenets and discipline as expressed in the quoted conference resolutions; each is a follower of the teachings of Jesus Christ; each accepts as a guide His teachings and those of the Bible and holds as a part of his religious and conscientious belief that war, training for war, and military training are immoral, wrong and contrary to the letter and spirit of His teaching and the precepts of the Christian religion.

Therefore these students, at the beginning of the fall term in 1933, petitioned the university for exemption from military training and participation in the activities of the training corps, upon the ground of their religious and conscientious objection to war and to military training. Their petition was denied. Thereupon, through that church's bishop in California, they and their fathers petitioned the regents that military training be made optional in order that conscientious and religious objectors to war, training for war and military training might not be confronted with the necessity of violating and foreswearing their beliefs or being denied the right of education in the state university to which these minors are entitled under the constitution and laws of the State of California and of the United States.

The regents refused to make military training optional or to exempt these students. Then, because of their religious and conscientious objections, they declined to take the prescribed course, and solely upon that ground the regents by formal notification suspended them from the university, but with leave to apply for readmission at any time, conditioned upon their ability and willingness to comply with all applicable regulations of the university governing the matriculation and attendance of students. The university affords opportunity for education such as may not be had at any other institution in California, except at a greater cost which these minors are not able to pay. And they, as appellees at the time of their suspension well knew, are willing to take as a substitute for military training such other courses as may be prescribed by the university.

Other allegations of the petition need not be stated as they merely go to show the grounds upon which appellants under the state practice sought the writ of mandate.

The university is a land grant college. An act of Congress (Morrill Act approved July 1, 1862, 12 Stat. 503; u U. S. C., §§ 301-308) donated public lands to the several states in order that upon the conditions specified all moneys derived from the sale of such lands or from the sale of land scrip issued under the act should be invested and constitute a perpetual fund the interest of which should be inviolably appropriated by each State accepting the benefits of the act "to the endowment, support, and maintenance of at least one college where the leading object shall be, without excluding the other scientific and classical studies, and including military tactics, to teach such branches of learning as are related to agriculture and the mechanic arts, in such manner as the legislatures of the States may respectively prescribe, in order to promote the liberal and practical education of the industrial classes in the several pursuits and professions in life"...

The state court, without announcing an opinion, denied the petition for a writ of mandate. Appellants applied for a rehearing. The court, denying the application, handed down an opinion in which it held that Art. IX, § 9, reposes in the regents full powers of organization and government of the university subject to legislative control in respect of its endowments and funds; that by § 6 of the organic act and Art. IX, § 9, military tactics is expressly required to be included among the subjects which shall be taught at the univeristy and that it is the duty of the regents to prescribe the nature and extent of the courses to be given and to determine what students shall be required to pursue them, and that the suspension of the petitioning students because of their refusal to pursue the compulsory courses in military training.involved no violation of their rights under the Constitution of the United States.

By their assignment of errors, appellants call upon this court to decide whether the challenged provisions of the state constitution, organic act and regents' order, in so far as they impose compulsory military training, are repugnant to the privileges and immunities clause of the Fourteenth Amendment, the due process clause of that amendment or the treaty that is generally called the Briand-Kellogg Peace Pact. 46 State. 2343...

The clauses of the Fourteenth Amendment invoked by appellants declare: "No State shall make or enforce any law which shall abridge the privileges or immunities of citizens of the United States; nor shall any State deprive any person of life, liberty or property, without due process of law." Appellants' contentions are that the enforcement of the order prescribing instruction in military science and tactics abridges some privilege or immunity covered by the first clause and deprives of liberty safeguarded by the second. The "privileges and immunities" protected are only those that belong to citizens of the United States as distinguished from citizens of the States - those that arise from the Constitution and laws of the United States as contrasted with those that spring from other sources. Slaughter-House Cases, 16 Wall. 36, 72-74, 77-80. MePherson v. Blacker, 146 U. S. 1, 38. Duncan v. Missouri, 152 U. S. 377, 382. Twining v. New Jersey, 211 U. S. 78, 97. Maxwell v. Bugbee, 250 U. S. 525, 538. Prudential Ins. Co. v. Cheek, 259 U. S. 530, 539. Appellants assert - unquestionably in good faith - that all war, preparation for war, and the training required by the university, are repugnant to the tenets and discipline of their church, to their religion and to their consciences. The "privilege" of attending the university as a student comes not from federal sources but is given by the State. It is not within the asserted protection. The only "immunity" claimed by these students is freedom from obligation to comply with the rule prescribing military training. But that "immunity" cannot be regarded as not within, or as distinguishable from, the "liberty" of which they claim to have been deprived by the enforcement of the regents' order. If the regents' order is not repugnant to the due process clause, then it does not violate the privileges and immunities clause. Therefore we need only decide whether by state action the "liberty" of these students has been infringed.

There need be no attempt to enumerate or comprehensively to define what is included in the "liberty" protected by the due process clause. Undoubtedly it does include the right to entertain the beliefs, to adhere to the principles and to teach the doctrines on which these students base their objections to the order prescribing military training. Meyer v. Nebraska,

262 U. S. 390, 399. Pierce v. Society of Sisters, 268 U. S. 510. Stromberg v. California, 283 U. S. 359, 368-369. Near v. Minnesota, 283 U. S. 697, 707. The fact that they are able to pay their way in this university but not in any other institution in California is without significance upon any constitutional or other question here involved. California has not drafted or called them to attend the university. They are seeking education offered by the State and at the same time insisting that they be excluded from the prescribed course solely upon grounds of their religious beliefs and conscientious objections to war, preparation for war and military education. Taken on the basis of the facts alleged in the petition, appellants' contentions amount to no more than an assertion that the due process clause of the Fourteenth Amendment as a safeguard of "liberty" confers the right to be students in the state university free from obligation to take military training as one of the conditions of attendance.

Viewed in the light of our decisions that proposition must at once be put aside as untenable.

Government, federal and state, each in its own sphere owes a duty to the people within its jurisdiction to preserve itself in adequate strength to maintain peace and order and to assure the just enforcement of law. And every citizen owes the reciprocal duty, according to his capacity, to support and defend government against all enemies. Selective Draft Law Cases, supra, p. 378. Minor v. Happersett, 21 Wall. 162, 166.

United States v. Schwimmer, 279 U. S. 644, involved a petition for naturalization by one opposed to bearing arms in defense of country. Holding the applicant not entitled to citizenship, we said (p. 650): "That it is the duty of citizens by force of arms to defend our government against all enemies whenever necessity arises is a fundamental principle of the Constitution. . . . Whatever tends to lessen the willingness of citizens to discharge their duty to bear arms in the country's defense detracts from the strength and safety of the Government."

In United States v. Macintosh, 283 U. S. 605, a later naturalization case, the applicant was unwilling, because of the conscientious objections, to take unqualifiedly the statutory oath of allegiance which contains this statement: "That he will support and defend the Constitution and laws of the United States against all enemies, foreign or domestic, and bear true faith and allegiance to the same." 8 U. S. C., § 381. His petition stated that he was willing if necessary to take up arms in defense of this country, "but I should want to be free to judge of the necessity." In amplification he said: "I do not undertake to support 'my country, right or wrong' in any dispute which may arise, and I am not willing to promise beforehand, and without knowing the cause for which my country may go to war, either that I will or that I will not 'take up arms in defense of this country,' however 'necessary' the war may seem to be the government of the day." The opinion of this Court quotes from petitioner's brief a statement to the effect that it is a "fixed principle of our Constitution, zealously guarded by our laws, that a citizen cannot be forced and need not bear arms in a way if he has conscientious religious scruples against doing so." And, referring to that part of the argument in behalf of the applicant, this Court said (p. 623), "This, if it means what it seems to say, is an astonishing statement. Of course, there is no such principle of the Constitution, fixed or otherwise. The conscientious objector is relieved from the obligation to bear arms in obedience to no constitutional provision, express or implied; but because, and only because, it has accorded with the policy of Congress thus to relieve him... The privilege of the native-born conscientious objector to avoid bearing arms comes not from the Constitution but from the acts of Congress. That body may grant or withhold the exemption as in its wisdom it sees fit; and if it be withheld, the native-born conscientious objector cannot successfully assert the privilege. No other conclusion is compatible with the well-nigh limitless extent of the war powers as above illustrated, which include, by necessary implication, the power, in the last extremity, to compel the armed service of any citizen in the land, without regard to his objections or his views in respect to the justice or morality of the particular war or of war in general. In Jacobson v. Massachusetts, 197 U.S. 11, 29, this Court (upholding a state compulsory vaccination law) speaking of the liberties guaranteed to the individual by the Fourteenth Amendment, said: '... and yet he may be compelled, by force if need be, against his will and without regard to his personal wishes or his pecuniary interests, or even his religious or political convictions, to take his place in the ranks of the army of his country and risk the chance of being shot down in its defense.' "

And see University of Maryland v. Coale, 165 Md. 224, 167 Atl. 54, a case, similar to that now before us, decided against the contention of a student in the University of Maryland who on conscientious grounds objected to military training there required. His appeal to this Court was dismissed for the want of a substantial federal question. 290 U. S. 597.

Plainly there is no ground for the contention that the regents' order, requiring able-bodied male students under the age of twenty-four as a condition of their enrollment to take the prescribed instruction in military science and tactics, transgresses any constitutional right asserted by these appellants.

The contention that the regents' order is repugnant to the Briand-Kellogg Peace Pact requires little consideration. In that instrument the United States and the other high contracting parties declare that they condemn recourse to war for the solution of international controversies and renounce it as an instrument of national policy in their relations with one another and agree that the settlement or solution of all disputes or conflicts which may arise among them shall never be sought except by pacific means. Clearly there is no conflict between the regents' order and the provisions of this treaty.

Affirmed.

United States v. Kauten
Court of Appeals, 2nd Circuit, 1943
133 Fed 2 703

AUGUSTUS N. HAND, Circuit Judge.

The defendant, Mathias Kauten, was convicted for neglecting to appear for induction into the United States Army pursuant to the Selective Training and Service Act of 1940, 50 U.S.C.A. Appendix, § 301 et seq. He claims that the conviction was erroneous because he was exempt as a conscientious objector under Section 5 (g) of the Selective Training and Service Act.[1]

The following is an outline of the facts: On March 10, 1941, the defendant was classified by the Local Draft Board as 1A. On April 3, 1941, he appealed from the classification on the ground that "by reason of religious training and belief" he was "conscientiously opposed to participation in war in any form." On May 19, 1942, the Board of Appeal affirmed the classification and on June 6, 1942, an order to report for induction on the following June 19th was mailed to him, which he received and knowingly neglected to obey.

Thereafter he was indicted and convicted under Section 11 of the Selective Training and Service Act, for knowingly failing to perform a duty required by the Act. At the trial, which on the motion of his attorney and upon his own consent in writing, was had before the court without a jury, he offered to prove that he had made a claim of exemption before his Local Board on the ground that he was a conscientious objector. This claim had been rejected both by the Local Board and by the Appeal Board because both boards concluded that his opposition was not based upon "religious training and belief." In support of the offer of proof he sought to introduce at the trial the findings of Honorable Lamar Hardy who had been appointed Hearing Officer of claims of conscientious objectors by the Department of Justice. This offer was made on the ground that the Appeal Board in reaching its conclusion had adopted the findings and conclusions of Lamar Hardy. The trial judge rejected the offer of evidence for the reason that the order to report for induction could not be attacked collaterally. In so ruling the court followed the decisions of the Third Circuit in United States v. Grieme, 128 F. 2d 811, and the Fifth Circuit in Fletcher v. United States, 129 F. 2d 262. A still more recent decision to the same effect was rendered by the Court of Appeals of the Third Circuit in United States v. Bowles, 131 F. 2d 818. By each decision it was held that the failure of a Draft Board to afford a fair hearing was not a defense to a prosecution for failure to report for induction and that the only procedure by which an inductee might procure judicial review of such an order or of an improper classification was by applying for a writ of habeas corpus after he had submitted to induction. . .

It results from the foregoing that the registrant was bound to obey the order to report for induction even if there had been error of law in his classification. The Administrative Board had jurisdiction of his case and its order could not be wilfully disregarded.

It seems proper, however, to say that we find no error of law on the part of the Appeal Board. The only error suggested is the adoption by the latter of the Report of the Hearing Commissioner whose conclusions are

[1] "Nothing contained in this Act shall be construed to require any person to be subject to combatant training and service in the land or naval forces of the United States who, by reason of religious training and belief, is conscientiously opposed to participation in war in any form..."

appended in the margin.[2] No question is raised about the facts which he and the Appeal Board found, but only whether the statute was properly interpreted as excluding from the exemption of Section 5(g) a person having such beliefs as the defendant expressed.

We hold that Mr. Hardy's interpretation was well founded. In order to avail himself of his privilege a registrant must establish that his objection to participation in war is due to "religious training and belief." It must ex vi termini be a general scruple against "participation in war in any form" and not merely an objection to participation in this particular war. Moreover, the conviction that war is a futile means of righting wrongs or of protecting the state, that it is not worth the sacrifice, that it is waged for base ends, or is otherwise indefensible is not necessarily a ground of opposition based on "religious training and belief." They, therefore, were properly overruled, but not because he lacked membership of any sect or organization whose religious convictions were against war. Such a status was necessary to obtain exemption under the Act of 1917, but the provisions of the present statute are more generous for they take into account the characteristics of a skeptical generation and make the existence of a conscientious scruple against war in any form, rather than allegiance to a definite religious group or creed, the basis of exemption. We are not convinced by anything in the record that the registrant did not report for induction because of a compelling voice of conscience, which we should

---

[2]The Registrant was brought up in the Catholic faith but has gotten away from it and from all religion. The Registrant admitted that he was an atheist or at least an agnostic. It is his belief that organized religion is detrimental and a hindrance to science.

In his questionnaire, the Registrant has circled the word "religious" with a notation on the side "This is not my case." The Registrant makes it quite clear that his religious training and belief is not the basis of his present opposition to war.

There is no doubt that the Registrant is sincerely opposed to war but this belief emanates from personal philosophical conceptions arising out of his nature and temperament, and which is to some extent, political.

The Registrant is an artist, who has travelled abroad and finally believes in a great deal of individual freedom. He denies the right of our Congress to pass laws which would infringe upon the "individual qualities of a person." During his travels the Registrant has witnessed the animosity which exists among the different peoples of Europe and this has strengthened his opposition to war as a solution to our problems.

It is quite obvious that the Registrant's opposition to the present war is greatly influenced by his dislike of our present administration. He has voiced his objections to its policies and has even stated that the Selective Service Act is a scheme devised by the President to solve the unemployment problem.

The Registrant believes in passive resistance as the only solution to our present situation. He has stated it is not right to have acted unfriendly to Japan and now seek to protect ourselves from the consequences of our own wrongdoing. He also believes that France did the right thing in submitting to Germany. Thus it appears that the Registrant believes in Ghandi's policy of passive resistance.

A report of the F.B.I. indicates that the Registrant is regarded very highly and is a sincere person. He has voiced his opinions about war to various people. However, some of the people interviewed stated that they regard as a religious impulse, but his declarations and reasoning seem to indicate that he was moved by convictions, however sincere, of quite a different character.

In the early days of the draft, many thousands of the American people distrusted our foreign policy. If men holding such views had been ipso facto classed as conscientious objectors, the military effort might well have been seriously hampered. In granting such exemption, we think Congress intended to satisfy the consciences of the very limited class we have described and not to give exemption to the great number of persons who might object to a particular war on philosophical or political grounds.

It is unnecessary to attempt a definition of religion; the content of the term is found in the history of the human race and is incapable of compression into a few words. Religious belief arises from a sense of the inadequacy of reason as a means of relating the individual to his fellow-men and to his universe - a sense common to men in the most primitive and in the most highly civilized societies. It accepts the aid of logic but refuses to be limited by it. It is a belief finding expression in a conscience which categorically requires the believer to disregard elementary self-interest and to accept martyrdom in preference to transgressing its tenets. A religious obligation forbade Socrates, even in order to escape condemnation, to entreat his judges to acquit him, because he believed that it was their sworn duty to decide questions without favor to anyone and only according to law. Such an obligation impelled Martin Luther to nail his theses on the door of the church at Wittenberg and, when he was summoned before Emperor Charles and the Diet at Worms, steadfastly to hold his ground and to utter the often quoted words: "I neither can nor will recant anything, since it is neither right nor safe to act against conscience. Here I stand. I cannot do other. God help me. Amen."

Recognition of this obligation moved the Greek poet Menander to write almost twenty-four hundred years ago: "Conscience is a God to all mortals"; impelled Socrates to obey the voice of his "Daimon" and led Wordsworth to characterize "Duty" as the "Stern Daughter of the Voice of God."

There is a distinction between a course of reasoning resulting in a conviction that a particular war is inexpedient or disastrous and a conscientious objection to participation in any war under any circumstances. The latter, and not the former, may be the basis of exemption under the Act. The former is usually a political objection, while the latter, we think, may justly be regarded as a response of the individual to an inward mentor, call it conscience or God, that is for many persons at the present time the equivalent of what has always been thought a religious impulse.

Even if the Board might have found that the registrant's objections to

---

did not believe the Registrant's objection to war was of a religious nature but rather of a personal nature because of his art work.

I conclude, therefore, from the personal observation and examination of the Registrant that although he may be sincere in his opposition to war, his belief does not emanate from any "religious training and belief" but from his philosophical and political convictions.

I recommend that the appeal of the Registrant based upon grounds of conscientious objections, be not sustained.

reporting for induction were based "on religious training and belief," rather than on personal predilection or political and social philosophy respecting the folly and futility of war, yet the record contained substantial indications that the objections were not because of "religious training and belief" in the sense those words are used in the statute, and the weight of the evidence was a matter for the Appeal Board.

For the foregoing reasons we find no error in the decision of the trial court and the judgment of conviction is accordingly affirmed.

<u>United States</u> v. <u>Ballard</u>
Supreme Court of the United States, 1944
322 U. S. 78

MR. JUSTICE DOUGLAS delivered the opinion of the Court.

Respondents were indicted and convicted for using, and conspiring to use, the mail to defraud. § 215 Criminal Code, 18 U.S.C. §333.[1] The indictment was in twelve counts. It charged a scheme to defraud by organizing and promoting the I Am movement through the use of the mails. The charge was that certain designated corporations were formed, literature distributed and sold, funds solicited, and memberships in the I Am movement sought "by means of false and fraudulent representations, pretenses and premises." The false representations charged were eighteen in number. It is sufficient at this point to say that they covered respondents' alleged religious doctrines or beliefs. They were all set forth in the first count. The following are representative:

"that Guy W. Ballard, now deceased, alias Saint Germain, Jesus, George Washington, and Godfre Ray King, had been selected and thereby designated by the alleged 'ascertained masters,' Saint Germain, as a divine messenger; and that the words of 'ascended masters' and the words of the alleged divine entity, Saint Germain, would be transmitted to mankind through the medium of the said Guy W. Ballard;

"that Guy W. Ballard, during his lifetime, and Edna W. Ballard, and Donald Ballard, by reason of their alleged high spiritual attainments and righteous conduct, had been selected as divine messengers through which the words of the alleged 'ascended masters,' including the alleged Saint Germain, would be communicated to mankind under the teachings commonly known as the 'I Am' movement;

"thay Guy W. Ballard, during his lifetime, and Edna W. Ballard and Donald Ballard had, by reason of supernatural attainments, the power to heal persons of ailments and diseases and to make well persons afflicted with any diseases, injuries, or ailments, and did falsely represent to persons intended to be defrauded that the three designated persons had the ability and power to cure persons of those diseases normally classified as curable and also of diseases which are ordinarily classified by the medical profession as being incurable diseases; and did further represent that the three designated persons had in fact cured either by the activity of one, either, or all of said persons, hundreds of persons afflicted with diseases and ailments;"

---

[1] § 37 Criminal Code, 18 U.S.C. §88.

Each of the representations enumerated in the indictment was followed by the charge that respondents "well knew" it was false. After enumerating the eighteen misrepresentations the indictment also alleged:

"At the time of making all of the afore-alleged representations by the defendants, and each of them, the defendants, and each of them, well knew that all of said aforementioned representations were false and untrue and were made with the intention on the part of the defendants, and each of them, to cheat, wrong, and defraud persons intended to be defrauded, and to obtain from persons intended to be defrauded by the defendants, money, property, and other things of value and to convert the same to the use and the benefit of the defendants, and each of them;"

The indictment contained twelve counts, one of which charged a conspiracy to defraud. The first count set forth all of the eighteen representations, as we have said. Each of the other counts incorporated and realleged all of them and added no additional ones. There was a demurrer and a motion to quash, each of which asserted, among other things, that the indictment attacked the religious beliefs of respondents and sought to restrict the free exercise of their religion in violation of the Constitution of the United States. These motions were denied by the District Court. Early in the trial, however, objections were raised to the admission of certain evidence concerning respondents' religious beliefs. The court conferred with counsel in absence of the jury and with the acquiescence of counsel for the United States and for respondents confined the issues on this phase of the case to the question of the good faith of respondents. At the request of counsel for both sides the court advised the jury of that action in the following language:

"Now, gentlemen, here is the issue in this case: First, the defendants in this case made certain representations of belief in a divinity and in a supernatural power. Some of the teachings of the defendants, representations, might seem extremely improbable to a great many people. For instance, the appearance of Jesus to dictate some of the works that we have had introduced in evidence, as testified to here at the opening transcription, or shaking hands with Jesus, to some people that might seem highly improbable. I point that out as one of the many statements.

"Whether that is true or not is not the concern of this Court and is not the concern of the jury - and they are going to be told so in their instructions. As far as this Court sees the issue, it is immaterial what these defendants preached or wrote or taught in their classes. They are not going to be permitted to speculate on the actuality of the happening of those incidents. Now, I think I have made that as clear as I can. Therefore, the religious beliefs of those defendants cannot be an issue in this court.

"The issue is: Did these defendants honestly and in good faith believe those things? If they did, they should be acquitted. I cannot make it any clearer than that.

"If those defendants did not believe those things, they did not believe that Jesus came down and dictated, or that Saint Germain came down and dictated, did not believe the things that they wrote, the things that they preached, but used the mail for the purpose of getting money, the jury should find them guilty. Therefore, gentlemen, religion cannot come into this case."

The District Court reiterated that admonition in the charge to the jury and made it abundantly clear. The following portion of the charge is typical:

"The question of the defendants' good faith is the cardinal question in this case. You are not to be concerned with the religious belief of the defendants, or any of them. The jury will be called upon to pass on the question of whether or not the defendants honestly and in good faith believed the representations which are set forth in the indictment, and honestly and in good faith believed that the benefits which they represented would flow from their belief to those who embraced and followed their teachings, or whether these representations were more pretenses without honest belief on the part of the defendants or any of them, and, were the representations made for the purpose of procuring money, and were the mails used for this purpose."

As we have said, counsel for the defense acquiesced in this treatment of the matter, made no objection to it during the trial, and indeed treated it without protest as the law of the case throughout the proceedings prior to the verdict. Respondents did not change their position before the District Court after verdict and contend that the truth or verity of their religious doctrines or beliefs should have been submitted to the jury. In their motion for new trial they did contend, however, that the withdrawal of these issues from the jury was error because it was in effect an amendment of the indictment. That was also one of their specifications of error on appeal. And other errors urged on appeal included the overruling of the demurrer to the indictment and the motion to quash, and the disallowance of proof of the truth of respondents' religious doctrines or beliefs.

The Circuit Court of Appeals reversed the judgment of conviction and granted a new trial, one judge dissenting. 138 F. 2d 549. In its view the restriction of the issue in question to that of good faith was error. Its reason was that the scheme to defraud alleged in the indictment was that respondents made the eighteen alleged false representations; and that to prove that defendants devised the scheme described in the indictment "it was necessary to prove that they schemed to make some, at least, of the (eighteen) representations . . . and that some, at least, of the representations which they schemed to make were false." 138 F. 2d 545. One judge thought that the ruling of the District Court was also error because it was "as prejudicial to the issue of honest belief as to the issue of purposeful misrepresentation." Id., p. 546.

The case is here on a petition for a writ of certiorari which we granted because of the importance of the question presented.

The United States contends that the District Court withdrew from the jury's consideration only the truth or falsity of those representations which related to religious concepts or beliefs and that there were representations charged in the indictment which fell within a different category. The argument is that this latter group of representations was submitted to the jury, that they were adequate to constitute an offense under the Act, and that they were supported by the requisite evidence. It is thus sought to bring the case within the rule of Hall v. United States, 168 U. S. 632, 639-640, which held that where an indictment contained "all the necessary averments to constitute an offense created by the statute," a conviction would not be set aside because a "totally immaterial fact" was averred but not proved. We do not stop to ascertain the relevancy of that rule to this case, for we are of the view that all of the representations charged in the indictment which related at least in part to the religious doctrines or beliefs of respondents were withheld from the jury. The trial judge did not differentiate them. He referred in the charge to the "religious beliefs" and "doctrines taught by the defendants" as matters withheld from the jury. And in stating that the issue of good faith was the "cardinal question" in the case he charged, as already noted, that "The jury will be called upon to pass on the question of whether or not the defendants honestly and in good faith believed the representations which are set forth in the indictment." Nowhere in the charge were any of the separate representations submitted to the jury. A careful reading of the whole charge leads us to agree with the Circuit Court of Appeals on this phase of the case that the only issue submitted to the jury was the question as stated by the District Court, of respondents' "belief in their representations and promises."

The United States contends that respondents acquiesced in the withdrawal from the jury of the truth of their religious doctrines or beliefs and that their consent bars them from insisting on a different course once that one turned out to be unsuccessful. Reliance for that position is sought in Johnson v. United States, 318 U.S. 189. That case stands for the proposition that, apart from situations involving an unfair trial, an appellate court will not grant a new trial to a defendant on the ground of improper introduction of evidence or improper comment by the prosecutor, where the defendant acquiesced in that course and made no objection to it. In fairness to respondents that principle cannot be applied here. The real objection of respondents is not that the truth of their religious doctrines or beliefs should have been submitted to the jury. Their demurrer and motion to quash made clear their position that that issue should be withheld from the jury on the basis of the First Amendment. Moreover, their position at all times was and still is that the court should have gone the whole way and withheld from the jury both that issue and the issue of their good faith. Their demurrer and motion to quash asked for dismissal of the entire indictment. Their argument that the truth of their religious doctrines or beliefs should have gone to the jury when the question of their good faith was submitted was and is merely an alternative argument. They never forsook their position that the indictment should have been dismissed and that none of it was good. Moreover, respondents' motion for new trial challenged the propriety of the action of the District Court in withdrawing from the jury the issue of the truth of their religious doctrines or beliefs without also withdrawing the question of their good faith. So we conclude that the rule of Johnson v. United States, supra, does not prevent respondents from reasserting now that no part of the indictment should have been submitted to the jury.

As we have noted, the Circuit Court of Appeals held that the question of the truth of the representations concerning respondents' religious doctrines or beliefs should have been submitted to the jury. And it remanded the case for a new trial. It may be that the Circuit Court of Appeals took that action because it did not think that the indictment could be properly construed as charging a scheme to defraud by means other than misrepresentations of respondents' religious doctrines or beliefs. Or that court may have concluded that the withdrawal of the issue of the truth of those religious doctrines or beliefs was unwarranted because it resulted in a substantial change in the character of the crime charged. But on whichever basis that court rested its action, we do not agree that the truth or verity of respondents' religious doctrines or beliefs should have been submitted to the jury. Whatever this particular indictment might require, the First Amendment precludes such a course, as the United States seems to concede. "The law knows no heresy, and is committed to the support of no dogma, the establishment of no sect." Watson v. Jones, 13 Wall. 679, 728. The First Amendment has a dual aspect. It not only "forestalls compulsion by law of the acceptance of any creed or the practice of any form of worship" but also "safeguards the free exercise of the chosen form of religion." Cantwell v. Connecticut, 310 U.S. 296, 303. "Thus the Amendment embraces two concepts, - freedom to believe and freedom to act. The first is absolute but, in the nature of things, the second cannot be." Id., pp. 303-304. Freedom of thought, which includes freedom of religious belief, is basic in a society of free men. Board of Education v. Barnette, 310 U.S. 624. It embraces the right to maintain theories of life and of death and of the hereafter which are rank heresy to followers of the orthodox faiths. Heresy trials are foreign to our Constitution. Men may believe what they cannot prove. They may not be put to the proof of their religious doctrines or beliefs. Religious experiences which are as real as life to some may be incomprehensible to others. Yet the fact that they may be beyond the ken of mortals does not mean that they can be made suspect before the law. Many take their gospel from the New Testament. But it would hardly be supposed that they could be tried before a jury charged with the duty of determining whether those teachings contained false representations. The miracles of the New Testament, the Divinity of Christ, life after death, the power of prayer are deep in the religious convictions of many. If one could be sent to jail because a jury in a hostile environment found those teachings false, little indeed would be left of religious freedom. The Fathers of the Constitution were not unaware of the varied and extreme views of religious sects, of the violence of disagreement among them, and of the lack of any one religious creed on which all men would agree. They fashioned a charter of government which envisaged the widest possible toleration of conflicting views. The religious views espoused by respondents might seem incredible, if not preposterous, to most people. But if those doctrines are subject to trial before a jury charged with finding their truth or falsity, then the same can be done with the religious beliefs of any sect. When the triers of fact undertake that task, they enter a forbidden domain. The First Amendment does not select any one group of any one type of religion for preferred treatment. It puts them all in that position. Murdock v. Pennsylvania, 319 U.S. 105. As stated in Davis v. Beason, 133 U.S. 333, 342, "With man's relations to his Maker and the obligations he may think they impose, and the manner in which an expression shall be made by him of his belief on those subjects, no interference can be permitted, provided always the laws of society, designed to secure its peace and prosperity, and the morals of its people, are not interfered with." See Prince v. Massachusetts, 321 U.S. 158. So we conclude that the District Court ruled properly when it withheld from the jury all questions concerning the truth or falsity of the religious beliefs of doctrines of respondents.

Respondents maintain that the reversal of the judgment of conviction was justified on other distinct grounds. The Circuit Court of Appeals did not reach those questions. Respondents may, of course, urge them here in support of the judgment of the Circuit Court of Appeals. Langnes v. Green, 282 U.S. 531, 538-539; Story Parchment Co. v. Paterson Co., 282 U.S. 555, 560, 567-568. But since attention was centered on the issues which we have discussed, the remaining questions were not fully presented to this Court either in the briefs or oral argument. In view of these circumstances we deem it more appropriate to remand the cause of the Circuit Court of Appeals so that it may pass on the questions reserved. Lutcher & Moore Lumber Co. v. Knight, 217 U.S. 257, 267-268; Brown v. Fletcher, 237 U.S. 583. If any questions of importance survive and are presented here, we will then have the benefit of the views of the Circuit Court of Appeals. Until that additional consideration is had, we cannot be sure that it will be necessary to pass on any of the other constitutional issues which respondents claim to have reserved.

The judgment is reversed and the cause is remanded to the Circuit Court of Appeals for further proceedings in conformity to this opinion.

Reversed.

MR. CHIEF JUSTICE STONE, dissenting:

I am not prepared to say that the constitutional guaranty of freedom of religion affords immunity from criminal prosecution for the fraudulent procurement of money by false statements as to one's religious experiences, more than it renders polygamy or libel immune from criminal prosecution. Davis v. Beason, 133 U.S. 333; see Chaplinsky v. New Hampshire, 315 U.S. 568, 572; cf. Patterson v. Colorado, 205 U.S. 454, 462; Near v. Minnesota, 283 U.S. 697, 715. I cannot say that freedom of thought and worship includes freedom to procure money by making knowingly false statements about one's religious experiences. To go no further, if it were shown that a defendant in this case had asserted as a part of the alleged fraudulent scheme, that he had physically shaken hands with St. Germain in San Francisco on a day named, or that, as the indictment here alleges, by the exertion of his spiritual power he "had in fact cured . . . hundreds of persons afflicted with diseases and ailments," I should not doubt that it would be open to the Government to submit to the jury proof that he had never been in San Francisco and that no such cures had ever been effected. In any event I see no occasion for making any pronouncement on this subject in the present case.

The indictment charges respondents' use of the mails to defraud and a conspiracy to commit that offense by false statements of their religious experiences which had not in fact occurred. But it also charged that the representations were "falsely and fraudulently" made, that respondents "well knew" that these representations were untrue, and that they were made by respondents with the intent to cheat and defraud those to whom they were made. With the assent of the prosecution and the defense the trial judge withdrew from the consideration of the jury the question whether the alleged religious experiences had in fact occurred, but submitted to the jury the single issue whether petitioners honestly believed that they had occurred, with the instruction that if the jury did not so find, then it should return a verdict of guilty. On this issue the jury, on ample evidence that respondents were without belief in the statements which they had made to their victims, found a verdict of guilty. The state of one's mind is a fact as capable of fraudulent misrepresentation as is one's physical condition or the state of his bodily health. See Seven Cases v. United States, 239 U.S. 510, 517; cf. Durland v. United States, 161 U.S. 306, 313. There are no exceptions to the charge and no contention that the trial court rejected any relevant evidence which petitions sought to offer. Since the indictment and the evidence support the conviction, it is irrelevant whether the religious experiences alleged did or did not in fact occur or whether that issue could or could not, for constitutional reasons, have been rightly submitted to the jury. Certainly none of respondents' constitutional rights are violated if they are prosecuted for the fraudulent procurement of money by false representations as to their beliefs, religious or otherwise.

Obviously if the question whether the religious experiences in fact occurred could not constitutionally have been submitted to the jury the court rightly withdrew it. If it could have been submitted I know of no reason why the parties could not, with the advice of counsel, assent to its withdrawal from the jury. And where, as here, the indictment charges two sets of false statements, each independently sufficient to sustain the conviction, I cannot accept respondents' contention that the withdrawal of one set and the submission of the other to the jury amounted to an amendment of the indictment.

An indictment is amended when it is so altered as to charge a different offense from that found by the grand jury. Ex parte Bain, 121 U.S. 1. But here there was no alteration of the indictment, Salinger v. United States, 272 U.S. 542, 549, nor did the court's action, in effect, add anything to it by submitting to the jury matters which it did not charge. United States v. Norris, 281 U.S. 619, 622. In Salinger v. United States, supra, 548-9, we explicitly held that where an indictment charges several offenses, or the commission of one offense in several ways, the withdrawal from the jury's consideration of one offense or one alleged method of committing it does not constitute a forbidden amendment of the indictment. See also Goto v. Lane, 265 U.S. 393, 402-3; Ford v. United States, 273 U.S. 593, 602. Were the rule otherwise the common practice of withdrawing from the jury's consideration one count of an indictment while submitting others for its verdict, sustained in Dealy v. United States, 152 U.S. 539, 542, would be a fatal error.

We may assume that under some circumstances the submission to the jury of part only of the matters alleged in the indictment might result in such surprise to the defendant as to amount to the denial of a fair trial. But, as in the analogous case of a variance between pleading and proof, a conviction can be reversed only upon a showing of injury to the "substantial rights" of the accused. Berger v. United States, 295 U.S. 78, 82. Here no claim of surprise has been or could be made. The indictment plainly charged both falsity of, and lack of good faith belief in the representations made, and it was agreed at the outset of the trial, without objection from the defendants, that only the issue of respondents' good faith belief in the representations of religious experiences would be submitted to the jury. Respondents, who were represented by counsel, at no time in the course of the trial offered any objection to this limitation of the issues, or any contention that it would result in a prohibited amendment of the indictment. So far as appears from the record before us the point was raised for the first time in the specifications of errors in the Circuit Court of Appeals. It is asserted that it was argued to the District Court on motions for new trial and in arrest of judgment. If so, there was still no surprise by a ruling to which, as we have said, respondents' counsel assented when it was made.

On the issue submitted to the jury in this case it properly rendered a verdict of guilty. As no legally sufficient reason for disturbing it appears, I think the judgment below should be reversed and that of the District Court reinstated.

Mr. Justice ROBERTS and Mr. Justice FRANKFURTER join in this opinion.

Mr. Justice JACKSON, dissenting:

I should say the defendants have done just that for which they are indicted. If I might agree to their conviction without creating a precedent, I cheerfully would do so. I can see in their teachings nothing but humbug, untainted by any trace of truth. But that does not dispose of the constitutional question whether misrepresentation of religious experience or belief is proscutable; it rather emphasizes the danger of such prosecutions.

The Ballard family claimed miraculous communication with the spirit world and supernatural power to heal the sick. They were brought to trial for mail fraud on an indictment which charged that their representations were false and that they "well knew" they were false. The trial judge, obviously troubled, ruled that the court could not try whether the statements were untrue, but could inquire whether the defendants knew them to be untrue; and, if so, they could be convicted.

I find it difficult to reconcile this conclusion with our traditional religious freedoms.

In the first place, as a matter of either practice or philosphy I do not see how we can separate an issue as to what is believed from considerations as to what is believable. The most convincing proof that one believes his statements is to show that they have been true in his experience. Likewise, that one knowingly falsified is best proved by showing that what he said happened never did happen. How can the Government prove these persons knew something to be false which it cannot prove to be false? If we try religious sincerity severed from religious verity, we isolate the dispute from the very considerations which in common experience provide its most reliable answer.

In the second place, any inquiry into intellectual honesty in religion raises profound psychological problems. William James, who wrote on these matters as a scientist, reminds us that it is not theology and ceremonies which keep religion going. Its vitality is in the religious experiences of many people. "If you ask what these experiences are, they are conversations with the unseen, voices and visions, responses to prayer, changes of heart, deliverances from fear, inflowings of help, assurances of support, whenever certain persons set their own internal attitude in certain appropriate ways." If religious liberty includes, as it must, the right to communicate such experiences to others, it seems to me an impossible task for juries to separate fancied ones from real ones, dreams from happenings, and hallucinations from true clairvoyance. Such experiences, like some tones and colors, have existence for one, but none at all for another. They cannot be verified to the minds of those whose field of consciousness does not include religious insight. When one comes to trial which turns on any aspect of religious belief or representation, unbelievers among his judges are likely not to understand and are almost certain not to believe him.

And then I do not know what degree of skepticism or disbelief in a religious representation amounts to actionable fraud. James points out that "Faith means belief in something concerning which doubt is still theoretically possible." Belief in what one may demonstrate to the senses is not faith. All schools of religious thought make enormous assumptions, generally on the basis of revelations authenticated by some sign or miracle. The appeal in such matters is to a very different plane of credulity than is invoked by representations of secular fact in commerce. Some who profess belief in the Bible read literally what others read as allegory or metaphor, as they read Aesop's fables. Religious symbolism is even used by some with the same mental reservations one has in teaching of Santa Claus or Uncle Sam or Easter bunnies or dispassionate judges. It is hard in matters so mystical to say how literally one is bound to believe the doctrine he teaches and even more difficult to say how far it is reliance upon a teacher's literal belief which induces followers to give him money.

There appear to be persons - let us hope not many - who find refreshment and courage in the teachings of the "I Am" cult. If the members of the sect get comfort from the celestial guidance of their "Saint Germain," however doubtful it seems to me, it is hard to say that they do not get what they pay for. Scores of sects flourish in this country by teaching what to me are queer notions. It is plain that there is wide variety in American religious taste. The Ballards are not alone in catering to it with a pretty dubious product.

The chief wrong which false prophets do to their following is not financial. The collections aggregate a tempting total, but individual payments are not ruinous. I doubt if the vigilance of the law is equal to making money stick by over-credulous people. But the real harm is on the mental and spiritual plane. There are those who hunger and thirst after higher values which they feel wanting in their humdrum lives. They live in mental confusion or moral anarchy and seek vaguely for truth and beauty and moral support. When they are deluded and then disillusioned, cynicism and confusion follow. The wrong of these things, as I see it, is not in the money the victims part with half so much as in the mental and spiritual poison they get. But that is precisely the thing the Constitution put beyond the reach of the prosecutor, for the price of freedom of religion or of speech or of the press is that we must put up with, and even pay for, a good deal of rubbish.

Prosecutions of this character easily could degenerate into religious persecution. I do not doubt that religious leaders may be convicted of fraud for making false representations on matters other than faith or experience, as for example if one represents that funds are being used to construct a church when in fact they are being used for personal purposes. But that is not this case, which reaches into wholly dangerous ground. When does less than full belief in a professed creed become actionable fraud if one is soliciting gifts or legacies? Such inquiries may discomfort orthodox as well as unconventional religious teachers, for even the most regular of them are sometimes accused of taking their orthodoxy with a grain of salt.

I would dismiss the indictment and have done with this business of judicially examining other people's faiths.

Ex parte Newman
Supreme Court of California 1858
9 California 502

TERRY, C. J. - The petitioner was tried and convicted before a justice of the peace for a violation of the act of April, 1858, entitled "An Act for the better observance of the Sabbath," and, upon his failure to pay the fine imposed, was imprisoned.

The counsel for petitioner moves his discharge, on the ground that the act under which these proceedings were had is in conflict with the first and fourth sections of the first article of the State Constitution, and therefore void.

The first section declares "all men are by nature free and independent, and have certain inalienable rights, among which are those of enjoying and defending life and liberty; acquiring, possessing, and protecting property, and pursuing and obtaining safety and happiness."

The fourth section declares "the free exercise and enjoyment of religious profession and worship, without discrimination or preference, shall for ever be allowed in this State."

The questions which arise in the consideration of the case, are:

1. Does the act of the Legislature make a discrimination or preference favorable to one religious profession, or is it a mere civil rule of conduct?

2. Has the Legislature the power to enact a municipal regulation which enforces upon the citizen a compulsory abstinence from his ordinary lawful and peaceable avocations for one day in the week?

There is no expression in the act under consideration which can lead to the conclusion that it was intended as a civil rule, as contradistinguished from a law for the benefit of religion. It is entitled "An Act for the better observance of the Sabbath," and the prohibitions in the body of the act are confined to the "Christian Sabbath."

It is, however, contended, on the authority of some of the decisions of other States, that notwithstanding the pointed language of the act, it may be construed into a civil rule of action, and that the result would be the same, even if the language were essentially different.

The fault of this argument is that it is opposed to the universally admitted rule which requires a law to be construed according to the intention of the law-maker, and this intention to be gathered from the language of the law, according to its plain and common acceptation.

It is contended that a civil rule requiring the devotion of one-seventh of the time to repose is an absolute necessity, and the want of it has been dilated upon as a great evil to society. But have the Legislature so considered it? Such an assumption is not warranted by anything contained in the Sunday law. On the contrary, the intention which pervades the whole act is to enforce, as a religious institution, the observance of a day held sacred by the followers of one faith, and entirely disregarded by all the other denominations within the State. The whole scope of the act is expressive of an intention on the part of the Legislature to require a periodical cessation from ordinary pursuits, not as a civil duty, necessary for the repression of any existing evil, but in furtherance of the interests, and in aid of the devotions of those who profess the Christian religion.

Several authorities, affirming the validity of similar statutes, have been cited from the reports of other States. While we entertain a profound respect for the Courts of our sister States, we do not feel called upon to yield our convictions of right to a blind adherence to precedent; especially when they are, in our opinion, opposed to principle; and the reasoning by which they are endeavored to be supported is by no means satisfactory or convincing. In Bryan v. Berry, (6 Cal. 398) in reference to the decisions of other States, we said, "decided cases are, in some sense, evidence of what the law is. We say in some sense, because it is not so much the decision as it is the reasoning upon which the decision is based, which makes it authority, and requires it to be respected." /Discussion of cases omitted.\

Now, does our Constitution, when it forbids discrimination or preference in religion, mean merely to guaranty toleration? For that, in effect, is all which the cases cited seem to award, as the right of a citizen. In a community composed of persons of various religious denominations, having different days of worship, each considering his own as sacred from secular employment, all being equally considered and protected under the Constitution, a law is passed which in effect recognizes the sacred character of one of these days, by compelling all others to abstain from secular employment, which is precisely one of the modes in which its observance is manifested and required by the creed of that sect to which it belongs as a Sabbath. Is not this a discrimination in favor of the one? Does it require more than an appeal to one's common sense to decide that this is a preference? And when the Jew, or Seventh-Day Christian complains of this, is it any answer to say, your conscience is not constrained, you are not compelled to worship or to perform religious rites on that day, nor forbidden to keep holy the day which you esteem as a Sabbath? We think not, however high the authority which decides otherwise.

When our liberties were acquired, our republican form of government adopted, and our Constitution framed, we deemed that we had attained not only toleration, but religious liberty in its largest sense - a complete separation between Church and State, and a perfect quality without distinction between all religious sects. "Our Government," said Mr. Johnson, in his celebrated Sunday-mail report, "is a civil and not a religious institution; whatever may be the religious sentiments of citizens, and however variant, they are alike entitled to protection from the government, so long as they do not invade the rights of other." And again, dwelling upon the danger of applying the powers of government to the furtherance and support of sectarian objects, he remarks, in language which should not be forgotten, but which ought to be deeply impressed on the minds of all who desire to maintain the supremacy of our republican system: "Extensive religious combinations to effect a political object, were, in the opinion of the committee, always dangerous. The first effort of the kind calls for the establishment of a principle which would lay the foundation for dangerous innovation upon the spirit of the Constitution, and upon the religious rights of the citizen. If admitted, it may be justly apprehended that the future measures of the Government will be strangely marked, if not eventually controlled by the same influence. All religious depotism commences by combination and influence, and when that influence begins to operate upon the political institution of a country, the civil power soon bends under it, and the catastrophe of other nations furnishes an awful warning of the consequences. *** What other nations call religious toleration, we call religious rights; they were not exercised in virtue of governmental indulgency, but as rights of which the government cannot deprive any portion of her citizens, however small. Despotic power may invade those rights, but justice still confirms them. Let the National Legislature once perform an act which involves the decision of a religious controversy, and it will have passed its legitimate bounds. The precedent will then be established, and the foundation laid for that usurpation of the divine prerogative in this country, which has been the desolating scourge of the fairest portions of the old world. Our Constitution recognizes no other power than that of persuasion for enforcing religious observances."

We come next to the question whether, considering the Sunday law as a civil regulation, it is in the power of the Legislature to enforce a compulsory abstinence from lawful and ordinary occupation for a given period of time, without some apparent civil necessity for such action; whether a pursuit, which is not only peaceable and lawful, but also praiseworthy and commendable, for six days in the week, can be arbitrarily converted into a penal offence or misdemeanor on the seventh. As a general rule, it will be admitted that men have a natural right to do anything which their inclinations may suggest, if it be not evil in itself, and in no way impairs the rights of others. When societies are formed, each individual surrenders certain rights, and as an equivalent for that surrender has secured to him the enjoyment of certain others appertaining to his person and property, without the protection of which society cannot exist. All legislation is a restraint on individuals, but it is a restraint which must be submitted to by all who would enjoy the benefits derived from the institutions of society...

Now, when we come to inquire what reason can be given for the claim of power to enact a Sunday law, we are told, looking at it in its purely civil aspect, that it is absolutely necessary for the benefit of his health and the restoration of his powers, and in aid of this great social necessity, the Legislature may, for the general convenience, set apart a particular day of rest, and require its observance by all.

This argument is founded on the assumption that mankind are in the habit of working too much, and thereby entailing evil upon society, and that without compulsion they will not seek the necessary repose which their exhausted natures demand. This is to us a new theory, and is contradicted by the history of the past and the observations of the present. We have heard, in all ages, of declamations and reproaches against the vice of indolence, but we have yet to learn that there has ever been any general complaint of an intemperate, vicious, unhealthy or morbid industry. On the contrary, we know that mankind seek cessation from toil from the natural influences of self-preservation, in the same manner and as certainly as they seek slumber, relief from pain, or food to appease their hunger . . .

The truth is, however much it may be disguised, that this one day of rest is a purely religious idea. Derived from the Sabbatical institutions of the ancient Hebrew, it has been adopted into all the creeds of succeeding religious sects throughout the civilized world; and whether it be the Friday of the Mohammedan, the Saturday of the Israelite, or the Sunday of the Christian, it is alike fixed in the affections of its followers, beyond the power of eradication, and in most of the States of our Confederacy, the aid of the law to enforce its observance has been given, under the pretence of a civil, municipal, or police regulation.

But it has been argued that this is a question exclusively for the Legislature; that the law-making power alone has the right to judge of the necessity and character of all police rules, and that there is no power in the judiciary to interfere with the exercise of this right.

One of the objects for which the judicial department is established is the protection of the constitutional rights of the citizen. The question presented in this case is not merely one of expediency or abuse of power; it is a question of usurpation of power. If the Legislature have the authority to appoint a time of compulsory rest, we would have no right to interfere with it, even if they required a cessation from toil for six days in the week instead of one. If they possess this power, it is without limit, and may extend to the prohibition of all occupations at all times . . .

It is the settled doctrine of this Court to enforce every provision of the Constitution in favor of the rights reserved to the citizen against a usurpation of power in any question whatsoever, and although in a doubtful case, we would yield to the authority of the Legislature, yet upon the question before us, we are contrained to declare that, in our opinion, the act in question is in conflict with the first section of article first of the Constitution, because, without necessity, it infringes upon the liberty of the citizen, by restraining his right to acquire property.

And that it is in conflict with the fourth section of the same article, because it was intended as, and is in effect, a discrimination in favor of one religious profession, and gives it a preference over all others.

It follows that the petitioner was improperly convicted, and it is ordered that he be discharged from custody. [The concurring opinion of Burnett, J. is omitted.]

FIELD, J. - After a careful and repeated perusal of the opinions of my associates, I am unable to concur either in their reasoning or in their judgment. I can not perceive any valid ground for declaring the Act of

1858, for the better observance of the Sabbath, unconstitutional. In ordinary cases, I should be content with refraining from a concurrence, or expressing a simple dissent, but, in the present case, I feel compelled to state the reasons of my dissent, as the opinions of my associates appear to me to assert a power in the judiciary never contemplated by the Constitution, and of dangerous consequences; and to adopt a construction of constitutional provisions, which must deprive the Legislature of all control over a great variety of subjects, upon which its right to legislate, in the promotion of the public weal, has never been doubted. . .

In examining the questions raised by the petitioner, I will first consider the fourth section [of Article I of the State Constitution] and whether the statute is in any sense within its provisions. The statute is prohibitory in its character, and its constitutionality must be determined by the acts it forbids. The inquiry is as to the power of the Legislature, not as to the motives which induced the enactment. The power is exhibited in the clause which provides that no person shall, on the Christian Sabbath, or Sunday, keep open any store, warehouse, mechanic-shop, work-ship, banking-house, manufacturing establishment, or other business house, for business purposes; or sell, or expose for sale, any goods, wares, or merchandise on that day, and fixes the penalty for the violation of the provision. If the exercise of this power is not prohibited to the Legislature by the Constitution, either in express terms, or by necessary implication, it is our duty to uphold the statute. Of its wisdom or policy, it is not within our province to judge. In what manner it conflicts with the fourth section I am unable to perceive. What have the sale of merchandise, the construction of machines, the discount of notes, the drawing of bills of exchange, the purchase of gold, or the business of the artisan, mechanic, or manufacturer, to do with religious profession or worship? There is no necessary connection between them. The petitioner is an israelite, engaged in the sale of clothing, and his complaint is, not that his religious profession or worship is interfered with, but that he is not permitted to dispose of his goods on Sunday; not that any religious observance is imposed upon him, but that his secular business is closed on a day on which he does not think proper to rest. In other words, the law, as a civil regulation, by the generality of its provisions, interrupts his acquisitions on a day which does not suit him. The law treats of business matters, not religious duties. In fixing a day of rest, it establishes only a rule of civil conduct. In limiting its command to secular pursuits, it necessarily leaves religious profession and worship free. It is absurd to say that the sale of clothing, or other goods, on Sunday, is an act of religion or worship; and it follows that the inhibition of such sale does not interfere with either. Religious profession springs from matters of faith, and religious worship is the adoration of the soul. As to the forms in which that profession or worship shall be exhibited, the law is silent; it utters no command, and it imposes no restraint. It makes no discrimination or preference between the Hebrew and Gentile, the Mussulman and Pagan, the Christian and Infidel, but leaves to all the privilege of worshipping God, or of denying His existence, according to the conclusions of their own judgments, or the dictates of their own consciences. It does not even allude to the subject of religious profession or worship, in any of its provisions. It establishes, as a civil regulation, a day of rest from secular pursuits, and that is its only scope and purpose. Its requirement is a cessation from labor. In its enactment, the Legislature has given the sanction of law to a rule of conduct, which the entire civilized world recognizes as essential to the physical and moral well-being of society. Upon no subject is there such a concurrence of opinion, among philosophers, moralists, and statesmen of all nations, as on the necessity of periodical cessations from labor. One day in seven is the rule, founded in experience, and sustained by science. There is no nation, possessing any degree of civilization, where the rule is not observed, either from the sanctions of the law, or the sanctions of religion. This fact has not escaped the observation of men of science, and distinguished philosophers have not hesitated to pronounce the rule founded upon a law of our race. . .

But it is urged that the intention of the law is to enforce the Sabbath as a religious institution. This position is assumed from the description of the day and the title of the act, but is not warranted by either. The terms "Christian Sabbath or Sunday," are used simply to designate the day selected by the Legislature. The same construction would obtain and the same result follow if any other terms were employed, as "the Lord's day, commonly called Sunday," contained in the statute of Pennsylvania, or simply "the Sabbath day," or "the first day of the week," as in several statutes. The power of selection being in the Legislature, there is no valid reason why Sunday should not be designated as well as any other day. Probably no day in the week could be taken which would not be subject to some objection. That the law operates with inconvenience to some is no argument against its constitutionality. Such inconvenience is an incident to all general laws. A civil regulation can not be converted into a religious institution because it is enforced on a day which a particular religious sect regards as sacred. . .

The fact that the civil regulation finds support in the religious opinions of a vast majority of the people of California is no argument against its establishment. It would be fortunate for society if all wise civil rules obtained a ready obedience from the citizen, not merely from the requirements of the law, but from conscientious or religious convictions of their obligation. The law against homicide is not the less wise and necessary because the Divine command is, "thou shalt do no murder." The legislation against perjury is not the less useful and essential for the due administration of justice because the injunction comes from the Most High, "thou shalt not bear false witness against they neighbor." The establishment by law of Sunday as a day of rest from labor, is none the less a beneficent and humane regulation, because it accords with the Divine precept that upon that day "thou shalt do no manner of work; thou, and thy son and thy daughter, thy man-servant and thy maid-servant, thy cattle, and the stranger that is within thy gates". . .

The law in question is free from all ambiguity. Its purview, or body, speaks a command which no one can mistake. Its title, therefore, is not a subject for consideration. The law would be equally obligatory if entitled "An Act to promote the general health." The section of the Constitution being directory in its character, can operate only on the conscience of the law-maker. Like the provision that the laws shall be published in Spanish, it creates a duty of imperfect obligation, which the judiciary can not enforce.

But, aside from these views, there is nothing in the title of the act open to criticism. It reads, "an Act to provide for the better observance of the Sabbath," which means nothing more or less than an act to provide for the better observance of a day of the week called the Sabbath . It does not indicate the manner of observance; that is exhibited in the body of the act. It is there commanded to be by cessation from labor, not by religious worship.

With the motives which operated upon the Legislature to pass the act, we have nothing to do. They may have been as varied as the different minds of its members. With some, religious convictions may have controlled; with others, a sense of the necessity of protecting labor; with some, a belief that it would be a popular law with their constituents; and with others, less worthy considerations. It is a question of power that we are determining, and whether that power was wisely or unwisely exercised, or from pure or impure motives, is of no moment. If we admit that the law had its origin in the religious opinions of the members of the Legislature, we advance nothing in favor of its constitutionality, and concede nothing against it. It would be, indeed, singular if a wise and beneficent law were the subject of objection, because suggested by the principles of a pure religion. Christianity is the prevailing faith of our people; it is the basis of our civilization; and that its spirit should infuse itself into and humanize our laws, is as natural as that the national sentiment of liberty should find expression in the legislation of the country. . . [Discussion of cases from other states omitted.]

This concurrence of opinion by the tribunals of so many different States, composed, in most instances, of Judges of distinguished ability and profound learning, ought to conclude the question before us. I do not assent to the proposition announced in Bryan v. Betty (6 Cal. 398) that the decisions of other Courts are authority and to be respected only from the reasoning upon which they are based. The proposition is not sound, except in a very restricted sense. The law is a science, whose leading principles are settled. They are not to be opened for discussion upon the elevation to the bench of every new Judge, however subtle his intellect, or profound his learning, or logical his reasoning. Upon their stability men rest their property, make their contracts, assert their rights, and claim protection. It is true that the law is founded upon reason, but by this is meant that it is the result of the general intelligence, learning, and experience of mankind, through a long succession of years, and not of the individual reasoning of one or of several judges. "Reason," says Lord Coke, "is the life of the law, nay, the common law itself is nothing else but reason, gotten by long study, observation and experience, and not of every man's natural reason," It is possible that some intellects may rise to the perception of absolute truth, and be justified in questioning the general judgment of the learned of mankind. But before the legitimate and just inference arising from the general acquiescence of the learned can be avoided, the error in the principles recognized should be clearly shown. We should not blindly adhere to precedents, nor should we more blindly abandon them as guides.

In the present case, the question under consideration is one of power dependent upon the construction of sections of the Constitution. The rules of construction are settled, and possess all the certainty which can exist out of the exact sciences; they do not vary in different Courts; they are the same now that they were a century ago; they are the same now that they will be a century hence; and a concurrence upon their application, of highest tribunals of every State where a Sunday law exists, in the same judgment, ought to inspire confidence in its soundness. [Discussion of the 1st Section of the Constitution omitted.]

I am of opinion that the "Act for the better observance of the Sabbath," is constitutional, and that the petitioner ought to be remanded.

Cantwell v. Connecticut
Supreme Court of the United States, 1940.
310 U.S. 296

Appeal from and Certiorari to the Supreme Court of Errors of Connecticut.

Newton, Jesse, and Russell Cantwell were convicted of violating a Connecticut statute prohibiting the solicitation of money for alleged religious, charitable, or philanthropic causes without approval of the Secretary of Public Welfare, and of inciting a breach of the peace. The conviction of all three for violating the statute, and conviction of Jesse Cantwell for inciting a breach of the peace, was affirmed by the Supreme Court of Errors of Connecticut, 126 Conn. 1, 8 A.2d 533, and defendants appeal and bring certiorari.

MR. JUSTICE ROBERTS delivered the opinion of the Court.

Newton Cantwell and his two sons, Jesse and Russell, members of a group known as Jehovah's witnesses, and claiming to be ordained ministers, were arrested in New Haven, Connecticut, and each was charged by information in five counts, with statutory and common law offenses. After trial in the Court of Common Pleas of New Haven County each of them was convicted on the third count, which charged a violation of § 6294 of the General Statutes of Connecticut, and on the fifth count, which charged commission of the common law offense of inciting a breach of the peace. On appeal to the Supreme Court the conviction of all three on the third count was affirmed. The conviction of Jesse Cantwell, on the fifth count, was also affirmed, but the conviction of Newton and Russell on that count was reversed and a new trial ordered as to them.

By demurrers to the information, by requests for rulings of law at the trial, and by their assignments of error in the State Supreme Court, the appellants pressed the contention that the statute under which the third count was drawn was offensive to the due process clause of the Fourteenth Amendment because, on its face and as construed and applied, it denied them freedom of speech and prohibited their free exercise of religion. In like manner they made the point that they could not be found guilty on the fifth count, without violation of the Amendment.

We have jurisdiction on appeal from the judgments on the third count, as there was drawn in question the validity of a state statute under the Federal Constitution, and the decision was in favor of validity. Since the conviction on the fifth count was not based upon a statute, but presents a substantial question under the federal Constitution, we granted the writ of certiorari in respect of it.

The facts adduced to sustain the convictions on the third count follow. On the day of their arrest the appellants were engaged in going singly from house to house on Cassius Street in New Haven. They were individually equipped with a bag containing books and pamphlets on religious subjects, a portable phonograph and a set of records, each of which, when played introduced, and was a description of, one of the books. Each appellant asked the person who responded to his call for permission to play one of the records. If permission was granted he asked the person to buy the book described and upon refusal, he solicited such contribution towards the publication of the pamphlets as the listener was willing to make. If a contribution was received a pamphlet was delivered upon condition that it would be read.

Cassius Street is in a thickly populated neighborhood, where about ninety per cent of the residents are Roman Catholics. A phonograph record, describing a book entitled "Enemies," included an attack on the Catholic religion. None of the persons interviewed were members of Jehovah's Witnesses.

The statute under which the appellants were charged provides:

"No person shall solicit money, services, subscriptions of any valuable thing for any alleged religious, charitable or philanthropic cause, from other than a member of the organization for whose benefit such person is soliciting or within the county in which such person or organization is located unless such cause shall have been approved by the secretary of the public welfare council. Upon application of any person in behalf of such cause, the secretary shall determine whether such cause is a religious one or is a bona fide object of charity or philanthropy and conforms to reasonable standards of efficiency and integrity, and if he shall so find, shall approve the same and issue to the authority in charge a certificate to that effect. Such certificate may be revoked at any time. Any person violating any provision of this section shall be fined not more than one hundred dollars or imprisoned not more than thirty days or both."

The appellants claimed that their activities were not within the statute but consisted only of distribution of books, pamphlets, and periodicals. The State Supreme Court construed the finding of the trial court to be that "in addition to the sale of the books and the distribution of the pamphlets the defendants were also soliciting contributions or donations of money for an alleged religious cause, and thereby came within the purview of the statute." It overruled the contention that the Act, as applied to the appellants, offends the due process clause of the Fourteenth Amendment, because it abridges or denies religious freedom and liberty of speech and press. The court stated that it was the solicitation that brought the appellants within the sweep of the Act and not their other activities in the dissemination of literature. It declared the legislation constitutional as an effort by the State to protect the public against fraud and imposition in the solicitation of funds for what purported to be religious, charitable, or philanthropic causes.

The facts which were held to support the conviction of Jesse Cantwell on the fifth count were that he stopped two men in the street, asked, and received, permission to play a phonograph record, and played the record "Enemies," which attacked the religion and church of the two men, who were Catholics. Both were incensed by the contents of the record and were tempted to strike Cantwell unless he went away. On being told to be on his way he left their presence. There was no evidence that he was personally offensive or entered into any argument with those he interviewed.

The court held that the charge was not assault or breach of the peace or threats on Cantwell's part, but invoking or inciting others to breach of the peace, and that the facts supported the conviction of that offense.

First. We hold that the statute, as construed and applied to the appellants, deprives them of their liberty without due process of law in contravention of the Fourteenth Amendment. The fundamental concept of liberty embodied in that Amendment embraces the liberties guaranteed by the First Amendment. The First Amendment declares that Congress shall make no law respecting an establishment of religion or prohibiting the free exercise thereof. The Fourteenth Amendment has rendered the legislatures of the states as incompetent as Congress to enact such laws.

The constitutional inhibition of legislation on the subject of religion has a double aspect. On the one hand, it forestalls compulsion by law of the acceptance of any creed or the practice of any form of worship. Freedom of conscience and freedom to adhere to such religious organization or form of worship as the individual may choose cannot be restricted by law. On the other hand, it safeguards the free exercise of the chosen form of religion. Thus the Amendment embraces two concepts,—freedom to believe and freedom to act. The first is absolute but, in the nature of things, the second cannot be. Conduct remains subject to regulation for the protection of society. The freedom to act must have appropriate definition to preserve the enforcement of that protection. In every case the power to regulate must be so exercised as not, in attaining a permissible end, unduly to infringe the protected freedom. No one would contest the proposition that a State may not, by statute, wholly deny the right to preach or to disseminate religious views. Plainly such a previous and absolute restraint would violate the terms of the guarantee. It is equally clear that a State may by general and non-discriminatory legislation regulate the times, the places, and the manner of soliciting upon its streets, and of holding meetings thereon; and may in other respects safeguard the peace, good order and comfort of the community, without unconstitutionally invading the liberties protected by the Fourteenth Amendment. The appellants are right in their insistence that the Act in question is not such a regulation. If a certificate is procured, solicitation is permitted without restraint but, in the absence of a certificate, solicitation is altogether prohibited.

The appellants urge that to require them to obtain a certificate as a condition of soliciting support for their views amounts to a prior restraint on the exercise of their religion within the meaning of the Constitution. The State insists that the Act, as construed by the Supreme Court of Connecticut, imposes no previous restraint upon the dissemination of religious views or teaching but merely safeguards against the perpetration of frauds under the cloak of religion. Conceding that this is so, the question remains whether the method adopted by Connecticut to that end transgresses the liberty safeguarded by the Constitution.

The general regulation, in the public interest, of solicitation, which does not involve any religious test and does not unreasonably obstruct or delay the collection of funds, is not open to any constitutional objection, even though the collection be for a religious purpose. Such regulation would not constitute a prohibited previous restraint on the free exercise of religion or interpose an inadmissible obstacle to its exercise.

It will be noted, however, that the Act requires an application to the secretary of the public welfare council of the State; that he is empowered to determine whether the cause is a religious one, and that the issue of a certificate depends upon his affirmative action. If he finds that the cause is not that of religion, to solicit for it becomes a crime. He is not to issue or refuse it involves appraisal of facts, the exercise of judgment, and the formation of an opinion. He is authorized to withhold his approval if he determines that the cause is not a religious one. Such censorship of religion as the means of determining its right to survive is a denial of liberty protected by the First Amendment and included in the liberty which is within the protection of the Fourteenth.

The State asserts that if the licensing officer acts arbitrarily, capriciously, or corruptly, his action is subject to judicial correction. . . It is suggested that the statute is to be read as requiring the officer to issue a certificate unless the cause in question is clearly not a religious one; and that if he violates his duty his action will be corrected by a court.

To this suggestion there are several sufficient answers. The line between a discretionary and a ministerial act is not always easy to mark and the statute has not been construed by the State court to impose a mere ministerial duty on the secretary of the welfare council. Upon his decision as to the nature of the cause, the right to solicit depends. Moreover, the availability of a judicial remedy for abuses in the system of licensing still leaves that system one of previous restraint which, in the field of free speech and press, we have held inadmissible. A statute authorizing previous restraint upon the exercise of the guaranteed freedom by judicial decision after trial is as obnoxious to the Constitution as one providing for like restraint by administrative action.

Nothing we have said is intended even remotely to imply that, under the cloak of religion, persons may, with impunity, commit frauds upon the public. Certainly penal laws are available to punish such conduct. Even the exercise of religion may be at some slight inconvenience in order that the State may protect its citizens from injury. Without doubt a State may protect its citizens from fraudulent solicitation by requiring a stranger in the community, before permitting him publicly to solicit funds for any purpose, to establish his identity and his authority to act for the cause which he purports to represent. The State is likewise free to regulate the time and manner of solicitation generally, in the interest of public safety, peace, comfort or convenience. But to condition the solicitation of aid for the perpetuation of religious views or systems upon a license, the grant of which rests in the exercise of a determination by state authority as to what is a religious cause, is to lay a forbidden burden upon the exercise of liberty protected by the Constitution.

Second. We hold that, in the circumstances disclosed, the conviction of Jesse Cantwell on the fifth count must be set aside. Decision as to the lawfulness of the conviction demands the weighing of two conflicting interests. The fundamental law declares the interest of the United States that the free exercise of religion be not prohibited and that freedom to communicate information and opinion be not abridged. The State of Connecticut has an obvious interest in the preservation and protection of peace and good order within her borders. We must determine whether the alleged protection of the State's interest, means to which end would, in the absence of limitation by the Federal Constitution, lie wholly within the State's discretion, has been pressed, in this instance, to a point where it has come into fatal collision with the overriding interest protected by the federal compact.

Conviction on the fifth count was not pursuant to a statute evincing a legislative judgment that street discussion of religious affairs, because of its tendency to provoke disorder, should be regulated, or a judgment that the playing of a phonograph on the streets should in the interest of comfort or privacy be limited or prevented. Violation of an Act exhibiting such a legislative judgment and narrowly drawn to prevent the supposed evil, would pose a question differing from that we must here answer. Such a declaration of the State's policy would weigh heavily in any challenge of the law as infringing constitutional limitations. Here however, the judgment is based on a common law concept of the most general and undefined nature. The court below has held that the petitioner's conduct constituted the commission of an offense under the state law, and we accept its decision as binding upon us to that extent.

The offense known as breach of the peace embraces a great variety of conduct destroying or menacing public order and tranquility. It includes not only violent acts but acts and words likely to produce violence in others. No one would have the hardihood to suggest that the principle of freedom of speech sanctions incitement to riot or that religious liberty connotes the privilege to exhort others to physical attack upon those belonging to another sect. When clear and present danger of riot, disorder, interference with traffic upon the public streets, or other immediate threat to public safety, peace, or order, appears, the power of the State to prevent or punish is obvious. Equally obvious is it that a State may not unduly suppress free communication of views, religious or other, under the guise of conserving desirable conditions. Here we have a situation analogous to a conviction under a statute sweeping in a great variety of conduct under a general and indefinite characterization, and leaving to the executive and judicial branches too wide a discretion in its application.

Having these considerations in mind, we note that Jesse Cantwell, on April 26, 1938, was upon a public street, where he had a right to be, and where he had a right peacefully to impart his views to others. There is no showing that his deportment was noisy, truculent, overbearing or offensive. He requested of two pedestrians permission to play to them a phonograph record. The permission was granted. It is not claimed that he intended to insult or affront the hearers by playing the record. It is plain that he wished only to interest them in his propaganda. The sound of the phonograph is not shown to have disturbed residents of the street, to have drawn a crowd, or to have impeded traffic. Thus far he had invaded no right or interest of the public or of the men accosted.

The record played by Cantwell embodies a general attack on all organized religious systems as instruments of Satan and injurious to man; it then singles out the Roman Catholic Church for strictures couched in terms which naturally would offend not only persons of that persuasion, but all others who respect the honestly held religious faith of their fellows. The hearers were in fact highly offended. One of them said he felt like hitting Cantwell and the other that he was tempted to throw Cantwell off the street. The one who testified he felt like hitting Cantwell said, in answer to the question "Did you do anything else or have any other reaction?" "No, sir, because he said he would take the victrola and he went." The other witness testified that he told Cantwell he had better get off the street before something happened to him and that was the end of the matter as Cantwell picked up his books and walked up the street.

Cantwell's conduct, in the view of the court below, considered apart from the effect of his communication upon his hearers, did not amount to a breach of the peace. One may, however, be guilty of the offense if he commit acts or make statements likely to provoke violence and disturbance of good order, even though no such eventuality be intended. Decisions to this effect are many, but examination discloses that, in practically all, the provocative language which was held to amount to a breach of the peace consisted of profane, indecent, or abusive remarks directed to the person of the hearer. Resort to epithets or personal abuse is not in any proper sense communication of information or opinion safeguarded by the Constitution, and its punishment as a criminal act would raise no question under that instrument.

We find in the instant case no assault or threatening of bodily harm, no truculent bearing, no intentional discourtesy, no personal abuse. On the contrary, we find only an effort to persuade a willing listener to buy a book or to contribute money in the interest of what Cantwell, however misguided others may think him, conceived to be true religion.

In the realm of religious faith, and in that of political belief, sharp differences arise. In both fields the tenets of one man may seem the rankest error to his neighbor. To persuade others to his own point of view, the pleader, as we know, at times, resorts to exaggeration, to vilification of men who have been, or are, prominent in church or state, and even to false statement. But the people of this nation have ordained in the light of history, that, in spite of the probability of excesses and abuses, these liberties are, in the long view, essential to enlightened opinion and right conduct on the part of the citizens of a democracy.

The essential characteristic of these liberties is, that under their shield many types of life, character, opinion and belief can develop unmolested and unobstructed. Nowhere is this shield more necessary than in our own country for a people composed of many races and of many creeds. There are limits to the exercise of these liberties. The danger in these times from the coercive activities of those who in the delusion of racial or religious conceit would incite violence and breaches of the peace in order to deprive others of their equal right to the exercise of their liberties, is emphasized by events familar to all. These and other transgressions of those limits the States appropriately may punish.

Although the contents of the record not unnaturally aroused animosity, we think that, in the absence of a statute narrowly drawn to define and punish specific conduct as constituting a clear and present danger to a substantial interest of the State, the petitioner's communication, considered in the light of the constitutional guarantees, raised no such clear and present menace to public peace and order as to render him liable to conviction of the common law offense in question.

The judgment affirming the convictions on the third and fifth counts is reversed and the cause is remanded for further proceedings not inconsistent with this opinion.

Reversed.

Murdock v. Pennsylvania[1]
Supreme Court of the United States, 1943
319 U.S. 105

Mr. Justice Douglas delivered the opinion of the Court.

The City of Jeannette, Pennsylvania, has an ordinance, some forty years old, which provides in part:

"That all persons canvassing for or soliciting within said Borough, orders for goods, paintings, pictures, wares, or merchandise of any kind, or persons delivering such articles under orders so obtained or solicited, shall be required to procure from the Burgess a license to transact said business and shall pay to the Treasurer of said Borough therefor the following sums according to the time for which said license shall be granted.

"For one day $1.50, for one week seven dollars ($7.00), for two weeks twelve dollars ($12.00), for three weeks twenty dollars ($20.00), provided that the provisions of this ordinance shall not apply to persons selling by sample to manufacturers or licensed merchants or dealers doing business in said Borough of Jeannette."

Petitioners are "Jehovah's Witnesses." They went about from door to door in the City of Jeannette distributing literature and soliciting people to "purchase" certain religious books and pamphlets, all published by the Watch Tower Bible & Tract Society. The "price" of the books was twenty-five cents each, the "price" of the pamphlets five cents each. In connection with these activities, petitioners used a phonograph on which they played a record expounding certain of their views on religion. None of them obtained a license under the ordinance. Before they were arrested each had made "sales" of books. There was evidence that it was their practice in making these solicitations to request a "contribution" of twenty-five cents each for the books and five cents each for the pamphlets,

---

[1]Footnotes to the opinions in the Murdock, Martin, and Douglas cases are omitted.

but to accept lesser sums or even to donate the volumes in case an interested person was without funds. In the present case, some donations of pamphlets were made when books were purchased. Petitioners were convicted and fined for violation of the ordinance. Their judgments of conviction were sustained by the Superior Court of Pennsylvania, 149 Pa. Super. Ct. 175, 27 A. 2d 666, against their contention that the ordinance deprived them of the freedom of speech, press, and religion guaranteed by the First Amendment. Petitions for leave to appeal to the Supreme Court of Pennsylvania were denied. The cases are here on petitions for writs of certiorari which we granted along with the petitions for rehearing of Jones v. Opelika, 316 U.S. 584, and its companion cases.

The First Amendment, which the Fourteenth makes applicable to the states, declares that "Congress shall make no law respecting an establishment of religion, or prohibiting the free exercise thereof; or abridging the freedom of speech, or of the press . . ." It could hardly be denied that a tax laid specifically on the exercise of those freedoms would be unconstitutional. Yet the license tax imposed by this ordinance is, in substance, just that.

Petitioners spread their interpretations of the Bible and their religious beliefs largely through the hand distribution of literature by full or part time workers. They claim to follow the example of Paul, teaching "publickly, and from house to house." Acts 20:20. They take literally the mandate of the Scriptures, "Go yet into all the world, and preach the gospel to every creature." Mark 16:15. In doing so they believe that they are obeying a commandment of God.

The hand distribution of religious tracts is an age-old form of missionary evangelism - as old as the history of printing presses. It has been a potent force in various religious movements down through the years. This form of evangelism is utilized today on a large scale by various religious sects whose colporteurs carry the Gospel to thousands upon thousands of homes and seek through personal visitations to win adherents to their faith. It is more than preaching; it is more than distribution of religious literature. It is a combination of both. Its purpose is as evangelical as the revival meeting. This form of religious activity occupies the same high estate under the First Amendment as do worship in the churches and preaching from the pulpits. It has the same claim to protection as the more orthodox and conventional exercises of religion. It also has the same claim as the others to the guarantees of freedom of speech and freedom of the press ...

The alleged justification for the exaction of this license tax is the fact that the religious literature is distributed with a solicitation of funds. Thus it was stated, in Jones v. Opelika, supra, p. 597, that when a religious sect uses "ordinary commercial methods of sales of articles to raise propaganda funds," it is proper for the state to charge "reasonable fees for the privilege of canvassing." Situations will arise where it will be difficult to determine whether a particular activity is religious or purely commercial. The distinction at times is vital. As we stated only the other day, in Jamison v. Texas, 318 U.S. 413, 417, "The states can prohibit the use of the streets for the distribution of purely commercial leaflets, even though such leaflets may have 'a civic appeal, or a moral platitude' appended.

Valentine v. Chrestensen, 316 U.S. 52, 55. They may not prohibit the distribution of handbills in the pursuit of a clearly religious activity merely because the handbills invite the purchase of books for the improved understanding of the religion or because the handbills seek in a lawful fashion to promote the raising of funds for religious purposes." But the mere fact that the religious literature is "sold" by itinerant preachers rather than "donated" does not transform evangelism into a commercial enterprise. If it did, then the passing of the collection plate in church would make the church service a commercial project. The constitutional rights of those spreading their religious beliefs through the spoken and printed word are not to be gauged by standards governing retailers or wholesalers of books. The right to use the press for expressing one's views is not to be measured by the protection afforded commercial handbills. It should be remembered that the pamphlets of Thomas Paine were not distributed free of charge. It is plain that a religious organization needs funds to remain a going concern. But an itinerant evangelist however misguided or intolerant he may be, does not become a mere book agent by selling the Bible or religious tracts to help defray his expenses or to sustain him. Freedom of speech, freedom of the press, freedom of religion are available to all, not merely to those who can pay their own way. As we have said, the problem of drawing the line between a purely commercial activity and a religious one will at times be difficult. On this record it plainly cannot be said that petitioners were engaged in a commercial rather than a religious venture. It is a distortion of the facts of record to describe their activities as the occupation of selling books and pamphlets. And the Pennsylvania court did not rest the judgments of conviction on that basis, though it did find that petitioners "sold" the literature. The Supreme Court of Iowa in State v. Mead, 230 Iowa 1217, 300 N.W. 523, 524, described the selling activities of members of this same sect as "merely incidental and collateral" to their "main object which was to preach and publicize the doctrines of their order." And see State v. Meredith 197 S.C. 351, 15 S.E. 2d 678; People v. Barber, 289 N.Y. 378, 385-386, 46 N.E. 2d 329. That accurately summarizes the present record.

We do not mean to say that religious groups and the press are free from all financial burdens of government. See Grosjean v. American Press Co., 297 U.S. 233, 250. We have here something quite different, for example, from a tax on the income of one who engages in religious activities or a tax on property used or employed in connection with those activities. It is one thing to impose a tax on the income or property of a preacher. It is quite another thing to exact a tax from him for the privilege of delivering a sermon. The tax imposed by the City of Jeannette is a flat license tax, the payment of which is a conditon of the exercise of these constitutional privileges. The power to tax the exercise of a privilege is the power to control or suppress its enjoyment. Magnano Co. v. Hamilton, 292 U.S. 40, 44-45, and cases cited. Those who can tax the exercise of this religious practice can make its exercise so costly as to deprive it of the resources necessary for its maintenance. Those who can tax the privilege of engaging in this form of missionary evangelism can close its doors to all those who do not have a full purse. Spreading religous beliefs in this ancient and honorable manner would thus be denied the needy. Those who can deprive religious groups of their colporteurs can take from them a part of the vital power of the press which has survived from the Reformation.

It is contended, however, that the fact that the license tax can suppress or control this activity is unimportant if it does not do so. But that is to disregard the nature of this tax. It is a license tax - a flat tax imposed on the exercise of a privilege granted by the Bill of Rights. A state may not impose a charge for the enjoyment of a right granted by the Federal Constitution. Thus, it may not exact a license tax for the privilege of carrying on interstate commerce (McGoldrick v. Berwind-White Co., 309 U.S. 33, 56-58), although it may tax the property used in, or the income derived from, that commerce, so long as those taxes are not discriminatory. Id., p. 47 and cases cited. A license tax applied to activities guaranteed by the First Amendment would have the same destructive effect. It is true that the First Amendment, like the commerce clause, draws no distinction between license taxes, fixed sum taxes, and other kinds of taxes. But that is no reason why we should shut our eyes to the nature of the tax and its destructive influence. The power to impose a license tax on the exercise of these freedoms is indeed as potent as the power of censorship which this Court has repeatedly struck down. Lovell v. Griffin, 303 U.S. 444; Schneider v. State, supra; Cantwell v. Connecticut, 310 U.S. 296, 306; Largent v. Texas, 318 U.S. 418; Jamison v. Texas, supra. It was for that reason that the dissenting opinion in Jones v. Opelika, supra, stressed the nature of this type of tax. 316 U.S. pp. 607-609, 620, 623. In that case as in the present ones, we have something very different from a registration system under which those going from house to house are required to give their names, addresses and other marks of identification to the authorities. In all of these cases the issuance of the permit or license is dependent on the payment of a license tax. And the license tax is fixed in amount and unrelated to the scope of the activities of petitioners or to their realized revenues. It is not a nominal fee imposed as a regulatory measure to defray the expenses of policing the activities in question. It is in no way apportioned. It is a flat license tax levied and collected as a condition to the pursuit of activities whose enjoyment is guaranteed by the First Amendment. Accordingly, it restrains in advance those constitutional liberties of press and religion and inevitably tends to suppress their exercise. That is almost uniformly recognized as the inherent vice and evil of this flat license tax. As stated by the Supreme Court of Illinois in a case involving this same sect and an ordinance similar to the present one, a person cannot be compelled "to purchase, through a license fee or a license tax, the privilege freely granted by the constitution." Blue Island v. Kozul, 379 Ill. 511, 519, 41 N. E. 2d 515. So, it may not be said that proof is lacking that these license taxes either separately or cumulatively have restricted or are likely to restrict petitioners' religious activities. On their face they are a restriction of the free exercise of those freedoms which are protected by the First Amendment ...

The fact that the ordinance is "nondiscriminatory" is immaterial. The protection afforded by the First Amendment is not so restricted. A license tax certainly does not acquire constitutional validity because it classifies the privileges protected by the First Amendment along with the wares and merchandise of hucksters and peddlers and treats them all alike. Such equality in treatment does not save the ordinance. Freedom of press, freedom of speech, freedom of religion are in a preferred position.·

It is claimed, however, that the ultimate question in determining the constitutionality of this license tax is whether the state has given something for which it can ask a return. That principle has wide applicability. State Tax Commission v. Aldrich, 316 U.S. 174, and cases cited. But it is quite irrelevant here. This tax is not a charge for the enjoyment of a privilege or benefit bestowed by the state. The privilege in question exists apart from state authority. It is guaranteed the people by the Federal Constitution.

Considerable emphasis is placed on the kind of literature which petitioners were distributing - its provocative, abusive, and ill-mannered character and the assault which it makes on our established churches and the cherished faiths of many of us. See Douglas v. Jeannette, concurring opinion, post, p. 166. But those considerations are no justification for the license tax which the ordinance imposes. Plainly a community may not suppress, or the state tax, the dissemination of views because they are unpopular, annoying or distateful. If that device were ever sanctioned, there would have been forged a ready instrument for the suppression of the faith which any minority cherishes but which does not happen to be in favor. That would be a complete repudiation of the philosophy of the Bill of Rights.

Jehovah's Witnesses are not "above the law." But the present ordinance is not directed to the problems with which the police power of the state is free to deal. It does not cover, and petitioners are not charged with, breaches of the peace. They are pursuing their solicitations peacefully and quietly. Petitioners, moreover, are not charged with or prosecuted for the use of language which is obscene, abusive, or which incites retaliation. Cf. Chaplinsky v. New Hampshire, supra. Nor do we have here, as we did in Cox v. New Hampshire, supra, and Chaplinsky v. New Hampshire, supra, state regulation of the streets to protect and insure the safety, comfort, or convenience of the public. Furthermore, the present ordinance is not narrowly drawn to safeguard the people of the community in their homes against the evils of solicitations. See Cantwell v. Connecticut, supra, 306. As we have said, it is not merely a registration ordinance calling for an identification of the solicitors so as to give the authorities some basis for investigating strangers coming into the community. And the fee is not a nominal one, imposed as a regulator measure and calculated to defray the expense of protecting those on the streets and at home against the abuses of solicitors. See Cox v. New Hampshire, supra, pp. 576-577. Nor can the present ordinance survive if we assume that it has been construed to apply only to solicitation from house to house. The ordinance is not narrowly drawn to prevent or control abuses or evils arising from that activity. Rather, it sets aside the residential areas as a prohibited zone, entry of which is denied petitioners unless the tax is paid. That restraint and one which is city-wide in scope (Jones v. Opelika) are different only in degree. Each is an abridgement of freedom of press and a restraint on the free exercise of religion. They stand or fall together.

The judgment in Jones v. Opelika has this day been vacated. Freed from that controlling precedent, we can restore to their high, constitutional position the liberties of itinerant evangelists who disseminate their religious beliefs and the tenets of their faith through distribution of literature. The judgments are reversed and the causes are remanded to the Pennsylvania Superior Court for proceedings not inconsistent with this opinion.

Reversed.

The following dissenting opinions are applicable to Nos. 280, 314, and 966 (October Term, 1941(, Jones v. Opelika, ante, p. 103; and to Nos. 480-487, Murdock v. Pennsylvania, ante, p. 105. See also opinion of Mr. Justice Jackson, post, p. 166.

Mr. Justice Reed, dissenting: . . .

The First Amendment reads as follows:

"Congress shall make no law respecting an establishment of religion, or prohibiting the free exercise thereof; or abridging the freedom of speech, or of the press; or the right of the people peaceably to assemble, and to petition the Government for a redress of grievances."

It was one of twelve proposed on September 25, 1789, to the States by the First Congress after the adoption of the Constitution. Ten were ratified. They were intended to be and have become our Bill of Rights. By their terms, our people have a guarantee that so long as law as we know it shall prevail, they shall live protected from the tyranny of the despot or the mob. None of the provisions of our Constitution is more venerated by the people or respected by legislatures and the courts than those which proclaim for our country the freedom of religion and expression. While the interpreters of the Constitution find the purpose was to allow the widest practical scope for the exercise of religion and the dissemination of information, no jurist has ever conceived that the prohibition of interference is absolute. Is subjection to nondiscriminatory, nonexcessive taxation in the distribution of religious literature, a prohibition of the exercise of religion or an abridgment of the freedom of the press?

Nothing has been brought to our attention which would lead to the conclusion that the contemporary advocates of the adoption of a Bill of Rights intended such an exemption. The words of the Amendment do not support such a construction. "Free" cannot be held to be without cost but rather its meaning must accord with the freedom guaranteed. "Free" means a privilege to print or pray without permission and without accounting to authority for one's actions. In the Constitutional Convention the proposal for a Bill or Rights of any kind received scant attention. In the course of the ratification of the Constitution, however, the absence of a Bill of Rights was used vigorously by the opponents of the new government. A number of the states suggested amendments. Where these suggestions have any hearing at all upon religion or free speech, they indicate nothing as to any feeling concerning taxation either of religious bodies or their evangelism. This was not because freedom of religion or free speech was not understood. It was because the subjects were looked upon from standpoints entirely distinct from taxation.

The available evidence of Congressional action shows clearly that the draftsmen of the amendments had in mind the practice of religion and the right to be heard rather than any abridgment or interference with either by taxation in any form. The amendments were proposed by Mr. Madison. He was careful to explain to the Congress the meaning of the amendment on religion. The draft was commented upon by Mr. Madison when it read: "no religion shall be established by law, nor shall the equal rights of conscience be infringed." 1 Annals of Congress 729.

He said that he apprehended the meaning of the words on religion to be that Congress should not establish a religion and enforce the legal observation of it by law, nor compel men to worship God in any manner contrary to their conscience. Id., 730. No such specific interpretation of the amendment on freedom of expression has been found in the debates. The clearest is probably from Mr. Benson, who said that

"The committee who framed this report proceeded on the principle that these rights belonged to the people; they conceived them to be inherent; and all that they meant to provide against was their being infringed by the Government." Id., 731-32.

There have been suggestions that the English taxes on newspapers, springing from the tax act of 10 Anne, c. 19, § CI, influenced the adoption of the First Amendment. These taxes were obnoxious but an examination of the sources of the suggestion is convincing that there is nothing to support in except the fact that the tax on newspapers was in existence in England and was disliked. The simple answer is that, if there had been any purpose of Congress to prohibit any kind of taxes on the press, its knowledge of the abominated English taxes would have led it to ban them unequivocally.

It is only in recent years that the freedoms of the First Amendment have been recognized as among the fundamental personal rights protected by the Fourteenth Amendment from impairment by the states. Until then these liberties were not deemed to be guarded from state action by the Federal Constitution. The states placed restraints upon themselves in their own constitutions in order to protect their people in the exercise of the freedoms of speech and of religion. Pennsylvania may be taken as a fair example. Its constitution reads:

"All men have a natural and indefeasible right to worship Almighty God according to the dictates of their own consciences; no man can of right be compelled to attend, erect or support any place of worship, or to maintain any ministry against his consent; no human authority can, in any case whatever, control or interfere with the rights of conscience and no preference shall ever be given by law to any religious establishments or modes of worship." Purdon's Penna. Stat., Const., Art. I, § 3.

"No person who acknowledges the being of a God, and a future state of rewards and punishments shall, on account of his religious sentiments, be disqualified to hold any office or place of trust or profit under this Commonwealth." Id., Art. I, § 4.

"The printing press shall be free to every person who may undertake to examine the proceedings of the Legislature or any branch of the government, and no law shall ever be made to restrain the right thereof. The free communication of thoughts and opinions is one of the invaluable rights of man, and every citizen may freely speak, write and print on any subject, being responsible for the abuse of that liberty . . .'' Id., Art. I, § 7.

It will be observed that there is no suggestion of freedom from taxation, and this statement is equally true of the other state constitutional provisions. It may be concluded that neither in the state or the federal constitutions was general taxation of church or press interdicted.

Is there anything in the decisions of this Court which indicates that church or press is free from the financial burdens of government? We find nothing. Religious societies depend for their exemptions from taxation upon state constitutions or general statutes, not upon the Federal Constitution. Gibbons v. District of Columbia, 116 U.S. 404. This Court has held that the chief purpose of the free press guarantee was to prevent previous restraints upon publication. Near v. Minnesota, 283 U.S. 697, 713. In Grosjean v. American Press Co., 297 U.S. 233, 250, it was said that the predominant purpose was to preserve ''an untrammeled press as a vital source of public information.'' In that case, a gross receipts tax on advertisements in papers with a circulation of more than twenty thousand copies per week was held invalid because ''a deliberate and calculated device in the guise of a tax to limit the circulation . . .'' There was this further comment:

''It is not intended by anything we have said to suggest that the owners of newspapers are immune from any of the ordinary forms of taxation for support of the government. But this is not an ordinary form of tax, but one single in kind, with a long history of hostile misuse against the freedom of the press.'' Id., 250.

It may be said, however, that ours is a too narrow, technical and legalistic approach to the problem of state taxation of the activities of church and press; that we should look not to the expressed or historical meaning of the First Amendment but to the broad principles of free speech and free exercise of religion which pervade our national way of life. It may be that the Fourteenth Amendment guarantees these principles rather than the more definite concept expressed in the First Amendment. This would mean that as a Court, we should determine what sort of liberty it is that the due process clause of the Fourteenth Amendment guarantees against state restrictions on speech and church.

But whether we give content to the literal words of the First Amendment or to principles of the liberty of the press and the church, we conclude that cities or states may levy reasonable, non-discriminatory taxes on such activities as occurred in these cases. Whatever exemptions exist from taxation arise from the prevailing law of the various states. The constitutions of Alabama and Pennsylvania, with substantial similarity to the exemption provisions of other constitutions, forbid the taxation of lots and buildings used exclusively for religious worship. Alabama (1901), § 91; Pennsylvania (1874), Art. IX, § 1. There are the only exemptions of religious bodies from taxes would not have occurred throughout our history, if it had been conceived that the genius of our institutions, as expressed in the First Amendment, was incompatible with the taxation of church or press.

Nor do we understand that the Court now maintains that the Federal Constitution frees press or religion of any tax except such occupational taxes as those here levied. Income taxes, ad valorem taxes, even occupational taxes are presumably valid, save only a license tax on sales of religious books. Can it be that the Constitution permits a tax on the printing presses and the gross income of a metropolitan newspaper but denies the right to lay an occupational tax on the distributors of the same papers? Does the exemption apply to booksellers or distributors of magazines or only to religious publications? And, if the latter, to what distributors? Or to what books? Or is this Court saying that a religious practice of book distribution is free from taxation because a state cannot prohibit the "free exercise thereof" and a newspaper is subject to the same tax even though the same Constitutional Amendment says the state cannot abridge the freedom of the press? It has never been thought before that freedom from taxation was a perquisite attaching to the privileges of the First Amendment. The National Government grants exemptions to ministers and churches because it wishes to do so, not because the Constitution compels. Internal Revenue Code, §§ 22 (b) (6), 101 (6), 812 (d), 1004 (a) (2) (B). Where camp meetings or revivals charge admissions, a federal tax would apply, if Congress had not granted freedom from the exaction. Id., § 1701.

It is urged that such a tax as this may be used readily to restrict the dissemination of ideas. This must be conceded but the possibility of misuse does not make a tax unconstitutional. No abuse is claimed here. The ordinances in some of these cases are the general occupation license type covering many businesses. In the Jeannette prosecutions, the ordinance involved lays the usual tax on canvassing or soliciting sales of goods, wares and merchandise. It was passed in 1898. Every power of taxation or regulation is capable of abuse. Each one, to some extent, prohibits the free exercise of religion and abridges the freedom of the press, but that is hardly a reason for denying the power. If the tax is used oppressively, the law will protect the victims of such action.

This decision forces a tax subsidy notwithstanding our accepted belief in the separation of church and state. Instead of all bearing equally the burdens of government, this Court now fastens upon the communities the entire cost of policing the sales of religious literature. That the burden may be heavy is shown by the record in the Jeannette cases. There are only eight prosecutions, but one hundred and four Witnesses solicited in Jeannette the day of the arrests. They had been requested by the authorities to await the outcome of a test case before continuing their canvassing. The distributors of religious literature, possibly of all informatory publications, become today privileged to carry on their occupations without contributing their share to the support of the government which provides the opportunity for the exercise of their liberties.

Nor do we think it can be said, properly, that these sales of religious books are religious exercises. The opinion of the Court in the Jeannette cases emphasizes for the first time the argument that the sale of books and pamphlets is in itself a religious practice. The Court says the Witnesses "spread their interpretations of the Bible and their religious beliefs largely through the hand distribution of literature by full or part time workers." "The hand distribution of religious tracts is an age-old form of missionary evangelism - as old as the history of printing presses."

"It is more than preaching; it is more than distribution of religious literature. It is a combination of both. Its purpose is as evangelical as the revival meeting. This form of religious activity occupies the same high estate under the First Amendment as do worship in the churches and preaching from the pulpits." "Those who can tax the exercise of this religious practice can make its exercise so costly as to deprive it of the resources necessary for its maintenance." "The judgment in Jones v. Opelika has this day been vacated. Freed from that controlling precedent, we can restore to their high, constitutional position the liberties of itinerant evangelists who disseminate their religious beliefs and the tenets of their faith through distribution of literature." The record shows that books entitled "Creation" and "Salvation", as well as Bibles, were offered for sale. We shall assume the first two publications, also, are religious books. Certainly there can be no dissent from the statement that selling religious books is an age-old practice, or that it is evangelism in the sense that the distributors hope the readers will be spiritually benefited. That does not carry us to the conviction, however, that when distribution of religious books is made at a price, the itinerant colporteur is performing a religious rite, is worshipping his Creator in his way. Many sects practice healing the sick as an evidence of their religious faith or maintain orphanages or homes for the aged or teach the young. These are, of course, in a sense, religious practices but hardly such examples of religious rites as are encompassed by the prohibition against the free exercise of religion.

And even if the distribution of religious books was a religious practice protected from regulation by the First Amendment, certainly the affixation of a price for the article would destroy the sacred character of the transaction. The evangelist becomes also a book agent.

The rites which are protected by the First Amendment are in essence spiritual - prayer, mass, sermons, sacrament - not sales of religious goods. The card furnished each Witness to identify him as an ordained minister does not go so far as to say the sale is a rite. It states only that the Witnesses worship by exhibiting to people "the message of said gospel in printed form, such as the Bible, books, booklets and magazines, and thus afford the people the opportunity of learning of God's gracious provision for them." On the back of the card appears: "You may contribute twenty-five cents to the Lord's work and receive a copy of this beautiful book." The sale of these religious books has, we think, relation to their religious exercises, similar to the "information march," said by the Witnesses to be one of their "ways of worship" and by this Court to be subject to regulation by license in Cox v. New Hampshire, 312 U.S. 569, 572, 573, 576...

The limitations of the Constitution are not maxims of social wisdom but definite controls on the legislative process. We are dealing with power, not its abuse. This late withdrawal of the power of taxation over the distribution activities of those covered by the First Amendment fixes what seems to us an unfortunate principle of tax exemption, capable of indefinite extension. We had thought that such an exemption required a clear and certain grant. This we do not find in the language of the First and Fourteenth Amendments. We are therefore of the opinion the judgments below should be affirmed.[2]

Martin v. Struthers
Supreme Court of the United States, 1943
319 U.S. 141

Mr. Justice Black delivered the opinion of the Court.

For centuries it has been a common practice in this and other countries for persons not specifically invited to go from home to home and knock on doors or ring doorbells to communicate ideas to the occupants or to invite them to political, religious, or other kinds of public meetings. Whether such visiting shall be permitted has in general been deemed to depend upon the will of the individual master of each household, and not upon the determination of the community. In the instant case, the City of Struthers, Ohio, has attempted to make this decision for all its inhabitants. The question to be decided is whether the City, consistently with the federal Constitution's guarantee of free speech and press, possesses this power.

The appellant, espousing a religious cause in which she was interested - that of the Jehovah's Witnesses - went to the homes of strangers, knocking on doors and ringing doorbells in order to distribute to the inmates of the homes leaflets advertising a religious meeting. In doing so, she pro ceeded in a conventional and orderly fashion. For delivering a leaflet to the inmate of a home, she was convicted in the Mayor's Court and was fined $10,00 on a charge of violating the following City ordinance:

"It is unlawful for any person distributing handbills, circulars or other advertisements to ring the doorbell ... or otherwise summon the inmate ... to the door for the purpose of receiving such handbills, circulars or other advertisements they or any person with them may be distributing."

The appellant admitted knocking at the door for the purpose of delivering the invitation, but seasonably urged in the lower Ohio state court that the ordinance as construed and applied was beyond the power of the State because in violation of the right of freedom of press and religion as guaranteed by the First and Fourteenth Amendments.

The right of freedom of speech and press has broad scope. The authors of the First Amendment knew that novel and unconventional ideas might disturb the complacent, but they chose to encourage a freedom which they believed essential if vigorous enlightenment was ever to triumph over slothful ignorance. This freedom embraces the right to distribute literature, Lovell v. Griffin, 303 U.S. 444, 452, and necessarily protects the right to receive it. The privilege may not be withdrawn even if it creates the minor nuisance for a community of cleaning litter from its streets. Schneider v. State, 308 U.S. 147, 162. Yet the peace, good order, and comfort of the community may imperatively require regulation of the time, place and manner of distribution. Cantwell v. Connecticut, 310 U.S. 296, 304. No one supposes, for example, that a city need permit a man with a communicable disease to distribute leaflets on the street or to homes, or that the First Amendment prohibits a state from prevent the distribution of leaflets in a church against the will of the church authorities.

---

[2]The dissenting opinion of Frankfurter, J. is omitted.

We are faced in the instant case with the necessity of weighing the conflicting interests of the appellant in the civil rights she claims, as well as the right of the individual householder to determine whether he is willing to receive her message, against the interest of the community which by this ordinance offers to protect the interests of all of its citizens, whether particular citizens want that protection or not. The ordinance does not control anything but the distribution of literature, and in that respect it substitutes the judgment of the community for the judgment of the individual householder. It submits the distributer to criminal punishment for annoying the person on whom he calls, even though the recipient of the literature distributed is in fact glad to receive it. In considering legislation which thus limits the dissemination of knowledge, we must "be astute to examine the effect of the challenged legislation" and must "weigh the circumstances and . . . appraise the substantiality of the reasons advanced in support of the regulation." Schneider v. State, supra, 161.

Ordinances of the sort now before us may be aimed at the protection of the householders from annoyance, including intrusion upon the hours of rest, and at the prevention of crime. Constant callers, whether selling pots or distributing leaflets, may lessen the peaceful enjoyment of a home as much as a neighborhood glue factory of railroad year which zoning ordinances may prohibit. In the instant case, for example, it is clear from the record that the householder to whom the appellant gave the leaflet which led to her arrest was more irritated than pleased with her visitor. The City, which is an industrial community most of whose residents are engaged in the iron and steel industry, has vigorously argued that its inhabitants frequently work on swing shifts, working nights and sleeping days so that casual bell pushers might seriously interfere with the hours of sleep although they call at high noon. In addition, burglars frequently pose as canvassers, either in order that they may have a pretense to discover whether a house is empty and hence ripe for burglary, or for the purpose of spying out the premises in order that they may return later. Crime prevention may thus be the purpose of regulatory ordinances.

While door to door distributers of literature may be either a nuisance or a blind for criminal activities, they may also be useful members of society engaged in the dissemination of ideas in accordance with the best tradition of free discussion. The widespread use of this method of communication by many groups espousing various causes attests its major importance. "Pamphlets have proved most effective instruments in the dissemination of opinion. And perhaps the most effective way of bringing them to the notice of individuals is their distribution at the homes of the people." Schneider v. State, supra, 164. Many of our most widely established religious organizations have used this method of disseminating their doctrines, and laboring groups have used it in recruiting their members. The federal government, in its current war bond selling campaign, encourages groups of citizens to distribute advertisements and circulars from house to house. Of course, as every person acquainted with political life knows, door to door campaigning is one of the most accepted techniques of seeking popular support, while the circulation of nominating papers would be greatly handicapped if they could not be taken to the citizens in their homes. Door to door distribution of circulars is essential to the poorly financed causes of little people.

Freedom to distribute information to every citizen wherever he desires to receive it so clearly vital to the preservation of a free society that, putting aside reasonable police and health regulations of time and manner of distribution, it must be fully preserved. The dangers of distribution can so easily be controlled by traditional legal methods, leaving to each householder the full right to decide whether he will receive strangers as visitors, that stringent prohibition can serve no purpose but that forbidden by the Constitution, the naked restriction of the dissemination of ideas.

Traditionally the American law punishes persons who enter onto the property of another after having been warned by the owner to keep off. General trespass after warning statutes exist in at least twenty states, while similar statutes of narrower scope are on the books of at least twelve states more. We know of no state which, as does the Struthers ordinance in effect, makes a person a criminal trespasser if he enters the property of another for an innocent purpose without an explicit command from the owners to stay away. The National Institute of Municipal Law Officers has proposed a form of regulation to its member cities which would make it an offense for any person to ring the bell of a householder who has appropriately indicated that he is unwilling to be disturbed. This or any similar regulation leaves the decision as to whether distributers of literature may lawfully call at a home where it belongs - with the homeowner himself. A city can punish those who call at a home in defiance of the previously expressed will of the occupant, and, in addition, can by identification devices control the abuse of the privilege by criminals posing as canvassers. In any case, the problem must be worked out by each community for itself with due respect for the constitutional rights of those desiring to distribute literature and those desiring to receive it, as well as those who choose to exclude such distributers from the home.

The Struthers ordinance does not safeguard these constitutional rights. For this reason, and wholly aside from any other possible defects, on which we do not pass but which are suggested in other opinion filed in this case, we conclude that the ordinance is invalid because in conflict with the freedom of speech and press.

The judgment below is reversed for further proceedings not inconsistent with this opinion.

Reversed[1]

Mr. Justice Frankfurter:

From generation to generation, fresh vindication is given to the prophetic wisdom of the framers of the Constitution in casting it in terms so broad that it has adaptable vitality for the drastic changes in our society which they knew to be inevitable, even though they could not foresee them. Thus it has come to be that the transforming consequences resulting from the pervasive industrialization of life find the Commerce Clause appropriate, for instance, for national regulation of an aircraft flight wholly within a single state. Such exertion of power by the national gov-

[1]A concurring opinion by Murphy J., and a dissent by Reed, J. are omitted.

ernment over what might seem a purely local transaction would, as a matter of abstract law, have been as unimaginable to Marshall as to Jefferson, precisely because neither could have foreseen the present conquest of the air by man. But law, whether derived from acts of Congress or the Constitution, is not an abstraction. The Constitution cannot be applied in disregard of the external circumstances in which men live and move and have their being. Therefore, neither the First nor the Fourteenth Amendment is to be treated by judges as though it were a mathematical abstraction, an absolute having no relation to the lives of man.

The habits and security of life in sparsely settled rural communities, or even in those few cities which a hundred and fifty years ago had a population of a few thousand, cannot be made the basis of judgment for determining the area of allowable self-protection by present-day industrial communities. The lack of privacy and the hazards to peace of mind and body caused by people living not in individual houses but crowded together in large human beehives, as they so widely do, are facts of modern living which cannot be ignored.

Concededly, the Due Process Clause of the Fourteenth Amendment did not abrogate the power of the states to recognize that homes are sanctuaries from intrusions upon privacy and of opportunities for leading lives of health and safety. Door-knocking and bell-ringing by professed peddlers of things or ideas may therefore be confined within specified hours and otherwise circumscribed so as not to sanctify the rights of these peddlers in disregard of the rights of those within doors. Acknowledgement is also made that the City of Struthers, the particular ordinance of which presents the immediate issue before us, is one of those industrial communities the residents of which have a working day consisting of twenty-four hours, so that for some portions of the city's inhabitants opportunities for sleep and refreshment require during day as well as night whatever peace and quiet is obtainable in a modern industrial town. It is further recognized that the modern multiple residences give opportunities for pseudo-canvassers to ply evil trades - dangers to the community pursued by the few but far-reaching in their success and in the fears they arouse.

The Court's opinion apparently recognizes these factors as legitimate concerns for regulation by those whose business it is to legislate. But it finds, if I interpret correctly what is wanting in explicitness, that instead of aiming at the protection of householders from intrusion upon needed hours of rest or from those plying evil trades, whether pretending the sale of pots and pans or the distribution of leaflets, the ordinance before us merely penalizes the distribution of "literature." To be sure, the prohibition of this ordinance is within a small circle. But it is not our business to require legislatures to extend the area of prohibition or regulation beyond the demands of revealed abuses. And the greatest leeway must be given to the legislative judgment of what those demands are. The right to legislate implies the right to classify. We should not, however unwittingly, slip into the judgment seat of legislatures. I myself cannot say that those in whose keeping is the peace of the City of Struthers and the right of privacy of its home dwellers could not single out, in circumstances of which they may have knowledge and I certainly have not, this class of canvassers as the particular source of mischief. The Court's opinion leaves one in doubt whether prohibition of all bell-ringing and door-knocking would be deemed an infringement of the constitutional protection of speech. It would be fantastic to suggest that a city has power, in the circumstances of modern urban life, to forbid house-to-house canvassing generally, but that the Constitution prohibits the inclusion in such prohibition of door-to-door vending of phylacteries or rosaries or of any printed matter. If the scope of the Court's opinion, apart from some of its general observations, is that this ordinance is an invidious discrimination against distributors of what is politely called literature, and therefore is deemed an unjustifiable prohibition of freedom of utterance, the decision leaves untouched what are in my view controlling constitutional principles, if I am correct in my understanding of what is held, and I would not be disposed to disagree with such a construction of the ordinance.

Douglas v. Jeannette
Supreme Court of the United States, 1943
319 U.S. 157

Mr. Chief Justice Stone delivered the opinion of the Court.

Petitioners brought this suit in the United States District Court for Western Pennsylvania to restain threatened criminal prosecution of them in the state courts by respondents, the City of Jeannette (a Pennsylvania municipal corporation) and its Mayor, for violation of a city ordinance which prohibits the solicitation of orders for merchandise without first procuring a license from the city authorities and paying a license tax. The ordinance as applied is held to be an unconstitutional abridgment of free speech, press and religion in Murdock v. Pennsylvania, ante, p. 105. The questions decisive of the present case are whether the district court has statutory jurisdiction as a federal court to entertain the suit, and whether petitioners have by their pleadings and proof established a cause of action in equity.

The case is not one of diversity of citizenship, since some of the petitioners, like respondents, are citizens of Pennsylvania. The bill of complaint alleges that the named plaintiffs are Jehovah's Witnesses, persons who entertain religious beliefs and engage in religious practices which it describes; that the suit is a class suit brought in petitioners' own behalf and in behalf of all other Jehovah's Witnesses in Pennsylvania and adjoining states to restrain respondents from enforcing ordinance No. 60 of the City of Jeannette against petitioners and all other Jehovah's Witnesses because, as applied to them, the ordinance abridges the guaranties of freedom of speech, press, and religion of the First Amendment made applicable to the states by the Fourteenth.

The suit is alleged to arise under the Constitution and laws of the United States, including the Civil Rights Act of 1871. The complain sets up that in the practice of their religion and in conformity to the teachings of the Bible, Jehovah's Witnesses make, and for many years have made, house to house distribution, among the people of the City of Jeannette, of certain printed books and pamphlets setting forth the Jehovah's Witnesses- interpretations of the teachings of the Bible. Municipal Ordinance No. 60 provides: "That all persons canvassing for or soliciting within said

Borough (now City of Jeannette), orders for goods . . . wares or merchandise of any kind, or persons delivering such articles under orders so obtained or solicited" without first procuring a license and paying prescribed license taxes, shall be punished by fine not exceeding $100 and costs, or if the fine is not paid, by imprisonment from five to thirty days. It is alleged that in April, 1939, respondents arrested and prosecuted petitioners and other Jehovah's Witnesses for violation of the ordinance because of their described activities in distributing religious literature, without the permits required by the ordinance, and that respondents threaten to continue to enforce the ordinance by arrests and prosecutions - all in violation of petitioners' civil rights.

No preliminary or interlocutory injunction was granted but the district court, after a trial, held the ordinance invalid, 38 F. Supp. 30, in that it deprived petitioners of the rights of freedom of press and religion guaranteed by the First and Fourteenth Amendments. The court enjoined respondents from enforcing the ordinance against petitioners and other Jehovah's Witnesses.

The Court of Appeals for the Third Circuit sustained the jurisdiction of the district court, but reversed on the merits, 130 F. 2d 652, on the authority of Jones v. Opelika, 316 U.S. 584. One judge dissented on the ground that the complaint did not sufficiently allege a violation of the Due Process Clause of the Fourteenth Amendment so as to entitle petitioners to relief under the Civil Rights Act. We granted certiorari, 318 U.S. 749, and set the case for argument with Murdock v. Pennsylvania, supra.

We think it plain that the district court had jurisdiction as a federal court to hear and decide the question of the constitutional validity of the ordinance, although there was no allegation or proof that the matter in controversy exceeded $3,000. By 8 U. S. C. § 43 (derived from § 1 of the Civil Rights Act of April 20, 1871, 17 Stat. 13, continued without substantial change as R. S. § 1979) it is provided that "every person who, under color of any statute, ordinance, regulation, custom, or usage, of any State or Territory, subjects, or causes to be subjected, any citizen of the United States or other person within the jurisdiction thereof to the deprivation of any rights, privileges, or immunities secured by the Constitution and laws, shall be liable to the party injured in an action at law, suit in equity, or other proper proceedings for redress."

As we held in Hague v. C. I. O., 307 U.S. 496, 507-14, 527-32, the district courts of the United States are given jurisdiction by 28 U. S. C. § 41 (14) over suits brought under the Civil Rights Act without the allegation or proof of any jurisdictional amount. Not only do petitioners allege that the present suit was brought under the Civil Rights Act, but their allegations plainly set out an infringement of its provisions. In substance, the complaint alleges that respondents, proceeding under the challenged ordinance, by arrest, detention and by criminal prosecutions of petitioners and other Jehovah's Witnesses, had subjected them to deprivation of their rights of freedom of speech, press and religion secured by the Constitution, and the complaint seeks equitable relief from such deprivation in the future.

The particular provision of the Constitution on which petitioners rely is the Due Process Clause of the Fourteenth Amendment, violation of which the dissenting judge below though was not sufficiently alleged to establish a bais for relief under the Civil Rights Act. But we think this overlooks the special relationship of the Fourteenth Amendment to the rights of freedom of speech, press, and religion guaranteed by the First. We have repeatedly held that the Fourteenth Amendment has made applicable to the states the guaranties of the First. Schneider v. State, 308 U.S. 147, 160, n. 8 and cases cited; Jamison v. Texas, 318 U.S. 413. Allegations of fact sufficient to show deprivation of the right of free speech under the First Amendment are sufficient to establish deprivation of a constitutional right guaranteed by the Fourteenth, and to state a cause of action under the Civil Rights Act, whenever it appears that the abridgement of the right is effected under color of a state statute or ordinance. It follows that the bill, which amply alleges the facts relied on to show the abridgment by criminal proceedings under the ordinance, sets out a case or controversy which is within the adjudicatory power of the district court.

Notwithstanding the authority of the district court, as a federal court, to hear and dispose of the case, petitioners are entitled to the relief prayed only if they establish a cause of action in equity. Want of equity jurisdiction, while not going to the power ot the court to decide the cuase, Di Giovanni v. Camden Ins. Assn., 296 U.S. 64, 69; Pennsylvania v. Williams, 294 U.S. 176, 181-82, may nevertheless, in the discretion of the court, be objected to on its own motion. Twist v. Prairie Oil Co., 274 U.S. 684, 690; Pennsylvania v. Williams, supra, 185. Especially should it do so where its powers are invoked to interfere by injunction with threatened criminal prosecutions in a state court.

The power reserved to the states under the Constitution to provide for the determination of controversies in their courts may be restricted by federal district courts only in obedience to Congressional legislation in conformity to the judiciary Article of the Constitution. Congress, by its legislation, has adopted the policy, with certain well defined statuory exceptions, of leaving generally to the state courts the trial of criminal cases arising under state laws, subject to review by this Court of any federal questions involved. Hence, courts of equity in the exercise of their discretionary powers should conform to this policy by refusing to interfere with or embarrass threatened proceedings in state courts save in those exceptional cases which call for the interposition of a court of equity to prevent irreparable injury which is clear and imminent; and equitable remedies infringing this independence of the states - though they might otherwise be given - should be withheld if sought on slight or inconsequential grounds. Di Giovanni v. Camden Ins. Assn., supra, 73; Matthews v. Rodgers, 294 U.S. 521, 525-26; cf. United States ex rel. Kennedy v. Tyler, 269 U.S. 13; Massachusetts State Grange v. Benton, 272 U.S. 525.

It is a familiar rule that courts of equity do not ordinarily restrain criminal prosecutions. No person is immune from prosecution in good faith for his alleged criminal acts. Its imminence, even though alleged to be in violation of constitutional guaranties, is not a ground for equity relief since the lawfulness or constitutionality of the statute or ordinance on which the prosecution is based may be determined as readily in the criminal case as in a suit for an injunction. Davis & Farnum Mfg. Co. v. Los Angeles, 189 U.S. 207; Fenner v. Boykin, 271 U. S. 240. Where the threatened prosecution is by state officers for alleged violations of a state law, the state courts are the final arbiters of its meaning and application, subject only to review by this Court on federal grounds appropriately asserted. Hence the arrest by the federal courts of the processes of the criminal law within the states, and the determination of questions of criminal liability under state law by a federal court of equity, are to be supported only on a showing of danger of irreparable injury "both great and immediate." Spielman Motor Co. v. Dodge, 295 U.S. 89, 95, and cases cited; Beal v. Missouri Pacific R. Corp., 312 U.S. 45, 49, and cases cited; Watson v. Buck, 313 U. S. 387; Williams v. Miller, 317 U.S. 599.

The trial court found that respondents had prosecuted certain of petitioners and other Jehovah's Witnesses for distributing the literature described in the complaint without having obtained the license required by the ordinance, and had declared their intention further to enforce the ordinance against petitioners and other Jehovah's Witnesses. But the Court made no finding of threatened irreparable injury to petitioners or others, and we cannot say that the declared intention to institute other prosecutions is sufficient to establish irreparable injury in the circumstances of this case.

Before the present suit was begun, convictions had been obtained in the state courts in cases Nos. 480-487, Murdock et al. v. Pennsylvania, supra, which were then pending on appeal and which were brought to this Court for review by certiorari contemporaneously with the present case. It does not appear from the record that petitioners have been threatened with any injury other than that incidental to every criminal proceeding brought lawfully and in good faith, or that a federal court of equity by withdrawing the determination of guilt from the state courts could rightly afford petitioners any protection which they could not secure by prompt trial and appeal pursue to this Court. In these respects the case differs from Hague v. C. I. O., supra, 501-02, where local officials forcibly broke up meetings of the complainants and in many instances forcibly deported them from the state without trial.

There is not allegation here and no proof that respondents would not, nor can we assume that they will not, acquiesce in the decision of this Court holding the challenged ordinance unconstitutional as applied to petitioners. If the ordinance had been held constitutional, petitioners could not complain of penalties which would have been but the consequence of their violation of a valid state law.

Nor is it enough to justify the exercise of the equity jurisdiction in the circumstances of this case that there are numerous members of a class threatened with prosecution for violation of the ordinance. In general the jurisdiction of equity to avoid multiplicity of civil suits at law is restricted to those cases where there would otherwise be some necessity for the maintenance of numerous suits between the same parties and the issues between them and the adverse party - here the state - are not necessarily identical. Matthews v. Rodgers, supra, 529-30, and cases cited. Far less should a federal court of equity attempt to envisage in advance all the diverse issues which could engage the attention of state courts in prosecutions of Jehovah's Witnesses for violations of the present ordinance, or assume to draw to a federal court the determination of those issues in advance, by a decree saying in what circumstances and conditions the application of the city ordinance will be deemed to abridge freedom of speech and religion.

In any event, an injunction looks to the future. Texas Co. v. Brown, 258 U. S. 466, 474; Standard Oil Co. v. United States, 283 U.S. 163, 182. And in view of the decision rendered today in Murdock v. Pennsylvania, supra, we find no ground for supposing that the intervention of a federal court, in order to secure petitioners' constitutional rights, will be either necessary or appropriate.

For these reasons, establishing the want of equity in the cause, we affirm the judgment of the circuit court of appeals directing that the bill be dismissed.

Affirmed.

Mr. Justice Jackson, concurring in the result in this case and dissenting in Nos. 480-487, Murdock v. Pennsylvania, ante, p. 105, and No. 238, Martin v. Struthers, ante, p. 141:

Except the case of Douglas et al. v. Jeannette, all of these cases are decided upon the record of isolated prosecutions in which information is confined to a particular act of offense and to the behavior of an individual offender. Only the Douglas record gives a comprehensive story of the broad plan of campaign employed by Jehovah's Witnesses and its full impact on a living community. But the facts of this case are passed over as irrelevant to the theory on which the Court would decide its particular issue. Unless we are to reach judgments as did Plato's men who were chained in a cave so that they saw nothing but shadows, we should consider the facts of the Douglas case at least as an hypothesis to test the validity of the conclusions in the other cases. This record shows us something of the strings as well as the marionettes. It reveals the problem of those in local authority when the right to proselyte comes in contact with what many people have an idea is their right to be let alone. The Chief Justice says for the Court in Douglas that "in view of the decision rendered today in Murdock v. Pennsylvania, supra, we find no ground for supposing that the intervention of a federal court, in order to secure petitioners' constitutional rights, will be either necessary or appropriate," which could hardly be said if the constitutional issues presented by the facts of this case are not settled by the Murdock case. The facts of record in the Douglas case and their relation to the facts of the other cases seem to me worth recital and consideration if we are realistically to weigh the conflicting claims of rights in the related cases today decided.

From the record in Douglas we learn:

In 1939, a "Watch Tower Campaign" was instituted by Jehovah's Witnesses in Jeannette, Pennsylvania, an industrial city of some 16,000 inhabitants. Each home was visited, a bell was rung or the door knocked upon, and the householder advised that the Witness had important information. If the householder would listen, a record was played on the phonograph. Its subject was "Snare and Racket." The following words are representative of its contents: "Religion is wrong and a snare because it deceives the people, but that does not mean that all who follow religion are willingly bad. Religion is a racket because it has been long used and is still used to extract money from the people upon the theory and promise that the paying over of money to a priest will serve to relieve the party paying from punishment after death and further insure his salvation.'' This line of attack is taken by the Witnesses generally upon all denominations, especially the Roman Catholic. The householder was asked to buy a variety of literature for a price or contribution. The price would be twenty-five cents for the books and smaller sums for the pamphlets. Oftentimes, if he was unwilling to purchase, the book or pamphlet was given to him anyway.

When this campaign began, many complaints from offended householders were received, and three or four of the Witnesses were arrested. Thereafter, the ''zone servant'' in charge of the campaign conferred with the Mayor. He told the Mayor it was their right to carry on the campaign and showed him a decision of the United States Supreme Court, said to have that effect, as proof of it. The Mayor told him that they were at liberty to distribute their literature in the streets of the city and that he would have no objection if they distributed the literature free of charge at the houses, but that the people objected to their attempt to force these sales, and particularly on Sunday. The Mayor asked whether it would not be possible to come on some other day and to distribute the literature without selling it. The zone servant replied that that was contrary to their method of ''doing business'' and refused. He also told the Mayor that he would bring enough Witnesses into the City of Jeannette to get the job done whether the Mayor liked it or not. The mayor urged them to await the outcome of an appeal which was then pending in the other cases and let the matter take its course through the courts. This, too, was refused, and the threat to bring more people than the Mayor's police force could cope with was repeated.

On Palm Sunday of 1939, the threat was made good. Over 100 of the Witnesses appeared. They were strangers to the city and arrived in upwards of twenty-five automobiles. The automobiles were parked outside the city limits, and headquarters were set up in a gasoline station with telephone facilities through which the director of the campaign could be notified when trouble occurred. He furnished bonds for the Witnesses as they were arrested. As they began their work, around 9:00 o'clock in the morning, telephone calls began to come in to the Police Headquarters, and complaints in large volume were made all during the day. They exceeded the number that the police could handle, and the Fire Department was called out to assist. The Witnesses called at homes singly and in groups, and some of the home complained that they were called upon several times. Twenty-one Witnesses were arrested. Only those were arrested where definite proof was obtainable that the literature had been offered for sale or a sale had been made for a price. Three were later discharged for inadequacies in this proof, and eighteen were convicted. The zone servant furnished appeal bonds.

The national structure of the Jehovah's Witness movement is also somewhat revealed in this testimony. At the head of the movement in this country is the Watch Tower Bible and Tract Society, a corporation organized under the laws of Pennsylvania, but having its principal place of business in Brooklyn, N. Y. It prints all pamphlets, manufactures all books, supplies all phonographs and records, and provides other materials for the Witnesses. It "ordains" these Witnesses by furnishing each, on a basis which does not clearly appear, a certificate that he is a minister of the Gospel. Its output is large and its revenues must be considerable. Little is revealed of its affairs. One of its "zone servants" testified that its correspondence is signed only with the name of the corporation and anonymity as to its personnel is its policy. The assumption that it is a "non-profit charitable" corporation may be true, but it is without support beyond mere assertion. In none of these cases has the assertion been supported by such usual evidence as a balance sheet or an income statement. What its manufacturing costs and revenues are, what salaries or bonuses it pays, what contracts it has for supplies or services we simply do not know. The effort of counsel for Jeannette to obtain information, books and records of the local "companies" of Witnesses engaged in the Jeannette campaign in the trial was met by contradictory statements as to the meaning of such meager accounts as were produced.

The publishing output of the Watch Tower corporation is disposed of through converts, some of whom are full-time and some part-time ministers. These are oganized into groups or companies under the direction of "zone servants." It is their purpose to carry on in a thorough manner so that every home in the communities in which they work may be regularly visited three or four times a year. The full-time Witnesses acquire their literature from the Watch Tower Bible & Tract Society at a figure which enables them to distribute it at the prices printed thereon with a substantial differential. Some of the books they acquire for 5¢ and dispose of for a contribution of 25¢. On others, the margin is less. Part-time ministers have a differential between the 20¢ which they remit to the Watch Tower Society and the 25¢ which is the contribution they ask for the books. We are told that many of the Witnesses give away a substantial quantity of the literature to people who make no contributions. Apart from the fact that this differential exists and that it enables the distributors to meet in whole or in part their living expenses, it has proven impossible in these cases to learn the exact results of the campaigns from a financial point of view. There is evidence that the group accumulated a substantial amount from the differentials, but the tracing of the money was not possible because of the failure to obtain records and the failure, apparently, to keep them.

The literature thus distributed is voluminous and repetitious. Characterization is risky, but a few quotations will indicate something of its temper.

Taking as representative the book "Enemies", of which J. F. Rutherford, the lawyer, who long headed this group, is the author, we find the following: "The greatest racket ever invented and practiced is that of religion. The most cruel and seductive public enemy is that which employs religion to carry on the racket, and by which means the people are deceived and the name of Almighty God is reproached. There are numerous systems of religion, but the most subtle, fraudulent and injurious to humankind is that which is generally labeled the 'Christian religion,' because it has the appearance of a worshipful devotion to the Supreme Being, and thereby easily misleads many honest and sincere persons."

Id. at 144-145. It analyzes the income of the Roman Catholic hierarchy and announces that it is "the great racket, a racket that is greater than all other rackets combined." Id. at 178. It also says under the chapter heading "Song of the Harlot," "Referring now to the foregoing Scriptural definition of harlot: What religious system exactly fits the prophecies recorded in God's Word? There is but one answer, and that is, The Roman Catholic Church organization." Id. at 204-205. "Those close or nearby and dependent upon the main organization, being of the same stripe, picture the Jewish and Protestant clergy and other allies of the Hierarchy who tag along behind the Hierarchy at the present time to do the bidding of the old 'whore'." Id. at 222. "Says the prophet of Jehovah: 'It shall come to pass in that day, that Tyre (modern Tyre, the Roman Catholic Hierarchy organization) shall be forgotten.' Forgotten by whom? By her former illicit paramours who have committed fornication with her." Id. at 264. Throughout the literature, statements of this kind appear amidst scriptural comment and prophecy, denunciation of demonology, which is used to characterize the Roman Catholic religion, criticism of government and those in authority, advocacy of obedience of the law of God instead of the law of man, and an interpretation of the law of God as they see it.

The spirit and temper of this campaign is most fairly states perhaps in the words, again of Rutherford, in his book "Religion," pp. 196-198:

"God's faithful servants go from house to house to bring the message of the kingdom to those who reside there, omitting none, not even the houses of the Roman Catholic Hierarchy, and there they give witness to the kingdom because they are commanded by the Most High to do so. 'They shall enter in at the windows like a thief.' They do not loot nor break into the houses, but they set up their phonographs before the doors and windows and send the message of the kingdom right into the houses into the ears of those who might wish to hear; and while those desiring to hear are hearing, some of the 'sour-pusses' are compelled to hear. Locusts invade the homes of the people and even eat the varnish off the wood and eat the wood to some extent. Likewise God's faithful witnesses, likened unto locusts, get the kingdom message right into the house and they take the veneer off the religious things that are in that house, including candles and 'holy water', remove the superstition from the minds of the people, and show them that the doctrines that have been taught to them are wood, hay and stubble, destructible by fire, and they cannot withstand the heat. The people are enabled to learn that 'purgatory' is a bogeyman, set up by the agents of Satan to frighten the people into the religious organizations, where they may be fleeced of their hard-earned money. Thus the kingdom message plagues the religionists, and the clergy find that they are unable to prevent it. Therefore, as described by the prophet, the message comes to them like a thief that enteres in at the windows, and this message is a warning to those who are on the inside that Jesus Christ has come, and they remember his warning words, to wit: 'Behold, I come as a thief.' (Revelation 16:15.) The day of Armageddon is very close, and that day comes upon the world in general like a thief in the night."

The day of Armageddon, to which all of this is prelude, is to be a violent and bloody one, for then shall be slain all "demonologists," including most of those who reject the teachings of Jehovah's Witnesses.

In the Murdock case, on another Sunday morning of the following Lent, we again find the Witnesses in Jeannette, travelling by twos and threes and carrying cases for the books and phonographs. This time eight were arrested, as against the 21 arrested on the preceding Palm Sunday involved in the Douglas case.

In the Struthers case, we find the Witness knocking on the door of a total stranger at 4:00 on Sunday afternoon, July 7th. The householder's fourteen year old son answered, and, at the Witness's request, called his mother from the kitchen. His mother had previously become "very much disgusted about going to the door" to receive leaflets, particularly since another person had on a previous occasion called her to the door and told her, as she testified, "that I was doomed to go to hell because I would not let this literature in my home for my children to read." She testified that the Witness "shoved in the door" the circular being distributed, and that she "couldn't do much more than take" it, and she promptly tore it up in the presence of the Witness, for while she believed "in the worship of God," she did not "care to talk to everybody" and did not "believe that anyone needs to be sent from door to door to tell us how to worship." The record in the Struthers case is even more sparse than that in the Murdock case, but the householder did testify that at the time she was given the circular the Witness "told me that a number of them were in jail and would I call the Chief of Police and ask that their workers might be released."

Such is the activity which it is claimed no public authority can either regulate or tax. This claim is substantially, if not quite, sustained today. I dissent - a disagreement induced in no small part by the facts recited.

As individuals many of us would not find this activity seriously objectionable. The subject of the disputes involved may be a matter of indifference to our personal creeds. Moreover, we work in offices affording ample shelter from such importunities and live in homes where we do no personally answer such calls and bear the burden of turning away the unwelcome. But these observations do not hold true for all. The stubborn persistence of the officials of smaller communities in their efforts to regulate this conduct indicates a strongly held conviction that the Court's many decisions in this field are at odds with the realities of life in those communities where the householder himself drops whatever he may be doing to answer the summons to the door and is apt to have positive religious convictions of his own. Three subjects discussed in the opinions in Murdock v. Pennsylvania and Martin v. Struthers tend to obscure the effect of the decisions. The first of these relates to the form of the ordinances in question. One cannot determine whether this is mere makeweight or whether it is an argument addressed to the constitutionality of the ordinances; and whatever it is, I cannot reconcile the treatment of the subject by the two opinions. In Murdock the Court says "the present ordinance is not narrowly drawn to safeguard the people of the community in their homes against the evils of solicitations," and again "the ordinance is not narrowly drawn to prevent or control abuses or evils arising from" solicitation from house to house. It follows the recent tendency to invalidate ordinances in this general field that are not "narrowly drawn."

But in Struthers the ordinance is certainly narrowly drawn. Yet the Court denies the householder the narrow protection it gives. The city points out that this ordinance was narrowly drawn to meet a particular evil in that community where many men must work nights and rest by day. I had supposed that our question, except in respect to ordinances invalid on their face, is always whether the ordinance as applied denies constitutional rights. Nothing in the Constitution says or implies that real rights are more vulnerable to a narrow ordinance than to a broad one. I think our function is to take municipal ordinances as they are construed by the state courts and applied by local authorities and to decide their constitutionality accordingly, rather than to undertake censoring their draftsmanship.

Secondly, in neither opinion does the Court give clear-cut consideration to the particular activities claimed to be entitled to constitutional immunity, but in one case blends with them conduct of others not in question, and in the other confuses with the rights in question here certain alleged rights of others which these petitioners are in no position to assert as their own.

In the Murdock case, the Court decides to "restore to their high, constitutional position the liberties of itinerant evangelists." That it does without stating what those privileges are, beyond declaring that "This form of religious activity occupies the same high estate under the First Amendment as do worship in the churches and preaching from the pulpits." How can we dispose of the questions in this case merely by citing the unquestioned right to minister to congregations voluntarily attending services?

Similarly, in the Struthers case the Court fails to deal with the behavior of the Witnesses on its own merits. It reaches its decision by weighing against the ordinance there in question not only the rights of the Witness but also "the right of the individual householder to determine whether he is willing to receive her message"; concludes that the ordinance "substitutes the judgment of the community for the judgment of the individual householder"; and decides the case on the basis that "it submits the distributer to criminal punishment for annoying the person on whom he calls, even though the recipient of the literature distributed is in fact glad to receive it." But the hospitable householder thus thrown in the balance with the Witness to make weight against the city ordinance is wholly hypothetical and the assumption is contrary to the evidence we have recited. Doubtless there exist fellow spirits who welcome these callers, but the issue here is what are the rights of those who do not and what is the right of the community to protect them in the exercise of their own faith in peace. That issue - the real issue - seems not to be dealt with.

Third, both opinions suggest that there are evils in this conduct that a municipality may do something about. But neither identifies it, nor lays down any workable guide in so doing. In Murdock the Court says that "the ordinance is not narrowly drawn to prevent or control abuses or evils arising" from house-to-house solicitation. What evils or abuses? It is also said in Murdock that we "have something very different from a registration system under which those going from house to house are required to give their names, addresses and other marks of identification to the authorities." What more? The fee of course. But we are told the fee is not "a nominal fee imposed as a regulatory measure to defray the expenses of policing the activities in question." Is it implied that such a registration for such a fee would be valid? Wherein does the suggestion differ from the ordinance we are striking down? This ordinance did nothing more, it did not give discretion to refuse the license nor to censor the literature. The fee ranged from $1.50 a day for one day to less than a dollar a day for two weeks. There is not a syllable of evidence that this amount exceeds the cost ot the community of policing this activity. If this suggestion of new devices is not illusory, why is the present ordinance invalid? The City of Struthers decided merely that one with no more business at home than the delivery of advertising matter should not obtrude himself farther by announcing the fact of delivery. He was free to make the distribution if he left the householder undisturbed, to take it in his own time. The Court says the City has not even this much leeway in ordering its affairs, however complicated they may be as the result of round-the-clock industrial activity. If the local authorities must draw closer aim at evils than they did in these cases I doubt that they ever can hit them. What narrow area of regulation exists under these decisions? The Struthers opinion says, "the dangers of distribution can so easily be controlled by traditional legal methods." It suggests that the City may "by identification devices control the abuse of the privilege by criminals posing as canvassers." Of course to require registration and license is one of the few practical "identification devices." Merely giving one's name and his address to the authorities would afford them basis for investigating who the strange callers are and what their record has been. And that is what Murdock prohibits the city from asking. If the entire course of concerted conduct revealed to us is immune, I should think it neither fair nor wise to throw out to the cities encouragement to try new restraints. If some part of it passes the boundary of immunity, I think we should say what part and why in these cases we are denying the right to regulate it. The suggestion in Struthers that "the problem must be worked out by each community for itself" is somewhat ironical in view of the fate of the ordinances here involved.

Our difference of opinion cannot fairly be given the color of a disagreement as to whether the constitutional rights of Jehovah's Witnesses should be protected in so far as they are rights. These Witnesses, in common will all others, have extensive rights to proselyte and propagandize. These of course include the right to oppose and criticize the Roman Catholic Church or any other denomination. These rights are, and should be held to be, as extensive as any orderly society can tolerate in religious disputation. The real question is where their rights end and the rights of others begin. The real task of determining the extent of their rights on balance with the rights of others is not met by pronouncement of general propositions with which there is no disagreement.

If we should strip these cases to the underlying questions, I find them too difficult as constitutional problems to be disposed of by a vague but fervent transcendentalism.

In my view, the First Amendment assures the broadest tolerable exercise of free speech, free press, and free assembly, not merely for religious purposes, but for political, economic, scientific, news , or informational ends as well. When limits are reached which such communications must observe, can one go father under the cloak of religious evangelism? Does what is obscene, or commercial, or abusive, or inciting become less so if employed to promote a religious theology? I had not supposed that the rights of secular and non-religious communications were more narrow or in any way inferior to those of avowed religious groups.

It may be asked why then does the First Amendment separately mention free exercise of religion? The history of religious persecution gives the answer. Religion needed specific protection because it was subject to attack from a separate quarter. It was often claimed that one was an heretic and guilty of blasphemy because he failed to conform in mere belief or in support of prevailing institutions and theology. It was to assure religious teaching as much freedom as secular discussion, rather than to assure it greater license, that led to its separate statement.

The First Amendment grew out of an experience which taught that society cannot trust the conscience of a majority to keep its religious zeal within the limits that a free society can tolerate. I do not think it any more intended to leave the conscience of a minority to fix its limits. Civil government cannot let any group ride rough-shod over others simply because their "consciences" tell them to do so.

A common-sense test as to whether the Court has struck a proper balance of these rights is to ask what the effect would be if the right given to these Witnesses should be exercised by all sects and denominations. If each competing sect in the United States went after the householder by the same methods, I should think it intolerable. If a minority can put on this kind of drive in a community, what can a majority resorting to the same tactics do to individuals and minorities? Can we give to one sect a privilege that we could not give to all, merely in the hope that most of them will not resort to it? Religious freedom in the long run does not come from this kind of license to each sect to fix its own limits, but comes of hard-headed fixing of those limits by neutral authority with an eye to the widest freedom of proselyte compatible with the freedom of those subject to proselyting pressures.

I cannot accept the holding in the Murdock case that the behavior revealed here "occupies the same high estate under the First Amendment as do worship in the churches and preaching from the pulpits." To put them on the same constitutional plane seems to me to have a dangerous tendency towards discrediting religious freedom.

Neither can I think it an essential part of freedom that religious differences be aired in language that is obscene, abusive, or inciting to retaliation. We have held that a Jehovah's Witness may not call a public officer a "God damned racketeer" and a "damned Fascist," because that is to use "fighting words," and such are not privileged. Chaplinsky v. New Hampshire, 315 U.S. 568. How then can the Court today hold it a "high constitutional privilege" to go to homes, including those of devout Catholics on Palm Sunday morning, and thrust upon them literature calling their church a "whore" and their faith a "racket"?

Nor am I convinced that we can have freedom of religion only by denying the American's deep-seated conviction that his home is a refuge from the pulling and hauling of the market place and the street. For a stranger to corner a man in his home, summon him to the door and put him in the position either of arguing his religion or of ordering one of unknown disposition to leave is a questionable use of religious freedom.

I find it impossible to believe that the Struthers case can be solved by reference to the statement that "The authors of the First Amendment knew that novel and unconventional ideas might disturb the complacent, but they chose to encourage a freedom which they believed essential if vigorous enlightenment was ever to triumph over slothful ignorance." I doubt if only the slothfully ignorant wish repose in their homes, or that the forefathers intended to open the door to such forced "enlightenment" as we have here.

In these case, local authorities caught between the offended householders and the drive of the Witnesses, have been hard put to keep the peace of their communities. They have invoked old ordinances that are crude and clumsy for the purpose. I should think that the singular persistence of the turmoil about Jehovah's Witnesses, one which seems to result from the work of no other sect, would suggest to this Court a thorough examination of their methods to see if they impinge unduly on the rights of others. Instead of that the Court has, in one way after another, tied the hands of all local authority and made the aggressive methods of this group the law of the land.

This Court is forever adding new stories to the temples of constitutional law, and the temples have a way of collapsing when one story too many is added. So it was with liberty of contract, which was discredited by being overdone. The Court is adding a new privilege to override the rights of others to what has before been regarded as religious liberty. In so doing it needlessly creates a risk of discrediting a wise provision of our Constitution which protects all - those in homes as well as those out of them - in the peaceful, orderly practice of the religion of their choice but which gives no right to force it upon others.

Civil liberties had their origin and must find their ultimate guaranty in the faith of the people. If that faith should be lost, five or nine men in Washington could not long supply its want. Therefore we must do our utmost to make clear and easily understandable the reasons for deciding these cases as we do. Forthright observance of rights presupposes their forthright definition.

I think that the majority has failed in this duty. I therefore dissent in Murdock and Struthers and concur in the result in Douglas.

I join in the opinions of Mr. Justice Reed in Murdock and Struthers, and in that of Mr. Justice Frankfurter in Murdock.

Mr. Justice Frankfurter joins in these views.

In the Matter of Joseph Burstyn, Inc., Appellant, against Lewis A. Wilson, as Commissioner of Education of the State of New York, et al., Respondents.
New York Court of Appeals, 1951
- N. Y. -

Froessel, J. A license for the exhibition of a motion picture film entitled "The Miracle" together with two other films, described in their combination as a trilogy and called "Ways of Love," was issued to petitioner on November 30, 1950, by the Motion Picture Division of the Department of Education of the State of New York, under the governing statute (Education Law, art. 3, part II). "The Miracle" was produced in Italy as "Il Miracolo," and English subtitles were later added. A prior license had been issued to the original owner of the distribution rights for exhibition, with Italian subtitles alone, but the film was never shown under the license.

The first public exhibition of "The Miracle" as part of the trilogy, "Ways of Love," was shown in New York City on December 12, 1950. It provoked an immediate and substantial public controversy, and the Education Department was fairly flooded with protests against its exhibition. Others expressed a contrary view. In consequence thereof, the Board of Regents of the University of the State of New York (hereinafter called the Regents) proceeded promptly to review the action of its motion picture division. It appointed a subcommittee, and directed a hearing requiring petitioner to show cause why the licenses should not be rescinded and cancelled.

After viewing the film and giving petitioner an opportunity to be heard, its subcommittee reported that there was basis for the claim that the picture is sacrilegious, and recommended that the Regents view the film. Petitioner declined to participate in the hearing other than to appear specially before the subcommittee for the purpose of challenging the jurisdiction of the Regents to cancel the licenses, but its sole stockholder, Joseph Burstyn, appeared as an individual and filed a brief.

Thereupon and on February 16, 1951, after reviewing the picture and the entire record, the Regents unanimously adopted a resolution rescinding and canceling the licenses upon their determination that "The Miracle" is sacrilegious, and not entitled to a license under the law. Thereafter petitioner instituted the present article 78 proceeding to review that determination, and now urges that (1) the Regents were powerless to review the action of its motion picture division or to revoke the licenses; (2) the word "sacrilegious" does not provide a sufficiently definite standard for action; (3) the Regents exceeded their authority; (4) the statute is unconstitutional as in violation of the First and Fourteenth Amendments of the Constitution of the United States in that denial or revocation of a license on account of sacrilege interferes with religious liberty and breaches the wall between Church and State; and (5) the statute is unconstitutional in toto as a prior restraint on the right of free speech guaranteed by the First and Fourteenth Amendments of the Federal Constitution. The Appellate Division unanimously confirmed the determination of the Regents.

First: The principal argument advanced by petitioner is directed toward the claim that the Regents have no power under the statute to rescind a license once issued by the motion picture division, unless upon a charge of fraud in the procurement thereof or subsequent misconduct by the licensee. Any other construction of the statute, it is said, would be inequitable to petitioner, which has spent money relying upon the license as issued. The Regents, on the other hand, contend that they were empowered under the Education Law and our State Constitution to make the determination here challenged.

[The Court here reviews the contention of the Regents.]

Accordingly, we are of the opinion that the Regents have power to review the action of its motion picture division in granting a license to exhibit motion pictures, and rightfully exercised its jurisdiction in this case.

Second: To the claim that the statute delegates legislative power without adequate standards, a short answer may be made. Section 122 of the Education Law provides that a license shall be issued for the exhibition of a submitted film, "unless such film or a part thereof is obscene, indecent, immoral, inhuman, sacrilegious, or is of such character that its exhibition would tend to corrupt morals or incite to crime." Only the word "sacrilegious" is attacked for indefiniteness. The dictionary, however, furnishes a clear definition thereof, were it necessary to seek one, as, e.g., "the act of violating or profaning anything sacred" (Funk & Wagnall's New Standard Dictionary [1937 ed.]). There is no difficulty in recognizing the limits of the criterion thus established, and the courts have had no problem either with the word "sacrilegious" or with its synonym, "profane."

In Mutual Film Corp. v. Hodges (236 U.S. 248, supra), the contention that there was an invalid delegation of legislative power was rejected where the statute provided that the censor should approve such films as were found to be "moral and proper and disapprove such as are sacrilegious, obscene, indecent or immoral, or such as tend to corrupt the morals" (p. 257, emphasis supplied). In Winters v. New York (333 U.S. 507, 510) it is stated that publications are "subject to control if they are lewd, indecent, obscene or profane" (emphasis supplied). In Chaplinsky v. New Hampshire (315 U.S. 568, 571-572) Mr. Justice Murphy declared for a unanimous court: "There are certain well-defined and narrowly limited classes of speech, the prevention and punishment of which have never been though to raise any Constitutional problem. These include the lewd and obscene, the profane" (emphasis supplied). Indeed, Congress itself has found in the word "profane" a useful standard for both administrative and criminal sanctions against those uttering profane language or meaning by means of radio (Dumont Laboratories v. Carroll, 184 F. 2d 153, 156, certiorari denied 340 U.S. 929; U. S. Code, tit. 47, § 303, subd. [m], par. [1], cl. [D]; U. S. Code, tit. 18, z 1464; see, also, Penal Law, § 2072).

Accordingly, the claim that the word "sacrilegious" does not provide a sufficiently definite standard may be passed without further consideration, since it is without substance.

Third: We turn now to the contention that the Regents exceeded their powers.

Petitioner urges that, even if the board had the power, there was no justification for revocation. Of course, as the Appellate Division below, in its opinion, said (278 App. Div. 253, 260): "Under the familiar rule, applicable to all administrative proceedings, we may not interfere unless the determination made was one that no reasonable mind could reach." This rule applies to the courts and not to administrative agencies, as the Regents. (Matter of Fay Productions, Ltd., v. Graves, 253 App. Div. 475, affd. 278 N.Y. 498.)

We have all viewed the film in question. The so-called exhibits, which are simply unsworn communications expressing personal opinions, are of little help to us. The principal basis for the charge of sacrilege is found in the picture itself, the personalities involved, the use of scriptural passages as a background for the portrayal of the characters, and their actions, together with other portions of the script and the title of the film itself. It is featured as a "way of love." At the very outset, we are given this definition: "ardent affection, passionate attachment, men's adoration of God, sexual passion, gratification, devotion."

While the film in question is called "The Miracle", no miracle is shown; on the contrary, we have the picture of a demented peasant girl meeting a complete stranger whom she addresses as "Saint Joseph." At the very beginning of the script, reference is made to "Jesus, Joseph, Mary." "Saint Joseph" first causes her to become intoxicated. Scriptural passages referring to the Holy Sacrament (Luke 22:19), and to the nativity of Christ (Matthew 1:20), are freely employed immediately after she states she is not well. A blackout in the film, in its association with the story, compels the inference that sexual intercourse and conception ensue. "Saint Joseph" abandons her immediately following the seduction, she is later found pregnant, and a mock religious procession is staged in her honor; she is "crowned" with an old wash-basin, is thrown out by her former lover, and the picture concludes with a realistic portrayal of her labor pains and the birth in a church courtyard of her child, whom she addresses as "my blessed son," "My holy son."

Christ is the heart and core of the Christian faith. Two personalities most closely related to Him in life were His mother, Mary, and Joseph. They are deeply revered by all Christians. Countless millions over the centuries have regarded their relationship as sacred, and so do millions living today. "The Miracle" not only encroaches upon this sacred relationship and the Biblical presentation thereof in respect to the birth of Christ, but utterly destroys it, associating it, as the Regents found, "with drunkenness, seduction, mockery and lewdness," and, in the language of the script itself, "with passionate attachment, sexual passion and gratification," as a way of love.

In the light of the foregoing, we conclude, as did the Appellate Division, (1) that we cannot say that the determination complained of "was one that no reasonable mind could reach"; and (2) that the board did not act arbitrarily or capriciously.

Fourth: It is further urged that a license may not be denied or revoked on the ground of sacrilege, because that would require a religious judgment on the part of the censoring authority and thus constitute an interference in religious matters by the State. In this connection, it is also urged that freedom of religion is thereby denied, since one man's sacrilege is another man's dogma, and one may thus be prevented from propagating his own religious views by means of motion pictures. The latter argument is specious when applied to motion pictures offered to the public for general exhibition as a form of entertainment, as we shall hereafter point out. Religious presentations, as ordinarily understood, as well as other educational and scientific films, are exempt (Education Law, §123). Thus freedom of religion is not impaired in the slightest, as anyone may express any religious or antireligious sentiment he chooses through a proper use of the films.

Nor is it true that the Regents must form religious judgments in order to find that a film is sacrilegious. As hereinbefore indicated, there is nothing mysterious about the standard to be applied. It is simply this: that no religion, as that word is understood by the ordinary, reasonable person, shall be treated with contempt, mockery, scorn and ridicule to the extent that it has been here, by those engaged in selling entertainment by way of motion pictures. As the court below said of the statute in question, "All it purports to do is to bar a visual caricature of religious beliefs held sacred by one sect or another, and such a bar, in our opinion, is not a denial of religious freedom." (278 App. Div. 253, 258.)

Although it is claimed that the law benefits all religions and thus breaches the wall of separation between Church and State, the fact that some benefit may incidentally accrue to religion is immaterial from the constitutional point of view if the statute has for its purpose a legitimate objective within the scope of the police power of the State (Everson v. Board of Educ., 330 U.S. 1; Cochran v. Louisiana State Bd. of Educ., 281 U.S. 370; Bradfield v. Roberts, 175 U.S. 291; People v. Friedman, 302 N.Y. 75, appeal dismissed for want of substantial Federal question 341 U.S. 907). Cases such as Illinois ex rel. McCollum v. Board of Educ. (333 U.S. 203) and Cantwell v. Connecticut (310 U.S. 296) are not to the contrary. The former case dealt with the use of State property for religious purposes (Matter of Zorach v. Clauson, 302 N.Y. 161), while the latter held (p. 305) that "a censorship of religion as the means of determinings its right to survival is a denial of liberty protected by the" First and Fourteenth Amendments. Yet even in those cases it was recognized that the States may validly regulate the manner of expressing religious views if the regulation bears reasonable relation to the public welfare. Freedom to believe - or not to believe - is absolute; freedom to act is not. "Conduct remains subject to regulation for the protection of society" (Cantwell v. Connecticut, supra, p. 304; American Communications Assn. v. Douds, 339 U.S. 382, 393).

The statute now before us is clearly directed to the promotion of the public welfare, morals, public peace and order. These are the traditionally recognized objects of the exercise of police power. For this reason, any incidental benefit conferred upon religion is not sufficient to render this statute unconstitutional. There is here no regulation of religion, nor restriction thereof or other interference with religious beliefs except insofar as the picture itself does so, nor is there any establishment of religion or preference of religion or use of State property or funds in aid of religion. There is nothing more than a denial of the claimed right to hurl insults as the deepest and sincerest religious beliefs of others through the medium of a commercial entertainment spectacle.

We are essentially a religious nation (Church of Holy Trinity v. United States, 143 U.S. 457, 465), of which it is well to be reminded now and then, and in the McCollum case (supra) the Supreme Court paused to note that a manifestation of governmental hostility to religion or religious teachings "would be at war with our national tradition" (p. 211). The preamble to our State Constitution expresses our gratitude as a people to Almighty God for our freedom. To say that government may not intervene to protect religious beliefs from purely private or commercial attacks or persecution, whatever the underlying motive, and however skillfully accomplished, as distinguished from the assertion of conflicting beliefs, is to deny not only its power to keep the peace, but also the very right to "the free exercise" of religion, guaranteed by the First Amendment. The offering of public gratuitous insult to recognized religious beliefs by means of commercial motion pictures is not only offensive to decency and morals, but constitutes in itself an infringement of the freedom of others to worship and believe as they choose. Insult, mockery, contempt and ridicule can be a deadly form of persecution - often far more so than more direct forms of action. The prohibition of such conduct comes within the legitimate sphere of State action, and this State has recognized this principle, not only in the Education Law but in other respects as well (see, e.g., Penal Law, art. 186; Civil Rights Law, art. 4). We are not aware that this power has ever been even impliedly denied to the States.

This nation is a land of religious freedom; it would be strange indeed if our Constitution, intended to protect that freedom, were construed as an instrument to uphold those who publicly and sacrilegiously ridicule and lampoon the most sacred beliefs of any religious denomination to provide amusement and for commercial gain.

For the foregoing reasons, we conclude that the challenged portion of the statute in no way violates the provisions of the First Amendment relating to religious freedom.

Fifth: Petitioner finally argues that the statute is unconstitutional in toto; that motion pictures are to be treated as the press generally, and may not be subjected to censorship or prior restraint. While it may not be heard in this respect, inasmuch as it has sought and obtained benefits under the statute, and even now seeks to retain the licenses granted (Fahey v. Mallonee, 332 U.S. 245, 255; Shepherd v. Mount Verson Trust Co., 269 N.Y. 234, 244-247), we shall dispose of this argument upon the merits.

The contention urged is made in the face of direct holdings to the contrary (Mutual Film cases, supra; RD-DR Corp. v. Smith, 183 F. 2d 562, certiorari denied 340 U.S. 853; Pathe Exch., Inc., v. Cobb, 202 App. Div. 450, affd. 236 N.Y. 539, supra; 64 A.L.R. 505).

The rationale of these decisions is that motion pictures are primarily a form of entertainment, a spectacle or show, and not such vehicles of thought as to bring them within the press of the country. On this basis, petitioner's contention that the Mutual Film cases (supra) lack authority today, because it was not the Federal Constitution against which the statute was there tested, is unsound, for the Ohio Constitution guarantees free speech and a free press as does the Federal Constitution. Essentially, what petitioner would have us do is to predict that the Supreme Court will overrule the Mutual Film cases and so disregard them here, as well as our own holding in the Pathe Exchange case (supra). But such was the position squarely taken in the RD-DR Corp. case (supra), where the same arguments were presented as are here urged, and they were unequivocally rejected.

On the same footing is the contention that technical developments have made a difference in the essential nature of motion pictures since the Mutual Film decisions. Such development was foreseen in the Mutual Film cases (see p. 242), and was realized at the time of the RD-DR Corp. case (p. 565), decided a year ago. We have already pointed out that scientific and educational films, among others of kindred nature, are not within the general licensing statute, and are thus not concerned with any problem that might be raised by an attempt to impose general censorship upon such films.

Some comfort is found by petitioner in a statement in United States v. Paramount Pictures, Inc. (334 U.S. 131, 166) to the effect that "moving pictures, like newspapers and radio, are included in the press." That was an antitrust case, freedom of the press was not involved, and the statement was pure dictum. Moreover, it may be observed that when certiorari was sought in the RD-DR Corp. case (supra), it was denied by the same court; the only Justice voting to grant was the one who wrote that dictum. Were we to rely upon dictum, the concurring remarks of Mr. Justice Frankfurter in a subsequently decided free speech case (Kovacs v. Cooper, 336 U.S. 77, 96), would be appropriate: "Movies have created problems not presented by the circulation of books, pamphlets, or newspapers, and so the movies have been constitutionally regulated." (Citing the Mutual Film cases, supra.) However, dictum is a fragile bark in which to sail the constitutional seas.

The fact is that motion pictures do create problems not presented by other media of communication, visual or otherwise, as already indicated. It should be emphasized, however, that technical developments which increase the force of impact of motion pictures simply render the problem more acute. It does not avail to argue that there is now greater ability of transmission, when it is precisely that ability which multiplies the dangers already inherent in the particular form of expression. Whether motion pictures are sui generis or a very special classification of the press becomes a question for the academicians, once it is recognized that there is a danger presented and met by legislation appropriate to protect the public safety, yet narrow enough as not otherwise to limit freedom of expression. If there is any one proposition for which the free speech cases may be cited, from Schenck v. United States (249 U.S. 47) to Dennis v. United States (341 U.S. 494) and Breard v. Alexandria (341 U.S. 622), it is that freedom of speech is not absolute, but may be limited when the appropriate occasion arises. We are satisfied that the dangers present and foreseen at the time of the Mutual Film cases (supra) are just as real today.

The order of the Appellate Division should be affirmed, with costs.[1]

Fuld, J. (dissenting). It may lend perspective to recall that we are here concerned with a motion picture that has passed the rigid scrutiny of a numerous array of critics of undenied religiousness. There is, of course, no suggestion that "The Miracle" is a product of heathen hands. The story was written by a Roman Catholic and the picture produced, directed and acted solely by Roman Catholics. It was filmed in Italy, and first exhibited in Rome, where religious censorship exists. There, the Vatican Newspaper, L'Osservatore Romano, in reviewing it, alluded to the story and weighed the artistry of the production without condemning the film or even intimating that there was any impropriety in its being viewed by Catholics. And thereafter the film passed the United States Customs with no voice raised against it.

In 1949 and again in 1950, successive directors of the motion picture division of the State Education Department licensed the film for statewide exhibition. It won the approval of the National Board of Review of Motion Pictures. It drew general acclaim from the press and was designated, as part of a trilogy, the best foreign language film of 1950 by the New York Film Critics, an association of critics of the major metropolitan newspapers. Finally, one important Roman Catholic publication, after deploring "these highly arbitrary invocations of a police censorship," noted that the film "is not obviously blasphemous or obscene, either in its intention or execution" (The Commonwealth, March 16, 1951, pp. 567-568; also, March 2, 1951, pp. 507-508), and all Protestant clergymen who expressed themselves publicly - and they constituted a large number representing various sects - found nothing in the film either irreverent or irreligious.

However, as Judge Froessel reminds us, the contrary opinion also found strong voice, eventually reaching the ears of the board of regents. After viewing the film, that body revoked and rescinded the license - some two years after it had been granted - invoking as authority therefor section 122 of the Education Law. That statute provides that the motion picture division shall license each moving picture submitted to it unless it is "obscene, indecent, immoral, inhuman, sacrilegious, or is of such character that its exhibition would tend to corrupt morals or incite to crime." The board of regents decided that the film is "sacrilegious," and its decision was confirmed by the Appellate Division.

Laying to one side for the moment the question as to the constitutionality of a statute which sanctions the banning of a moving picture on the ground that it is "sacrilegious," I am of opinion that the regents' action was without legislative warrant.

[Discussion of this problem is omitted.]

Even if I were to assume, however, that the statute does confer a power to review and revoke, I would still conclude for reversal. In my view, that portion of the statute here involved must fall before the constitutional guarantee that there be freedom of speech and press. The early decision of Mutual Film Corp. v. Industrial Comm. of Ohio (236 U.S. 230), is urged as establishing that motion pictures are not within the First

---

[1] A concurring opinion of Desmond, J. is omitted.

Amendment's coverage or protection. The consistent course of decision by the Supreme Court of the United States in recent years, however, persuades me that that early decision no longer has the force or authority here claimed for it.

We are confronted in this case with censorship in its baldest form - a licensing system requiring permission in advance for the exercise of the right to disseminate ideas via motion pictures, and committing to the licensor a broad discretion to decide whether that right may be exercised. Insofar as the statute permits the state to censor a moving picture labelled "sacrilegious," it offends against the First and Fourteenth Amendments of the Federal Constitution, since it imposes a prior restraint - and, at that, a prior restraint of broad and undefined limits - on freedom of discussion of religious matters. And, beyond that, it may well be that the restraint on the "sacrilegious" constitutes an attempt to legislate orthodoxy in matters of religious belief, contrary to the First Amendment's prohibition against laws "respecting an establishment of religion." (Cf. Everson v. Board of Educ., 330 U.S. 1, 15; Illinois ex rel. McCollum v. Board of Educ., 333 U.S. 203, 210.)

The freedoms of the First Amendemtn are not, I appreciate, absolutes, although they are as near to absolutes as our judicial and political system recognizes. But insofar as these freedoms are qualified, the qualification springs from the necessity of accommodating them to some equally pressing public need. Thus, some limited measure of restraint upon freedom of expression may be justified where the forum is the public street or the public square, where the audience may be a "captive" one, and where breaches of the peace may be imminent as the result of the use, or rather the abuse, of fighting words. (Cf. Dennis v. United States, 341 U.S. 494, 593 et seq.; Feiner v. New York, 340 U.S. 315, 319; Niemotko v. Maryland, 340 U.S. 268; Terminiello v. Chicago, 337 U.S. 1; Chaplinsky v. New Hampshire, 315 U.S. 568, 571-572; Cantwell v. Connecticut, 310 U.S. 296; Schneider v. State, 308 U.S. 147, 160.) Here, there is no "captive" audience; only those see the picture who wish to do so, and, then, only if they are willing to pay the price of admission to the theatre. Moreover, if subject matter furnishes any criterion for the exercise of a restraint, I know of no subject less proper for censorship by the state than the one here involved.

The Supreme Court has "consistently condemned licensing systems which vest in an administrative official discretion to grant or withhold a permit upon broad criteria unrelated to proper regulation of public places." (Kunz v. New York, 340 U.S. 290, 294; see, also, Niemotko v. Maryland, supra, 340 U.S. 268; Saia v. New York, 334 U.S. 558; Cantwell v. Connecticut, supra, 310 U.S. 296; Hague v. C.I.O., 307 U.S. 496; Lovell v. City of Griffin, 303 U.S. 444.) "The State cannot of course forbid public proselyting or religious argument merely because public officials disapprove the speaker's views. It must act in patent good faith to maintain the public peace, to assure the availability of the street for their primary purpose of passenger and vehicular traffic, or for equally indispensable ends of modern community life." (See Niemotko v. Maryland, supra, 340 U.S. 268, 282, per Frankfurter, J., concurring.)

Invasion of the right of free expression must, in short, find justification in some overriding public interest, and the restricting statute must be narrowly drawn to meet an evil which the state has a substantial interest in correcting. (See Feiner v. New York, supra, 340 U.S. 315, 319; Niemotko v. Maryland, supra, 340 U.S. 268; Winters v. New York, 333 U.S. 507, 509; Cantwell v. Connecticut, supra, 310 U.S. 296, 307-308; thornhill v. Alabama, 310 U.S. 88, 97-98, 105.) The statute before us is not one narrowly drawn to meet such a need as that of preserving the public peace or regulating public places. On the contrary, it imposes a general and pervasive restraint on freedom of discussion of religious themes in moving pictures, which cannot be justified on the basis of any substantial interest of the state. (Cf. Kunz v. New York, supra, 340 U.S. 290; Dennis v. United States, supra, 341 U.S. 494, 508-509.)

Over a century ago, the Supreme Court declared that "The law knows no heresy, and is committed to the support of no dogma". (Watson v. Jones, 13 Wall. [U.S.] 679, 728.) Just as clearly, it is beyond the competency of government to prescribe norms of religious conduct and belief. That follows inevitably from adherence to the principles of the First Amendment. "In the realm of religious faith, and in that of political belief," it has been said (Cantwell v. Connecticut, supra, 310 U.S. 296, 310), "sharp differences arise. In both fields the tenets of one man may seem the rankest error to his neighbor. To persuade others to his own point of view, the pleader, as we know, at times, resorts to exaggeration, to vilification of men who have been, or are, prominent in church or state, and even to false statement. But the people of this nation have ordained in the light of history, that, in spite of the probability of excesses and abuses, these liberties are, in the long view, essential to enlightened opinion and right conduct on the part of the citizens of a democracy."

The inherent indefinability, in its present context, of the term "sacrilege" is apparent upon the merest inquiry. At what point, it may be asked, does a search for the eternal verities, a questioning of particular religious dogma, take on the aspect of "sacrilege"? At what point does expression or portrayal of a doubt of some religious tenet become "sacrilegious"? Not even authorities or students in the field of religion will have a definitive answer, and certainly not the same answer. There are more than two hundred and fifty different religious sects in this country, with varying religious beliefs, dogmas and principles. (See Illinois ex rel. McCollum v. Board of Educ., supra, 333 U.S. 203, 227, per Frankfurter, J., concurring.) With this great contrariety of religious views, it has been aptly observed that one man's heresy is another's orthodoxy, one's "sacrilege," another's consecrated belief. How and where draw the line between permissible theological disputation and "sacrilege"? What is orthodox, what sacrilegious? Whose orthodoxy, to whom sacrilegious? In the very nature of thing, what is "sacrilegious," will of necessity differ with the philosophy, the training, the education and the background of the particular censor of the moment; the determination whether a film is "sacrilegious" or not, must necessarily rest in the undiscoverable recesses of the official's mind.

Any possible doubt that the term is essentially vague is dispelled by a reference to the variant and inconsistent definitions ascribed to it by the board of regents and by the Appellate Division and Judge Froessel.

Thus, the regents, frowning upon the dictionary definition as "technical",[2] nevertheless assure us that "everyone knows what is meant by this term" and, by way of demonstrating that fact, proceed to define the word as describing a film which "affronts a large segment of the population"; offends the sensibilities by ridiculing and burlesquing anything "held sacred by the adherents of a particular religious faith"; is "offensive to the religious sensibilities of any element of society." (Italics supplied.) Indeed, any semblance of either general meaning or specific content is, I suggest, abandoned by the regents themselves when they assert that, since "anything is only sacrilegious to those persons who hold the concept sacred" the opinions of nonbelievers are "worthless." By such reasoning, the adherents of a particular doma become the only judges as to whether that dogma has been offended! And, if that is so, it is impossible to fathom how any governmental agency such as the board of regents, composed as it is of laymen of different faiths, could possibly discharge the function of determining whether a particular film is "sacrilegious."

Judge Froessel and the Appellate Division state that the statutory proscription against the "sacrilegious" is intended to bar any "visual caricature of religious beliefs held sacred by one sect or another" (opinion of Froessel, J., p.---, italics supplied). Though Judge Froessel also defines "sacrilegious" in terms of "attacking" or "insulting" religious beliefs or treating them with "contempt, mockery, scorn and ridicule" - all words of ephemeral and indefinite content - the basic criterion appears to be whether the film treats a religious theme in such a manner as to offend the religious beliefs of any group of persons. If the film does have that effect, and it is "offered as a form of entertainment," it apparently falls within the statutory ban regardless of the sincerity and good faith of the producer of the film, no matter how temperate the treatment of the theme, and no matter how unlikely a public disturbance or breach of the peace.

The drastic nature of such a ban is highlighted by the fact that the film in question makes no direct attack on, or criticism of, any religious dogma or principle, and it is not claimed to be obscene, scurrilous, intemperate or abusive. Nor is there any evidence of any malicious purpose or intention on the part of the producers of the film to revile or even attack Catholic doctrine or dogma, nor any suggestion of any reasonable likelihood of a breach of the peace resulting from the film's exhibition. So broad, indeed, is the suggested criterion of "sacrilege" that it might be applied to any fair and temperate treatment of a psychological, ethical, moral or social theme with religious overtones which some group or other might find offensive to its "religious beliefs."

It is claimed that "the courts have had no problem either with the word 'sacrilegious' or with its synonym, 'profane'" (opinion of Froessel,

---

[2] A typical definition of "sacrilege" is that found in Webster's New International Dictionary (2d Ed., 1948): "the crime of stealing, misusing, violating or desecrating that which is sacred, or holy, or dedicated to sacred uses." (See, also, the New Catholic Dictionary [Vatican ed., 1929].)

J., supra. The cases to which reference is made, however, involved niether the "profane" in religion nor the "sacrilegious," and the simple fact is that the Supreme Court has never had occasion to pass upon either the one term or the other. The context in which the word "profane" appears in the cases cited (Winters v. New York, supra, 333 U.S. 507, 510; Chaplinsky v. New Hampshire, supra, 315 U.S. 568, 572; as well as the authorities there relied upon (Cantwell v. Connecticut, supra, 310 U.S. 296, 309-310; Chafee, Free Speech in the United States [1941], pp. 149-150), make it evident that the term was used, not as a synonym for "sacrilegious," but as a substitute for "epithets or personal abuse", for swear words and for the other "insulting or 'fighting' words", which "by their very utterance inflict injury or tend to incite an immediate breach of the peace" and "are no essential part of any exposition of ideas". (Chaplinsky v. New Hampshire, supra, 315 U.S. 568, 572; see, also, Cantwell v. Connecticut, supra, 310 U.S. 296, 310; Chafee, op. cit., p. 150.) In short, the cases cited have nothing whatsoever to do with the "profane" in religion, and the judges who sat in them were not called upon to give the slightest thought or consideration to the subject with which we are now concerned.

The shortcomings of ambiguous epithets as rigid boundaries for free expression are great enough in temporal and political matters (cf., e.g., Winters v. New York, supra, 333 U.S. 507; Dennis v. United States, supra, 341 U.S. 494; Jordan v. De George, 341 U.S. 223; Musser v. Utah, 333 U.S. 95), but they are all the greater when the epithets trench upon areas of religious belief. (See, e.g., Kunz v. New York, supra, 340 U.S. 290; Saia v. New York, supra, 334 U.S. 558, 567; Cantwell v. Connecticut, supra, 310 U.S. 296.) Indeed, the Supreme Court has gone so far as to hold that the First Amendment's guarantee forbids prior restraint of public discussion that even "ridicules" or "denounces" any form of religious belief. (See Kunz v. New York, supra, 340 U.S. 290, and see, particularly, concurring opinion of Frankfurter, J., reported in 340 U.S., at pp. 285-286.) In a free society "all sects and factions, as the price of their own freedom to preach their views, must suffer that freedom in others." (Kunz v. New York, supra, 340 U.S., at p. 301, per Jackson, J., dissenting; see, also, Murdock v. Pennsylvania, 319 U.S. 105, 116.)

Were we dealing with speeches, with handbills, with newspapers or with books, there could be no doubt as to the unconstitutionality of that portion of the statute here under consideration. The constitutional guarantee of freedom of expression, however, is neither limited to the oral word uttered in the street or the public hall nor restricted to the written phrase printed in newspaper or book. It protects the transmission of ideas and beliefs, whether popular or not, whether orthodox or not. A belief does not lose its character as a belief, an idea does not become less of an idea, because, instead of being expressed by the "air-borne voice," the printed word or the "still" picture, it is put forward by a "moving" picture. The First Amendment does not ask whether the medium is visual, acoustic, electronic, or some yet unheard-of device. It has readily accommodate itself to other products of inventive genius, to other advances in technology, such as the radio and television. If "The Constitution deals with substance, not shadows", if "Its inhibition was levelled at the thing, not the name" (Cummings v. State of Missouri, 4 Wall. [U.S.] 277, 325), then, surely, its meaning and vitality are not to be conditioned upon the mechanism involved. Of course, it may well be that differences in medium will give rise to different problems of accommodation of conflicting interests. (See Kovacs v. Cooper, 336 U.S. 77, 96, per Frankfurter, J., concurring.) But any such accommodation must necessarily be made in the light of fundamental constitutional safeguards.[3]

One reason for denying free expression to motion pictures, we are told, is that the movies are commercial. But newspapers, magazines and books are likewise commercially motivated, and that has never been an obstacle to their full protection under the First Amendment. (See, e.g., Grosjean v. American Press Co., 297 U.S. 23.) Again, it is said, the fact that the moving picture conveys its though or message in dramatic episodes or by means of a story or in a form that is entertaining, makes the difference. But neither novels, magazines nor comic books are made censorable because they are designed for entertainment or amusement. (See e.g., Winters v. New York, supra, 333 U.S. 507, 510; Hannegan v. Esquire, Inc., 327 U.S. 146, 153.) The Supreme Court made that plain in the Winters case, when it declared: "We do not accede to appellee's suggestion that the constitutional protection for a free press applies only to the exposition of ideas. The line between the informing and the entertaining is too elusive for the protection of that basic right. Everyone is familiar with instances of propaganda through fiction. What is one man's amusement, teaches another's doctrine. Though we can see nothing of any possible value to society in these magazines, they are as much entitled to the protection of free speech as the best of literature." (333 U.S., p. 510.)

Whatever may have been true thirty-six years ago when the Mutual Film case (supra, 236 U.S. 230), was decided, there is no reason today for casting the motion picture beyond the barriers of protected expression. Learned and thoughtful writers so opine (see Chafee, Free Speech in the United States [1942], pp. 544 et seq.; Ernst, The First Freedom, p. 268; Kupferman & O'Brien, Motion Picture Censorship, 36 Cornell L. Q. 273; Note, 60 Yale L. J. 696; Note, 49 Yale L. J. 87), and the Supreme Court itself has recently so declared (See United States v. Paramount Pictures, Inc., 334 U.S. 131, 166; see, also, Kovacs v. Cooper, supra, 336 U.S. 77, 102, per Black, J., dissenting.) As Chafee put it (op. cit., p. 545), "In an age when 'commerce' in the Constitution has been construed to include airplanes and electromagnetic waves, 'freedom of speech' in the First Amendment and 'liberty' in the Fourteenth should be similarly applied to new media for the communication of ideas and facts. Freedom of speech should not be limited to the air-borne voice, the pen, and the printing press, any more than interstate commerce is limited to stage-

---

[3]Whether, for instance, the statute (Education Law, § 122) may be sustained as valid even as a censorship measure insofar as its criterion is the narrow one of "obscenity," is not, of course, before us and need not be considered. (Cf. Chaplinsky v. New Hampshire, supra, 315 U.S. 568, 572; Near v. Minnesota, 283 U.S. 697; Ex parte Jackson, 96 U.S. 727, 736.)

coaches and sailing vessels." And, wrote the Supreme Court (United States v. Paramount Pictures, Inc., supra, 334 U.S. 131, 166;), "We have no doubt that moving pictures, like newspapers and radio are included in the press whose freedom is guaranteed by the First Amendment."

Every consideration points that conclusion. The Mutual Film case (supra) should be relegated to its place upon the history shelf. Rendered in a day before the guarantees of the Bill of Rights were held to apply to the states, and when moving pictures were in their infancy, the decision was obviously a product of the view that motion pictures did not express or convey opinions or ideas. Today, so far have times and the films changed, some would deny protection for the opposite reason, for the reason that films are too effective in their presentation of ideas and points of view. The latter motion is as unsupportable as the other and antiquated view; that the moving picture is a most effective mass medium for spreading ideas is, of course, no reason for refusing it protection. If only ineffectual expression is shielded by the Constitution, free speech becomes a fanciful myth. Few would dispute the anomaly of a doctrine that protects as freedom of expression comic books that purvey stories and pictures of "bloodshed and lust" (see Winters v. New York, supra, 333 U.S. 507, 510), light and racy magazine reading (see Hannegan v. Esquire, Inc., supra, 327 U.S. 146, 153) and loudspeaker harangues (see Saia v. New York, supra, 334 U.S. 558), and yet denies that same protection to the moving picture.

Sincere people of unquestioned good faith may, as in this case find a moving picture offensive to their religious sensibilities, but that cannot justify a statute which empowers licensing officials to censor the free expression of ideas or beliefs in the field of religion. "If there is any fixed star in our constitutional constellation," the Supreme Court has said (West Virginia State Bd. of Educ. v. Barnette, 319 U.S. 624, 642), "It is that no official, high or petty, can prescribe what shall be orthodox in politics, nationalism, religion or other matters of opinion."

The order of the Appellate Division should be reversed and the determination of the board of regents annulled.

Loughran, Ch. J., Lewis and Conway, JJ., concur with Froessel, J.; Desmond, J., concurs in separate opinion; Fuld, J., dissents in opinion in which Dye, J., concurs.

Order affirmed.

The following article from the New York Times for Sunday, October 21, 1951, is reproduced with the permission of the publisher and the author.

Pressure Problem
Director Discusses Cuts Compelled in
"A Streetcar Named Desire"
By Elia Kazan

This newspaper has asked me for a statement about a reported dispute between Warner Brothers and myself with regard to cuts which the studio made in "A Streetcar Named Desire," directed by me.

The cuts, it must be said at once, are minor although, to me, painful. They do not hurt the total impact of the picture.

Even if it were otherwise, I can think of nothing of less general interest than a conflict between a director and a picture studio. However, I met a situation here which extended beyond the studio. The producers have implored me to keep silent about it, for they regard it as a passing headache with a happy ending at the box office. On sober thought, I cannot see it that way. I feel the public should hear this kind of story and make its own conclusions. I want to tell it, although, ironically, I was in the position of an outsider as it occurred.

Warner Brothers and Charles K. Feldman, who jointly produced "Streetcar," had shown courage in purchasing a fine and unusual play. They had been extremely cooperative and exceptionally generous throughout the making of the picture. They had provided me with the best possible scenic designer, cameraman, cutter, composer—and cast. What differences we had had were normal differences of taste and opinion, and were resolved as such.

Background. By last summer the picture was finished. We had received the seal of approval of the Breen Office, certifying that it conformed to the requirement of the picture industry's moral code. Prevues were behind us. The last cuts had been agreed upon. "Streetcar" was booked into Radio City Music Hall, and I was in Hollywood once more, at work on another picture, for another studio.

Then I heard that Warners had canceled the booking.

Then one day, quite by accident, I learned that the cutter who had worked with me on "Streetcar" had been sent to New York.

I began to ask questions. After delays and evasions, which are significant only for the nervousness they betrayed, I received reluctant answers. An executive of Warners was kind enough to explain to me, at least in part, what was going on:

Warners had learned that the Legion of Decency was about to give the picture a "C" or "Condemned" rating. This would mean that people of the Roman Catholic faith would be instructed not to see it.

The studio's reaction was one of panic. They had a sizable investment in the picture, and they at once assumed that no Catholic would buy a ticket. They feared further that theatres showing the picture would be picketed, might be threatened with boycotts of as long as a year's duration if they dared to show it, that priests would be stationed in the lobbies to take down the names of parishioners who attended. I was told that all these things had happened in Philadelphia when a picture with a "C" rating was shown there, and, further, that the rating was an invitation for every local censor board in the country to snipe at a picture, to require cuts or to ban it altogether.

Legion's Position. The explanation continued: the Legion of Decency did not want to appear as censors. They simple view finished work and pronounce their verdict. As nearly as I could gather, Warners were begging to be told what changes might be made in order to avoid the dreaded rating, while the Legion repeated that it was not theirs to censor, but only to say if the picture was decent for Catholic eyes and ears. But of course if a new version were submitted, they could not refuse to rule upon it.

The next thing I knew was the cutter, David Weisbart, was back in Hollywood with a cut print which either subsequently received, or already had, the desired "B" rating.

I was then allowed to see it.

I decided to get to New York as fast as I could. Here I was introduced to a prominent Catholic layman, who informed me that he himself, giving time and thought and great care to the matter, had suggested the cuts in my picture. His presence was at the invitation of Warner Brothers, and he had striven to bridge between the picture's artistic achievement—which he praised highly — and "the primacy of the moral order" as interpreted by himself, in conformity with the Legion's standards. There had been no overt involvement of the Legion, which had then passed the cut version.

I could not help wondering where this process left the moral responsibility of the makers of the picture, including the author and myself, or how the end result differed from direct censorship by the Legion.

However that may be, I—and for that matter the public—was presented with a finished fact. My picture had been cut to fit the specifications of a code which is not my code, is not the recognized code of the picture industry, and is not the code of the great majority of the audience.

And that was that. There was no recourse, as I discovered when I tried to reopen the matter.

As to the cuts themselves, I believe that if the audience—any audience—could see projected on the screen the footage which was cut out of "A Streetcar Named Desire" in order to protect the morals of that portion of them who are Roman Catholics, they would be overwhelmed by a bewilderment which would leave them, ever after, suspicious of censorship. For when something is cut out of a picture on such grounds, it is only natural to assume that it is something of special and daring character, somehow very different from what is permitted to remain. If you could see the banned footage, you would find it just about indistinguishable from the body of the picture, which you are allowed to see. You might even echo the producers' anxious and repeated and almost reasonable question: What difference does it make?

Director's View. As the director of the picture I see the deleted film somewhat differently. It does make a difference. I see it as small but necessary bits that built mood or motivation as I needed them, and whose rough excision leaves small holes or unprepared climaxes that make my work appear cruder than it was. I see it as lost fragments of a subtly told story, whose omission leaves the characters less fully explained than the author intended and than the actors, before, conveyed.

There were twelve cuts altogether, which remove some three or four minutes from the film. They range from a trivial cut of three words, "—on the mouth" (following the words, "I would like to kiss you softly and sweetly—"), to a recutting of the wordless scene in which Stella, played by Kim Hunter, comes down the stairway to Stanley after a quarrel.

This scene was carefully worked out in an alternation of close and medium shots, to show Stella's conflicting revulsion and attraction to her husband, and Miss Hunter played it beautifully. The censored version protects the audience from the close shots and stubstitutes a long shot of her descent. It also, by explicit instruction, omits a wonderful piece of music. It was explained to me that both the close shots and the music made the girl's relation to her husband "too carnal."

Another cut comes directly before Stanley attacks Blanche. It takes out his line, "You know, you might not be bad to interfere with." Apart from forcing a rather jerky transition, this removes the clear implication that only here, for the first time, does Stanley have any idea of harming the girl. This obviously changes the interpretation of the character, but how it serves the cause of morality is obscure to me, though I have given it much thought.

Other Deletions. The other cuts are of like nature. Certain of them were interpreted to me as stemming from the though that if one character—Stella was the candidate—could be shown as "good," the film would be redeemed. Such a thought, of course, is directly opposed to Tennessee Williams' thought. All his characters are a mixture of the qualities we label "good" and "bad," and that is their humanity.

A final incident: I asked Warner Brothers if we could not send the original version of "Streetcar" to the Venice Film Festival where, in international competition, American films are often at a disadvantage because of their removal from life as Europeans (and the rest of us) know it. The producers reported back to me that if the uncut version were shown, even once, in Venice, the Legion would be compelled to give the (cut) picture a "C" rating this country.

Now Warner Brothers, as the owners of the film, had the right to make these—or any other—cuts. From a business standpoint, it is easy to understand why they acceded to them. The Legion's point of view is also clear: they believe that certain things should be seen and others should not be seen by those who follow their dictates. If a picture, especially an important picture, can be brought into line with their code, they are naturally pleased.

That leaves the public, the author and myself to be considered.

Meanwhile the box office is breaking records.

CHAPTER V

EDUCATION

Commonwealth v. Cooke
Police Court of Boston, Massachusetts, 1859
7 Am. L. Reg. 417

MAINE, J. - The complaint in this case was made on the 16th day of March last, and charges that "McLaurin F. Cooke, teacher, on the 14th day of March, 1859, committed an assault and battery on Thomas J. Wall, son of the complainant, under circumstances of aggravation; that Thomas was eleven years of age, a pupil in the Eliot School, and defendant a teacher, and that defendant struck, beat and wounded Thomas with a stick for the space of thirty minutes, inflicting serious wounds."

Upon this complaint a warrant was issued by order of the court, the defendant Cook arrested, and in open court pleaded not guilty to the complaint.

Upon this issue, evidence was introduced on the part of the Commonwealth to prove the assault, and by the defendant explanatory of the matter, and from the evidence so introduced, the following facts appeared:

That the defendant was the first Assistant Teacher in the Eliot School, Samuel W. Mason, Principal; that Thomas J. Wall was a scholar in said school, and had been for six or seven years last past. That during his attendance the Bible in the common English version was read in the school, and that the scholars sufficiently advanced were required to read or commit to memory the Lord's Prayer and the Ten Commandments.

That by the rules and regulations of the school, the Commandments were repeated by the scholars every Monday morning, and that the boy Wall had repeated them without objection until Monday, March the 7th, when he refused, and was discharged from the school. That an interview was had between the father of the boy and the Principal of the school, and the boy returned to the school.

That on Monday, the 14th of March, he refused again to read or repeat the Commandments, giving as reasons for so doing, that his father had agreed with Mr. Mason that he should not say them. That his father had told him for his life not to say them, and that his priest had also told him not to say them, and that on the Sunday previous to the 14th the priest (Father Wiget) while addressing nine hundred children of St. Mary's Church, of whom Wall was one, told them not to be cowards to their religion, and not to read or repeat the Commandments in school, that if they did he would read their names from the altar.

That Wall came to the school on Monday with the determination not to read or repeat them.

That before the 14th, Father Wiget had promised to give him a medal, blessed, and that since the 14th he had given it to him; that he had given them to other boys, and he knew no reason for his giving it to him; that Father Wiget said at the time he was a good boy.

It further appeared, from the evidence, that there was a concerted plan of action on Monday, the 14th, between many of the boys to refuse to obey the orders of the school, if required to read or repeat the Lord's Prayer or the Commandments, and that two-thirds of the scholars composing the school where Wall attended, and numbering about sixty, declared their intention not to comply with the rules of the school in that particular. And from all the evidence it was manifest that Wall was one of, if not the principal actor. He refused to repeat the Commandments for the reasons given. He was told by Mr. Mason that his father had requested him to make him repeat them, and that if he did not, to punish him severely. Wall still refusing, was punished by the defendant with a rattan stick, some three feet in length, and three-eighths of an inch thick, by whipping upon his hands. From the time when the punishment commenced to the time when it ended, repeated inquiries were made of Wall if he would comply with the requirements of the school. Some thirty minutes' time was occupied in the whole. During this time there were several intervals at two of which the defendant was absent from the room some little time. The blows were not given in quick succession, but with deliberation. During the chastisement Wall was encouraged by others, who told him not to give up. This was while defendant was absent from the room. The master ceased to punish, when Wall submitted to the requirements of the school.

From the effect of the punishment Wall's hands were swollen, he was taken to the sink by the defendant twice, and his hands held in water. The physician who saw his hands in the afternoon of Monday, and prescribed for them, after describing their appearance, says that he did not think the injury very severe; that at the time he thought he would recover from it in twenty-four hours.

Now, was the punishment so inflicted without jurisdiction, and in violation of the constitutional rights of Wall? and was the punishment excessive? Before considering the constitutional rights of the pupil while in school, it may be proper to see by what right or authority the schools themselves exist.

The constitution recognizes the existence of schools, and declares that "all moneys raised by taxation in the towns and cities for the support of public schools, and all moneys that may be appropriated by the State for the support of common schools, shall be applied to and expended to no other schools than those which are conducted according to law, under the order and superintendence of the authorities of the town or city in which the money is to be expended; and such moneys shall never be appropriated to any religious sect, for the maintenance, exclusively, of its own schools." The schools recognized by the constitution are those which are to be conducted according to law, under the order and superintendence of the authorities of the town or city where the moneys are to be expended.

The statutes by which our schools are established and governed, provide "that it shall be the duty of the President, Professors, and Tutors of the University at Cambridge, and of the several colleges, and of all preceptors and teachers of academies, and of all other instructors of youth, to exert their best endeavors to impress on the minds of children and youth, committed to their care and instruction, the principles of piety, justice, and a sacred regard to truth, love to their country, humanity and universal benevolence, sobriety, industry, and frugality, chastity, moderation, and temperance, and those other virtues which are the ornaments of human society, and the basis upon which a republican constitution is founded."

By statute it is also provided, "that the School Committee of each town and city in the Commonwealth, shall require the daily reading of some portion of the Bible in the common English version, and shall direct what other books shall be used in the public schools."

The School Committee for the city of Boston, in their published regulations, direct and recommend as follows:

"The morning exercises of all the schools shall commence with reading a portion of the Scripture in each room by the teachers, and the Board recommend that the reading be followed with the Lord's Prayer repeated by the teacher alone, or chanted by the teacher and the children in concert, and that the afternoon session close with appropriate singing, and also that the pupils learn the Ten Commandments, and repeat them once a week."

Do these laws and regulations, when carried out, conflict with the constitutional rights of any pupil? It is claimed that they do, and the constitution is cited, or that portion of it supposed to apply to the case, which is as follows: -

"That it is the right as well as the duty of all men in society publicly and at stated seasons to worship the Supreme Being, the great Creator and Preserver of the universe. And no subject shall be hurt, molested, or restrained in his person, liberty, or estate, for worshipping God in the manner and seasons most agreeably to the dictates of his own conscience, or for his religious professions or sentiments, provided he doth not disturb the public peace, or obstruct others in their religious worship."

Can the position assumed be a correct one? Our schools are the granite foundation on which our republican form of government rests. They were created and are now sustained by our constitution and laws, and the almost unanimous voice of the people. But a pupil in one of them has religious scruples of conscience, and cannot read or repeat the Commandments, unless from that version of the Bible which his parent may approve. Now what is to be done in such a case? If he has a constitutional right to refuse to read or to repeat them from books furnished for the school by statute law, then to punish him in any way would be a great wrong. He could not be expelled from school for standing upon his constitutional rights. Neither could he be punished by corporal punishment; and if the plea of conscience and his constitutional rights would protect him from reading the Bible, is it not equally clear that he could not be compelled to hear it read?

If, then, these are constitutional rights, secured to the children in our common schools, at any time when one pupil can be found in each public school in the Commonwealth with conscientious scruples against reading the Bible, or hearing it read, the Bible may be banished from them, and so the matter of education may be taken from the State government and placed in the hands of a few children.

Not Roman Catholic children alone. For if the plea of conscience is good for one form of sectarian religion, it is good for another. The child of a Protestant may say, "I am a conscientious believer in the doctrine of universal salvation. There are portions of the Bible read in school which it is claimed by others tend to prove a different doctrine; my conscience will not allow me to hear it read, or to read it." Another objects as a believer in baptism by sprinkling. "There are passages in the Bible which are believed by some to teach a different doctrine. I cannot read it, conscience is in the way." Still another objects as a believer in one God. "The Bible, it is claimed by some, teaches a different doctrine; my conscience will not allow me to read it or to hear it read." And so, every denomination may object for conscience sake, and war upon the Bible and its use in common schools.

Those who drafted and adopted our constitution, could never have intended it to meet such narrow and sectarian views. That section of the constitution was clearly intended for higher and nobler purposes. It was for the protection of all religions - The Buddhist and the Brahim, the Pagan and the Jew, the Christian and the Turk, that all might enjoy an unrestricted liberty in their religion, and feel an assurance that for their religion alone, they should never, by legislative enactments, be subjected to fines, cast into prisons, starved in dungeons, burned at the stake, or make to feel the power of the inquisition.

It was intended to prevent persecution by punishing for religious opinions. The Bible has long been in our common schools. It was placed there by our fathers, not for the purpose of teaching sectarian religion, but a knowledge of God and of his will, whose practice is religion. It was placed there as the book best adapted from which to "teach children and youth the principles of piety, justice, and a sacred regard to truth, love to their country, humanity, and a universal benevolence, sobriety, moderation and temperance, and those other virtues which are the ornaments of human society, and the basis upon which a republican constitution is founded."

But, in doing this, no scholar is requested to believe it, none to receive it as the only true version of the laws of God. The teacher enters into no argument to prove its correctness, and gives no instructions in theology from it. To read the Bible in school for these and like purposes, or to require it to be read without sectarian explanations, is no interference with religious liberty.

If the plea of conscience is good against the reading or use of the Bible, why is it not equally good against any other book, or the language in which the book may be printed?

The Jew, for conscience sake, will only read the Scriptures from the Torah, and why may not the pupils in our schools refuse to read the Bible, until they are sufficiently learned to read it in the original Hebrew? If tender consciences may rightfully claim such unlimited power, what constitutional injustice is daily done in our courts of law, by swearing the Protestant by the uplifted hand, the Roman Catholic upon the Evangelists, the Jew upon the Pentateuch, while facing the East, with his head covered, and refusing to admit the Infidel as a witness at all!

There is another part of the case, which should here be considered. It is the argument, that in disobeying the commands of the school, Wall was acting under the lawful authority of his father.

Can the authority of the parent, and that of the teacher, over the pupil, exist at the same time, in and during the hours of school? That school approaches nearest to perfection that most resembles a well governed family, where nothing is required excepting that which is believed to be for the best interests of every member, and where all requirements are obeyed, and where all are subjects to one head. If "a house be divided against itself, the house cannot stand;" so will it ever be with our schools, if the authority of the master and that of the parent enter the school-room together. The master is there by authority of law. He is also there by the implied authority and consent of the parent, who sends his child to him for instruction, knowing at the same time the duties of both master and pupil. By sending his child to school he surrenders so much of his parental rights over the child as would, if exercised, conflict with the reasonable rules and regulations of the school. If this is not so, why may not the parent command his child while in school to read from one book and to reject another. And what are the rights and what the authority of the master in such a case? What becomes of the power of the School Committee, whose business it is to direct what books shall be used in the public schools?

From the argument it is understood that in this case there are conflicting rights, the rights of conscience of the scholar, the rights of the parent over him, and the rights of the defendant as master, and that these rights are to be upheld by compromises. What the compromise is to be, the court is not informed. Can it be that those pupils whose religion teaches them that the Douay version of the Bible is the only true record of the Scriptures, shall be permitted to read and repeat the Lord's Prayer and the Ten Commandments from his own Bible? Grant the request, and what follows?

It is enacted by the statute "that the School Committee shall never direct to be purchased or used in any of the two schools any school books which are calculated to favor the tenets of any particular sect of Christians." So by such a compromise, we see the very thing would be done which is now complained of, that of favoring the tenets of a particular religion.

Is the compromise to be that of a division of the school moneys, allowing separate schools to be carried on in accordance with religious views? Our Constitution declared that no money raised by taxation for the support of schools shall ever be appropriated to any religious sect for the maintenance, exclusively, of its own schools.

The last point for the consideration of the court is, was the offence one which required punishment? Had the matter the right to inflict corporal punishment? and, if he had, was the punishment excessive, or inflicted through malice? The apparent magnitude of the offence depends somewhat upon the stand-point from which it is viewed. From one aspect, it appears to be of the most innocent and simple nature. A child desired the privilege in school of reading the Commandments from his Bible, the only one that his religion would allow him to read. It would seem to be a generous mind tyrannical, to deny so simple and innocent a request; and it would indeed be so, were that the whole of the matter.

That most wonderful speciment of human skill and human invention, the Suspension Bridge, that spans the dark, deep waters at Niagara, with strength to support the heaviest engines with cars laden with their freight, and defying the whirlwind and the tempest, is but the perfection of strength from the most feeble beginning. A tiny thread was but safely secured across the abyss, and final success became certain. Thread after thread were interchanged, until iron cables bound opposite shores together. May not the innocent pleading of a little child for its religion in school, if granted, be used like a silken thread, to first pass that heretofore impassable gulf which lies between Church and State, and when once secured, may not stronger cords be passed over it, until cables, which human hands cannot sever, shall have bound Church and State together forever?

As for the right of inflicting punishment in schools by the teacher, it has been conceded ever since our schools were established, if in severity it does not exceed the nature and magnitude of the offence, and it is not inflicted in haste, or with malice on the part of the teacher. The case finds that the father of Wall had requested that he should be punished severely if he refused. It was not necessary that the father should give his consent for the inflicting of reasonable punishment, neither can the teacher justify and excessive punishment by authority from the father. The parent cannot delegate a power that he does not possess, and as he could not punish his child severely without a sufficient cause, neither could the teacher do it without sufficient cause. The nature and extent of the punishment have already been considered. It now becomes necessary to look at the provocation.

The mind and the will of Wall had been prepared for insubordination and revolt by his father and the priest. His refusal to obey the commands of the school was deliberate. His offence became the more aggravated by reason of many others acting in concert with him, to put down the authority of the school. The extent of the punishment was left as it were to his own choice. From the first blow that fell upon his hands from the master's rattan, to the last that was given, it was in his power to make every one the last.

He was punished for insurbordination, and a determination to stand out against the lawful commands of the school. Every blow given was for a continued resistance and a new offence. The offence and the punishment went hand in hand together. The punishment ceased when the offence ceased.

By this the court is not to be understood as justifying the inflicting of punishment upon a scholar so long as he holds out against the commands of the school. The punishment must not be extended beyond the limits of sound discretion, and this every master must decide at his peril. In this case the punishment inflicted, when compared with the offence committed, and all the attendant circumstances as they appeared upon the trial, was neither excessive, nor inflicted through malice by the defendant.

The defendant is discharged.[1]

---

[1]Cf., Doremus v. Board of Education, 5 N.J. 435 (1950).

Board of Education v. Minor et al
Supreme Court of Ohio, 1872
23 Oh. St. 211

Error to the Superior Court of Cincinnati.

The defendants in error are tax-payers of the city of Cincinnati, and the city solicitor having refused to institute any proceeding for that purpose, they brought their action in the Superior Court of Cincinnati to enjoin the plaintiffs in error, the board of education and certain of its members and officers, from carrying into effect, or enforcing, two resolutions then lately adopted by the board. These resolutions are as follows:

"Resolved, That religious instruction and the reading of religious books, including the Holy Bible, are prohibited in the common schools of Cincinnati, it being the true object and intent of this rule to allow the children of the parents of all sects and opinions, in matters of faith and worship, to enjoy alike the benefit of the common-school fund.

"Resolved, That so much of the regulations of the course of study and the text-books in the intermediate and district schools (page 213, annual report), as reads as follows, 'The opening exercise in every department shall commence by reading a portion of the Bible by or under the direction of the teacher, and appropriate singing by the pupils,' be repealed."

The entire rule thus quoted from is in the following words: "The opening exercise in ever department shall commence by reading a portion of the Bible by or under the direction of the teacher, and appropriate singing by the pupils. The pupils of the common schools may read such version of the Sacred Scriptures as their parents or guardians may prefer, provided that such preference of any version, except the one now in use, be communicated by the parents and guardians to the principal teachers, and that no notes or marginal readings be allowed in the schools, or comments made by the teachers on the text of any version that is or may be introduced."

The plaintiffs below allege in their petition, that the rule last above quoted was adopted in 1852, and has ever since that time been in full force and effect, as one of the rules for the conduct of the schools of the city, and that the version of the Holy Bible generally used in said schools, and referred to in the rule above quoted as "the one now in use," is that published by the "American Bible Society," and commonly known as King James' version. They further say, "that the reading of the Holy Bible, without note or comment, has been one of the daily exercises of said schools from the time of their first establishment under the general school laws of Ohio, to wit, from about the year 1820 till now, and that instruction in the elemental truths and principles of religion has always been given in said schools, but no sectarian teaching, nor any interference with the rights of conscience, has at any time been permitted."

They further say, "that a large number of the textbooks used in said schools contain selections and passages from the Holy Bible, and from other books and writings which inculcate religious truths; that this is especially true as to the readers in common use in said schools; ... and that the enforcement of the rule proposed by said board of education will exclude from the schools large numbers of valuable text-books, which have been recently purchased by parents or guardians for the use of children attending said schools in compliance with the requirements of said board of education."

They further say, "that a large majority of the children in said city who receive any education are educated in said schools, and of said children large numbers receive no religious instruction or knowledge of the Holy Bible, except that communicated as aforesaid in said schools, and that the enforcement of the resolutions first aforesaid will result in leaving such children without any religious instruction whatever. And the plaintiffs allege that such instruction is necessary and indispensable to fit said children to be good citizens of the State of Ohio and of the United States, and is required by the third article of the act passed by the Congress of the United States, July 13, 1787, entitled 'an ordinance for the government of the territory of the United States northwest of the river Ohio,' to be forever encouraged."

By this answer the defendants, among other things, say: ... "It is true that there are books other than the Bible, now in use in the common schools of Cincinnati, which contain passages and selections from the Bible, and from writing inculcating truths, which, by many persons are designated as religious truths, but that such books are not religious books, and are not used for the purpose of conveying religious instruction; that these defendants believe it to be true that a number of children, who are educated in the common schools, receive no religious instruction or knowledge of the Bible except that communicated in said schools; that while the defendants do not deny that religious instruction is necessary and indispensable to fit said children to be good citizens of the State of Ohio and of the United States, they deny that such instruction can or ought to be imparted in the schools established by the state."

And the defendants further say, "that the citizens of Cincinnati, who are taxed for the support of the schools under the management of said board of education, and all of whom are equally entitled to the benefits thereof by having their children instructed therein, are very much divided in opinion and practice upon matters connected with the religious belief, worship, and education; that a considerable number thereof are Israelites who reject the Christian religion altogether and believe only in the inspired truth of what is known as the Old Testament, and this only in the original Hebrew tongue, and such other religious truths and worship as are perpetuated in their body by tradition; that, also, many of said citizens do not believe the writings embraced in the Bible to be entitled to be considered as containing an authoritative declaration of religious truth; that a still greater number of said citizens, together with their children, are members of the Roman Catholic Church, and conscientiously believe in its doctrines, faith, and forms of worship, and that by said church the version of the Scriptures referred to in the petition, is taught and believed to be incorrect as a translation and incomplete; ... and furthermore, inasmuch as said church has divine authority as the only infallible teacher and interpreter of the same, that the reading of the same without note or comment, and without being properly expounded by the only authorized teachers and interpreters thereof, is not only not beneficial to the children in said schools, but likely to lead to the adoption of dangerous errors, and that by reason thereof the practice of reading the King James' version of the Bible, commonly and only received as inspired and true by the Protestant religious sects, in the presence and hearing of Roman Catholic children, is regarded by the members of the Roman Catholic Church as contrary to their rights of conscience; ... that there are other religious sects and denominations and bodies of citizens who either do not regard the Bible as the authoritative source of religious truth, or who regard themselves as possessed of the only true sense thereof; that furthermore, a large number of persons in this community who are ready and qualified to act as teachers in said public schools, object to the reading of the Bible in the version in use (or, indeed, in any version without note or comment) on conscientious grounds, and are thereby precluded from employment as teachers in said schools; that in consideration of these facts, said board of education has concluded that it was not possible for it to take upon itself any instruction in religion, and that it is neither right nor expedient to continue in use as said public schools the reading of any version of the Bible as a religious exercise, or any other religious exercise whatever, and therefore has passed the resolutions now complained of by the plaintiffs."

No reply was filed, and the cause was submitted to the court, substantially, upon the facts thus appearing in the petition and answer. A bill of exceptions setting forth the evidence forms part of the record, but it does not substantially vary the case thus made in the pleadings.

Upon hearing, the court gave judgment for the plaintiff and granted a perpetual injunction against the enforcement of the resolutions in question, or of either of them. And now, to reverse this judgment, the defendants file their petition in error here, assigning for error that the court should have rendered a judgment for them, and not for the plaintiffs below. ...

WELCH, J. The arguments in this case have taken a wide range, and counsel have elaborately discussed questions of state policy, morality, and religion, which, in our judgment, do not belong to the case. We are not called upon as a court, nor are we authorized to say whether the Christian religion is the best and only true religion. There is no question before us of the wisdom or unwisdom of having "the Bible in the schools," or of withdrawing it therefrom. Nor can we, without usurping legislative functions, undertake to decide what religious doctrines, if any, ought to be taught, or where, when, by whom, or to whom it would be best they should be taught. These are questions which belong to the people and to other departments of the government.

The case, as we view it, presents merely or mainly a question of the courts' rightful authority to interfere in the managment and control of the public schools of the state. In other words, the real question is, has the court jurisdiction to interfere in the management and control of such schools, to the extent of enforcing religious instructions, or the reading of religious books therein? ...

If this power exists, it must be found in our state or federal constitution, or in statutes of the state enacted in conformity therewith. We know of no law enforceable by courts of the state above or beyond these.

We are referred to no provision of the federal constitution, nor to any enactment of the state legislature, confering such a power.

Counsel for the defendants in error, as we understand them, claim to derive this authority of the court from the last clause in section 7, article 1, in connection with section 2, article 6, of the state constitution, which are as follows:

Sec. 7. "All men have a natural and indefeasible right to worship Almighty God according to the dictates of their own conscience. No person shall be compelled to attend, erect, or support any place of worship, or maintain any form of worship, against his consent; and no preference shall be given, by law, to any religious society; nor shall any interference with the rights of conscience be permitted. No religious test shall be required as a qualification for office, nor shall any person be incompetent to be a witness on account of his religious belief; but nothing herein shall be construed to dispense with oaths and affirmations. Religion, morality, and knowledge, however, being essential to good government, it shall be the duty of the general assembly to pass suitable laws to protect every religious denomination in the peaceable enjoyment of its own mode of public worship, and to encourage schools and the means of instruction."

"Sec. 2. The general assembly shall make such provisions, by taxation or otherwise, as, with the income arising from the school trust fund, will secure a thorough and efficient system of common schools throughout the state; but no religious or other sect or sects shall ever have any exclusive right to, or control of, any part of the school funds of this state."

If we rightly comprehend the arguments, it is claimed on behalf of the defendants in error, (1) that these provisions in the constitution require and enjoin religious instructions, or the teaching of religious doctrines in the public schools, irrespective of the wishes of the people concerned therein; and (2) that this requirement and injunction rests, not upon the legislature alone, but, in the absence of legislative action for that purpose, is a law of the state, proprio vigore, binding upon the courts and people.

If it is not conceded, it must be conceded that the legislature have never passed any law enjoining or requiring religious instructions in the public schools, or giving the courts power in any manner, or to any extent, to direct or determine the particular branches of learning to be taught therein, or to enforce instructions in any particular branch or branches. The extent of legislative action, either under the present constitution, or under that of 1802, which contained a provision quite similar to the present, has been, to establish and maintain a general system of common schools for the state, and to place their management and control exclusively in the hands of directors, trustees, or boards of education, other than the courts of the state. The laws establishing this system date back to 1825, and form an important part of the legislation of the state. They have from time to time been changed, amended, repealed, and re-enacted. While these laws do refer to other branches of learning in the schools, they nowhere enjoin or speak of religious instruction therein. They speak of the "morals" and "good conduct" of the pupils, and of the "moral character" of the teachers, but they nowhere require the pupil to be taught religion, or the teacher to be religious; much less do they require this to be done against the will of the people interested ...

There is a total absence, therefore, of any legislation looking to the enforcement of religious instruction, or the reading of religious books in the public schools; and we are brought back to the question, what is the true meaning and effect of these constitutional provisions on this subject? Do they enjoin religious instructions in the schools? and does this injunction bind the courts, in the absence of legislation? We are unanimous in the opinion that both these questions must be answered in the negative.

The clause relied upon as enjoining religious instructions in the schools declares three things to be essential to good government, and for that reason requires the legislature to encourage "means of instruction" generally, and among other means, that of "schools." The three things so declared to be essential to good government are "religion, morality. and knowledge." These three words stand in the same category, and in the same relation to the context; and if one of them is used in its generic or unlimited sense, so are all three. That the word "knowledge" and the word "morality" are used in that sense, is very plain. The meaning is, that true religion, true morality, and true knowledge shall be promoted, by encouraging schools and means of instruction. The last named of these three words, "knowledge," comprehends in itself all that is comprehended in the other two words, "religion" and "morality," and which can be the subject of human "instructions," must be included under the general term "knowledge." Nothing is enjoined, therefore, but the encouragement of means of instruction in general "knowledge" - the knowledge of truth. The fair interpretation seems to be, that true "religion" and "morality" are aided and promoted by the increase and diffusion of "knowledge" on the theory that "knowledge is the hand-maid of virtue," and that all three - religion, morality, and knowledge - are essential to good government. But there is no direction given as to what system of general knowledge, or of religion or morals, shall be taught; nor as to what particular branches of such system or systems shall be introduced into the "schools;" nor is any direction given as to what other "means of instruction" shall be employed; to enjoin "instructions" in "knowledge," the knowledge of truth in all its branches - religious, moral, or otherwise - is one thing; and to declare what is truth - truth in any one, or in all departments of human knowledge - and to enjoin the teaching of that, as truth, is quite another thing. To enjoin the latter, would be to declare that human knowledge had reached its ultimatum. This the constitution does not undertake to do, neither as to "religion," "morality," nor any other branch or department of human "knowledge." And even had it so declared what was to be received and taught as religious truth, to the exclusion of all else, it would still be necessary, in order to make the case here claimed, to go fruther, and show what branches embraced in the injunction are required to be taught in the schools, and that those to be so taught include the subject of religion.

The truth is that these are matters left to legislative discretion, subject to the limitations on legislative power, regarding religious freedom, contained in the bill of rights; and subject also to the injunction that laws shall be passed, such as in the judgment of the legislature are "suitable" to encourage general means of instruction, including, among other means, a system of common schools.

Equally plain is it to us, that if the supposed injunction to provide for religious instructions is to be found in the clauses of the constitution in question, it is one that rests exclusively upon the legislature. In both sections the duty is expressly imposed upon the "general assembly." The injunction is, to "pass suitable laws." Until these "laws" are passed, it is quite clear to us that the courts have no power to interpose. The courts can only execute the laws when passed. They cannot compel the general assembly to pass them.

This opinion might well end here. Were the subject of controversy any other branch of instructions in the schools than religion, I have no doubt it might safely end here, and the unanimous opinion of the court thus rendered be satisfactory to all. The case is of peculiar importance, however, in the fact that it touches our religious convictions and prejudices, and threatens to disturb the harmonious working of the state government, and particularly of the public schools of the state. I deem it not improper, therefore, to consider briefly some of the points and matters so ably and elaborately argued by counsel, although really lying outside of the case proper, or only bearing on it remotely.

The real claim here is, that by "religion," in this clause of the constitution, is mean "Christian religion," and that by "religious denomination" in the same clause is meant "Christian denomination." If this claim is well founded, I do not see how we can consistently avoid giving a like meaning to the same words and their congnates, "worship," "religious society," "sect," "consicence," "religious belief," throughout the entire section. To do so, it will readily be seen, would be to withdraw from every person not of Christian belief the guaranties therein vouchsafed, and to withdraw many of them from Christians themselves. In that sense the clause of section 7 in question would read as follows:

"Christianity, morality, and knowledge, however, being essential to good government, it shall be the duty of the general assembly to pass suitable laws to protect every christian denomination in the peaceable enjoyment of its own mode of public worship, and to encourage schools and the means of instruction" . . .

We are told that this word "religion" must mean "Christian religion" because "Christianity is a part of the common law of this country," lying behind and above its constitutions. Those who make this assertion can hardly be serious, and intend the real import of their language. If Christianity is a law of the state, like every other law, it must have a sanction. Adequate penalties must be provided to enforce obedience to all its requirements and precepts. No one seriously contends for any such doctrine in this country, or, I might almost say, in this age of the world. The only foundation - rather, the only excuse - for the proposition, that Christianity is part of the law of this country, is the fact that it is a Christian country, and that its constitutions and laws are made by a Christian people. And is not the very fact that those laws do not attempt to enforce Christianity, or to place it upon exceptional or vantage ground, itself a strong evidence that they are the laws of a Christian people, and that their religion is the best and purest of religions? It is strong evidence that their religion is indeed a religion "without partiality," and therefore a religion "without hypocrisy." True Christianity asks no aid from the sword of civil authority. It began without the sword, and wherever it has taken the sword it has perished by the sword. To depend on civil authority for its enforcement is to acknowledge its own weakness, which it can never afford to do. It is able to fight its own battles. Its weapons are moral and spiritual, and not carnal. Armed with these, and these alone, it is not afraid nor "ashamed" to be compared with other religions, and to withstand them single-handed. And the very reason why it is not so afraid or "ashamed" is, that it is not the "power of man," but "the power of God," on which it depends. True Christianity never shields itself behind majorities. Nero, and the other persecuting Roman emperors, were amply supported by majorities; and yet the pure and peaceable religion of Christ in the end triumphed over them all; and it was only when it attempted itself to enforce religion by the arm of authority, that it began to wane. A form of religion that cannot live under equal and impartial laws ought to die, and sooner or later must die.

Legal Christianity is a solecism, a contradiction of terms. When Christianity asks the aid of government beyond mere impartial protection, it denies itself. Its laws are divine, and not human. Its essential interests lie beyond the reach and range of human governments. United with government, religion never rises above the merest superstition; united with religion, government never rises above the merest despotism; and all history shows us that the more widely and completely they are separated, the better it is for both ...

If it be true that our law enjoins the teaching of the Christian religion in the schools, surely, then, all its teachers should be Christians. Were I such a teacher, while I should instruct the pupils that the Christian religion was true and all other religions false, I should tell them that the law itself was an unchristian law. One of my first lessons to the pupils would show it to be unchristian. That lesson would be: "Whatsoever ye would that men should do to you, do yet even so to them; for this is the law and the prophets." I could not look the veriest infidel or heathen in the face, and say that such a law was just, or that it was a fair specimen of Christian republicanism. I should have to tell him that it was an outgrowth of false Christianity, and not one of the "lights" which Christians are commanded to shed upon an unbelieving world. I should feel bound to acknowledge to him, moreover, that it violates the spirit of our constitutional guaranties, and is a state religion in embryo; that if we have no right to tax him to support "worship," we have no right to tax him to support religion instructions; that to tax a man to put down his own religion is of the very essence of tyranny; that however small the tax, it is a first step in the direction of an "establishment of religion"; and I should add, that the first step in that direction is the fatal step, because it logically involves the last step ...

Counsel say that to withdraw all religious instruction from the schools would be to put them under the control of "infidel sects." This is by no means so. To teach the doctrines of infidelity, and thereby teach that Christianity is false, is one thing; and to give no instructions on the subject is quite another thing. The only fair and impartial method, where serious objection is made, is to let each sect give its own instructions, elsewhere than in the state schools, where of necessity all are to meet; and to put disputed doctrines of religion among other subjects of instruction, for there are many others, which can more conveniently satisfactorily, and safely be taught elsewhere. Our charitable, punitive, and disciplinary institutions stand on an entirely different footing. There the state takes the place of the parent, and may well act the part of a parent or guardian in directing what religious instructions shall be given.

The principles here expressed are not new. They are the same, so far as applicable, enunciated by this court in Bloom v. Richards, 2 Ohio St. 387, and in McGatrick v. Wason, 4 Lb. 566. They are as old as Madison, and were his favorite opinions. Madison, who had more to do with framing the constitution of the United States than any other man, and whose purity of life and orthodoxy of religious belief no one questions, himself says:

"Religion is not within the purview of human government." And again he says: "Religion is essentially distinct from human government, and exempt from its cognizance. A connection between them is injurious to both. There are causes in the human breast which insure the perpetuity of religion without the aid of law."

In his letter to Governor Livingston, July 10, 1822, he says: "I observe with particular pleasure the view you have taken of the immunity of religion from civil government, in every case where it does not trespass on private rights or the public peace. This has always been a favorite doctrine with me."

I have made this opinion exceptionally and laboriously long. I have done so in the hope that I might thereby aid in bringing about a harmony of views and a fraternity of feeling between different classes of society, who have a common interest in a great public institution of the state, which, if managed as sensible men ought to manage it, I have no doubt, will be a principal instrumentality in working out for us what all desire - the best form of government and the purest system of religion.

I ought to observe that, in our construction of the first named of the two resolutions in questions, especially in the light of the answer of the board, we do not understand that any of the "readers," so called, or other books used as mere lesson-books, are excluded from the schools, or that any inconvenience from the necessity of procuring new books will be occasioned by the enforcement of the resolutions.

It follows that the judgment of the Superior Court will be reversed, and the original petition dismissed.

Judgment accordingly

State ex rel. Weiss et al. v. District Board, etc.
Supreme Court of Wisconsin, 1890
76 Wis. 177

LYON, J. The petitioners are residents and tax-payers of the city of Edgerton, and their children are pupils in the public schools of that city. They allege in their petition that certain of the teachers, employed by the district board having charge of such schools, read daily to the pupils therein, during school hours, certain portions of King James' version of the Bible, selected by the teachers; and that the petitioners have requested the district board to require the teachers to discontinue such practice, but the board refuses to do so. The petitioners further allege that such practice is a violation of certain provisions of the constitution of this state, hereinafter more particularly mentioned, and pray that a writ of mandamus may issue from the circuit court to the school board, commanding such board to cause the teachers to discontinue the practice and exercises complained of.

Upon the filing of such petition in the circuit court, the usual alternative writ of mandamus was issued and served upon the school board. The board made return to such writ by filing an answer to the petition, admitting the existence of the practice complained of and the refusal of the board to cause it to be discontinued, denying the authority of the board to interfere with the practice, and alleging that the practice is legal and proper, and that the Bible is a duly authorized and selected text-book for use in said schools. Further statement of the contents of the petition and answer is hereinafter made. The petitioners demurred to the answer of the school board, alleging, as gound of demurrer, that the answer fails to state facts showing that a peremptory writ of mandamus as prayed should not issue. The circuit court overruled the demurrer, and the petitioners appealed to this court from the order in that behalf ...

The constitutional objections urged by the petitioners to the reading of the Bible in the district schools are that (1) it violates the rights of conscience; (2) it compels them to aid in the support of a place of worship against their consent (sec. 18, art. I, Const.); (3) it is sectarian instruction (Const. art. X, sec. 3).

This opinion will be confined quite closely to a discussion of the question whether the adoption of the Protestant, or King James, version of the Bible, or any version thereof, in the public schools in the city of Edgerton, as a textbook, and the reading of selections therefrom in those schools at the times and in the manner stated in the answer, is sectarian instruction, within the meaning of that term as used in sec. 3, art. X, of the constitution, which ordains that no sectarian instruction shall be allowed in the district schools of this state ...

The petitioners are members of the Roman Catholic Church and believers in its doctrines. Hence it is quite natural that most of the averments in their petition should be made, as they in fact are, from the standpoint of such doctrines. But should it be held that members of that church have no valid grounds, as such, for their objections to the reading of the Bible in the district schools, still the petition contains general averments sufficiently broad to cover any valid objection to such reading which might be made by any citizen of the state aggrieved by the action of the school board. These averments are "that the residents of said city of Edgerton, who are taxed for the support of said schools, are equally entitled to the benefits thereof, by having their children instructed therein according to law;" and that such reading of the Bible "is contrary to the rights of conscience, and wholly contrary to and in violation of the law; and that your petitioners believe such exercises as above set forth, and each and all of them, are sectarian instruction, and in violation of section 3, article X, of the constitution of the state of Wisconsin."

The answer contains several averments which counsel claim are admitted by the demurrer, but which are mere legal conclusions from facts stated therein; such as that the reading of the Bible in schools is not sectarian instruction, or that the school board have lawful right to permit, and none to prevent, such reading of the same. Averments of this kind or of facts not well pleaded are not admitted by a general demurrer to the pleading. 5 Am. & Eng. Ency. of Law, 551, and cases cited in note 6.

It is averred in the return that there is no material difference between the King James version of the Bible, used in the Edgerton schools, and the Douay version, which is the only one recognized by the Catholic Church as correct and complete. It is universally known that there are differences between these two versions in many particulars which the respective sects regard as material. Hence the averment is against common knowledge, and therefore not well pleaded.

Our conclusion is that if such reading of the Bible is sectarian instruction, or if it violates any other constitutional right of any citizen or sect, the petition is sufficient ...

4. Counsel for the school board maintain, in their argument, that the Christian religion is part of the common law of England; that the same was brought to this country by the colonists, and by virtue of the various colonial charters was embodied in the fundamental laws of the colonies; that this religious element or principle was incorporated in the various state constitutions, and in the Ordinance of 1787 for the government of the Northwest Territory, by virtue of which ordinance it became the fundamental law of the territory of Wisconsin. Numerous quotations are given by him from the above documents, from the utterances of Congress and legislatures, and from the writings of our early statesmen, to prove these propositions. That the learned counsel have fairly demonstrated their accuracy is freely conceded. More than that, counsel have proved that many, probably most, of those charters, and some of the state constitutions, not only ordained and enforced some of the principles of the Christian religion, but sectarian doctrines as well.

They have also attempted, at considerable length, to show that the Church of Rome is hostile to our common-school system. This court neither affirms nor denies the accurary of this position. Moreover, counsel on both sides have argued, to some extent, as to whether certain religious dogmas are true or false.

None of these matters are material or pertinent to the questions to be determined on this appeal. This case must be decided under the constitution and laws of this state now in force; and it is entirely immaterial to the decision thereof whether the interference of the courts to compel a faithful execution of the law by school boards is invoked by those who are hostile or friendly to our common school system. The question is, What is the law of the case? not what opinions are entertained by those who demand its enforcement? It is scarcely necessary to add that we have no concern with the truth or error of the doctrines of any sect. We are only concerned to know whether instruction in sectarian doctrines has been, or under existing regulations, is liable to be, given in the district schools of the state, and especially in the public schools of the city of Edgerton.

5. We come now to the more direct consideration of the merits of the controversy. The term "sectarian instruction," in the constitution, manifestly refers exclusively to instruction in religious doctrines, and the pro-

hibition is only aimed at such instruction as is sectarian; that is to say, instruction in religious doctrines which are believed by some religious sects and rejected by others. Hence, to teach the existence of a Supreme Being, of infinite wisdom, power, and goodness, and that it is the highest duty of all men to adore, obey, and love Him, is not sectarian, because all religious sects so believe and teach. The instruction becomes sectarian when it goes further, and inculcates doctrine or dogma concerning which the religious sects are in conflict. This we understand to be the meaning of the constitutional prohibition.

That the reading from the Bible in the schools, although unaccompanied by any comment on the part of the teacher, is "instruction," seems to us too clear for argument. Some of the most valuable instruction a person can receive may be derived from reading alone, without any extrinsic aid by way of comment or exposition. The question, therefore, seems to narrow down to this: Is the reading of the Bible in the schools - not merely selected passages therefrom, but the whole of it - sectarian instruction of the pupils? In view of the fact already mentioned, that the Bible contains numerous doctrinal passages, upon some of which the peculiar creed of almost every religious sect is based, and that such passages may reasonably be understood to inculcate the doctrines predicated upon them, an affirmative answer to the question seems unavoidable. Any pupil of ordinary intelligence who listens to the reading of the doctrinal portions of the Bible will be more or less instructed thereby in the doctrines of the divinity of Jesus Christ, the eternal punishment of the wicked, the authority of the priesthood, the binding force and efficacy of the sacraments, and many other conflicting sectarian doctrines. A most forcible demonstration of the accuracy of this statement is found in certain reports of the American Bible Society of its work in Catholic countries (referred to in one of the arguments), in which instances are given of the conversion of several persons from "Romanism" through the reading of the Scriptures alone; that is to say, the reading of the Protestant or King James version of the Bible converted Catholics to Protestants without the aid of comment or exposition. In those cases the reading of the Bible certainly was sectarian instruction. We do not know how to frame an argument in support of the proposition that the reading thereof in the district schools is not also sectarian instruction ...

7. The answer of the respondent states that the relators' children are not compelled to remain in the school-room while the Bible is being read, but are at liberty to withdraw therefrom during the reading of the same. For this reason it is claimed that the relators have no good cause for complaint, even though such reading be sectarian instruction. We cannot give our sanction to this position. When, as in this case, a small minority of the pupils in the public school is excluded, for any cause, from a stated school exercise, particularly when such cause is apparent hostility to the Bible which a majority of the pupils have been taught to revere, from that moment the excluded pupil loses caste with his fellows, and is liable to be regarded with aversion and subjected to reproach and insult. But is it a sufficient refutation of the argument that the practice in question tends to destroy the equality of the pupils which the constitution seeks to establish and protect, and puts a portion of them to serious disadvantage in many ways with respect to the others ...

11. The drift of some remarks in the argument of counsel for the respondent, and perhaps also in the opinion of Judge Bennett, is that the exclusion of Bible reading from the district schools is derogatory to the value of the Holy Scriptures, a blow to their influence upon the conduct and consciences of men, and disastrous to the cause of religion. We most emphatically reject these views. The priceless truths of the Bible are best taught to our youth in the church, the Sabbath and parochial schools, the social religious meetings, and, above all, by parents in the home circle. There, those truths may be explained and enforced, the spiritual welfare of the child guarded and protected, and his spiritual nature directed and cultivated, in accordance with the dictates of the parental conscience. The constitution does not interfere with such teaching and culture. It only banishes theological polemics from the district schools. It does this, not because of any hostility to religion, but because the people who adopted it believed that the public good would thereby be promoted, and they so declared in the preamble. Religion teaches obedience to law, and flourishes best where good government prevails. The constitutional prohibition was adopted in the interests of good government; and it argues but little faith in the vitality and power of religion to predict disaster to its progress because a constitutional provision, enacted for such a purpose, is faithfully executed.

By the Court - The order of the circuit court overruling the demurrer of the relators to the answer of the school board must be reversed, and the cause remanded with directions to that court to give judgment for the relators on the demurrer, awarding a peremptory writ of mandamus as prayed in the petition...

[The concurring opinions of Cassoday and Orton, JJ. are omitted.]

Scopes v. State
Supreme Court of Tennessee, 1927
154 Tenn. 105

Chief Justice Green delivered majority opinion; Judge Chambliss concurring opinion, and Justice Cook concurred; Judge Colin P. McKinney, opinion dissenting, and Judge Swiggart did not participate.

Scopes was convicted of a violation of chapter 27 of the Acts of 1925 for that he did teach in the public schools of Rhea county a certain theory that denied the story of the divine creation of man, as taught in the Bible, and did teach instead thereof that man had descended for a lower order of animals. After a verdict of guilty by the jury, the trial judge imposed a fine of $100, and Scopes brought the case to this court by an appeal in the nature of a writ of error ....

Chapter 27 of the Acts of 1925, known as the Tennessee Anti-evolution Act is set out in the margin.[1]

---

[1] "Be it enacted ... that it shall be unlawful for any teacher in any of the universities, normals and all other public schools of the state which are supported in whole or in part by the public school funds of the state, to teach any theory that denies the story of the Divine creation of man as taught in the Bible, and to teach instead that man has descended from a lower order of animals."

While the Act was not drafted with as much care as could have been desired, nevertheless, there seems to be no great difficulty in determining its meaning. It is entitled "An Act prohibiting the teaching of the evolution theory in all the Universities, Normals and all other public schools of Tennessee, which are supported in whole or in part by the public school funds of the State, and to provide penalties for the violations thereof."

Evolution like prohibition is a broad term. In recent bickering, however, evolution has been understood to mean the theory which holds that man has developed from some pre-existing lower type. This is the popular significance of evolution, just as the popular significance of prohibition is prohibition of the traffic in intoxicating liquors. It was in this sense that evolution was used in this Act. It is in this sense that the word will be used in this opinion, unless the context otherwise indicates. It is only to the theory of the evolution of man from a lower type that the Act before us was intended to apply, and much of the discussion we have heard is beside this case. The words of a Statute, if in common use, are to be taken in their natural and ordinary sense. O'Neill v. State, 115 Tenn., 427; State ex rel. v. Turnpike Co., 34 Tenn. (2 Sneed), 90.

Thus defining evolution the Act's title clearly indicates the purpose of the Statute to be the prohibition of teaching in the Schools of the State that man has developed or descended from some lower type or order of animals.

When the draftsman came to express this purpose in the body of the Act he first forbade the teaching of "any theory that denies the story of the divine creation of man as taught in the Bible" - his conception evidently being that to forbid the denial of the Bible story would ban the teaching of evolution. To make the purpose more explicit he added that it should be unlawful to teach "that man has descended from a lower order of animals" ...

It thus seems plain that the Legislature in this enactment only intended to forbid teaching that man descended from a lower order of animals. The denunciation of any theory denying the Bible story of creation is restricted by the caption and by the final clause of section 1. So interpreted the Statute does not seem to be uncertain in its meaning nor incapable of enforcement for such a reason, notwithstanding the great argument to the contrary. The indictment herein follows the language of the Statute. The Statute being sufficiently definite in its terms, such an indictment is good. State v. Odom, 70 Tenn., (2 Lea), 220; Villines v. State, 96 Tenn. 141; Griffin v. State, 109 Tenn., 17. The assignments of error which challenge the sufficiency of the indictment and the certainty of the Act are accordingly overruled.

It is contended that the Statute violates section 8 of article 1 of the Tennessee Constitution, and section 1 of the Fourteenth Amendment to the Constitution of the United States - the Law of the Land clause of the State Constitution, and the Due Process of Law clause of the Federal Constitution, which are practically equivalent in meaning.

We think there is little merit in this contention. The plaintiff in error was a teacher in the public schools of Rhea county. He was an employee of the State of Tennessee or of a municipal agency of the State. He was under contract with the State work in an institution of the State. He had no right or privilege to serve the State except upon such terms as the State prescribed. His liberty, his privilege, his immunity to teach and proclaim the theory of evolution, elsewhere than in the service of the State, was in no wise touched by this law.

The Statute before us is not an exercise of the police power of the State undertakings to regulate the conduct and contracts of individuals in their dealings with each other. On the other hand it is an Act of the State as a corporation, a proprietor, an employer. It is a declaration of a master as to the character of work the master's servant shall, or rather shall not, perform. In dealing with its own employees engaged upon its own work, the State is not hampered by the limitations of Section 8 or article 1 of the Tennessee Constitution, nor of the Fourteenth Amendment to the Constitution of the United States ...

Since the State may prescribe the character and the hours of labor of the employees on its works, just as freely may it say what kind of work shall be performed in its service - what shall be taught in its schools, so far at least as section 8 of article 1 of the Tennessee Constitution, and the Fourteenth Amendment to the Constitution of the United States are concerned.

But it is urged that chapter 27 of the Acts of 1925 conflicts with section 12 of article 11, the Education clause, and section 3 of article 1, the Religious Preference clause of the Tennessee Constitution. It is to be doubted if the plaintiff in error, before us only as the State's employee, is sufficiently protected by these constitutional provisions to justify him in raising such questions. Nevertheless as the State appears to concede that these objections are properly here made, the court will consider them.

The relevant portion of section 12 of article 11 of the Constitution is in these words:

"... It shall be the duty of the General Assembly in all future periods of this government to cherish Literature and Science."

The argument is that the theory of the descent of man from a lower order of animals is now established by the preponderance of scientific thought and that the prohibition of the teaching of such theory is a violation of the legislative duty to cherish Science.

While this clause of the Constitution has been mentioned in several of our cases, there references have been casual, and no Act of the Legislature has ever been held inoperative by reason of such provision. In one of the opinions in Green v. Allen, 24 Tenn. (5 Humph.) 170, the provision was said to be directory. Although this court is loath to say that any language of the Constitution is merely directory, State v. Burrow, 119 Tenn., 376; Webb v. Carter, 129 Tenn., 182, we are driven to the conclusion that this particular admonition must be so treated. It is too vague to be enforced by any court. To cherish Science means to nourish, to encourage, to foster Science.

In no case can the court directly compel the Legislature to perform its duty. In a plain case the court can prevent the Legislature from transgressing its duty under the Constitution by declaring ineffective such a legislative Act. The case, however, must be plain and the legislative Act is always given the benefit of any doubt ...

If the Legislature thinks that by reason of popular prejudice, the cause of education and the study of Science generally will be promoted for forbidding the teaching of evolution in the schools of the State, we can conceive of no ground to justify the court's interference. The courts cannot sit in judgment on such Acts of the Legislature or its agents and determine whether, or not, the omission or addition of a particular course of study tends "to cherish Science."

The last serious criticism made of the Act is that it contravenes the provision of section 3 of article 1 of the Constitution, "that no preference shall ever be given by law to any religious establishment or mode of worship."

The language quoted is a part of our Bill of Rights, was contained in the first Constitution of the State adopted in 1796, and has been brought down into the present Constitution.

At the time of the adoption of our first Constitution, this government had recently been established and the recollection of previous conditions was fresh. England and Scotland maintained State churches as did some of the Colonies, and it was intended by this clause of the Constitution to prevent any such undertaking in Tennessee.

We are not able to see how the prohibition of teaching the theory that man has descended from a lower order of animals gives preference to any religious establishment or mode of worship. So far as we know there is no religious establishment or organized body that has its creed or confession of faith any article denying or affirming such a theory. So far as we know the denial or affirmation of such a theory does not enter into any recognized mode of worship. Since this cause has been pending in this court, we have been favored, in addition to briefs of counsel and various amici curiae, with a multitude of resolutions, addresses and communications from scientific bodies, religious factions, and individuals giving us the benefit of their views upon the theory of evolution. Examination of these contributions indicates that Protestants, Catholics, and Jews are divided among themselve in their beliefs, and that there is no unanimity among the members of any religious establishment as to this subject. Belief or unbelief in the theory of evolution is no more a characteristic of any religious establishment or mode of worship than is belief or unbelief in the wisdom of the prohibition laws. It would appear that members of the same churches quite generally disagree as to these things.

Furthermore, chapter 27 of the Acts of 1925 requires the teaching of nothing. It only forbids the teaching of the evolution of man from a lower order of animals. Chapter 102 of the Acts of 1915 requires that ten verses from the Bible be read each day at the opening of every public school, without comment and provided the teacher does not read the same verses more than twice during any session. It is also provided in this Act that pupils may be excused from the Bible readings upon the written request of their parents.

As the law thus stands, while the theory of evolution of many may not be taught in the schools of the State, nothing contrary to that theory is required to be taught. It could scarcely be said that the statutory scriptural reading just mentioned would amount to the teaching of a contrary theory.

Our school authorities are, therefore, quite free to determine how they shall act in this state of the law. Those in charge of the educational affairs of the State are men and women of discernment and culture. If they believe that the teaching of the Science of Biology has been so hampered by chapter 27 of the Acts of 1925 as to render such an effort no longer desirable, this course of study may be entirely omitted from the curriculum of our schools. If this be regarded as a misfortune, it must be charged to the Legislature. It should be repeated that the Act of 1925 deals with nothing but the evolution of man from a lower order of animals.

It is not necessary now to determine the exact scope of the Religious Preference clause of the Constitution and other language of that section. The situation does not call for such an attempt. Section 3 of article 1 is binding alike on the Legislature, and the school authorities. So far, we are clear that the Legislature has not crossed these constitutional limitations. If hereafter, the school authorities should go beyond such limits, a case can then be brought to the courts.

Much has been said in argument about the motives of the Legislature in passing this Act. But the validity of a Statute must be determined by its natural and legal effect, rather than proclaimed motives. Lochner v. New York, 198 U. S. 45; Grainger v. Douglas Park Jockey Club, 148 Feb. 513, 6 R. C. L. 111, 81.

Some other questions are made but in our opinion they do not merit discussion, and the assignments of error raising such questions are overruled.

This record discloses that the jury found the defendant below guilty but did not assess the fine. The trial judge himself undertook to impose the minimumfine of $100 authorized by the Statute. This was error. Under section 14 of article 6 of the Constitution of Tennessee, a fine in excess of $50 must be assessed by a jury. The Statute before us does not permit the imposition of a smaller fine than $100.

Since a jury alone can impose the penalty this Act requires and as a matter of course no different penalty can be inflicted, the trial judge exceeded his jurisdiction in levying this fine and we are without power to correct his error. The judgment must accordingly be reversed. Upchurch v. The State, 153 Tenn. 198.

The court is informed that the plaintiff in error is no longer in the service of the State. We see nothing to be gained by prolonging the life of this bizarre case. On the contrary we think the peace and dignity of the State, which all criminal prosecutions are brought to redress, will be the better conserved by the entry of a nolle prosequi herein. Such a course is suggested to the Attorney-General.[2]

---

[2]The concurring opinion of Chambliss, J. and a dissenting opinion of Mc-Kinney, J. are omitted.

Pierce v. Society of Sisters
Supreme Court of the United States, 1925
268 U.S. 510

Mr. Justice McReynolds delivered the opinion of the Court.

These appeals are from decrees, based upon undenied allegations, which granted preliminary orders restraining appellants from threatening or attempting to enforce the Compulsory Education Act adopted November 7, 1922, under the initiative provision of her Constitution by the voters of Oregon. Jud. Code, § 266. They present the same points of law; there are no controverted questions of fact. Rights said to be guaranteed by the federal Constitution were specially set up, and appropriate prayers asked for their protection.

The challenged Act, effective September 1, 1926, requires every parent, guardian or other person having control or charge or custody of a child between eight and sixteen years to send him "to a public school for the period of time a public school shall be held during the current year" in the district where the child resides; and failure so to do is declared a misdemeanor. There are exemptions - not specially important here - for children who are not normal, or who have completed the eighth grade, or who reside at considerable distances from any public school, or whose parents or guardians hold special permits from the County Superintendent. The manifest purpose is to compel general attendance at public schools by normal children, between eight and sixteen, who have not completed the eighth grade. And without doubt enforcement of the statute would seriously impair, perhaps destroy, the profitable features of appellees' business and greatly diminish the value of their property.

Appellee, the Society of Sisters, is an Oregon corporation, organized in 1880, with power to care for orphans, educate and instruct the youth, establish and maintain academies or schools, and acquire necessary real and personal property. It has long devoted its property and effort to the secular and religious education and care of children, and has acquired the valuable good will of many parents and guardians. It conducts interdependent primary and high schools and junior colleges, and maintains orphanages for the custody and control of children between eight and sixteen. In its primary schools many children between those ages are taught the subjects usually pursued in Oregon public schools during the first eight years. Systematic religious instruction and moral training according to the tenets of the Roman Catholic Church are also regularly provided. All courses of study, both temporal and religious, contemplate continuity of training under appellee's charge; the primary schools are essential to the system and the most profitable. It owns valuable buildings, especially constructed and equipped for school purposes. The business is remunerative - the annual income from primary schools exceeds thirty thousand dollars - and the successful conduct of this requires long time contracts with teachers and parents. The Compulsory Education Act of 1922 has already caused the withdrawal from its schools of children who would otherwise continue, and their income has steadily declined. The appellants, public officers, have proclaimed their purpose strictly to enforce the statute.

After setting out the above facts the Society's bill alleges that the enactment conflicts with the right of parents to choose schools where their children will receive appropriate mental and religious training, the right of the child to influence the parents' choice of a school, the right of schools and teachers therein to engage in a useful business or profession, and is accordingly repugnant to the Constitution and void. And, further, that unless enforcement of the measure is enjoined the corporation's business and property will suffer irreparable injury.

Appellee, Hill Military Academy, is a private corporation organized in 1908 under the laws of Oregon, engaged in owning, operating and conducting for profit an elementary, college preparatory and military training school for boys between the ages of five and twenty-one years. The average attendance is one hundred, and the annual fees received for each student amount to some eight hundred dollars. The elementary department is divided into eight grades, as in the public schools: the college prepatory department has four grades, similar to those of the public high schools; the courses of study conform to the requirements of the State Board of Education. Military instruction and training are also given, under the supervision of an Army officer. It owns considerable real and personal property, some useful only for school purposes. The business and incident good will are very valuable. In order to conduct its affairs long time contracts must be made for supplies, equipment, teachers and pupils. Appellants, law officers of the State and County, have publicly announced that the Act of November 7, 1922, is valid and have declared their intention to enforce it. By reason of the statute and threat of enforcement appellee's business is being destroyed and its property depreciated; parents and guardians are refusing to make contracts for the future instuction of their sons, and some are being withdrawn.

The Academy's bill states the foregoing facts and then alleges that the challenged Act contravenes the corporation's rights guaranteed by the Fourteenth Amendment and that unless appellants are restrained from proclaiming its validity and threatening to enforce it irreparable injury will result. The prayer is for an appropriate injunction.

No answer was interposed in either cause, and after proper notices they were heard by three judges (Jud. Code # 266) on motions for preliminary injunctions upon the specifically alleged facts. The court ruled that the Fourteenth Amendment guaranteed appellees against the deprivation of their property without due process of law consequent upon the unlawful interference by appellants with the free choice of patrons, present and prospective. It declared the right to conduct schools was property and that parents and guardians, as a part of their liberty, might direct the education of children by selecting reputable teachers and places. Also, that these schools were not unfit or harmful to the public, and that enforcement of the challenged statute would unlawfully deprive them of patronage and thereby destroy their owners' business and property. Finally, that the threats to enforce the Act would continue to cause irreparable injury; and the suits were not premature.

No question is raised concerning the power of the State reasonably to regulate all schools, to inspect, supervise and examine them, their teachers and pupils; to require that all children of proper age attend some school, that teachers shall be of good moral character and patriotic disposition, that certain studies plainly essential to good citizenship must be taught, and that nothing be taught which is manifestly inimical to the public welfare.

The inevitable practical result of enforcing the Act under consideration would be destruction of appellees' primary schools, and perhaps all other private primary schools for normal children within the State of Oregon. These parties are engaged in a kind of undertaking not inherently harmful, but long regarded as useful and meritorious. Certainly there is nothing in the present records to indicate that they have failed to discharge their obligations to patrons, students or the State. And there are no peculiar circumstances or present emergencies which demand extraordinary measures relative to primary education.

Under the doctrine of Meyer v. Nebraska, 262 U.S. 390, we think it entirely plain that the Act of 1922 unreasonably interferes with the liberty of parents and guardians to direct the upbringing and education of children under their control. As often, heretofore pointed out, rights guaranteed by the Constitution may not be abridged by legislation which has no reasonable relation to some purpose within the competency of the State. The fundamental theory of liberty upon which all governments in this Union repose excludes any general power of the State to standardize its children by forcing them to accept instruction from public teachers only. The child is not the mere creature of the State; those who nurture him and direct his destiny have the right, coupled with the high duty, to recognize and prepare him for additional obligations.

Appellees are corporations and therefore, it is said, they cannot claim for themselves the liberty which the Fourteenth Amendment guarantees. Accepted in the proper sense, this is true. Northwestern Life Ins. Co. v. Riggs, 203 U.S. 243, 255; Western Turf Association v. Greenberg, 204 U. S. 359, 363. But they have business and property for which they claim protection. These are threatened with destruction through the unwarranted compulsion which appellants are exercising over present and prospective patrons of their schools. And this court has gone very far to protect against loss threatened by such action. Truax v. Raich, 239 U.S. 33; Truax v. Corrigan, 257 U.S. 312; Terrace v. Thompson, 263 U.S. 197.

The courts of the State have not construed the Act, and we must determine it meaning for ourselves. Evidently it was expected to have general application and cannot be construed as though merely intended to amend the charters of certain private corporations, as in Berea College v. Kentucky, 211 U.S. 45. No argument in favor of such view has been advanced.

Generally it is entirely true, as urged by counsel, that no person in any business has such an interest in possible customers as to enable him to restrain exercise of proper power of the State upon the ground that he will be deprived of patronage. But the injunctions here sought are not against the exercise of any proper power. Plaintiffs asked protection against arbitrary, unreasonable and unlawful interference with their patrons and the consequent destruction of their business and property. Their interest is clear and immediate, within the rule approve in Truax

v. Raich, Truax v. Corrigan and Terrace V. Thompson, supra, and many other cases where injunctions have issued to protect business enterprises against interference with the freedom of patrons or customers. Hitchman Coal & Coke Co. v. Mitchell, 245 U.S. 229; Duplex Printing Press Co. v. Deering, 254 U.S. 443; American Steel Foundries v. Tri-City Central Trades Council, 257 U.S. 184; Nebraska District v. McKelvie, 262 U.S. 404; Truax v. Corrigan, supra, and cases there cited.

The suits were not premature. The injury to appellees was present and very real, not a mere possibility in the remote future. If no relief had been possible prior to the effective date of the Act, the injury would have become irreparable. Prevention of impending injury by unlawful action is a well recognized function of courts of equity.

The decrees below are Affirmed.

Cochran v. Board of Education
Supreme Court of the United States, 1930
281 U.S. 370

MR. CHIEF JUSTICE HUGHES delivered the opinion of the Court.

The appellants, as citizens and taxpayers of the State of Louisiana, brought this suit to restrain the State Board of Education and other state officials from expending any part of the severance tax fund in purchasing school books and in supplying them free of cost to the school children of the State, under Acts No. 100 and No. 143 of 1928, upon the ground that the legislation violated specified provisions of the constitution of the State and also section 4 of Article IV and the Fourteenth Amendment of the Federal Constitution. The Supreme Court of the State affirmed the judgment of the trial court, which refused to issue an injunction. 168 La. 1030.

Act No. 100 of 1928 provided that the severance tax fund of the State, after allowing funds and appropriations as required by the state constitution, should be devoted "first, to supplying school books to the school children of the State." The Board of Education was directed to provide "school books for school children free of cost to such children." Act No. 143 of 1928 made appropriations in accordance with the above provisions.

The Supreme Court of the State, following its decision in Borden v. Louisiana State Board of Education, 168 La. 1005, held that these acts were not repugnant to either the state or the Federal Constitution.

No substantial Federal question is presented under section 4 of Article IV of the Federal Constitution guaranteeing to every State a republican form of government, as questions arising under this provision are political, not judicial, in character. State of Ohio ex rel. Bryant v. Akron Metropolitan Park District, ante, p. 74, and cases there cited.

The contention of the appellant under the Fourteenth Amendment is that taxation for the purchase of school books constituted a taking of private property for a private purpose. Loan Association v. Topeka, 20 Wall. 655. The purpose is said to be to aid private, religious, sectarian, and other schools not embraced in the public educational system of the State by furnishing text-books free to the children attending such private schools. The operation and effect of the legislation in question were described by the Supreme Court of the State as follows (168 La. p. 1020):

"One may scan the acts in vain to ascertain where any money is appropriated for the purchase of school books for the use of any church, private, sectarian, or even public school. The appropriations were made for the specific purpose of purchasing school books for the use of the school children of the state, free of cost to them. It was for their benefit and the resulting benefit to the state that the appropriations were made. True, these children attend some school, public or private, the latter, sectarian or nonsectarian, and that the books are to be furnished them for their use, free of cost, whichever they attend. The schools, however, are not the beneficiaries of these appropriations. They obtain nothing from them, nor are they relieved of a single obligation, because of them. The school children and the state alone are the beneficiaries. It is also true that the sectarian schools, which some of the children attend, instruct their pupils in religion, and books are used for that purpose, but one may search diligently the acts, though without result, in an effort to find anything to the effect that it is the purpose of the state to furnish religious books for the use of such children ... What the statutes contemplate is that the same books that are furnished children attending public schools shall be furnished by children attending private schools. This is the only practical way of interpreting and executing the statutes, and this is what the state board of education is doing. Among these books, naturally, none is to be expected, adapted to religious instruction."

The Court also states, although the point is not of importance in relation to the Federal question, that it was "only the use of the books that is granted to the children, or, in other words, the books are lent to them."

Viewing the statute as having the effect thus attributed to it, we can not doubt that the taxing power of the State is exerted for a public purpose. The legislation does not segregate private schools, or their pupils, as its beneficiaries or attempt to interfere with any matters of exclusively private concern. Its interest is education, broadly; its method, comprehensive. Individual interests are aided only as the common interest is safeguarded.

Judgment affirmed.

Nicholls, Jr., v. Mayor and School Committee of Lynn
Supreme Judicial Court of Massachusetts, 1937
297 Mass. 65

RUGG, C. J. This petition for a writ of mandamus was submitted without evidence upon agreement that the facts stated in the petition and answer are taken to be true, the answer to control in case of inconsistencies. The single justice reported the case without decision with the statement that he should not exercise his discretion against the issuance of the writ if in other respects the petitioner was entitled to it. The object of this petition is to secure reinstatement as a pupil in a public school from which the petitioner has been expelled.

The essential facts are these: The petitioner is about eight years old, a resident of Lynn, and in his third year as a pupil in the public schools of that city. During all this time and for many years theretofore, there was in effect a rule as to the conduct of the schools in Lynn of this tenor:

"Rule 18. Salute To The Flag. - The following salute to the flag shall be given in every school at least once a week and at such other times as occasion may warrant: I pledge allegiance to the Flag of the United States of America and to the Republic for which it stands, one Nation indivisible, with liberty and justice for all." During his first two years in school, the petitioner joined with his teachers and room classmates in the salute to the flag and the recitation of the pledge of allegiance. After the opening of the school in 1935, it was observed that the petitioner, while standing during the salute and the recitation of the pledge, was otherwise taking no part therein. Upon inquiry it was said by the petitioner and his father that the petitioner would not take part in the ceremony "because he was being called upon to adore the flag and to bow down to the flag and that according to his religious views, he could only adore and bow down to Jehovah." Courteous requests by the teacher and principal of the school failed to change the decision of the petitioner not to participate in the ceremony. On September 30, 1935, there was repeated a refusal by the petitioner to join in the salute to the flag and the pledge of allegiance as a part of the opening exercises of the school, but he remained seated and refused to rise. The father of the petitioner was present at the time. After due notice to the petitioner and his father, a hearing was held before the respondents on October 8, 1935, on the question why the petitioner should not be expelled from school because of his conduct. The father was present and was represented by counsel, who made an explanation of the reasons for the refusal of the petitioner to salute the flag and to recite the pledge of allegiance in that they constituted an act of adoring and of bowing down to the flag, which is contrary to the religious beliefs of the petitioner. The respondents as members of the school committee of Lynn then voted to exclude the petitioner from attending the Lynn public schools "until he, of his own free will, shall be willing to subscribe to the laws of the Lynn School Committee and Commonwealth of Massachusetts." This petition was then seasonably brought.

By G. L. (Ter. Ed.) c. 71, § 37, the school committee is given general charge of all the public schools in Lynn and is authorized to make regulations as to attendance therein. In Leonard v. School Committee of Springfield, 241 Mass. 325, 329, 330, it was said: "The school committee is an independent body, entrusted by law with broad powers, important duties and large discretion ... The school committee may make all reasonable rules and regulations for the government, discipline and management of the schools under their charge" ... The discretion of the school committee was diminished by St. 1935, C. 258, amending G. L. (Ter. Ed.) c. 71 § 69. It was thereby enacted that the school committee shall provide flags for each school-house under its control and that a flag of the United States "shall be displayed in each assembly hall or other room in each such schoolhouse where the opening exercises on each school day are held. Each teacher shall cause the pupils under his charge to salute the flag and recite in unison with him at said opening exercises at least once each week the 'Pledge of Allegiance to the Flag.'" Failure to comply with this mandate by the school committee or by a teacher is made punishable by fine. No penalty is imposed on pupils for refusing to participate in the ceremony. The respondents are required to cause to be given instruction in the public schools in American history and civics, the Constitution of the United States, and the duties of citizenship. All instructors of youth are required to "exert their best endeavors to impress on the minds of children and youth committed to their care and instruction the principles of piety and justice and a sacred regard for truth, love of their country, humanity and universal benevolence ..." G. L. (Ter. Ed.) c. 71, §§ 1, 2, 30.

The general rule of the school committee of Lynn, already quoted is within the power conferred by G. L. (Ter. Ed.) c. 71, s 27, and is expressly authorized by St. 1935, c. 258. The latter statute established no penalty for a disobedient pupil, but is directed to the school committee and to the teacher. Power to enforce the rule is implied in the grant of power to establish it. It necessarily follows that, if said c. 258 and the rule are valid, the school committee was acting within its jurisdiction in excluding the petitioner from attending school. Antell v. Stokes, 287 Mass. 103. Sherman v. Charlestown, 8 Cush. 160, 164. Hodgkins v. Rockport, 105 Mass. 475. Hammond v. Hyde Park, 195 Mass. 29. Watson v. Cambridge, 157 Mass. 561. The rigidity of this rule extends no latitude to the pupils who refuse to obey it because of religious objections. Said c. 258 is clear in its command that "Each teacher shall cause the pupils under his charge to salute the flag and recite in unison with him" the pledge of allegiance ...

As justification for his conduct, the petitioner appeals to art. 2 of the Declaration of Rights of the Constitution of this Commonwealth. It is there provided that "no subject shall be hurt, molested, or restrained, in his person, liberty, or estate, for worshipping God in the manner and season most agreeable to the dictates of his own conscience; or for his religious profession or sentiments; provided he doth not disturb the public peace, or obstruct others in their religious worship." He invokes, also, § 1 of art. 18 of the Amendments to the Constitution, as found in art. 46 of the Amendments: "No law shall be passed prohibiting the free exercise of religion." He further relies on G. L. (Ter. Ed.) c. 76, § 5, to the effect that "No child shall be excluded from a public school of any town on account of race, color or religion."

Neither the Constitution of this Commonwealth nor that of the United States contains any definition of religion. Reynolds v. United States, 98 U. S. 145, 162. Nevertheless, a deep reverence for religion permeates several parts of the Constitution of this Commonwealth. That Constitution guarantees "absolute freedom as to religious belief and liberty unrestrained as to religious practices, subject only to the conditions that the public peace must not be disturbed nor others obstructed in their religious worship or the general obligations of good citizenship violated." Opinion of the Justices, 214 Mass. 599, 601.

In Davis v. Beason, 133 U. S. 333, 342, it was said: "The term 'religion' has reference to one's views of his relations to his Creator, and to the obligations they impose of reverence for his being and character, and of obedience to his will. ... With man's relations to his Maker and the obligations he may think they impose, and the manner in which an expression shall be made by him of his belief on those subjects, no interferences can be permitted, provided always the laws of society, designed to secure its peace and prosperity, and the morals of its people, are not interfered with." The flag salute and pledge of allegiance here in question do not in any just sense relate to religion. They are not observances which are religious in nature. They do not concern the views of any one as to his Creator. They do not touch upon his relations with his Maker. They impose no obligations as to religious worship. They are wholly patriotic in design and purpose.

The petitioner has made no disturbance in school and has simply stood mute during the ceremony of flag salute and pledge of allegiance, except that he remained seated on the single occasion on September 30, 1935, when his father was present. He refused to recognize the rule. It is assumed that the statement of beliefs of the petitioner made by him is genuine and true and constitutes the ground of his conduct.

It has been assumed by both sides in the argument of the case at bar that the petitioner and his parents belong to the group known as "Jehovah's Witnesses." A member of that group, as stated in the brief of the petitioner, through a literal reading of the Bible, and especially of the frist two Commandments as found in Exodus XX, entertains the belief that he "must express reverence to God alone and not to the flag, which is not the symbol of God." According to his belief, a salutation is equivalent to an act of reverence or adoration, or idolatry, and in violation of the Commandments of Scripture. The pledge of allegiance to the flag, as set forth in the rule of the school committee and referred to in said c. 258, is an acknowledgment of sovereignty, a promise of obedience, a recognition of authority above the will of the individual, to be respected and obeyed. It has nothing to do with religion.

The salute and pledge do not go beyond that which, according to generally recognized principles, is due to government. There is nothing in the salute or the pledge of allegiance which constitutes an act of idolatry, or which approaches to any religious observance. It does not in any reasonable sense hurt, molest, or restrain a human being in respect to "worshipping God" within the meaning of words in the Constitution. The rule and the statute are well within the competency of legislative authority. They exact nothing in opposition to religion. They are directed to a justifiable end in the conduct of education in the public schools. The practice of the petitioner was in contravention of them. It was said in Reynolds v. United States, 98 U. S. 145, 166: "Laws are made for the government of actions, and while they cannot interfere with mere religious belief and opinions, they may with practices." In Fraina v. United States, 255 Fed. 28, 36, the statement occurs: "the most profound religious conviction that compliance with statute is wrong will not by law save any one from conviction ... for violating that statute." In Spiller v. Woburn, 12 Allen, 127, a pupil sought damages for her alleged illegal expulsion from school. A rule had been passed that the schools should be opened each morning with reading from the Bible and prayer, and that during the prayer the scholars should bow their heads; with a proviso that any pupil whose parent so requested should be excused from taking part in the ceremony. The father of the plaintiff refused to make such request, but instructed her to refuse to bow her head. As a result, she was expelled from school. Judgment was rendered for the defendant and the rule was upheld as a reasonable exercise of the power of the school committee. In the opinion, at page 129, it was stated: "We do not mean to say that it would be competent for a school committee to pass an order or regulation requiring pupils to conform to any religious rite or observance, or to go through with any religious forms or ceremonies, which were inconsistent with or contrary to their religious convictions or conscientious scruples ... But we are unable to see that the regulation with which the plaintiff was required to comply can be justly said to fall within this category" ...

The result is that, in our opinion, the rule and said c. 258 are not invalid and the petitioner fails to show that any of his rights have been invaded.

Matters of policy or wisdom are not open for our consideration. Our descision is confined to the question of law whether the petitioner is entitled to the writ.

Petition dismissed.

Minersville School District v. Gobitis
Supreme Court of the United States, 1940
310 U. S. 586

MR. JUSTICE FRANKFURTER delivered the opinion of the Court.[1]

A grave responsibility confronts this Court whenever in course of litigation it must reconcile the conflicting claims of liberty and authority. But when the liberty invoked is liberty of conscience, and the authority is authority to safeguard the nation's fellowship, judicial conscience is put to its severest test. Of such a nature is the present controversy.

Lillian Gobitis, aged twelve, and her brother William, aged ten, were expelled from the public schools of Minersville, Pennsylvania, for refusing to salute the national flag as part of a daily school exercise. The local Board of Education required both teachers and pupils to participate in this ceremony. The ceremony is a familiar one. The right hand is placed on the breast and the following pledge recited in unison: "I pledge allegiance to my flag, and to the Republic for which it stands; one nation indivisible, with liberty and justice for all." While the words are spoken, teachers and pupils extend their right hands in salute to the flag. The Gobitis family are affiliated with "Jehovah's Witnesses," for whom the Bible as the Word of God is the supreme authority. The children had been brought up conscientiously to believe that such a gesture of respect for the flag was forbidden by command of Scripture.

The Gobitis children were of an age for which Pennsylvania makes school attendance compulsory. Thus they were denied a free education, and their parents had to put them into private schools. To be relieved of the financial burden thereby entailed, their father, on behalf of the children and in his own behalf, brought this suit. He sought to enjoin the authorities from continuing to exact participation in the flag-salute ceremony as a condition of his children's attendance at the Minersville school. After trial of the issues Judge Maris gave relief in the District Court, 24 F. Supp. 271, on the basis of a thoughtful opinion at a preliminary stage of the

---

[1]Footnotes of the Court are omitted.

litigation, 21 F. Supp. 581; his decree was affirmed by the Circuit Court of Appeals, 108 F. 2d 683. Since this decision ran counter to several per curiam dispositions of this Court, we granted certiorari to give the matter full reconsideration. 309 U.S. 645. By their able submissions, the Committee on the Bill of Rights of the American Bar Association and the American Civil Liberties Union, as friend of the Court, have helped us to our conclusion.

We must decide whether the requirement of participation in such a ceremony, exacted from a child who refuses upon sincere religious grounds, infringes without due process of law the liberty guaranteed by the Fourteenth Amendment.

Centuries of strife over the erection of particular dogmas as exclusive or all-comprehending faiths led to the inclusion of a guarantee for religious freedom in the Bill of Rights. The First Amendment, and the Fourteenth through its absorption of the First, sought to guard against repetition of those bitter religious struggles by prohibiting the establishment of a state religion and by securing to every sect the free exercise of its faith. So pervasive is the acceptance of this precious right that its scope is brought into question, as here, only when the conscience of individuals collides with the felt necessities of society.

Certainly the affirmative pursuit of one's convictions about the ultimate mystery of the universe and man's relation to it is placed beyond the reach of law. Government may not interfere with organized or individual expression of belief or disbelief. Propagation of belief - or even disbelief - in the supernatural is protected, whether in church or chapel, mosque or synagogue, tabernacle or meeting-house. Likewise the Constitution assures generous immunity to the individual from imposition of penalties for offending, in the course of his own religious activities, the religious views of others, be they a minority or those who are dominant in government. Cantwell v. Connecticut, ante, p. 196.

But the manifold character of man's relations may bring his conception of religious duty into conflict with the secular interests of his fellow-men. When does the constitutional guarantee compel exemption from doing what society thinks necessary for the promotion of some great common end, or from a penalty for conduct which appears dangerous to the general good? To state the problem is to recall the truth that no single principle can answer all of life's complexities. The right to freedom of religious belief, however dissident and however obnoxious to the cherished beliefs of others - even of a majority - is itself the denial of an absolute. But to affirm that the freedom to follow conscience has itself no limits in the life of a society would deny that very plurality of principles which, as a matter of history, underlies protection of religious toleration. Compate Mr. Justice Holmes in Hudson Water Co. v McCarter, 209 U. S. 349, 355. Our present task, then, as so often the case with courts, is to reconcile two rights in order to prevent either from destroying the other. But, because in safe-guarding conscience we are dealing with interests so subtle and so dear, every possible leeway should be given to the claims of religious faith.

In the judicial enforcement of religious freedom we are concerned with a historic concept. See Mr. Justice Cardozo in Hamilton v. Regents, 293

U. S. at 265. The religious liberty which the Constitution protects has never excluded legislation of general scope not directed against doctrinal loyalties of particular sects. Judicial nullification of legislation cannot be justified by attributing to the framers of the Bill of Rights views for which there is no historic warrant. Conscientious scruples have not, in the course of the long struggle for religious toleration, relieved the individual from obedience to a general law not aimed at the promotion or restriction of religious beliefs. The mere possession of religious convictions which contradict the relevant concerns of a political society does not relieve the citizen from the discharge of political responsibilities. The necessity for this adjustment has again and again been recognized. In a number of situations the exertion of political authority has been sustained, while basic considerations of religious freedom have been left inviolate. Reynolds v. United States, 98 U. S. 145; Davis V. Beason, 133 U. S. 333; Selective Draft Law Cases, 245 U. S. 366; Hamilton v. Regents, 293 U. S. 245. In all these cases the general laws in question, upheld in their application to those who refused obedience from religious conviction, were manifestations of specific powers of government deemed by the legislature essential to secure and maintain that orderly, tranquil, and free society without which religious toleration itself is unattainable. Nor does the freedom of speech assured by Due Process move in a more absolute circle of immunity than that enjoyed by religious freedom. Even if it were assumed that freedom of speech goes beyond the historic concept of full opportunity to utter and to disseminate views, however heretical or offensive to dominant opinion, and includes freedom from conveying what may be deemed an implied but rejected affirmation, the question remains whether school children, like the Gobitis children, must be excused from conduct required of all the other children in the promotion of national cohesion. We are dealing with an interest inferior to none in the hierarchy of legal values. National unity is the basis of national security. To deny the legislature the right to select appropriate means for its attainment presents a totally different order of problem from that of the propriety of subordinating the possible ugliness of littered streets to the free expression of opinion through distribution of handbills. Compare Schneider v. State, 308 U. S. 147.

Situations like the present are phases of the profoundest problem confronting a democracy - the problem which Lincoln case in memorable dilemma: "Must a government of necessity be too strong for the liberties of its people, or too weak to maintain its own existence?" No mere textual reading or logical talisman can solve the dilemma. And when the issue demands judicial determination, it is not the personal notion of judges of what wise adjustment requires which must prevail.

Unlike the instances we have cited, the case before us is not concerned with an exertion of legislative power for the promotion of some specific need or interest of secular society - the protection of the family, the promotion of health, the common defense, the raising of public revenues to defray the cost of government. But all these specific activities of government presuppose the existence of an organized political society. The ultimate foundation of a free society is the binding tie of cohesive sentiment. Such a sentiment is fostered by all those agencies of the mind and spirit which may serve to gather up the traditions of a people, transmit them from generation to generation, and thereby create that continuity of a treasured common life which constitutes a civilization. "We live by symbols." The flag is the symbol of our national unity, transcending all internal differences, however large, within the framework of the Constitution. This Court has had occasion to say that "... the flag is the symbol of the Nation's power, the emblem of freedom in its truest, best sense ... it signifies government resting on the consent of the governed; liberty regulated by law; the protection of the weak against the strong; security against the exercise of arbitrary power; and absolute safety for free institutions against foreign aggression." Halter v. Nebraska, 205 U. S. 34, 43. And see United States v. Gettysburg Electric Ry. Co., 160 U. S. 668.

The case before us must be viewed as though the legislature of Pennsylvania had itself formally directed the flag-salute for the children of Minersville; had made no exemption for children whose parents were possessed of conscientious scruples like those of the Gobitis family; and had indicated its belief in the desirable ends to be secured by having its public school children share a common experience at those periods of development when their minds are supposedly receptive to its assimilation, by an exercise appropriate in time and place and setting, and one designed to evoke in them appreciation of the nation's hopes and dreams, its sufferings and sacrifices. The precise issue, then, for us to decide is whether the legislatures of the various states and the authorities in a thousand counties and school districts of this country are barred from determining the appropriateness of various means to evoke that unifying sentiment without which there can ultimately be no liberties, civil or religious. To stigmatize legislative judgment in providing for this universal gesture of respect for the symbol of our national life in the setting of the common school as a lawless inroad on that freedom of conscience which the Constitution protects, would amount to no less than the pronouncement of pedagogical and psychological dogma in a field where courts possess no marked and certainly no controlling competence. The influences which help toward a common feeling for the common country are manifold. Some may seem harsh and others no doubt are foolish. Surely, however, the end is legitimate. And the effective means for its attainment are still so uncertain and so unauthenticated by science as to preclude us from putting the widely prevalent belief in flag-saluting beyond the pale of legislative power. It mocks reason and denies our whole history to find in the allowance of a requirement to salute our flag on fitting occasions the seeds of sanction for obeisance to a leader.

The wisdom of training children in patriotic impulses by those compulsions which necessarily pervade so much of the educational process is not for our independent judgment. Even were we convinced of the folly of such a measure, such belief would be no proof of its unconstitutionality. For ourselves, we might be tempted to say that the deepest patriotism is best engenedered by giving unfettered scope to the most crochety beliefs. Perhaps it is best even from the standpoint of those interests which ordinances like the one under review seek to promote, to give to the least popular sect leave from conformities like those here in issue. But the courtroom is not the arena for debating issues of educational policy. It is not our province to choose among competing considerations in the subtle process of securing effective loyalty to the traditional ideals of democracy, while respecting at the same time individual idiosyncracies among a people so diversified in racial origins and religious allegiances. So to hold would in effect make us the school board for the country. That authority has not been given to this Court, nor should we assume it.

We are dealing here with the formative period in the development of citizenship. Great diversity of psychological and ethical opinion exists among us concerning the best way to train children for their place in society. Because of these differences and because of reluctance to permit a single, ironcast system of education to be imposed upon a nation compounded of so many strains, we have held that, even though public education is one of our most cherished democratic institutions, the Bill of Rights bars a state from compelling all children to attend the public schools. Pierce v. Society of Sisters, 268 U. S. 510. But it is a very different thing for this Court to exercise censorship over the conviction of legislatures that a particular program or exercise will best promote in the minds of children who attend the common schools an attachment to the institutions of their country.

What the school authorities are really asserting is the right to awaken in the child's mind considerations as to the significance of the flag contrary to those implanted by the parent. In such an attempt the state is normally at a disadvantage in competing with the parent's authority, so long - and this is the vital aspect of religious toleration - as parents are unmolested in their right to counteract by their own persuasiveness the wisdom and rightness of those loyalties which the state's educational system is seeking to promote. Except where the transgression of constitutional liberty is too plain for argument, personal freedom is best maintained - so long as the remedial channels of the democratic process remain open and unobstructed - when it is ingrained in a people's habits and not enforced against popular policy by the coercion of adjudicated law. That the flag-salute is an allowable portion of a school program for those who do not invoke conscientious scruples is surely not debatable. But for us to insist that, though the ceremony may be required, exceptional immunity must be given to dissidents, is to maintain that there is no basis for a legislative judgment that such an exemption might introduce elements of difficulty into the school discipline, might cast doubts in the minds of the other children which would themselves weaken the effect of the exercise.

The preciousness of the family relation, the authority and independence which give dignity to parenthood, indeed the enjoyment of all freedom, presuppose the kind of ordered society which is summarized by our flag. A society which is dedicated to the preservation of these ultimate values of civilization may in self-protection utilize the educational process for inculcating those almost unconscious feelings which bind men together in a comprehending loyalty, whatever may be their lesser difference and difficulties. That is to say, the process may be utilized so long as men's right to believe as they please, to win others to their way of belief, and their right to assemble in their chosen places of worship for the devotional ceremonies of their faith, are all fully respected.

Judicial review, itself a limitation on popular government, is a fundamental part of our constitutional scheme. But to the legislature no less than to courts is committed the guardianship of deeply-cherished liberties. See Missouri, K. & T. Ry. Co. v. May, 194 U. S. 267, 270. Where all the effective means of inducing political changes are left free from interference, education in the abandonment of foolish legislation is itself a training in liberty. To fight out the wise use of legislative authority in the forum of public opinion and before legislative assemblies rather than to transfer such a contest to the judicial arena, serves to vindicate the self-confidence of a free people.

Reversed.

MR. JUSTICE McREYNOLDS concurs in the result.

MR. JUSTICE STONE, dissenting:

I think the judgment below should be affirmed.

Two youths, of fifteen and sixteen years of age, are by the judgment of this Court held liable to expulsion from the public schools and to denial of all publicly supported educational privileges because of their refusal to yield to the complusion of a law which commands their participation in a school ceremony contrary to their religious convictions. They and their father are citizens and have not exhibited by any action or statement of opinion, any disloyalty to the Government of the United States. They are ready and willing to obey all its laws which do not conflict with what they sincerely believe to be the higher commandments of God. It is not doubted that these convictions are religious, that they are genuine, or that the refusal to yield to the compulsion of the law is in good faith and with all sincerity. It would be a denial of their faith as well as the teachings of most religions to say that children of their age could not have religious convictions.

The law which is thus sustained is unique in the history of Anglo-American legislation. It does more than suppress freedom of speech and more than prohibit the free exercise of religion, which concededly are forbidden by the First Amendment and are violations of the liberty guaranteed by the Fourteenth. For by this law the state seeks to coerce these children to express a sentiment which, as they interpret it, they do not entertain, and which violates their deepest religious convictions. It is not denied that such compulsion is a prohibited infringement of personal liberty, freedom of speech and religion, guaranteed by the Bill of Rights, except in so far as it may be justified and supported as a proper exercise of the state's power over public education. Since the state, in competition with parents, may through teaching in the public schools indoctrinate the minds of the young, it is said that in aid of its undertaking to inspire loyalty and devotion to constituted authority and the flag which symbolizes it, it may coerce the pupil to make affirmation contrary to his belief and in violation of his religious faith. And, finally, it is said that since the Minersville School Board and others are of the opinion that the country will be better served by conformity than by the observance of religious liberty which the Constitution prescribes, the courts are not free to pass judgment on the Board's choice.

Concededly the constitutional guaranties of personal liberty are not always absolutes. Government has a right to survive and powers conferred upon it are not necessarily set at naught by the express prohibitions of the Bill of Rights. It may make war and raise armies. To that end it may compel citizens to give military service. Selective Draft Law Cases, 245 U. S. 366, and subject them to military training despite their religious objections. Hamilton v. Regents, 293 U. S. 245. It may suppress religious practices dangerous to morals, and presently those also which are inimical to public safety, health and good order. Davis v. Beason, 133 U. S. 333. But it is a long step, and one which I am unable to take, to the position that government may, as a supposed educational measure and as a means of disciplining the young, compel public affirmations which violate their religious conscience.

The very fact that we have constitutional guaranties of civil liberties and the specificity of their command where freedom of speech and of religion are concerned require some accommodation of the powers which government normally exercises, when no question of civil liberty is involved, to the constitutional demand that those liberties be protected against the action of government itself. The state concededly has power to require and control the education of its citizens, but it cannot by a general law compelling attendance at public schools preclude attendance at a private school adequate in its instruction, where the parent seeks to secure for the child the benefits of religious instruction not provided by the public school. Pierce v. Society of Sisters, 268 U. S. 510. And only recently we have held that the state's authority to control its public streets by generally applicable regulations is not an absolute to which free speech must yield, and cannot be made the medium of its suppression Hague v. Committee for Industrial Organization, 307 U. S. 406, 514, et. seq., any more than can its authority to penalize littering of the streets by a general law be used to suppress the distribution of handbills as a means of communicating ideas to their recipients. Schneider v. State, 308 U. S. 147.

In these cases it was pointed out that where there are competing demands of the interests of government and of liberty under the Constitution, and where the performance of governmental functions is brought into conflict with specific constitutional restrictions, there must, when that is possible, be reasonable accommodation between them so as to preserve the essentials of both and that it is the function of courts to determine whether such accommodation is reasonably possible. In the cases just mentioned the Court was of opinion that there were ways enough to secure the legitimate state end without infringing the asserted immunity, or that the inconvenience caused by the inability to secure that end satisfactorily through other means, did not outweigh freedom of speech or religion. So here, even if we believe that such compulsions will contribute to national unity, there are other ways to teach loyalty and patriotism which are the sources of national unity, than by compelling the pupil to affirm that which he does not believe and by commanding a form of affirmance which violates his religious convictions. Without recourse to such compulsion the state is free to compel attendance at school and require teaching by instruction and study of all in our history and in the structure and organization of our government, including the guaranties of civil liberty which tend to inspire patriotism and love of country. I cannot say that government here is deprived of any interest or function which it is entitled to maintain at the expense of the protection of civil liberties by requiring it to resort to the alternatives which do not coerce an affirmation of belief.

The guaranties of civil liberty are but guaranties of freedom of the human mind and spirit and of reasonable freedom and opportunity to express them. They presuppose the right of the individual to hold such opinions as he will and to give them reasonably free expression, and his freedom, and that of the state as well, to teach and persuade others by the communication of ideas. The very essence of the liberty which they guaranty is the freedom of the individual from compulsion as to what he shall think and what he shall say, at least where the compulsion is to bear false witness to his religion. If these guaranties are to have any meaning they must, I think, be deemed to withhold from the state any authority to compel belief or the expression of it where that expression violates religious convictions, whatever may be the legislative view of the desirability of such compulsion.

History teaches us that there have been but few infringements of personal liberty by the state which have not been justified, as they are here, in the name of righteousness and the public good, and few which have not been directed, as they are now, at politically helpless minorities. The framers were not unaware that under the system which they created most governmental curtailments of personal liberty would have the support of a legislative judgment that the public interest would be better served by its curtailment than by its constitutional protection. I cannot conceive that in prescribing, as limitations upon the powers of government, the freedom of the mind and spirit secured by the explicit guaranties of freedom of speech and religion, they intended or rightly could have left any latitude for a legislative judgment that the compulsory expression of belief which violates religious convictions would better serve the public interest than their protection. The Constitution may well elicit expressions of loyalty to it and to the government which it created, but it does not command such expressions or otherwise give any indication that compulsory expressions of loyalty play any such part in our scheme of government as to override the constitutional protection of freedom of speech and religion. And while such expressions of loyalty, when voluntarily given, may promote national unity, it is quite another matter to say that their compulsory expression by children in violation of their own and their parents' religious convictions can be regarded as playing so important a part in our national unity as to leave school boards free to exact it despite the constitutional guarantee of freedom of religion. The very terms of the Bill of Rights preclude, it seems to me, any reconciliation of such compulsions with the constitutional guaranties by a legislative declaration that they are more important to the public welfare than the Bill of Rights.

But even if this view be rejected and it is considered that there is some scope for the determination by legislatures whether the citizen shall be compelled to give public expression of such sentiments contrary to his religion, I am not persuaded that we should refrain from passing upon the legislative judgment "as long as the remedial channels of the democratic process remain open and unobstructed." This seems to me no less than the surrender of the constitutional protection of the liberty of small minorities to the popular will. We have previously pointed to the importance of a searching judicial inquiry into the legislative judgment in situations where prejudice against discrete and insular minorities may tend to curtail the operation of those political processes ordinarily to be relied on to protect minorities. See United States v. Carolene Products Co., 304 U. S. 144, 152, note 4. And until now we have not hesitated similarly to scrutinize legislation restricting the civil liberty of racial and religious minorities although no political process was affected. Meyer v. Nebraska, 262 U. S. 390; Pierce v. Society of Sisters, supra; Farrington v. Tokushige, 273 U. S. 284. Here we have such a small minority entertaining in good faith a religious belief, which is such a departure from the usual course of human conduct, that most persons are disposed to regard it with little toleration or concern. In such circumstances careful scrutiny of legislative efforts to secure conformity of belief and opinion by a compulsory affirmation of the desired belief, is especially needful if civil rights are to receive any protection. Tested by this standard, I am not prepared to say that the right of this small and helpless minority, including children having a strong religious conviction, whether they understand its nature or not, to refrain from an expression obnoxious to their religion, is to be overborne by the interest of the state in maintaining discipline in the schools.

The Constitution expresses more than the conviction of the people that democratic processes must be preserved at all costs. It is also an expression of faith and a command that freedom of mind and spirit must be preserved, which government must obey, if it is to adhere to that justice and moderation without which no free government can exist. For this reason it would seem that legislation which operates to repress the religious freedom of small minorities, which is admittedly within the scope of the protection of the Bill of Rights, must at least be subject to the same judicial scrutiny as legislation which we have recently held to infringe the constitutional liberty of religious and racial minorities.

With such scrutiny I cannot say that the inconveniences which may attend some sensible adjustment of school discipline in order that the religious convictions of these children may be spared, presents a problem so momentous or pressing as to outweigh the freedom from compulsory violation of religious faith which has been thought worthy of constitutional protection.

Board of Education v. Barnette

In Board of Education v. Barnette, 319 U. S. 624 (1943) the Gobitis case was overruled. Mr. Justice Jackson, for the majority, followed closely the direction indicated in Mr. Justice Stone's dissenting opinion in the Gobitis case. One phase of the issue received new emphasis, however, in the following portion of Mr. Justice Jackson's opinion:

In weighing arguments of the parties it is important to distinguish between the due process clause of the Fourteenth Amendment as an instrument for transmitting the principles of the First Amendment and those cases in which it is applied for its own sake. The test of legislation which collides with the Fourteenth Amendment, because it also collides with the principles of the First, is much more definite than the test when only the Fourteenth is involved. Much of the vagueness of the due process clause disappears when the specific prohibitions of the First become its standard. The right of a State to regulate, for example, a public utility may well include, so far as the due process test is concerned, power to impose all of the restrictions which a legislature may have a "rational basis" for adopting. But freedoms of speech and of press, of assembly, and of worship may not be infringed on such slender grounds. They are susceptible of restriction only to prevent grave and immediate danger to interests which the State may lawfully protect. It is important to note that while it is the Fourteenth Amendment which bears directly upon the State it is the more specific limiting principles of the First Amendment that finally govern this case.

Nor does our duty to apply the Bill of Rights to assertions of official authority depend upon our possession of marked competence in the field where the invasion of rights occurs. True, the task of translating the majestic generalities of the Bill of Rights, conceived as part of the pattern of liberal government in the eighteenth century, into concrete restraints on officials dealing with the problems of the twentieth century, is one to disturb self-confidence. These principles grew in soil which also produced a philosophy that the individual was the center of society, that his liberty was attainable through mere absence of governmental restraints, and that government should be entrusted with few controls and only the mildest supervision over men's affairs. We must transplant these rights to a soil in which the laissez-faire concept or principle of non-interference has withered at least as to economic affairs, and social advancements are increasingly sought through closer integration of society and through expanded and strengthened governmental controls. These changed conditions often deprive precedents of reliability and cast us more than we would choose upon our own judgment. But we act in these matters not by authority of our competence but by force of our commissions. We cannot, because of modest estimates of our competence in such specialties as public education, withhold the judgment that history authenticates as the function of this Court when liberty is infringed.

Lastly, and this is the very heart of the Gobitis opinion, it reasons that "National unity is the basis of national security," that the authorities have "the right to select appropriate means for its attainment," and hence reaches the conclusion that such compulsory measures toward "national unity" are constitutional. Id. at 595. Upon the verity of this assumption depends our answer in this case.

National unity as an end which officials may foster by persuasion and example is not in question. The problem is whether under our Constitution compulsion as here employed is a permissible means for its achievement.

Struggles to coerce uniformity of sentiment in support of some end thought essential to their time and country have been waged by many good as well as by evil men. Nationalism is a relatively recent phenomenon but at other times and places the ends have been racial or territorial security, support of a dynasty or regime, and particular plans for saving souls. As first and moderate methods to attain unity have failed, those bent on its accomplishment must resort to an ever-increasing severity. As governmental pressure toward unity becomes greater, so strife becomes more bitter as to whose unity it shall be. Probably no deeper division of our people could proceed from any provocation than from finding it necessary to choose what doctrine and whose program public educational officials shall compel youth to unite in embracing. Ultimate futility of such attempts to compel coherence is the lesson of every such effort from the Roman drive to stamp out Christianity as a disturber of its pagan unity, the Inquisition, as a means to religious and dynastic unity, the Siberian exiles as a means to Russian unity, down to the fast failing efforts of our present totalitarian enemies. Those who begin coercive elimination of dissent soon find themselves exterminating dissenters. Compulsory unification of opinion achieves only the unanimity of the graveyard.

It seems trite but necessary to say that the First Amendment to our Constitution was designed to avoid these ends by avoiding these beginnings. There is no mysticism in the American concept of the State or of the nature or origin of its authority. We set up government by consent of the governed, and the Bill of Rights denies those in power any legal opportunity to coerce that consent. Authority here is to be controlled by public opinion, not public opinion by authority.

The case is made difficult not because the principles of its decision are obscure but because the flag involved is our own. Nevertheless, we apply the limitations of the Constitution with no fear that freedom to be intellectually and spiritually diverse or even contrary will disintegrate the social organization. To believe that patriotism will not flourish if patriotic ceremonies are voluntary and spontaneous instead of a compulsory routine is to make an unflattering estimate of the appeal of our institutions to free minds. We can have intellectual individualism and the rich cultural diversities that we owe to exceptional minds only at the price of occasional eccentricity and abnormal attitudes. When they are so harmless to others or to the State as those we deal with here, the price is not too great. But freedom to differ is not limited to things that do not matter much. That would be a mere shadow of freedom. The test of its substance is the right to differ as to things that touch the heart of the existing order. . .

In the course of his dissenting opinion in the Barnette case, Mr. Justice Frankfurter discussed the purposes of the First and Fourteenth Amendments in the following passage:

What one can say with assurance is that the history out of which grew constitutional provisions for religious equality and the writings of the great exponents of religious freedom - Jefferson, Madison, John Adams, Benjamin Franklin - are totally wanting in justification for a claim by dissidents of exceptional immunity from civic measures of general applicability, measures not in fact disguised assaults upon such dissident views. The great leaders of the American Revolution were determined to remove political support from every religious establishment. They put on an equality the different religious sects - Episcopalians, Presbyterians, Catholics, Baptists, Methodists, Quakers, Huguenots - which, as dissenters, had been under the heel of the various orthodoxies that prevailed in different colonies. So far as the state was concerned, there was to be neither orthodoxy nor heterodoxy. And so Jefferson and those who followed him wrote guaranties of religious freedom into our constitutions. Religious minorities as well as religious majorities were to be equal in the eyes of the political state. But Jefferson and the others also knew that minorities may disrupt society. It never would have occurred to them to write into the Constitution the subordination of the general civil authority of the state to sectarian scruples.

The constitutional protection of religious freedom terminated disabilities, it did not create new privileges. It gave religious equality, not civil immunity. Its essence is freedom from conformity to religious dogma, not freedom from conformity to law because of religious dogma. Religious loyalties may be exercised without hindrance from the state, not the state may not exercise that which except by leave of religious loyalties is within the domain of temporal power. Otherwise each individual could set up his own censor against obedience to laws conscientiously deemed for the public good by those whose business it is to makes laws.

The prohibition against any religious establishment by the government placed denominations on an equal footing - it assured freedom from support by the government to any mode of worship and the freedom of individuals to support any mode of worship. Any person may therefore believe or disbelieve what he pleases. He may practice what he will in his own house of worship or publicly within the limits of public order. But the lawmaking authority is not circumscribed by the variety of religious beliefs, otherwise the constitutional guaranty would be not a protection of the free exercise of religion but a denial of the exercise of legislation.

The essence of the religious freedom guaranteed by our Constitution is therefore this: no religion shall either receive the state's support or incur its hostility. Religion is outside the sphere of political government. This does not mean that all matters on which religious organizations or beliefs may pronounce are outside the sphere of government. Were this so, instead of the separation of church and state, there would be the subordination of the state on any matter deemed within the sovereignty of the religious conscience. Much that is the concern of temporal authority affects the spiritual interests of men. But it is not enough to strike down a non-discriminatory law that it may hurt or offend some dissident view. It would be too easy to cite numerous prohibitions and injunctions to which laws run counter if the variant interpretations of the Bible were made the tests of obedience of law. The validity of secular laws cannot be measured by their conformity to religious doctrines. It is only in a theocratic state that ecclesiastical doctrines measure legal right or wrong.

An act compelling profession of allegiance to a religion, no matter how subtly or tenuously promoted, is bad. But an act promoting good citizenship and national allegiance is within the domain of governmental authority and is therefore to be judged by the same considerations of power and of constitutionality as those involved in the many claims of immunity from civil obedience because of religious scruples.

That claims are pressed on behalf of sincere religious convictions does not of itself establish their constitutional validity. Nor does waving the banner of religious freedom relieve us from examining into the power

·e asked to deny the states. Otherwise the doctrine of separation of
:h and state, so cardinal in the history of this nation and for the
:y of our people, would mean not the disestablishment of a state
:h but the establishment of all churches and of all religious groups ...
'hen dealing with religious scruples we are dealing with an almost
erless variety of doctrines and beliefs entertained with equal sin-
y by the particular groups for which they satisfy man's needs in his
:on to the mysteries of the universe. There are in the United States
than 250 distinctive established religious denominations. In the
of Pennsylvania there are 120 of these, and in West Virginia as
as 65. But if religious scruples afford immunity from civic obedi-
to laws, they may be invoked by the religious beliefs of any individual
though he holds no membership in any sect or organized denomination.
inly this Court cannot be called upon to determine what claims of
:ience should be recognized and what should be rejected as satisfying
religion" which the Constitution protects. That would indeed resur-
:he very discriminatory treatment of religion which the Constitution
it forever to forbid. And so, when confronted with the task of con-
ing the claims of immunity from obedience to a law dealing with
affairs because of religious scruples, we cannot conceive religion
narrowly than in the terms in which Judge Augustus N. Hand recently
.cterized it:
It is unnecessary to attempt a definition of religion; the content of
:rm is found in the history of the human race and is incapable of com-
;ion into a few words. Religious belief arises from a sense of the in-
iacy of reason as a means of relating the individual to his fellowmen
) his universe ... (It) may justly be regarded as a response of the
.dual to an inward mentor, call it conscience or God, that is for many
ns at the present time the equivalent of what has always been thought
.gious impulse." United States v. Kauten, 133 F. 2d 703, 708.
onsider the controversial issue of compulsory Bible-reading in public
ls. The educational policies of the states are in great conflict over
and the state courts are divided in their decisions on the issue
ier the requirement of Bible-reading offends constitutional provisions
ıg with religious freedom. The requirement of Bible-reading has
justified by various state courts as an appropriate means of inculcat-
:hical precepts and familiarizing pupils with the most lasting expres-
of great English literature. Is this Court to overthrow such variant
educational policies by denying states the right to entertain such
ctions in regard to their school systems, because of a belief that the
James version is in fact a sectarian text to which parents of the
lic and Jewish faiths and of some Protestant persuasions may rightly
t to having their children exposed? On the other hand the religious
iences of some parents may rebel at the absence of any Bible-read-
the schools. See Washington ex rel. Clithero v. Showalter, 284 U.S.
Or is this Court to enter the old controversy between science and
on by unduly defining the limits within which a state may experiment
ts school curricula? The religious consciences of some parents may
ended by subjecting their children to the Biblical account of creation,

while another state may offend parents by prohibiting a teacher of biology that contradicts such Biblical account. Compare Scopes v. State, 154 Tenn. 105, 289 S. W. 363. What of conscientious objections to what is devoutly felt by parents to be the poisoning of impressionable minds of children by chauvinistic teaching of history? This is very far from a fanciful suggestion for in the belief of many thoughtful people nationalism is the seed-bed of war.

There are other issues in the offing which admonish us of the difficulties and complexities that confront states in the duty of administering their local school systems. All citizens are taxed for the support of public schools although this Court has denied the right of a state to compel all children to go to such schools and has recognized the right of parents to send children to privately maintained schools. Parents who are dissatisfied with the public schools thus carry a double educational burden. Children who go to public school enjoy in many states derivative advantages such as free textbooks, free lunch, and free transportation in going to and from school. What of the claims for equality of treatment of those parents who, because of religious scruples, cannot send their children to public schools? What of the claim that if the right to send children to privately maintained schools is partly an exercise of religious conviction, to render effective this right it should be accompanied by equality of treatment by the state in supplying free textbooks, free lunch, and free transportation to children who go to private schools? What of the claim that such grants are offensive to the cardinal constitutional doctrine of separation of church and state?

These questions assume increasing importance in view of the steady growth of parochial schools both in number and in population. I am not borrowing trouble by adumbrating these issues nor am I parading horrible examples of the consequences of today's decision. I am aware that we must decide the case before us and not some other case. But that does not mean that a case is dissociated from the past and unrelated to the future. We must decide this case with due regard for what went before and no less regard for what may come after. Is it really a fair construction of such a fundamental concept as the right freely to exercise one's religion that a state cannot choose to require all children who attend public school to make the same gesture of allegiance to the symbol of our national life because it may offend the conscience of some children, but that it may compel all children to attend public school to listen to the King James version although it may offend the consciences of their parents? And what of the larger issue of claiming immunity from obedience to a general civil regulation that has a reasonable relation to a public purpose within the general competence of the state? See Pierce v. Society of Sisters, 268 U. S. 510, 535. Another member of the sect now before us insisted that in forbidding her two little girls, aged nine and twelve, to distribute pamphlets Oregon infringed her and their freedom of religion in that the children were engaged in "preaching the gospel of God's Kingdom." A procedural technicality led to the dismissal of the case, but the problem remains. McSparran v. Portland, 318 U. S. 768.

These questions are not lightly stirred. They touch the most delicate issues and their solution challenges the best wisdom of political and religious statesmen. But it presents awful possibilities to try to encase the solution of these problems within the rigid prohibitions of unconstitutionality...

Everson v. Board of Education
330 U. S. 1 (1947)

A majority of the Supreme Court in a taxpayer's suit sustained the validity of the action of a New Jersey School Board which had reimbursed parents for payments which they had made for the transportation of their children to Catholic parochial schools. The majority of the Court was satisfied that the record did not show discrimination in favor of Catholics as against Protestants whose children attended private schools not conducted for profit. The opinion of Mr. Justice Black, for the majority, concluded with the following paragraph:

"The First Amendment has erected a wall between church and state. The wall must be kept high and impregnable. We could not approve the slightest breach. New Jersey has not breached it here."

Passages from the dissenting opinion of Mr. Justice Rutledge have already been reprinted, supra, p. 59. Other considerations than those discussed by Rutledge, J. were emphasized in the dissenting opinion of Mr. Justice Jackson, in which Frankfurter, J. concurred.

MR. JUSTICE JACKSON, dissenting.

I find myself, contrary to first impressions, unable to join in this decision. I have a sympathy, though it is not ideological, with Catholic citizens who are compelled by law to pay taxes for public schools, and also feel constrained by conscience and discipline to support other schools for their own children. Such relief to them as this case involves is not in itself a serious burden to taxpayers and I had assumed it to be as little serious in principle. Study of this case convinces me otherwise. The Court's opinion marshals every argument in favor of state aid and puts the case in its most favorable light, but much of its reasoning confirms my conclusions that there are no good grounds upon which to support the present legislation. In fact, the undertones of the opinion, advocating complete and uncompromising separation of Church from State, seem utterly discordant with its conclusion yielding support to their commingling in educational matters. The case which irresistibly comes to mind as the most fitting precedent is that of Julia who, according to Byron's reports, "whispering 'I will ne'er consent,' - consented" ...

Whether the taxpayer constitutionally can be made to contribute aid to parents of students because of their attendance at parochial schools depends upon the nature of those schools and their relation to the Church. The Constitution says nothing of education. It lays no obligation on the states to provide schools and does not undertake to regulate state systems of education if they see fit to maintain them. But they cannot, through school policy any more than through other means, invade rights secured to citizens by the Constitution of the United States. West Virginia State Board of Education v. Barnette, 319 U. S. 624. One of our basic rights is to be free of taxation to support a transgression of the constitutional command that the authorities "shall make no law respecting an establishment of religion, or prohibiting the free exercise thereof ..." U. S. Const. Amend. I; Cantwell v. Connecticut, 310 U. S. 296.

The function of the Church school is a subject on which this record is meager. It shows only that the schools are under superintendence of a priest and that "religion is taught as part of the curriculum." But we know that such schools are parochial only in name - they, in fact, represent a worldwide and age-old policy of the Roman Catholic Church. Under the rubric "Catholic Schools," the Canon Law of the Church, by which all Catholics are bound, provides:

"1215. Catholic children are to be educated in schools where not only nothing contrary to Catholic faith and morals is taught, but rather in schools where religious and moral training occupy the first place ... (Canon 1372.)"

"1216. In every elementary school the children must, according to their age, be instructed in Christian doctrine.

"The young people who attend the higher schools are to receive a deeper religious knowledge, and the bishops shall appoint priests qualified for such work by their learning and piety. (Canon 1373.)"

"1217. Catholic children shall not attend non-Catholic, indifferent, schools that are mixed, that is to say, schools open to Catholics and non-Catholics alike. The bishop of the diocese only has the right, in harmony with the instructions of the Holy See, to decide under what circumstances, and with what safeguards to prevent loss of faith, it may be tolerated that Catholic children go to such schools. (Canon 1374.)"

"1224. The religious teaching of youth in any schools is subject to the authority and inspection of the Church.

"The local Ordinaries have the right and duty to watch that nothing is taught contrary to faith or good morals, in any of the schools of their territory.

"They, moreover, have the right to approve the books of Christian doctrine and the teachers of religion, and to demand, for the sake of safeguarding religion and morals, the removal of teachers and books. (Canon 1381.)" (Woywod, Rev. Stanislaus, The New Canon Law, under imprimatur of Most Rev. Francis J. Spellman, Archbishop of New York and others, 1940).

It is no exaggeration to say that the whole historic conflict in temporal policy between the Catholic Church and non-Catholics comes to a focus in their respective school policies. The Roman Catholic Church, counseled by experience in many ages and many lands and with all sorts and conditions of men, takes what, from the viewpoint of its own progress and the success of its mission, is a wise estimate of the importance of education to religion. It does not leave the individual to pick up religion by chance. It relies on early and indelible indoctrination in the faith and order of the Church by the word and example of persons consecrated to the task.

Our public school, if not a product of Protestantism, at least is more consistent with it than with the Catholic culture and scheme of values. It is a relatively recent development dating from about 1840. It is organized on the premise that secular education can be isolated from all religious teaching so that the school can inculcate all needed temporal knowledge and also maintain a strict and lofty neutrality as to religion. The assumption is that after the individual has been instructed in worldly wisdom he will be better fitted to choose his religion. Whether such a disjunction is possible, and if possible whether it is wise, are questions I need not try to answer.

I should be surprised if any Catholic would deny that the parochial school is a vital, if not the most vital, part of the Roman Catholic Church. If put to the choice, that venerable institution, I should expect, would forego its whole service for mature persons before it would give up education of the young, and it would be a wise choice. Its growth and cohesion, discipline and loyalty, spring from its schools. Catholic education is the rock on which the whole structure rests, and to render tax aid to its Church school is indistinguishable to me from rendering the same aid to the Church itself.

It is of no importance in this situation whether the beneficiary of this expenditure of tax-raised funds is primarily the parochial school and incidentally the pupil, or whether the aid is directly bestowed on the pupil with indirect benefits to the school. The state cannot maintain a Church and it can no more tax its citizens to furnish free carriage to those who attend a Church. The prohibition against establishment of religion cannot be circumvented by a subsidy, bonus or reimbursement of expense to individuals for receiving religious instruction and indoctrination.

The Court, however, compares this to other subsidies and loans to individuals and says, "Nor does it follow that a law has a private rather than a public purpose because it provides that tax-raised funds will be paid to reimburse individuals on account of money spent by them in a way which furthers a public program. See Carmichael v. Southern Coal & Coke Co., 301 U. S. 495, 518." Of course, the state may pay out tax-raised funds to relieve pauperism, but it may not under our Constitution do so to induce or reward piety. It may spend funds to secure old age against want, but it may not spend funds to secure religion against skepticism. It may compensate individuals for loss of employment, but it cannot compensate them for adherence to a creed.

It seems to me that the basic fallacy in the Court's reasoning, which accounts for its failure to apply the principles it avows, is in ignoring the essentially religious test by which beneficiaries of this expenditure are selected. A policeman protects a Catholic, of course - but not because he is a Catholic; it is because he is a man and a member of our society. The fireman protects the Church school - but not because it is a Church school; it is because it is property, part of the assets of our society. Neither the fireman nor the policeman has to ask before he renders aid "Is this man or building identified with the Catholic Church?" But before these school authorities draw a check to reimburse for a student's fare they must ask just that question, and if the school is a Catholic one they may render aid because it is such, while if it is of any other faith or is run for profit, the help must be withheld. To consider the converse of the Court's reasoning will best disclose its fallacy. That there is no parallel between police and fire protection and this plan of reimbursement is apparent from the incongruity of the limitation of this Act if applied to police and fire service. Could we sustain an Act that said the police shall protect pupils on the way to or from public schools and Catholic schools but not while going to and coming from other schools, and firemen shall extinguish a blaze in public or Catholic school buildings but shall not put out a blaze in Protestant Church schools or private schools operated for profit? That is the true analogy to the case we have before us and I should think it pretty plain that such a scheme would not be valid.

The Court's holding is that this taxpayer has no grievance because the state has decided to make the reimbursement a public purpose and therefore we are bound to regard it as such. I agree that this Court has left, and always should leave to each state, great latitude in deciding for itself, and the light of its own conditions, what shall be public purposes in its scheme of things. It may socialize utilities and economic enterprises and make taxpayers' business out of what conventionally had been private business. It may make public business of individual welfare, health, education, entertainment or security. But it cannot make public business of religious worship or instruction, or of attendance at religious institutions of any character. There is no answer to the proposition, more fully expounded by Mr. Justice Rutledge, that the effect of the religious freedom Amendment to our Constitution was to take every form of propagation of religion out of the realm of things which could directly or indirectly be made public business and thereby be supported in whole or in part at Taxpayer's expense. That is a difference which the Constitution sets up between religion and almost every other subject matter of legislation, a difference which goes to the very root of religious freedom and which the Court is overlooking today. This freedom was first in the Bill of Rights because it was first in the forefathers' minds; it was set forth in absolute terms, and its strength is its rigidity. It was intended not only to keep the states' hands out of religion, but to keep religion's hands off the state, and, above all, to keep bitter religious controversy out of public life by denying to every denomination any advantage from getting control of public policy or the public purse. Those great ends I cannot but think are immeasurably compromised by today's decision.

This policy of our Federal Constitution has never been wholly pleasing to most religious groups. They all are quick to invoke its protections; they all are irked when they feel its restraints. This Court has gone a long way, if not an unreasonable way, to hold that public business of such paramount importance as maintenance of public order, protection of the privacy of the home, and taxation may not be pursued by a state in a way that even indirectly will interfere with religious proselyting. See dissent in Douglas v. Jeannette, 319 U. S. 157, 166; Murdock v. Pennsylvania, 319 U. S. 105; Martin v. Struthers, 319 U. S. 141; Jones v. Opelika, 316 U. S. 584, reversed on rehearing, 319 U. S. 103.

But we cannot have it both ways. Religious teaching cannot be a private affair when the state seeks to impose regulations which infringe on it indirectly, and a public affair when it comes to taxing citizens of one faith to aid another, or those of no faith to aid all. If these principles seem harsh in prohibiting aid to Catholic education, it must not be forgotten that it is the same Constitution that alone assures Catholics the right to maintain these schools at all when predominant local sentiment would forbid them. Pierce v. Society of Sisters, 268 U. S. 510. Nor should I think that those who have done so well without this aid would want to see this separation between Church and State broken down. If the state may aid these religious schools, it may therefore regulate them. Many groups have sought aid from tax funds only to find that it carried political controls with it. Indeed this Court has declared that "It is hardly lack of due process for the Government to regulate that which it subsidizes." Wickard v. Filburn, 317 U. S. 111, 131.

But in any event, the great purposes of the Constitution do not depend on the approval or convenience of those they restrain. I cannot read the history of the struggle to separate political from ecclesiastical affairs, well summarized in the opinion of Mr. Justice Rutledge in which I generally concur, without a conviction that the Court today is unconsciously giving the clock's hands a backward turn.

McCollum v. Board of Education
Supreme Court of the United States, 1948
333 U. S. 203

MR. JUSTICE BLACK delivered the opinion of the Court.

This case relates to the power of a state to utilize its tax-supported public school system in aid of religious instruction insofar as that power may be restricted by the First and Fourteenth Amendments to the Federal Constitution.

The appellant, Vashti McCollum, began this action for mandamus against the Champaign Board of Education in the Circuit Court of Champaign County, Illinois. Her asserted interest was that of a resident and taxpayer of Champaign and of a parent whose child was then enrolled in the Champaign public schools. Illinois has a compulsory education law which, with exceptions, requires parents to send their children, aged seven to sixteen, to its tax-supported public schools where the children are to remain in attendance during the hours when the schools are regularly in session. Parents who violate this law commit a misdemeanor punishable by fine unless the children attend private or parochial schools which meet educational standards fixed by the State. District boards of education are given general supervisory powers over the use of the public school buildings within the school districts. Ill. Rev. Stat. ch. 122, §§ 123, 301 (1943).

Appellant's petition for mandamus alleged that religious teachers, employed by private religious groups, were permitted to come weekly into the school buildings during the regular hours set apart for secular teaching, and then and there for a period of thirty minutes substitute their religious teaching for the secular education provided under the compulsory education law. The petitioner charged that this joint public-school religious-group program violated the First and Fourteenth Amendments to the United States Constitution. The prayer of her petition was that the Board of Education be ordered to "adopt and enforce rules and regulations prohibiting all instruction in and teaching of religious education in all public schools in Champaign School District Number 71, ... and in all public school houses and buildings in said district when occupied by public schools."

The board first moved to dismiss the petition on the ground that under

Illinois law appellant had no standing to maintain the action. This motion was denied. An answer was then filed, which admitted that regular weekly religious instruction was given during school hours to those pupils whose parents consented and that those pupils were released temporarily from their regular secular classes for the limited purpose of attending the religious classes. The answer denied that this coordinated program of religious instruction violated the State or Federal Constitution. Much evidence was heard, findings of fact were made, after which the petition for mandamus was denied on the ground that the school's religious instruction program violated neither the federal nor state constitutional provisions invoked by the appellant. On appeal the State Supreme Court affirmed. 396 Ill. 14, 71 N. E. 2d 161. Appellant appealed to this Court under 28 U.S.C. § 344 (a), and we noted probable jurisdiction on June 2, 1947 ...

Although there are disputes between the parties as to various inferences that may or may not properly be drawn from the evidence concerning the religious program, the following facts are shown by the record without dispute. In 1940 interested members of the Jewish, Roman Catholic, and a few of the Protestant faiths formed a voluntary association called the Champaign Council on Religious Education. They obtained permission from the Board of Education to offer classes in religious instruction to public school pupils in grades four to nine inclusive. Classes were made up of pupils whose parents signed printed cards requesting that their children be permitted to attend; they were held weekly, thirty minutes for the lower grades, forty-five minutes for the higher. The council employed the religious teachers at no expense to the school authorities, but the instructors were subject to the approval and supervision of the superintendent of schools. The classes were taught in three separate religious groups by Protestant teachers, Catholic priest, and a Jewish rabbi, although for the past several years there have apparently been no classes instructed in the Jewish religion. Classes were conducted in the regular classrooms of the school building. Students who did not choose to take the religious instruction were not released from public school duties; they were required to leave their classrooms and go to some other place in the school building for pursuit of their secular studies. On the other hand, students who were released from secular study for the religious instructions were required to be present at the religious classes. Reports of their presence or absence were to be made to their secular teachers.

The foregoing facts, without reference to others that appear in the record, show the use of tax-supported property for religious instruction and the close cooperation between the school authorities and the religious council in promoting religious education. The operation of the State's compulsory education system thus assists and is integrated with the program of religious instruction carried on by separate religious sects. Pupils compelled by law to go to school for secular education are released in part from their legal duty upon the condition that they attend the religious classes. This is beyond all question a utilization of the tax-established and tax-supported public school system to aid religious groups to spread their faith. And it falls squarely under the ban of the First Amendment (made applicable to the States by the Fourteenth) as we interpreted it in <u>Everson</u> v. <u>Board of Education</u>, 330 U. S. 1 ...

Recognizing that the Illinois program is barred by the First and Fourteenth Amendments if we adhere to the views expressed both by the majority and the minority in the Everson case, counsel for the respondents challenge those views as dicta and urge that we reconsider and repudiate them. They argue that historically the First Amendment was intended to forbid only government preference of one religion over another, not an impartial governmental assistance of all religions. In addition they ask that we distinguish or overrule our holding in the Everson case that the Fourteenth Amendment made the "establishment of religion" clause of the First Amendment applicable as a prohibition against the States. After giving full consideration to the arguments presented we are unable to accept either of these contentions.

To hold that a state cannot consistently with the First and Fourteenth Amendments utilize its public school system to aid any or all religious faiths or sects in the dissemination of their doctrines and ideals does not, as counsel urge, manifest a governmental hostility to religion or religious teachings. A manifestation of such hostility would be at war with our national tradition as embodied in the First Amendment's guaranty of the free exercise of religion. For the First Amendment rests upon the premise that both religion and government can best work to achieve their lofty aims if each is left free from the other within its respective sphere. Or, as we said in the Everson case, the First Amendment has erected a wall between Church and State which must be kept high and impregnable.

Here not only are the State's tax-supported public school buildings used for the dissemination of religious doctrines. The State affords sectarian groups an invaluable aid in that it helps to provide pupils for their religious classes through use of the State's compulsory public school machinery. This is not separation of Church and State.

The cause is reversed and remanded to the State Supreme Court for proceedings not inconsistent with this opinion.

Reversed and remanded.

MR. JUSTICE FRANKFURTER delivered the following opinion, in which Mr. Justice Jackson, Mr. Justice Rutledge and Mr. Justice Burton join.

We dissented in Everson v. Board of Education, 330 U. S. 1, because in our view the Constitutional principle requiring separation of Church and State compelled invalidation of the ordinance sustained by the majority. Illinois has here authorized the commingling of sectarian with secular instruction in the public schools. The Constitution of the United States forbids this ...

To understand the particular program now before us as a conscientious attempt to accommodate the allowable functions of Government and the special concerns of the Church within the framework of our Constitution and with due regard to the kind of society for which it was designed, we must put this Champaign program of 1940 in its historic setting. Traditionally, organized education in the Western world was Church education. It could hardly be otherwise when the education of children was primarily study of the Word and the ways of God. Even in the Protestant countries, where there was a less close identification of Church and State, the basis of education was largely the Bible, and its chief purpose inculcation of piety. To the extent that the State intervened, it used its authority to further aims of the Church.

The emigrants who came to these shores brought this view of education with them. Colonial schools certainly started with a religious orientation. When the common problems of the early settlers of the Massachusetts Bay Colony revealed the need for common schools, the object was the defeat of "one chief project of that old deluder, Satan, to keep men from the knowledge of the Scriptures." The Laws and Liberties of Massachusetts, 1648 edition (Cambridge 1929) 47.

The evolution of colonial education, largely in the service of religion, into the public school system of today is the story of changing conceptions regarding the American democratic society, of the functions of State-maintained education in such a society, and of the role therein of the free exercise of religion by the people. The modern public school derived from a philosophy of freedom reflected in the First Amendment. It is appropriate to recall that the Remonstrance of James Madison, an event basic in the history of religious liberty, was called forth by a proposal which involved support to religious education. See Mr. Justice Rutledge's opinion in the Everson case, supra, 330 U. S. at 36-37. As the momentum for popular education increased and in turn evoked strong claims for State support of religious education, contests not unlike that which in Virginia had produced Madison's Remonstrance appeared in various forms in other States. New York and Massachusetts provide famous chapters in the history that established dissociation of religious teaching from State-maintained schools. In New York, the rise of the common schools led, despite fierce sectarian opposition, to the barring of tax funds to church schools, and later to any school in which sectarian doctrine was taught. In Massachusetts, largely through the efforts of Horace Mann, all sectarian teachings were barred from the common school to save it from being rent by denominational conflict. The upshot of these controversies, often long and fierce, is fairly summarized by saying that long before the Fourteenth Amendment subjected the States to new limitations, the prohibition of furtherance by the State of religious instruction became the guiding principle, in law and feeling, of the American people. In sustaining Stepehn Girard's will, this Court referred to the inevitable conflicts engendered by matters "connected with religious polity" and particularly "in a country composed of such a variety of religious sects as our country." Vidal v. Girard's Executors, 2 How, 127, 198. That was more than one hundred years ago.

Separation in the field of education, then, was not imposed upon unwilling States by force of superior law. In this respect the Fourteenth Amendment merely reflected a principle then dominant in our national life. To the extent that the Constitution thus made it binding upon the States, the basis of the restriction is the whole experience of our people. Zealous watchfulness against fusion of secular and religious activities by Government itself, through any of its instruments but especially through its educational agencies, was the democratic response of the American community to the particular needs of a young and growing nations, unique in the composition of its people. A totally different situation elsewhere, as illustrated for instance by the English provisions for religious education in

State maintained schools, only serves to illustrate that free societies are not cast in one mould. See the Education Act of 1944, 7 and 8 Geo. VI, c. 31. Different institutions evolve from different historic circumstances ...

Enough has been said to indicate that we are dealing not with a full-blown principle, nor one having the definiteness of a surveyor's metes and bounds. But by 1875 the separation of public education from Church entanglements, of the State from the teaching of religion, was firmly established in the consciousness of the nation. In that year President Grant made his famous remarks to the Convention of the Army of the Tennessee: "Encourage free schools, and resolve that not one dollar appropriated for their support shall be appropriated to the support of any sectarian schools. Resolve that neither the State nor nation, nor both combined, shall support institutions of learning other than those sufficient to afford every child growing up in the land the opportunity of a good common-school education, unmixed with sectarian, pagan, or atheistical dogmas. Leave the matter of religion to the family altar, the church, and the private school, supported entirely by private contributions. Keep the church and the state forever separate." "The President's Speech at Des Moines," 22 Catholic World 433, 434-35 (1876).

So strong was this conviction, that rather than rest on the comprehensive prohibitions of the First and Fourteenth Amendments, President Grant urged that there be written into the United States Constitution particular elaborations, including a specific prohibition against the use of public funds for sectarian education, such as had been written into many State constitutions. By 1894, in urging the adoption of such a provision in the New York Constitution, Elihu Root was able to summarize a century of the nation's history: "It is not a question of religion, or of creed, or of party; it is a question of declaring and maintaining the great American principle of eternal separation between Church and State." Root, Addresses on Government and Citizenship, 137, 140. The extent to which this principle was deemed a presupposition of our Constitutional system is strikingly illustrated by the fact that every State admitted into the Union since 1876 was compelled by Congress to write into its constitution a requirement that it maintain a school system "free from sectarian control."

Prohibition of the commingling of sectarian and secular instruction in the public school is of course only half the story. A religious people was naturally concerned about the part of the child's education entrusted "to the family altar, the church, and the private school." The promotion of religious education took many forms. Laboring under financial difficulties and exercising only persuasive authority, various denominations felt handicapped in their task of religious education. Abortive attempts were therefore frequently made to obtain public funds for religious schools. But the major efforts of religious inculcation were a recognition of the principle of Separation by the establishment of church schools privately supported. Parochial schools were maintained by various denominations. These, however, were often beset by serious handicaps, financial and otherwise, so that the religious aims which they represented found other directions. There were experiments with vacation schools, with Saturday as well as Sunday schools. They all fell short of their purpose. It was urged that by appearing to make religion a one-day-a-week matter, the

Sunday School, which acquired national acceptance, tended to relegate the child's religious education, and thereby his religion, to a minor role not unlike the enforced piano lesson.

Out of these inadequate efforts evolved the week-day church school, held on one or more afternoons a week after the close of the public school. But children continued to be children; they wanted to play when school was out, particularly when other children were free to do so. Church leaders decided that if the week-day church schools was to succeed, a way had to be found to give the child his religious education during what the child conceived to be his "business hours."

The initiation of the movement may fairly be attributed to Dr. George U. Wenner. The underlying assumption of his proposal, made at the Interfaith Conference on Federation held in New York City in 1905, was that the public school unduly monopolized the child's time and that the churches were entitled to their share of it. This, the schools should "release." Accordingly, the Federation, citing the example of the Third Republic of France, urged that upon the request of their parents children be excused from public school on Wednesday afternoon, so that the churches could provide "Sunday school on Wednesday." This was to be carried out on church premises under church authority. Those not desiring to attend church schools would continue their normal classes. Lest these public school classes unfairly compete with the church education, it was requested that the school authorities refrain from scheduling courses or activities of compelling interest or importance.

The proposal aroused considerable opposition and it took another decade for a "released time" schemed to become part of a public school system. Gary, Indiana, inaugurated the movement. At a time when industrial expansion strained the communal facilities of the city, superintendent of Schools Wirt suggested a fuller use of the school buildings. Building on theories which had become more or less current, he also urged that education was more than instruction in a classroom. The school was only one of several educational agencies. The library, the playground, the home, the church, all have their function in the child's proper unfolding. Accordingly, Wirt's plan sought to rotate the schedules of the children during the school-day so that some were in class, others were in the library, still others in the playground. And some, he suggested to the leading ministers of the City, might be released to attend religious classes if the churches of the City cooperated and provided them. They did, in 1914, and thus was "released time" begun. The religious teaching was held on church premises and the public schools had no hand in the conduct of these church schools. They did not supervise the choice of instructors or the subject matter taught. Nor did they assume responsibility for the attendance, conduct or achievement of the child in a church school; and he received no credit for it. The period of attendance in the religious schools would otherwise have been a play period for the child, with the result that the arrangement did not cut into public school instruction or truly affect the activities or feelings of the children who did not attend the church schools.

From such a beginning "released time" has attained substantial proportions. In 1914-15, under the Gary program, 619 pupils left the public schools for the church schools during one period a week. According to responsible figures almost 2,000,000 in some 2,200 communities participated in "released time" programs during 1947. A movement of such scope indicates the importance of the problem to which the "released time" programs are directed. But to the extent that aspects of these programs are open to Constitutional objection, the more extensively the movement operates, the more ominous the breaches in the wall of separation ...

Religious education so conducted on school time and property is patently woven into the working scheme of the school. The Champaign arrangement thus presents powerful elements of inherent pressure by the school system in the interest of religious sects. The fact that this power has not been used to discriminate is beside the point. Separation is a requirement to abstain from fusing functions of Government and of religious sects, not merely to treat them all equally. That a child is offered an alternative may reduce the constraint; it does not eliminate the operation of influence by the school in matters sacred to conscience and outside the school's domain. The law of imitation operates, and non-conformity is not an outstanding characteristic of children. The result is an obvious pressure upon children to attend. Again, while the Champaign school population represents only a fraction of the more than two hundred and fifty sects of the nation, not even all the practicing sects in Champaign are willing or able to provide religious instruction. The children belonging to these non-participating sects will thus have inculcated in them a feeling of separatism when the school should be the training ground for habits of community, or they will have religious instruction if a faith which is not that of their parents. As a result, the public school system of Champaign actively furthers inculcation in the religious tenets of some faiths, and in the process sharpens the consciousness of religious differences at least among some of the children committed to its care. These are consequences not amenable to statistics. But they are precisely the consequences against which the Constitution was directed when it prohibited the Government common to all from becoming embroiled, however innocently, in the destructive religious conflicts of which the history of even this country records some dark pages ...

Separation means separation, not something less. Jefferson's metaphor in describing the relation between Church and State speaks of a "wall of separation," not of a fine line easily overstepped. The public school is at once the symbol of our democracy and the most pervasive means for promoting our common destiny. In no activity of the State is it more vital to keep out divisive forces than in its schools, to avoid confusing, not to say fusing, what the Constitution sought to keep strictly apart. "The great American principle of eternal separation" - Elihu Root's phrase bears repetition - is one of the vital reliances of our Constitutional system for assuring unities among our people stronger than our diversities. It is the Court's duty to enforce this principle in its full integrity.

We renew our conviction that "we have staked the very existence of our country on the faith that complete separation between the state and religion is best for the state and best for religion." Everson v. Board of

Education, 330 U. S. at 59. If nowhere else, in the relation between Church and State, "good fences made good neighbors."

MR. JUSTICE REED, dissenting.

The decisions reversing the judgment of the Supreme Court of Illinois interpret the prohibition of the First Amendment against the establishment of religion, made effective as to the states by the Fourteenth Amendment, to forbid pupils of the public schools electing, with the approval of their parents, courses in religious education. The courses are given, under the school laws of Illinois as approved by the Supreme Court of that state, by lay or clerical teachers supplied and directed by an interdenominational, local council of religious education. The classes are held in the respective school buildings of the pupils at study or released time periods so as to avoid conflict with recitations. The teachers and supplies are paid for by the interdenominational group. As I am convinced that this interpretation of the First Amendment is erroneous, I feel impelled to express the reasons for my disagreement. By directing attention to the many instances of close association of church and state in American society and be recalling that many of these relations are so much a part of our tradition and culture that they are accepted without more, this dissent may help in an appraisal of the meaning of the clause of the First Amendment concerning the establishment of religion and of the reasons which lead to the approval or disapproval of the judgment below ...

The phrase "an establishment of religion" may have been intended by Congress to be aimed only at a state church. When the First Amendment was pending in Congress in substantially its present form, "Mr. Madison said, he apprehended the meaning of the words to be, that Congress should not establish a religion, and enforce the legal observation of it by law, nor compel men to worship God in any manner contrary to their conscience." Passing years, however, have brought about acceptance of a broader meaning, although never until today, I believe, has this Court widened its interpretation to any such degree as holding that recognition of the interest of our nation in religion, through the granting, to qualified representatives of the principal faiths, of opportunity to present religion as an optional, extracurricular subject during released school time in public school buildings, was equivalent to an establishment of religion. A reading of the general statements of eminent statesmen of former days, referred to in the opinions in this case and in Everson v. Board of Education, supra, will show that circumstances such as those in this case were far from the minds of the authors. The words and spirit of those statements may be wholeheartedly accepted without in the least impugning the judgment of the State of Illinois.

Mr. Jefferson, as one of the founders of the University of Virginia, a school which from its establishment in 1819 has been wholly governed, managed and controlled by the State of Virginia, was faced with the same problem that is before this Court today: the question of the constitutional limitation upon religious education in public schools. In his annual report

---

[1] A concurring opinion of Mr. Justice Jackson is omitted.

as Rector, to the President and Directors of the Literary Fund, dated October 7, 1822, approved by the Visitors of the University of whom Mr. Madison was one, Mr. Jefferson set forth his views at some length. These suggestions of Mr. Jefferson were adopted and ch. II, § 1, of the Regulations of the University of October 4, 1824, provided that: "Should the religious sects of this State, or any of them, according to the invitation held out to them, establish within, or adjacent to, the precincts of the University, schools for instruction in the religion of their sect, the students of the University will be free, and expected to attend religious worship at the establishment of their respective sects, in the morning, and in time to meet their school in the University at its stated hour."

Thus, the "wall of separation between church and State" that Mr. Jefferson built at the University which he founded did not exclude religious education from that school. The difference between the generality of his statements on the separation of church and state and the specificity of his conclusions on education are considerable. A rule of law should not be drawn from a figure of speech.

Mr. Madison's Memorial and Remonstrance against Religious Assessments, relied upon by the dissenting Justices in Everson, is not applicable here. Mr. Madison was one of the principal opponents in the Virginia General Assembly of A Bill Establishing a Provision for Teachers of the Christian Religion. The monies raised by the taxing section of that bill were to be appropriated "by the Vestries, Elders, or Directors of each religious society, ... to a provision for a Minister or Teacher of the Gospel of their denomination, or the providing places of diving worship, and to none other use whatsoever ..." The conclusive legislative struggle over this act took place in the fall of 1785, before the adoption of the Bill of Rights. The Remonstrance had been issued before the General Assembly convened and was instrumental in the final defeat of the act, which died in committee. Throughout the Remonstrance, Mr. Madison speaks of the "establishment" sought to be effected by the act. It is clear from its historical setting and its language that the Remonstrance was a protest against an effort by Virginia to support Christian sects by taxation. Issues similar to those raised by the instant cases were not discussed. Thus, Mr. Madison's approval of Mr. Jefferson's report as Rector gives, in my opinion, a clearer indication of his views on the constitutionality of religious education in public schools than his general statements on a different subject.

This Court summarized the amendment's accepted reach into the religious field, as I understand its scope, in Everson v. Board of Education, supra. The Court's opinion quotes the gist of the Court's reasoning in Everson. I agree, as there stated, that none of our governmental entities can "set up a church." I agree that they cannot "aid" all or any religious or prefer one "over another." But "aid" must be understood as a purposeful assistance directly to the church itself or to some religious group or organization doing religious work of such a character that it may fairly be said to be performing ecclesiastical functions. "Prefer" must give an advantage to one "over another." I agree that pupils cannot "be released in part from their legal duty" of school attendance upon condition that they attend religious classes. But as Illinois has held that it is within the discretion of the School Board to permit absence from school for religious instruction no legal duty of school attendance is violated. 396 Ill. 14, 71 N. E. 2d 161. If the sentence in the Court's opinion, concerning the pupils' release from legal duty, is intended to mean that the Constitution forbids a school to excuse a pupil from secular control during school hours to attend voluntarily a class in religious education, whether in or out of school buildings, I disagree. Of course, no tax can be levied to support organizations intended "to teach or practice religion." I agree too that the state cannot influence one toward religion against his will or punish him for his beliefs. Champaign's religious education course does none of these things.

It seems clear to me that the "aid" referred to by the Court in the Everson case could not have been those incidental advantages that religious bodies, with other groups similarly situated, obtain as a by-product of organized society. This explains the well-known fact that all churches receive "aid" from government in the form of freedom from taxation. The Everson decision itself justified the transportation of children to church schools by New Jersey for safety reasons. It accords with Cochran v. Louisiana State Board of Education, 281 U. S. 370, where this Court upheld a free textbook statute of Louisiana against a charge that it aided private schools on the ground that the books were for the education of the children, not to aid religious schools. Likewise the National School Lunch Act aids all school children attending tax-exempt schools. In Bradfield v. Roberts, 175 U. S. 291, this Court held proper the payment of money by the Federal Government to build an addition to a hospital, chartered by individuals who were members of a Roman Catholic sisterhood, and operated under the auspices of the Roman Catholic Church. This was done over the objection that it aided the establishment of religion. While obviously in these instances the respective churches, in a certain sense, were aided, this Court has never held that sud "aid" was in violation of the First or Fourteenth Amendment.

Well-recognized and long-established practices support the validity of the Illinois statute here in question. That statute, as construed in this case, is comparable to those in many states. All differ to some extent. New York may be taken as a fair example. In many states the program is under the supervision of a religious council composed of delegates who are themselves communicants of various faiths. As is shown by Bradfield v. Roberts, supra, the fact that the members of the council have religious affilications is not significant. In some, instruction is given outside of the school buildings; in others, within these buildings. Metropolitan centers like New York usually would have available quarters convenient to schools. Unless smaller cities and rural communities use the school building at times that do not interfere with recitations, they may be compelled to give up religious education. I understand that pupils not taking religious education usually are given other work of a secular nature within the schools. Since all these states use the facilities of the schools to aid the religious education to some extent, their desire to permit religious education to school children is thwarted by this Court's judgment. Under it, as I understand its language, children cannot be released or dismissed from school to attend classes in religion while other children must remain to pursue secular education. Teachers cannot keep the records as to which pupils are to be dismissed and which retained. To do so is said to be an "aid" in establishing religion; the use of public money for religion.

Cases running into the scores have been in the state courts of last resort that involved religion and the schools. Except where the exercises with religious significance partook of the ceremonial practice of sects or groups, their constitutionality has been generally upheld. Illinois itself promptly struck down as violative of its own constitution required exercises partaking of a religious ceremony. People ex rel. Ring v. Board of Education, 245 Ill. 334, 92 N. E. 251. In that case compulsory religious exercises - a reading from the King James Bible, the Lord's Prayer and the singing of hymns - were forbidden as "worship services." In this case, the Supreme Court of Illinois pointed out that in the Ring case, the activities in the school were ceremonial and compulsory; in this, voluntary and educational. 396 Ill. 14, 20-21, 71 N. E. 2d 161, 164.

The practices of the federal government offer many examples of this kind of "aid" by the state to religion. The Congress of the United States has a chaplain for each House who daily invokes divine blessings and guidance for the proceedings. The armed forces have commissioned chaplains from early days. They conduct the public services in accordance with the liturgical requirements of their respective faiths, ashore and afloat, employing for the purpose property belonging to the United States and dedicated to the services of religion. Under the Servicemen's Readjustment Act of 1944, eligible veterans may receive training at government expense for the ministry in denominational schools. The schools of the District of Columbia have opening exercises which include a reading from the Bible without note or comment, and the Lord's prayer.

In the United States Naval Academy and the United States Military Academy, schools wholly supported and completely controlled by the federal government, there are a number of religious activities. Chaplains are attached to both schools. Attendance at church services on Sunday is compulsory at both the Military and Naval Academies. At West Point the Protestant services are held in the Cadet Chapel, the Catholic in the Catholic Chapel, and the Jewish in the Old Cadet Chapel; at Annapolis only Protestant services are held on the reservation, midshipmen of other religious persuasions attend the churches of the city of Annapolis. These facts indicate that both schools since their earliest beginnings have maintained and enforced a pattern of participation in formal worship.

With the general statements in the opinions concerning the constitutional requirement that the nation and the states, by virtue of the First and Fourteenth Amendments, may "make no law respecting an establishment of religion," I am in agreement. But, in the light of the meaning given to those words by the precedents, customs, and practices which I have detailed above, I cannot agree with the Court's conclusion that when pupils compelled by law to go to school for secular education are released from school so as to attend the religious classes, churches are unconstitutionally aided. Whatever may be the wisdom of the arrangement as to the use of the school buildings made with the Champaign Council of Religious Education, it is clear to me that past practice shows such cooperation between the schools and a non-ecclesiastical body is not forbidden by the First

Amendment. When actual church services have always been permitted on government property, the mere use of the school buildings by a non-sectarian group for religious education ought not to be condemned as an establishment of religion. For a non-sectarian organization to give the type of instruction here offered cannot be said to violate our rule as to the establishment of religion by the state. The prohibition of enactments respecting the establishment of religion do not bar every friendly gesture between church and state. It is not an absolute prohibition against every conceivable situation where the two may work together, any more than the other provisions of the First Amendment - free speech, free press - are absolutes. If abuses occur, such as the use of the instruction hour for sectarian purposes, I have no doubt, in view of the Ring case, that Illinois will promptly correct them. If they are of a kind that tend to the establishment of a church or interfere with the free exercise of religion, this Court is open for a review of any erroneous decision. This Court cannot be too cautious in upsetting practices embedded in our society by many years of experience. A state is entitled to have great leeway in its legislation when dealing with the important social problems of its population. A definite violation of legislative limits must be established. The Constitution should not be stretched to forbid national customs in the way courts act to reach arrangements to avoid federal taxation. Devotion to the great principle of religious liberty should not lead us into a rigid interpretation of the constitutional guarantee that conflicts with accepted habits of our people. This is an instance where, for me, the history of past practices is determinative of the meaning of a constitutional clause, not a decorous intoduction to the study of its text. The judgment should be affirmed.

<u>Zorach et al</u>. v. <u>Clauson et al</u>.
Court of Appeals of New York, 1951
100 N.E.2d 463

FROESSEL, Judge

This appeal challenges the constitutionality of the long-standing "released time" program in New York City, whereby parents may withdraw their children from the public schools one hour a week to receive religious instruction in the faith of their acceptance.

For many years released time existed in this State without express statutory authority. Then in 1940, the State Legislature, by an almost unanimous vote and with the approval of Governor Lehman, 1940 Public Papers of Governor Lehman, p. 328, added, L.1940, ch. 305 to the Education Law, which governs, among other things, the attendance of minors in schools, the following provision: "Absence for religious observance and education shall be permitted under rules that the commissioner [of education] shall establish."

Pursuant to this provision, which is now found in paragraph b of subdivision 1 of section 3210 of the Education Law, Consol. Laws, c. 16, the State Commissioner of Education has promulgated the following rules Regulations of Comr. of Educ., art. 17, § 154. 1 N.Y. Official Compilation of Codes, Rules and Regulations, p. 683:

"1. Absence of a pupil from school during school hours for religious observance and education to be had outside the school building and grounds will be excused upon the request in writing signed by the parent of guardian of the pupil.

"2. The courses in religious observance and education must be maintained and operated by or under the control of duly constituted religious bodies.

"3. Pupils must be registered for the courses and a copy of the registration filed with the local public school authorities.

"4. Reports of attendance of pupils upon such courses shall be filed with the principal or teacher at the end of each week.

"5. Such absence shall be for not more than one hour each week at the close of a session at a time to be fixed by the local school authorities.

"6. In the event that more than one school for religious observance and education is maintained in any district, the hour for absence for each particular public school in such district shall be the same for all such religious schools."

Additional rules have been established by the New York City Board of Education:

"1. A program for religious instruction may be initiated by any religious organization, in cooperation with the parents of pupils concerned. There will be no announcement of any kind in the public schools relative to the program.

"2. When a religious organization is prepared to initiate a program for religious instruction, the said organization will notify parents to enroll their children with the religious organization, and will issue to each enrolled pupil a card countersigned by the parent and addressed to the principal of the public school, requesting the release of the pupil from school for the purpose of religious instruction at a specific location. The said cards will be filed in the office of the public school as a record of pupils entitled to be excused, and will not be available or used for any other purpose.

"3. Religious organizations, in cooperation with parents, will assume full responsibility for attendance at the religious center and will file with the school principal, weekly, a card attendance record and in cases of absence from religious instruction, a statement of the reason therefor.

"4. Upon the presentation of a proper request as above prescribed, pupils of any grade will be dismissed from school for the last hour of the day's session on one day of each week to be designated by the Superintendent of Schools: A different day may be designated for each borough.

"5. Pupils released for religious instruction will be dismissed from school in the usual way and the school authorities have no responsibility beyond that assumed in regular dismissals.

"6. There shall be no comment by any principal or teacher on the attendance or non-attendance of any pupil upon religious instruction."

Appellants, parents of children attending public schools in New York City who do not avail themselves of this program and are in nowise obliged to do so, challenge by this article 78 proceeding the constitutionality of the foregoing statute and rules in toto upon the ground that they violate the prohibition against laws respecting an establishment of religion contained in the First Amendment of the Federal Constitution, as applied to the States by the Fourteenth Amendment, and prohibit the free exercise of religion in violation of the First and Fourteenth Amendments of the Federal Constitution and section 3 of article I of our State Constitution. The courts below have denied them relief and dismissed the proceeding.

In support of their contention, appellants rely primarily on People of State of Illinois ex rel. McCollum v. Board of Education of School Dist. No. 71, 333 U.S. 203, 68 S.Ct. 461, 92 L.Ed. 648. There, a local board of education in Champaign County, Illinois, participated in a released time program which differed radically from the one before us. There was no underlying State enabling act. Religious training took place in the school buildings and on school property. The place for instruction was designated by the school authorities. Pupils taking religious instruction were segregated by school authorities according to faiths. School officials supervised and approved the religious teachers. Pupils were solicited in school buildings for religious instruction. Registration cards were distributed by the school, and in one case printed by the school. None of these factors is present in the case before us, and, accordingly, the Supreme Court's holding that the Champaign released time program was constitutionally invalid is not controlling here.

In the New York City program there is neither supervision nor approval of religious teachers and no solicitation of pupils or distribution of cards. The religious instruction must be outside the school building and grounds. There must be no announcement of any kind in the public schools relative to the program and no comment by any principal or teacher on the attendance or nonattendance of any pupil upon religious instruction. All that the school does besides excusing the pupil is to keep a record—which is not available for any other purpose—in order to see that the excuses are not taken advantage of and the school deceived, which is, of course, the same procedure the school would take in respect of absence for any other reason.

It is manifest that the McCollum case, supra, is not a holding that all released time programs are per se unconstitutional. The Supreme Court's decision is limited to the fact situation before it. Thus, Mr. Justice Black, writing for the court, reviewed the evidence so far as undisputed and stated, 333 U.S. at page 209, 68 S.Ct. at page 464, that the "foregoing facts" (emphasis supplied) "show the use of tax-supported property for religious instruction and the close cooperation between the school authorities and the religious council in promoting religious education."

In the instant case, there is no "use" of tax-supported "property or credit or any public money" "directly or indirectly" "in aid of maintenance" of religious instruction, People ex rel. Lewis v. Graves, 245 N.Y. 195, 198, motion for reargument denied 245 N.Y. 620, affirming 219 App.Div. 233, affirming 127 Misc. 135, and there is no such co-operation as in the McCollum case, supra, between the school authorities and the religious committee in promoting religious education.

Other Justices who wrote in the McCollum case, supra, were even more explicit in placing boundaries on the determination. Mr. Justice Frankfurter, in a concurring opinion in which three other Justices joined, stated:

"Of course, 'released time' as a generalized conception, undefined by differentiating particularities, is not an issue for Constitutional adjudication." 333 U.S. at page 225.

"The substantial differences among arrangements lumped together as 'released time' emphasize the importance of detailed analysis of the facts to which the Constitutional test of Separation is to be applied. How does 'released time' operate in Champaign?" 333 U.S. at page 226.

"We do not consider, as indeed we could not, school programs not before us which, though colloquially characterized as 'released time,' present situations differing in aspects that may well be constitutionally crucial. Different forms which 'released time' has taken during more than thirty years of growth include programs which, like that before us, could not withstand the test of the Constitution; others may be found unexceptionable." 333 U.S. at page 231, 68 S.Ct. at page 475.

Mr. Justice Jackson, in addition to agreeing with the limitations expressed by Mr. Justice Frankfurter, added reservations of his own, and stated: "we should place some bounds on the demands for interference with local schools that we are empowered or willing to entertain", 333 U.S. at page 232, 68 S.Ct. at page 475, and that "it is important that we circumscribe our decision with some care." 333 U.S. at page 234, 68 S.Ct. at page 476.

Mr. Justice Reed, who dissented from the court's holding, pointed out 333 U.S. at pages 239-240, 68 S.Ct. at page 479, that expressions in the opinions of his colleagues "seem to leave open for further litigation variations from the Champaign plan." Thus, in addition to the reference in the court's opinion to the "foregoing facts" of the Champaign plan as showing is unconstitutionality, we have five other Justices expressly agreeing that released time as such is not unconstitutional.

Binding precedent must therefore be found in our own decision of nearly twenty-five years ago in People ex rel. Lewis v. Graves, supra, which involved a released time program in the city of White Plains. Such program, except for the absence of a State enabling act, was substantially the same as the one now in issue. Judge Pound, writing for a unanimous court, its other distinguished members having been Chief Judge Cardozo, and Judges Crane, Andrews, Lehman, Kellogg and O'Brien, there said, 245 N.Y. at pages 198, 199.

"A child otherwise regular in attendance may be excused for a portion of the entire time during which the schools are in session, to the extent at least of half an hour in each week, to take outside instruction in music or dancing without violating the provisions of the Compulsory Education Law, either in letter or spirit. Otherwise the word 'regularly' as used in the statute would be superfluous. Practical administration of the public schools calls for some elasticity in this regard and vests some discretion in the school authorities. Neither the Constitution nor the law discriminates against religion. Denominational religion is merely put in its proper place outside of public aid or support. * * *

"The separation of the public school system from religious denominational instruction is thus complete. Jealous sectaries may view with alarm the introduction in the schools of religious teaching which to the unobservant eye is but faintly tinted with denominationalism. Eternal vigilance is the price of constitutional rights. But it is impossible to say, as matter of law, that the slightest infringement of constitutional right or abuse of statutory requirement has been shown in this case"...

No metaphorical "wall" that mere words can build ever precisely and mathematically delineates a constitutional right. The Supreme Court has recognized, in a religious freedom case, that to "make accommodation between these freedoms" guaranteed by the First Amendment and "an exercise of state authority" is always "delicate", Prince v. Commonwealth of Massachusetts, 321 U.S. 158, 165. Such freedoms are not absolute, Prince v. Commonwealth of Massachusetts, supra, 321 U.S. at page 166. Dennis v. United States, 341 U.S. 494; Breard v. City of Alexandria, 341 U.S. 622; Schenck v. United States, 249 U.S. 47. Numerous situations involving some incidental benefit to religion have been found constitutionally unexceptionable, see, e. g., Everson v. Board of Education of Ewing Tp., 330 U.S. 1; Cochran v. Louisiana State Board of Education, 281 U.S. 370; Bradfield v. Roberts, 175 U.S. 291. Tax exemption of church properties, Tax Law, Consol.Laws, c. 60, § 4, subd. 6 is but another of many illustrations, and the practice is generally followed. Very recently, in upholding the Sunday law, we have recognized that separation of church and State does not mean that every State action remotely connected with religion must be outlawed. People v. Friedman, 302 N.Y. 75, appeal dismissed for want of a substantial Federal question, 341 U.S. 907.

It is thus clear beyond cavil that the Constitution does not demand that every friendly gesture between church and State shall be discountenanced. The so-called "wall of separation" may be built so high and so broad as to impair both State and church, as we have come to know them. Indeed, we should convert this "wall", which in our "religious nation", Church of Holy Trinity v. United States, 143 U.S. 457, 470, is designed as a reasonable line of demarcation between friends, into an "iron curtain" as between foes, were we to strike down this sincere and most scrupulous effort of our State legislators, the elected representatives of the People, to find an accommodation between constitutional prohibitions and the right of parental control over children. In so doing we should manifest "a governmental hostility to religion" which would be "at war with our national tradition", People of State of Illinois ex rel. McCollum v. Board of Education of School Dist. No. 71, supra, 333 U.S. at page 211, and would disregard the basic tenet of constitutional law that "the public interests imperatively demand—that legislative enactments should be recognized and enforced by the courts as embodying the will of the people, unless they are plainly and palpably, beyond all question, in violation of the fundamental law of the Constitution," Atkin v. State of Kansas, 191 U.S. 207, 223.

While extreme care must, of course, be exercised to protect the constitutional rights of these appellants, it must also be remembered that the First Amendment not only forbids laws "respecting an establishment of religion" but also laws "prohibiting the free exercise thereof." We must not destroy one in an effort to preserve the other. We cannot, therefore, be unmindful of the constitutional rights of those many parents in our State (we are told that some 2000,000 children are enrolled in the released time programs in this jurisdiction, and ten times as many throughout the nation) who participate in and subscribe to such programs. The right of parents to direct the rearing and education of their children, free from any general power of the State to standardize children by forcing them to accept instruction from public school teachers only, is an unquestioned one, Pierce v. Society of the Sisters of the Holy Names of Jesus and Mary, 268 U.S. 510, and, more recently, the nation's highest judicial tribunal has declared: "It is cardinal with us that the custody care and nurture of the child reside first in the parents, whose primary function and freedom include preparation for obligations the state can neither supply nor hinder." Prince v. Commonwealth of Massachusetts, supra, 321 U.S. at page 166, 64 S.Ct. at page 442.

Because the public school must be kept separate and apart from the church, pupils may not constitutionally receive religious instruction therein. All that New York parents ask then is that their children may be excused one hour a week for that purpose. The New York City Board of Education provides more days for secular instruction than required by law. Education Law, s 3204, subd. 4. The Education Law does not fix the number of hours that constitute a school day. Excuses from attendance are permitted for many good reasons; among others, children are excused from school on holy days set apart by their respective faiths, thus producing a most obvious form of divisiveness, not paralleled in the released time program. Indeed we are all agreed that refusal to excuse children for that reason would be an unconstitutional abridgement of freedom of religion. If it be constitutional to excuse children of a particular faith for entire days for such a religious purpose, it seems clear, by a parity of reasoning, that it is also constitutional, under the cirumstances here presented, to excuse children of whatever faith one hour a week for another and similar religious purpose. The statute, Education Law, §3210, subd. 1, par. b, authorizes absence for both "religious observance and education."

Moreover, parents have the right to educate their children elsewhere than in the public schools, provided the State's minimum requirements are met, Education Law, § 3204; Pierce v. Society of the Sisters, supra, of the Holy Names of Jesus and Mary, and thus, if they wish, choose a religious or parochial school where religious instruction if freely given. That being so, it follows that parents, who desire to have their children educated in the public schools but to withdraw them therefrom for the limited period of only one hour a week in order to receive religious instruction, may ask the public school for such permission, and the school may constitutionally accede to this parental request. There is nothing in the Constitution commanding that religious instruction may be given on the Sabbath alone, and on no other day...

LOUGHRAN, Chief Judge (concurring).

I vote to affirm the order of the Appellate Division upon the authority of People ex rel. Lewis v. Graves, 245 N.Y. 195, 156 N.E. 663.

DESMOND, Judge (concurring).

This is a mandamus-type procceding, Civ.Prac.Act, art. 78, brought to compel the New York City Board of Education and the State Commissioner of Education, to discontinue and abolish the so-called "released time program" in the city's public schools, on the alleged ground that the release of children from those schools, for one hour a week, at the request of parents, to attend outside religious instruction in their several faiths, violates the Federal Constitution as to its First Amendment, made applicable to the States by the Fourteenth Amendment. Specifically, it is the contention of petitioners that the program as conducted in New York City, and the State statute and State and local regulations under which it operates, "are violative of the U. S. Constitution within the principles set forth in the McCollum decision" that is, People of State of Illinois ex rel. McCollum v. Board of Education of School Dist. No. 71, 333 U.S. 203. I vote for affirmance, because I see no basis for any claim of unconstitutionality.

The First Amendment, which is not quoted at any place in the petition or in the briefs of petitioners and their supporters, forbids the making of laws "respecting an establishment of religion or prohibiting the free exercise thereof". Neither of those prohibitions, in language or meaning, has anything whatever to do with this released time system. The McCollum case, supra, is not controlling on us here, since the Champaign, Illinois plan, there struck down as unconstitutional, differed from the New York program in a number of important respects, principally in that religious training took place in the classrooms of the Champaign public schools (one of the "chief reasons" for the decision, says Justice Jackson in a note in the Kunz v. People of State of New York dissent, 340 U.S. 290,) some public funds were spent in Champaign, the religious teachers there were chosen with the approval of the public school officials, and pupils were, in the Champaign school buildings, solicited for religious instruction. If we are to decide this case on precedent, we must follow our own decision in People ex rel. Lewis v. Graves, 245 N.Y. 195, where we upheld as against claims that it contravened both the Federal and State Constitutions, a released time plan identical with the one now before this court. It must be conceded, of course, that there are, scattered through the several lengthy opinions in McCollum, expressions which can be read to proscribe all released time programs, including this one. But stare decisis does not mean stare verbis, and until the New York plan, or one just like it, confronts the Supreme Court, there will be no precedent binding on us.

Before turning to a somewhat more thorough discussion of the constitutional question, I mention another separate ground for affirmance. Petitioners are, according to the petition, the parents of pupils in New York City schools where this plan operates. Their children do not take part in the program but each receives religious instructions at religious schools, outside public school hours. It is indeed difficult to see how the release of other parents' children impinges in any way at all, on any "right" of petitioners. True, they allege that the operation of the released time program "inevitably results" in coercion on parents and children to attend religious instruction, but it is clear that no such "inevitable" result has befallen petitioners or their children. The Lewis case, supra, in this court can, I suppose, be read as holding that these petitioners, as citizens, have standing to bring this mandamus proceeding, but I suggest the point will bear investigation. It is farfetched to say that petitioners are aggrieved by the continuance of a program which has no effect on them or their children, and which does not involve the use of public buildings, property or funds.

I return to the alleged constitutional question, which needs must be one under the Federal Bill of Rights, since an extramural religious education project, just like this one, was expressly held, in the Lewis case, supra, not to be interdicted by our State Constitution, art. XI, § 4. Our duty then (unhampered by McCollum which is not controlling) is to lay the plain facts of this released time system over against the plain words of the First Amendment. The amendment, lavishly alluded to but seldom quoted, bans, in lucid, specific words, the making of any law "respecting an establishment of religion, or prohibiting the free exercise thereof." The New York released time setup is authorized by a statute, Education Law, § 3210, which permits absences from public schools "for religious observance and education," under rules to be established by the State Commissioner. In approving its passage, Governor Lehman, whose devotion to constitutional liberties needs no encomium, characterized as groundless the fears expressed by some that it "violates principles of our Government" and stated; "The bill does not introduce anything new into our public school system nor does it violate the principles of our public educational system," 1940 Public Papers of Governor Lehman, p. 328. The regulations adopted by the State Education Commissioner, and by respondent New York City board (taking both sets of regulations together) excuse the absence from school, for one hour a week at the close of a daily session of any pupil, whose absence is requested by his parent or guardian for attendance at, and, who does attend, a religious education course conducted under the control of one or more duly constituted religious bodies, each such pupil to be registered for the religious course with, and his attendance thereat reported to, the public school authorities, no announcement of any kind relative to the program to be made in the public school, but notification to come to parents from the religious organization only, no comment to be made by any principal or teacher of attendance or nonattendance of any pupil at the religion classes, and no responsibility for attendance thereat to be assumed by the public school but solely by the religious organizations, which, co-operating with parents, must file with the public school principal weekly, a statement of attendance at, or absence from the religion classes, of any pupil enrolled in the latter, with a statement of reasons for absences therefrom. Just where in all that is there "an establishment of religion" or a prohibition of "the free exercise thereof"? Characterization of such a program as "divisive" or "oppressive" or "coercive" is meaningless on a question of constitutional law. What petitioners are saying is that they dislike the whole enterprise, and consider it socially undesirable. Those are predilections, not questions of law.

The basic fundamental here at hazard is not, it should be made clear, any so-called (but nonexistent, as I shall try to show) "principle" of complete separation of religion from government. Such a total separation has never existed in America, and none was ever planned or considered by the founders. The true and real principle that calls for assertion here is that of the right of parents to control the education of their children, so long as they provide them with the State-mandated minimum of secular learning, and the right of parents to raise and instruct their children in any religion chosen by the parents, Pierce v. Society of the Sisters of the Holy Names of Jesus and Mary, 268 U.S. 510; Meyer v. State of Nebraska, 262 U.S. 390, 625; Packer Collegiate Inst. v. University of State of New York, 298 N.Y. 184, 192. Those are true and absolute rights under natural law, antedating, and superior to, any human constitution or statute.

I cannot believe that the Chief Justice of the United States, in his opinion for the Supreme Court majority in Dennis v. United States, 341 U.S. 494, 508, meant, literally, what he wrote: "that there are no absolutes" and that "all concepts are relative." Of course, even the constitutional rights of freedom of speech and freedom of religion are, to a degree, nonabsolute, since their disorderly or dangerous exercise may be forbidden by law. But embodied within "freedom of religion" is a right which is absolute and not subject to any governmental interference whatever. Absolute, I insist, is the right to practice one's religion without hindrance, and that necessarily comprehends the right to teach that religion, or have it taught, to one's children. That anything in the United States Constitution means, or could ever be tortured into meaning, that our basic law is violated by an arrangement whereby parents take their own children from the common schools, for one hour a week for instruction in their religion, is beyond my comprehension. As Dean Pound has lately reminded us, our American bills of rights "in their significant provisions are bills of liberties" New Paths of the Law, p. 7. The New York released time system is a mere method for the exercise of the religious liberties of the parents of public school pupils, and infringes on no rights of anyone, since no one else's rights are in any affected.

By what process, then, in the teeth of those fundamentals, is an argument contrived for the proposition that this release of children from secular schools for religious education amounts to "an establishment of religion" or prohibits the free exercise thereof? The answer is: the argument construes the First Amendment by ignoring its language, its history and its obvious meaning, and by substituting, for its plain wording, and intendment, the metaphor, Frankfurter, J., in the McCollum case, 333 U.S. 203, 231, supra, or loose colloquialism of "a wall between church and State." That the "wall" has never been more than a figure of speech, is clear from the context in which it was first used by Jefferson, see as quoted by Justice Reed in the dissent in People of State of Education of School Dist. No. 71, supra, 333 U.S. at page 245, n. Quite recently, the Supreme Court itself, in two of its careful opinions in the Dennis case, supra, has warned us against encasing truth in a "semantic straitjacket" (Chief Justice's opinion, p. 508) or attempting to decide great constitutional issues by the use of a "sonorous formula" (concurring opinion of Justice Frankfurter, 341 U.S. at page 519). To dispose of this "unbreachable wall" or "impassable gulf" idea, we need only apply here the simple, lucid test proposed by Justice Frankfurter in that same Dennis opinion: "Not what words did Madison and Hamilton use, but what was in their minds which they conveyed?" 341 U.S. pat page 523. What was in the minds of the founders is writ as large and plain as anything on history's pages, and there is not the slightest possible warrant for ascribing to them an intent to interfere (in the guise of a "Bill of Rights"!), with parents' religious indoctrination of their own children.

One of the curiosities of history is the enlarged and distorted meaning currently being given, by some, to the simple phrase of the First Amendment: "an establishment of religion." It must be the rule as to constitutions, just as to statutes, that there is "no occasion for construction" when the phrasing "is entirely free from ambiguity," Wright v. United States, 302 U.S. 583, 589; 1 Cooley's Const. Limitations [8th ed], pp. 124-126; Carey v. Morton, 297 N.Y. 361, 366. The language of a constitution is to be given its ordinary meaning, Wright v. United States, and Carey v. Morton, supra. The fundamental purpose in construing it is to ascertain and give effect to the intent of the framers and of the people who adopted it, keeping in mind the objects sought to be accomplished and the evils sought to be prevented or remedied. Under any or all those rules and tests (and they are all one), what is the meaning of "an establishment of religion"? The Supreme Court itself gave us the answer in Cantwell v. State of Connecticut, 310 U.S. 296, 303: "it forestalls compulsion by law of the acceptance of any creed or the practice of any form of worship." "Established" churches were well known to the colonists, who had experienced them in Europe and America. They knew that the phrase meant "a state church, such as for instance existed in Massachusetts for more than forty years after the adoption of the Constitution," Corwin, Constitution and What it Means Today [9th ed] pp. 155-156.

When the Constitution was adopted there were still established churches in five of the States, and a few years earlier there had been nine of them in the thirteen colonies, O'Neill, Religion and Education under the Constitution p. 97. "Establishment" of a church or religion always and necessarily means an act of government favoring one particular church or group of churches. Historically, that is exactly what the amendment meant to the framers of the Constitution and to the Congress and the people who adopted it. Despite all the "historical" gloss, there is one only exposition in the Annals of Congress of the meaning, and no comtemporary proofs to the contrary. Madison, the author, said during the First Congress, Annals of Congress for August 15, 1789, Vol. 1, p. 758, that the amendment mandated: "that Congress should not establish a religion, and enforce the legal observation of it by law, nor compel men to worship God in any manner contrary to their conscience." The necessity for the amendment, he went on to say, was a fear by some that Congress might otherwise have power to "make laws of such a nature as might infringe the rights of conscience, and establish a national religion" and he repeated that the amendment was intended "to prevent these effects." Finally, he noted that the amendment was being added because "the people feared one sect might obtain a pre-eminence, or two combine together and establish a religion to which they would compel others to conform." Such fears had indeed been expressed during the campaign to ratify the Constitution as originally drawn, see Van Doren. The Great Rehearsal, pp. 217, 237. No one at that time, or for years thereafter, so far as I can discover, ever attributed to the First Amendment any broader meaning. It is inconceivable that it was ever meant to prohibit governmental encouragement of, or cooperation with, religions generally. As Judge Story pointed out in his Commentaries, Vol. II [5th ed], pp. 630-631 the "general if not the universal sentiment in America was, that Christianity ought to receive encouragement."

I realize that much broader scope may seem to have been accorded to the First Amendment, by the Supreme Court in the Everson v. Board of Education of Ewing Tp., 330 U.S. 1, and McCollum decisions. But if such a broadening was intended in McCollum and Everson, supra, it has, I say with respect, no basis in the only history which is pertinent: the history of the drafting and adoption of the amendment itself. Indeed, that seems to have been conceded by the Justices who were in the majority in the Mc-Collum case (see Justice Frankfurter, concurring, pages 217-220 of 333 U.S. So experienced and proficient a modern commentator as Charles P. Curtis says, while approving the McCollum holding, that the court reached its decision without "any justification whatever in what the Constitution says, and even less in what those who write it intended it to mean," Custis, Modern Supreme Court, Vanderbilt L. Rev., Vol. 4, No. 3, p. 438. Indeed, Curtis surmises "that the First Congress would have rephrased the First Amendment to exclude the release of school time for religious teaching, if it had then been one of the issues of the day." The surmise is not a particularly daring one, as to those early Americans, nearly all of whose schools were religious in spirit and foundation, and who then, or just before or after, invoked the Deity in their Declaration of Independence, established chaplaincies, expressed their trust in God on their coins, and sang "America" part of which is a prayer to God to "protect us by Thy might." The spirit of those times was that of Washington telling us in his Farewell Address that national morality cannot "prevail in exclusion of religious principle" and Edmund Burke, across the sea, warning that "religion is the basis of civil society, and the source of all good and comfort." (Reflections on The Revolution in France.) Mr. Curtis says that Everson and McCollum represent judicial work "wise and well done" but his reason for that personal judgment is that he thinks that "such a use of release time would have a bad effect on our public schools" inculcating a feeling of separatism, etc. Perhaps so, but what has all that to do with the Constitution, and is it anything more than a disguished plea that the court be allowed to rewrite or amend the Constitution, to accomplish what seems, at the moment and to the incumbents, the better social policy?

Learned writers on law justify this sort of constitutional exegesis, and urge that "a written constitution, which is frequently thought to give ridigity to a system, must provide flexibility if judicial supremacy is to be permitted." Levi, An Introduction to Legal Reasoning, p. 42. Rejected by them is the suggestion that "the interpretation ought to remain fixed in order to permit the people through legislative machinery, such as the constitutional convention, or the amending process, to make a change," Levi, id. The answer, says the same author, is that "a written constitution must be enormously ambiguous in its general provisions." General and sweeping, yes. But not ambiguous. Being a constitution, it should state basic law in broadest outline, available for specific applications as needed. But it cannot, I suggest, be ambiguous and be at the same time a constitution. And, regardless of all this, a particular constituion may use definite, one-shot, one-meaning words, and when such are found, as we find them here in the First Amendment, no process of legal reasoning can make them mean something else, or serve some new and unintended purpose.

Petitioners, lacking support in precedent or history, fall back on assertions that this released time method gives religion "active cooperation" and "aid in obtaining pupils" for the off-campus religious classes. If proof of such co-operation, aid and encouragement could lead to a conclusion of law that the scheme is unconstitutional, then a trial of those allegations would be in order, and the dismissal of the petition below, without a trial, would be wrong. But governmental aid to, and encouragement of, religions generally, as distinguished from establishment or support of separate sects, has never been considered offensive to the American constitutional system. If they are inimical to our fundamental law, then every President has offended by invoking the Deity in his oath of office, by issuing Thanksgiving proclamations and calling on our people to pray for victory in war, or for peace, or for our soliders' safety. If petitioners are right, then there is a violation every time a chaplain opens a Congressional session with prayer, or an army bugler sounds "Church call." If petitioners are right; then the Pilgrims were wrong, as was every President who officially urged our people to train themselves in, and practice, religion. Our own State Constitution, on petitioners' theory, offends against American constitutionalism at the point in its preamble where it expresses gratitude "to Almighty God" for our freedom. Petitioners would have this court now deny the declarations of the Supreme Court in the Church of Holy Trinity v. United States case, 143 U.S. 457, and of Chief Justice Kent in the People v. Ruggles case, 8 Johns. 290, in 1811, that ours is a religious nation. I stand on Chief Justice Kent's declaration, long ago in the Ruggles case, 8 Johns. at page 296, that the Constitution "never meant to withdraw religion in general, and with it the best sanctions of moral and social obligation, from all consideration and notice of the law."

The order should be affirmed, with costs.

FULD, Judge (dissenting).

On federal constitutional questions, the Supreme Court of the United States is, of course, the final arbiter, and, concerning the impact of the First Amendment upon religious instruction and the public school, it has recenly spoken. That Amendment, the Supreme Court declared, "rests upon the premise that both religion and government can best work to achieve their lofty aims if each is left free from the other within its respective sphere. * * * the First Amendment has erected a wall between Church and State which must be kept high and impregnable." People of State of Illinois ex rel. McCollum v. Board of Education of School Dist. No. 71, 333 U.S. 203, 212. In the light of that principle, the court ruled, the Amendment prevents the passage of any laws "which aid one religion, aid all religions, or prefer one religion over another." People of State of Illinois ex rel. McCollum v. Board of Education of School Dist. No. 71, supra, 333 U.S. 203; Everson v. Board of Education of Ewing Tp., 330 U.S. 1, 15.

Drawing authority and direction from section 3210, paragraph b, subd. 1, of the Education Law, as amended in 1940, and rules and regulations promulgated by the New York State Commissioner of Education, Regulations of Comr. of Educ., art. 17, § 154; 1 N. Y. Official Compilation of Codes, Rules and Regulations, p. 683, the New York City Board of Education has made provision for a plan of religious instruction by individual sects for the training of public school students. The instruction is given on public school time, but not on public school property. The rules direct that, upon the written request to the school by a parent and a "duly constituted religious body" "prepared to initiate a program for religious instruction," a child is to be released from his regular classes for such instruction for one hour a week; and the public schools are required to maintain records of attendance at these religious courses and of the reasons for absence therefrom . Those children whose parents do not wish them to attend or whose religious sect has not set up a program of instruction in co-operation with the public school's regimen are kept in school to receive what the Superintendent of Schools of the City of New York refers to as "significant education work."

Petitioners challenge that program as a breach of the wall of separation erected by the First Amendment. Their standing is not questioned by respondents and many of the allegations of their petition are not disputed. They are United States citizens, residents, taxpayers and property owners in Kings County and parents of children attending public schools in the Borough of Brooklyn, New York City, where the "released time" program is in operation. Their children do not utilize that program, but instead receive regular religious instruction outside of public school hours at religious schools of their respective faiths—Zorach's child at a Protestant Episcopal religious school and Gluck's children at a Jewish religious school. Asserting that other children in the public schools are released regularly from classes for one hour each week on condition that they attend courses for sectarian religious instruction at religious centers, petitioners seek an order directing the State Commissioner and the City Board to discontinue the program and rescind their regulations.

Denied, but deemed admitted for the purposes of this motion to dismiss the petition, see, e. g., Hines v. State Board of Parole, 293 N.Y. 254, 258; Schwab v. McElligott, 282 N.Y. 182, 185-186, are the further allegations of the petition that the Greater New York Coordinating Committee on Released Time of Jews, Protestants and Roman Catholics "cooperates closely with the public school authorities" in managing the program and in "promoting religious instruction"; that "the system necessarily entails use of the public school machinery and time of public school principals, teachers and administrative staff"; that "the compulsory education system * * * assists and is integrated with the program of sectarian religious instruction carried on by separate religious sects"; that it "has resulted and inevitable results in the exercise of pressure and coercion upon parents and children to secure attendance by the children for religious instruction"; that it "has resulted and evitably will result in divisiveness because of difference in religious belies and disbeliefs"; and that "limiting" participation in the "program to 'duly constituted religious bodies' effects an unlawful censorship of religion and preference in favor of certain religious sects."

In its present posture, the case before us presents the simple question whether the program just described is infected with the same constitutional infirmity that the United States Supreme Court found in People of State of Illinois ex rel. McCollum v. Board of Education of School Dist.

No. 71, supra, 333 U.S. 203. And, though it is ultimately upon the meaning of the First Amendment that the answer to that question depends, we are no longer free since the McCollum decision to place our own meaning or gloss upon that Amendment, but must read it as has the Supreme Court.

While the Champaign "released time" system which was condemned in that case differed in details from that here complained of, the court's conclusion and the principles which it enunciated are broad in scope and clearly reach far beyond the precise fact situation there presented.

In fixing upon the exact holding of the Supreme Court, there may be room for argument as to which phrase, separated from context, best reflects the sense to be distilled from the several opinions written, but there can be no doubt whatsoever as to the net result. Mr. Justice Reed, dissenting alone, recorded the common ground and ultimate conclusion of his brethren's opinions with the statement, 333 U.S. at page 240: "From the tenor of the opinions I conclude * * * that any use of a pupil's school time whether that use is on or off the school grounds, with the necessary school regulations to facilitate attendance, falls under the ban." (Emphasis supplied.)

Regarding the principles enunciated by the court, the first tenet was that the First Amendment has erected a wall "high and impregnable" between Church and State and that the state must maintain a strict neutrality, neither suppressing nor supporting religion. Speaking for a majority of six judges, Mr. Justice Black wrote, 333 U.S. at pages 210-211: "Neither a state nor the Federal Government can set up a church. Neither can pass laws which aid one religion, aid all religions, or prefer one religion over another. * * * In the words of Jefferson, the clause against establishment of religion by law was intended to erect 'a wall of separation between Church and State.' "

That wall was breached by the released time program in Champaign, according to the court, since by it the state effectively aided religion in two respects—(1) by making the public school buildings available and (2) by providing pupils for this or that sect's religious classes. Mr. Justice Black made this exceedingly plain in the following passages, 333 U.S. at pages 209-210, 212.

"Pupils compelled by law to go to school for secular education are released in part from their legal duty upon the condition that they attend the religious classes. This is beyond all question a utilization of the tax-established and tax-supported public school system to aid religious groups to spread their faith. And it falls squarely under the ban of the First Amendment. [333 U.S. at pages 209-210.]

* * * * * * * * *

"Here not only are the state's tax-supported public school buildings used for the dissemination of religious doctrines. The State also affords sectarian groups an invaluable aid in that it helps to provide pupils for their religious classes through use of the state's compulsory public school machinery. This is not separation of Church and State. [333 U.S. at page 212]"

Not only by direct command, but also by the pressures inherent in the functioning of the program did the Champaign system effect a breach of the wall. "The Champaign arrangement," Mr. Justice Frankfurter, concurring, said, "thus presents powerful elements of inherent pressure by the school system in the interest of religious sects. The fact that this power has not been used to discriminate is beside the point. * * * That a child is offered an alternative may reduce the constraint; it does not eliminate the operation of influence by the school in matters sacred to conscience and outside the school's domain. The law of imitation operates, and nonconformity is not an outstanding characteristic of children. The result is an obvious pressure upon children to attend," 333 U.S. at page 227.

It is not that the First Amendment begrudges the use of a portion of the school day for religious instruction that condemned the Champaign program. Rather, the objection was the utilization by state authority of the "momentum of the whole school atmosphere and school planning" behind released time: "If it were merely a question of enabling a child to obtain religious instruction with a receptive mind the thirty or forty-five minutes could readily be found on Saturday or Sunday. If that were all, Champaign might have drawn upon the French system, known in its American manifestation as 'dismissed time', whereby one school day is shortened to allow all children to go where they please leaving those who desire to go to a religious school. The momentum of the whole school atmosphere and school planning is presumably put behind religious instruction, as given in Champaign, precisely in order to secure for the religious instruction such momentum and planning. To speak of 'released time' as being only half or three quarters of an hour is to draw a thread from a fabric" (per Frankfurter, J., concurring, 333 U.S., at pages 230-231).

The statute, the regulations and the pleadings in the record before us similarly make plain the use of the state's compulsory public school machinery, its atmosphere and its momentum. The vice in the use of such machinery to provide pupils for the religious classes is as predominant a factor in the present case as it was in McCollum, 333 U.S., at page 212. As in that case, so here, pupils compelled by law to go to school for secular education, are released for an hour on condition that they attend religious classes. Accordingly, there is no denying that the program enables religious denominations to divert to sectarian instruction pupils assembled, and time set aside, for secular education by the state's compulsory attendance laws. Moreover, while it is true that the regulations prohibit comment on a pupil's failure to attend the religious classes, the program itself seems bound to exert certain inherent pressures on the pupils to attend. For one thing, there results an inevitable of "separation" in pupils "left behind"—to avoid which, few will hesitate to conform to the practices of their fellow students, 333 U.S. at page 227. In addition, the release from the obligation to attend public school for the one hour a week is unquestionably an inducement to register for such courses, for, it has been observed, religious instruction can compete more successfully with arithmetic than with recreation.

The co-operation of the public school system further serves to assure the attendance at the religious classes of the pupils enrolled therein. The regulations require that "Reports of attendance of pupils upon such courses shall be filed with the principal or teacher at the end of each week" together with a statement of the reason for any absence. Knowledge that an official record is kept of his attendance necessarily places pressures on the child—accustomed as he is to the discipline of school—to attend these religious classes.

Indeed, the entire vitality of the program lies in the prestige, planning, co-operation and assistance lent by the public school system, which is exactly that fusion and integration of state and religion prohibited by the First Amendment as interpreted by the Supreme Court. While, therefore, there may here be no use of public school buildings and—I am willing to assume—no use of public school funds and but little of the time of public school personnel, no one may dispute that the state affords sectarian groups "invaluable aid" in helping to provide pupils for their religious classes through the use of its compulsory public school machinery. This is more than a "friendly gesture"—the phrase is Judge Froessel's—between Church and State. If "Separation means separation, not something less", if the relation between Church and State is "a 'wall * * *' not * * a fine line easily overstepped" (per Frankfurter, J., concurring, 333 U.S. at page 231), then, certainly, the New York City program violates the First Amendment.

And, as was true of the Champaign plan, so here in this case, the program is necessarily divisive in its effect. As Justice Frankfurter forcefully noted:

"Again, while the Champaign school population represents only a fraction of the more than two hundred and fifty sects of the nation, not even all the practicing sects in Champaign are willing or able to provide religious instruction. The children belonging to these non-participating sects will thus have inculcated in them a feeling of separatism when the school should be the training ground for habits of community, or they will have religious instruction in a faith which is not that of their parents. As a result, the public school system of Champaign actively furthers inculcation in the religious tenets of some faiths, and in the process sharpens the consciousness of religious differences at least among some of the children committed to its care. These are consequences not amenable to statistics. But they are precisely the consequences against which the Constitution was directed when it prohibited the Government common to all from becoming embroiled, however innocently, in the destructive religious conflicts of which the history of even this country records some dark pages. [333 U.S. at pages 227-228, 68 S.Ct. at page 473]

* * * * * * * * *

"Designed to serve as perhaps the most powerful agency for promoting cohesion among a heterogeneous democratic people, the public school must keep scrupulously free from entanglement in the strife of sects. The preservation of the community from divisive conflicts, of Government from irreconcilable pressures by religious groups, of religion from censorship and coercion however subtly exercised, requires strict confinement of the State to instruction other than religious, leaving to the individuals' church and home, indoctrination in the faith of his choice. [333 U.S. at pages 216-217, 68 S.Ct. at page 468] "

Present a program where some children are released from their usual attendance at public school on condition that they attend courses in religious observance and education under the control of duly constituted religious bodies, it cannot matter, insofar as the impact of the First Amendment is concerned, that such religious instruction is given off the school grounds. What is vital and operative is, not where the religious teaching is given, but that it secures its pupils through the instrumentality of the state and through the machinery and momentum of the public school system. No one disputes the power of the legislature to shorten the school day so as to afford greater opportunity for week-day religious instruction, but it may not go beyond that and lend its aid to coerce or encourage enrollment for such instruction. There is a vital distinction between coercion and what the court chooses to term "an accommodation" between "constitutional prohibitions and the right of parental control over children." Opinion of Judge Froessel, supra, 303 N.Y. at page 172, 100 N.E.2d 468.

In sum, then, what the First Amendment forbids is the fusing, through state action, of the secular and the sectarian in the field of public education. The circumstance that any sect may participate in the program is immaterial. It is not discrimination alone that the Constitution prohibits; as the Supreme Court made indisputably clear, neither the state nor its public schools may be used to "'aid one religion, aid all religions, or prefer one religion over another.'" 333 U.S. 203, 210-211, 68 S.Ct. 461, 465.

I perceive no merit in the contention for which Pierce v. Society of the Sisters of the Holy Names of Jesus and Mary, 268 U.S. 510, 45 S.Ct. 571, 69 L.Ed. 1070, is cited—that a challenge to the released time program is a challenge to the right of parents to control the rearing and education of their children. More specifically, it is urged that, if a parent may insist upon the complete "release" of a child from any attendance at a public school so as to permit him to pursue his studies in a parochial school, the parent has, a fortiori, a right to insist on the release of the child for but a small percentage of school time.

The argument goes too far. It assumes that, even though the child is enrolled in a public school, the parent has a constitutional right to remove him therefrom for any period and at any time for instruction in sectarian religious courses. The Pierce case stands for no such proposition. The Supreme Court there held only that the state cannot constitutionally prevent parents from determining for themselves where their children shall be educated and whether that education shall be sectarian or nonsectarian. No one questions the right of parents to send their children to private or parochial schools of their own choosing. Parents do not however, have any constitutional right to interfere with the functioning of the public school system or to demand that it serve as an adjunct to a plan of religious instruction. Moreover, what the McCollum case concerned itself with, and what is here involved, is not the right of a parent, but rather a basic limitation on the power of the state. The McCollum case, as we have noted, invoked the doctrine of separation, not against the parent's right, but against the state's power, and held that the state may not commingle a program of religious instruction with the secular education given in its public schools. Nothing in the Pierce case either negates that doctrine or suggests a contrary conclusion.

It may well be that there are children growing up untutored in matters religious and, if that be so, it is a matter for grave concern. Considerations of fundamental principle, however, are involved when an attempt is made to enable religious groups to cure that lack through the instrumentality of the public school. Our constitutional policy, it has been said, "does not deny the value or the necessity for religious training, teaching or observance. Rather it secures their free exercise. But to that end it does deny that the state can undertake or sustain them in any form or degree. For this reason the sphere of religious activity, as distinguished from the secular intellectual liberties, has been given the twofold protection and, as the state cannot forbid, neither can it perform or aid in performing the religious function. The dual prohibition makes that function altogether private. It cannot be made a public one by legislative act. This was the very heart of Madison's Remonstrance, as it is of the [First] Amendment itself.

"It is not because religious teaching does not promote the public or the individual's welfare, but because neither is furthered when the state promotes religious education, that the Constitution forbids it to do so." Rutledge, J., dissenting in Everson v. Board of Education of Ewing Tp., supra, 330 U.S., at page 52.

Nor may the released time program be justified as merely another application of the immemorial and unchallenged practice or releasing children from school attendance to permit them to observe their religious Holy Days. The suggested analogy confuses two entirely different and distinct matters. Religious observance of Holy Days necessarily requires attendance at church or temple at stated times which may coincide with the hours otherwise prescribed by law for school attendance. To refuse to excuse children for such religious observance would be a restraint of that freedom of religion, an interference with that liberty of worship, which the Constitution guarantees. Cf. West Virginia State Board of Education v. Barnette, 319 U.S. 624, passim. Obviously, no such issue is here involved.

People ex rel. Lewis v. Graves, 245 N. Y. 195, upon which respondents heavily rely, did involve a scheme for released time for religious instruction somewhat similar to the one before us: on the written request of the parent alone—and not, as in this case, by a clergyman of a "duly constituted religious bodies" as well—the child was released for a half hour a week of what would normally have been a study session at school. However, in view of the Supreme Court's interpretation in the McCollum case of the controlling First Amendment, the Lewis case can no longer be deemed decisive, and no useful purpose is served by considering whether an appraisal of the factual differences between the New York City program and the White Plains program in the Lewis case would make the Lewis decision inapplicable even under the Constitution of New York State. In addition, and I mention it but in passing, the petitioner in the Lewis case relied upon article IX, section 4 (now art. XI, § 4), of the State Constitution, and neither the court nor any of the parties even referred to the constitutional provision, art. I, § 3, here invoked.

It is impossible to justify the determination made below that the petition be dismissed for insufficiency. At the very least, there should be a trial to afford petitioners an opportunity to establish by proof, if they can, such allegations as those that assert the "close cooperation" between public school authorities and those conducting the classes in religious instruction; the use of public school machinery and the time of public school personnel "necessarily entailed" by the program; the "exercise of pressure and coercion" upon parents and children to secure attendance of children at such classes; the divisive nature of the program; and the "unlawful censorship of religion and preference in favor of certain religious sects" "effected" by the program. However, I believe—as did two of the justices in the Appellate Division—that, on the basis of statute, regulations and the admitted allegations of the petition, petitioners are entitled to a decision, on the pleadings, that the released time program under consideration falls within the ban of the Federal Constitution.

Time, has taught, and the Supreme Court, by its McCollum decision has reaffirmed, the wisdom and necessity of maintaining "a wall * * * high and impregnable" between Church and State, between public school secular education and religious observance and teaching. Maintenance of that barrier was regarded by the Supreme Court, as earlier it had been by the Foundling Fathers, not as a demonstration of hostility to religion, but rather as a means of assuring complete freedom of religious worship. In my opinion, the conclusion is inescapable that the released time program in New York City breaches that barrier.

Accordingly, I would reverse and direct entry of a final order granting the relief sought in the petition.

LEWIS, CONWAY and DYE, JJ., concur with FROESSEL, J.

LOUGHRAN, C. J., concurs for affirmance upon the authority of People ex rel. Lewis v. Graves, 245 N.Y. 195, 156 N.E. 663.

DESMOND, J., concurs for affirmance in a separate opinion.

FULD, J., dissents in opinion.

Order affirmed.

Bei Fragen zur Produktsicherheit wenden Sie sich bitte an:
If you have any questions regarding product safety,
please contact:

Walter de Gruyter GmbH
Genthiner Straße 13
10785 Berlin
productsafety@degruyterbrill.com